Code Check®
Complete

3rd Edition

An Illustrated Guide to the Building, Plumbing, Mechanical, and Electrical Codes

BUILDING **PLUMBING** **MECHANICAL** **ELECTRICAL**

Douglas Hansen / Redwood Kardon / Skip Walker

C*ode Check Complete 3rd Edition* **is a compilation of the individual Code Check field guides to codes, including *Code Check Building 5th Edition, Code Check Plumbing & Mechanical 6th Edition,* and *Code Check Electrical 9th Edition.***

By Douglas Hansen, Redwood Kardon & Skip Walker • Illustrations by Paddy Morrissey, Douglas Hansen & Kaia Mathewson

ISBN 978-1-63186-945-7

Printed in China 10 9 8 7 6 5 4 3 2

For updates and information related to this book, visit www.codecheck.com.

TABLE OF CONTENTS

Special thanks to Larry Johnson, Tom Trainor, Glenn Mathewson, Ryan Jackson & Peter Chapman
For additional information, or to contact the authors, visit **www.codecheck.com** and **www.taunton.com**

Part 1 of **Code ✓ Check Complete** Third Edition

An Illustrated Reference for Planning, Building & Inspecting Residential Light-Frame Construction

Based on Chapters 1–11 of the 2021 edition of the International Residential Code®
including annotated changes from the 2018 edition

BY DOUGLAS HANSEN, REDWOOD KARDON & SKIP WALKER

Illustrations by Paddy Morrissey, Douglas Hansen & Kaia Mathewson

BUILDING

TABLE OF CONTENTS

KEY

Code Check Building 5th edition is a condensed guide to codes used for light-frame residential construction. The primary references are the building portions of the *2021 International Residential Code (IRC)* and the *2021 International Building Code (IBC)*. The IRC is used for 1- & 2-family dwellings and townhouses, while the IBC is used for structural issues beyond the scope of the IRC, and for multifamily and commercial buildings.

This book can also be used in areas where the 2018 model codes are still in effect. Significant changes from the 2018 code editions have a different color in the code citation and a comment on the change at the bottom of the page. If a particular code line does not have those features, it also applied in the 2018 IRC. Check with the local building department to determine which model codes are used in your area and for local code amendments.

The information in this book is believed to be accurate; however, it is provided for informational purposes only and is not intended as a substitute for the full text of the referenced codes. Publication by the The Taunton Press, ICC, and the authors should not be considered by the user to be a substitute for the enforceable interpretation of the local building department.

Benjamin Franklin was chosen as the main character in our illustrations for a number of reasons. His insatiable curiosity, scientific genius, and civic-mindedness drove him to promote fire safety, public sanitation, heating methods that improved efficiency and reduced pollution, safe exits, and, of course, electricity. Franklin made major contributions to each of the four main disciplines of building inspection: Building, Plumbing, Mechanical, and Electrical.

codecheck.com/why-ben/

Code ☑ Check

INTERNATIONAL CODE COUNCIL®

KEY TO USING THIS BOOK

Each line that starts with a checkbox ends with a code reference. The code being referenced is shown in the top of the column at the right side, as in this example from page 30:

Required Egress Doors — **21 IRC**

- ☐ Min 1 egress door reqd each dwelling unit ______ 311.2

This line tells us that each dwelling requires an egress door, and the IRC code reference is section 311.2. The actual reference is R311.2, and we drop the R in order to save space throughout the book. Not all of the code references are from the IRC; see page 8 for a list of other references used in this book.

When a line ends with the letters EXC, it means that an exception to the code rule follows in the next line, as in this example from page 9 regarding work that does not require a building permit:

Work Exempt from Permits — **21 IRC**

- ☐ 1-story detached accessory structures ≤ 200 sq. ft. floor area EXC _ 105.2#1
  - • Storm shelters ______ 105.2#1[2]

This line tells us that building permits are not required for accessory structures up to 200 sq. ft. except for storm shelters, which do require permits. The code line ends with a different color and the superscript "2", indicating it is code change #2, and that change is further explained at the bottom of the page (see below).

There are 100 illustrations and 79 tables in this book. They are referenced in the text as in this example from page 52:

- ☐ Notching & boring per **T23** & **F53** ______ 502.8.1

This line tells us that the limits for notching and boring of joists are found in table 23 and that these are illustrated in figure 53.

Code Check uses abbreviations to save space, as in this example from page 15:

- ☐ L&L fire-rated boxes (plastics) allowed in walls AMI **F4** ______ 302.4.2X2

This line tells us that "listed and labeled" (L&L) electrical boxes are allowed in rated wall membranes if installed "in accordance with manufacturer's instructions" (AMI). The "X" in the code citation references an exception in the code, i.e., it refers here to exception 2 to section 302.4.2. A full list of the abbreviations in this book appears on the following page. Specialized terms used in the book are found in the glossary on pages 6 and 7.

2 Storm shelters now require permits regardless of size.

ABBREVIATIONS

1&2FD = 1- & 2-family dwellings
AAMA = American Architectural Manufacturers Association
ABW = alternate braced wall
ACH = air changes per hour
AFF = above finished floor
ACI = American Concrete Institute
AMI = in accordance with manufacturer's instructions
ASCE = American Society of Civil Engineers
ASTM = ASTM International (formerly American Society for Testing & Materials)
BFE = base flood elevation
BIPV = building-integrated photovoltaic
BO = building official
BWL = braced wall line
BWP = braced wall panel
BUR = built-up roof
BV-WSP = WSP w/ stone/masonry veneer
cfm = cubic feet per minute
CMU = concrete masonry unit
CPSC = Consumer Product Safety Commission
CS = continuous sheathing (wall bracing)
CS-G = CS-WSP adjacent garage openings
CS-PF = continuously sheathed portal frame
CS-SFB = CS structural fiberboard
CS-WSP = CS wood structural panel
DFE = design flood elevation
DWB = diagonal wood boards
EERO = emergency escape & rescue opening
EXC = except, exception
FM = FM Approvals (factory mutual)
FRT = fire-retardant treated
FSD = fire separation distance
ft. = foot / feet
ga = gauge
GB = gypsum board
HPS = hardboard panel siding
hr., hrs. = hour, hours
IBC = International Building Code
ICC = International Code Council
ICF = insulating concrete form
in. = inch(es)
L&L = listed & labeled
lav = lavatory basin
lb. = pound(s)
LIB = let-in bracing
LL = lot line
LVL = laminated veneer lumber
max. = maximum
MEP = mechanical, electrical & plumbing
MFR = manufacturer
mil = thousands of an inch
min. = minimum
mph = miles per hour
NDW = naturally durable wood
NFPA = National Fire Protection Association
NP = not permitted
NRTL = Nationally Recognized Testing Laboratory
o.c. = on center
OSB = oriented strand board
p. = page, as in "*see p. 5*"
PBS = particleboard sheathing
PCP = Portland cement plaster
PFG = portal frame at garage
PFH = portal frame w/ hold-downs
PPT = pressure-preservative treated
psf = pounds per square foot
psi = pounds per square inch
PT = preservative treated
PV = photovoltaic
req, reqs = require, requires, requirements
reqd = required
SDC = Seismic Design Category
SDC D = Seismic Design Categories D_0, D_1 & D_2 inclusive
SFB = structural fiberboard sheathing
SHGC = solar heat gain coefficient
spec = specification
sq. = square, as in sq. ft.
T&G = tongue & groove
temp = temperature
UDWS = ultimate design wind speed
UL = UL (formerly Underwriters Laboratories)
w/ = with
w/o = without
WC = water closet (toilet)
WRB = water-resistive barrier
WSP = wood structural panel
X = in code citation, refers to "exception"
Zi = zinc, galvanized

GLOSSARY

Several definitions here have been abridged. See IRC section 202 for complete definitions.

Access (to): That which enables a device, appliance, or equipment to be reached either readily or by first removing a panel, door, or similar obstruction.

Approved: Acceptable to the building official (BO).

Approved agency: An independent entity regularly engaged in conducting tests, inspections, or product certifications and that is approved by the building official.

Aspect ratio: The ratio of longest to shortest perpendicular dimensions, or for wall sections, the ratio of height to length.

Attic: The unfinished space between the ceiling assembly of the top story and the roof assembly.

Attic, habitable: A finished or unfinished habitable space within an attic.

Basement: A story that is not a story above grade plane.

Braced wall line (BWL): A straight line through the building plan representing the location of lateral resistance provided by wall bracing. **F63**

Braced wall panel (BWP): A full-height section of wall constructed to resist shear loads through interaction of framing members, sheathing material, and anchors.

Building official (BO): The officer or their duly authorized representative charged with administration and enforcement of codes.

Building thermal envelope: The basement walls, exterior walls, floor, roof, and other building elements that enclose conditioned space.

Cement plaster (stucco): A mixture of Portland or blended cement and aggregate, lime, masonry cement, plastic cement, and other approved materials. **F91**

Change of occupancy: A change in the use of the building or portion thereof that involves a change in the application of the requirements of the code.

Connector: A device such as a joist hanger, post base, hold-down, mudsill anchor, or hurricane tie used to connect structural components—also see *Fastener*.

Crawlspace: An underfloor space that is not a basement.

Cripple wall: A framed wall extending from the top of the foundation to the underside of the floor framing of the first story above grade plane. **F67**

Dampproofing: A coating intended to protect against the passage of water vapor through walls or other building elements. It is a lesser degree of protection than *waterproofing*.

Dead load: The weight of all materials and fixed service equipment incorporated into the building.

Diaphragm: A horizontal or nearly horizontal system, such as a floor or low-slope roof, acting to transmit lateral forces to the vertical resisting elements. The term also refers to horizontal bracing systems.

Draft stop: A material, device, or construction installed to restrict the movement of air within open spaces of concealed areas of building components, such as crawlspaces, floor-ceiling assemblies, roof-ceiling assemblies, and attics.

Dwelling unit: A single unit providing complete independent living facilities for one or more persons, including provisions for living, sleeping, eating, cooking, and sanitation.

Emergency escape and rescue opening: An operable exterior door, window, or similar device that provides a means of escape and access for rescue in an emergency. Also see *Grade floor emergency escape & rescue opening.* **F29**

Exterior Insulation Finish Systems (EIFS): Nonstructural exterior wall cladding systems that consist of an adhered and/or anchored insulation board, and an integrally reinforced base coat, and a textured finish coat. EIFS with drainage incorporates a means of drainage over a water-resistive barrier.

Fastener: Generic category that includes nails, screws, bolts, or anchors—also see *Connector.*

Fire separation distance: The distance measured perpendicularly from the building face to the closest interior lot line or to the centerline of a street, alley, or public way, or to an imaginary line between two buildings on the same lot. **F2,3**

Fireblocking: Materials installed to resist the free passage of flame to other areas of the building through concealed spaces. **F8–11**

Flight (of stairs): A continuous run of treads from one landing to another.

Grade: The finished ground level adjoining the building at all exterior walls.

Grade floor emergency escape & rescue opening: An *emergency escape and rescue opening* located such that the bottom of the opening is not more than 44 in. above or below the finished ground level adjacent to the opening. **F29**

Grade plane: The averaged finished ground level adjoining the building exterior walls. Where sloping away from the building, the reference plane is established by the lowest points within 6 ft. of the building or the lot line, whichever is less.

Guard: A building component or system near the open sides of elevated walking surfaces that minimizes the possibility of a fall to a lower level. **F27–28**

Habitable space: Space in a building for living, sleeping, eating, or cooking. Bathrooms, toilet rooms, closets, hallways, storage, or utility spaces and similar areas are not considered habitable space.

Insulating concrete form (ICF): A concrete forming system using stay-in-place forms of rigid foam or other insulating material for cast-in-place concrete walls.

Labeled: An identifying mark applied to a product by the manufacturer indicating that a sample of the product has met appropriate standards for the product to be listed by an approved agency or organization. Manufacturer's instructions are by default a part of the listing of products that are listed and labeled.

Light-frame construction: Construction whose vertical elements are primarily formed by repetitive wood or cold-formed steel framing members.

Listed: Equipment, materials, products, or services included in a list by an agency or organization (typically a NRTL) that performs evaluations and periodic testing of products or services for conformity to identified standards or suitability for specific purposes.

Live loads: Loads produced by use and occupancy of the building and not including wind, snow, rain, earthquake, flood, or *dead loads*.

Live/Work unit: A dwelling unit or sleeping unit in which a significant portion of the space includes a nonresidential use that is operated by the tenant.

Living space: Space within a dwelling unit utilized for living, sleeping, eating, cooking, bathing, washing, and sanitation purposes.

Monolithic: Concrete cast in one continuous operation with no joints, such as a footing and floor slab or a footing and foundation stem wall.

Naturally durable wood (NDW): Heartwood of specific species of wood that resist decay (redwood, cedar, black locust, black walnut) or termites (Alaska yellow cedar, redwood, red cedar). Occasional sapwood is allowed if ≥ 90% of width on each side where such occurs is heartwood. Sapwood of Western red cedar is termite-resistant.

Perm: The unit of measurement of water vapor transmission through a material, based on the number of grains of water vapor at a given pressure differential. *Vapor retarders* are rated in perms.

Ready access (to): That which enables a device, appliance, or equipment to be directly reached without removal or movement of any panel, door, or obstruction.

Registered design professional: An individual licensed to practice their design profession as defined by the professional registration laws of the state or jurisdiction in which the project is to be constructed.

Retaining wall: A wall that resists lateral soil load and is not laterally supported at the top. Basement walls are typically restrained walls, not retaining walls.

Seismic Design Category (SDC): Classification assigned to buildings based on the occupancy category and severity of earthquake ground motion expected at the site.

Shear wall: Walls designed and constructed to resist racking from seismic or wind. In wood framing, shear walls are constructed of *Braced wall panels*.

Sill: The lowest horizontal member of a framed opening or of a frame for a window.

Sill plate: A horizontal wood member resting directly on a foundation. **F41**

Sole plate (bottom plate): The horizontal wall member at the bottom of a framed wall.

Stair: A change of elevation consisting of 1 or more risers. **F23–25**

Story: That portion of a building that is between the upper surface of one floor and below the upper surface of the next floor above or the roof.

Story above grade plane: Any story having its finished surface entirely above grade plane, or in which the finished surface of the next floor above is either more than 6 ft. above grade plane or more than 12 ft. above the ground level at any point.

Top plate: A horizontal wall member(s) at the top of a framed wall.

Townhouse: A building containing 3 or more attached *townhouse units*.

Townhouse unit: A single-family dwelling unit in a *townhouse* that extends from foundation to roof and that has a yard or public way on at least two sides.

Vapor diffusion port: An assembly constructed or installed with a roof assembly at an opening in the roof deck to convey water vapor from an unvented attic to the outside atmosphere.

Vapor permeable: Material that permits the passage of water vapor, having a permeance rating of 5 perms or greater when tested to ASTM E96.

Vapor retarder class: A measure of the ability of a material or assembly to limit the amount of moisture that passes through it using procedure A of ASTM E96:

Class I: ≤ 0.1 perm rating

Class II: > 0.1 to ≤ 1.0 perm rating

Class II: > 1.0 to ≤ 10 perm rating

Water-resistive barrier: A material behind an exterior wall covering that is intended to resist liquid water that has penetrated behind the exterior covering from intruding further into the exterior wall assembly. **F91**

Waterproofing: Materials that protect walls or other building elements from the passage of moisture as either vapor or liquid under hydrostatic pressure.

Wood structural panel (WSP): A panel manufactured from veneers (plywood) or wood strands (OSB) and bonded with waterproof synthetic resins. Wood structural panels must bear a grade stamp **F55** and are used in floors, roof diaphragms, and shear walls.

REFERENCED STANDARDS

TABLE 1	REFERENCED ORGANIZATIONS, STANDARDS & ALTERNATIVE DESIGN DOCUMENTS USED IN THIS BOOK	
Abbreviation	**Organization**	**Document Name**
AAMA	American Architectural Manufacturers Association	AAMA/WDMA/CSA 101/I.S.2/A440–17 North American Fenestration Standards/Specifications for Windows, Doors & Skylights
ACI	American Concrete Institute	ACI 318–19 Building Code Requirements for Structural Concrete
ACI	American Concrete Institute	ACI 332–20 Code Requirements for Residential Concrete
AISI	American Iron & Steel Institute	AISI S230–18 Standard for Cold-Formed Steel Framing—Prescriptive Method for 1&2FD
ANSI	American National Standards Institute	ANSI A108 American National Standard Specifications for the Installation of Ceramic Tile Material & Installation Standards
ASCE	American Society of Structural Engineers Structural Engineering Institute	ASCE 7-16 with Supplement 1—Minimum Design Loads and Associated Criteria for Buildings and other Structures
ASHRAE	American Society of Heating, Refrigeration & Air Conditioning Engineers	ASHRAE 62.2–2019 Ventilation & Acceptable Indoor Air Quality in Residential Buildings
ASTM	ASTM International	ASTM C926–21 Standard Specification for Application of Portland Cement-Based Plaster
ASTM	ASTM International	ASTM C1063–22 Standard Specification for Installation of Lathing and Furring to Receive Interior and Exterior Portland Cement Plaster
SBCA	Structural Building Components Association	BCSI—2018 Building Component Safety Information Guide to Good Practice for Handling, Installing, Restraining & Bracing of Metal Plate Connected Wood Trusses
ICC	International Code Council	2021 International Building Code
ICC	International Code Council	2021 International Residential Code
NFPA	National Fire Protection Association	NFPA 13D Standard for the Installation of Sprinkler Systems in 1- & 2-Family Dwellings
NFPA	National Fire Protection Association	NFPA 72 National Fire Alarm and Signaling Code
NFPA	National Fire Protection Association	NFPA 211 Standard for Chimneys, Fireplaces, Vents & Solid Fuel-Burning Appliances
TMS	The Masonry Society	TMS 402–16 Building Code Requirements for Masonry Structures
TMS	The Masonry Society	TMS 602–16 Specifications for Masonry Structures
TPI	Truss Plate Institute	TPI 1–2014 National Design Standard for Metal Plate Connected Wood Truss Construction
AWC	American Wood Council	NDS–2018 National Design Specification for Wood Construction
AWC	American Wood Council	WFCM–2018 Wood Frame Construction Manual for One- and Two-Family Dwellings

PLANNING, PERMITS & INSPECTIONS

Planning department approval is the first step for a new building or a project that changes the use of a building. Requirements vary from one jurisdiction to another and may include regulations for setbacks, easements, daylight plane restrictions, and lot coverage. Plans must conform to applicable climatic and geographic design criteria and must include setbacks from the property lines and adjacent slopes. The plans may require a signature and stamp from a licensed design professional if required by the local jurisdiction or if special conditions exist that require professional design.

Plans — 21 IRC

- ☐ Plans & other construction documents reqd to be submitted EXC ____ 106.1
  - Minor work that does not req design (e.g., replacing water heater) ___ 106.1X
- ☐ Local statutes may req plans by registered design professional ____ 106.1
- ☐ Special conditions may req plans by registered design professional ___ 106.1
- ☐ Electronic submittals OK if allowed by BO ____ 106.1.1
- ☐ MFR's installation instructions must be on job site ____ 106.1.2
- ☐ BWLs must be identified on plans ____ 106.1.3
- ☐ If in flood hazard area, delineate boundaries & elevations (*p. 11*) ____ 106.1.4
- ☐ Site plan reqd including distances of structures to lot lines ____ 106.2
- ☐ Approved plans reqd to be on site ____ 106.3.1
- ☐ Alternative materials, design & methods OK when approved by BO __ 104.11
- ☐ BO must provide written explanation for rejection of applications for alternative materials, design & methods ____ 104.11
- ☐ Additions, alterations, repairs & relocations may not cause a structure to be less code-compliant than existing building was prior to such work _ 102.7.1[1]

Permits

- ☐ Permits reqd for new work, additions, repairs & alterations ____ 105.1
- ☐ Permit or copy reqd to be on site until project completion ____ 105.7
- ☐ C of O (Certificate of Occupancy) reqd prior to use or occupancy ____ 110.1

1. Previous wording of this section prohibited making existing building "unsafe."

Work Exempt from Permits — 21 IRC

- ☐ 1-story detached accessory structures ≤200-sq.-ft. floor area EXC _ 105.2#1
  - Storm shelters ____ 105.2#1[2]
- ☐ Fences ≤7 ft. high* ____ 105.2#2
- ☐ Retaining walls ≤ 4 ft. bottom of footing to top of wall & no surcharge 105.2#3
- ☐ Water tanks on grade ≤5,000 gallons & ≤2:1 aspect ratio ____ 105.2#4
- ☐ Sidewalks & driveways ____ 105.2#5
- ☐ Painting, countertops, cabinets, tile, carpet, similar finish work ____ 105.2#6
- ☐ Prefab pools <24 in. deep ____ 105.2#7
- ☐ Swings & other playground equipment ____ 105.2#8
- ☐ Window awnings ≤54 in. projection & supported solely by wall ____ 105.2#9
- ☐ Decks ≤200 sq. ft. & ≤30 in. above grade & not attached & not serving the reqd exit door ____ 105.2#10

(Note: in Wildland-Urban Interface Areas or Very High Fire Hazard Severity Zones, deck construction may have local restrictions and requirements.)

Required Inspections

- ☐ Inspection & approval prior to concealing any work ____ 109.4
- ☐ Foundation inspection (rebar, Ufer**, forms) prior to placing concrete _ 109.1.1
- ☐ Rough MEP inspections prior to framing & before concealment (including concealment by concrete) ____ 109.1.2
- ☐ In flood hazard areas, registered design professional reqd to document lowest floor elevation before construction above it ____ 109.1.3
- ☐ Frame & masonry after roof, masonry, firestopping, draftstopping & bracing in place & after MEP inspection ____ 109.1.4
- ☐ Other inspections as reqd by BO (e.g., 3rd party for insulation) ____ 109.1.5
- ☐ GB nailing of fire resistance-rated walls prior to taping ____ 109.1.5.1
- ☐ In flood hazard areas, documentation of elevations reqd to be submitted to BO prior to final inspection ____ 109.1.6.1
- ☐ Final inspection prior to occupancy ____ 109.1.6

2. Storm shelters now require permits regardless of size.

* In many areas, the allowance for 7-ft.-high fences conflicts with zoning regulations or is subject to modification. Check with your local jurisdiction.

** Concrete-encased grounding electrodes are referred to by the name of the system's founder, Herbert Ufer.

DESIGN

Construction following the prescribed guidelines of the IRC does not require design by a licensed design professional. When aspects of a building exceed the prescriptive limits of the IRC, design is required in conformance with the IBC. Some projects might be in wind, snow, or seismic areas that require structural aspects to be built to the IBC, while the nonstructural aspects are built to the IRC.

The IRC includes maps for *Ultimate Design Wind Speeds* and regions where *Wind Design* is required. A more precise determination of the status of a particular area can be obtained from the Applied Technology Council (ATC) Hazard Locations' web engine @ hazards.atcouncil.org.

Design Criteria — 21 IRC

- ☐ Construction per IRC to safely support all loads (dead & live loads, roof, flood, snow, wind & seismic loads) & transfer loads to foundation _____ 301.1
- ☐ OK to use AWC or AISI **T1** as alternatives if within IRC scope _____ 301.1.1
- ☐ IRC basis of design is platform & balloon-frame light-frame buildings _ 301.1.2
- ☐ Structural elements exceeding IRC limits req design per accepted engineering practice _____ 301.1.3
- ☐ Design in accordance w/ IBC is acceptable alternative to IRC _____ 301.1.3
- ☐ Construct in accordance w/ climatic & geographic design criteria **T2** __ 301.2

The *Ultimate Design Wind Speed* obtained from IRC figure 301.2(2) or the ATC website is used to help determine the *Component and Cladding Pressure Loads* of IRC figure 301.2.1 and table 301.2.1(1). These are adjusted for height and exposure by table 301.2.1(2). These results are then used to determine the performance standard for wall coverings, windows, exterior doors, roof coverings, skylights, and garage doors. These tables are too large to summarize in this book but can be viewed on line at codes.iccsafe.org. Table 301.2.1(2) uses *exposure categories* that are defined in 301.2.1.4 as follows:

- **Exposure B**: Areas w/ numerous closely spaced obstructions having the size of single-family dwellings or larger—may be urban, suburban, wooded area, or similar. This exposure category is the typical default.
- **Exposure C**: Open terrain w/ scattered obstructions w/ heights <30 ft. extending > 1,500 ft. from building site. Also applies to buildings in Exposure B when directly adjacent to Exposure C terrain for a distance of ≥ 600 ft.
- **Exposure D**: Flat unobstructed areas exposed to wind over open water or smooth mud or salt flats for a distance of 5,000 ft.

When mapping per IRC figure 301.2.1.1 indicates that *Wind Design* is required or when the *Ultimate Design Wind Speed* is ≥140mph, the project is beyond the design limits of the IRC and a design in accordance with accepted engineering practice is required.

TABLE 2 — CLIMATIC & GEOGRAPHIC DESIGN CRITERIA (FILL-IN TABLE) ◆ T301.2

Ground Snow Load[A]	Wind Design				Seismic Design Category[B]	Subject to Damage From			Ice Barrier Reqd[B,C]	Flood Hazards[B,E]	Air Freezing Index[B,F]	Mean Annual Temp[B,F]
	Speed (mph)[B]	Topo-graphic Effects[B,C]	Special Wind Region[B,C]	Wind-borne Debris Zone[B,C]		Weathering (Concrete)[D]	Frost Line Depth[B]	Termites[B]				

A. From IRC figure 301.2(3&4) or local information.
B. To be filled in by the building jurisdiction.
C. These questions can be answered yes or no.
D. From IRC figure 301.2(1).
E. Include jurisdiction's date of entry into National Flood Insurance Program.
F. Obtain from National Climatic Data Center Air-Freezing Index.

Flood hazard areas are shown on a FIRM (flood insurance rate map) prepared by FEMA (the Federal Emergency Management Agency) including zones designated as A zones or V zones (where breaking waves are higher than 3 ft.).

Flood-Resistant Construction — 21 IRC

- ☐ Design, connect & anchor to resist flotation, collapse, or permanent lateral movement due to flooding at DFE ____ 322.1.2
- ☐ Flood Hazard Area = area ≥1% chance of flooding any given year ____ 322.1.4
- ☐ Coastal High Hazard Area = subject to wave heights >3 ft. (V zones) & designated Coastal A Zones (wave heights ≥1.5 ft. & ≤3 ft.) ____ 322.2&3
- ☐ Design per flood hazard area EXC ____ 301.2.4 & 322.1
  - ASCE 24 OK as alternative to IRC ____ 322.1.1
  - Buildings in identified floodways (e.g., river channels) req design per ASCE 24 Flood Resistant Design & Construction ____ 301.2.4 & 322.1
- ☐ BFE = peak flood elevation including wave height ____ 322.1.4
- ☐ Establish DFE by BFE w/ 1% chance of occurrence in any given year or by locally adopted map or data source ____ 322.1.4
- ☐ "Lowest floor" = floor of lowest enclosed area including basement excluding flood-resistant areas solely for parking, access, or storage ____ 322.1.5
- ☐ Min. elevation of lowest floor in flood hazard area must be base flood elevation + 1 ft. or the DFE, whichever is higher ____ 322.2.1
- ☐ Buildings w/substantial damage of any origin w/ repair costs > 50% of value require 100% compliance w/flood-resistant design ____ 105.3.1.1

Flood-Resistance – Coastal A Zones & High Hazard Areas

- ☐ Registered design professional reqd for design & documents ____ 322.3.3&9
- ☐ Building reqs anchorage to pilings or columns ____ 322.3.3
- ☐ Design soil penetration of pilings to resist combined wave & wind lateral & uplift loads; factor in scouring of surrounding soil strata ____ 322.3.3
- ☐ No fill incorporated into structural support ____ 322.3.2
- ☐ Horizontal structural members above BFE + 1 ft. or above DFE ____ 322.3.2
- ☐ Garages & basements req min. one side above grade ____ 322.3.2

Flood-Resistance: Enclosed Areas below DFE — 21 IRC

- ☐ Uses limited to parking, building access, or storage ____ 322.2.2
- ☐ Flood openings reqd for min. 1 sq. in / sq. ft of enclosed area ____ 322.2.2
- ☐ Min. 2 openings reqd, must be on different sides ____ 322.2.2.1
- ☐ Openings max. height 1 ft. above final interior & exterior grade ____ 322.2.2.1
- ☐ Openings may be installed in windows & doors ____ 322.2.2.1
- ☐ Windows & doors w/o openings do not count as openings ____ 322.2.2.1

Flood-Resistance: Structure below Required Elevation

- ☐ Walls below reqd elevation not part of structural support ____ 322.3.5
- ☐ Walls must be designed to break away; max. resistance 20 psf
- ☐ No MEP components attached to or through break-away walls ____ 322.3.5
- ☐ Slabs for parking, decks, walkways, etc., structurally independent of building foundation system, max. 4 in. thick, no reinforcement, control joints max. 4 ft. o.c., no turned-down edges ____ 322.3.4

Wind Design

- ☐ Determine UDWS ____ 301.2.1 & F301.2(2)
- ☐ If history of damage due to wind speed-up at hills, modify map values to consider topographic effects ____ 301.2.1.5
- ☐ If wind design reqd or if UDWS ≥140mph in a special wind region, design per ICC-600, ASCE-7, WFCM, AISI S230, or IBC **T2** ____ 301.2.1.1
- ☐ Wall & roof coverings & fenestration must meet performance reqs for component & cladding pressure loads ____ 301.2.1
- ☐ Asphalt shingles req classification for wind resistance ____ 905.2.4.1
- ☐ Metal shingles req classification for wind resistance ____ 905.4.4.1[3]
- ☐ Exterior glazed openings in windborn debris regions to meet ASTM E1886 & E1996 as modified by 301.2.1.2.1 EXC ____ 301.2.1.2
  - Pre-drilled wood structural panels OK for opening protection; must fit on permanently installed anchors on building ____ 301.2.1.2X
- ☐ Provide continuous load path to transmit uplift forces from roof assembly to foundation **F78** ____ 301.2.1

3. Added req for metal shingle wind-resistance classification in this edition.

SEISMIC DESIGN

The IRC assigns a seismic design category (SDC) from A to E, with A the least seismic risk and E considerable risk. Category D is further broken down into parts, D_0, D_1, and D_2. Buildings in SDC E must be designed to the IBC. The BO can allow an E to be designated as D_2 (and therefore within the prescriptive scope of the IRC) if the building has no "irregular" portions and has wall bracing continuous in one plane from the foundation to the uppermost story with no cantilevers.

Seismic Provisions — 21 IRC

- ☐ Assign seismic design category per F301.2.2.1(1-6) EXC ________ 301.2.2.1
  - IBC 1613.2 OK as basis for soils w/ Site Class A, B, or D ____ 301.2.2.1.1
- ☐ Seismic provisions apply to 1&2FD & townhouses in SDC D & to townhouses in SDC C ________ 301.2.2
- ☐ Buildings in SDC E req design per IBC EXC ________ 301.2.2.1
  - Reclassification as D_2 OK w/ detailed evaluation per IBC or ___ 301.2.2.1.2
    1. All exterior shear lines or BWP in one plane vertically foundation to roof &
    2. Floors not cantilevered past exterior walls &
    3. Building not classified as irregular per 301.2.2.6
- ☐ Irregular buildings or irregular portions thereof req design ________ 301.2.2.6
- ☐ SIP buildings max. 2 stories above grade plane ________ 301.2.2.7
- ☐ Cold-formed steel-frame buildings max. 3 stories above grade plane ________ 301.2.2.7
- ☐ Wood-framed buildings >2 stories in SDC D_2 req design for wind & seismic loads in accordance w/ standard engineering practice ___ 301.2.2.7[4]
- ☐ Cold-formed steel buildings in SDC D also to comply w/ AISI S230 ________ 301.2.2.8
- ☐ Masonry chimneys in SDC D req reinforcement & anchorage *(p. 115)* ________ 301.2.2.9
- ☐ Water heaters & thermal storage tanks req anchorage in SDC D, also townhouses in SDC C & D ________ 301.2.2.10

4. Engineered design for bracing of 3-story buildings in SDC D_2 was previously triggered by reqs in T602.10.3(3) and now specifically reqs engineered design.

Conditions Considered Irregular — 21 IRC

- ☐ Shear wall lines or BWPs not in same vertical plane from foundation to uppermost story where reqd **F1A** EXC ________ 301.2.2.6 #1
  - Cantilevers or setbacks ≤4× joist depth (min. 2x10 joists ≤16 in. o.c.) OK if cantilever backspan ≥2:1, joists at ends of BWPs doubled, continuous rim joist, and gravity loads at end of cantilever only uniform wall/roof loads & reactions of headers ≤8 ft. ________ 301.2.2.6 #1X
- ☐ Floor or roof not laterally supported by BWL on all edges EXC _301.2.2.6 #2
  - Floors not supporting BWPs OK if ≤6 ft. beyond BWP ____ 301.2.2.6 #2X
- ☐ BWPs in same vertical plane (or offset per exc to item #1) extending >1 ft. over openings in wall below **F1B** EXC ________ 301.2.2.6 #3
  - Over a header exceeding **T36** (see details in code text) ____ 301.2.2.6 #3X
- ☐ Diaphragm (floor or roof) openings w/ a dimension >12 ft. or >50% of the least floor or roof dimension ________ 301.2.2.6 #4
- ☐ Floor levels are vertically offset **F1C** EXC ________ 301.2.2.6 #5
  - Framing supported by continuous perimeter foundations or where floor framing is lapped or tied ________ 301.2.2.6 #5X
- ☐ Shear walls & BWLs not in two perpendicular directions ______ 301.2.2.6 #6
- ☐ Walls that include masonry or concrete construction & have wood or cold-formed steel wall bracing EXC ________ 301.2.2.6 #7
  - Fireplaces, chimneys & masonry veneer ________ 301.2.2.6 #7X
- ☐ Hillside light-frame construction where average grade slope >1:5, tallest cripple wall clear height >7 ft. or post & beam has posts >7 ft., total plan area below lowest framed floor is <50% living space w/ interior wall finish **F1D** EXC ______ 301.2.2.6 #8[5]
  - Lowest framed floor directly supported on concrete or masonry full length of all sides except downhill side ______ 301.2.2.6 #8X[5]

5. Definition of hillside irregular construction new in 2021 edition.

FIG. 1

Irregular Construction Outside Scope of IRC Prescriptive Rules

A Braced wall panels not in same plane:

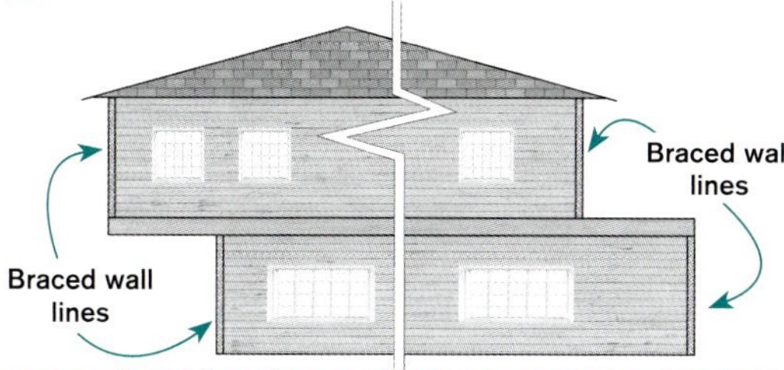

Exceptions allowed if cantilever or setback ≤4× nominal joist depth and
1) joists min. nominal 2×10 max. spacing 16 in. o.c.
2) backspan ratio of cantilever min. 2:1
3) joists doubled at ends of BWPs
4) continuous rim joist at ends of cantilever joists
5) gravity loads only and reactions from headers ≤ 8 ft.

Irregular structures require engineered design. Where the forces associated with the irregularity are resisted by such design, the remainder of the building is permitted to use the prescriptive provisions of the code.

B Braced wall panels in same plane end over opening in wall below:

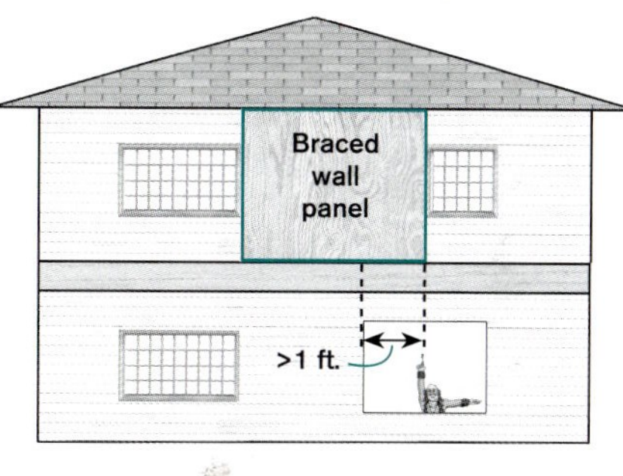

C Floor level offset:

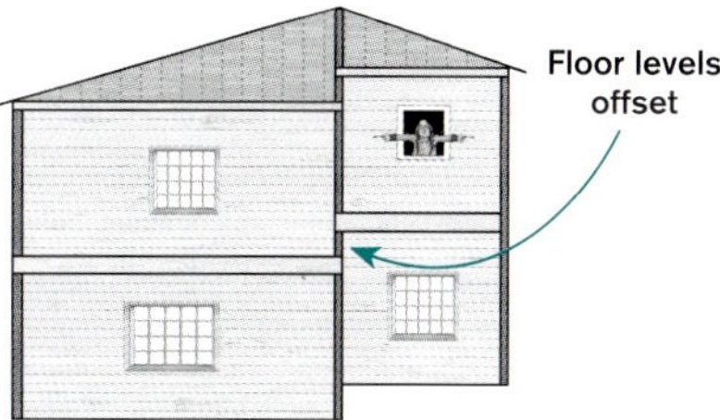

Exceptions allowed if floor framing can be lapped or tied, or if framing supported by continuous foundations at building perimeter.

D Hillside light-frame construction:

When all 3 conditions below exist, design reqd for entire story above cripple walls and for structural elements connecting floor diaphragm to foundation.

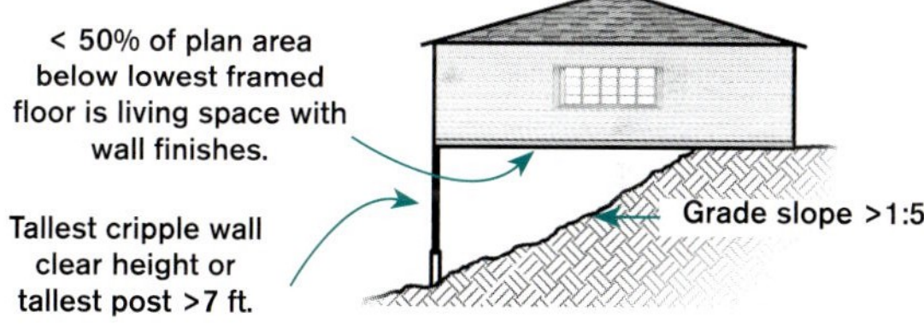

Exception is allowed if lowest-framed floor supported entirely on concrete or masonry walls for full length except downhill side (walkout basement).

LOCATION ON SITE

Lot Line Setbacks — 21 IRC

- ☐ Exterior walls, projections & openings to comply w/ FSD **F3** ________ 302.1
- ☐ 1-hour rated walls **F3** per ASTM E119, UL 263, or IBC 703.3 w/ exposure from outside (both sides if not sprinklered) _______ T302.1(1&2)
- ☐ FSD is measured perpendicular to face of wall **F2** ________ 202
- ☐ Rating not reqd for walls facing accessory structures on same lot ___ 302.1X2
- ☐ Rating not reqd for accessory structures exempted from permits ____ 302.1X3
- ☐ No eave or other projections over the LL _________ 302.1X3 & T302.1(1&2)

FIG. 2 Fire Separation Distance Measurement

A

Lot lines

A

B

A

Fire separation distance (A) is measured perpendicular to building walls. Distance (B) to the lot line can be less than the required fire separation distance.

Openings F3 — 21 IRC

- ☐ No openings in walls < 3 ft. from LL EXC ________ T302.1(1&2)
  - Openings OK in walls perpendicular to line determining FSD ____ 302.1X1
  - Foundation vents not counted as openings ________ 302.1X5
- ☐ Openings in walls < 5 ft. from LL max. 25% of wall area EXC ____ T302.1(1)
  - Openings ≥ 3 ft. from LL unrestricted in dwellings w/ fire sprinklers T302.1(2)

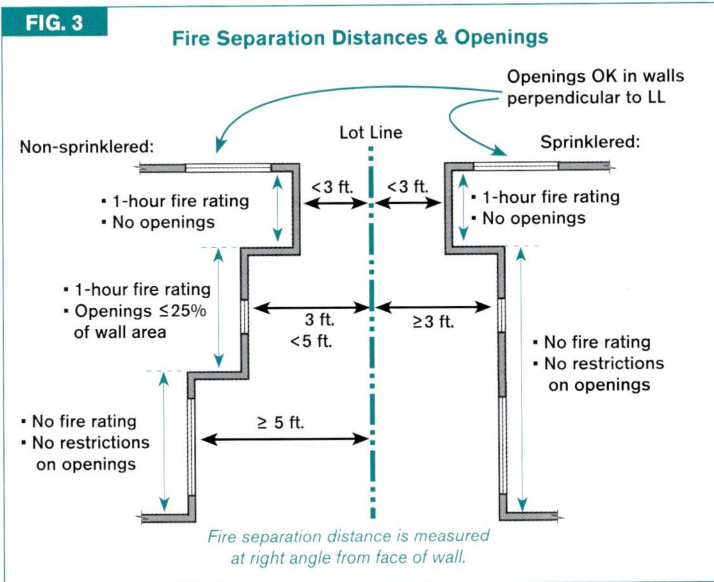

Fire separation distance is measured at right angle from face of wall.

Projections — 21 IRC

- ☐ No projections (eaves) <2 ft. of LL EXC ________ T302.1(1&2)
  - Detached garages within 2 ft. of LL eave projections ≤4 in. OK ___ 302.1X4
- ☐ Underside of eaves reqs 1-hr. rating or heavy timber or fire-retardant treated wood if FSD ≥2 ft. to <5 ft. EXC ________ T302.1(1)
  - In sprinkler-protected building unrated OK if > 3 ft. to LL ______ T302.1(2)
  - Unrated OK if fireblocking between top wall plate & roof sheath T302.1(1&2)b
  - Unrated rake OK if sprinkler-protected & no gable vent opening T302.1(2)c

Subdivisions 21 IRC

- ☐ Unrated walls, unlimited openings & fire-rated projections OK to 0 ft. in subdivisions where all dwellings sprinklered & adjoining lot has open setback yard ≥ 6 ft. on opposite side of the property line ___T302.1(2)a

Site Identification

- ☐ Address numbers visible from street & contrasting background EXC __ 319.1
  - If access from private road & address not visible from street, provide pole or sign to identify the structure ______ 319.1
- ☐ Min 4-in.-high Arabic numerals, min. ½-in. stroke width ______ 319.1

FIRE SEPARATIONS

Fire-resistive construction materials such as gypsum board provide passive protection against the rapid spread of a fire. Generic rated assemblies are described in IBC Tables 721.1(1–3). Proprietary rated assemblies are described in GA-600-2021, *The Gypsum Association Fire Resistance and Sound Control Design Manual.*

Separation in Two-Family Dwellings 21 IRC

- ☐ 1-hr. common wall & floor separation reqd EXC ______ 302.3
  - ½-hr. OK if building protected by automatic sprinkler system ______ 302.3X1[6]
- ☐ Separation reqs apply regardless of whether LL exists between the 2 units_ 302.3[7]
- ☐ Fire-resistance rated floor/ceiling & wall assemblies must extend to & be tight against exterior wall ______ 302.3
- ☐ Wall assembly continuous from foundation to underside of roof EXC ______ 302.3
  - Attic separation can be draft stop if ceilings ⅝-in. Type X GB & framing supporting ceiling protected by ½-in. GB or equivalent ______ 302.3X2
- ☐ Floor/ceiling assemblies must extend to & be tight against exterior walls ___ 302.3
- ☐ Supporting construction below rated floor/ceiling assemblies reqs rating ≥ that of the floor/ceiling assembly ______ 302.3.1

6. 2018 reqd sprinkler system to comply w/ NFPA 13 rather than 13D.
7. New clarification that building can be considered a duplex rather than 2 separate SFDs or townhouses even if lot line exists at the separation line.

Penetrations of Rated Assemblies 21 IRC

Membrane penetrations are through only one side of a rated assembly. A through-penetration passes through both sides of the assembly.

- ☐ Through penetrations req installation as tested in approved rated assembly or as part of penetration firestop system EXC ______ 302.4.1.1&2
  - Steel, iron, or copper pipes, tubes, or conduit or water-filled sprinkler piping w/ annular space around them sealed w/ approved material______ 302.4.1X[8]
- ☐ Steel electrical boxes allowed as membrane penetrations if max. 16 sq. in. & aggregate area of openings ≤ 100 sq. in. over 100-sq.-ft. area **F4** ___302.4.2X1
- ☐ Steel boxes on opposite sides of wall OK if one of the following **F4** ___302.4.2X1
  1. Min. 24-in. horizontal separation if located in non-communicating stud cavities
  2. Horizontal separation ≥ wall depth & protected by cellulose or rock wool
  3. Solid fireblocking per 302.11 between the cavities w/ the boxes
  4. Both boxes protected w/ listed putty pads
  5. Other listed materials & methods
- ☐ L&L fire-rated boxes (plastics) allowed in walls AMI **F4** ______302.4.2X2
- ☐ Listed boxes on opposite sides of wall OK if one of the following **F4** __302.4.2X2
  1. Horizontal separation per terms of listing
  2. Solid fireblocking between the cavities w/ the boxes
  3. Both boxes protected w/ listed putty pads
  4. Other listed materials & methods
- ☐ Annular space between membrane & penetration box ⅛ in. max.___ 302.4.2X1&2
- ☐ Fire sprinklers or water-filled piping OK as membrane penetration if annular space covered by metal escutcheon plate ____ 302.4.2X3[8]
- ☐ Ceiling membrane penetrations by luminaires (recessed lights) allowed if protected w/ listed materials installed AMI ______302.4.2X4

8. Plastic sprinkler piping now allowed in through-penetrations and membrane penetrations when piping is filled with water.

FIRE SEPARATIONS

FIG. 4 **Membrane Penetrations of Rated Walls**

A 1-hr. rated wall typically has 1 layer of 5/8-in. Type X GB on each side. Walls with staggered studs reduce sound transmission between units.

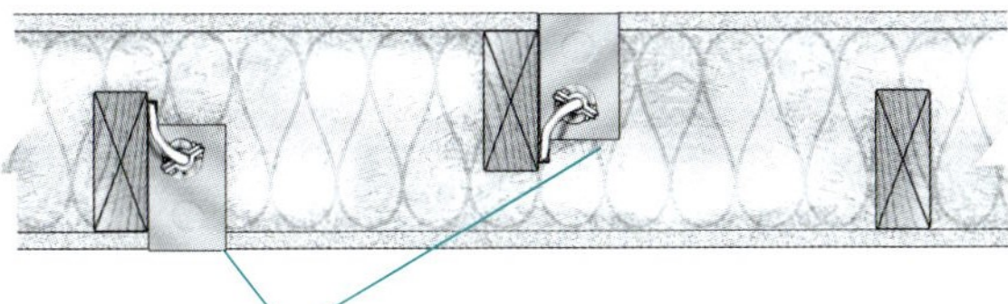

Steel electrical boxes on opposite sides of wall:

- Min. 24-in. horizontal separation in separate stud cavities, or
- Putty pads on both boxes, or
- Solid fireblocking, or
- Cellulose or mineral wool insulation ≥ distance as wall depth.

Same rules apply for listed plastic boxes except that horizontal separation is in accordance with the listing of the boxes.

Walls Separating Townhouse Units 21 IRC

- ☐ Construct w/ either common wall or 2 separate 1-hr. walls **F4** ___________ 302.2
- ☐ Common walls rated for fire exposure from both sides _______________ 302.2.2
- ☐ Common walls 1-hr. rated if automatic sprinklers, 2-hr. rated if not ______ 302.2.2
- ☐ No plumbing, mechanical equipment, ducts or vents in common walls EXC 302.2.2
  - Water-filled sprinkler piping OK in common wall___________________ 302.2.2[9]
- ☐ Electrical boxes meeting penetration rules OK in common wall **F4** ______ 302.2.2
- ☐ Extend common walls to exterior sheathing of frame exterior walls EXC _ 302.2.2[10]
  - OK to end at inside of exterior walls if cavity between end of common wall & exterior sheathing filled w/ min. 2 2-in. nominal wood studs ___ 302.2.2X[10]

9. Sprinkler piping was not allowed in common walls in the 2018 IRC.
10. Clarification on the common wall termination at building exterior.

Parapets for Townhouses 21 IRC

- ☐ Common & exterior walls separating townhouse units req parapets _____ 302.2.4
- ☐ Parapets req same fire resistance rating as supporting walls___________ 302.2.5
- ☐ Parapets min. 30 in. above roof if roof surfaces at same elevation **F5** __302.2.4#1
- ☐ If roof surfaces at different elevations & higher roof ≤30 in. above lower roof, parapet to extend min. 30 in. above lower roof surface **F5** _302.2.4#2
- ☐ Parapets not reqd in above 2 items if no roof openings within 4 ft. each side of common wall, roof covering min. Class C & sheathing noncombustible or FRT min. 4 ft. each side or min. 5/8-in. Type X GB on 2 × 2 ledgers **F5** ______ 302.2.4X
- ☐ If roof surfaces at different elevations & higher roof > 30 in. above lower roof, parapet not reqd, common wall above lower roof 1-hr. rated_____302.2.4#3

FIG. 5 **Townhouse Parapets**

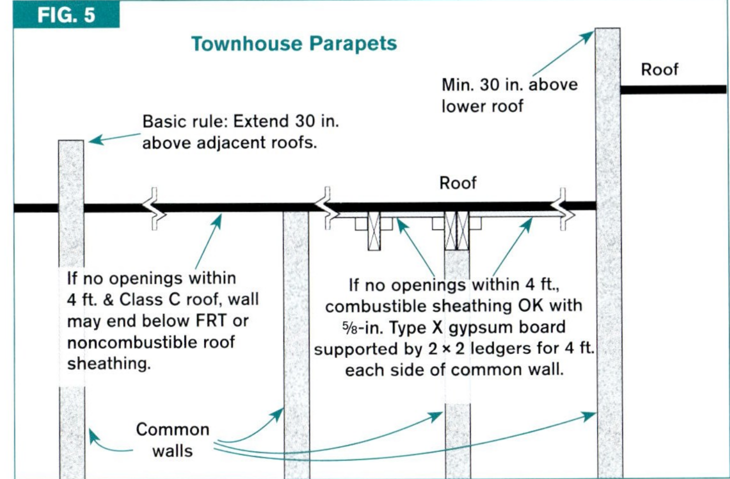

Separation from Garages — 21 IRC

- ☐ Min. ½-in. GB or equivalent on garage side of walls & ceilings common to house or shared attic space EXC **F6**,**7** ________ T302.6
  - Min. ⅝-in. Type X GB on ceiling under habitable room **F7** ________ T302.6
- ☐ Min. ½-in. GB on walls, beams, or other structures that support ceilings providing separation between house & garage ________ T302.6
- ☐ Garage walls perpendicular to dwelling OK unprotected unless supporting floor/ceiling separations ________ 302.6
- ☐ No direct openings between garage & sleeping rooms **F6** ________ 302.5.1
- ☐ Door to house either 20-minute fire-rated, solid wood min. 1⅜ in. thick, or solid or honeycomb steel min. 1⅜ in. thick **F6** ________ 302.5.1
- ☐ Door must be self-latching & self-closing **F6** ________ 302.5.1[11]
- ☐ Detached garages closer than 3 ft. to dwelling on same lot req ½-in. GB on interior side of garage walls facing house ________ T302.6

Garage Penetrations

- ☐ Ducts in garage & penetrating common walls min. 26-ga steel ________ 302.5.2
- ☐ No duct openings in garage ________ 302.5.2
- ☐ Seal penetrations of common walls with approved material ________ 302.5.3
- ☐ Sealant does not have to comply with ASTM E 136 ________ 302.11#4

FIG. 6 **Door Between House & Garage**

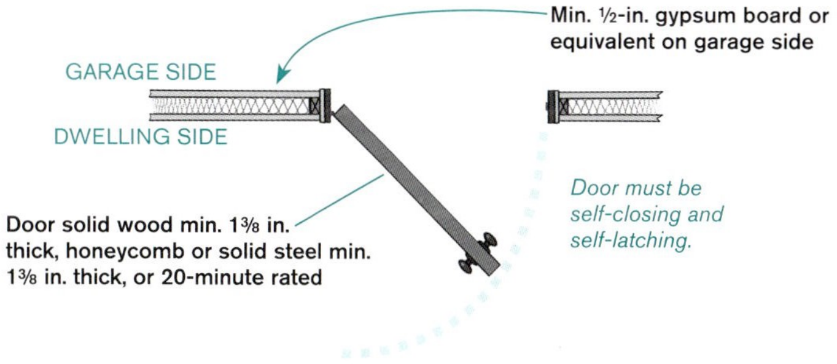

Min. ½-in. gypsum board or equivalent on garage side

GARAGE SIDE

DWELLING SIDE

Door solid wood min. 1⅜ in. thick, honeycomb or solid steel min. 1⅜ in. thick, or 20-minute rated

Door must be self-closing and self-latching.

FIG. 7 **Fire Separation from Garage**

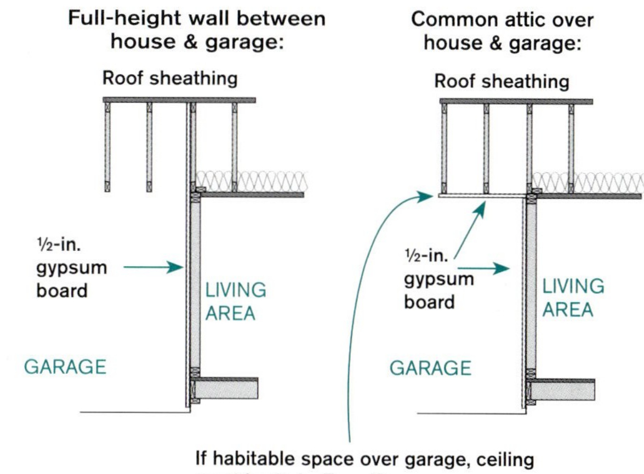

If habitable space over garage, ceiling must be ⅝-in. Type X.

*See **T75** for fastening reqs for GB.*

Note: The IRC does not directly address the question of whether an electrical panel can penetrate the reqd ½-in. GB on the garage side of the common wall. Many jurisdictions interpret this to mean that the panel must either be in a chase outside the GB or, if recessed into the wall, be "5-sided" with GB around & behind the panel.

11. Doors must now be self-latching as well as self-closing.

FIREBLOCKING & DRAFTSTOPPING

Fireblocking slows the spread of fire in small concealed spaces, and draftstopping accomplishes the same function in larger concealed areas.

Fireblocking — 21 IRC

- ☐ Purpose is to cut off concealed draft openings **F9** ______ 302.11
- ☐ Materials can be 2-in. lumber, 2 thicknesses 1-in. lumber w/ joints lapped, 23/32-in. WSP w/ joints backed, 3/4-in. particleboard w/ joints backed, 1/2-in. GB, 1/4-in. cement-based millboard, mineral wool or glass fiber batts securely retained, or cellulose per ASTM E199 or UL 263 ___ 302.11.1
- ☐ 10 ft. horizontal OK w/ mineral or glass fiber batts **F4** ______ 302.11.1.1
- ☐ Unfaced fiberglass must fill entire cavity to height of 16 in. & be tightly packed around pipes or similar obstructions **F11** ______ 302.11.1.2
- ☐ Loose-fill insulation as fireblocking must meet test reqs for ability to remain in place & retard spread of fire & hot gases ______ 302.11.1.3
- ☐ Approved caulking does not have to comply w/ ASTM E-136 ____ 302.11#4
- ☐ Required locations of fireblocking in wood-frame construction: ______ 302.11
  - In walls vertically at ceiling & floor levels, horizontally max. 10-ft. intervals
  - Intersections of concealed vertical/horizontal spaces such as occur at coved ceilings **F8** & soffits **F9**
  - Concealed spaces between stair stringers at top & bottom of run
  - Openings around vents, ducts, pipes & cables at ceilings & floors **F10**
  - In space between chimneys & combustible framing **F11**
  - In two-family dwelling cornices at line of unit separation

Draftstopping

- ☐ If usable space above & below a floor/ceiling assembly using open-web trusses or a suspended ceiling, draftstopping reqd to limit concealed space to approximately equal areas 1,000 sq. ft. each ______ 302.12
- ☐ Materials min. 1/2-in. GB, 3/8-in. WSP, or equivalent ______ 302.12.1
- ☐ Install parallel to floor framing members ______ 302.12.1

FIG. 8

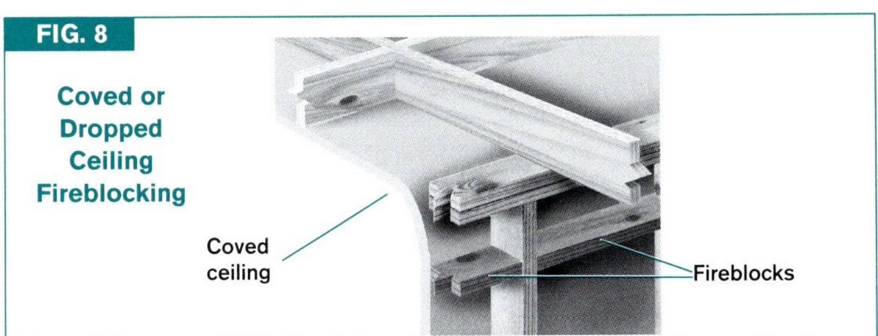

FIG. 9

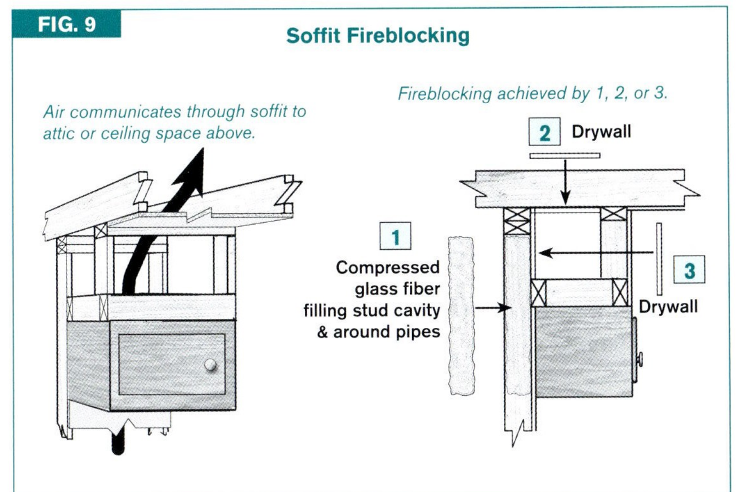

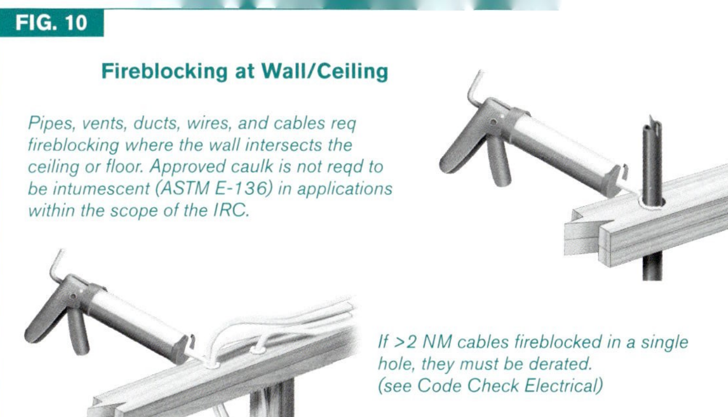

FIG. 10 Fireblocking at Wall/Ceiling

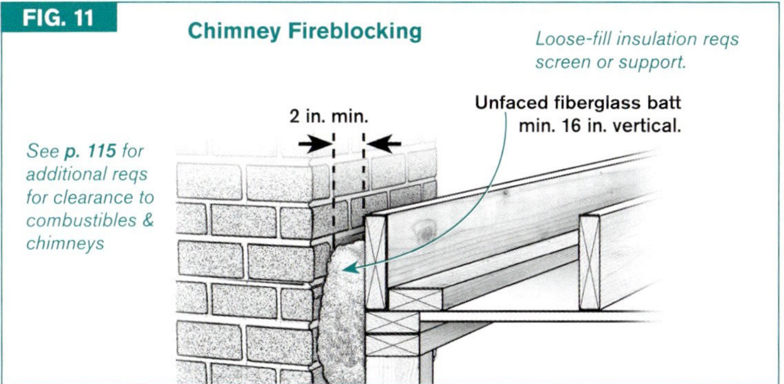

FIG. 11 Chimney Fireblocking

Fire Protection of Floors & Underside of Stairs 21 IRC

- ☐ Underside of floor assembly reqs ½-in. GB or ⅝-in. WSP EXC **F12** _ 302.13
  - Over a space protected with approved fire sprinkler system _____ 302.13X1
  - Over crawlspace w/ no storage or heating appliances __________ 302.13X2
  - Unprotected portion of crawlspace ≤ 80 sq. ft. & separated by fireblocking from remainder of floor assembly ________________ 302.13X3
  - Floor constructed of dimensional or structural composite lumber ≥ 2 × 10 nominal or floor assemblies of equal fire performance ___ 302.13X4
- ☐ OK to penetrate floor for ducts, wires, piping, etc. **F12** _____________ 302.13
- ☐ Accessible enclosed areas under stairs reqs min. ½-in. GB __________ 302.7

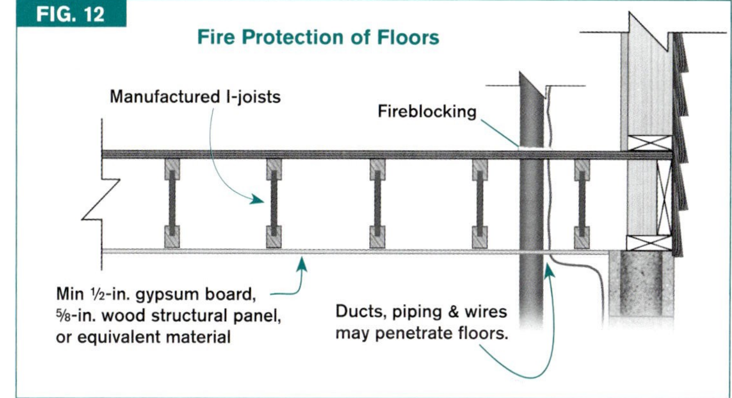

FIG. 12 Fire Protection of Floors

LOADS & ALLOWABLE DEFLECTION

General — 21 IRC

- ☐ Dead load = actual weights of materials + fixed service equipment ___ 301.4
- ☐ Live loads per **T4** ___ 301.5
- ☐ Roof loads = greater of ground snow load **T2** or live load in **T4** ___ 301.6
- ☐ Allowable deflections under gravity loads or wind loads **T3** ___ 301.7

TABLE 3 — ALLOWABLE DEFLECTION OF STRUCTURAL MEMBERS[A] ◆ T301.7

Structural Member	Deflection
Rafters > 3:12 slope & no finished ceiling attached to rafters	*L*/180
Interior walls and partitions	*H*/180
Floors	*L*/360
Ceilings w/ brittle finishes – including plaster & stucco	*L*/360
Ceilings w/ flexible finishes – including gypsum board	*L*/240
All other structural members	*L*/240
Exterior walls – wind loads w/ plaster or stucco finishes	*H*/360
Exterior walls – wind loads w/ other brittle finishes	*H*/240
Exterior walls – wind loads w/ flexible finishes & GB interior	*H*/180
Exterior walls – wind loads w/ flexible finishes & no GB	*H*/120
Lintels supporting masonry veneer walls	*L*/600

A. For cantilevers, *L* shall be considered twice the length of the cantilever.

TABLE 4 — MINIMUM LIVE LOADS[12] ◆ T301.5

Use	Uniform Load (psf)	Concentrated Load (lb)
Uninhabitable attic without storage **F73**	10	
Uninhabitable attic with limited storage[A] **F73**	20	
Habitable attics & attics with fixed stairs	30	
Sleeping rooms	30	
Rooms other than sleeping rooms	40	
Exterior balconies & decks[B]	40	
Guards		200[C]
Guard infill components		50[D]
Handrails		200[E]
Passenger vehicle garages	50[F]	2,000[F]
Sleeping areas[G]	30	
Other than sleeping areas[G]	40	
Stairs	40[H]	300[H]

A. 10 psf for portions of joists or truss bottom chords not in limited storage area.
B. Per snow load if > 40 psf, also check w/ local jurisdiction for amendments.
C. If top of guard is a handrail, loads are applied in any direction. If not a handrail, loads are considered in vertical downward direction or horizontally away from walking surface.[13]
D. Load applied horizontally over a 1-sq.-ft. area.
E. Single concentrated load applied in any direction.
F. Elevated garages must be capable of supporting either the uniformly distributed load or a 2,000-lb. load over a 4.5-in. × 4.5-in. area, whichever produces the greater stress.
G. Determines whether **T53** or **T54** is to be applied.
H. Individual treads must be capable of supporting either the uniformly distributed load or a 300-lb. load over a 2-in. × 2-in. area, whichever produces the greater stress.

12. Table reformatted in 2021 to distinguish concentrated loads from uniform loads that were previously explained through footnotes in the 2018 edition. Though other minor clarifications were made, the table basically applies equally to the 2018 IRC.

13. Previous code applied loads in any direction on guard as well as on handrail guard.

STORY HEIGHT & ROOM DIMENSIONS

Maximum Story Heights — 21 IRC

- ☐ Max. story height for wood-frame walls 11 ft. 7 in. EXC ________ 301.3#1
  - 13 ft. 7 in. OK if max. stud height 12 ft. & in accordance w/ exceptions 2 & 3 to section 602.3.1 *(p. 58)* & in compliance w/ bracing reqs *(p. 69)* or if engineered design ________ 301.3#1X[14]
- ☐ Cold-formed steel 11 ft. 7 in., max. bearing wall stud height 10 ft. __ 301.3#2
- ☐ Masonry walls 13 ft. 7 in., bearing wall clear height max. 12 ft., additional 8 ft. of bearing wall clear height OK at gable ends ______ 301.3#3
- ☐ ICF walls 11 ft. 7 in., max. unsupported wall height 10 ft. ________ 301.3#4
- ☐ SIP walls 11 ft. 7 in., bearing wall height per story max. 10 ft. ______ 301.3#5
- ☐ Engineered design per IBC reqd when exceeding above heights _____ 301.3

Room Areas

- ☐ Habitable room floor areas min. 70 sq. ft.—except kitchens ________ 304.1
- ☐ Min. horizontal dimension in any direction 7 ft.—except kitchens _____ 304.2
- ☐ Areas w/ sloping ceilings <5 ft. & areas w/ furred ceiling <7 ft. in height do not count toward reqd room dimensions ____________ 304.3

Bathroom Fixture Clearances

(See Code Check Plumbing for reqs in areas using the UPC.)

- ☐ 21 in. clearance in front of toilets and lavatory sinks/vanities ________ 307.1
- ☐ Shower min. 30 × 30 in. w/ 24 in. clearance in front of opening ______ 307.1
- ☐ Hinged shower doors must open outward ____________________ 2708.1
- ☐ 15 in. clearance each side of centerline of toilet or bidet __________ 307.1
- ☐ Tub/shower floors & walls nonabsorbent surface to 6 ft. above floor ___ 307.2

14. New allowance for taller stories w/o engineering if meeting these framing reqs. These include location in an area w/ a ground snow load ≤30 psf.

Minimum Ceiling Height — 21 IRC

- ☐ Bathrooms, toilet rooms & laundries min. 6 ft. 8 in.______________ 305.1
- ☐ Habitable space, hallways & such areas in basements: 7 ft. EXC _____ 305.1
  - Reqd floor area of rooms w/ sloped ceilings min. 50% ≥7 ft. AFF, portions <5 ft. do not count toward reqd room area **F13** ________ 305.1X1
  - Height above bathroom & toilet room fixtures not to interfere w/ use of fixture, height above shower min. 6 ft. 8 in. for 30-in. × 30-in. area _305.1X2
  - Beams, ducts, etc. in habitable space of basements OK 6 ft. 4 in. _305.1X3
  - Beams & girders OK to project to 6 ft. 6 in. AFF if clear width between them min. 36 in. ______________ 305.1X4[15]

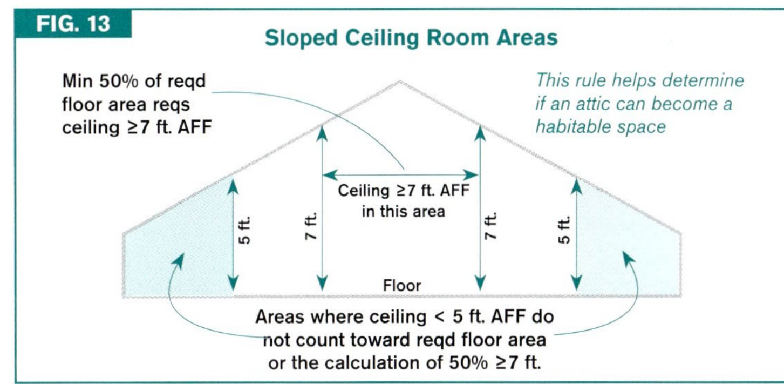

FIG. 13 Sloped Ceiling Room Areas

15. New allowance for height to beams is same height as the reqd egress door.

HABITABILITY

Light — 21 IRC

- ☐ Habitable rooms req natural light w/ glazing ≥8% floor area EXC — 303.1
  - Artificial light & whole-house mechanical ventilation system present — 303.1X3
- ☐ Artificial light reqd for interior stairs — 303.7

Ventilation

- ☐ Habitable rooms req natural ventilation openings to outdoor air — 303.1
- ☐ Natural ventilation reqd by windows, doors, skylights, louvers, or other approved openings min. 4% of floor area of room or area EXC — 303.1
  - (Habitable rooms other than kitchens) Whole-house mechanical ventilation system or mechanical ventilation capable of 0.35 room ACH — 303.1X1[16]
  - Kitchen windows need not be openable if local exhaust installed — 303.1X2[17]

Light & Ventilation from Adjoining Rooms

- ☐ Light & ventilation OK from adjoining rooms if opening between them is ≥½ of common wall, min. 25 sq. ft. & min. 10% interior room area — 303.2
- ☐ Reqd ventilation openings can be to sunroom additions if >40% of the sunroom is open or only enclosed by screening — 303.1X4
- ☐ Light & ventilation OK from adjoining sunroom or patio cover if opening between them is min. 20 sq. ft. & min. 10% of area of interior room — 303.2X
- ☐ Reqd glazed openings permitted to open onto sunroom additions if sunroom is 40% open or screened & has min. 7-ft. ceiling — 303.9.1

Heat

- ☐ Habitable rooms req heating capable of maintaining 68°F at 3 ft. above floor & 2 ft. from exterior walls (exc Hawaii) — 303.10
- ☐ Portable space heaters not OK as means of compliance — 303.10

Sanitation — 21 IRC

- ☐ Every dwelling reqs a WC, lav & a tub or shower — 306.1
- ☐ Every dwelling reqs a kitchen w/ a sink — 306.2
- ☐ Connection reqd to sanitary sewer or private sewage disposal system — 306.3
- ☐ Sinks, lavs, tubs, showers, bidets & laundry req hot & cold water — 306.3

Bathrooms

- ☐ Bathrooms & toilet rooms req min. 3-sq.-ft. glazing 50% openable EXC — 303.3
  - Glazed areas not reqd if artificial light & local exhaust installed; exhaust air must go directly to out of doors — 303.3X

ASHRAE 62.2 and many state energy codes recommend mechanical ventilation for all kitchens, bathrooms, and toilet rooms. *See **p. 217***

FINISH SURFACES & INSULATION

General — 21 IRC

- ☐ Wall & ceiling finishes max. flame spread index 200, max. smoke-developed index 450 in accordance with ASTM E-84 / UL 723 EXC — 302.9.1–3
  - Baseboards, trim, moldings, handrails, windows, doors, etc. — 302.9.1X
- ☐ Insulation & facing max. flame spread index 25, max. smoke-developed index 450 in accordance with ASTM E-84 / UL 723 EXC — 302.10.1
  - Facing material exempt when in substantial contact with unexposed surface of wall, floor, or ceiling—i.e., not visible in finished job — 302.10.1X1

GARAGES & CARPORTS

General — 21 IRC

- ☐ Floor surfaces approved noncombustible material EXC — 309.1&2
- ☐ • Asphalt OK at ground level in carports — 309.2X
- ☐ Floor sloped to a drain or to main vehicle entry doorway — 309.1&2
- ☐ Carports not open on 2 sides considered a garage — 309.2
- ☐ Garage doors req permanent MFR label — 609.4.1[18]

16. The 2018 IRC did not have the option of the system w/ 0.35 ACH.
17. The 2018 IRC did not have a separate rule for kitchens.

18. Labeling now reqd and must include positive and negative design wind pressure rating.

FOAM PLASTICS

While foam plastic insulation has a flame spread and smoke-developed index, it is still considered flammable, and in most applications requires either a thermal or ignition barrier (a slightly lesser degree of protection than a thermal barrier). Aside from these prescriptive barriers, equivalent or alternative materials or assemblies are often used. These require acceptance by the AHJ, typically on the basis of an ICC Evaluation Report. The prescriptive barriers in the code are as follows:

- A ***thermal barrier*** = min. ½-in. GB or 23/32-in. WSP or NFPA 275 equivalent.
- An ***ignition barrier*** = 1½-in. mineral fiber insulation, ¼-in. WSP, ⅛-in. particle board, ¼-in. hardboard, ⅜-in. GB, min. 0.016-in. steel, or ¼-in. fiber cement board.

Approvals & Labeling — 21 IRC

- ☐ Materials delivered to job site req labeling by an approved agency ________ 316.2
- ☐ Max. flame spread index 75, max. smoke-developed index 450 ___________ 316.3

Areas of Very Heavy Probability of Termite Infestation

- ☐ No foam plastics on exterior face or under foundation walls or slab foundations below grade; plastic min. 6 in. above grade & exposed earth EXC _316.7 & 318.4
  - Buildings w/ noncombustible structural members or PPT wood _____ 318.4X1
  - Approved protection method *(see p. 51)* is used ________________ 318.4X2
  - Interior side of basement walls ______________________________ 318.4X3
- ☐ Not reqd on walking surface of structural floor where covered by min. ½-in. WSP or equivalent ______________________ 316.5.13

Thermal Barriers — 21 IRC

- ☐ Thermal barrier reqd to separate foam from building interior EXC ______ 316.4
  - Foam approved on basis of approved tests (NFPA 286, FM 4880, UL 1040, or UL 1715) in assemblies equal to end use configuration or as evidenced by ICC Evaluation Report per ICC AC 377 _______________ 316.6

Thermal Barrier Exemptions

- ☐ Where separated from building interior by ≥1-in. masonry or concrete _ 316.5.1
- ☐ In roof assemblies where separated from building interior by T&G wood planks or min. 15/32-in. WSP w/ edges supported ____ 316.5.2
- ☐ In attic or crawlspace w/ access, not for storage & where entered only for purposes of repair or maintenance (e.g., maintenance of heating equipment) & where plastic protected by ignition barrier ____316.5.3&4
- ☐ Foam-filled exterior door & garage doors exempt _______________316.5.5&6
- ☐ Foam backer board exempt where separated from building interior by ≥2-in. mineral fiber insulation or over existing wall finish (residing) 316.5.7&8
- ☐ Interior trim w/ min. density 20 lb./cu. ft., max. ½ in. thick × 8 in. wide, max. 10% of aggregate area of wall or ceiling area any room or space ____ 316.5.9
- ☐ OK to apply foam to sills & headers in perimeter joist space max. 3¼ in. thick, density 0.5 – 2.0 lb./cu. ft., flame spread index max. 25 ___________316.5.11
- ☐ Foam sheathing exposed to attic reqs ignition barrier _____________316.5.12

AUTOMATIC FIRE SPRINKLER SYSTEMS

The building section of the IRC tells us *when* we need to install automatic fire sprinklers. The methods for *how* we do this are in the plumbing section of the code. NFPA has different standards for different occupancy types. NFPA 13D is for townhouses and 1- & 2-family dwellings and is the basis of the IRC fire sprinkler requirements. NFPA 13 is the standard for commercial systems, and NFPA 13R is for low-rise multifamily residential.

Residential systems differ from commercial systems. Residential systems operate at much lower flows than commercial and are designed to provide the occupants time to escape before a dwelling reaches "flashover"; their purpose is to protect the occupants rather than the building. Residential sprinkler piping systems are designed to provide flow to 2 sprinkler heads at the same time, whereas commercial systems are required to supply water flow to larger areas. Residential sprinklers have faster response times than commercial. Their spray pattern is to the sides, rather than the "umbrella" pattern of commercial sprinklers. UL 1626 requires residential sprinklers to discharge water uniformly on the walls within 28 in. of the ceiling.

Local rules vary on the extent of an addition or remodel that might trigger a need for full compliance. In some jurisdictions the rule will be based on crossing a threshold amount of overall area or the percentage of building being remodeled. Always check with the local jurisdiction on the rules adopted in your area.

General — 21 IRC

- ☐ Required in new townhouses & 1&2FD EXC ____ 313.1&2
  - Additions or alterations to existing dwellings w/o sprinklers ____ 313.1X&2X
- ☐ Partial systems only allowed when sprinklers not reqd ____ 2904.1
- ☐ IRC 2904 considered equivalent to NFPA 13D ____ 2904.1
- ☐ May be multipurpose system or stand-alone system ____ 2904.1
- ☐ Stand-alone system = independent from potable water ____ 2904.1
- ☐ Multipurpose system = shared w/ potable water system **F14** ____ 2904.1

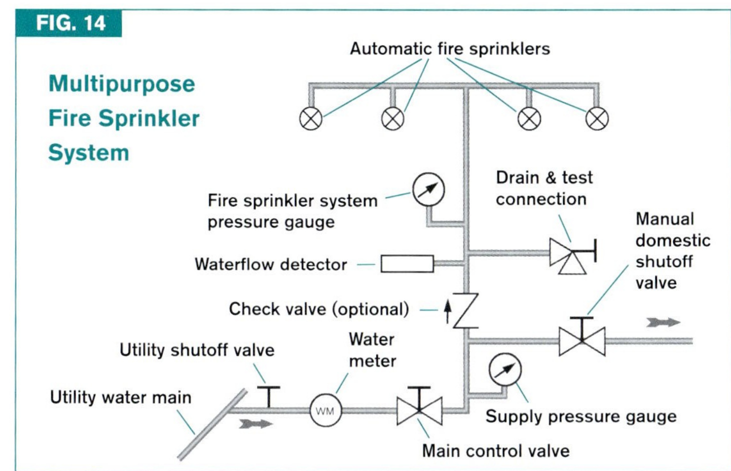

Required Locations of Protection — 21 IRC

- ☐ Must protect all areas of dwelling unit EXC ____ 2904.1.1
  - Attics, crawlspaces & normally unoccupied concealed spaces w/o fuel-fired appliances ____ 2904.1.1X1
  - Attics, crawlspaces, etc. with fuel-fired appliances req sprinklers directly over appliance, not elsewhere in that space ____ 2904.1.1X1
  - Pantries, clothes closets & linen closets ≤24 sq. ft. w/ smallest dimension ≤3 ft. & GB surfaces on walls & ceilings ____ 2904.1.1X2
  - Bathrooms ≤55 sq. ft ____ 2904.1.1X3
  - Garages, carports, exterior porches & unheated entry areas (e.g., mud rooms) that are adjacent to an exterior door ____ 2904.1.1X4

Coverage & Obstructions — 21 IRC

- ☐ Coverage area of a single sprinkler AMI & not >400 sq. ft. ______2904.2.4.1
- ☐ Install additional sprinklers to cover obstructed areas **F15, T5** ____2904.2.4.2
- ☐ Ceiling (pendant) sprinklers ≤3 ft. of center of ceiling paddle fan considered obstructed ____ 2904.2.4.2.1
- ☐ Sidewall sprinklers within 5 ft. of ceiling paddle fan considered obstructed ____ 2904.2.4.2.2
- ☐ Painting, caulking, or modifying sprinklers prohibited____ 2904.2.6
- ☐ MFR published flow rates for 8-ft. ceilings also allowed for sprinklers in areas w/ sloped ceiling w/o significant irregularities in surface; sprinklers above any communicating openings. See MFR instructions ____ 2904.4.1.1[19]

TABLE 5 — CLEARANCES TO OBSTRUCTIONS ◆ F2904.2.4.2

Distance A_1 does not exceed	Min. distance of B_1	Distance A_2 does not exceed	Min. distance of B_2
1 in.	1½ ft.	1 in.	8 ft.
3 in.	3 ft.	2 in.	10 ft.
5 in.	4 ft.	3 in.	11 ft.
7 in.	4½ ft.	4 in.	12 ft.
9 in.	6 ft.	6 in.	13 ft.
11 in.	6½ ft.	7 in.	14 ft.
14 in.	7 ft.	9 in.	15 ft.
		11 in.	16 ft.
		14 in.	17 ft.

19. A new section in the 2021 IRC allows standard flow rates to apply to sprinklers in sloped ceiling areas in accordance with instructions in sprinkler MFR's cut sheets.

FIG. 15 Sprinkler Clearances to Obstructions

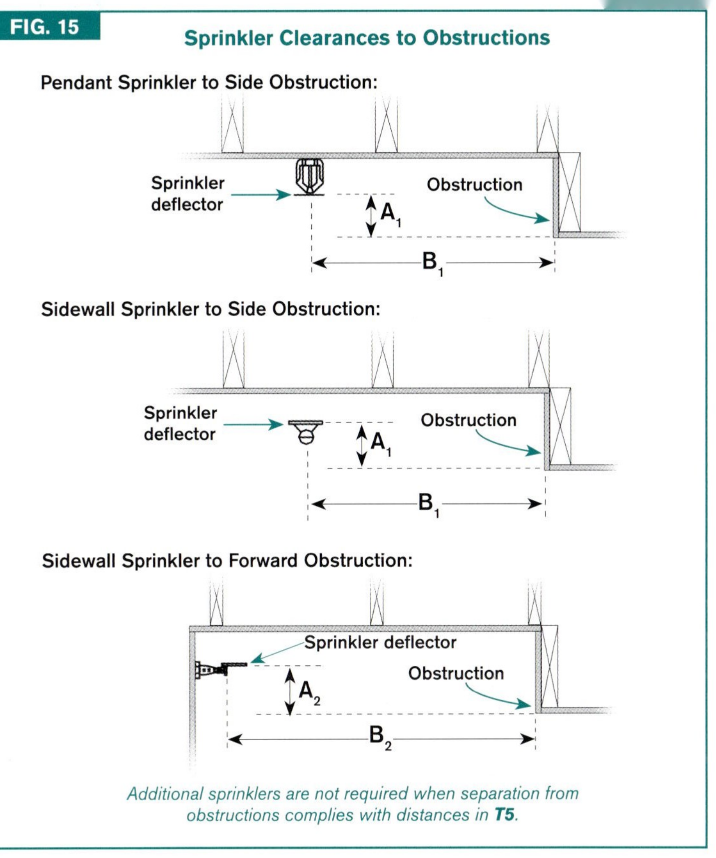

*Additional sprinklers are not required when separation from obstructions complies with distances in **T5**.*

Sprinklers — 21 IRC

- ☐ Must be new, rated as residential type & installed AMI ____________ 2904.2
- ☐ Temperature rating ≥135°F & ≤225°F ____________ 2904.2.1[20]
- ☐ Separation from heat sources AMI ____________ 2904.2.1
- ☐ Intermediate temperature sprinklers (rating 175°F - 225°F) reqd in attics, under skylights where sprinkler exposed to direct sunlight, in concealed spaces directly beneath roof, or within distance in **T6**, **F16** ________ 2904.2.2

TABLE 6 — REQUIRED LOCATIONS OF INTERMEDIATE TEMPERATURE SPRINKLERS ◆ T2904.2.2

Type of Heat Source	Min. Distance[A]	Max. Distance[A]
Coal & wood burning stoves	12 in.	42 in.
Front of recessed fireplace	36 in.	60 in.
Side of open or recessed fireplace	12 in.	36 in.
Front of wall mounted warm air register	18 in.	36 in.
Heating duct—not insulated	9 in.	18 in.
Hot water pipe—not insulated	6 in.	12 in.
Kitchen range top	9 in.	18 in.
Luminaire up to 250 watts	3 in.	6 in.
Luminaire >250 watts to 499 watts	6 in.	12 in.
Oven	9 in.	18 in.
Side of ceiling or wall warm air register	12 in.	24 in.
Vent connector or chimney connector	9 in.	18 in.
WH, furnace, or boiler	3 in.	6 in.

A. Distances are measured in a straight line from nearest edge of heat source to nearest edge of sprinkler.

FIG. 16 Example of Distance to Heat Source

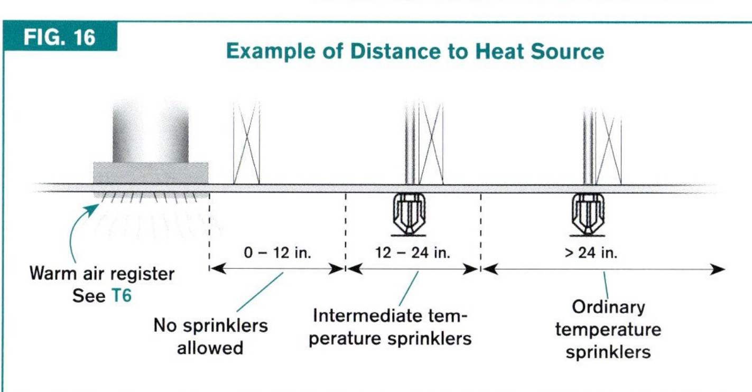

Piping Systems — 21 IRC

- ☐ Pipe support reqs same as water supply pipe ____________ 2904.3
- ☐ Nonmetallic pipe reqs listing as sprinkler pipe (CPVC is orange) __ 2904.3.1
- ☐ Protect nonmetallic pipe from exposure to living space w/ GB or plywood w/ 15-min. finish EXC ____________ 2904.3.1.1
  - Not reqd in areas where sprinkler protection not reqd ______ 2904.3.1.1X1
  - Not reqd when permitted by pipe listing ____________ 2904.3.1.1X2
- ☐ No valves ahead of sprinkler exc main shutoff ____________ 2904.3.2
- ☐ Only one dwelling unit after main shutoff ____________ 2904.3.3
- ☐ Provide means to drain down system **F14** ____________ 2904.3.4

*Pipe layouts can be a tree system, such as **F14**, or a loop system (where more than one path supplies each sprinkler), or a network system shared with the plumbing fixtures (where water flows through all of the network when any fixture is opened).*

20. The 2018 IRC had a maximum temperature rating of 170°F for "ordinary temperature" sprinkler locations. NFPA 13D now allows intermediate temperature sprinklers in all areas.

Freezing Areas — 21 IRC

- ☐ Protect from freezing by insulation, heat, or both EXC ____________ 2904.2.3
  - Dry-pipe system listed for residential applications __________ 2904.2.3#1[21]
  - Dry-type sprinklers from a non-freezing area into a freezing area 2904.2.3#2

Flow Rates

- ☐ Determine rate for each sprinkler based on coverage area, ceiling configuration & temperature rating AMI ________________ 2904.4.1
- ☐ Rate for room w/ 1 sprinkler = rate for that sprinkler _____________ 2904.4.2
- ☐ Rate for room w/ 2 sprinklers = 2× highest-rated sprinkler _______ 2904.4.2
- ☐ System design flow rate based on room w/ largest flow rate ______ 2904.4.2
- ☐ Flow rate AMI for ceilings not smooth, flat & horizontal ___________ 2904.4.2

Water Supply & Pipe Size

- ☐ Water supply to provide reqd flow rate for 7 minutes for 1-story dwelling units <2,000 sq. ft. ________________________ 2904.5.2
- ☐ Water supply to provide reqd flow rate for 10 minutes for dwelling units ≥2 stories or ≥2,000 sq. ft. __________________ 2904.5.2
- ☐ Pipe sizes to meet reqd flow rate to sprinklers—flow to plumbing fixtures need not be added to sprinkler design flow ________________ 2904.6
- ☐ Sizing method prescriptive per IRC/NFPA 13D or hydraulic calculation _ 2904.6.1
- ☐ Min. pipe size to any sprinkler ¾ in.; threaded adapter fittings attaching sprinklers to piping min. ½ in. nominal _________________ 2904.6.1
- ☐ Prescriptive calculation method based on static pressure at water purveyor (or pressure control setting of well), pipe size & friction losses, device losses (e.g., filter) & elevation losses _____________________ 2904.6.2

The IRC and NFPA 13D contain tables based on flow rate, diameter, and length of pipe for water service pipe, meter losses, and distribution piping, as well as a table for elevation losses. The tables can be viewed at codes.iccsafe.org.

21. The option of a listed dry-pipe system is new.

Preconcealment Inspection (Rough Inspection) — 21 IRC

- ☐ Verify the following prior to concealment of any sprinkler piping ____ 2904.8.1
  1. Sprinklers installed in all reqd areas.
  2. Additional sprinklers as necessitated by obstructions.
  3. Sprinklers are correct temperature rating & distance from heat sources.
  4. Pipe size ≥ size determined by prescriptive or hydraulic calculation.
  5. Pipe length not exceeding length permitted in prescriptive tables.
  6. Nonmetallic piping is listed for use w/ fire sprinklers.
  7. Pipes supported AMI per pipe MFR & sprinkler MFR.
  8. Pressure test of system @ working pressure 15 min. or air test for nonplastic pipe 50 psi 15 min., or gas test of PEX AMI

Final Inspection

- ☐ Provide owner's manual for the system ________________ 2904.7 & 2904.8.2
- ☐ Provide warning sign at main shutoff **F17** ______________ 2904.7 & 2904.8.2
- ☐ Verify the following upon completion of the system _____________ 2904.8.2
  1. Sprinklers not painted, damaged, or otherwise hindered from operating.
  2. Where system supplied by pump, verify automatic start.
  3. No added components, such as pressure-reducing valves, water softeners, or water filters that were not part of the original design.

FIG. 17

Required Text of Fire Sprinkler Warning Sign

Sign must be installed at main water shutoff (typically white lettering on red background).

WARNING

The water system for this home supplies fire sprinklers that require certain flows and pressures to fight a fire. Devices that restrict the flow or decrease the pressure or automatically shut off the water to the fire sprinkler system, such as water softeners, filtration systems, and automatic shutoff valves, shall not be added to this system without a review of the fire sprinkler system by a fire protection specialist.

DO NOT REMOVE THIS SIGN

SMOKE ALARMS

Smoke alarms and detectors can have photoelectric or ionization technology. See www.codecheck.com/videos for Skip Walker's comparison of the two, and the reason we recommend smoke alarms using photoelectric technology.

General — 21 IRC

- ☐ Alarms must comply w/ NFPA 72 ____ 314.1
- ☐ Alarms must be listed to UL 217 ____ 314.1.1
- ☐ Combination smoke & CO alarms must also be listed to UL 2034 ____ 314.1.1

Required Locations

- ☐ Each sleeping room **F18 A** ____ 314.3#1
- ☐ In immediate vicinity outside each sleeping room **F18 B** ____ 314.3#2
- ☐ Min 1 on each story, including basements & habitable attics ____ 314.3#3
- ☐ If open split level < 1 story below upper level, only upper alarm reqd 314.3#3
- ☐ Min 3 ft. from door to bath w/ tub or shower EXC **F18 C** ____ 314.3#4
  - When this rule would prevent placement in a reqd location ____ 314.3#4
- ☐ 1 additional alarm reqd in a room open to a hallway serving bedrooms where ceiling height exceeds that of the hallway by 24 in. or more ____ 314.3#5[22]
- ☐ When alterations, repairs & additions that req a permit occur alarms are reqd in same locations as for new construction EXC ____ 314.2.2
  - Work only on exterior (e.g., roofing, windows, decks) or installation or repairs of plumbing or mechanical systems ____ 314.2.2X

Horizontal Distances from Cooking Appliances — 22 NFPA 72

- ☐ Prior to 1/1/23, if 10 ft. – 20 ft., either photoelectric or hush button, or listed per UL 217 8th or newer edition or UL 268 7th edition for resistance to common nuisance sources from cooking **F18 D** ____ 29.11.3.4(4)(a)
- ☐ After 1/1/23, if 10 ft. – 20 ft., above listing mandatory **F18 D** ____ 29.11.3.4(4)(b)
- ☐ If <10 ft. would prohibit placement of reqd alarms, radial distance of 6 ft. OK prior to 1/1/23 w/ photoelectric, or if listed as above. After 1/1/23, listing is mandatory **F18 E** ____ 29.11.3.4(5)[23]

Additional Required Locations — 22 NFPA 72

- ☐ Within 21 ft. path of travel outside of door to each sleeping area ____ 29.8.1.1(2)
- ☐ Every level of residential board & care occupancy ____ 29.8.1.1(4)
- ☐ In living areas of guest suites ____ 29.8.1.1(5)
- ☐ If area outside sleeping area is separated from adjacent living areas by a door, alarm also reqd on living area side of door ____ 29.8.1.2
- ☐ Where interior floor area >1,000 sq. ft. for given level, max. travel distance to alarm from any point 30 ft., or min. 1 alarm per 500 ft. 29.8.1.3.1
- ☐ Within 36 in. horizontal of high side of peaked ceiling or ceiling w/ rise greater than 1:8, min. 4 in. from peak or adjoining wall **F19** ____ 29.11.3.1&2
- ☐ Wall-mounted detectors max. 12 in. below adjoining ceiling **F19** ____ 29.11.3.3
- ☐ Where stairs lead to occupiable levels, locate such that smoke rising in stairway not prevented by a door from reaching the alarm ____ 29.11.3.4(9)
- ☐ Locate basement alarm on ceiling near entry to stairs ____ 29.11.3.4(10)
- ☐ For coffered ceilings, locate on highest portion or on sloped portion max. 12 in. vertically down from highest point ____ 29.11.3.4(11)
- ☐ Beam ceilings or intersecting beams (waffle type) normal spacing OK if beam depths <10% of ceiling height ____ 29.11.3.4(12)

Restricted Locations

- ☐ Not in garages, unfinished attics, or other spaces where temperatures can be <40°F or >100°F ____ 29.11.3.4(2)
- ☐ Not where mounting surface could be warmer or cooler than room, such as ceiling w/ uninsulated attic—mount on an inside wall ____ 29.11.3.4(3)
- ☐ Not within 3 ft. of door to bath w/ tub or shower EXC **F18 C** ____ 29.11.3.4(6)
  - When listed for installation in close proximity to such locations 29.11.3.4(6)
- ☐ Min. 3 ft. from supply registers of heating or cooling system & outside direct air flow from registers **F18 F** ____ 2911.3.4(7)
- ☐ Min. 3 ft. from tip of ceiling paddle fan blade **F18 G** ____ 2911.3.4(8)

22. New reqd location for rooms and hallways arranged as described.
23. This UL standard change and marking req is new in the 21 IRC and NFPA 72.

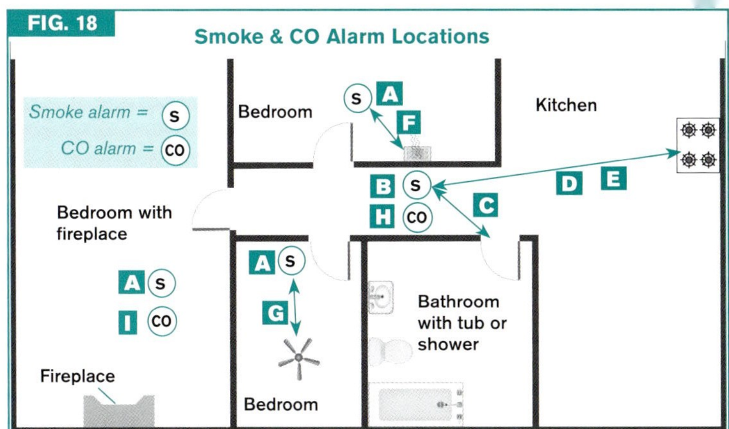

CARBON MONOXIDE ALARMS

Carbon monoxide (CO) alarms are important life-safety devices. CO is roughly the same molecular weight as air. Warm CO will therefore rise, but it can also stratify. The placement of CO alarms should be in accord with manufacturer's instructions.

General — 21 IRC

- ☐ Alarms must comply w/ UL 2034 ____ 315.1.1
- ☐ Combo smoke/CO alarms OK if L&L to UL 217 & UL 2034 ____ 315.1.1
- ☐ Reqd in dwellings w/ fuel-fired appliances or attached garages that communicate w/ the dwelling unit ____ 315.2.1
- ☐ Alterations, repairs, additions req compliance same as new EXC ____ 315.2.2
  - Work limited to exterior or to plumbing/mechanical alterations/repairs that are not fuel-fired appliances ____ 315.2.2X[24]
- ☐ Install outside each separate sleeping area **F18 H** & in bedrooms w/ a fuel-burning appliance in the bedroom or attached bath **F18 I** ____ 315.3

24. 2018 IRC exempted repairs for plumbing and mechanical systems; 2021 IRC reqs CO alarms when such work involves fuel-fired appliances.

Power Sources & Interconnection (Smoke & CO) — 21 IRC

- ☐ All alarms req interconnection so activation of one activates all 314.4 & 315.5
- ☐ Interconnection can be listed wireless connection ____ 314.4 & 315.5
- ☐ Power source from building wiring + battery backup EXC ____ 314.6 & 315.6
  - Battery-only OK for additions, alterations & repairs ____ 314.6X2 & 315.6X2
- ☐ No disconnect allowed other than branch circuit breaker ____ 314.6 & 315.6

Fire Alarm & Carbon Monoxide Alarm Systems

- ☐ Fire alarm systems (separate alarm & detectors) allowed; must comply w/ NFPA 72 & detectors listed to UL 268 ____ 314.7.1
- ☐ Detector locations same as for alarms **F18** ____ 314.7.2 & 315.7.2
- ☐ Alarm system becomes permanent fixture of property ____ 314.7.3 & 315.7.3
- ☐ CO alarm systems (separate alarm & detectors) allowed; must comply w/ NFPA 720 & detectors listed to UL 2075 ____ 315.7.1
- ☐ Combo smoke & CO detectors listed UL 268 & UL 2075 ____ 314.7.4 & 315.7.4

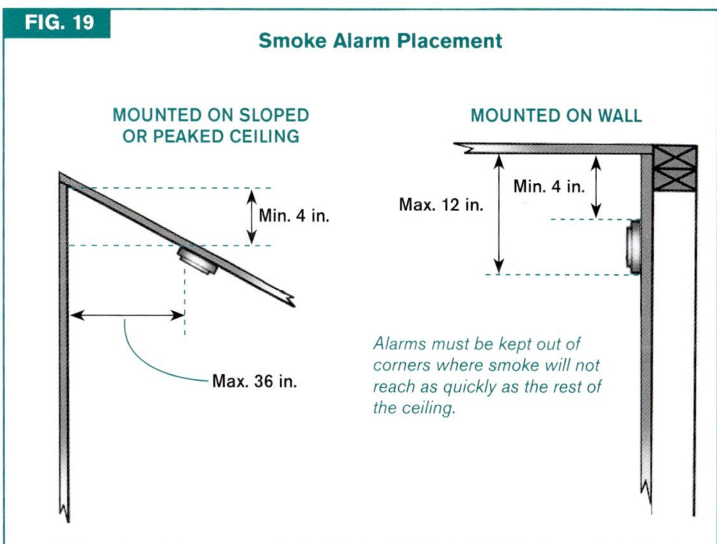

MEANS OF EGRESS

Required Egress Doors — 21 IRC

- ☐ Min. 1 egress door reqd each dwelling unit ____ 311.2
- ☐ Egress door side-hinged & min. net clear width 32 in. **F20** ____ 311.2
- ☐ Min. clear height of egress door 78 in. top of threshold to bottom of stop ____ 311.2
- ☐ Other doors do not need to comply w/ these min. dimensions ____ 311.2
- ☐ Egress doors req keyless operation from interior side ____ 311.2
- ☐ Reqd egress door must open directly to public way or equivalent ____ 311.1
- ☐ Reqd egress travel cannot be through garage ____ 311.1

FIG. 20

Egress Door Minimum Width

A standard 3′–0″ door meets the reqd size.

Thresholds & Landings at Exterior Doors — 21 IRC

- ☐ Threshold max. 1½ in. above landing or floor EXC **F21** ____ 311.3.1
  - Landing 7¾ in. below if door does not swing over landing **F21** ____ 311.3.1X
- ☐ Floor or landing min. 36 in. deep on each side of exterior door EXC ____ 311.3
  - Balconies <60 sq. ft. OK for landing to be <36 in. deep ____ 311.3X
  - OK to omit landing for stair of 1 or 2 risers at exterior door other than the reqd egress door provided door does not swing over stair ____ 311.3.2X
- ☐ Landing width at least the width of door served by landing ____ 311.3
- ☐ Max. slope of exterior landings 2% **F21** EXC ____ 311.3
  - Max. 5% if exterior landing reqd to drain surface water **F33** ____ 311.7.7X[25]
- ☐ Storm & screen doors may swing over lower landing ____ 311.3.3
- ☐ Landings req independent support or positive anchor to structure **F80** 311.5

25. Section 401.3 reqs 5% slope within first 10 ft. This new exception allows 401.3 to take precedence over the limitation of 2% for landing slope where applicable.

FIG. 21

Threshold Height

Applicable to occupancies within scope of IRC and to individual units of R-2 occupancies, such as apartments

Thresholds & Landings at Exterior Doors: Multifamily — 21 IBC

- ☐ Thresholds of sliding doors of dwelling units max. ¾ in. above landing or floor; thresholds of doors in public areas max. ½ in. above landing or floor **F22** EXC ____ 1010.1.6
  - **F21** height allowed if not part of reqd means of egress & not serving accessible route or unit ____ 1010.1.6X1
- ☐ Bevel edges of threshold & floor elevation changes >¼ in. **F22** ____ 1010.1.6
- ☐ Floor or landing min. length ≥ width of door & min. 44 in. on each side of door **F22** EXC ____ 1010.1.5
  - 36-in. length OK in individual units ____ 1010.1.5X
- ☐ Landing width at least the width of door served by landing ____ 1010.1.5
- ☐ Max. slope of exterior landings 2% ____ 1010.1.4

FIG. 22

R-2 Common Area Landings & Thresholds

Landing length min. 36 in. in individual dwelling units

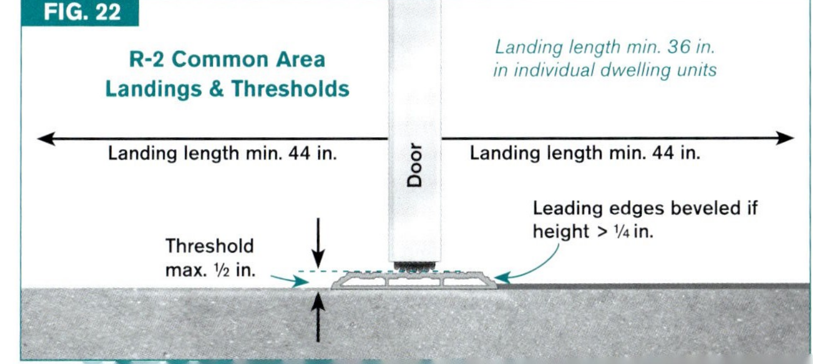

Landings at Stairs & Interior Doors — 21 IRC

- ☐ Min. 36 in.-deep landing reqd at top & bottom each stairway EXC **F27** ____ 311.7.6
  - Not reqd for door at top of interior stairs (including stairs to a garage) provided door does not swing over stairs ____ 311.7.6X
- ☐ Max. 12 ft. 7 in. vertical between landings or floor levels ____ 311.7.3[26]
- ☐ Max. 2% slope on walking surface of treads & landings ____ 311.7.7

Stairs & Ramps: Scope of Code Requirements

- ☐ Egress by stair or ramp reqd from all habitable levels ____ 311.4
- ☐ Stairways not within or serving a building, porch, or deck are not within scope of code ____ 311.7X1[27]
- ☐ Stairways to crawlspaces & nonhabitable attics not in scope ____ 311.7X2&3[27]

Stair Dimensions

- ☐ Min. width 36 in. **F23** measured above handrail height EXC ____ 311.7.1
  - Spiral stairways ____ 311.7.1X
- ☐ Min. width 31½ in. measured at or below handrail height if handrail on one side, 27 in. if handrails on both sides EXC ____ 311.7.1
  - Spiral stairways ____ 311.7.1X
- ☐ Min. headroom 6 ft. 8 in. **F23** EXC ____ 311.7.2
  - Floor openings above stair OK to project max. 4¾ in. into reqd headroom at the side of a flight of stairs ____ 311.7.2X1
  - Spiral stairways ____ 311.7.2X2

Treads & Risers

- ☐ Riser height max. 7¾ in., tread depth min. 10 in. **F24** ____ 311.7.5.1&2
- ☐ Tallest riser not > ⅜ in. taller than shortest riser **F24** ____ 311.7.5.1
- ☐ Deepest tread not > ⅜ in. more than shortest **F24** ____ 311.7.5.2
- ☐ Tread depth min. 11 in. if no nosing projection on treads **F24** ____ 311.7.5.3X
- ☐ Measure rise & run exclusive of carpets, rugs, or runners ____ 311.7.5
- ☐ Risers vertical or sloped from tread above max. 30° from vertical ____ 311.7.5.1
- ☐ Open riser treads must prevent passage of 4 in. sphere EXC ____ 311.7.5.1
  - No limit on opening size when ≤ 30 in. above floor or ground ____ 311.7.5.1
  - No limit on opening size on spiral stairways ____ 311.7.5.1X1

26. Changed from 12 ft. 4 in. in previous code edition.
27. Clarification regarding items that are outside the scope of the code.

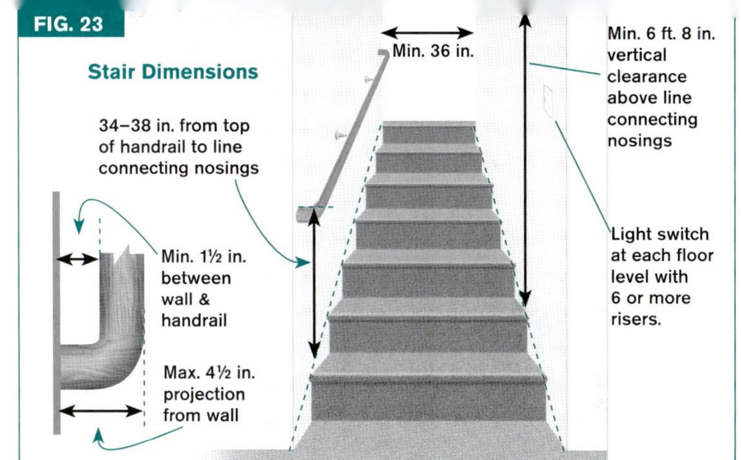

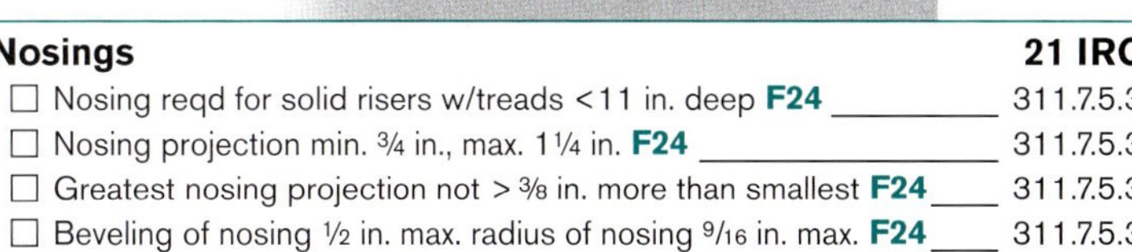

Nosings — 21 IRC

- ☐ Nosing reqd for solid risers w/treads <11 in. deep **F24** ____ 311.7.5.3
- ☐ Nosing projection min. ¾ in., max. 1¼ in. **F24** ____ 311.7.5.3
- ☐ Greatest nosing projection not > ⅜ in. more than smallest **F24** ____ 311.7.5.3
- ☐ Beveling of nosing ½ in. max. radius of nosing 9/16 in. max. **F24** ____ 311.7.5.3

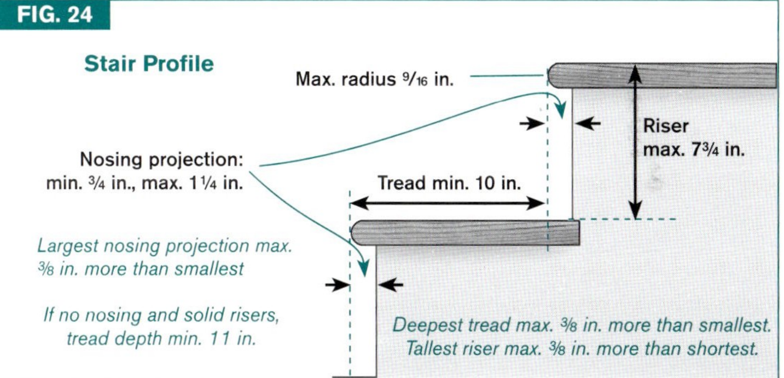

Winding Stairs F25 — 21 IRC

- ☐ Walkline is concentric to turn & measured 12 in. from first clear stair width at inside of turn ______ 311.7.4
- ☐ Min. tread depth 10 in. at walkline ______ 311.7.5.2.1
- ☐ Deepest tread not > ⅜ in. than shortest measured at walkline ______ 311.7.5.2.1
- ☐ OK for consistent rectangular treads in same flight of stairs as winders to not be within ⅜ in. of depth of winders ______ 311.7.5.2.1

FIG. 25 **Winding Stairs**

Walkline of winder treads is concentric to turn and parallel to direction of travel.

Walkline measured 12 in. from inside of turn.

Tread depth at walkline must be uniform; deepest tread may not exceed shortest by > ⅜ in.

12 in.

Min. 10-in. tread depth at walkline

Min. 6-in. tread depth at all points within clear width of stair

The uniform depth of rectangular treads in the same flight as winders is allowed to be different from the uniform depth of winders at the walkline.

Spiral Stairways — 21 IRC

- ☐ Spiral stairways permitted for all means of egress stairs ______ 311.7.10
- ☐ Max. rise between treads 9½ in. ______ 311.7.10.1
- ☐ Min. width 26 in. measured at & below handrail ______ 311.7.10.1
- ☐ All treads identical, min. headroom 6 ft. 6 in. ______ 311.7.10.1
- ☐ Min. tread depth 6¾ in. measured at walkline ______ 311.7.10.1
- ☐ Walkline radius max. 24½ in. from center point ______ 311.7.10.1

Handrails — 21 IRC

- ☐ Reqd on at least one side of flights of stairs w/ ≥ 4 risers **F23,27** ______ 311.7.8
- ☐ Top of rail 34–38 in. above line connecting nosings **F27** EXC ______ 311.7.8.1
  - Volute, turnout, or starting easing OK over lowest tread **F27** ______ 311.7.8.1X1
  - Fitting or bending OK to exceed 38 in. at continuous transition between flights, start of flight, or from handrail to guard **F27** ______ 311.7.8.1X2
- ☐ Max. handrail projection into stairway 4½ in. **F23,26** ______ 311.7.8.2
- ☐ Min. 1½-in. space between wall and handrail **F23,26** EXC ______ 311.7.8.3
  - Ends must return to wall, post, or guard walking surface **F23,27** ______ 311.7.8.4
- ☐ Handrail continuous for full length each flight of stairway EXC ______ 311.7.8.4
  - OK interrupted by newel post at turn, landing, or lowest tread ______ 311.7.8.4X1
  - Volute or turnout OK over lowest tread & over top landing **F27** ______ 311.7.8.4X2
- ☐ Round Type I handrails min. 1¼ in.–max. 2 in. diameter **F26** ______ 311.7.8.5
- ☐ Non-round Type I handrails perimeter min. 4 in. max. 6¼ in. **F26** ______ 311.7.8.5
- ☐ If perimeter > 6¼ in. (Type II), finger recess reqd both sides **F26** ______ 311.7.8.5

FIG. 26 **Handrail Profiles**

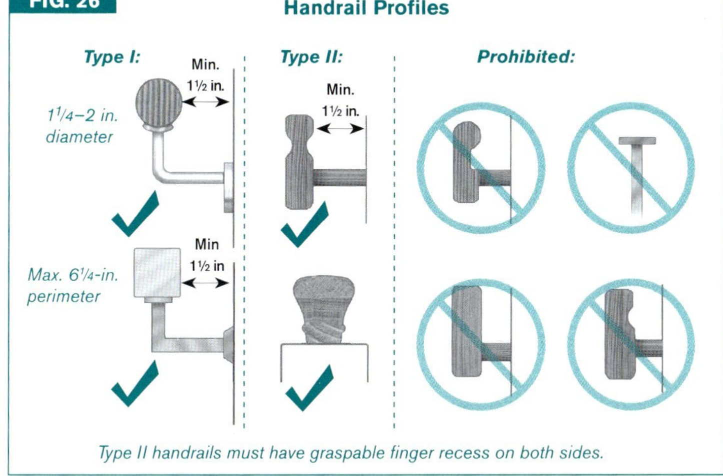

Type II handrails must have graspable finger recess on both sides.

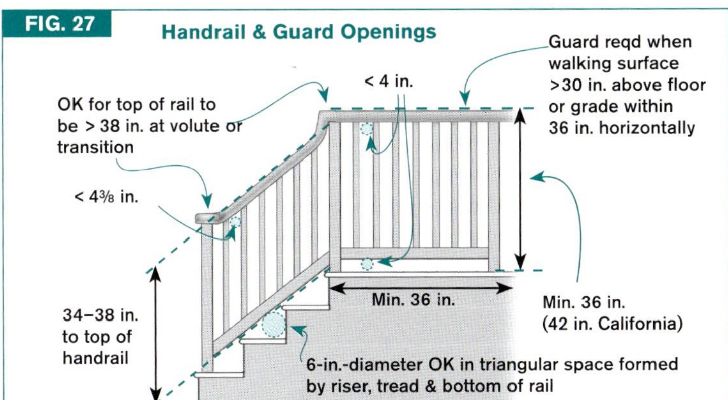

Ramps — 21 IRC

- ☐ Code applies where ramps reqd or provided EXC ____ 311.8[28]
  - Ramps not serving a building, porch, or deck ____ 311.8X[28]
- ☐ Ramps serving reqd egress door max. slope 1:12 (8.3%) EXC ____ 311.8.1
  - Where technically not feasible due to site constraints, 1:8 OK ____ 311.8.1X
- ☐ Ramps serving other areas max. slope 1:8 (12.5%) ____ 311.8.1
- ☐ Landing or floor reqd top & bottom each ramp & at change of direction 311.8.2
- ☐ Width of landing ≥ width of ramp ____ 311.8.2
- ☐ Depth of landing in direction of slope min. 36 in. ____ 311.8.2
- ☐ Handrails reqd one side of ramps exceeding 1:12 slope ____ 311.8.3

Alternating Tread Devices & Ship's Ladders

- ☐ Not considered an element of a means of egress EXC ____ 311.7.11 & 311.7.12
  - From lofts, mezzanines, etc. ≤200 sq. ft. & not providing the exclusive access to a kitchen or a bathroom ____ 311.7.11X & 311.7.12X
- ☐ Tread depth min. 5 in., nosing projection + tread depth min. 8½ in., riser height ≤9½ in. ____ 311.7.11.1 & 311.7.12.1
- ☐ Handrails per **F26** except height uniform & 30–34 in. ____ 311.7.11.2 & 311.7.12.2
- ☐ Alternating tread device clear width between handrails ≥20 in. ____ 311.7.11
- ☐ Alternating tread device angle of ascent 50°–70° ____ 311.7.11.1

28. Clarification on when ramps become within scope of code.

Lighting at Stairs — 21 IRC

- ☐ Illumination reqd for stairs & landings ____ 303.7&8
- ☐ Exterior stairs req artificial light at top landing ____ 303.8
- ☐ Basement w/ exterior stairs to grade req artificial light at bottom landing 303.8
- ☐ Interior stairs req artificial light min. 1 ft. candle at treads ____ 303.7
- ☐ Interior stair switch at each floor level if ≥ 6 risers **F23** EXC ____ 303.7
  - When remote, central, or automatic lighting controls provided ____ 303.7X

GUARDS

Location & Height — 21 IRC

- ☐ Reqd at open-sided walking surfaces including stairs, ramps & landings > 30 in. above lower floor or grade within 36 in. horizontally **F28** ____ 312.1.1
- ☐ Guard min. 36 in. above walking surface EXC ____ 312.1.2
  - Guard on open side of stair can be 34-in.-high handrail **F27** ____ 312.1.2X1
  - Top of handrail 34–38 in. above line connecting nosings **F27** ____ 312.1.2X2
  - California guard height min. 42 in. except handrail guards ____ 312.1.2

Strength, Infill & Openings

- ☐ Guard to resist 200-lb. point load applied downward or outward **T4** ____ T301.5
- ☐ Infill must resist 50-lb. load applied horizontally over 1 sq. ft. area **F28** ____ T301.5
- ☐ Openings must prevent passage of 4 in. sphere **F27** EXC ____ 312.1.3
  - Prevent passage of 4⅜ in. sphere at open sides of stairs **F27** ____ 312.1.3X2
  - Prevent 6 in. sphere at triangle of tread, riser & bottom rail **F27** ____ 312.1.3X1

FIG. 28

Guards

36 in.

36 in.

Min. 36-in. (42-in. California) guard reqd when walking surface > 30 in. above any point within 36 in.

>30 in.

TABLE 7	ESCAPE & RESCUE: MIN. HEIGHT & WIDTH REQUIREMENTS TO MEET REQD 5.7-SQ.-FT. OPENING SIZE (SQ. IN.)																												
Width	20	20½	21	21½	22	22½	23	23½	24	24½	25	25½	26	26½	27	27½	28	28½	29	29½	30	30½	31	31½	32	32½	33	33½	34
Height	41	40	39½	38½	37½	36½	35½	35	34½	33½	33	32½	32	31	30½	30	29½	29	28½	28	27½	27	26½	26½	26	25½	25	24½	24

TABLE 8	ESCAPE & RESCUE: 5.0-SQ.-FT. OPENING: GRADE-FLOOR OPENINGS ONLY (SQ. IN.)																				
Width	20	20½	21	21½	22	22½	23	23½	24	24½	25	25½	26	26½	27	27½	28	28½	29	29½	30
Height	36	35	34½	33½	33	32	31½	31	30	29½	29	28½	28	27½	27	26½	26	25½	25	24½	24

EMERGENCY ESCAPE & RESCUE OPENINGS

Required Locations & Egress Paths — 21 IRC

- ☐ Reqd for every sleeping room, basements & habitable attics EXC **F29** _ 310.1
  - Storm shelters & mechanical equipment basements ≤ 200 sq. ft. _ 310.1X1
  - In sprinklered dwellings w/ basement sleeping rooms: either 1 EERO + a means of egress path, or 2 means of egress paths (stairs) ____ 310.1X2
- ☐ Open to public way or yard or court or min. 36-in.-width path to same _ 310.1[29]
- ☐ Path under decks min. 36-in. clear height & width to yard or court _ 310.2.4[29]
- ☐ Additions req opening in each sleeping room ____ 310.6
- ☐ Existing basements undergoing alterations or repairs exempt EXC ____ 310.7
  - New basement sleeping rooms req escape & rescue openings ____ 310.7

Operation & Dimensions of Openings

- ☐ Opening operation cannot req keys, tools, or special knowledge ____ 310.1.1
- ☐ Security bars must be openable from the interior w/o use of keys, tools, special knowledge, or greater force than normal operation of opening 310.4.4
- ☐ Window fall prevention devices per ASTM F2090 max. 70 in. AFF _ 310.1.1[30]
- ☐ Min. net clear area 5.7 sq. ft. **T7** EXC ____ 310.2.1
  - 5.0 sq. ft. OK for grade floor openings **T8** ____ 310.2.1X
  - 4.0 sq. ft. OK for additions, min. height 22 in., min. width 20 in. _ 310.6X3[31]
- ☐ Bottom of clear opening max. 44 in. AFF **F29** ____ 310.2.3[32]
- ☐ Min. net clear height 24 in., min. net clear width 20 in. **T7,8** ____ 310.2.2
- ☐ Replacement windows exempt from height & size reqs if replacement is MFR's largest size that will fit into existing frame or rough opening __ 310.5

29. Added width req.
30. New rule on max. height of hardware to unlatch window fall-prevention devices.
31. New allowance for smaller openings for additions and basement alterations.
32. Height now measured to actual opening, not simply the window sill.

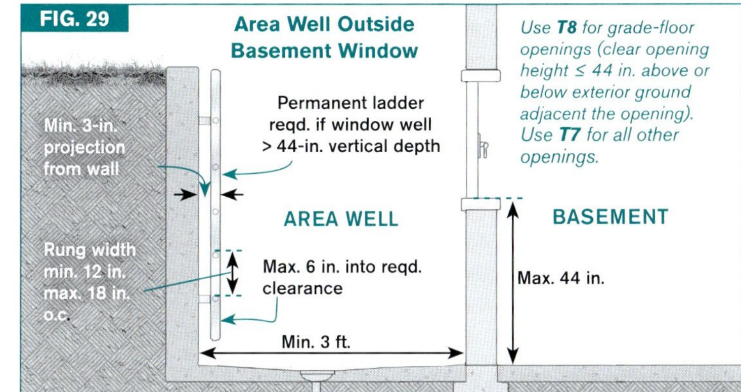

Area Wells — 21 IRC

- ☐ Openings w/ finished sill below grade req area well ____ 310.4
- ☐ Area wells min. 9 sq. ft. & 36 in. min. horizontal dimensions **F29** ____ 310.4.1
- ☐ Permanent ladder or stair reqd if > 44-in. vertical depth **F29** ____ 310.4.2
- ☐ Window or door in open position shall not obstruct ladder or stair ___ 310.4.2
- ☐ Ladder or steps max. projection 6 in. into reqd well space **F29** ____ 310.4.1X
- ☐ Ladder or steps min. width 12 in. ____ 310.4.2.1&2
- ☐ Ladder rungs 12 – 18 in. o.c., min. 3-in. projection from wall **F29** __ 310.4.2.1
- ☐ Steps min. tread depth 5-in. max. riser height 18 in. ____ 310.4.2.2[33]
- ☐ Covers or bulkheads over wells min. 9 sq. ft. & operable from inside _ 310.4.4
- ☐ Area wells req drainage system unless well-draining Group 1 soils _ 310.4.3

33. Rise and run of area well stairs was not specified in previous code.

Construction Adjacent to Slopes 21 IRC

*The presumed (non-engineered) angle of repose of sloped soils is 45°, which is the basis of the setback from slopes in **F30** & **F31**. Construction closer than those clearances requires an investigation and supervision by a qualified engineer. Filled soils must be designed, installed, and tested in accordance with accepted engineering practice.*

- ☐ Building placement near slopes >1:3 & ≤1:1per **F30** ______________ 403.1.7
- ☐ Provide sufficient distance from ascending slopes to provide protection from drainage, erosion & shallow slope failures ________ 403.1.7.1
- ☐ Provide sufficient distance from descending slopes to provide vertical & lateral support for footing w/o settlement ______________ 403.1.7.1
- ☐ If slope >1:1, setbacks from slope per **F31** __________________ 403.1.7.1&2
- ☐ Measure height from top of retaining walls at toe of ascending slope 403.1.7.1
- ☐ BO may approve alternate setbacks per engineering investigation _ 403.1.7.4

Retaining Walls

A foundation wall supporting a building is a restrained wall, held in place at the top by the floor system and at the bottom by a footing and/or floor slab. Retaining walls as described in this section are unrestrained and do not include foundation walls that support building loads.

- ☐ Retaining walls ≤48 in. from bottom of footing to top of wall exempt from permit reqs unless supporting a surcharge ___________ 105.2#3
- ☐ Design reqd for retaining walls w/o lateral support & retaining >48-in. unbalanced backfill or >24-in. if also resisting lateral loads ___ 404.4
- ☐ Design against overturning, sliding, excessive pressure & water uplift __ 404.4
- ☐ Design for safety factor of 1.5 against lateral sliding & overturning ____ 404.4
- ☐ Does not apply to walls supporting buildings ______________________ 404.4

FIG. 30

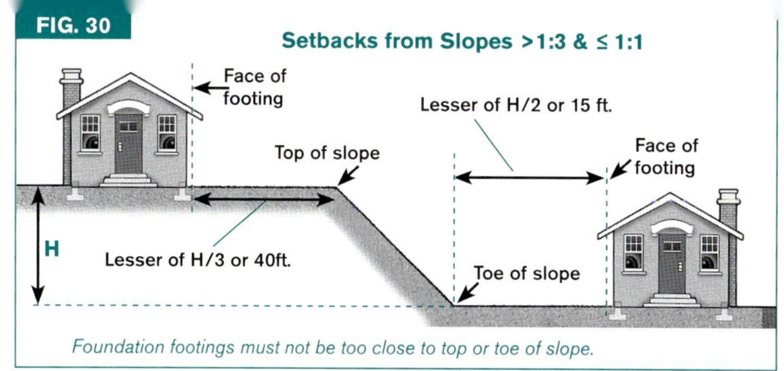

Foundation footings must not be too close to top or toe of slope.

FIG. 31

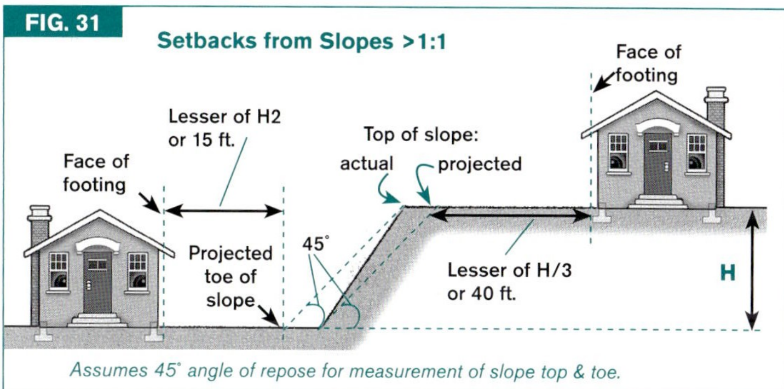

Assumes 45° angle of repose for measurement of slope top & toe.

SOILS, GRADING & DRAINAGE

Soils — 21 IRC

*In lieu of a complete soil investigation, the building official may allow **T9** for sites where the soil type is known. When the official determines that soils with a bearing capacity <1,500 psf are likely to be present, the bearing capacity must be determined by a soils investigation by a licensed design professional.*

- ☐ BO may req soil tests if expansive, compressible, or questionable ____ 401.4
- ☐ BO may allow **T9** in lieu of complete geotechnical evaluation (typical where satisfactory data from adjacent areas is available) ____401.4.1
- ☐ Foundation design per IBC 1808.6 for sites w/ expansive soils EXC 403.1.8
  - BO may allow systems known to perform on similar sites _______ 403.1.8X
- ☐ Compressible or shifting soils must be removed to stable level **T10** __401.4.2
- ☐ Filled soils layered & compacted per accepted engineering practice __ 401.2

TABLE 9 — PRESUMPTIVE LOAD-BEARING VALUES ◆ T401.4.1

Class of Materials	Load-Bearing Pressure (psf)
Crystalline bedrock	12,000
Sedimentary & foliated rock	4,000
Sandy gravel &/or gravel	3,000
Sand, silty sand, clayey sand, silty gravel & clayey gravel	2,000
Clay, sandy clay, silty clay, clayey silt, silt & sandy siltclay	1,500

Grading — 21 IRC

- ☐ Grade surface to storm drain or other approved collection point(s) **F32** 401.3
- ☐ Grade away from foundation: min. 6 in. fall within 1st 10 ft. **F33** EXC _ 401.3
  - Use swale if physical barrier or lot line prohibits 6 in. fall in 10 ft. ___ 401.3X
- ☐ Hardscape within 10 ft. min. 2% slope from building **F33** __________ 401.3X
- ☐ Grading to provide 6-in. clearance of non-PT wood & siding to soil, 2-in. clearance to hardscape **F33** ______________________________ 317.1#5
- ☐ For graded sites (such as subdivisions), elevation of top of foundation min. elevation above street gutter 12 in. + 2% slope **F32** EXC ____ 403.1.7.3
  - Alternate elevations if approved by BO & reqd drainage to point of discharge provided at all locations on site_ 401.1.7.3

FIG. 32 — Site Grading: Elevation View

Graded sites, such as subdivisions, must establish positive drainage to the point of discharge.

Foundation elevation above street gutter 12 in. + 2%

Grade must fall 6 in. within first 10 ft.

FIG. 33 — Site Grading: Plan View

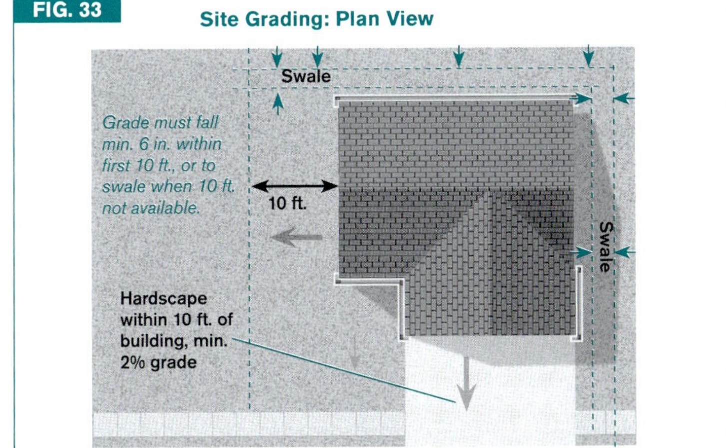

TABLE 10 SOIL PROPERTIES ACCORDING TO THE UNIFIED SOIL CLASSIFICATION SYSTEM ◆ T405.1

Soil Group	Symbol[A]	Soil Description	Drainage Characteristics[B]	Frost-Heave Potential	Expansion Potential[C]
Group I	GW	Well-graded gravels, gravel sand mixtures, little or no fines	Good	Low	Low
	GP	Poorly graded gravels or gravel sand mixtures, little or no fines	Good	Low	Low
	SW	Well-graded sands, gravelly sands, little or no fines	Good	Low	Low
	SP	Poorly graded sands or gravelly sands, little or no fines	Good	Low	Low
	GM	Silty gravels, gravel-sand-silt mixtures	Good	Medium	Low
	SM	Silty sand, sand-silt mixtures	Good	Medium	Low
Group II	GC	Clayey gravels, gravel-sand-clay mixtures	Medium	Medium	Low
	SC	Clayey sands, sand-clay mixture	Medium	Medium	Low
	ML	Inorganic silts & very fine sands, rock flour, silty or clayey fine sand, or clayey silts with slight plasticity	Medium	High	Low
	CL	Inorganic clays low to medium plasticity, gravelly clays, sandy clays, silty clays, lean clays	Medium	Medium	Medium to low
Group III	CH	Inorganic clays of high plasticity, fat clays	Poor	Medium	High
	MH	Inorganic silts, micaceous or diatomaceous fine sandy or silty soils, elastic silts	Poor	High	High
Group IV	OL	Organic silts and organic silty clays of low plasticity	Poor	Medium	Medium
	OH	Organic clays of medium to high plasticity, organic silts	Unsatisfactory	Medium	High
	Pt	Peat and other highly organic soils	Unsatisfactory	Medium	High

A. Letter codes: G = Gravel, S = Sand, M = Silt, C = Clay, O = Organic, P = Poorly graded, W = Well graded (many different particle sizes), H = High plasticity, L = Low plasticity
B. The percolation rate for good drainage is over 4 in. per hour, medium drainage is 2 in. to 4 in. per hour, and poor is less than 2 in. per hour.
C. Soils with a low potential expansion typically have a plasticity index (PI) of 0 to 15, soils with a medium potential expansion have a PI of 10 to 35, and soils with a high potential expansion have a PI greater than 20.

It is possible for a soils test to determine a combination of the soil types listed in this table, such as GW-GM (well-graded gravel with silt). In addition to the characteristics addressed in this table, soil chemistry may need to be considered, such as sulfates or seawater.

Sand, Silt, and Clay

Drainage — 21 IRC

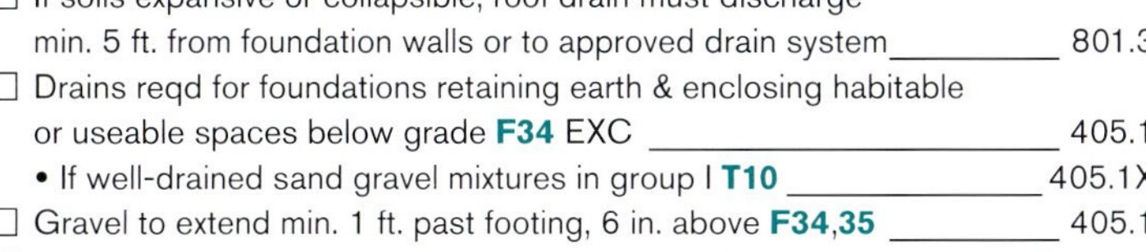

- ☐ If groundwater table can rise to within 6 in. of finished floor at perimeter, or if water does not readily drain from site, crawlspace to be as high as outside grade or approved drainage system must be installed ________ 408.6
- ☐ If soils expansive or collapsible, roof drain must discharge min. 5 ft. from foundation walls or to approved drain system __________ 801.3
- ☐ Drains reqd for foundations retaining earth & enclosing habitable or useable spaces below grade **F34** EXC __________ 405.1
  - If well-drained sand gravel mixtures in group I **T10** __________ 405.1X
- ☐ Gravel to extend min. 1 ft. past footing, 6 in. above **F34,35** __________ 405.1
- ☐ Perforated drain pipe "sock" or filter fabric reqd **F34,35** __________ 405.1

FIG. 34 Basement Walls

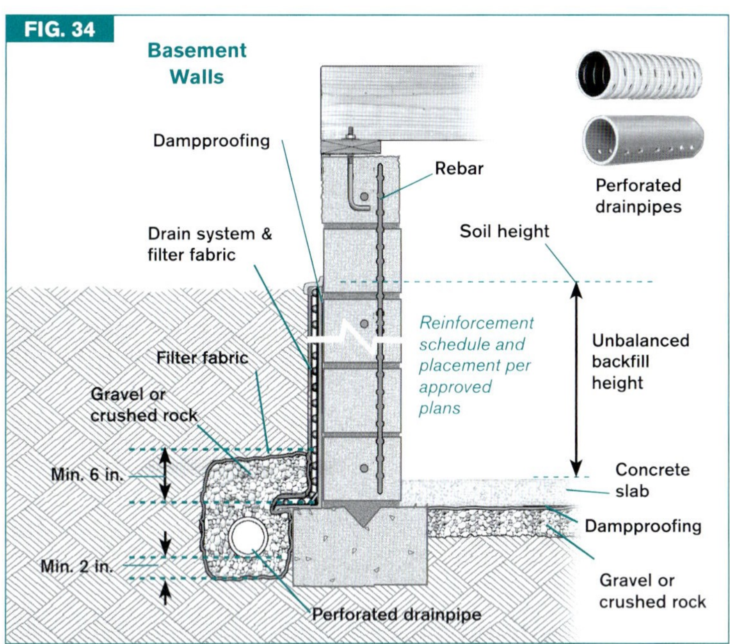

FIG. 35 Foundation Drain

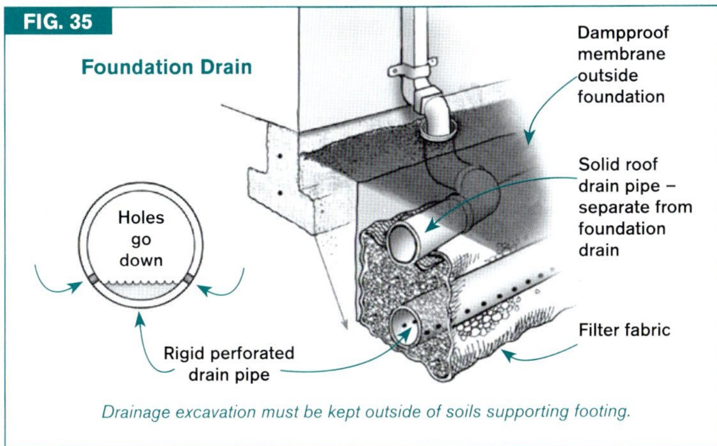

Drainage excavation must be kept outside of soils supporting footing.

Waterproofing & Dampproofing — 21 IRC

- ☐ Dampproofing or waterproofing reqd for foundations retaining earth & enclosing interior spaces & floors below grade **F34** ________ 406.1&2
- ☐ Extend from finished grade to top of footing or 6 in. below the top of the basement floor **F34** __________ 406.1&2
- ☐ CMU walls req min. ⅜-in. parging prior to dampproofing EXC ________ 406.1
  - When using material approved for direct application __________ 406.1X
- ☐ Dampproofing material = bituminous coating, 3 lb. sq. yd. acrylic modified cement, ⅛-in. surface bonding cement per ASTM C 887, or any material approved as waterproofing **F34** __________ 406.1
- ☐ If high water table exists, waterproofing reqd __________ 406.2
- ☐ Design per accepted engineering practice reqd if walls subject to hydrostatic pressure from ground water __________ 404.1.1#1
- ☐ Waterproofing material = Two-ply hot-mop felt, 55-lb. roll roofing, 40-mil poly-modified asphalt, 60-mil poly cement, ⅛-in. cement-based fiber-reinforced waterproof coating, or 60-mil liquid-applied synthetic rubber __________ 406.2[34]

34. 6-mil polyvinyl chloride or 6-mil polyethylene no longer allowed as waterproofing.

FOOTINGS & FOUNDATIONS

Footings transmit the structural loads and forces to the supporting soils. They can be cast monolithically with a foundation wall, as in **F36**, or separately, as is the case when the foundation wall consists of CMUs. With CMU foundations, a "key" is typically set into the footing, as in **F34**, to resist lateral displacement.

General — 21 IRC

- ☐ All exterior walls req support on footings ____ 403.1
- ☐ Support on undisturbed natural soils or engineered fill **F34** ____ 403.1
- ☐ ACI 332 OK as alternative code for concrete footings ____ 403.1
- ☐ Placement min. 12 in. below previously undisturbed ground surface ____ 403.1.4
- ☐ Extend below frost line **F34** if not frost-protected *(p. 40)* EXC ____ 403.1.4.1
  - Light-frame accessory structures ≤600 sq. ft. eave height ≤10 ft. _ 403.1.4.1X
- ☐ Top surface of all footings level ____ 403.1.5
- ☐ Bottom surface of footings max. 10% slope (stepped when > 10%) _ 403.1.5
- ☐ Footings for fireplaces per 1001.2 *(p. 115)* ____ 403.1.1

FIG. 36

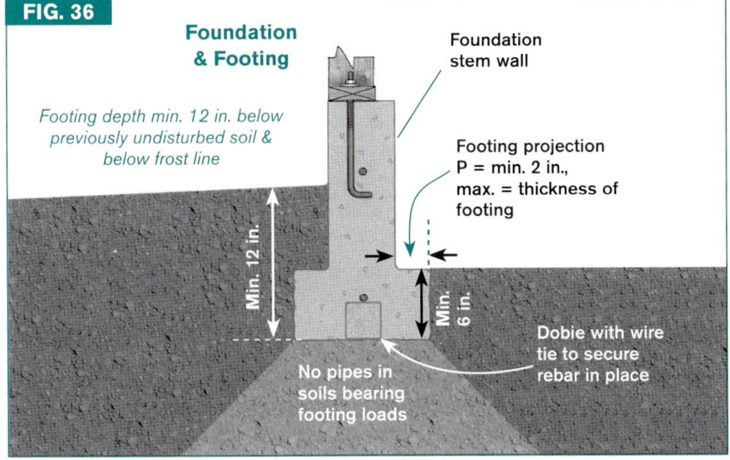

Footing Size — 21 IRC

- ☐ Width dependent on soil type & snow load **T2,9** ____ 403.1.1
- ☐ Min. width 12 in. min. thickness 6 in. & per **T11** ____ 403.1.1[35]
- ☐ Projection past foundation min. 2 in., max. = footing thickness **F36**__ 403.1.1

TABLE 11 — MIN WIDTH OF FOOTINGS FOR LIGHT FRAME[A] T403.1(1)

Light-Frame Construction[B]	# of Stories	Load-Bearing Value of Soil			
		1,500	2,000	2,500	≥ 3,000
Slab-on-grade	1	12	12	12	12
	2	13	12	12	12
	3	16	12	12	12
Crawlspace	1	12	12	12	12
	2	15	12	12	12
	3	18	14	12	12
Basement	1	16	12	12	12
	2	19	14	12	12
	3	22[C]	16	13	12

A. Based on 20 psf roof live load (or 25 psf snow load). See full code tables for values in snow country.
B. See code tables for values with masonry veneer or concrete/masonry walls.
C. 7 in. footing thickness — all other cells in this table require 6 in. thickness.

Footings in SDC D — 21 IRC

- ☐ Continuous concrete or masonry footings reqd at exterior walls ____ 403.1.2
- ☐ Continuous footings reqd below interior braced wall panels EXC ____ 403.1.2
  - SDC D_0 & D_1 w/ no plan dimensions >50 ft. ____ 403.1.2
  - 2-story buildings in SDC D w/ no plan dimensions >50 ft., cripple walls ≤4 ft., first-floor BWPs supported on beams or double joists & distance between BWPs ≤ twice building width parallel to BWPs ____ 403.1.2X

35. Several changes in table values from previous edition.

Frost-Protected Shallow Foundations — 21 IRC

While the most common design in freezing climates is to extend the foundation below the frost line, another option is a frost-protected shallow foundation. These use insulation in such a way that heat from the building prevents freezing of the soil below the footing. According to the National Oceanic & Atmospheric Administration, these have been used successfully on over a million homes in Scandinavian countries. An excellent article on the subject can be found at finehomebuilding.com/project-guides/insulation/protecting-foundations-from-frost.

- ☐ Monthly mean building temp must be maintained ≥64°F ____ 403.3
- ☐ Determine air-freezing index per F403.3(2) or T403.3(2) **T2** ____ T403.3(1)
- ☐ Footing depth, insulation size & R-value per T403.3(1) ____ 403.3
- ☐ Insulation materials below grade labeled compliant w/ ASTM C578 ____ 403.3
- ☐ 4-in. gravel/ crushed stone below footing & horizontal insulation **F37** F403.3(1)
- ☐ Provide drain to daylight for gravel layer **F37** ____ F403.3.3
- ☐ If unheated slab-on-grade structure abuts frost-protected foundation, provide insulation under slab & between slab & protected foundation 403.3.1.1

FIG. 37 **Frost-Protected Footing in Heated Building**

A frost-protected footing uses heat from the building to prevent soils from freezing, thereby raising the frostline elevation.

See full code text for distances of insulation from foundation walls and building corners.

Heat

Insulation protection

4 in. of screened & washed gravel or crushed stone – drain must be provided.

Isolated Footings & Piers — 21 IRC

- ☐ Isolated plain concrete footings allowed for column support **F38** ____ 403.1.3.6
- ☐ Footings for isolated hollow masonry piers same as other footings **F36, T11** (min. 6 in. deep 12 in. width) ____ 404.1.9
- ☐ Isolated hollow masonry piers min. 8 in. thick, height max. 4X nominal thickness, length max. 3 times nominal thickness ____ 404.1.9
- ☐ Hollow piers req min. 4-in. cap of solid masonry or filled top course 404.1.9.1
- ☐ Masonry piers supporting wood girders min. dimension 12 in. max. height 10 ft. top of footing to bottom of plate or girder EXC ____ 404.1.9.2
  - 4 ft. max. if girder supporting exterior bearing wall ____ 404.1.9.2
- ☐ Masonry piers supporting braced wall panels or in SDC D or for townhouses in SDC C req professional design ____ 404.1.9.3&4

Columns & Posts

- ☐ Steel columns corrosion-resistant or provided w/ rust-inhibiting paint ____ 407.2
- ☐ Wood posts <8 in. above ground req protection against decay **F38** ____ 407.1
- ☐ Wood posts min. nominal 4-in. × 4-in., steel min. 3 in. diameter ____ 407.3
- ☐ Restrain bottom to prevent lateral displacement **F38** EXC ____ 407.3
  - Not reqd in SDC A, B & C if ≤48 in. & enclosed by foundation ____ 407.3X

FIG. 38 **Posts on Isolated Footings**

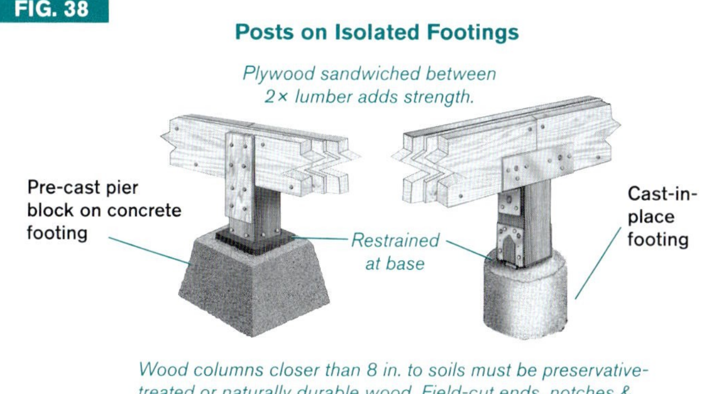

Wood columns closer than 8 in. to soils must be preservative-treated or naturally durable wood. Field-cut ends, notches & drilled holes must be treated in accordance with AWPA M4.

Forms **21 IRC**

- ☐ Pipe penetrations through foundations must be sleeved ____________ 2603.4
- ☐ Sleeve min. 2 pipe sizes larger than pipe passing through __________ 2603.4
- ☐ Wood beam connections min. ½-in. air space 3 sides **F39** ________ 317.1#4
- ☐ Accurately position & secure forms before placing concrete ___ 404.1.3.3.6[36]
- ☐ Form ties can be steel, plastic, or other material to resist forces created by fluid pressure of concrete ____________ 404.1.3.3.6
- ☐ Forms must resist deflection during concrete placement _______ 404.1.3.3.6

Stay-in-Place Forms

- ☐ Flat ICF wall system forms to conform to ASTM E2634 ____ 404.1.3.3.6.1#5
- ☐ Surface-burning characteristics of ICF to comply w/ 316.3 _ 404.1.3.3.6.1#1
- ☐ Protect surface on interior of building ____________________ 404.1.3.3.6.1#2
- ☐ Protect exposed surfaces on exterior of building __________ 404.1.3.3.6.1#3
- ☐ Provide approved method of termite protection for below-grade forms in areas prone to infestation_ 404.1.3.3.6.1#4 & 318.4X2

Anchorage to Foundations

- ☐ Anchors reqd all wood sill plates & walls supported on foundations _ 403.1.6
- ☐ Anchors reqd all monolithic slab exterior wall wood sole plates & interior wall sole plates at BWPs __________________ 403.1.6
- ☐ Anchors = min. ½-in. anchor bolts or approved anchor straps (*see comment on* ***p. 42***) providing equivalent anchorage **F40–42** ____ 403.1.6
- ☐ Bolts min. 7 in. into concrete or grouted CMU cell **F41** ___________ 403.1.6
- ☐ Nut & washer on each bolt **F41** _______________________________ 403.1.6
- ☐ Bolt distance from end of plate min. 7 bolt diameters, max. 12 in. **F41** 403.1.6
- ☐ Bolt in middle third of width of plate **F41**________________________ 403.1.6
- ☐ Max. spacing 6 ft. o.c. & min. 2 bolts per plate EXC **F41**____________ 403.1.6
  - Walls ≤24 in. connecting offset BWs 1 bolt in center ⅓ _______ 403.1.6X1
  - Walls ≤12 in. connecting offset BWs no bolt OK_____________ 403.1.6X2

  Wood structural panel sheathing continuous through offset for above 2 exceptions.
- ☐ Where bolts "wet set" into soft concrete resist placement or if concrete consolidation impaired, vibrate concrete to ensure full contact_____ 403.1.6[37]

36. Req added that forms be accurately positioned and secured.
37. Code now permits "wet set" of bolts – a practice that has long been questioned, and that is specifically not permitted by ACI 318-19 section 26.7.2. See further explanation in **F40**.

FIG. 39 **Beam Pocket**

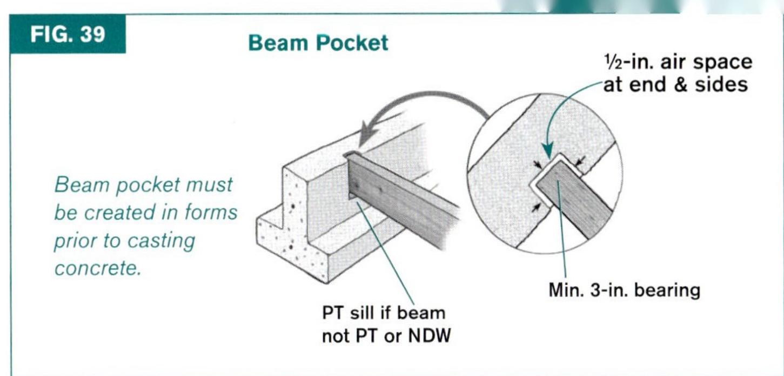

FIG. 40 **Anchor Bolt Holder**

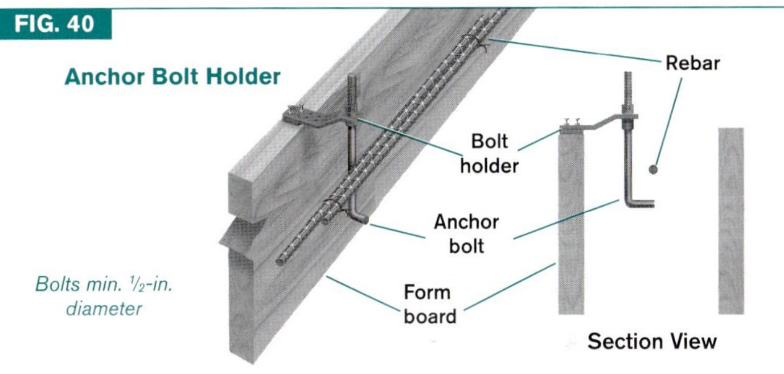

Anchor bolt holders help ensure the bolt will be in the reqd center ⅓ of the plate and also hold the bolt vertical. ACI 318-19 section 26.7.2 reqs bolts to be securely positioned in the formwork. Bolts "wet set" into soft concrete are often crooked, incorrectly placed, or not in full contact w/ concrete.

In addition to the requirements for a bolt within 12 in. of the end of each sill plate and the maximum spacing of 6 ft. between bolts, plan ahead for the length of the sill plates and the placement of beams, studs, or other framing members so that they do not have to be notched over the bolts.

Additional Anchorage in SDC D & Townhouses in SDC C 21 IRC

- ☐ Plate washers or approved* anchor straps full length of BWLs _ 403.1.6.1#1
- ☐ Slotted plate washers permitted if standard washer also used **F41** _ 602.11.1
- ☐ Bolts reqd 6 ft. o.c. & max. 12 in. from ends of interior braced wall plates or sole plates on continuous foundations ______ 403.1.6.1#2&3
- ☐ Max. bolt spacing 4 ft. o.c. if >2 stories in height __________ 403.1.6.1#4
- ☐ Stepped cripple walls req drag straps **F67** ________________ 403.1.6.1

**Anchor straps can be approved as an alternative to bolts. Products such as Simpson Strong-Tie® MABs and MASBs have evaluation reports from 3rd party agencies that state the values of loads parallel to plates that can be resisted by these products. Their instructions state that the calculated forces must be submitted to the BO and that installation instructions be on site. They are more commonly used with CMUs than cast concrete, and in SDCs A and B, not C or D. Care must also be taken when setting these products to not bend them "out of the way" prior to installing sills; they are only designed to be bent once.*

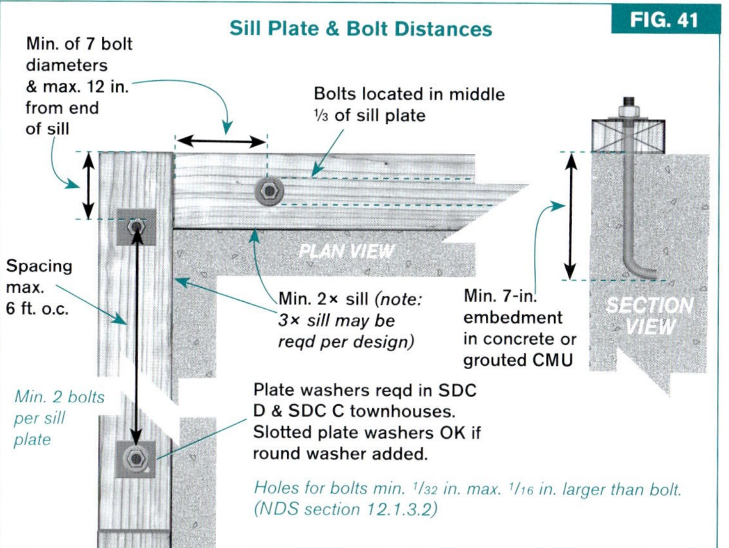

Concrete Slabs on Ground 21 IRC

- ☐ Min. 3½ in. thick **F42** ________________ 506.1
- ☐ Remove foreign material, vegetation & topsoil __________ 506.2
- ☐ Max. fill 24-in. clean sand/gravel or 8-in. earth __________ 506.2.1
- ☐ Below-grade slabs req min. 4 in. base course **F42** EXC __________ 506.2.2
  - Group I well-drained or sand/gravel mixtures **T10** __________ 506.2.2X
- ☐ Min. 10-mil vapor retarder conforming to ASTM E1745 Class A w/ joints lapped min. 6 in. below concrete floor slab **F42** EXC ______ 506.2.3[38]
  - Garages, unheated accessory structures, unheated storage rooms <70 sq. ft., carports, driveways, walks, patios, other unenclosed flatwork, or where approved by BO based on local site conditions 506.2.3X
- ☐ Wire chairs or dobies reqd to hold reinforcement in place between center & upper ⅓ of slab during concrete placement **F42** ________ 506.2.4

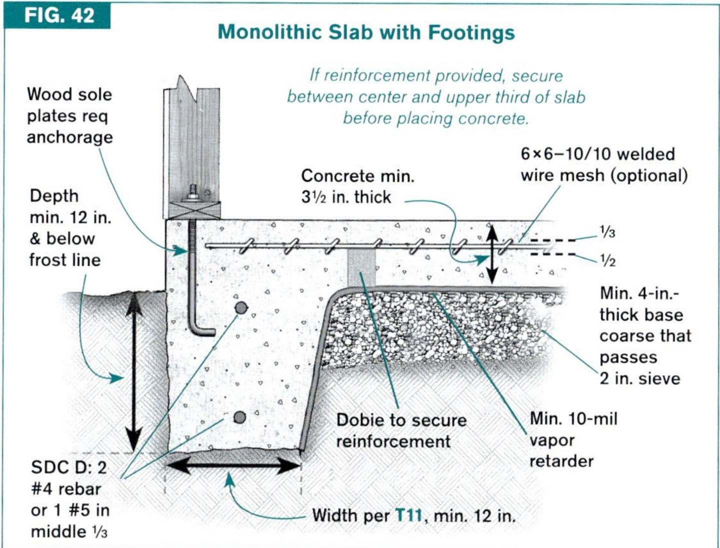

38. 6 mil vapor retarders no longer allowed. They must be Class A: Maximum of 0.1 perms, minimum 45 lb/in tensile strength, and 2200 grams puncture resistance.

Foundation (Basement) Walls — 21 IRC

- ☐ Design reqd if supporting >48 in. unbalanced backfill or if subject to hydrostatic pressure from ground water ______ 404.1.1
- ☐ Concrete & masonry walls must extend above grade min. 4 in. where masonry veneer used & min. 6 in. elsewhere ______ 404.1.6
- ☐ No backfill until walls anchored to floor above ______ 404.1.7
- ☐ Concrete foundation walls req lateral support at top & bottom ______ 404.1.3.2
- ☐ Masonry wall thickness not < thickness of wall supported EXC ______ 404.1.5.1
  - 8 in. walls OK under brick-veneered frame walls or 10 in. cavity walls where total height of wall (including gables) ≤ 20 ft. ______ 404.1.5.1
- ☐ Concrete wall thickness not < thickness of wall in story above ______ 404.1.5.2

REINFORCEMENT

Foundation walls below the first story above grade plane & enclosing a crawlspace are referred to as *stem walls.* As used in section 404 of the IRC, the term "foundation wall" refers to *basement walls.* The tables for reinforcement in these walls start at a height of 5 ft. or more, and are based upon unsupported wall height, unbalanced backfill height, and soil class. The tables for masonry foundations all include a schedule for vertical reinforcing steel at prescribed distances from the soil side, with the steel placed close to the inside face (tension side) of the wall. For concrete foundations, there are tables for plain concrete, tables where the vertical steel is in the centerline of the wall, and an alternate table for steel on the tension side of the wall. The tables are too large for this book and can be viewed in chapter 4 of the IRC at codes.iccsafe.org/content/IRC2021P1.

Reinforced Masonry Foundation Walls — 21 IRC

- ☐ Design per TMS 402 not reqd to bear seal of licensed design professional unless otherwise reqd by law or local AHJ ______ 404.1.2
- ☐ Mortar Type M or S ______ 606.2.8.1 & T404.1.1(2–4)note a
- ☐ Masonry in running bond ______ T404.1.1(2–4)note a
- ☐ Distance face of soil to center of vertical reinforcement 8-in. CMU: 5 in., 10-in. CMU: 6.75 in, 12-in. CMU: 8.75 in. ______ T404.1.1(2–4)note c
- ☐ Table values for vertical steel all based on grade 60 ___ T404.1.1(2–4)note c
- ☐ Alternate bar sizes & spacing w/ equivalent cross-sectional area OK provided max. spacing ≤ 72 in. SDC A, B, C & ≤ 48 in. SDC D _ T404.1.1(2–4)note b

Footing + Stem Wall Reinforcement in SDC D — 21 IRC

- ☐ Concrete footings req reinforcement ______ 403.1.3
- ☐ Min. 1 #4 vertical bar max. 4 ft. o.c. min. 14 in. into stem wall __ 403.1.3.1&2
- ☐ Vertical bars to have standard hook into footing ______ 403.1.3.1&2
- ☐ Min. 1 #4 horizontal bar in upper 12 in. of stem wall ______ 403.1.3.1&2
- ☐ Min. 1 #4 horizontal bar in 3 – 4 in. from bottom of footing ______ 403.1.3.1&2
- ☐ Masonry stem walls req solid grout **F43** ______ 403.1.3.2
- ☐ Steel reinforcement min. grade 40 (40,000 psi yield strength) ___ 403.1.3.5.1
- ☐ Locate vertical reinforcement at centerline of stem wall ______ 403.1.3.5.2
- ☐ Support & cover per **T12** ______ 403.1.3.5.3
- ☐ Where splices necessary, splice length per **T14** ______ 403.1.3.5.4
- ☐ Gap between bars at lap splice lesser of 6 in. or ⅕ splice length 403.1.3.5.4

Slab-on-Ground Footings in SDC D

- ☐ Slab-on-ground w/ turned-down footings req min. 1 #4 bar at top & bottom of footing or 1 #5 or 2 #4 bar in middle ⅓ of footing depth **F42** ___ 403.1.3.3
- ☐ If slab not monolithic w/ footing, #3 hooks at max. 4 ft. o.c. ______ 403.1.3.3
- ☐ Interior footings cast monolithically w/ slab ≥12 in. below top of slab _ 403.1.3.4

TABLE 12 — REINFORCEMENT COVER ◆ 403.1.3.5.3 & 404.1.3.3.7.4

Foundation Surface	Min. Cover
Concrete cast against & permanently exposed to earth	3 in.
Concrete exposed to earth or weather after forms removed	1½ in.[A]
Not exposed to weather (e.g., top of slab)	¾ in.
Concrete in stay-in-place forms (ICF)	¾ in.

A. 2-in. min. cover reqd for #6 or larger bars.

TABLE 13 — MIN. HORIZONTAL REINFORCEMENT FOR CONCRETE BASEMENT WALLS ◆ T404.1.2(1)

Max. Unsupported Wall Height	Location of Horizontal Reinforcement
≤8 ft.	1 #4 bar ≤ 12 in. of top of wall story & 1 #4 near mid-height
>8 ft.	1 #4 bar ≤ 12 in. of top of wall story & 1 #4 near ⅓ points

Concrete Foundation Wall Reinforcement — 21 IRC

- ☐ Horizontal reinforcement min. per **T13** ____ 404.1.3.2
- ☐ Horizontal reinforcement min. grade 40 ____ T404.1.2(1)
- ☐ Reinforcement in SDC A, B & C permitted to be grade 40 ____ 404.1.3.3.7.1
- ☐ Vertical reinforcement in SDC D reqd to be min. grade 60 ____ 404.1.3.3.7.1
- ☐ Table values for vertical steel all based on grade 60 ____ T404.1.2(2–8)
- ☐ Different grades of steel permitted in lieu of grade 60 if spacing adjusted to provide equivalent per lineal foot ____ T404.1.2(9) & 404.1.3.3.7.6
- ☐ Vertical bars in centerline of wall if using tables 404.1.2(2–7) ____ 404.1.3.3.7.2
- ☐ Max. cover of vertical bars from inside face of wall 1¼ in. if using table 404.1.2(8) ____ 404.1.3.3.7.2
- ☐ Secure w/ tie wire, dobies, etc., to prevent displacement ____ 404.1.3.3.7.4
- ☐ Min. concrete cover of reinforcement per **T12** ____ 404.1.3.3.7.4
- ☐ Tolerances in **T12** ⅜ in. or ⅓ reqd cover, whichever is less ____ 404.1.3.3.7.4
- ☐ Splice lap min. 20 in. #4 bar, 25 in. #5 bar, 30 in. #6 bar **T14** ____ 404.1.3.3.7.5
- ☐ Spacing between lapped bars max. ⅕ lap splice length ____ 404.1.3.3.7.5
- ☐ Plain concrete or masonry OK if complying w/ following: ____ 404.1.4.1&2
  - Min. wall thickness for plain concrete 7½ in., plain masonry 8 in.
  - Max. height 8 ft., max. unbalanced backfill 4 ft.
  - Plain masonry reqs 2 #4 horizontal bars in upper 12 in. of wall
  - Plain concrete reqs #4 horizontal bars upper 12 in. & mid-height of wall

TABLE 14 LAP SPLICE & TENSION DEVELOPMENT LENGTHS ◆ T608.5.4(1)

Condition	Bar Size	Grade 40	Grade 60
		Splice or Development Length (in.)	
Tension development length for straight bar (when reqd by other provisions of code)	4	15	23
	5	19	28
	6	23	34
Lap splice length-tension	4	20	30
	5	25	38
	6	30	45

MASONRY WALLS (CMUs)

The IRC reqs for above-grade masonry walls include details for grouting, mortar, reinforcement, and tolerances that also apply to masonry foundation walls. TMS 402 and TMS 602 are applicable to both. High-lift grouting refers to a pour height in excess of 64 in. Low-lift grouting reqs separate inspections for each lift; high-lift grouting reqs continuous special inspection during the pour.

General — 21 IRC

- ☐ Where IRC or TMS 402 appendix A used to design masonry, the project drawings, details & specs not reqd to bear seal of licensed design professional unless otherwise reqd by state law of AHJ ____ 606.1.1
- ☐ Min. 8-in. thickness > 1-story bearing walls ____ 606.4.1
- ☐ 6-in.-thick walls OK for 1 story to 9 ft. + 6 ft. to peak of gable ____ 606.4.1

Mortar

- ☐ Mortar proportions per ASTM C270 ____ 606.2.8
- ☐ Mortar Type M or S in masonry foundation walls ____ 606.2.8.1
- ☐ Mortar Type M, S or N if resisting lateral force in SDC A, B, or C ____ 606.2.8.2
- ☐ Mortar Type M or S if resisting lateral force in SDC D ____ 606.2.8.3
- ☐ Bed & head joints ⅜ in. thick EXC ____ 606.3.1
  - Starting course over foundations min. ¼ in. max. ¾ in. ____ 606.3.1
  - Where otherwise listed on shop drawings ____ 606.3.1
- ☐ Joint thickness tolerances for load-bearing masonry: ____ 606.3.1
  - Bed joints + ⅛ in.
  - Head joints −¼ in.+ ⅜ in.
  - Collar joints −¼ in.+ ⅜ in.
- ☐ Place units w/ sufficient pressure that mortar extrudes from joints ____ 606.3.2
- ☐ Solid masonry unit all joints filled (ends buttered not slushed) ____ 606.3.2.1
- ☐ Hollow masonry unit solid fill not less than thickness of face shell ____ 606.3.2.2

Piers & Columns — 21 IRC

- ☐ Unsupported height of masonry piers max. 10× their least dimension __ 606.7
- ☐ Hollow CMUs supporting beams & girders req solid fill of grout or Type M or S mortar EXC ________________ 606.7
  - Unfilled hollow OK in SDC A & B up to 4× height of least dimension __606.7
- ☐ Hollow piers req cap of solid masonry or concrete or top course filled _ 606.7.1
- ☐ Masonry piers & columns in SDC C & D req reinforcement ___ F606.11(2&3)

Lateral Support

- ☐ Lateral support reqd vertically or horizontally per **T15** ____ 606.4.1 & 606.6.4
- ☐ Horizontal lateral support by cross walls, pilasters, buttresses, or structural frame, vertical lateral support by floors & roofs ________ 606.6.4
- ☐ Horizontal lateral support by intersecting masonry walls can be laid in overlapping bond pattern min. bearing 3 in. on unit below or by anchoring w/ galvanized mesh or metal ties or other anchors ___606.6.4.1
- ☐ Vertical lateral support by anchoring to floor diaphragms or roof structures w/ strap anchors installed AMI, bolts ≤ 6 ft. o.c., or other means __606.6.4.2

Reinforcement & Coverage — TMS 402

- ☐ Joint reinforcement wires min. W1.1 (11 gauge); max. ½ the joint thickness (e.g., 3/16 wire in 3/8 joint) ______________ 6.1.2.3
- ☐ Joint reinforcement min. 5/8-in. setback from face exposed to earth or weather, ½-in. setback when not so exposed____________ 6.1.4.2
- ☐ Reinforcing bars must be completely embedded in grout ____________ 6.1.1
- ☐ Area of vertical reinforcement max. 6% area of the grout space______ 6.1.2.4
- ☐ Clear distance between parallel bars min. 1 in. & min. 1 bar diameter_ 6.1.3.1
- ☐ In columns & pilasters, clear distance between parallel bars min. 1½ in. & min. 1½ bar diameters______________________ 6.1.3.2
- ☐ Clear distances in 6.1.3.1 & 6.1.3.2 also apply to lap splices **T14** & adjacent splices or bars ____________________ 6.1.3.3
- ☐ Groups of parallel bars bundled to act as a unit limited to 2 bars_____ 6.1.3.4
- ☐ Grout thickness between bars & CMUs min. ¼ in. for fine grout, ½ in. for coarse grout ________________ 6.1.3.5
- ☐ Min 1½ in. between reinforcement & face of masonry EXC _________ 6.1.4.1
  - 2 in. for bars > #5 from masonry face exposed to earth or weather _ 6.1.4.1

TABLE 15 — MASONRY WALL LATERAL SUPPORT SPACING T606.6.4

Construction	Max. Length to Thickness or Height to Thickness Ratio[A,B]
Bearing walls – solid or solid grouted	20
All other bearing walls	18
Nonbearing exterior walls	18
Nonbearing interior walls	36

A. Thickness = nominal thickness perpendicular to face of wall. For cavity walls, thickness = sum of thicknesses of wythes.
B. An additional unsupported height of 6 ft. permitted for gable end walls.

Reinforcement in SDC C Townhouses — 21 IRC

- ☐ Horizontal joint reinforcement wires min. W1.7 (9 gauge)______ 606.12.2.2.3
- ☐ Min solid wall length on exterior wall lines per **T16** ____________606.12.2.1
- ☐ Vertical reinforcement min. #4 bars at corners, ≤ 16 in. each side of openings, ≤8 in. of movement joints, ≤of ends & max. 10 ft. o.c. 606.12.2.3.3
- ☐ Horizontal reinforcement at bottom & top of wall openings & extending 24 in. past, continuously at structurally connected roof & floor levels & within 16 in. of top of walls ____________ 606.12.2.3.3

Reinforcement in SDC D

- ☐ Reqs for SDC C townhouses apply to all structures in SDC D ____ 606.12.3
- ☐ Design reqd in accordance w/ TMS 402 1-7 + 8.1 & 8.3 _________ 606.12.3
- ☐ Uniformly distributed reinforcement reqd vertical & horizontal_____606.12.3.2
- ☐ Max. spacing of vertical & horizontal reinforcement smaller of ⅓ length of shear wall, ⅓ height of shear wall, or 48 in. _______ 606.12.3.2.1
- ☐ Min vertical reinforcement ⅓ of total reqd reinforcement ______ 606.12.3.2.1
- ☐ Shear reinforcement reqs standard hooks around vertical bars __ 606.12.3.2.1
- ☐ Lateral ties reqd in columns min. diameter at max. 8 in. o.c. _______ 606.12.3.3
- ☐ SDC D_2 stack bond masonry max. horizontal reinforcement 16 in. 606.12.4.2

MASONRY WALLS

Grout — 21 IRC

- ☐ Cells containing reinforcement req solid grout fill ______ 606.3.5.3
- ☐ If construction stopped for ≥1 hr. in grouted masonry walls, all tiers stop at same elevation & grout within 1 in. of top ______ 606.3.5.1
- ☐ Pour in max. height 8 ft. lifts **F43** ______ 606.3.5.1
- ☐ Higher than 8-ft. pours must be placed in lifts ≤64 in. **F43** ______ 606.3.5.1
- ☐ High-lift grouting reqs special inspection **F43** ______ 606.3.5.1
- ☐ Cleanouts max. 32 in. o.c. reqd for high-lift grouting (> 64 in.) **F43** ______ 606.3.5.2
- ☐ Cleanouts sealed before grouting & after inspection **F43** ______ 606.3.5.2
- ☐ Max ½-in. projection of mortar into grout space ______ 606.3.5.2
- ☐ Vertical reinforcement held in position at top & bottom & at max. intervals of 200 bar diameters ______ 606.3.5.3
- ☐ Min. ¼-in. grout coverage between reinforcement & masonry EXC ______ 606.3.5.3
  - ¼-in. bars OK in ½-in. horizontal mortar joints, wire OK in horizontal joints 2× wire thickness ______ 606.3.5.3

FIG. 43

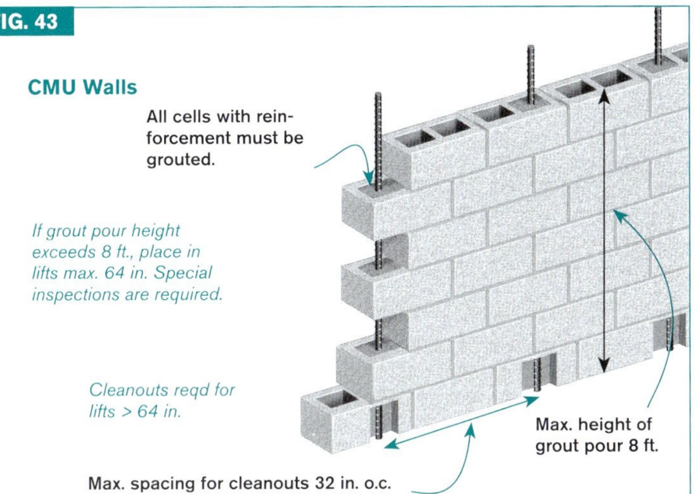

TABLE 16	MIN. PERCENTAGE OF SOLID MASONRY WALL LENGTH[A] ON EXTERIOR WALL LINES ◆ T606.12.2.1		
SDC	1 story or top of 2-story	Wall supporting light-frame 2nd story + roof	Wall supporting masonry 2nd story + roof
C[B]	20	25	35
D_0 or D_1	25	NP[C]	NP[C]
D_2	30	NP[C]	NP[C]

A. Based on length parallel to wall direction of rectangle inscribing overall building plan.
B. Applies only to townhouses.
C. NP = not permitted except by design in accordance w/ IBC.

Ledgers & Sills — 21 IRC

- ☐ Beam supports min. bearing 3 in. on 4 in. solid masonry or metal plate ______ 606.6.3
- ☐ Joist support on wood sill min. bearing 1½ in. ______ 606.6.3.1
- ☐ Bolt embedment min. 4 in. ______ F606.11.1

Floor & Roof Diaphragm Construction SDC C&D

- ☐ WSP diaphragms req blocking at edges perpendicular to framing 606.12.1.1
- ☐ WSP nailing 4 in. o.c. if diaphragm dimensions > 2:1 ratio ______ 606.12.1.1
- ☐ Secure to CMU walls in accordance w/ F606.11(1-3) **F44** ______ 606.12.1

FIG. 44

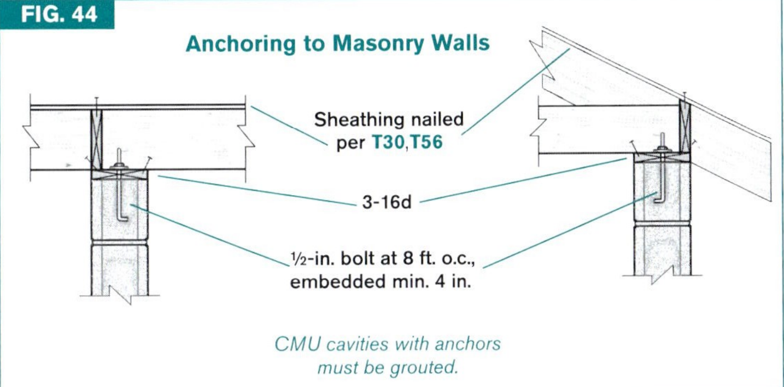

CONCRETE

As an alternative to the prescriptive reqs of the IRC, concrete foundation walls can be designed to ACI 318 or ACI 332. Those references also contain information on construction techniques and allowable tolerances that apply even without a complete adoption of them as an alternative code. Examples of the need for those documents include areas where soluble sulfates in the soil will be in contact with concrete or where adverse environmental conditions exist. ACI documents provide guidelines for admixtures to deal with these conditions. Slab-on-grade construction of single-family homes and townhouses is sometimes done with post-tensioned concrete, which then falls under the requirements of the IBC and ACI 318-19.

Materials & Placement — 21 IRC

- ☐ Materials & testing to conform to ACI 318 & ACI 332 **T1** ____________ 402.2
- ☐ Min. compressive strength 2,500 psi & per **T17** ________ 402.2 & 404.1.3.3.1
- ☐ Cements per ASTM C150, C595 & C1157 ___________ 402.2.1 & 608.5.1.1
- ☐ Mixing & delivery per ASTM C94 & C685 _____________ 402.2.1 & 608.5.1.2
- ☐ Max. aggregate size 1/5 distance between forms or 3/4 distance between reinforcement bars or between bar & side of form __ 404.1.3.3.3 & 608.5.1.3
- ☐ Max. slump if removable forms 6 in. **F45** __________ 404.1.3.3.4 & 608.5.1.4
- ☐ Slump w/ stay-in-place forms >6 in. per ASTM C143 404.1.3.3.4 & 608.5.1.4
- ☐ Thoroughly work around rebar & into corners ______ 404.1.3.3.5 & 608.5.1.6
- ☐ Immersion-vibrate stay-in-place forms (ICF) _______ 404.1.3.3.5 & 608.5.1.6
- ☐ Cold joint reinforcement min. 12 in. each side of joint 404.1.3.3.7.8 & 608.5.5

ACI 318-19

- ☐ Remove debris & ice prior to placement of concrete ____________ 26.5.2.1(a)
- ☐ Standing water removed (unless tremie is to be used) __________ 26.5.2.1(b)
- ☐ No pumping concrete through aluminum or aluminum alloy pipes _ 26.5.2.1(d)
- ☐ Select materials, methods, delivery, handling, placement & curing within specified temperature limits (max. temp of concrete 95°) _ 26.5.4.2 & 26.5.5.2

Curing

- ☐ Maintain concrete at min. 50°F & in moist condition 7 days EXC __ 26.5.3.2(a)
  - High-early-strength concrete 3 days OK _________________ 26.5.3.2(b)
  - Accelerated curing at direction of licensed design professional _ 26.5.3.2(c)

FIG. 45 — Slump Test: ASTM C143

1. Dampen mold and place on flat nonabsorbent rigid surface. Hold mold in place by standing on foot pieces (preferred) or by clamping to a base plate.

2. Fill mold in 3 layers from concrete sample, each approximately 1/3 cone volume. Third layer is heaped above the top of the mold.

3. Rod each layer with strokes of tamping rod, uniformly distributed over cross section of each layer. Rod each layer to its depth, barely penetrating the underlying layer. Heap concrete above mold for top layer; keep excess of concrete above top.

4. Strike excess concrete off surface by screeding and rolling motion of the tamping rod.

5. Immediately remove mold with smooth vertical lift. Complete entire test from start of filling to removal of mold without interruption within elapsed time of 2 1/2 minutes.

6. Vertical distance between top of mold and displaced center of slumped concrete is measured and reported to the nearest 1/4 in.

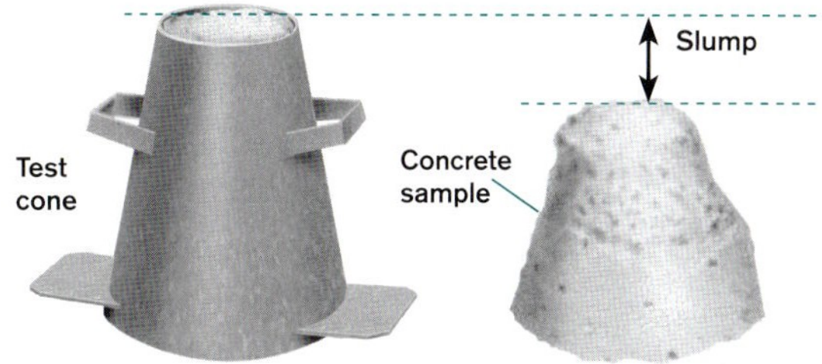

If a decided falling away or shearing off of a portion of concrete or portion of the mass occurs, disregard test and make a new test on another sample. Two consecutive failed tests are grounds to reject the concrete.

In general, concrete >2,500 psi requires special inspections and tests conducted by an approved agency, except for concrete that supports light-frame construction ≤3 stories above grade plane. The IRC does not address the question of testing for areas requiring >2,500 psi concrete in **T17**, and pumped concrete will be >2,500 psi. Environmental, climate, or soils issues may necessitate testing even for buildings within the scope of the IRC, and testing is reqd for commercial construction. A design professional will specify which tests are needed, and building jurisdictions typically have a list of approved agencies qualified to perform special testing. ICC provides certification for special inspectors of concrete work.

Special Inspections — 21 IBC

- ☐ Approved agency to be independent of contractor performing work _1703.1.1
- ☐ Special inspections of concrete reqd EXC ______________1705.3 & 1901.6
  - Fully supported footings supporting ≤3 stories above grade plane of light-frame construction, prescriptively designed & based on specified compressive strength ≤2,500 psi ______________1705.3X2
  - Nonstructural slabs supported directly on the ground __________1705.3X3
  - Prescriptive concrete foundation walls per IBC T1807.1.6.2_____1705.3X4
  - Patios, sidewalks & driveways on grade ____________________1705.3X5
- ☐ No welding of reinforcing bars w/o special inspection____________1705.3.1

FIG. 46

Test Cylinders

Strength tests are taken from the average of at least two 6×12-in. cylinders (or three 4×8 cylinders). Extra cylinders are usually made. Care must be taken in the storage and transporting of cylinders. They must be kept at a temperature between 60°F and 80°F and be taken to the lab within 48 hours.

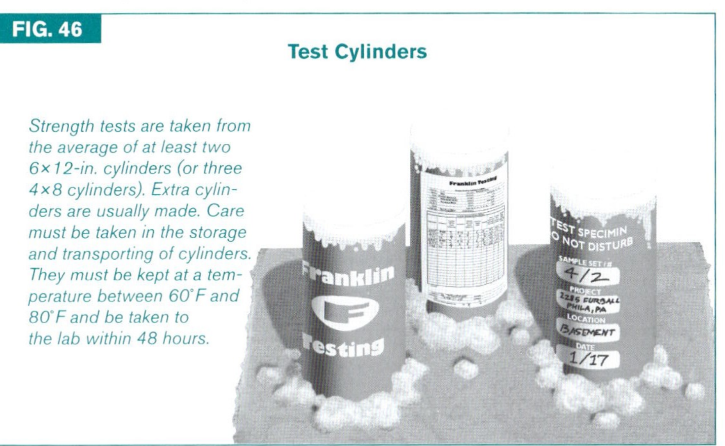

TABLE 17 — MIN. SPECIFIED COMPRESSIVE STRENGTH OF CONCRETE ◆ T402.2 & 404.1.3.3.1

Type or Location of Construction	Min. Compressive Strength[A]		
	Weathering Potential (from **T2**)		
	Negligible	Moderate	Severe
Basement walls, foundation & other concrete not exposed to weather	2,500	2,500	2,500[B]
Basement slabs and interior slabs on grade, except garage floor slabs	2,500	2,500	2,500[B]
Basement walls, foundation walls, exterior walls & other vertical concrete work exposed to the weather	2,500	3,000[C]	3,000[C]
Porches, carport slabs & steps exposed to the weather & garage floor slabs	2,500	3,000[C,D,E]	3,500[C,D,E]
Foundation walls in SDC A, B & C	2,500		
Foundation walls in SDC D	3,000		

A. Strength at 28 days psi.
B. Must be air entrained per note C if subject to freeze-thaw during construction.
C. Must be air entrained. Total air content by volume min. 5% max. 7%.
D. Max. cementitious materials content per ACI 332 T5.4.2 or ACI 318 T26.4.2.2(b).
E. Steel-trowel finished garage slab OK to reduce air entrainment to ≥3% if concrete is ≥4,000 psi.

Testing — ACI 318-19

- ☐ Strength test = average of at least two 6×12 cylinders or three 4 × 8 cylinders from same sample & tested at 28 days **F46** __________26.12.1.1(a)
- ☐ Samples min. once per day, once per 150 cu. yd. & once for each 5,000 sq. ft. of slabs or walls **F46** ______________26.12.2.1(a)
- ☐ Min. of 5 randomly selected batches for testing _____________26.12.2.1(b)
- ☐ If total quantity < 50 cu. yd. BO may accept other evidence of satisfactory strength & waive testing_____________26.12.2.1(c)
- ☐ If strength test fails, core testing per ASTM C42 ______________ 26.12.6.1

Cycles of freezing and thawing, exposure to sulfates in soils, and exposure to de-icing chemicals or other salt or seawater all can deteriorate concrete and reinforcement. These conditions req higher strengths of concrete as well as limitations on admixtures that might otherwise be used for applications such as accelerated curing. We recommend consulting the full text of ACI 318-19 or ACI 332-20 when these conditions are encountered.

Special Exposure Conditions — ACI 332-20

- ☐ Assign to classes in **T18** based on severity of anticipated exposure ____ 5.1.1
- ☐ Calcium chloride admixtures prohibited in **T18** RS2&3 condition ______ T5.3.2
- ☐ Min. psi per **T19** ______ T5.3.2
- ☐ Category RF1–4 reqd to be air entrained per **T20** ______ T5.4.1
- ☐ Max. quantity of pozzolans, fly ash, silica fume & slag in RF3&4 **T21** ___ T5.4.2

TABLE 18 — EXPOSURE CATEGORIES & CLASSES ◆ ACI 332-20 5.1.1

Category	Severity	Class	Condition
RF freezing & thawing	Not applicable	RF0	Not exposed to freeze-thaw cycles
	Moderate	RF1	Moisture exposure but unlikely saturation
	Severe	RF2	Reinforced, potential saturation, freeze-thaw
	Very severe	RF3	Plain concrete, moisture exposure, de-icing chemicals, saturation during freeze-thaw
	Most severe	RF4	Reinforced concrete, moisture exposure, de-icing chemicals, saturation during freeze-thaw
RS sulfate	Not applicable	RS0	$SO_4 < 0.10$[A]
	Moderate	RS1	$0.10 \le SO_4 < 0.20$[A]
	Severe	RS2	$0.20 \le SO_4 < 2.00$[A]
	Very severe	RS3	$SO_4 > 2.00$[A]
RC corrosion protection of reinforcement	Not applicable	RC0	Dry or protected from moisture
	Moderate	RC1	Reinforced concrete, moisture exposure, no exposure to external sources of chlorides
	Severe	RC2	Reinforced concrete, moisture exposure, exposure to chlorides, de-icing, salt, seawater, etc.

A. Soluble SO_4 in soil, % by mass.

TABLE 19 — MIN. PSI FOR EXPOSURE CLASSES ◆ ACI 332-20 T5.3.2

Class	Min. PSI	Class	Min. PSI	Class	Min. PSI
RF0	2,500	RF4	5,000	RS3	3,000
RF1	3,500	RS0	2,500	RC0	2,500
RF2	4,500	RS1	2,500	RC1	2,500
RF3	4,500	RS2	3,000	RC2	4,000

TABLE 20 — AIR CONTENT % IN CATEGORY RF ◆ ACI 332-20 T5.4.1

Max. Aggregate Size (in.)	Air Content[A] Class RF1	Air Content[A] Class RF2, 3 & 4
3/8	6	7.5
1/2	5.5	7
3/4	5	6
1	4.5	6
1 1/2	4.5	5.5
2	4	5
3	3.5	4.5

A. Tolerance on air content of + or − 1.5% is permissible.

TABLE 21 — MATERIALS IN CLASS RF3 & RF4 ◆ ACI 332-20 T5.4.2

Cementitious Materials	Max. % of total cementitious materials by weight
Fly ash or other pozzolans conforming to ASTM C618	25
Slag conforming to ASTM C989/C989M	50
Silica fume conforming to ASTM C1240	10
Total of fly ash or other pozzolans, slag & silica fume	50[A]
Total of fly ash or other pozzolans & silica fume	35[A]

A. Fly ash or other pozzolans and silica fume max. 25% and 10% respectively of total weight of cementitious materials.

UNDERFLOOR AREA (CRAWLSPACES)

Foundation Walls & Crawlspaces — 21 IRC

- ☐ Remove all vegetation, organic material & construction debris ________ 408.5
- ☐ Wood forms must be completely stripped off foundation ________ 408.5

Access Openings

- ☐ Access openings in floor min. 24 in. × 18 in. ________ 408.4
- ☐ Access openings in perimeter wall min. 24 in. × 16 in. **F47** ________ 408.4
- ☐ If any portion of perimeter wall opening below grade, provide min. 16-in. × 24-in. areaway **F47** ________ 408.4
- ☐ Bottom of areaway must be below threshold of access opening **F47** __ 408.4
- ☐ Through-wall openings not OK below a door to the residence ________ 408.4
- ☐ Opening large enough to remove underfloor mechanical equipment 1305.1.3

Ventilation

- ☐ Underfloor space reqs moisture control except space for basements __ 408.1
- ☐ Vent openings in foundation or exterior walls surrounding crawlspace _ 408.2
- ☐ One vent opening within 3 ft. of each external corner **F48** ________ 408.2[39]
- ☐ Openings req protective cover of screens, grates, or plates ________ 408.2
- ☐ Largest allowable opening dimension in covering elements ¼ in. _____ 408.2
- ☐ Min. net area of openings 1 sq. ft. per 150 sq. ft. of underfloor area EXC ________ 408.2
  - Reduction to 1/1500 OK w/ Class 1 vapor retarder ________ 408.2X1
  - If Class 1 vapor retarder covers ground, openings need not be within 3 ft. of external corners if openings provide cross ventilation ____ 408.2X2[40]
- ☐ Unvented crawlspaces allowed w/ Class I vapor retarder on ground & sealed to stem wall & space conditioned or provided w/ continuous mechanical ventilation or dehumidification system ________ 408.3

Underfloor Vapor Retarder

- ☐ In Climate Zones 1A, 2A & 3A (humid very hot to warm) continuous Class I or II vapor retarder reqd on exposed face of air-permeable insulation beneath joists & exposed to grade in ventilated crawlspace 408.8[41]

39. Clarification that vents only reqd within 3 ft. of external corners – not all corners.
40. New exception can exempt corner locations when cross ventilation provided.
41. New req for vapor retarders to protect insulation in warm, hot, and very hot humid climates.

FIG. 47

Underfloor Access Opening

Access opening through a perimeter wall opening not allowed beneath a door.

Min. 24 in.

Min. 16 in.

Min. 16 in.

Bottom of area way below threshold of access opening

Dimensions shown are for access through a perimeter wall opening. Access openings through floors must be min. 18 in. x 24 in.

FIG. 48

Crawlspace Ventilation

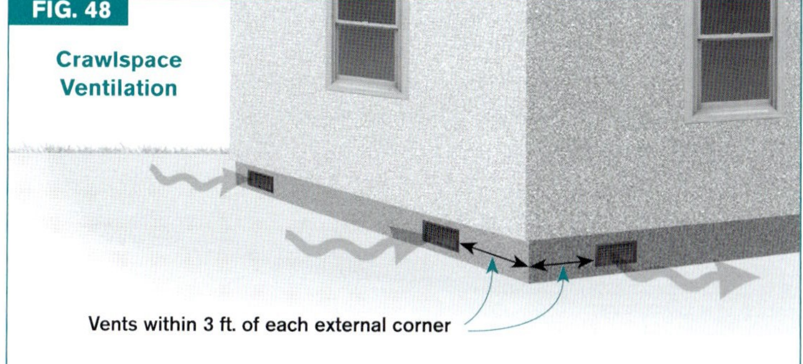

PROTECTION AGAINST DECAY & TERMITES

Naturally durable wood (NDW) refers to the heartwood of redwood, cedar, black locust, and black walnut. Fastener corrosion can be a major problem with preservative-treated (PT) wood or fire-retardant-treated (FRT) wood.

Protection Against Decay — 21 IRC

- ☐ Following areas req NDW or PT wood: ____ 317.1
  1. F49 In crawlspaces or unexcavated areas within building footprint, NDW or PT reqd if distance to exposed ground <18 in. for joists or underside of floor, <12 in. for girders, or <8 in. for wood columns[42]
  2. Framing on concrete or masonry exterior foundations < 8 in. above exposed ground F49
  3. Sills & sleepers on concrete slab w/o impervious moisture barrier
  4. Ends of wood girders in concrete or masonry walls F39
  5. Exterior siding/sheathing/framing <6 in. to soil or 2 in. to hardscape F49
  6. Wood supporting permeable structural members exposed to weather & w/o an impervious moisture barrier
  7. Wood furring on below-grade exterior walls w/o approved vapor retarder
  8. Structural supports of balconies, porches, etc., exposed to weather[43]
  9. Wood columns in direct contact w/ basement floor slabs[44]
- ☐ Field-cut ends, notches & holes to be field-treated ____ 317.1.1
- ☐ Wood in ground contact or embedded in concrete reqd to be PPT rated suitable for ground-contact ____ 317.1.2
- ☐ Quality mark from accredited agency reqd on PT lumber & plywood ____ 317.2
- ☐ Quality mark reqd on each piece & must include identification of treatment plant, preservative type, min. retention, end use for which product was treated, standard, identification of inspection agency & the designation "dry" if applicable EXC ____ 317.2.1
  - Small pieces (< nominal 1 in., <1 in. × 5 in., <2 in. × 4 in., or <36 in. length) stamp on exterior face or end label of bundled unit ____ 317.2.1X

Protection Against Termites

- ☐ In areas subject to termite damage T2, provide barriers, chemical treatment, PT or NDW wood, bait systems, or steel framing ____ 318.1

42. Wood columns added to this section; heights in this section are to exposed ground.
43. Items 8 and 9 are new. An example for #8 would be cantilevered support for an elevated balcony.
44. Exempt if column is on min. 1-in. metal pedestal and separated by impervious barrier.

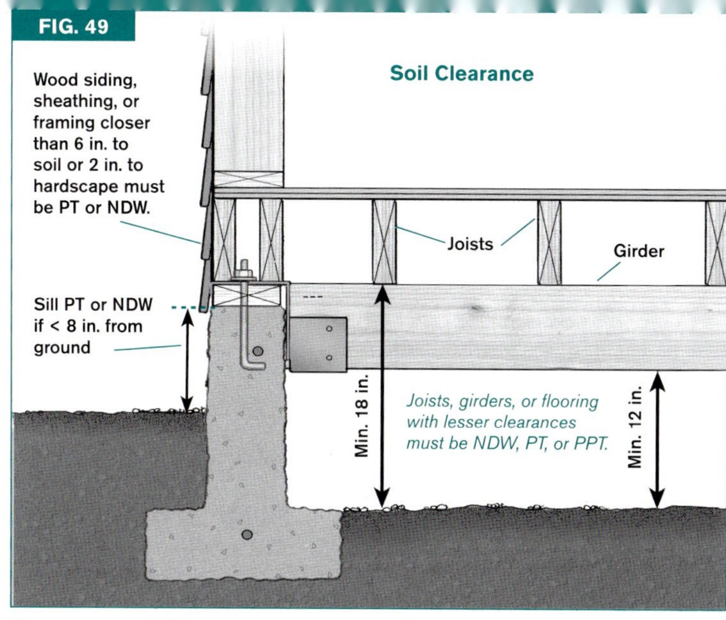

Connectors & Fasteners in Contact w/ Treated Wood — 21 IRC

- ☐ Fastener & connector coatings for PT or FRT wood either Zi weights per ASTM A153 or stainless steel per ASTM F1667 ____ 317.3
- ☐ Staples reqd to be stainless steel ____ 317.3.1
- ☐ Fasteners, nuts & washers for PT wood hot-dipped, Zi-coated Zi steel, stainless steel, silicon bronze, or copper installed AMI EXC ____ 317.3.1
  - Steel bolts ≥ ½ in. diameter ____ 317.3.1X1
  - Fasteners other than nails, staples & timber rivets Zi ≥ Class 55 317.3.1X2
  - Plain carbon steel fasteners in SBX/DOT or zinc-borate PT OK in an interior dry environment ____ 317.3.1X3
- ☐ In absence of MFR instructions, min. G185 Zi coating or equivalent ____ 317.3.1
- ☐ Same rules as above for fasteners in FRT wood ____ 317.3.3&4

FLOOR FRAMING

Prior to placing sill plates, sealants, vapor retarders, and termite shields can be put in place to improve the energy conservation features and protection of the house. Example videos can be found by a search for "sill plates" at FineHomebuilding.com. Manufactured lumber products, such as I-joists, do not use the same span tables as the tables for common lumber species. Follow the manufacturer's instructions and plans for these products. Substitutions should not be made without first consulting the specifying architect or other designer.

General — 21 IRC

- ☐ Sawn lumber reqs identifying grade mark or certificate of inspection 502.1.1
- ☐ Approved end-jointed lumber reqs identifying grade mark & can be used interchangeably w/ solid sawn lumber of same species & grade ___ 502.1.1.2
- ☐ Manufactured wood products per standards in **T22** ___ 502.1.2–7
- ☐ Fastening per **T29** ___ 502.9
- ☐ Wood sills min. 2 in. × 4 in. nominal, anchorage per **F41** ___ 404.3

TABLE 22 — MANUFACTURED WOOD PRODUCT STANDARDS

Product	Applicable Standards
Prefabricated wood I-joists	ASTM D5055
Structural glued laminated timbers	ANSI A190.1, 117 ASTM D3737
Structural composite lumber (e.g., LVL)	ASTM D5456
Cross-laminated timber	ANSI/APA PRG 320
Engineered wood rim board	ANSI/APA PRR 410 or ASTM D7672

Wood Girders — 21 IRC

- ☐ Girders directly supported on masonry piers req anchorage ___ 404.1.9.2
- ☐ Positive connection reqd between posts & girders **F38** ___ 502.9
- ☐ Built-up girder and header spans per T602.7(1,2&3) **T35,36** ___ 502.5
- ☐ Built-up girder nailing per **T29** ___ T602.3(1)
- ☐ End bearing min. 3 in. when direct on concrete or masonry; 1½ in. OK on sill plate w/ min. nominal bearing area 48 sq. in. ___ 502.6
- ☐ End bearing min. 1½ in. on wood or metal ___ 502.6
- ☐ Max. offset 1 joist depth from bearing wall above **F50** ___ 502.4
- ☐ Notching & boring per **F53** & **T23** ___ 502.8.1

FIG. 50 — Bearing Wall Support

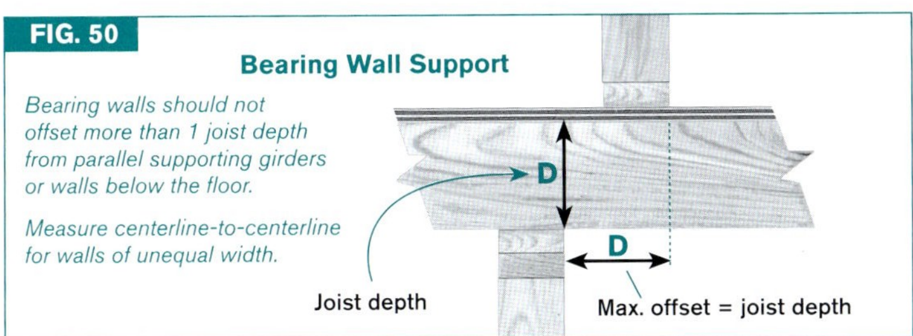

Bearing walls should not offset more than 1 joist depth from parallel supporting girders or walls below the floor.

Measure centerline-to-centerline for walls of unequal width.

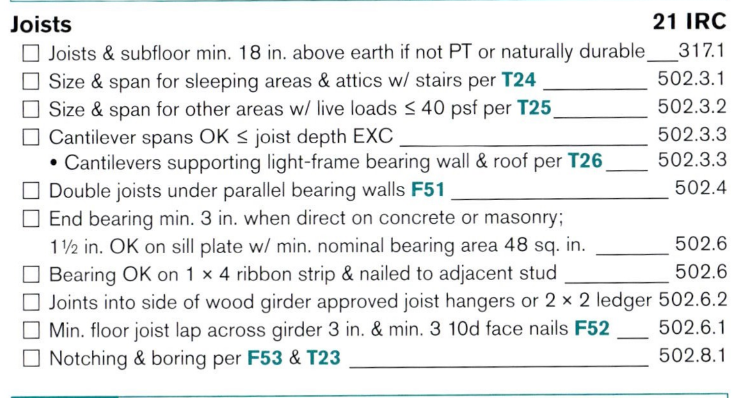

Joists — 21 IRC

- ☐ Joists & subfloor min. 18 in. above earth if not PT or naturally durable ___ 317.1
- ☐ Size & span for sleeping areas & attics w/ stairs per **T24** ___ 502.3.1
- ☐ Size & span for other areas w/ live loads ≤ 40 psf per **T25** ___ 502.3.2
- ☐ Cantilever spans OK ≤ joist depth EXC ___ 502.3.3
  - Cantilevers supporting light-frame bearing wall & roof per **T26** ___ 502.3.3
- ☐ Double joists under parallel bearing walls **F51** ___ 502.4
- ☐ End bearing min. 3 in. when direct on concrete or masonry; 1½ in. OK on sill plate w/ min. nominal bearing area 48 sq. in. ___ 502.6
- ☐ Bearing OK on 1 × 4 ribbon strip & nailed to adjacent stud ___ 502.6
- ☐ Joints into side of wood girder approved joist hangers or 2 × 2 ledger 502.6.2
- ☐ Min. floor joist lap across girder 3 in. & min. 3 10d face nails **F52** ___ 502.6.1
- ☐ Notching & boring per **F53** & **T23** ___ 502.8.1

FIG. 51 — Double Joists under Parallel Bearing Wall

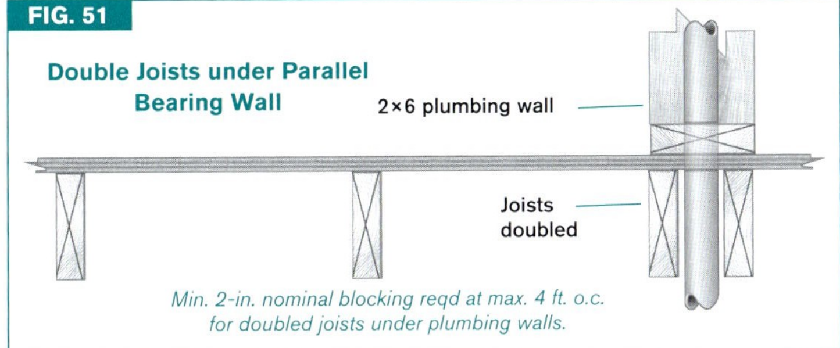

Min. 2-in. nominal blocking reqd at max. 4 ft. o.c. for doubled joists under plumbing walls.

Framing at Openings in Floors — 21 IRC

- ☐ Openings to be framed using headers & trimmers ________ 502.10
- ☐ Single header joist same size as floor joists allowed max. 4-ft. span __ 502.10
- ☐ Single trimmers carrying single headers max. 3 ft. to trimmer bearing _ 502.10
- ☐ Double trimmers for openings >3 ft. from trimmer bearing points ____ 502.10
- ☐ Double headers & trimmers when header span >4 ft. ________ 502.10
- ☐ Headers & trimmers req bearing support or approved joist hangers ___ 502.6
- ☐ Combustible framing min. 2 in. from masonry chimneys *(see p. 115)*_ 1003.18

Joist Blocking & Bridging

- ☐ All joist ends req lateral restraint: blocking, attachment to rim joists or full depth header, or attachment to adjoining stud **F52** ________ 502.7
- ☐ Blocking min. 2× material & full depth of joist **F52** ________ 502.7
- ☐ Blocking also reqd at intermediate supports in SDC D ________ 502.7X2
- ☐ Lateral restraint of engineered lumber AMI ________ 502.7X1
- ☐ Joists >2 × 12 req bridging or continuous 1-in. × 3-in. strip across bottom of joists at max. 8-ft. intervals ________ 502.7.1

FIG. 52 Joist Blocking

Blocking or other lateral restraint at all joist ends

Lap min. 3 in.

Min. 3 10d nails to tie joists together

Lateral restraint also reqd at intermediate supports in SDC D

Toenails into girder per **T29**

TABLE 23 — NOTCHING & BORING JOISTS & GIRDERS ◆ 502.8.1

Nominal[A] Dimension Joist or Girder	Max. Diameter Bored Hole	Max. Notch Length	Max. Notch Depth Outer 1/3	Max. Depth End Notch
6	1 1/2 in.[B]	1 13/16 in.	7/8 in.	1 3/8 in.
8	2 3/8 in.	2 3/8 in.	1 3/16 in.	1 13/16 in.
10	3 1/16 in.	3 1/16 in.	1 1/2 in.	2 5/16 in.
12	3 3/4 in.	3 3/4 in.	1 7/8 in.	2 13/16 in.

A. Table numbers based on actual dimensions: Typically 5 1/2, 7 1/4, 9 1/4, and 11 1/4.
B. Though 1/3 depth would be 1 13/16 in., a hole that size would be <2 in. from the edge in 5 1/2-in. material.

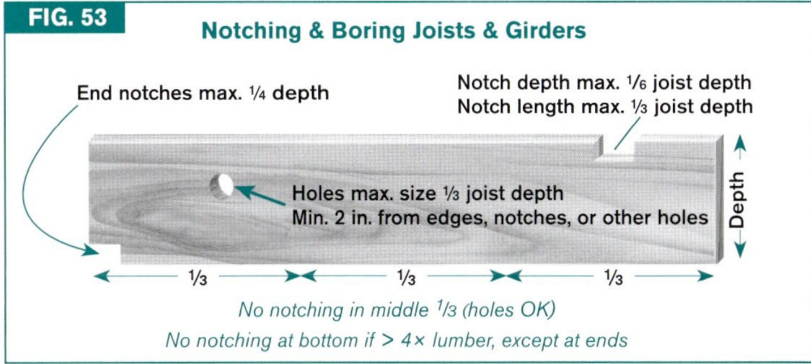

Engineered Wood Products & Floor Trusses — 21 IRC

- ☐ Cuts, notches & holes only AMI by MFR or where specified & considered in design by a registered design professional **F54** ______ 502.8.2
- ☐ Metal-plate connected wood trusses per ANSI/TPI 1 & req design drawings by a registered design professional ________ 502.11.1
- ☐ Truss drawings to include bracing requirements ________ 502.11.2
- ☐ No truss alterations or repairs w/o approval of registered design professional ________ 502.11.3
- ☐ Truss design drawings must be submitted & approved by BO prior to installation & design drawings to be provided w/ shipment to job site 502.11.4
- ☐ Design drawings to include same types of information as reqd for roof trusses—see *p. 95* ________ 502.11.4

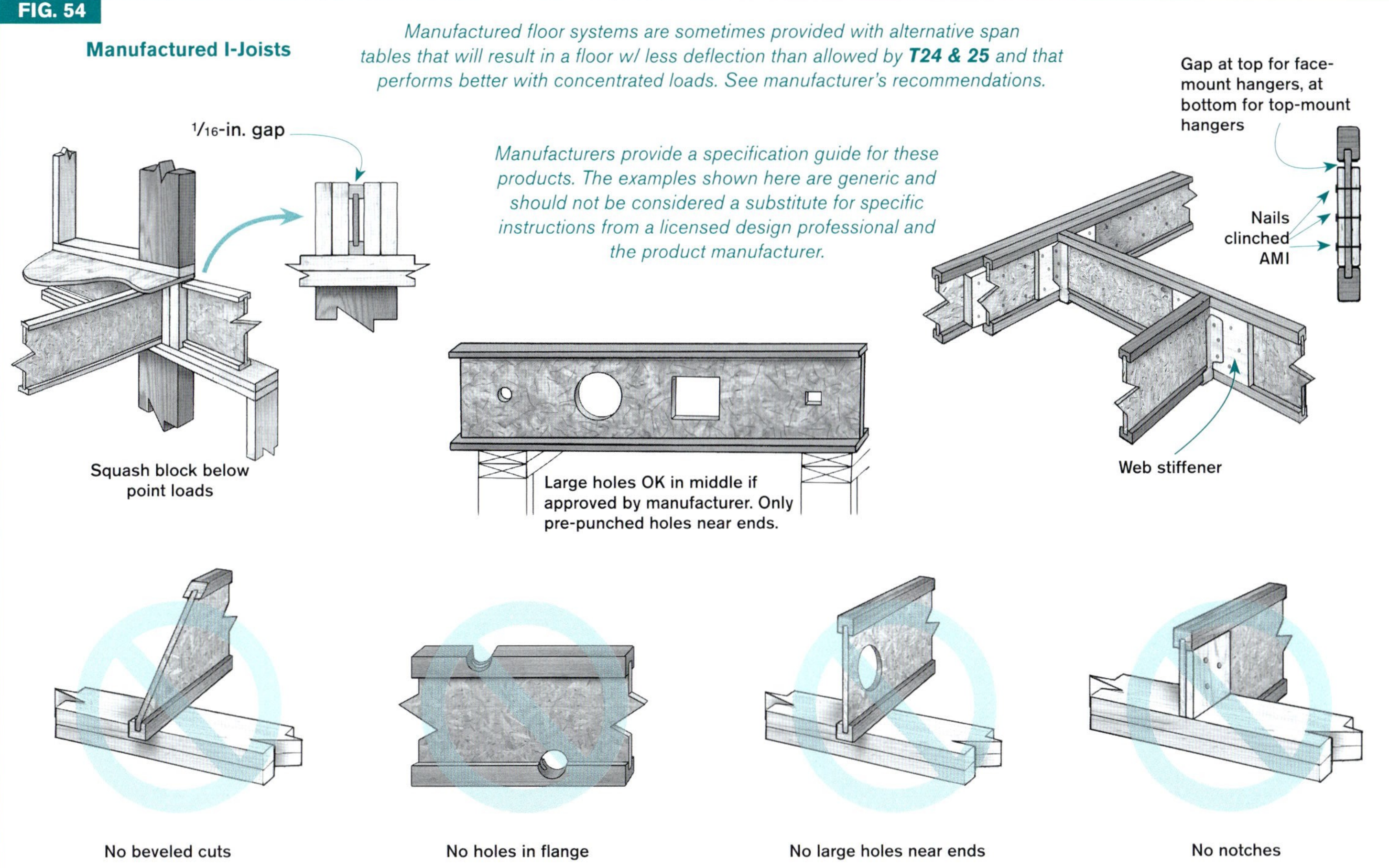
FIG. 54
Manufactured I-Joists
Manufactured floor systems are sometimes provided with alternative span tables that will result in a floor w/ less deflection than allowed by **T24 & 25** and that performs better with concentrated loads. See manufacturer's recommendations.
Manufacturers provide a specification guide for these products. The examples shown here are generic and should not be considered a substitute for specific instructions from a licensed design professional and the product manufacturer.
1/16-in. gap
Squash block below point loads
Large holes OK in middle if approved by manufacturer. Only pre-punched holes near ends.
Gap at top for face-mount hangers, at bottom for top-mount hangers
Nails clinched AMI
Web stiffener
No beveled cuts
No holes in flange
No large holes near ends
No notches

TABLE 24 JOIST SPANS FOR 30-PSF LIVE LOAD[A] (SLEEPING AREAS) ◆ T502.3.1(1) (IN FEET–INCHES)

Size	Spacing (in. o.c.)				Spacing (in. o.c.)			
	12	16	19.2	24	12	16	19.2	24
	Douglas Fir-Larch #2				Hem-Fir #2			
2×6	11–10	10–9	10–1	9–3	11–0	10–0	9–5	8–9
2×8	15–7	14–2	13–0	11–8	14–6	13–2	12–5	11–4
2×10	19–10	17–5	15–11	14–3	18–6	16–10	15–6	13–10
2×12	23–4	20–3	18–6	16–6	22–6	19–8	17–1	16–1
Size	Southern Pine #2				Spruce-Pine-Fir #2			
2×6	11–3	10–3	9–6	8–6	11–3	10–3	9–8	8–11
2×8	14–11	13–3	12–1	10–10	14–11	13–6	12–9	11–6
2×10	18–1	15–8	14–4	12–10	19–0	17–2	15–8	14–1
2×12	21–4	18–6	16–10	15–1	23–0	19–11	18–3	16–3

A. Dead load = 10 psf. For other grades or dead loads, see IRC Table R502.3.1(1).

TABLE 25 JOIST SPANS FOR 40-PSF LIVE LOAD[A] (LIVING AREAS) ◆ T502.3.1(2) (IN FEET–INCHES)

Size	Spacing (in. o.c.)				Spacing (in. o.c.)			
	12	16	19.2	24	12	16	19.2	24
	Douglas Fir-Larch #2				Hem–Fir #2			
2×6	10–9	9–9	9–2	8–3	10–0	9–1	8–7	7–11
2×8	14–2	12–9	11–8	10–5	13–2	12–0	11–3	10–2
2×10	18–0	15–7	14–3	12–9	16–10	15–2	13–10	12–5
2×12	20–11	18–1	16–6	14–9	20–4	17–7	16–1	14–4
Size	Southern Pine #2				Spruce-Pine-Fir #2			
2×6	10–3	9–4	8–6	7–7	10–3	9–4	8–9	8–1
2×8	13–6	11–10	10–10	9–8	13–6	12–3	11–6	10–3
2×10	16–2	14–0	12–10	11–5	17–3	15–5	14–1	12–7
2×12	19–1	16–6	15–1	13–6	20–7	17–10	16–3	14–7

A. Dead load = 10 psf. For other grades or dead loads, see IRC Table R502.3.1(2).

TABLE 26 CANTILEVER SPANS FOR JOISTS SUPPORTING LIGHT-FRAME EXTERIOR BEARING WALL + ROOF ONLY[A] ◆ T502.3.3(1)

Nominal Member Size & Spacing	Max. Cantilever Span in Inches (Uplift Force at Backspan in Pounds)											
	≤ 20 psf Ground Snow Load			30 psf Ground Snow Load			50 psf Ground Snow Load			70 psf Ground Snow Load		
	Roof Width			Roof Width			Roof Width			Roof Width		
	24 ft.	32 ft.	40 ft.	24 ft.	32 ft.	40 ft.	24 ft.	32 ft.	40 ft.	24 ft.	32 ft.	40 ft.
2×8 @ 12 in.	20 (177)	15(227)		18 (209)								
2×10 @ 16 in.	29 (228)	21 (297)	16 (364)	26(271)	18 (354)		20 (375)					
2×10 @ 12 in.	36 (166)	26 (219)	20 (270)	34 (198)	22 (263)	16 (324)	26 (277)			19 (356)		
2×12 @ 16 in.		32 (287)	25 (356)	36 (263)	29 (345)	21 (428)	29 (367)	20 (484)		23 (471)		
2×12 @ 12 in.		42 (209	31 (263)		37 (253)	27 (317)	36 (271)	27 (358)	17 (447)	31 (348)	19 (462)	
2×12 @ 8 in.		48 (136)	45 (169)		48 (164)	38 (206)		40 (233)	26 (294)	36 (230)	29 (304)	18 (379)

A. Based on #2 grade lumber; ratio of backspan to cantilever min. 3:1; uplift connections reqd at backspan support; see ***p. 12 and 13*** for limitations on SDC C & D; full-depth rim joist reqd at unsupported end of cantilever joists, solid blocking reqd at supported end. Linear interpolation of table values allowed.

FLOOR SHEATHING

The IRC allows lumber sheathing as subfloor material, though wood structural panels (plywood and OSB) are far more common. When used on roofs and floors, the allowable live load is based upon the panel rating, orientation, and support span in accordance w/ its grade stamp **F55**. Underlayment is a special grade of plywood attached on top of the subfloor to provide a more durable and dent-resistant layer under finish flooring. "Subfloor and combined subfloor underlayment" is a material that can be covered directly with carpeting or other finish floor materials. Products such as APA-rated "Sturd-I-Floor" **F56** are intended primarily as combination subfloor-underlayment, and are also rated as subfloor, roof, or diaphragm sheathing.

Lumber Sheathing — 21 IRC

- ☐ Allowable spans per **T27** _______ 503.1
- ☐ End joints over supports unless end-matched lumber used _______ 503.1.1
- ☐ No subfloor reqd for nominal 1 in. T&G perpendicular to 16 in. o.c. joists _ 503.1.1

TABLE 27 MIN. NET SIZE LUMBER FLOOR SHEATHING ◆ T503.1

Joist or Beam Spacing	Perpendicular to Joist	Diagonal to Joist
24 in.	11/16 in.	3/4 in.
16 in.	5/8 in.	5/8 in.
48 in.	1 1/2 in. T&G	n/a

Wood Structural Panel (WSP) Sheathing — 21 IRC

- ☐ WSP sheathing used for structural purposes reqs grade stamp from approved agency **F55** _______ 503.2.1
- ☐ Allowable spans & loads per T503.2.1.1(1) (see grade stamp) _______ 503.2.2
- ☐ Panels continuous over ≥ 2 spans _______ T503.2.1.1(1)
- ☐ Strength axis perpendicular to supports _______ T503.2.1.1(1)
- ☐ Unsupported edges T&G or blocked _______ T503.2.1.1(1)
- ☐ Fasten in accordance w/ **T30,31,F62** _______ 503.2.3

Subfloor & Combined Subfloor Underlayment

- ☐ Allowable span based on species grouping **T28** _______ 503.2.1.1
- ☐ Must be continuous over 2 or more spans, grain perpendicular to supports, tongue & groove edges or blocked _______ T503.2.1.1(2)

FIG. 55 Wood Structural Panel Grade Mark

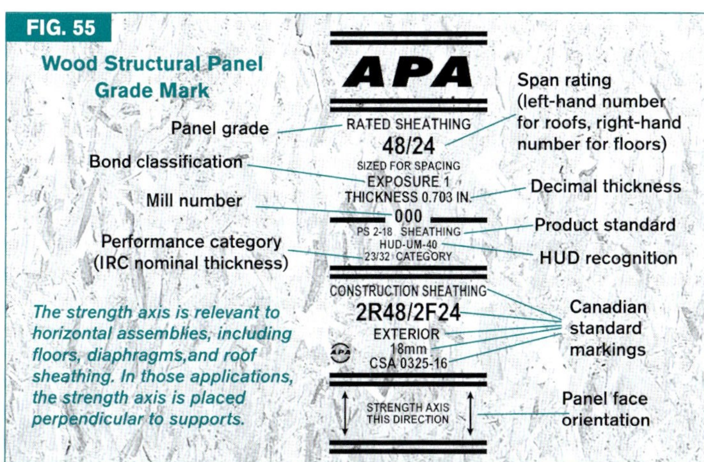

FIG. 56 Subfloor & Combined Subfloor Underlayment

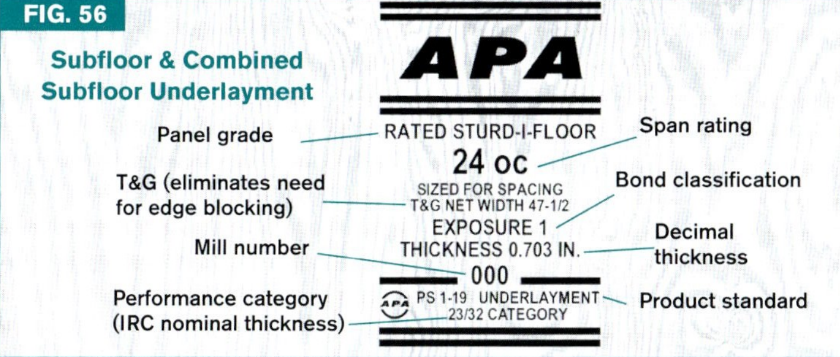

TABLE 28 ALLOWABLE SPANS SANDED PLYWOOD COMBINATION SUBFLOOR UNDERLAYMENT ◆ T503.2.1.1(2)

Species Group	16-in.-o.c. Joists	20-in.-o.c. Joists	24-in.-o.c. Joists
1	1/2	5/8	3/4
2,3	5/8	3/4	7/8
4	3/4	7/8	1

TABLE 29 FLOOR FRAMING FASTENER SCHEDULE ◆ T602.3(1)

Connection	Fastener	Method
Joist to sill, top plate, or girder	4 8d box; or 3 8d common or 3 10d box or 3 3-in. gun nails	Toenail
Rim joist, band joist, or blocking to sill or top plate (also roof)	8d box	4 in. o.c. toenail
	8d common or 10d box; or 3-in. gun nails	6 in. o.c. toenail
1 × 6 subfloor to joist	3 8d box or 2 8d common or 3 10d box or 2 1-in. crown 16-ga. staples 1¾ in. long	Face nail
2-in. plank subfloor to joist or girder	3 16d box or 2 16d common	Blind & face nail
2-in. planks to beams	3 16d box or 2 16d common	Each bearing, face nail
Band or rim joist to joist	3 16d common or 4 10d box or 4 3-in. gun nails or 4 3-in. 14-ga staples w/ 7/16 crown	End nail
Built-up girders & beams, 2-in. lumber layers	20d common	each layer 32 in. o.c. at top & bottom & staggered
	10d box or 3-in. gun nails	24 in. o.c. face nail top & bottom & staggered on opposite sides
Ends & splices of built-up girders and beams	2 20d common or 3 10d box or 3 3-in. gun nails	Face nail
Ledger strip supporting joists or rafters	4 16d box or 3 16d common or 4 10d box or 4 3-in. gun nails	At each joist or rafter, face nail
Bridging or blocking to joist or truss	2 10d box or 2 8d common or 2 3-in. gun nails	Each end, toenail

TABLE 30 WSP SUBFLOOR SHEATHING[A] TO FRAMING ◆ T602.3(1)

Nominal Thickness	Fastener	Spacing (in.)	
		Ends	Intermediate
⅜ – ½ in.	6d common or deformed or 2⅜ × 0.113 gun nail w/ 0.266 head	6	12
19/32 – ¾ in.	8d common	6	12
	Deformed 2⅜ × 0.113 gun nail w/ 0.266 head[45]	6	12
⅞ – 1¼ in.	10d common or deformed	6	12

A. See **F55.**

TABLE 31 WSP COMBINATION SUBFLOOR[A] TO FRAMING ◆ T602.3(1)

Nominal Thickness	Fastener	Spacing (in.)	
		Edges	Intermediate
≤ ¾ in.	Deformed 2-in. gun nail[45] or 8d common	6	12
⅞ – 1 in.	8d common or deformed 2 × 0.113-in. gun nail or 2½ × 0.120-in. gun nail[45]	6	12
1⅛ – 1¼ in.	10d common or deformed 2 × 0.113-in. gun nail or 2½ × 0.120-in. gun nail[45]	6	12

A. See **F56** & **T28.**

45. These methods added in the 2021 code edition.

WOOD WALL FRAMING

Grade marks on sawn lumber, finger-jointed lumber, and engineered wood products are necessary to ensure that appropriate materials are used in framing. End-jointed lumber, more commonly known as finger-jointed lumber, may include a grade mark that restricts its use to studs or other vertical members. The use of 2 × 6 studs for exterior walls is becoming more common to accommodate thicker insulation.

Lumber: General — 21 IRC

- ☐ Lumber reqs grade mark or certification by lumber-grading agency __ 602.1.1
- ☐ End-jointed ("finger joint") lumber OK if identified by grade mark __ 602.1.2
- ☐ End-jointed lumber in fire-rated assemblies reqs "HRA" mark ______ 602.1.2

Stud Walls

- ☐ Studs min. #3, standard, or stud grade lumber EXC ______ 602.2
  - Utility grade studs allowed max. 16 in. o.c., not supporting floors, max. 8 ft. high for exterior & load-bearing walls & 10 ft. for interior nonbearing walls ______ 602.2X & 602.3.1X1
- ☐ Studs continuous from sole plate to top plate EXC ______ 602.3
  - Jack studs, trimmer studs & cripple studs ______ 602.3X
- ☐ Size, height & spacing of studs per **T32** EXC ______ 602.3.1
  - #2 grade nominal 2 × 6 studs that support tributary roof load ≤ 6 ft. OK max. height 18 ft. if 16 in. o.c., 20 ft. if 12 in. o.c. ______ 602.3.1X2
  - #2 grade exterior load-bearing studs ≤12 ft. OK per **T32** ______ 602.3.1X3
- ☐ Studs req full bearing on nominal 2× sole plates ≥ stud width ______ 602.3.4
- ☐ Studs req full bearing on plate at least equal to stud width ______ 602.3.4
- ☐ Interior load-bearing walls req construction, framing & fireblocking as specified for exterior walls. ______ 602.4

Top Plates

- ☐ Double top plates reqd EXC ______ 602.3.2
  - Single plate OK w/ metal ties at joints per **T33** & joists/rafters centered over studs within 1 in. tolerance ______ 602.3.2X
- ☐ Plates min. 2 in. nominal thickness & at least same width as studs __ 602.3.2
- ☐ End joints offset min. 24 in., need not occur over studs **F61** ______ 602.3.2
- ☐ Plates must overlap at corners & intersections w/ bearing partitions _ 602.3.2
- ☐ Nailing per **T38**,**F62** ______ 602.3

TABLE 32 — STUD SIZE, HEIGHT & SPACING ◆ T602.3(5)

Bearing Walls to 10-ft. Laterally Unsupported Height[A]				
Load supported	Nominal stud size & max. o.c. spacing			
	2×4	3×4	2×5[B]	2×6
Roof + ceiling or habitable attic	24 in.[C]	24 in.	24 in.	24 in.
1 floor & roof+ceiling or habitable attic	16 in.[C]	24 in.	24 in.	24 in.
2 floors & roof+ceiling or habitable attic	NP[D]	16 in.	NP[D]	16 in.
1 floor	24 in.	24 in.	24 in.	24 in.
Nonbearing Walls				
Nominal stud size	2×3[E]	2×4 & 3×4	2×5	2×6
Max. spacing	16 in.	24 in.	24 in.	24 in.
Max. laterally unsupported height[A]	10 ft.	14 ft.	16 ft.	20 ft.

A. Lateral support refers to floor/ceiling or roof/ceiling assemblies.
B. May be a special-order product.
C. Habitable attic supported by 2×4 studs is limited to roof span of 32 ft.
D. NP = Not permitted.
E. Not allowed in exterior walls.

FIG. 57 Top Plate Notches

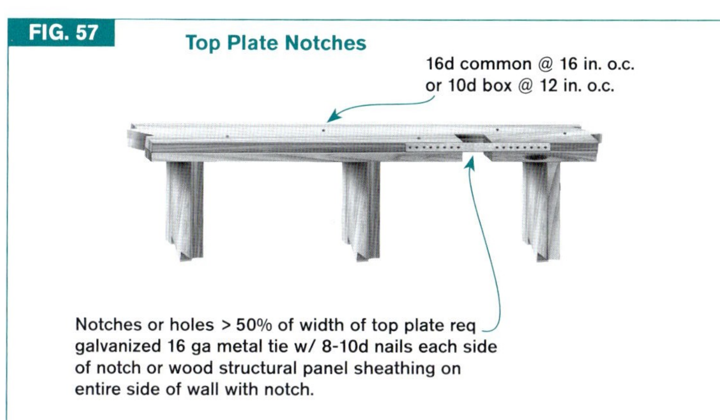

TABLE 33	SINGLE TOP PLATE SPLICES ◆ T602.3.2			
Condition	Corners & Intersecting Walls		Butt Joints in Straight Walls	
	Plate Size	Nails Each Side	Plate Size	Nails Each Side
SDC A-C & SDC D if BWL spacing < 25 ft.	3 in. × 6 in. × 0.036 Zi steel	6 8d box or 2½ gun nail	3 in. × 12 in. × 0.036 Zi steel	12 8d box or 2½ gun nail
SDC D if BWL spacing ≥ 25 ft.	3 in. × 8 in. × 0.036 Zi steel	9 8d box or 2½ gun nail	3 in. × 16 in. × 0.036 Zi steel	18 8d box or 2½ gun nail

Notching & Boring of Studs & Plates — 21 IRC

- ☐ Notching max. 25% of stud depth in exterior or bearing wall **F59** ___ 602.6#1
- ☐ Notching max. 40% of stud depth in nonbearing wall **F59** ___ 602.6#1
- ☐ Bored holes min. ⅝ in. from face of stud ___ 602.6#2
- ☐ Holes not OK in same area as notch ___ 602.6#2
- ☐ Bored holes 60% of stud depth max. EXC ___ 602.6#2
  - If >40% in exterior or bearing wall, studs doubled & max. 2 successive doubled studs **F59** ___ 602.6#2
  - Where approved stud shoes are installed AMI ___ 602.6X
- ☐ Cuts, notches, or bored holes >50% of top plate width req min. 1½-in. 16-ga Zi tie min. 6 in. past notch or hole w/ min. 8 10d nails each side of notch or hole **F57** EXC ___ 602.6.1
  - Not reqd if entire side of wall w/ notch/cut covered by WSP ___ 602.6.1X

TABLE 34	MAX. NOTCHES & BORED HOLES IN STUDS ◆ 602.6				
Wall Type	Exterior or Bearing Walls		Nonbearing Walls		
	2×4[A]	2×6[A]	2×3[A]	2×4[A]	2×6[A]
Notches	⅞ in.	1⅜ in.	1 in.	1⅜ in.	2³⁄₁₆ in.
Holes[A]	1⅜ in.	2³⁄₁₆ in.	1½ in.	2⅛ in.	3¼ in.

A. Nominal sizes – actual sizes ½ in. less each dimension
B. Holes min. ⅝ in. from edge of stud.

Corners

- ☐ 3 studs at corners **F58** EXC ___ F602.3(2)
  - 2 studs OK w/ devices as backing to secure face materials ___ F602.3(2)

FIG. 58 Corners & Partition Intersections

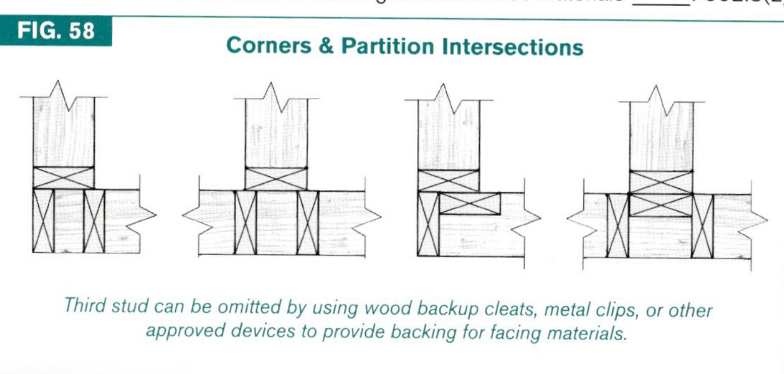

Third stud can be omitted by using wood backup cleats, metal clips, or other approved devices to provide backing for facing materials.

FIG. 59 Notching & Boring Studs

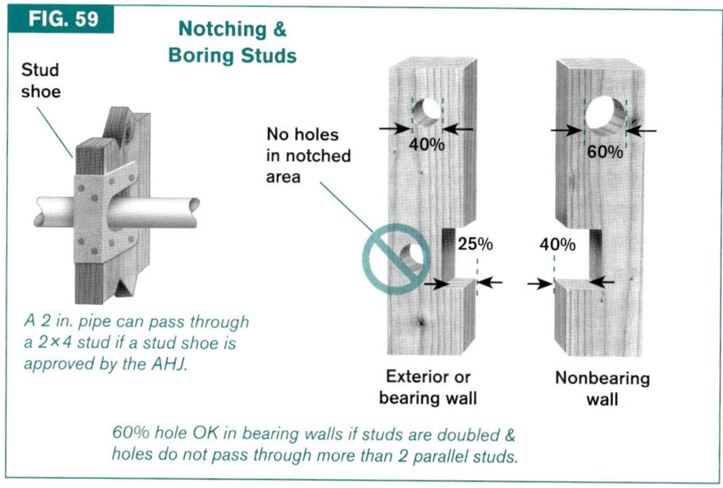

A 2 in. pipe can pass through a 2×4 stud if a stud shoe is approved by the AHJ.

60% hole OK in bearing walls if studs are doubled & holes do not pass through more than 2 parallel studs.

Headers — 21 IRC

- ☐ Header spans per **T35,36** ____ 602.7
- ☐ Min. number of full-height studs **F60** adjacent to headers per **T37** ____ 602.7.5
- ☐ Single member headers min. 2×material, face nail 12 in. o.c. top & bottom w/ 10d nails **F60** ____ 602.7.1
- ☐ Headers not reqd for nonbearing wall openings; single flat 2-in. × 4-in. member OK for span up to 8 ft. if ≤24 in. below nailing surface above 602.7.4

Rim Board Headers

- ☐ Rim board header (header above top plates w/ cripple studs below top plate to top of opening) spans per **T36** ____ 602.7.2
- ☐ Number of full-height studs each end of rim board headers must be at least the number of studs displaced by ½ the header span ____ 602.7.2
- ☐ Joists hangers reqd all joists above rim board header span ____ F602.7.2

FIG. 60 Headers

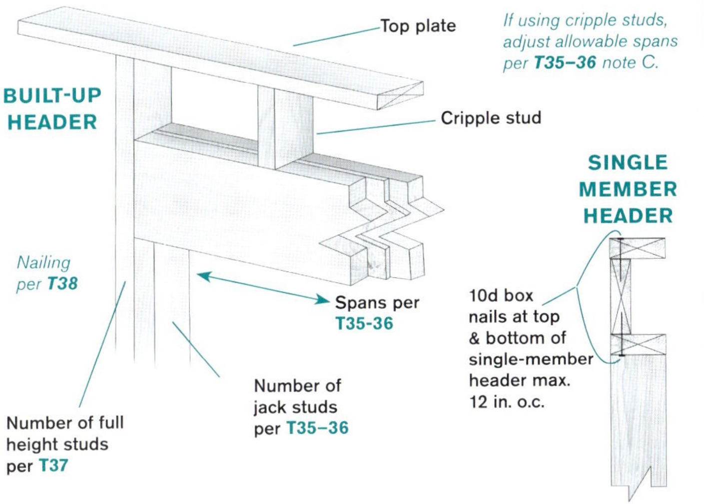

TABLE 35 ALLOWABLE GIRDER & HEADER SPANS FOR INTERIOR BEARING WALLS[A] ◆ T602.7(2)

No. of Floors Supported	Size	Building Width[B] 12 ft. Span[C]	12 ft. NJ[D]	24 ft. Span[C]	24 ft. NJ[D]	36 ft. Span[C]	36 ft. NJ[D]
1 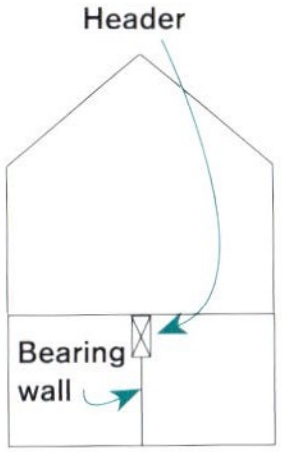	2–2×4	4–1	1	2–10	1	2–4	1
	2–2×6	6–1	1	4–4	1	3–6	1
	2–2×8	7–9	1	5–5	1	4–5	2
	2–2×10	9–2	1	6–6	2	5–3	2
	2–2×12	10–9	1	7–7	2	6–3	2
	3–2×8	9–8	1	6–10	1	5–7	1
	3–2×10	11–5	1	8–1	1	6–7	2
	3–2×12	13–6	1	9–6	2	7–9	2
	4–2×8	11–2	1	7–11	1	6–5	1
	4–2×10	13–3	1	9–4	1	7–8	1
	4–2×12	15–7	1	11–0	1	9–0	2
2 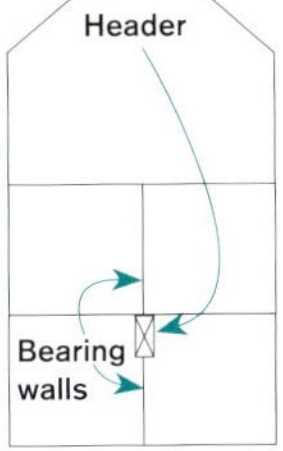	2–2×4	2–7	1	1–11	1	1–7	1
	2–2×6	3–11	1	2–11	2	2–5	2
	2–2×8	5–0	1	3–8	2	3–1	2
	2–2×10	5–11	2	4–4	2	3–7	2
	2–2×12	6–11	2	5–2	2	4–3	3
	3–2×8	6–3	1	4–7	2	3–10	2
	3–2×10	7–5	1	5–6	2	4–6	2
	3–2×12	8–8	2	6–5	2	5–4	2
	4–2×8	7–2	1	5–4	1	4–5	2
	4–2×10	8–6	1	6–4	2	5–3	2
	4–2×12	10–1	1	7–5	2	6–2	2

A. Based on No. 2 grade Douglas fir-larch, hem-fir, Southern pine, and spruce-pine-fir.
B. Building width is measured perpendicular to ridge. For building widths between those shown, spans listed in table are permitted to be interpolated.
C. Where top of header not laterally braced (e.g., cripple studs bearing on header as in **F60**), spans for 2 × 8, 2 × 10, or 2 × 12 to be multiplied by 0.70.
D. Number of jack studs reqd to support each end. If NJ=1, headers are permitted to be supported by an approved framing anchor to the full-height wall stud.

TABLE 36A GIRDER & HEADER SPANS IN FEET-INCHES FOR EXTERIOR BEARING WALLS[A] ◆ T602.7(1)

Header

Building width

Girders & headers supporting roof + ceiling

Nominal Sizes	Ground Snow Load																	
	30 psf						50 psf						70 psf					
	Building Width[B] (ft.)																	
	12		24		36		12		24		36		12		24		36	
	Span[C]	NJ[D]	Span[C]	NJ[D]	Span[C]	NJ[D]	Span[C]	NJ[D]	Span[C]	NJ[D]	Span[C]	NJ[D]	Span[C]	NJ[D]	Span[C]	NJ[D]	Span[C]	NJ[D]
1–2 × 6	4–0	1	3–1	2	2–7	2	3–5	1	2–8	2	2–3	2	3–0	2	2–4	2	2–0	2
1–2 × 8	5–1	2	3–11	2	3–3	2	4–4	2	3–4	2	2–10	2	3–10	2	3–0	2	2–6	3
1–2 × 10	6–0	2	4–8	2	3–11	2	5–2	2	4–0	2	3–4	3	4–7	2	3–6	3	3–0	3
1–2 × 12	7–1	2	5–5	2	4–7	3	6–1	2	4–8	3	3–11	3	5–5	2	4–2	3	3–6	3
2–2 × 4	4–0	1	3–1	1	2–7	1	3–5	1	2–7	1	2–2	1	3–0	1	2–4	1	2–0	1
2–2 × 6	6–0	1	4–7	1	3–10	1	5–1	1	3–11	1	3–3	2	4–6	1	3–6	2	2–11	2
2–2 × 8	7–7	1	5–9	1	4–10	2	6–5	1	5–0	2	4–2	2	5–9	1	4–5	2	3–9	2
2–2 × 10	9–0	1	6–10	2	5–9	2	7–8	2	5–11	2	4–11	2	6–9	2	5–3	2	4–5	2
2–2 × 12	10–7	2	8–1	2	6–10	2	9–0	2	6–11	2	5–10	2	8–0	2	6–2	2	5–2	3
3–2 × 8	9–5	1	7–3	1	6–1	1	8–1	1	6–3	1	5–3	2	7–2	1	5–6	2	4–8	2
3–2 × 10	11–3	1	8–7	1	7–3	2	9–7	1	7–4	2	6–2	2	8–6	1	6–7	2	5–6	2
3–2 × 12	13–2	1	10–1	2	8–6	2	11–3	2	8–8	2	7–4	2	10–0	2	7–9	2	6–6	2
4–2 × 8	10–11	1	8–4	1	7–0	1	9–4	1	7–2	1	6–0	1	8–3	1	6–4	1	5–4	2
4–2 × 10	12–11	1	9–11	1	8–4	1	11–1	1	8–6	1	7–2	2	9–10	1	7–7	2	6–4	2
4–2 × 12	15–3	1	11–8	1	9–10	2	13–0	1	10–0	2	8–5	2	11–7	1	8–11	2	7–6	2

A. Based on No. 2 grade Douglas fir-larch, hem-fir, Southern pine, and spruce-pine-fir.
B. Building width is measured perpendicular to ridge. For building widths between those shown, spans listed in table are permitted to be interpolated.
C. Where top of header not laterally braced (e.g., cripple studs bearing on header as in F60), spans for 2 × 8, 2 × 10, or 2 × 12 to be multiplied by 0.70.
D. Number of jack studs reqd to support each end. If NJ=1, headers are permitted to be supported by an approved framing anchor to the full-height wall stud.

TABLE 36B GIRDER & HEADER SPANS IN FEET-INCHES FOR EXTERIOR BEARING WALLS[A] ◆ T602.7(1)

Header

Building width

Girders & headers supporting roof + ceiling + 1 center bearing floor

Nominal Sizes	Ground Snow Load																	
	30 psf						50 psf						70 psf					
	Building Width[B] (ft.)																	
	12		24		36		12		24		36		12		24		36	
	Span[C]	NJ[D]	Span[C]	NJ[D]	Span[C]	NJ[D]	Span[C]	NJ[D]	Span[C]	NJ[D]	Span[C]	NJ[D]	Span[C]	NJ[D]	Span[C]	NJ[D]	Span[C]	NJ[D]
1–2 × 6	3–3	1	2–7	2	2–2	2	3–0	2	2–4	2	2–0	2	2–9	2	2–2	2	1–10	2
1–2 × 8	4–1	2	3–3	2	2–9	2	3–9	2	3–0	2	2–6	3	3–6	2	2–9	2	2–4	3
1–2 × 10	4–11	2	3–10	2	3–3	3	4–6	2	3–6	3	3–0	3	4–1	2	3–3	3	2–9	3
1–2 × 12	5–9	2	4–6	3	3–10	3	5–3	2	4–2	3	3–6	3	4–10	3	3–10	3	3–3	4
2–2 × 4	3–3	1	2–6	1	2–2	1	3–0	1	2–4	1	2–0	1	2–8	1	2–2	1	1–10	1
2–2 × 6	4–10	1	3–9	1	3–3	2	4–5	1	3–6	2	3–0	2	4–1	1	3–3	2	2–9	2
2–2 × 8	6–1	1	4–10	2	4–1	2	5–7	2	4–5	2	3–9	2	5–2	2	4–1	2	3–6	2
2–2 × 10	7–3	2	5–8	2	4–10	2	6–8	2	5–3	2	4–5	2	6–1	2	4–10	2	4–1	2
2–2 × 12	8–6	2	6–8	2	5–8	2	7–10	2	6–2	2	5–3	3	7–2	2	5–8	2	4–10	3
3–2 × 8	7–8	1	6–0	1	5–1	2	7–0	1	5–6	2	4–8	2	6–5	1	5–1	2	4–4	2
3–2 × 10	9–1	1	7–2	2	6–1	2	8–4	1	6–7	2	5–7	2	7–8	2	6–1	2	5–2	2
3–2 × 12	10–8	2	8–5	2	7–2	2	9–10	2	7–8	2	6–7	2	9–0	2	7–1	2	6–1	2
4–2 × 8	8–10	1	6–11	1	5–11	1	8–1	1	6–4	1	5–5	2	7–5	1	5–11	1	5–0	2
4–2 × 10	10–6	1	8–3	2	7–0	2	9–8	1	7–7	2	6–5	2	8–10	1	7–0	2	6–0	2
4–2 × 12	12–4	1	9–8	2	8–3	2	11–4	2	8–11	2	7–7	2	10–4	2	8–3	2	7–0	2

A. Based on No. 2 grade Douglas fir-larch, hem-fir, Southern pine, and spruce-pine-fir.
B. Building width is measured perpendicular to ridge. For building widths between those shown, spans listed in table are permitted to be interpolated.
C. Where top of header not laterally braced (e.g., cripple studs bearing on header as in F60), spans for 2 × 8, 2 × 10, or 2 × 12 to be multiplied by 0.70.
D. Number of jack studs reqd to support each end. If NJ=1, headers are permitted to be supported by an approved framing anchor to the full-height wall stud.

TABLE 36C GIRDER & HEADER SPANS IN FEET-INCHES FOR EXTERIOR BEARING WALLS[A] ◆ T602.7(1)

Header

Building Width

Girders & headers supporting roof + ceiling + 1 clear span floor

Nominal Sizes	Ground Snow Load																	
	30 psf						50 psf						70 psf					
	Building Width[B] (ft.)																	
	12		24		36		12		24		36		12		24		36	
	Span[C]	NJ[D]	Span[C]	NJ[D]	Span[C]	NJ[D]	Span[C]	NJ[D]	Span[C]	NJ[D]	Span[C]	NJ[D]	Span[C]	NJ[D]	Span[C]	NJ[D]	Span[C]	NJ[D]
1–2 × 6	2–11	2	2–3	2	1–11	2	2–9	2	2–1	2	1–9	2	2–7	2	2–0	2	1–8	2
1–2 × 8	3–9	2	2–10	2	2–5	3	3–6	2	2–8	2	2–3	3	3–3	2	2–6	3	2–2	3
1–2 × 10	4–5	2	3–5	3	2–10	3	4–2	2	3–2	3	2–8	3	3–11	2	3–0	3	2–6	3
1–2 × 12	5–2	2	4–0	3	3–4	3	4–10	3	3–9	3	3–2	4	4–7	3	3–6	3	3–0	4
2–2 × 4	2–11	1	2–3	1	1–10	1	2–9	1	2–1	1	1–9	1	2–7	1	2–0	1	1–8	1
2–2 × 6	4–4	1	3–4	2	2–10	2	4–1	1	3–2	2	2–8	2	3–10	1	3–0	2	2–6	2
2–2 × 8	5–6	2	4–3	2	3–7	2	5–2	2	4–0	2	3–4	2	4–10	2	3–9	2	3–2	2
2–2 × 10	6–7	2	5–0	2	4–2	2	6–1	2	4–9	2	4–0	2	5–9	2	4–5	2	3–9	3
2–2 × 12	7–9	2	5–11	2	4–11	3	7–2	2	5–7	2	4–8	3	6–9	2	5–3	3	4–5	3
3–2 × 8	6–11	1	5–3	2	4–5	2	6–5	1	5–0	2	4–2	2	6–1	1	4–8	2	4–0	2
3–2 × 10	8–3	2	6–3	2	5–3	2	7–8	2	5–11	2	5–0	2	7–3	2	5–7	2	4–8	2
3–2 × 12	9–8	2	7–5	2	6–2	2	9–0	2	7–0	2	5–10	2	8–6	2	6–7	2	5–6	3
4–2 × 8	8–0	1	6–1	1	5–1	2	7–5	1	5–9	2	4–10	2	7–0	1	5–5	2	4–7	2
4–2 × 10	9–6	1	7–3	2	6–1	2	8–10	1	6–10	2	5–9	2	8–4	1	6–5	2	5–5	2
4–2 × 12	11–2	2	8–6	2	7–2	2	10–5	2	8–0	2	6–9	2	9–10	2	7–7	2	6–5	2

A. Based on No. 2 grade Douglas fir-larch, hem-fir, Southern pine, and spruce-pine-fir.
B. Building width is measured perpendicular to ridge. For building widths between those shown, spans listed in table are permitted to be interpolated.
C. Where top of header not laterally braced (e.g., cripple studs bearing on header as in F60), spans for 2 × 8, 2 × 10, or 2 × 12 to be multiplied by 0.70.
D. Number of jack studs reqd to support each end. If NJ=1, headers are permitted to be supported by an approved framing anchor to the full-height wall stud.

TABLE 36D GIRDER & HEADER SPANS IN FEET-INCHES FOR EXTERIOR BEARING WALLS[A] ◆ T602.7(1)

Header

Building width

Girders & headers supporting roof + ceiling + 2 center bearing floors

Nominal Sizes	Ground Snow Load																	
	30 psf						50 psf						70 psf					
	Building Width[B] (ft.)																	
	12		24		36		12		24		36		12		24		36	
	Span[C]	NJ[D]	Span[C]	NJ[D]	Span[C]	NJ[D]	Span[C]	NJ[D]	Span[C]	NJ[D]	Span[C]	NJ[D]	Span[C]	NJ[D]	Span[C]	NJ[D]	Span[C]	NJ[D]
1–2 × 6	2–8	2	2–1	2	1–10	2	2–7	2	2–0	2	1–9	2	2–5	2	1–11	2	1–8	2
1–2 × 8	3–5	2	2–8	2	2–4	3	3–3	2	2–7	2	2–2	3	3–1	2	2–5	3	2–1	3
1–2 × 10	4–0	2	3–2	3	2–9	3	3–10	2	3–1	3	2–7	3	3–8	2	2–11	3	2–5	3
1–2 × 12	4–9	3	3–9	3	3–2	4	4–6	3	3–7	3	3–1	4	4–3	3	3–5	3	2–11	4
2–2 × 4	2–8	1	2–1	1	1–9	1	2–6	1	2–0	1	1–8	1	2–5	1	1–11	1	1–7	1
2–2 × 6	4–0	1	3–2	2	2–8	2	3–9	1	3–0	2	2–7	2	3–7	1	2–10	2	2–5	2
2–2 × 8	5–0	2	4–0	2	3–5	2	4–10	2	3–10	2	3–3	2	4–7	2	3–7	2	3–1	2
2–2 × 10	6–0	2	4–9	2	4–0	2	5–8	2	4–6	2	3–10	3	5–5	2	4–3	2	3–8	3
2–2 × 12	7–0	2	5–7	2	4–9	3	6–8	2	5–4	3	4–6	3	6–4	2	5–0	3	4–3	3
3–2 × 8	6–4	1	5–0	2	4–3	2	6–0	1	4–9	2	4–1	2	5–8	2	4–6	2	3–10	2
3–2 × 10	7–6	2	5–11	2	5–1	2	7–1	2	5–8	2	4–10	2	6–9	2	5–4	2	4–7	2
3–2 × 12	8–10	2	7–0	2	5–11	2	8–5	2	6–8	2	5–8	3	8–0	2	6–4	2	5–4	3
4–2 × 8	7–3	1	5–9	1	4–11	2	6–11	1	5–6	2	4–8	2	6–7	1	5–2	2	4–5	2
4–2 × 10	8–8	1	6–10	2	5–10	2	8–3	2	6–6	2	5–7	2	7–10	2	6–2	2	5–3	2
4–2 × 12	10–2	2	8–1	2	6–10	2	9–8	2	7–8	2	6–7	2	9–2	2	7–3	2	6–2	2

A. Based on No. 2 grade Douglas fir-larch, hem-fir, Southern pine, and spruce-pine-fir.
B. Building width is measured perpendicular to ridge. For building widths between those shown, spans listed in table are permitted to be interpolated.
C. Where top of header not laterally braced (e.g., cripple studs bearing on header as in F60), spans for 2 × 8, 2 × 10, or 2 × 12 to be multiplied by 0.70.
D. Number of jack studs reqd to support each end. If NJ=1, headers are permitted to be supported by an approved framing anchor to the full-height wall stud.

TABLE 36E GIRDER & HEADER SPANS IN FEET-INCHES FOR EXTERIOR BEARING WALLS[A] ◆ T602.7(1)

Header

Building width

Girders & headers supporting roof + ceiling + 2 clear span floors

Nominal Sizes	Ground Snow Load																	
	30 psf						50 psf						70 psf					
	Building Width[B] (ft.)																	
	12		24		36		12		24		36		12		24		36	
	Span[C]	NJ[D]	Span[C]	NJ[D]	Span[C]	NJ[D]	Span[C]	NJ[D]	Span[C]	NJ[D]	Span[C]	NJ[D]	Span[C]	NJ[D]	Span[C]	NJ[D]	Span[C]	NJ[D]
1–2 × 6	2–3	2	1–9	2	1–5	2	2–3	2	1–9	2	1–5	3	2–2	2	1–8	2	1–5	3
1–2 × 8	2–10	2	2–2	3	1–10	3	2–10	2	2–2	3	1–10	3	2–9	2	2–1	3	1–10	3
1–2 × 10	3–4	2	2–7	3	2–2	3	3–4	3	2–7	3	2–2	4	3–3	3	2–6	3	2–2	4
1–2 × 12	4–0	3	3–0	3	2–7	4	4–0	3	3–0	4	2–7	4	3–10	3	3–0	4	2–6	4
2–2 × 4	2–3	1	1–8	1	1–4	1	2–3	1	1–8	1	1–4	1	2–2	1	1–8	1	1–4	2
2–2 × 6	3–4	1	2–6	2	2–2	2	3–4	2	2–6	2	2–2	2	3–3	2	2–6	2	2–1	2
2–2 × 8	4–3	2	3–3	2	2–8	2	4–3	2	3–3	2	2–8	2	4–1	2	3–2	2	2–8	3
2–2 × 10	5–0	2	3–10	2	3–2	3	5–0	2	3–10	2	3–2	3	4–10	2	3–9	3	3–2	3
2–2 × 12	5–11	2	4–6	3	3–9	3	5–11	2	4–6	3	3–9	3	5–8	2	4–5	3	3–9	3
3–2 × 8	5–3	1	4–0	2	3–5	2	5–3	2	4–0	2	3–5	2	5–1	2	3–11	2	3–4	2
3–2 × 10	6–3	2	4–9	2	4–0	2	6–3	2	4–9	2	4–0	2	6–1	2	4–8	2	4–0	3
3–2 × 12	7–5	2	5–8	2	4–9	3	7–5	2	5–8	2	4–9	3	7–2	2	5–6	3	4–8	3
4–2 × 8	6–1	1	4–8	2	3–11	2	6–1	1	4–8	2	3–11	2	5–11	1	4–7	2	3–10	2
4–2 × 10	7–3	2	5–6	2	4–8	2	7–3	2	5–6	2	4–8	2	7–0	2	5–5	2	4–7	2
4–2 × 12	8–6	2	6–6	2	5–6	2	8–6	2	6–6	2	5–6	2	8–3	2	6–4	2	5–4	3

A. Based on No. 2 grade Douglas fir-larch, hem-fir, Southern pine, and spruce-pine-fir.
B. Building width is measured perpendicular to ridge. For building widths between those shown, spans listed in table are permitted to be interpolated.
C. Where top of header not laterally braced (e.g., cripple studs bearing on header as in F60), spans for 2 × 8, 2 × 10, or 2 × 12 to be multiplied by 0.70.
D. Number of jack studs reqd to support each end. If NJ=1, headers are permitted to be supported by an approved framing anchor to the full-height wall stud.

TABLE 37 MIN. NUMBER OF FULL-HEIGHT STUDS AT EACH END OF HEADERS IN EXTERIOR WALLS ◆ T602.7.5

Max. header span (ft.)	Ultimate Design Wind Speed & Exposure Category	
	< 140 mph Exposure B < 130 mph Exposure C	≤ 115 mph Exposure B[A]
4	1	1
6	2	1
8	2	1
10	3	2
12	3	2
14	3	2
16	4	2
18	4	2

A. If framing anchors used in lieu of jack studs (see note D in **T35-36**), min. number of full-height studs per center column, not right-hand column.

FIG. 61 Top Plate Splice Lap

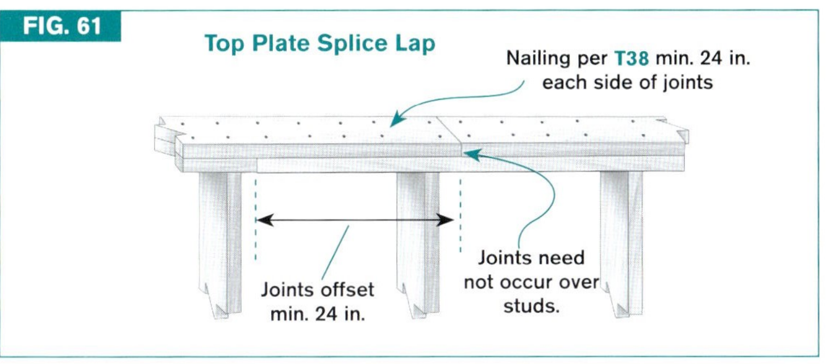

FIG. 62 Common Nails (actual sizes)

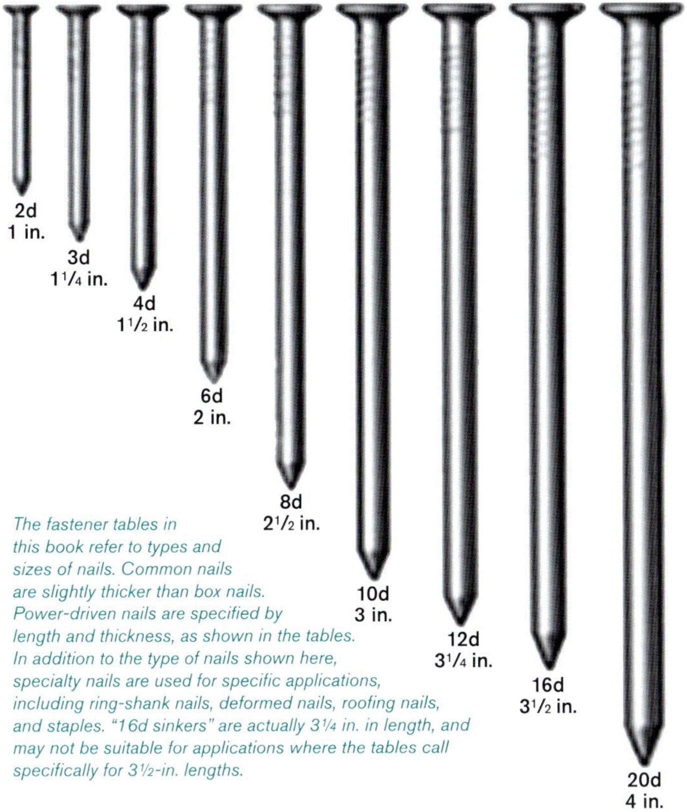

2d 1 in.

3d $1^1/_4$ in.

4d $1^1/_2$ in.

6d 2 in.

8d $2^1/_2$ in.

10d 3 in.

12d $3^1/_4$ in.

16d $3^1/_2$ in.

20d 4 in.

The fastener tables in this book refer to types and sizes of nails. Common nails are slightly thicker than box nails. Power-driven nails are specified by length and thickness, as shown in the tables. In addition to the type of nails shown here, specialty nails are used for specific applications, including ring-shank nails, deformed nails, roofing nails, and staples. "16d sinkers" are actually 3¼ in. in length, and may not be suitable for applications where the tables call specifically for 3½-in. lengths.

TABLE 38 WALL FRAMING FASTENER SCHEDULE ◆ T602.3(1)

Connection	Fastener	Method
Stud to stud (not at BWPs)	16d common	24 in. o.c. face nail
	10d box or 3-in. gun nails	16 in. o.c. face nail
Stud to stud & abutting studs at intersecting wall corners at BWPs	16d box or 3-in. gun nails	12 in. o.c. face nail
	16d common	16 in. o.c. face nail
Built-up header (2 in. to 2 in. w/½-in. spacer)	16d common	16 in. o.c. each edge face nail
	16d box	12 in. o.c. each edge face nail
Continuous header to stud	5 8d box or 4 8d common or 4 10d box	Toenail
Adjacent full-height stud to end of header[46]	3 16d common or 4 16d box or 4 10d box or 4 3-in. gun nails	End nail
Top plate to top plate	16d common	16 in. o.c. face nail
	10d box or 3-in. gun nails	12 in. o.c. face nail
Double top plate splice **F61**	8 16d common or 12 16d box or 12 10d box or 12 3-in. gun nails	Face nail on each side of end joint (min. 24-in. lap splice length each side of joint
Bottom plate to joist, rim joist, band joist, or blocking (not at BWPs)	16d common	16 in. o.c. face nail
	16d box or 3-in. gun nails	12 in. o.c. face nail
Bottom plate to joist, rim joist, band joist, or blocking at BWPs	3 16d box or 2 16d common or 4 3-in. gun nails	16 in. o.c. face nail
Top or bottom plate to stud	4 8d box or 4 10d box or 3 16d box or 4 8d common or 4 3-in. gun nails	Toenail
	3 10d or 16d box or 2 16d common or 3 3-in gun nails	End nail
Top plate laps at corners & intersections	3 10d box or 2 16d common or 3 3-in. gun nails	Face nail

46. New material in this code edition.

TABLE 39 WALL BRACING & SHEATHING FASTENER SCHEDULE ◆ T602.3(1)

Connection	Fastener	Method
1-in. brace to each stud & plate	3 8d box or 2 8d common or 2 10d box or 2 staples 1¾ in. long	Face nail
1-in. × 6 in. sheathing to each bearing	3 8d box or 2 8d common or 2 10d box or 2 staples 1 in. crown 16ga 1¾ in. long	Face nail
1-in. × 8 in. sheathing to each bearing	3 8d box or 3 8d common or 3 10d box or 3 staples 1 in. crown 16ga 1¾ in. long	Face nail
1-in. × > 8 in. sheathing to each bearing	4 8d box or 3 8d common or 3 10d box or 4 staples 1 in. crown 16ga 1¾ in. long	Face nail

Wall Sheathing — 21 IRC

- ☐ WSPs must be identified by grade mark **F55** — 604.1
- ☐ Allowable WSP spans per **T41** — 604.2
- ☐ WSP fastening per **T40** or **T43** — 604.3
- ☐ Particleboard to conform to ANSI A208.1 & grade marked **T42** — 605.1

TABLE 40 WSP-TO-WALL FASTENERS ◆ T602.3(1)

Nominal Thickness[A]	Fastener	Spacing (in. o.c.)	
		Edges	Field
⅜ in. – ½ in.	6d common or deformed or 2⅜ in. × 0.113 in. × 0.266 head nail	6	12
19/32 in. – ¾ in.	8d common or 2½ in. × 0.131 in.	6	12
⅞ in. – 1¼ in.	10d common or 2½ in. × 0.131 in. × 0.281 head deformed nail	6	12

A. Performance category – see **F55**.

WALL SHEATHING ◆ FASTENERS

TABLE 41 WSP SHEATHING USED TO RESIST WIND PRESSURES[A] ◆ T602.3(3)

Min. Nail Size	Min. WSP Span Rating F55	Min. Nominal Thickness	Max. Stud Spacing	Ultimate Design Wind Speed (mph)		
				Exposure Category (p. 10)		
				B	C	D
6d common	24/0[B]	3/8 in.	16	140	115	110
8d common	24/16[B]	7/16 in.	16	170	140	135
			24[C]	140	115	110

A. Assumes nail spacing of 6 in. o.c. edges, 12 in. o.c. in field.
B. WSPs w/ span rating of Wall-16 or Wall-24 OK as alternate to 24/0 span rating. Plywood siding rated 16 o.c. OK as alternate to 24/16 span rating. "Wall-16" and plywood "16 o.c." only OK w/ max. stud spacing of 16 in. o.c.
C. 3-ply plywood must have strength axis perpendicular to supports.

TABLE 42 ALLOWABLE SPANS FOR PARTICLEBOARD WALL SHEATHING ◆ T602.3(4)

Thickness	Grade	Stud Spacing (in. o.c.)	
		Siding nailed to studs[A]	Siding nailed to sheathing[A]
3/8 in.	M-1 Exterior Glue	16	Not Permitted
1/2 in.	M-2 Exterior Glue	16	16

A. Sheathing not to be exposed to weather. If panels applied horizontally, offset so that 4 panel corners will not meet. Leave 1/16-in. gap between panels and nail ≥ 3/8 in. from panel edges.

TABLE 43 OTHER WALL SHEATHING FASTENERS ◆ T602.3(1)

Nominal Thickness	Fastener	Spacing (in. o.c.)	
		Edges	Field
1/2-in. structural cellulosic fiberboard	1 1/2-in. × 0.120 Zi roofing nail w/ 7/16-in. head or 1 1/4-in. 16 ga staple	3	6
25/32-in. structural cellulosic fiberboard	1 3/4-in. × 0.120 Zi roofing nail w/ 7/16-in. head or 1 1/4-in. 16 ga staple	3	6
1/2-in. gypsum sheathing[A]	1 1/2-in. × 0.120 Zi roofing nail w/ 7/16-in. head diameter or 1 1/2-in. 16 ga Zi staple or 1 1/4-in. screws Type W or S	7	7
5/8-in. gypsum sheathing[A]	1 3/4-in. × 0.120 Zi roofing nail w/ 7/16-in. head diameter or 1 5/8-in. 16 ga Zi staple or 1 5/8-in. screws Type W or S	7	7

A. Panels to be applied vertically.

WALL BRACING

Wall bracing resists lateral forces imposed by earthquakes and wind. The reqd type, amount, and spacing of wall bracing are based on the SDC, the exposure category, and the ultimate design wind speed **T2**. The spacing between parallel BWLs and the length of bracing are the critical issues in resisting wind and earthquake forces. Overturning and uplift forces are also resisted by hardware and anchoring devices such as hold-downs.

In general, the IRC has provided prescriptive rules by which most buildings within its scope can be designed. These detailed rules often provide tradeoffs between methods and materials. We have included important rules and tables in this book to aid in plan review and for field use. These are not all of the essential material that is necessary to ensure compliance w/ the IRC prescriptive design, and we therefore encourage the use of the full text of the code. Another guide to using the IRC rules is ICC's *A Guide to the 2018 IRC Wood Wall Bracing Provisions*. Though that book is based on the previous code cycle, there were only a few changes in the 2021 IRC, and most of those are noted here. IRC tables T602.10.3(2) (wind adjustment factors) and 602.10.3(4) (seismic adjustment factors) have not been included in Code Check. These tables take into account wind exposure categories other than category B, tall roofs and stories, the added (or subtracted) bracing value of interior gypsum wall sheathing, the effect of added weight of veneers, and many other conditions. Design by a licensed professional engineer may be necessary when encountering those conditions, and when buildings exceed the prescriptive limits of the IRC they must be designed per the standards in **T1**.

Braced Wall Lines (BWLs) — 21 IRC

- ☐ BWLs reqd to be shown as straight lines on plans ______ 106.1.3 & 602.10.1
- ☐ Bracing methods, location & length of BWPs & foundation reqs at top & bottom of BWPs to be shown on plans ______ 106.1.3
- ☐ Length of BWL is distance between its ends, either at intersection w/ perpendicular BWL, an exterior wall, or a projected intersection w/ an angled BWL **F63** ______ 602.10.1.1
- ☐ BWPs can offset up to 4 ft. from designated BWL **F63** ______ 602.10.1.2
- ☐ Max. 2/3 of reqd BWP length on one side of BWL **F63** ______ 602.10.1.2[47]
- ☐ Intermediate BWLs through building interior permitted **F63** ______ 602.10.1.3

47. The entire length of the reqd BWP can no longer be entirely on one side of the BWL.

Angled Braced Wall Lines F63 — 21 IRC

- ☐ Any portion of wall along BWL can be angled up to 8 ft. ______ 602.10.1.4
- ☐ Length of BWL w/ angled wall = projected corner at angle ______ 602.10.1.4
- ☐ If angled wall > 8 ft., it must be considered as separate BWL ______ 602.10.1.4
- ☐ Projected length can be used to determine reqd min. length of BWPs 602.10.3

FIG. 63 Braced Wall Lines

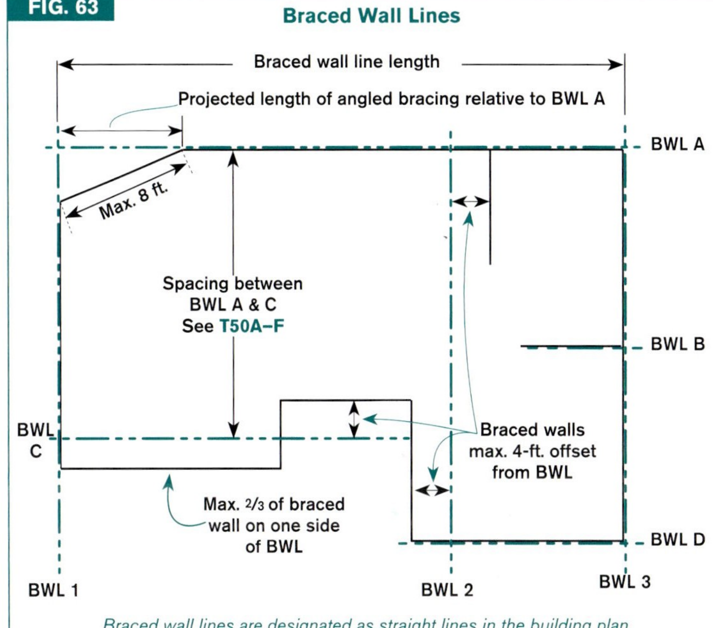

Braced wall lines are designated as straight lines in the building plan.

The projected length of braced wall panels on the angled wall at upper left can count toward the reqd bracing on either BWL 1 or BWL A, not both. If the angled wall is longer than 8 ft., it must count as its own braced wall line.

TABLE 44	INTERMITTENT BRACING METHODS ◆ T602.10.4		
Abbreviation/Name		Description	Connections[A]
LIB	Let-in bracing[B]	Wood 1x4 or metal straps at 45°–60 angles, max. 16 in. o.c. stud spacing	Wood: 2 8d common or 3 2½-in. gun nails each stud + top & bottom plates; metal straps AMI
DWB	Diagonal wood boards	1 in. nominal	2 8d (2½-in. gun nails) or 2 1¾-in. staples per stud
WSP	Wood structural panels	min. ⅜ in.	Per **T41** & **T43** or IRC T602.3(2)
BV-WSP	Wood structural panels w/ stone or masonry veneer[C]	SDC D: see IRC F602.10.6.5.2	8d common or 2½-in. gun nails 4 in. o.c. edges, 12 in. o.c. field, 4 in. o.c. at BWP end posts
SFB	Structural fiber-board sheathing	½ in. or 25/32 in. on max. 16 in. o.c. studs	Fastening per **T43**
GB	Gypsum board	min. ½ in.	7 in. o.c. edges & field at BWP locations (otherwise per **T75**)
PBS	Particleboard sheathing	⅜ in. or ½ in. on 16 in. o.c. studs	6d common for ⅜ in.; 8d common for ½ in.: 3 in. o.c. edges, 6 in. field
PCP	Portland cement plaster	max. 16 in. o.c. studs, see ***p. 108***	6 in. o.c. on all framing members
HPS	Hardboard panel siding	7/16 in. thickness, max. 16 in. o.c. studs	0.092 in. shank 0.225 in. head 1½-in. penetration, 4 in. o.c. edges 8 in. field
ABW	Alternate braced wall	⅜-in. WSP or per evaluation report	see F602.10.6.1 (or per evaluation report)
PFH	Portal frame w/ hold-downs	⅜-in. WSP	see F602.10.6.2 & **F64**
PFG	Portal frame at garage	7/16-in. WSP	see F602.10.6.3

A. Adhesive attachment of wall coverings (including GB) prohibited in SDC C & D.
B. Not allowed in SDC D per T602.10.3.(3).
C. Applies only to SDC D.

TABLE 45	CONTINUOUS SHEATHING BRACING METHODS ◆ T602.10.4		
Abbreviation/Name		Description	Connections[A]
CS-WSP	Continuously sheathed WSP	min. ⅜ in. exterior sheathing per **T40,41**	Interior sheathing per **T43** or per fasteners in 602.3(2)
CS-G	CS-WSP adjacent to garage openings[B]	same as CS-WSP	same as CS-WSP
CS-PF	Continuously sheathed portal frame	7/16-in. WSP	see F602.10.6.4 & **F64**
CS-SFB	Continuously sheathed structural fiberboard[C]	½-in. or 25/32-in. on 16 in. o.c. studs	Zi roofing nails 1½-in. for ½-in., 1¾-in. for 25/32-in. 3 in. o.c. edges 6 in. field

A. Applies only to panels next to garage door opening supporting gable end wall or roof. Only to be used on 1 wall of garage. Roof covering dead load max. 3 psf in SDC D.
B. Garage opening must have header; clear height wall opening not allowed on other side of panel.
C. Not applicable in SDC D.

FIG. 64 **Manufactured Shear Walls**

Manufactured products that use steel or wood shear panels in a tested assembly can be used as a substitute for IRC bracing methods. These products require an ICC Evaluation Services Report (ESR) that confirms their allowable equivalence to the IRC methods. Manufacturer's instructions are a part of the ESR and must be followed to obtain a code-compliant installation.

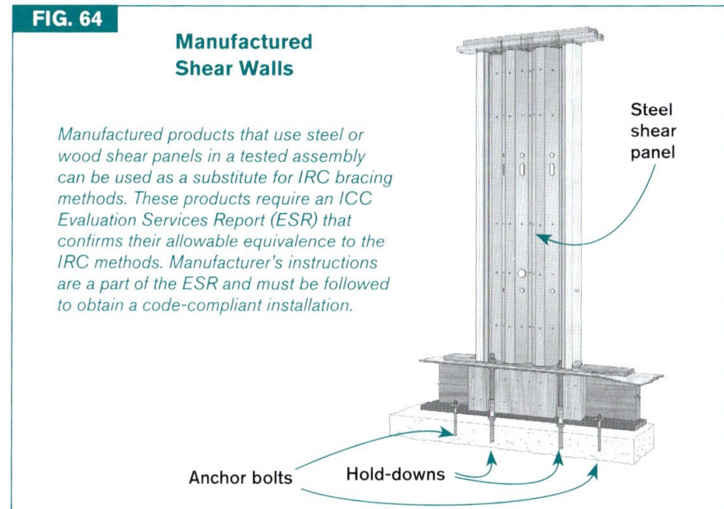

Braced Wall Panels (BWPs) — 21 IRC

- ☐ BWP methods per **T44,45** ____ 602.10.4
- ☐ Must be full height w/o vertical or horizontal offsets ____ 602.10.2
- ☐ Table lengths only applicable if uplift loads also resisted ____ 602.10.2.1
- ☐ Only BWPs parallel to BWL count for reqd bracing length EXC ____ 602.10.3
  - Angled walls may contribute projected length for 1 of the 2 intersecting BWLs **F63** ____ 602.10.3
- ☐ CS methods reqd to cover all sheathable surfaces on 1 side of BWL, including above & below openings & gable end walls ____ 602.10.4.2
- ☐ GB reqd on opposite side of wall from bracing material EXC ____ 602.10.4.3
  - Methods GB, BV-WSP, ABW, PFH, PFG & CS-PF ____ 602.10.4.3X1
  - Other in-plane finish w/ equivalent shear resistance ____ 602.10.4.3X2
  - Except for LIB, adjustment factor per T602.10.3(2&4) ____ 602.10.4.3X3
- ☐ Vertical joints of panel sheathing on common stud EXC ____ 602.10.4.4
  - Over double studs connected w/ 2 rows 10d box 10 in. o.c. _ 602.10.4.4X2
- ☐ Horizontal joints of panel sheathing on blocking EXC ____ 602.10.4.4
  - WSP & CS-WSP if T602.10.3(2&4) adjustment factors applied _ 602.10.4.4X1
  - Not reqd in segments not counted as BWPs ____ 602.10.4.4X3
  - Method GB panels installed horizontally ____ 602.10.4.4X4

Locations of BWPs

- ☐ In SDC A, B & C BWPs max. 20-ft. distance between adjacent edges of BWPs & begin within 10 ft. of each end of BWL EXC ___ 602.10.2.2
  - If method CS, 1 of 5 conditions in IRC F602.10.7: ____ 602.10.2.2X2
    1. BWP & return panel at corner at end of BWL **F65**
    2. BWP & 800-lb. hold-down device at corner at end of BWL
    3. Min. 48-in. BWP at corner at end of BWL
    4. 24-in. CS-WSP or 32-in. CS-SFB at corner + return panel of same & first BWP ≤ 10 ft. from corner
    5. 800-lb. hold-down at beginning of BWP ≤ 10 ft. from end of BWL **F65**
- ☐ In SDC D BWPs begin within 10 ft. of each end of BWL EXC 602.10.2.2X1
  - If method WSP, BV-WSP & CS, either of the following ____ 602.10.2.2.1X1
    1. WSP, CS-WSP, CS-G, or CS-PF: 24-in. return panels **F65**
    2. 1,800-lb. hold-down at beginning of BWP ≤ 10 ft. from end of BWL **F65**
  - Method PFH, ABW, BV-WSP: hold-downs per T602.10.6.5.4 _ 602.10.2.2.1X2

Permitted Mixing of BWP Methods

- ☐ Intermittent & CS methods can be intermixed story to story ___ 602.10.4.1#1
- ☐ Mixed intermittent methods from BWL to BWL within a story ___ 602.10.4.1#2
- ☐ In SDC A, B & C w/ UDWS ≤130 mph, OK to mix intermittent & CS from BWL to BWL within a story ____ 602.10.4.1#2
- ☐ In SDC A, B & detached structures in SDC C OK to mix intermittent methods within a BWL if reqd bracing length based on highest value of all methods used ____ 602.10.4.1#3
- ☐ CS-WSP, CS-G & CS-PF OK to mix within a BWL ____ 602.10.4.1#4
- ☐ ABW, PFH & PFG OK to mix w/ CS methods within a BWL if reqd bracing length based on highest value of all methods used ___ 602.10.4.1#4

FIG. 65

SDC D: Braced Wall Panel Locations at Ends of Braced Wall Line

Braced wall panels are allowed to begin 10 ft. from ends of braced wall lines if meeting either of the conditions shown below. These conditions would also comply for items 1 and 5 of F602.10.7 for SDC A, B & C if used with continuous sheathing.

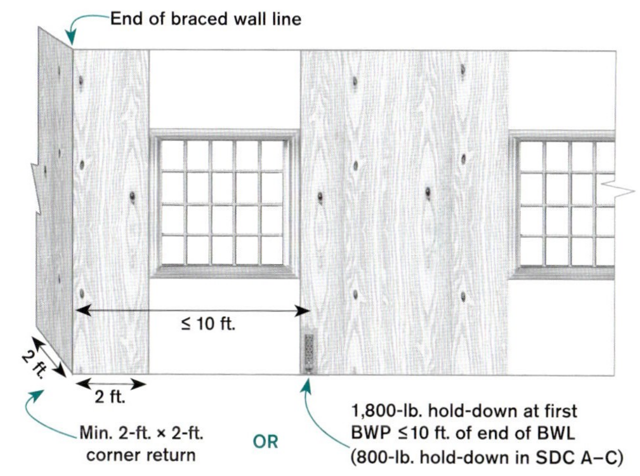

Spacing of Braced Wall Lines — 21 IRC

- ☐ Wind bracing max. 60 ft. (UDWS <140 mph) ____ T602.10.1.3
- ☐ Seismic bracing SDC A, B & C 1&2FD use wind bracing ____ T602.10.1.3
- ☐ Seismic bracing SDC C townhouse max. 35 ft. ____ T602.10.1.3
- ☐ Seismic bracing SDC D max. 25 ft. EXC ____ T602.10.1.3
  - 35 ft. max. single room ≤900 sq. ft. ____ T602.10.1.3

Braced Wall Panel Connections

- ☐ If joists perpendicular to & above or below BWP, band joist, rim joist, or blocking reqd along entire length ____ 602.10.8#1
- ☐ If joists parallel to & above or below BWP, attach to parallel framing members reqd directly above & below BWP or to full-depth blocking at max. 16 in. o.c. if no parallel members aligned w/ BWP ____ 602.10.8#2
- ☐ Top plates of BWPs to connect to rim, band, or header joist or to blocking between rafters or trusses EXC ____ 602.10.8.2
  - Blocking not reqd over openings in CS BWLs ____ 602.10.8.2
- ☐ In SDC D if top of BWP ≤15¼ in. from top of truss or rafter, blocking reqd w/ 8d nails at 6 in. o.c. full length of BWP ____ 602.10.8.2#2
- ☐ In SDC D if top of BWP >15¼ in. from top of truss or rafter, soffit blocking or vertical blocking per F602.10.8.2(3), or blocking per truss design, or in accordance w/ accepted engineering practice ____ 602.10.8.2#3
- ☐ Cantilevers ≤ joist depth permitted to support BWPs ____ 602.10.9

Minimum Length of Individual BWPs

- ☐ Min. length of a BWP per **T46,47** ____ 602.10.5
- ☐ BWP length that contributes to reqd length per **T47** ____ 602.10.5.1
- ☐ Methods CS-WSP & CS-SFB contribute actual length based on tallest height of openings adjacent to the BWP per **T46,F66** ____ 602.10.5
- ☐ In SDC A, B & C methods DWB, WSP, SFB, PBS, PCP & HPS panels 36–48 in. allowed partial credit per **T48** ____ 602.10.5.2

TABLE 46 — MIN. LENGTH (IN.) CS-WSP & CS-SFB ADJACENT TO OPENINGS ◆ T602.10.5

Adjacent Clear Opening Height (in.)	Wall Height				
	8 ft.	9 ft.	10 ft.	11 ft.	12 ft.
≤ 64	24	27	30	33	36
68	26	27	30	33	36
72	27	27	30	33	36
76	30	29	30	33	36
80	32	30	30	33	36
84	35	32	32	33	36
88	38	35	33	33	36
92	43	37	35	35	36
96	48	41	38	36	36
100	–	44	40	38	38
104	–	49	43	40	39
108	–	54	46	43	41
112	–	–	50	45	43
116	–	–	55	48	45
120	–	–	60	52	48
124	–	–	–	56	51
128	–	–	–	61	54
132	–	–	–	66	58
136	–	–	–	–	62
140	–	–	–	–	66
144	–	–	–	–	72

TABLE 47	MIN. LENGTH OF INDIVIDUAL BWPs ◆ T602.10.5						
Method		Min. Length (in.)					Contributing Length (in.)[A]
		Wall Height					
		8 ft.	9 ft.	10 ft.	11 ft.	12 ft.	
DWB, WSP, SFB, PBS, PCP, HPS, BV-WSP		48	48	48	53	58	Actual
GB		48	48	48	53	58	Both sides = Actual 1 side = 50%
LIB		55	62	69	NP	NP	Actual
ABW	SDC A, B, C	28	32	34	38	42	48
	SDC D	32	32	34	NP	NP	
CS-G		24	27	30	33	36	Actual
PF-H	Support roof	16	16	16	Note B		48
	1 story + roof	24	24	24	Note B		
PFG		24	27	30	Note B		1.5 × Actual
CS-PF	SDC A, B, C	16	18	20	Note B		1.5 × Actual
	SDC D	16	18	20	Note B		Actual

A. The actual length can be used when ≥ the reqd min. length.
B. Methods limit the header height to 10 ft. The wall height permitted to be 12 ft. w/ pony walls.

FIG. 66 Min. Length of BWPs: CS-WSP & CS-SFB

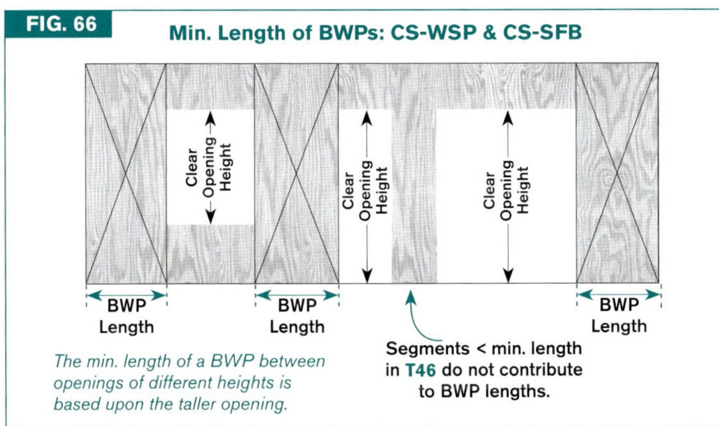

The min. length of a BWP between openings of different heights is based upon the taller opening.

TABLE 48	PARTIAL CREDIT FOR DWB, WSP, SFB, PBS, PCP, & HPS PANELS IN SDC A, B, C ◆ T602.10.5.2	
Actual BWP Length	Contributing Length Applied to Reqd Length[A]	
	8-ft. Wall Height	9-ft. Wall Height
48	48	48
42	36	36
36	27	n/a

A. Linear interpolation permitted.

- ☐ Methods ABW, PFH, PFG constructed per figures F602.10.6.1–3 __ 602.10.6
- ☐ Method CS-PF reqs tension strap for resisting wind pressures per T602.10.6.4 & F602.10.6.4 __ 602.10.6.4
- ☐ Methods ABW, PFH, PFG, CS-PF & BV-WSP in SDC D townhouses w/ stone or masonry veneer above first story & 1- & 2-family dwellings exceeding 2 stories req design in accord w/ accepted engineering practice __ 602.10.6.5[48]
- ☐ ABW hold-down force per **T49** __ 602.10.6.1

TABLE 49	MIN. HOLD-DOWN FORCES FOR ABW[A] ◆ T602.10.6.1					
SDC	Supporting/ Story	Height of Braced Wall Panel				
		8 ft.	9 ft.	10 ft.	11 ft.	12 ft.
A, B, C	One story	1,800	1,800	1,800	2,000	2,200
	1st of 2 stories	3,000	3,000	3,000	3,300	3,600
D	One story	1,800	1,800	1,800	NP	NP
	1st of 2 stories	3,000	3,000	3,000	NP	NP

A. Assumes UDWS < 140 mph.

48. Design req for 1- & 2-family dwellings was added, and there are several changes in 602.10.6.5 for those dwellings that are still within the prescriptive limits. See the full code text for structures w/ veneer in SDC D.

Minimum Number of BWPs — 21 IRC

- ☐ BWLs ≤ 16 ft. req min. 2 BWPs of any length or 1 min. 4 ft. _____ 602.10.2.3
- ☐ BWLs > 16 ft. req min. 2 BWPs _____ 602.10.2.3

Required Length of Bracing on Each Braced Wall Line

- ☐ All buildings in SDC A & B & detached buildings in SDC C per **T50** & adjustment factors per T602.10.3(2) _____ 602.10.3#1&2[49]
- ☐ Townhouses in SDC C & all buildings in SDC D req the greater value of **T50** or **T51** & adjustments per T602.10.3(2) & T602.10.3(4) EXC _602.10.3#3&4
  - SDC D buildings w/ stone or masonry veneer per 602.10.6.5 __ 602.10.3X

*Adjustment factors must be applied to tables **T50–T51** for a final determination on the reqd length of bracing. The adjustment factors are in IRC tables 602.10.3(2) and 602.10.3(4). Tables **T50A–F** are modified for exposure category, roof eave-to-ridge height, story height, number of BWLs per plan direction, additional hold-downs, presence of interior gypsum board, extra fastening for gypsum board, and absence of horizontal blocking. Tables **T51A–D** are modified for story height, BWL spacing, dead loads, walls w/ veneer, and absence of gypsum board or horizontal blocking. Refer to the full text of the IRC for these modifications.*

49. **T50A** is new in the 2021 code. In previous editions, these tables began at wind speeds under 110 mph, and the new table for < 95 mph allows for less bracing than previously reqd.

Stepped Foundations & Cripple Walls — 21 IRC

- ☐ Studs no smaller than size of studding above cripple wall _____ 602.9
- ☐ Exterior wall < 14 in. high reqs WSP sheathing or solid blocking ____ 602.9[50]
- ☐ If > 4 ft. high, size studs as reqd for additional story _____ 602.9
- ☐ SDC A, B & C bracing length 1.15× reqd length of wall above ___602.10.10
- ☐ SDC D_0 & D_1 bracing length 1.5× reqd length of wall above ___ 602.10.10.1
- ☐ SDC D_2 bracing per tables 602.10.3(3&4) _____ 602.10.10.2
- ☐ If any segment > 4 ft. high, entire cripple wall counts as additional story for bracing purposes & stories above redesignated _____ 602.10.10.3
- ☐ SDC C townhouses & SDC D_0 & D_1 only WSP & CS-WSP bracing, distance between adjacent BWP edges max. 14 ft. _____ 602.10.10.1
- ☐ When BWL height varies > 4 ft., cripple walls tied to stepped foundations w/ min. 8 ft. direct on foundation per **F67** considered braced _____ 602.11.2

FIG. 67 Stepped Foundation in SDC D

When the height of a reqd braced wall line varies >4 ft., the cripple walls are considered braced when tied to a sill of the lowest floor framing as depicted below.

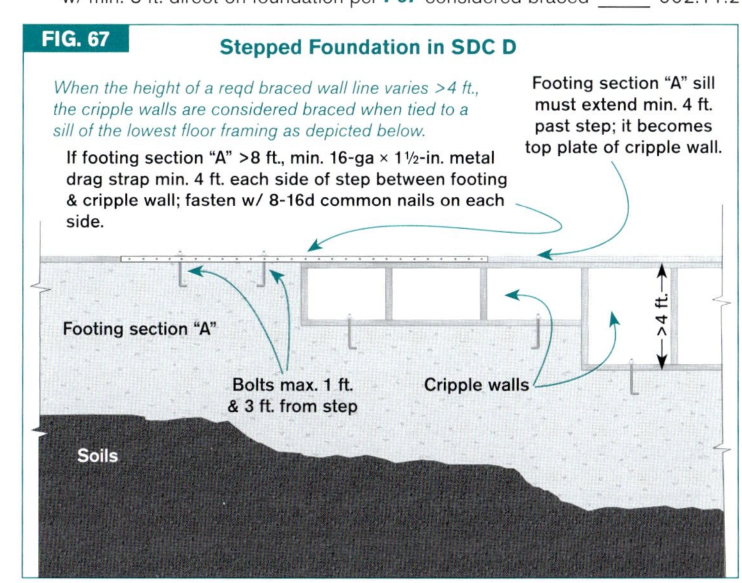

50. Prior code applied to all cripple walls, now only applies to exterior cripple walls.

TABLE 50A	MIN. BRACING LENGTH[A] BASED ON WIND SPEED <95 mph[49] ◆ T602.10.3(1)				
Story Location	BWL Spacing (ft.)[C]	Min. Total Length[B] of BWP at each BWL (ft.)			
		Bracing Methods			
		LIB[D]	GB	DWB, WSP, SFB, PCP, HPS, BV-WSP, PBS, ABW, PFH, PFG, CS-SFB	CS-WSP, CS-G, CS-PF
Top story (of 1, 2 or 3)	10	2.5	2.5	1.5	1.5
	20	4.5	4.5	2.5	2.5
	30	6.5	6.5	4.0	3.5
	40	8.5	8.5	5.0	4.0
	50	10.5	10.5	6.0	5.0
	60	12.5	12.5	7.0	6.0
Lower of 2 / middle of 3	10	5.0	5.0	3.0	2.5
	20	8.5	8.5	5.0	4.5
	30	12.5	12.5	7.0	6.0
	40	16.0	16.0	9.5	8.0
	50	20.0	20.0	11.5	10.0
	60	23.5	23.5	13.5	11.5
Bottom of 3	10	NP	7.0	4.0	3.5
	20	NP	13.0	7.5	6.5
	30	NP	18.5	10.5	9.0
	40	NP	24.0	13.5	11.5
	50	NP	29.5	17.0	14.5
	60	NP	35.0	20.0	17.0

A. Based on Exposure Category B, 30-ft. mean roof height, 10-ft. wall height, and 2 BWLs.
B. Linear interpolation permitted.
C. If ≥3 BWLs are present, the average dimension between them is permitted to be used.
D. Method LIB reqs GB attached to min. 1 side; spacing at panel edges ≤8 in.

TABLE 50B	MIN. BRACING LENGTH[A] BASED ON WIND SPEED ≤110 mph ◆ T602.10.3(1)				
Story Location	BWL Spacing (ft.)[C]	Min. Total Length[B] of BWP at each BWL (ft.)			
		Bracing Methods			
		LIB[D]	GB	DWB, WSP, SFB, PCP, HPS, BV-WSP, PBS, ABW, PFH, PFG, CS-SFB	CS-WSP, CS-G, CS-PF
Top story (of 1, 2 or 3)	10	3.5	3.5	2.0	1.5
	20	6.0	6.0	3.5	3.0
	30	8.5	8.5	5.0	4.5
	40	11.5	11.5	6.5	5.5
	50	14.0	14.0	8.0	7.0
	60	16.5	16.5	9.5	8.0
Lower of 2 / middle of 3	10	6.5	6.5	3.5	3.0
	20	11.5	11.5	6.5	5.5
	30	16.5	16.5	9.5	8.0
	40	21.5	21.5	12.5	10.5
	50	26.5	26.5	15.5	13.0
	60	31.5	31.5	18.0	15.5
Bottom of 3	10	NP	9.5	5.5	4.5
	20	NP	17.0	10.0	8.5
	30	NP	24.5	14.0	12.0
	40	NP	32.0	18.5	15.5
	50	NP	39.5	22.5	19.0
	60	NP	46.5	26.5	23.0

A. Based on Exposure Category B, 30-ft. mean roof height, 10-ft. wall height, and 2 BWLs.
B. Linear interpolation permitted.
C. If ≥3 BWLs are present, the average dimension between them is permitted to be used.
D. Method LIB reqs GB attached to min. 1 side; spacing at panel edges ≤8 in.

TABLE 50C — MIN. BRACING LENGTH[A] BASED ON WIND SPEED ≤115 mph ◆ T602.10.3(1)

Story Location	BWL Spacing (ft.)[C]	Min. Total Length[B] of BWP at each BWL (ft.) — Bracing Methods: LIB[D]	GB	DWB, WSP, SFB, PCP, HPS, BV-WSP, PBS, ABW, PFH, PFG, CS-SFB	CS-WSP, CS-G, CS-PF
	10	3.5	3.5	2.0	2.0
	20	6.5	6.5	3.5	3.5
	30	9.5	9.5	5.5	4.5
	40	12.5	12.5	7.0	6.0
	50	15.0	15.0	9.0	7.5
	60	18.0	18.0	10.5	9.0
	10	7.0	7.0	4.0	3.5
	20	12.5	12.5	7.5	6.5
	30	18.0	18.0	10.5	9.0
	40	23.5	23.5	13.5	11.5
	50	29.0	29.0	16.5	14.0
	60	34.5	34.5	20.0	17.0
	10	NP	10.0	6.0	5.0
	20	NP	18.5	11.0	9.0
	30	NP	27.0	15.5	13.0
	40	NP	35.0	20.0	17.0
	50	NP	43.0	24.5	21.0
	60	NP	51.0	29.0	25.0

A. Based on Exposure Category B, 30-ft. mean roof height, 10-ft. wall height, and 2 BWLs.
B. Linear interpolation permitted.
C. If ≥3 BWLs are present, the average dimension between them is permitted to be used.
D. Method LIB reqs GB attached to min. 1 side; spacing at panel edges ≤8 in.

TABLE 50D — MIN. BRACING LENGTH[A] BASED ON WIND SPEED ≤120 mph ◆ T602.10.3(1)

Story Location	BWL Spacing (ft.)[C]	Min. Total Length[B] of BWP at each BWL (ft.) — Bracing Methods: LIB[D]	GB	DWB, WSP, SFB, PCP, HPS, BV-WSP, PBS, ABW, PFH, PFG, CS-SFB	CS-WSP, CS-G, CS-PF
	10	4.0	4.0	2.5	2.0
	20	7.0	7.0	4.0	3.5
	30	10.5	10.5	6.0	5.0
	40	13.5	13.5	8.0	6.5
	50	16.5	16.5	9.5	8.0
	60	19.5	19.5	11.5	9.5
	10	7.5	7.5	4.5	3.5
	20	14.0	14.0	8.0	7.0
	30	20.0	20.0	11.5	9.5
	40	25.5	25.5	15.0	12.5
	50	31.5	31.5	18.0	15.5
	60	37.5	37.5	21.5	18.5
	10	NP	11.0	6.5	5.5
	20	NP	20.5	11.5	10.0
	30	NP	29.0	17.0	14.5
	40	NP	38.0	22.0	18.5
	50	NP	47.0	27.0	23.0
	60	NP	55.5	32.0	27.0

A. Based on Exposure Category B, 30-ft. mean roof height, 10-ft. wall height, and 2 BWLs.
B. Linear interpolation permitted.
C. If ≥3 BWLs are present, the average dimension between them is permitted to be used.
D. Method LIB reqs GB attached to min. 1 side; spacing at panel edges ≤8 in.

TABLE 50E — MIN. BRACING LENGTH[A] BASED ON WIND SPEED ≤130 mph ◆ T602.10.3(1)

Story Location	BWL Spacing (ft.)[C]	Min. Total Length[B] of BWP at each BWL (ft.)			
		Bracing Methods			
		LIB[D]	GB	DWB, WSP, SFB, PCP, HPS, BV-WSP, PBS, ABW, PFH, PFG, CS-SFB	CS-WSP, CS-G, CS-PF
Top story	10	4.5	4.5	2.5	2.5
	20	8.5	8.5	5.0	4.0
	30	12.0	12.0	7.0	6.0
	40	15.5	15.5	9.0	7.5
	50	19.5	19.5	11.0	9.5
	60	23.0	23.0	13.0	11.0
Story below top story	10	8.5	8.5	5.0	4.5
	20	16.0	16.0	9.5	8.0
	30	23.0	23.0	13.5	11.5
	40	30.0	30.0	17.5	15.0
	50	37.0	37.0	21.5	18.0
	60	44.0	44.0	25.0	21.5
Bottom of three stories	10	NP	13.0	7.5	6.5
	20	NP	24.0	13.5	11.5
	30	NP	34.5	19.5	17.0
	40	NP	44.5	25.5	22.0
	50	NP	55.0	31.5	26.5
	60	NP	65.0	37.5	31.5

A. Based on Exposure Category B, 30-ft. mean roof height, 10-ft. wall height, and 2 BWLs.
B. Linear interpolation permitted.
C. If ≥3 BWLs are present, the average dimension between them is permitted to be used.
D. Method LIB reqs GB attached to min. 1 side; spacing at panel edges ≤8 in.

TABLE 50F — MIN. BRACING LENGTH[A] BASED ON WIND SPEED ≤140 mph ◆ T602.10.3(1)

Story Location	BWL Spacing (ft.)[C]	Min. Total Length[B] of BWP at each BWL (ft.)			
		Bracing Methods			
		LIB[D]	GB	DWB, WSP, SFB, PCP, HPS, BV-WSP, PBS, ABW, PFH, PFG, CS-SFB	CS-WSP, CS-G, CS-PF
Top story	10	5.5	5.5	3.0	2.5
	20	10.0	10.0	5.5	5.0
	30	14.0	14.0	8.0	7.0
	40	18.0	18.0	10.5	9.0
	50	22.5	22.5	13.0	11.0
	60	26.5	26.5	15.0	13.0
Story below top story	10	10.0	10.0	6.0	5.0
	20	18.5	18.5	11.0	9.0
	30	27.0	27.0	15.5	13.0
	40	35.0	35.0	20.0	17.0
	50	43.0	43.0	24.5	21.0
	60	51.0	51.0	29.0	25.0
Bottom of three stories	10	NP	15.0	8.5	7.5
	20	NP	27.5	16.0	13.5
	30	NP	39.5	23.0	19.5
	40	NP	51.5	29.5	25.0
	50	NP	63.5	36.5	31.0
	60	NP	75.5	43.0	36.5

A. Based on Exposure Category B, 30-ft. mean roof height, 10-ft. wall height, and 2 BWLs.
B. Linear interpolation permitted.
C. If ≥3 BWLs are present, the average dimension between them is permitted to be used.
D. Method LIB reqs GB attached to min. 1 side; spacing at panel edges ≤8 in.

TABLE 51A MIN. BRACING LENGTH FOR TOWNHOUSES BASED ON SEISMIC DESIGN CATEGORY C ◆ T602.10.3(3)

Story Location	BWL Length (ft.)[B]	Min. Total Length[A] of BWP at each BWL (ft.)			
		Bracing Methods			
		LIB[C]	GB, DWB, SFB, PBS, PCP, HPS, CS-SFB	WSP, ABW,[D] PFH,[D] PFG[D]	CS-WSP, CS-G, CS-PF
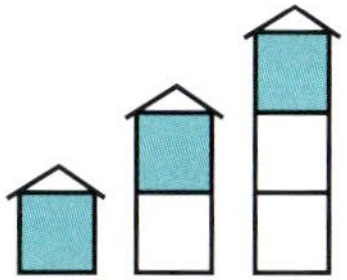	10	2.5	2.5	1.6	1.4
	20	5.0	5.0	3.2	2.7
	30	7.5	7.5	4.8	4.1
	40	10.0	10.0	6.4	5.4
	50	12.5	12.5	8.0	6.8
	10	NP	4.5	3.0	2.6
	20	NP	9.0	6.0	5.1
	30	NP	13.5	9.0	7.7
	40	NP	18.0	12.0	10.2
	50	NP	22.5	15.0	12.8
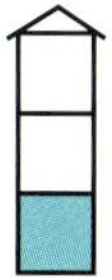	10	NP	6.0	4.5	3.8
	20	NP	12.0	9.0	7.7
	30	NP	18.0	13.5	11.5
	40	NP	24.0	18.0	15.3
	50	NP	30.0	22.5	19.1

A. Linear interpolation permitted.
B. BWLs >50 ft. can be divided into segments ≤50 ft. and amount of bracing in each segment then computed in accord w/ this table.
C. Method LIB reqs GB attached to min. 1 side; spacing at panel edges ≤8 in.
D. Methods ABW, PFH, and PFG only permitted on single story or first of 2 stories.

TABLE 51B MIN. BRACING LENGTH BASED ON SEISMIC DESIGN CATEGORY D_0 ◆ T602.10.3(3)

Story Location	BWL Length (ft.)[B]	Min. Total Length[A] of BWP at each BWL (ft.)		
		Bracing Methods[C]		
		GB, DWB, SFB, PBS, PCP, HPS	WSP, ABW,[D] PFH[D]	CS-WSP, CS-G, CS-PF
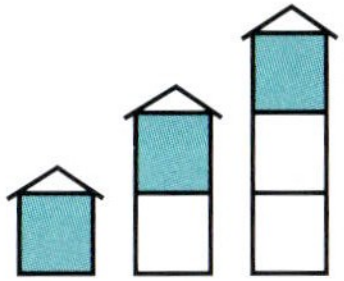	10	2.8	1.8	1.6
	20	5.5	3.6	3.1
	30	8.3	5.4	4.6
	40	11.0	7.2	6.1
	50	13.8	9.0	7.7
	10	5.3	3.8	3.2
	20	10.5	7.5	6.4
	30	15.8	11.3	9.6
	40	21.0	15.0	12.8
	50	26.3	18.8	16.0
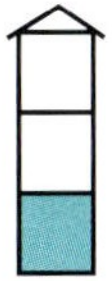	10	7.3	5.3	4.5
	20	14.5	10.5	9.0
	30	21.8	15.8	13.4
	40	29.0	21.0	17.9
	50	36.3	26.3	22.3

A. Linear interpolation permitted.
B. BWLs >50 ft. can be divided into segments ≤50 ft. and amount of bracing in each segment then computed in accord w/ this table.
C. Methods LIB, PFG, and CS-SFB are not applicable in SDC D.
D. Methods ABW and PFH only permitted on single story or 1st of 2 stories.

TABLE 51C — MIN. BRACING LENGTH BASED ON SEISMIC DESIGN CATEGORY D_1 ◆ T602.10.3(3)

Story Location	BWL Length (ft.)[B]	Min. Total Length[A] of BWP at each BWL (ft.)		
		Bracing Methods		
		GB, DWB, SFB, PCP, HPS===	WSP, ABW,[C] PFH[C]	CS-WSP, CS-G, CS-PF
	10	3.0	2.0	1.7
	20	6.0	4.0	3.4
	30	9.0	6.0	5.1
	40	12.0	8.0	6.8
	50	15.0	10.0	8.5
	10	6.0	4.5	3.8
	20	12.0	9.0	7.7
	30	18.0	13.5	11.5
	40	24.0	18.0	15.3
	50	30.0	22.5	19.1
	10	8.5	6.0	5.1
	20	17.0	12.0	10.2
	30	25.5	18.0	15.3
	40	34.0	24.0	20.4
	50	42.5	30.0	25.5

A. Linear interpolation permitted.
B. BWLs >50 ft. can be divided into segments ≤ 50 ft. and amount of bracing in each segment then computed in accord w/ this table.
C. Methods ABW and PFH only permitted on single story or 1st of 2 stories.
D. Methods LIB, PFG, and CS-SFB are not applicable in SDC D.

TABLE 51D — MIN. BRACING LENGTH BASED ON SEISMIC DESIGN CATEGORY D_2 ◆ T602.10.3(3)

Story Location	BWL Length (ft.)[B]	Min. Total Length[A] of BWP at each BWL (ft.)		
		Bracing Methods		
		GB, DWB, SFB, PCP, HPS	WSP, ABW,[C] PFH[C]	CS-WSP, CS-G, CS-PF
	10	4.0	2.5	2.1
	20	8.0	5.0	4.3
	30	12.0	7.5	6.4
	40	16.0	10.0	8.5
	50	20.0	12.5	10.6
	10	7.5	5.5	4.7
	20	15.0	11.0	9.4
	30	22.5	16.5	14.0
	40	30.0	22.0	18.7
	50	37.5	27.5	23.4
Cripple wall below 1- or 2-story dwelling	10	NP	7.5	6.4
	20	NP	15.0	12.8
	30	NP	22.5	19.1
	40	NP	30.0	25.5
	50	NP	37.5	31.9
3-story dwellings	Design in accordance w/ accepted engineering practice			

A. Linear interpolation permitted.
B. BWLs >50 ft. can be divided into segments ≤50 ft. and amount of bracing in each segment then computed in accord w/ this table.
C. Methods ABW and PFH only permitted on single story or 1st of 2 stories.
D. Methods LIB, PFG, and CS-SFB are not applicable in SDC D.

SIMPLIFIED WALL BRACING

Simplified wall bracing is permitted for qualifying structures. The method does not consider the contribution of interior walls to the required amount of bracing and does not use the conventional method of drawing braced wall lines as straight lines on plans. A circumscribed rectangle is drawn around the entire structure at each floor level, and a simplified formula determines the number of "bracing units."

General — 21 IRC

- ☐ Must meet all of the following qualifications ______ 602.12
  1. Max. 3 stories above concrete or masonry foundation or basement wall.
  2. Max. 24-in. cantilever beyond foundation or bearing wall below.
  3. Wall height max. 10 ft.
  4. Roof eave to ridge height max. 15 ft.
  5. Exterior walls must have min. ½-in. GB on interior side.
  6. Max. 130 mph ultimate wind speed design, Exposure Category B or C.
  7. Detached 1&2FD must be in SDC A, B, or C, townhouses in A or B.
  8. Cripple walls not permitted in 3-story buildings.
- ☐ Reqd bracing determined by circumscribed rectangle each floor **F68** 602.12.1
- ☐ Open carports & decks permitted to be excluded from rectangle __ 602.12.1
- ☐ Long side of rectangle max. 60 ft., max. ratio longer to shorter 3:1 _ 602.12.1

Bracing Units

- ☐ Bracing unit = full-height sheathed segment w/o openings or offsets 602.12.3
- ☐ Sheathing must be min. ⅜-in. WSP or min. ½-in. SFB ______ 602.12.2
- ☐ No mixing sheathing materials, fasten per **T40** or **T43** ______ 602.12.2
- ☐ Mixing bracing methods on same story not permitted ______ 602.12.3
- ☐ If exterior walls completely sheathed min., bracing unit 3 ft. **F70** ___ 602.12.3
- ☐ If exterior walls not completely sheathed min., bracing unit 4 ft. **F69** 602.12.3
- ☐ Segments of walls longer than min. bracing unit are considered multiple bracing units; their number of units determined by dividing actual length by min. bracing unit length **F69,70** ______ 602.12.3.1

Required Number & Distribution of Bracing Units

- ☐ Number of bracing units each side of rectangle per **T52** ______ 602.12.4
- ☐ Bracing units must begin within 12 ft. of corners **F69,70** ______ 602.12.5
- ☐ Max. 20 ft. between adjacent edges of bracing units **F69,70** ______ 602.12.5
- ☐ Wall segments >8 ft. min. 1 bracing unit ______ 602.12.5

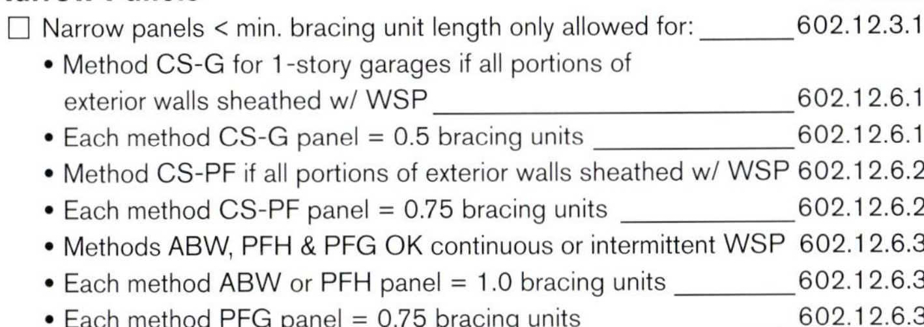

Narrow Panels — 21 IRC

- ☐ Narrow panels < min. bracing unit length only allowed for: ______ 602.12.3.1
  - Method CS-G for 1-story garages if all portions of exterior walls sheathed w/ WSP ______ 602.12.6.1
  - Each method CS-G panel = 0.5 bracing units ______ 602.12.6.1
  - Method CS-PF if all portions of exterior walls sheathed w/ WSP 602.12.6.2
  - Each method CS-PF panel = 0.75 bracing units ______ 602.12.6.2
  - Methods ABW, PFH & PFG OK continuous or intermittent WSP 602.12.6.3
  - Each method ABW or PFH panel = 1.0 bracing units ______ 602.12.6.3
  - Each method PFG panel = 0.75 bracing units ______ 602.12.6.3

FIG. 68 Circumscribed Rectangle for Simplified Bracing

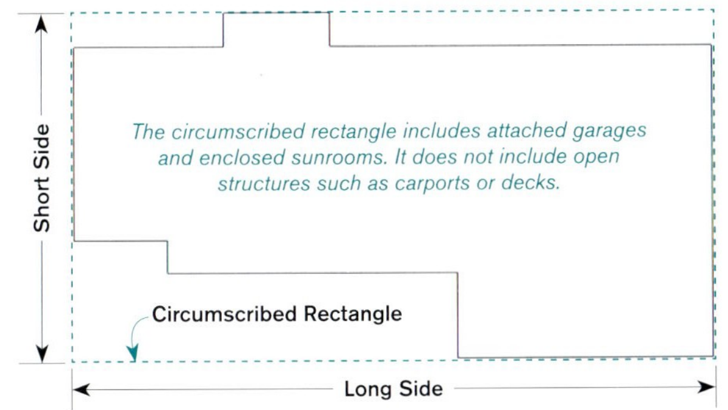

Example: Suppose that the building has continuous exterior sheathing including the areas that are not part of braced wall units, and the bracing units are 3 ft., 8 ft., 7 ft., and 2 ft. The 2-ft. segment does not count unless part of an allowed narrow panel (see methods above). The number of bracing units is determined by (3 ft. ÷ 3 ft.) + (8 ft. ÷ 3 ft.) + (7 ft. ÷ 3 ft.) = 6.

*Use **T52** to determine if 6 bracing units are sufficient. Note that the table bases the required number on the length of the perpendicular wall, not the wall containing the bracing units.*

FIG. 69 Areas Between Bracing not Sheathed with Bracing Material

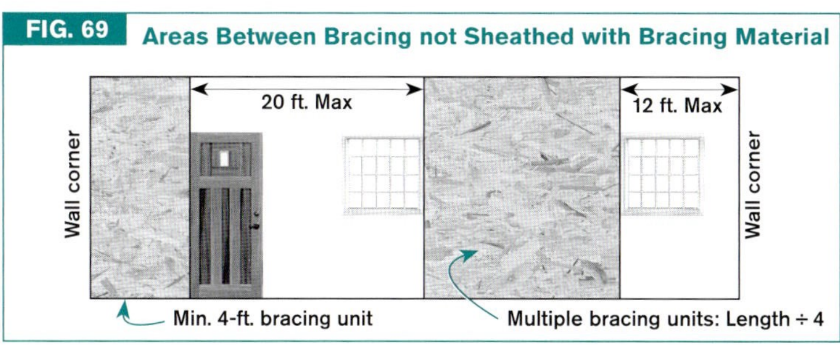

FIG. 70 Areas Between Bracing Sheathed with Bracing Material

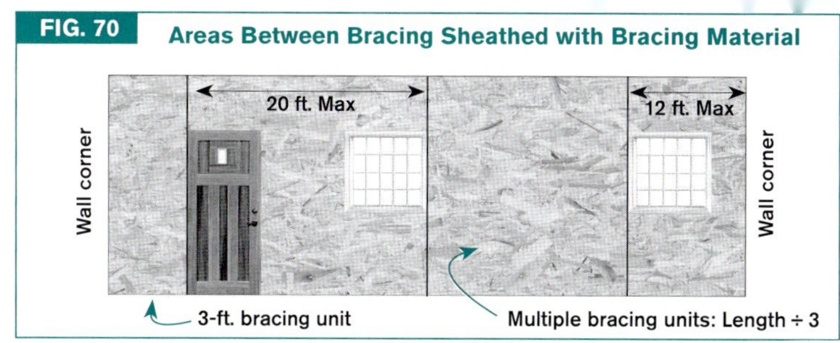

TABLE 52 MIN. NUMBER OF BRACING UNITS ON EACH SIDE OF CIRCUMSCRIBED RECTANGLE ◆ T602.12.4

Ultimate Design Wind Speed (mph)	Eave-to-Ridge Height (ft.)	Story Location	Min. Number of Bracing Units each Long Side[A,B]						Min. Number of Bracing Units each Short Side[A,B]					
			Length of Short Side (ft.)[C]						Length of Long Side (ft.)[C]					
			10	20	30	40	50	60	10	20	30	40	50	60
115	10	Single or top story	1	2	2	2	3	3	1	2	2	2	3	3
		Lowest 2 story, 2nd of 3 stories	2	3	3	4	5	6	2	3	3	4	5	6
		Lowest of 3-story	2	3	4	6	7	8	2	3	4	6	7	8
	15	Single or top story	1	2	3	3	4	4	1	2	3	3	4	4
		Lowest 2 story, 2nd of 3 stories	2	3	4	5	6	7	2	3	4	5	6	7
		Lowest of 3-story	2	4	5	6	7	9	2	4	5	6	7	9
130	10	Single or top story	1	2	2	3	3	4	1	2	2	3	3	4
		Lowest 2 story, 2nd of 3 stories	2	3	4	5	6	7	2	3	4	5	6	7
		Lowest of 3-story	2	4	5	7	8	10	2	4	5	7	8	10
	15	Single or top story	2	3	3	4	4	6	2	3	3	4	4	6
		Lowest 2 story, 2nd of 3 stories	3	4	6	7	8	10	3	4	6	7	8	10
		Lowest of 3-story	3	6	7	10	11	13	3	6	7	10	11	13

A. Cripple walls of walkout basements to be designated as first story and subsequent stories above redesignated.
B. In Exposure Category C, multiply reqd number of bracing units by 1.2 for 1-story building, 1.3 for 2-story, and 1.4 for 3-story.
C. Interpolation is not permitted; actual lengths of circumscribed rectangle to be rounded up to the nearest unit of 10 when using this table.

ROOF & CEILING FRAMING

Ceiling joists must be sized in anticipation of whether the attic space will be suitable for limited storage. Roof assemblies must be capable of supporting the maximum snow load and must resist the maximum wind loads, including uplift. Roof assemblies must be tied together to prevent them from exerting lateral thrust on supporting walls. The performance requirement for this is found in 802.2, and the specific means of achieving that goal are in section 802.5.2.

General — 21 IRC

- ☐ Sawn lumber reqs grade mark or agency approval certificate _______ 802.1.1
- ☐ Each piece of FRT lumber & WSP reqs label _______ 802.1.5.4
- ☐ Paints, coatings, or other surface treatment not OK as FRT _______ 802.1.5.2[51]
- ☐ Roof/ceiling assembly must provide continuous tie across structure __ 802.2[52]
- ☐ Rafter or joist end min. 1½ in. bearing on wood or metal, 3 in. on masonry EXC _______ 802.6
  - When continuous tension tie **F75** provided, vertical bearing against ridge satisfies bearing support reqt _______ 802.6
- ☐ Cutting, boring & notching dimensional lumber per **T23**, **F53** EXC ___ 802.7.1
  - Cantilevered eave rafters ≤2 ft. max. notch per **F72** _______ 802.7.1.1
  - Ceiling joist end cuts per **F71** _______ 802.7.1.2
- ☐ Cutting, boring & notching of engineered wood products AMI _______ 802.7.2
- ☐ Fastening per **T57** _______ 802.4.2, 802.5, 803.2.3
- ☐ > 5:1 nominal (e.g. 2 × 12) rafters & joists req blocking at bearing points 802.8
- ☐ > 6:1 nominal (e.g. 2 × 14) rafters or joists req solid blocking, diagonal bridging, or 1 × 3 backer at max. 8-ft. intervals _______ 802.8.1

51. Specific prohibition on use of applied coatings in lieu of FRT material unless approved.
52. The intent of this section did not change; the related sections were significantly re-worded for clarity and emphasis.

Openings — 21 IRC

- ☐ Openings to be framed w/ header & trimmer joists/rafters _______ 802.9
- ☐ Single-member header same size as joists/rafters OK up to 4 ft. _______ 802.9
- ☐ Single trimmer OK for single header within 3 ft. of trimmer bearing ____ 802.9
- ☐ Doubled header & trimmer joists reqd if header >4 ft. _______ 802.9
- ☐ Hangers reqd for header-trimmer connections if header >6 ft. _______ 802.9
- ☐ Hangers or ledger strips reqd at header for tail joists >12 ft.* _______ 802.9

**Note: Joists and rafters require min. 1½-in. bearing on wood or metal or 3 in. on masonry or concrete. Best practice is to use hangers at all openings.*

FIG. 71

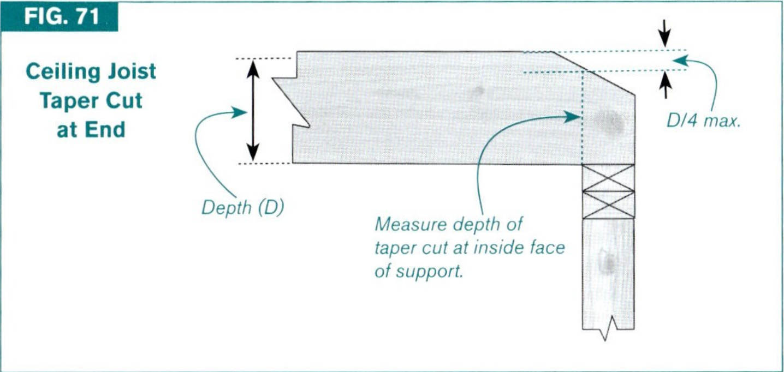

FIG. 72

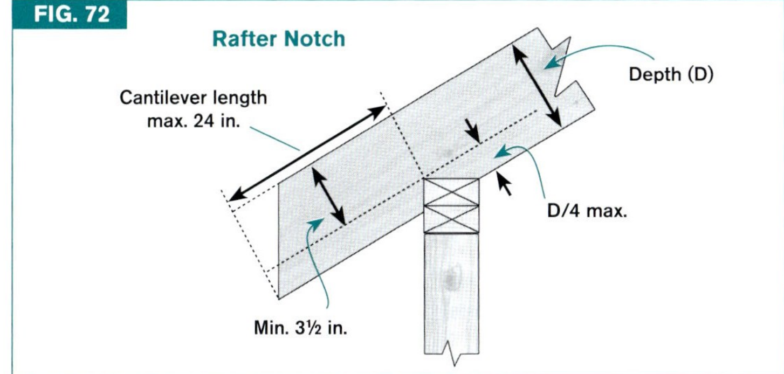

Ceiling Joists **21 IRC**

- ☐ Spans per **T53**,**54**, **F73** EXC ____ T301.5 & 802.5.1
  - Use **T24** for attics w/ fixed stairs ____ 502.3.1
- ☐ 3 in. lap over partitions or butted & toenailed to bearing member ____ 802.5.2.1
- ☐ Fastening per **T57** EXC ____ 802.5
  - Joists acting as rafter tie nailed to each other per **T60** ____ 802.5.2.1
  - Lapped joists not restraining rafters OK to nail per **T57** ____ 802.5.2.1
- ☐ End cuts max. ¼ joist depth at inside bearing face of wall **F71** ____ 802.7.1.2

TABLE 53 CEILING JOIST SPANS FOR 10-PSF LIVE LOAD T802.5.1(1) (IN FEET-INCHES) (UNINHABITABLE ATTICS WITHOUT STORAGE)

Size	Douglas Fir-Larch #2				Hem-Fir #2			
	Spacing (in. o.c.)				Spacing (in. o.c.)			
	12	16	19.2	24	12	16	19.2	24
2×4	12–5	11–3	10–7	9–10	11–7	10–6	9–11	9–2
2×6	19–6	17–8	16–8	15–0	18–2	16–6	15–7	14–5
2×8	25–8	23–4	21–4	19–1	24–0	21–9	20–6	18–6
2×10	A	A	26–0	23–3	A	A	25–3	22–7
Size	Southern Pine #2				Spruce–Pine-Fir #2			
	Spacing (in. o.c.)				Spacing (in. o.c.)			
	12	16	19.2	24	12	16	19.2	24
2×4	11–10	10–9	10–2	9–3	11–10	10–9	10–2	9–5
2×6	18–8	16–11	15–7	13–11	18–8	16–11	15–11	14–9
2×8	24–7	21–7	19–8	17–7	24–7	22–4	21–0	18–9
2×10	A	25–7	23–5	20–11	A	A	25–8	22–11

A. The span exceeds 26 ft.

TABLE 54 CEILING JOIST SPANS FOR 20-PSF LIVE LOAD T802.5.1(2) (IN FEET-INCHES) (UNINHABITABLE ATTICS WITH LIMITED STORAGE)

Size	Douglas Fir-Larch #2				Hem-Fir #2			
	Spacing (in. o.c.)				Spacing (in. o.c.)			
	12	16	19.2	24	12	16	19.2	24
2×4	9–10	8–11	8–2	7–3	9–2	8–4	7–10	7–1
2×6	15–0	13–0	11–11	10–8	14–5	12–8	11–7	10–4
2×8	19–1	16–6	15–1	13–6	18–6	16–0	14–8	13–1
2×10	23–3	20–2	18–5	16–5	22–7	19–7	17–10	16–0
Size	Southern Pine #2				Spruce-Pine–Fir #2			
	Spacing (in. o.c.)				Spacing (in. o.c.)			
	12	16	19.2	24	12	16	19.2	24
2×4	9–3	8–0	7–4	6–7	9–5	8–7	8–0	7–2
2×6	13–11	12–0	11–0	9–10	14–9	12–10	11–9	10–6
2×8	17–7	15–3	13–11	12–6	18–9	16–3	14–10	13–3
2×10	20–11	18–1	16–6	14–9	22–11	19–10	18–2	16–3

FIG. 73 Uninhabitable Attic with Limited Storage

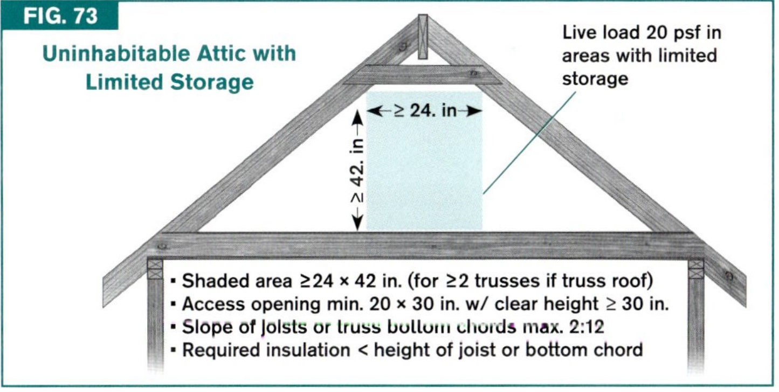

TABLE 55	MIN. ROOF LIVE LOADS LB. PER SQ. FT. OF HORIZONTAL PROJECTION ◆ T301.6		
Roof Slope	Tributary Loaded Area in sq. ft. for any structural member		
	0 – 200	201 – 600	> 600
Flat to <4:12	20	16	12
4:12 – <12:12	16	14	12
≥12:12	12	12	12

Roof Sheathing — 21 IRC

- ☐ Lumber sheathing min. ⅝ in. net thickness at 24-in.-o.c. supports ____ T803.1
- ☐ Min. 1½ in. net thickness if >24-in.-o.c. supports ____ T803.1
- ☐ Spaced lumber sheathing not allowed in SDC D_2 ____ 803.1
- ☐ WSP reqs grade mark from approved agency **F55** ____ 803.2.1
- ☐ WSP spans per **F55** ____ 803.2.2
- ☐ WSP fastening per **T56** ____ 602.3.1
- ☐ WSP sheathing OK to be permanently exposed on underside (such as eaves) if identified as Exposure 1 ____ 803.2.1.1
- ☐ FRT plywood reqs grading ____ 803.2.1.2
- ☐ Values for FRT plywood must consider humidity & temperature by approved method of investigation ____ 803.2.1.2

TABLE 56	WSP FASTENING TO ROOF FRAMING ◆ T602.3(1)		
Panel Thickness	Fastener[A]	Spacing (in.)	
		Edges	Intermediate
⅜ in. – ½ in.	8d common or RSRS-01 (2⅜ × 0.113 in.)	6[B]	6[B]
19/32 in. – ¾ in.	8d common or RSRS-01 (2⅜ × 0.113 in.)	6[B]	6[B]
⅞ in. – 1¼ in.	10d common or 2½ in. × 0.131 in. × 0.281 in. head deformed nail	6	12

A. Table T602.3(2) provides a schedule for alternate fastening methods w/ staples and gun nails in areas where the UDWS is ≤110 mph. It requires generally tighter spacing than this table.
B. 4 in. o.c. when attaching sheathing to roof and intermediate framing if within 48 in. of roof edges and ridges and >130 mph in Exposure B or if >110 mph in Exposure C.

TABLE 57	ROOF FRAMING FASTENER SCHEDULE ◆ T602.3(1)	
Connection	Fastener	Method
Blocking between joists, rafters, or trusses to top plate or other framing below	4 8d box or 3 8d common or 3 10d box or 3 3-in. gun nails	Toenail
Blocking at rafters or truss not at top wall plates, to rafter or truss	2 8d common or 2 3-in. gun nails	Each end toenail
	2 16d common or 3 3-in. gun nails	End nail
Flat blocking to truss & web filler	16d common or 3-in. gun nails	6 in. o.c. face nail
Ceiling joists to top plate	4 8d box or 3 8d common or 3 10d box or 3 3-in. gun nails	Per joist, toenail
Ceiling joist laps over partitions when joists not attached to parallel rafter	4 10d box or 3 16d common or 4 3-in. gun nails	Face nail
Ceiling joist laps over partitions & rafter heel joints when joists attached to form tie to parallel rafter	**T60**	Face nail
Collar tie to rafter, face nail	3 10d common or 4 10d box or 4 3-in. gun nails	Face nail each rafter
Rafter or roof truss to plate	3 16d box or 3 10d common or 4 10d box or 4 3-in. gun nails	Toenail
Roof rafters to ridge, valley, or hip rafters or roof rafter to min. 2-in. ridge beam	4 16d box or 3 10d common or 4 10d box or 4 3-in. gun nails	Toenail
	3 16d box or 2 16d common or 3 10d box or 3 3-in. gun nails	End nail

Rafters — 21 IRC

- ☐ If roof pitch < 3:12, ridges, valleys & hips req design as beams — 802.4.4
- ☐ Rafter min. 1½-in. bearing on ridges, valleys & hips designed as beams 802.6
- ☐ Rafter horizontal spans per **T61A–61P** EXC — 802.4.1
  - • Adjust allowed span per **F75** & **T59** — T802.4.1 note a
  - • Rafter span can be measured from purlin support **F74** — 802.4.5
- ☐ Purlin min. dimension same as supported rafters **F74** — 802.4.5
- ☐ Purlin braces (kickers) min. nominal 2 × 4, max. spacing 4 ft. o.c. **F74** 802.4.5
- ☐ Purlin supports min. 45° from horizontal **F74** — 802.4.5
- ☐ Max. unbraced length of kickers 8 ft. — 802.4.5
- ☐ Rafters must be framed opposite from each other to a ridge board — 802.4.2[53]
- ☐ Ridge min. 1 in nominal thickness & depth ≥ cut end of rafter — 802.3
- ☐ Max. 1½-in. offset allowed for rafters opposed at ridge — 802.4.2
- ☐ Collar ties, ridge straps, or gusset plate reqd to tie together rafters — 802.4.2
- ☐ Collar ties min. nominal 1 × 4 in. in upper ⅓ of attic space **F75** — 802.4.6
- ☐ Rafter ties min. nominal 2 × 4 in. in lower ⅓ of attic space **F75** — 802.5.2.2
- ☐ Ridge straps can substitute for collar ties — 802.4.6
- ☐ Ridge straps min. 1¼ in. × 20 ga nailed to top edge of each rafter — 802.4.6[54]
- ☐ Ridge strap nails min. 3 10d common, closest nail min. 2⅜ in. from rafter end — 802.4.6[55]
- ☐ Valley & hip rafters min. 2× material & full depth of cut rafter ends — 802.4.3
- ☐ Valley & hip rafters at ridge req brace to bearing partition or design to carry & distribute specific load at that point — 802.4.3
- ☐ Max. deflection of valley & hip rafters $L/\Delta=180$ — T301.7
- ☐ Cantilevered eave rafters ≤2 ft. max. notch ¼ depth **F72** — 802.7.1.1
- ☐ Heel joint connections per **T60** as adjusted by **T58** — 802.5.2

TABLE 58 — HEEL JOINT CONNECTION ADJUSTMENTS T802.5.2(2)

H_C / H_R	Adjustment	H_C / H_R	Adjustment
1/3	1.5	1/5	1.25
1/4	1.33	1/6	1.2

53. The 2018 IRC allowed the use of a collar ties, gusset plates, or ridge straps in lieu of a ridge board. The 2021 edition reqs collar ties or ridge straps in addition to a ridge board.
54. New specification for size and nailing of ridge straps.
55. This topic reorganized and now succinctly summarized in section 802.5.2 – see full code text.

FIG. 74

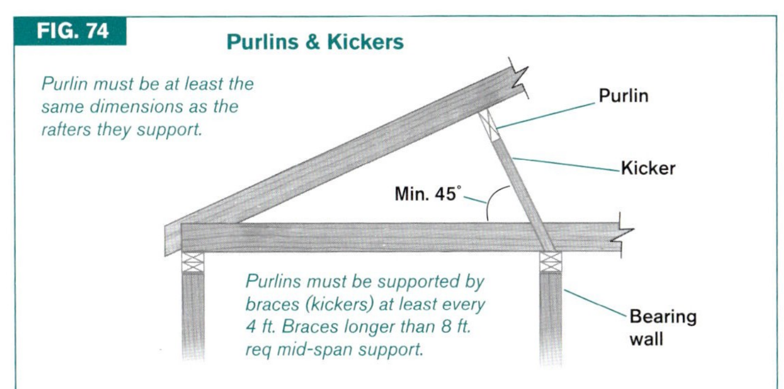

FIG. 75

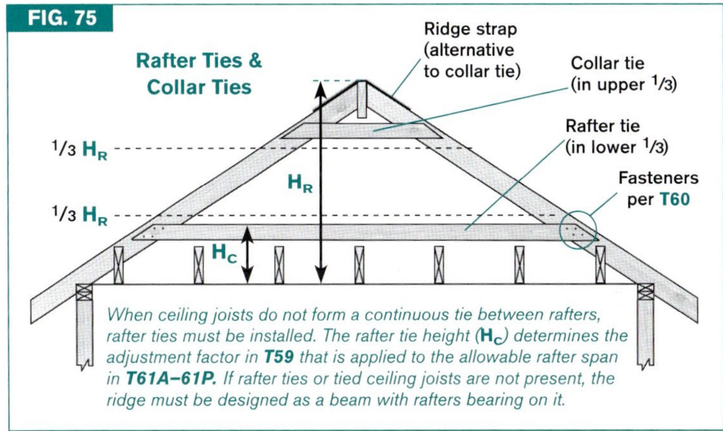

TABLE 59 — RAFTER SPAN ADJUSTMENT FACTORS T802.4.1(9)

H_C / H_R	Adjustment	H_C / H_R	Adjustment
1/3	0.67	1/5	0.83
1/4	0.76	1/6	0.90

TABLE 60	NUMBER OF 16d NAILS AT RAFTER/CEILING JOIST HEEL JOINT CONNECTIONS[A] ◆ T802.5.2(1)												
Rafter Slope	Rafter Spacing (in.)	Ground Snow Load 20 psf			Ground Snow Load 30 psf			Ground Snow Load 50 psf			Ground Snow Load 70 psf		
		Roof Span (ft.)											
		12	24	36	12	24	36	12	24	36	12	24	36
3:12	12	3	5	8	3	6	9	5	9	13	6	12	17
	16	4	7	10	4	8	12	6	12	17	8	15	23
	19.2	4	8	12	5	10	14	7	14	21	9	18	27
	24	5	10	15	6	12	18	9	17	26	12	23	34
4:12	12	3	4	6	3	5	7	4	7	10	5	9	13
	16	3	5	8	3	6	9	5	9	13	6	12	17
	19.2	3	6	9	4	7	11	6	11	16	7	14	21
	24	4	8	11	5	9	13	7	13	19	9	17	26
5:12	12	3	3	5	3	4	6	3	6	8	4	7	11
	16	3	4	6	3	5	7	4	7	11	5	9	14
	19.2	3	5	7	3	6	9	5	9	13	6	11	17
	24	3	6	9	4	7	11	6	11	16	7	14	21
7:12	12	3	3	4	3	3	4	3	4	6	3	5	8
	16	3	3	5	3	4	5	3	5	8	4	7	10
	19.2	3	4	5	3	4	6	3	6	9	4	8	12
	24	3	5	7	3	5	8	4	8	11	5	10	15
9:12	12	3	3	3	3	3	3	3	3	5	3	4	6
	16	3	3	4	3	3	4	3	4	6	3	5	8
	19.2	3	3	4	3	4	5	3	5	7	3	6	9
	24	3	4	5	3	4	6	3	6	9	4	8	12
12:12	12	3	3	3	3	3	3	3	3	4	3	3	5
	16	3	3	3	3	3	3	3	3	5	3	4	6
	19.2	3	3	3	3	3	4	3	4	6	3	5	7
	24	3	3	4	3	3	5	3	5	7	3	6	9

A. 10d nails can substitute for 16d if 1.2× as many nails are used. Equivalent nailings are reqd for ceiling joist lap splices. If joists or ties not at bottom of attic space, apply multiplier per **T58.**

IRC Rafter Span Tables: *The IRC provides 8 tables for rafter spans using common lumber species. Spans are measured as the horizontal distance between supports, including purlins. Each IRC table has separate sections for 10 psf and 20 psf dead load. Most roofing materials (including 2 layers of asphalt shingle) have a weight less than 10 psf, and the tables on the left side of these pages are used. Framing for tile or slate roofs weighing more than 10 psf should be sized using the 20 psf dead load columns on the right side of the page. The tables below are based on #2 grade lumber because it is the most common choice; the full IRC tables include other grades, including SS (select structural), #1, and #3. There are separate tables for 20 psf live loads, and for 30, 50, and 70 psf snow loads (see* ***T2****). There are also separate tables based on whether or not the ceiling is directly attached to the rafters.* ***T3*** *limits ceiling deflection to 1/240th the span, and the allowable spans in those tables are less than the tables that allow 1/180th deflection. If there is no tie at the bottom to connect the rafters, adjustment in accord with* ***T59*** *must be applied.*

TABLE 61A — RAFTER SPANS[A] ◆ T802.4.1(1)
20 PSF LIVE LOAD 10 PSF DEAD LOAD
CEILING NOT ATTACHED TO RAFTERS, $L/\Delta=180$

Rafter Nominal Size	Douglas Fir-Larch #2				Hem-Fir #2			
	Rafter Spacing (in. o.c.)				Rafter Spacing (in. o.c.)			
	12	16	19.2	24	12	16	19.2	24
	ft.–in.	ft.–in.	ft.–in.	ft.–in.	ft.–in.	ft.–in.	ft.–in.	ft.–in.
2×4	10–10	9–10	9–1	8–2	10–1	9–2	8–8	7–11
2×6	16–10	14–7	13–3	11–11	15–11	14–2	12–11	11–7
2×8	21–4	18–5	16–10	15–1	20–8	17–11	16–4	14–8
2×10	26–0	22–6	20–7	18–5	25–3	21–11	20–0	17–10
2×12	B	26–0	23–10	21–4	B	25–5	23–2	20–9

Rafter Nominal Size	Southern Pine #2				Spruce-Pine-Fir #2			
	Rafter Spacing (in. o.c.)				Rafter Spacing (in. o.c.)			
	12	16	19.2	24	12	16	19.2	24
	ft.–in.	ft.–in.	ft.–in.	ft.–in.	ft.–in.	ft.–in.	ft.–in.	ft.–in.
2×4	10–4	9–0	8–2	7–4	10–4	9–5	8–10	8–0
2×6	15–7	13–6	12–3	11–0	16–3	14–4	13–1	11–9
2×8	19–8	17–1	15–7	13–11	21–0	18–2	16–7	14–10
2×10	23–5	20–3	18–6	16–6	25–8	22–3	20–3	18–2
2×12	B	23–10	21–9	19–6	B	25–9	23–6	21–0

A. Multiply by **T59** adjustment factor if joists or rafter ties do not create a tie at the bottom of attic space.
B. The span exceeds 26 ft.

TABLE 61B — RAFTER SPANS[A] ◆ T802.4.1(1)
20 PSF LIVE LOAD 20 PSF DEAD LOAD
CEILING NOT ATTACHED TO RAFTERS, $L/\Delta=180$

Rafter Nominal Size	Douglas Fir-Larch #2				Hem-Fir #2			
	Rafter Spacing (in. o.c.)				Rafter Spacing (in. o.c.)			
	12	16	19.2	24	12	16	19.2	24
	ft.–in.	ft.–in.	ft.–in.	ft.–in.	ft.–in.	ft.–in.	ft.–in.	ft.–in.
2×4	10–0	8–7	7–10	7–0	9–8	8–5	7–8	6–10
2×6	14–7	12–7	11–6	10–4	14–2	12–3	11–2	10–0
2×8	18–5	16–0	14–7	13–0	17–11	15–6	14–2	12–8
2×10	22–6	19–6	17–10	15–11	21–11	18–11	17–4	15–6
2×12	26–0	22–7	20–8	18–6	25–5	22–0	20–1	17–11

Rafter Nominal Size	Southern Pine #2				Spruce-Pine-Fir #2			
	Rafter Spacing (in. o.c.)				Rafter Spacing (in. o.c.)			
	12	16	19.2	24	12	16	19.2	24
	ft.–in.	ft.–in.	ft.–in.	ft.–in.	ft.–in.	ft.–in.	ft.–in.	ft.–in.
2×4	9–0	7–9	7–1	6–4	9–10	8–6	7–9	6–11
2×6	13–6	11–8	10–8	9–6	14–4	12–5	11–4	10–2
2×8	17–1	14–9	13–6	12–1	18–2	15–9	14–4	12–10
2×10	20–3	17–6	16–0	14–4	22–3	19–3	17–7	15–8
2×12	23–10	20–8	18–10	16–10	25–9	22–4	20–4	18–3

A. Multiply by **T59** adjustment factor if joists or rafter ties do not create a tie at the bottom of attic space.

IRC Rafter Span Tables: *The IRC provides 8 tables for rafter spans using common lumber species. Spans are measured as the horizontal distance between supports, including purlins. Each IRC table has separate sections for 10 psf and 20 psf dead load. Most roofing materials (including 2 layers of asphalt shingle) have a weight less than 10 psf, and the tables on the left side of these pages are used. Framing for tile or slate roofs weighing more than 10 psf should be sized using the 20 psf dead load columns on the right side of the page. The tables below are based on #2 grade lumber because it is the most common choice; the full IRC tables include other grades, including SS (select structural), #1, and #3. There are separate tables for 20 psf live loads, and for 30, 50, and 70 psf snow loads (see **T2**). There are also separate tables based on whether or not the ceiling is directly attached to the rafters. **T3** limits ceiling deflection to 1/240th the span, and the allowable spans in those tables are less than the tables that allow 1/180th deflection. If there is no tie at the bottom to connect the rafters, adjustment in accord with **T59** must be applied.*

TABLE 61C — RAFTER SPANS[A] ◆ T802.4.1(2) — 20 PSF LIVE LOAD 10 PSF DEAD LOAD — CEILING ATTACHED TO RAFTERS, L/Δ=240

Rafter Nominal Size	Douglas Fir–Larch #2				Hem–Fir #2			
	Rafter Spacing (in. o.c.)				Rafter Spacing (in. o.c.)			
	12	16	19.2	24	12	16	19.2	24
	ft.–in.	ft.–in.	ft.–in.	ft.–in.	ft.–in.	ft.–in.	ft.–in.	ft.–in.
2×4	9–10	8–11	8–5	7–10	9–2	8–4	7–10	7–3
2×6	15–6	14–1	13–3	11–11	14–5	13–1	12–4	11–5
2×8	20–5	18–5	16–10	15–1	19–0	17–3	16–3	14–8
2×10	26–0	22–6	20–7	18–5	24–3	21–11	20–0	17–10
2×12	B	26–0	23–10	21–4	B	25–5	23–2	20–9

Rafter Nominal Size	Southern Pine #2				Spruce–Pine–Fir #2			
	Rafter Spacing (in. o.c.)				Rafter Spacing (in. o.c.)			
	12	16	19.2	24	12	16	19.2	24
	ft.–in.	ft.–in.	ft.–in.	ft.–in.	ft.–in.	ft.–in.	ft.–in.	ft.–in.
2×4	9–5	8–7	8–1	7–4	9–5	8–7	8–1	7–6
2×6	14–9	13–5	12–3	11–0	14–9	13–5	12–8	11–9
2×8	19–6	17–1	15–7	13–11	19–6	17–9	16–7	14–10
2×10	23–5	20–3	18–6	16–6	24–10	22–3	20–3	18–2
2×12	B	23–10	21–9	19–6	B	25–9	23–6	21–0

A. Multiply by **T59** adjustment factor if joists or rafter ties do not create a tie at the bottom of attic space.
B. The span exceeds 26 ft.

TABLE 61D — RAFTER SPANS[A] ◆ T802.4.1(2) — 20 PSF LIVE LOAD 20 PSF DEAD LOAD — CEILING ATTACHED TO RAFTERS, L/Δ=240

Rafter Nominal Size	Douglas Fir–Larch #2				Hem–Fir #2			
	Rafter Spacing (in. o.c.)				Rafter Spacing (in. o.c.)			
	12	16	19.2	24	12	16	19.2	24
	ft.–in.	ft.–in.	ft.–in.	ft.–in.	ft.–in.	ft.–in.	ft.–in.	ft.–in.
2×4	9–10	8–7	7–10	7–0	9–2	8–4	7–8	6–10
2×6	14–7	12–7	11–6	10–4	14–2	12–3	11–2	10–0
2×8	18–5	16–0	14–7	13–0	17–11	15–6	14–2	12–8
2×10	22–6	19–6	17–10	15–11	21–11	18–11	17–4	15–6
2×12	26–0	22–7	20–8	18–6	25–5	22–0	20–1	17–11

Rafter Nominal Size	Southern Pine #2				Spruce–Pine–Fir #2			
	Rafter Spacing (in. o.c.)				Rafter Spacing (in. o.c.)			
	12	16	19.2	24	12	16	19.2	24
	ft.–in.	ft.–in.	ft.–in.	ft.–in.	ft.–in.	ft.–in.	ft.–in.	ft.–in.
2×4	9–0	7–9	7–1	6–4	9–5	8–6	7–9	6–11
2×6	13–6	11–8	10–8	9–6	14–4	12–5	11–4	10–2
2×8	17–1	14–9	13–6	12–1	18–2	15–9	14–4	12–10
2×10	20–3	17–6	16–0	14–4	22–3	19–3	17–7	15–8
2×12	23–10	20–8	18–10	16–10	25–9	22–4	20–4	18–3

A. Multiply by **T59** adjustment factor if joists or rafter ties do not create a tie at the bottom of attic space.

IRC Rafter Span Tables: *The IRC provides 8 tables for rafter spans using common lumber species. Spans are measured as the horizontal distance between supports, including purlins. Each IRC table has separate sections for 10 psf and 20 psf dead load. Most roofing materials (including 2 layers of asphalt shingle) have a weight less than 10 psf, and the tables on the left side of these pages are used. Framing for tile or slate roofs weighing more than 10 psf should be sized using the 20 psf dead load columns on the right side of the page. The tables below are based on #2 grade lumber because it is the most common choice; the full IRC tables include other grades, including SS (select structural), #1, and #3. There are separate tables for 20 psf live loads, and for 30, 50, and 70 psf snow loads (see* ***T2****). There are also separate tables based on whether or not the ceiling is directly attached to the rafters.* ***T3*** *limits ceiling deflection to 1/240th the span, and the allowable spans in those tables are less than the tables that allow 1/180th deflection. If there is no tie at the bottom to connect the rafters, adjustment in accord with* ***T59*** *must be applied.*

TABLE 61E — RAFTER SPANS[A] ◆ T802.4.1(3) — 30 PSF GROUND SNOW LOAD 10 PSF DEAD LOAD — CEILING NOT ATTACHED TO RAFTERS, L/Δ=180

Rafter Nominal Size	Douglas Fir-Larch #2				Hem-Fir #2			
	Rafter Spacing (in. o.c.)				Rafter Spacing (in. o.c.)			
	12	16	19.2	24	12	16	19.2	24
	ft.–in.	ft.–in.	ft.–in.	ft.–in.	ft.–in.	ft.–in.	ft.–in.	ft.–in.
2×4	9–6	8–3	7–7	6–9	8–10	8–0	7–4	6–7
2×6	14–0	12–1	11–0	9–10	13–7	11–9	10–9	9–7
2×8	17–8	15–4	14–0	12–6	17–2	14–11	13–7	12–2
2×10	21–7	18–9	17–1	15–3	21–0	18–2	16–7	14–10
2×12	25–1	21–8	19–10	17–9	24–4	21–1	19–3	17–3
Rafter Nominal Size	Southern Pine #2				Spruce-Pine-Fir #2			
	Rafter Spacing (in. o.c.)				Rafter Spacing (in. o.c.)			
	12	16	19.2	24	12	16	19.2	24
	ft.–in.	ft.–in.	ft.–in.	ft.–in.	ft.–in.	ft.–in.	ft.–in.	ft.–in.
2×4	8–7	7–6	6–10	6–1	9–1	8–2	7–5	6–8
2×6	12–11	11–2	10–2	9–2	13–9	11–11	10–11	9–9
2×8	16–4	14–2	12–11	11–7	17–5	15–1	13–9	12–4
2×10	19–5	16–10	15–4	13–9	21–4	18–5	16–10	15–1
2×12	22–10	19–10	18–1	16–2	24–8	21–5	19–6	17–6

A. Multiply by **T59** adjustment factor if joists or rafter ties do not create a tie at the bottom of attic space.

TABLE 61F — RAFTER SPANS[A] ◆ T802.4.1(3) — 30 PSF GROUND SNOW LOAD 20 PSF DEAD LOAD — CEILING NOT ATTACHED TO RAFTERS, L/Δ=180

Rafter Nominal Size	Douglas Fir-Larch #2				Hem-Fir #2			
	Rafter Spacing (in. o.c.)				Rafter Spacing (in. o.c.)			
	12	16	19.2	24	12	16	19.2	24
	ft.–in.	ft.–in.	ft.–in.	ft.–in.	ft.–in.	ft.–in.	ft.–in.	ft.–in.
2×4	8–6	7–5	6–9	6–0	8–4	7–2	6–7	5–10
2×6	12–6	10–10	9–10	8–10	12–2	10–6	9–7	8–7
2×8	15–10	13–8	12–6	11–2	15–4	13–4	12–2	10–10
2×10	19–4	16–9	15–3	13–8	18–9	16–3	14–10	13–3
2×12	22–5	19–5	17–9	15–10	21–9	18–10	17–3	15–5
Rafter Nominal Size	Southern Pine #2				Spruce-Pine-Fir #2			
	Rafter Spacing (in. o.c.)				Rafter Spacing (in. o.c.)			
	12	16	19.2	24	12	16	19.2	24
	ft.–in.	ft.–in.	ft.–in.	ft.–in.	ft.–in.	ft.–in.	ft.–in.	ft.–in.
2×4	7–8	6–8	6–1	5–5	8–5	7–3	6–8	5–11
2×6	11–7	10–0	9–2	8–28	12–4	10–8	9–9	8–8
2×8	14–8	12–8	11–7	10–4	15–7	13–6	12–4	11–0
2×10	17–4	15–1	13–9	12–3	19–1	16–6	15–1	13–6
2×12	20–5	17–9	16–2	14–6	22–1	19–2	17–6	15–7

A. Multiply by **T59** adjustment factor if joists or rafter ties do not create a tie at the bottom of attic space.

IRC Rafter Span Tables: The IRC provides 8 tables for rafter spans using common lumber species. Spans are measured as the horizontal distance between supports, including purlins. Each IRC table has separate sections for 10 psf and 20 psf dead load. Most roofing materials (including 2 layers of asphalt shingle) have a weight less than 10 psf, and the tables on the left side of these pages are used. Framing for tile or slate roofs weighing more than 10 psf should be sized using the 20 psf dead load columns on the right side of the page. The tables below are based on #2 grade lumber because it is the most common choice; the full IRC tables include other grades, including SS (select structural), #1, and #3. There are separate tables for 20 psf live loads, and for 30, 50, and 70 psf snow loads (see **T2**). There are also separate tables based on whether or not the ceiling is directly attached to the rafters. **T3** limits ceiling deflection to 1/240th the span, and the allowable spans in those tables are less than the tables that allow 1/180th deflection. If there is no tie at the bottom to connect the rafters, adjustment in accord with **T59** must be applied.

TABLE 61G — RAFTER SPANS[A] ◆ T802.4.1(4) 30 PSF GROUND SNOW LOAD 10 PSF DEAD LOAD CEILING ATTACHED TO RAFTERS, L/Δ=240

Rafter Nominal Size	Douglas Fir-Larch #2				Hem-Fir #2			
	Rafter Spacing (in. o.c.)				Rafter Spacing (in. o.c.)			
	12	16	19.2	24	12	16	19.2	24
	ft.–in.	ft.–in.	ft.–in.	ft.–in.	ft.–in.	ft.–in.	ft.–in.	ft.–in.
2×4	8–7	7–10	7–4	6–9	8–0	7–3	6–10	6–4
2×6	13–6	12–1	11–0	9–10	12–7	11–5	10–9	9–7
2×8	17–8	15–4	14–0	12–6	16–7	14–11	13–7	12–2
2×10	21–7	18–9	17–1	15–3	21–0	18–2	16–7	14–10
2×12	25–1	21–8	19–10	17–9	24–4	21–1	19–3	17–3
Rafter Nominal Size	Southern Pine #2				Spruce-Pine-Fir #2			
	Rafter Spacing (in. o.c.)				Rafter Spacing (in. o.c.)			
	12	16	19.2	24	12	16	19.2	24
	ft.–in.	ft.–in.	ft.–in.	ft.–in.	ft.–in.	ft.–in.	ft.–in.	ft.–in.
2×4	8–3	7–6	6–10	6–1	8–3	7–6	7–0	6–6
2×6	12–11	11–2	10–2	9–2	12–11	11–9	10–11	9–9
2×8	16–4	14–2	12–11	11–7	17–0	15–1	13–9	12–4
2×10	19–5	16–10	15–4	13–9	21–4	18–5	16–10	15–1
2×12	22–10	19–10	18–1	16–2	24–8	21–5	19–6	17–6

A. Multiply by **T59** adjustment factor if joists or rafter ties do not create a tie at the bottom of attic space.

TABLE 61H — RAFTER SPANS[A] ◆ T802.4.1(4) 30 PSF GROUND SNOW LOAD 20 PSF DEAD LOAD CEILING ATTACHED TO RAFTERS, L/Δ=240

Rafter Nominal Size	Douglas Fir-Larch #2				Hem-Fir #2			
	Rafter Spacing (in. o.c.)				Rafter Spacing (in. o.c.)			
	12	16	19.2	24	12	16	19.2	24
	ft.–in.	ft.–in.	ft.–in.	ft.–in.	ft.–in.	ft.–in.	ft.–in.	ft.–in.
2×4	8–6	7–5	6–9	6–0	8–0	7–2	6–7	5–10
2×6	12–6	10–10	9–1	8–10	12–2	10–6	9–7	8–7
2×8	15–10	13–8	12–6	11–2	15–4	13–4	12–2	10–10
2×10	19–4	16–9	15–3	13–8	18–9	16–3	14–10	13–3
2×12	22–5	19–5	17–9	15–10	21–9	18–10	17–3	15–5
Rafter Nominal Size	Southern Pine #2				Spruce-Pine-Fir #2			
	Rafter Spacing (in. o.c.)				Rafter Spacing (in. o.c.)			
	12	16	19.2	24	12	16	19.2	24
	ft.–in.	ft.–in.	ft.–in.	ft.–in.	ft.–in.	ft.–in.	ft.–in.	ft.–in.
2×4	7–8	6–8	6–1	5–5	8–3	7–3	6–8	5–11
2×6	11–7	10–0	9–2	8–2	12–4	10–8	9–9	8–8
2×8	14–8	12–8	11–7	10–4	15–7	13–6	12–4	11–0
2×10	17–4	15–1	13–9	12–3	19–1	16–6	15–1	13–6
2×12	20–5	17–9	16–2	14–6	22–1	19–2	17–6	15–7

A. Multiply by **T59** adjustment factor if joists or rafter ties do not create a tie at the bottom of attic space.

IRC Rafter Span Tables: *The IRC provides 8 tables for rafter spans using common lumber species. Spans are measured as the horizontal distance between supports, including purlins. Each IRC table has separate sections for 10 psf and 20 psf dead load. Most roofing materials (including 2 layers of asphalt shingle) have a weight less than 10 psf, and the tables on the left side of these pages are used. Framing for tile or slate roofs weighing more than 10 psf should be sized using the 20 psf dead load columns on the right side of the page. The tables below are based on #2 grade lumber because it is the most common choice; the full IRC tables include other grades, including SS (select structural), #1, and #3. There are separate tables for 20 psf live loads, and for 30, 50, and 70 psf snow loads (see **T2**). There are also separate tables based on whether or not the ceiling is directly attached to the rafters. **T3** limits ceiling deflection to 1/240th the span, and the allowable spans in those tables are less than the tables that allow 1/180th deflection. If there is no tie at the bottom to connect the rafters, adjustment in accord with **T59** must be applied.*

TABLE 61I — RAFTER SPANS[A] ◆ T802.4.1(5) — 50 PSF GROUND SNOW LOAD 10 PSF DEAD LOAD — CEILING NOT ATTACHED TO RAFTERS, $L/\Delta=180$

Rafter Nominal Size	Douglas Fir-Larch #2				Hem-Fir #2			
	Rafter Spacing (in. o.c.)				Rafter Spacing (in. o.c.)			
	12	16	19.2	24	12	16	19.2	24
	ft.–in.	ft.–in.	ft.–in.	ft.–in.	ft.–in.	ft.–in.	ft.–in.	ft.–in.
2×4	7–10	6–9	6–2	5–6	7–5	6–7	6–0	5–4
2×6	11–5	9–10	9–0	8–1	11–1	9–7	8–9	7–10
2×8	14–5	12–6	11–5	10–3	14–0	12–2	11–1	9–11
2×10	17–8	15–3	13–11	12–6	17–2	14–10	13–7	12–1
2×12	20–5	17–9	16–2	14–6	19–11	17–3	15–9	14–1
Rafter Nominal Size	Southern Pine #2				Spruce-Pine-Fir #2			
	Rafter Spacing (in. o.c.)				Rafter Spacing (in. o.c.)			
	12	16	19.2	24	12	16	19.2	24
	ft.–in.	ft.–in.	ft.–in.	ft.–in.	ft.–in.	ft.–in.	ft.–in.	ft.–in.
2×4	7–0	6–1	5–7	5–0	7–8	6–8	6–1	5–5
2×6	10–6	9–2	8–4	7–5	11–3	9–9	8–11	7–11
2×8	13–4	11–7	10–7	9–5	14–3	12–4	11–3	10–1
2×10	15–10	13–9	12–6	11–3	17–5	15–1	13–9	12–4
2×12	18–8	16–2	14–9	13–2	20–2	17–6	15–11	14–3

A. Multiply by **T59** adjustment factor if joists or rafter ties do not create a tie at the bottom of attic space.

TABLE 61J — RAFTER SPANS[A] ◆ T802.4.1(5) — 50 PSF GROUND SNOW LOAD 20 PSF DEAD LOAD — CEILING NOT ATTACHED TO RAFTERS, $L/\Delta=180$

Rafter Nominal Size	Douglas Fir-Larch #2				Hem-Fir #2			
	Rafter Spacing (in. o.c.)				Rafter Spacing (in. o.c.)			
	12	16	19.2	24	12	16	19.2	24
	ft.–in.	ft.–in.	ft.–in.	ft.–in.	ft.–in.	ft.–in.	ft.–in.	ft.–in.
2×4	7–3	6–3	5–8	5–1	7–0	6–1	5–7	4–11
2×6	10–7	9–2	8–4	7–6	10–3	8–11	8–1	7–3
2×8	13–4	11–7	10–9	9–5	13–0	11–3	10–3	9–2
2×10	16–4	14–2	12–11	11–7	15–10	13–9	12–7	11–3
2×12	18–11	16–5	15–0	13–5	18–5	15–11	14–7	13–0
Rafter Nominal Size	Southern Pine #2				Spruce-Pine-Fir #2			
	Rafter Spacing (in. o.c.)				Rafter Spacing (in. o.c.)			
	12	16	19.2	24	12	16	19.2	24
	ft.–in.	ft.–in.	ft.–in.	ft.–in.	ft.–in.	ft.–in.	ft.–in.	ft.–in.
2×4	6–6	5–8	5–2	4–7	7–1	6–2	5–7	5–0
2×6	9–9	8–5	7–9	6–11	10–5	9–0	8–3	7–4
2×8	12–4	10–9	9–9	8–9	13–2	11–5	10–5	9–4
2×10	14–8	12–9	11–7	10–5	16–1	13–11	12–9	11–5
2×12	17–3	15–0	13–8	12–3	18–8	16–2	14–9	13–2

A. Multiply by **T59** adjustment factor if joists or rafter ties do not create a tie at the bottom of attic space.

IRC Rafter Span Tables: *The IRC provides 8 tables for rafter spans using common lumber species. Spans are measured as the horizontal distance between supports, including purlins. Each IRC table has separate sections for 10 psf and 20 psf dead load. Most roofing materials (including 2 layers of asphalt shingle) have a weight less than 10 psf, and the tables on the left side of these pages are used. Framing for tile or slate roofs weighing more than 10 psf should be sized using the 20 psf dead load columns on the right side of the page. The tables below are based on #2 grade lumber because it is the most common choice; the full IRC tables include other grades, including SS (select structural), #1, and #3. There are separate tables for 20 psf live loads, and for 30, 50, and 70 psf snow loads (see* ***T2****). There are also separate tables based on whether or not the ceiling is directly attached to the rafters.* ***T3*** *limits ceiling deflection to 1/240th the span, and the allowable spans in those tables are less than the tables that allow 1/180th deflection. If there is no tie at the bottom to connect the rafters, adjustment in accord with* ***T59*** *must be applied.*

TABLE 61K — RAFTER SPANS[A] ◆ T802.4.1(6) — 50 PSF GROUND SNOW LOAD 10 PSF DEAD LOAD — CEILING ATTACHED TO RAFTERS, L/Δ=240

Rafter Nominal Size	Douglas Fir-Larch #2				Hem-Fir #2			
	Rafter Spacing (in. o.c.)				Rafter Spacing (in. o.c.)			
	12	16	19.2	24	12	16	19.2	24
	ft.–in.	ft.–in.	ft.–in.	ft.–in.	ft.–in.	ft.–in.	ft.–in.	ft.–in.
2×4	7–3	6–7	6–2	5–6	6–9	6–2	5–9	5–4
2×6	11–5	9–10	9–0	8–1	10–8	9–7	8–9	7–10
2×8	14–5	12–6	11–5	10–3	14–0	12–2	11–1	9–11
2×10	17–8	15–3	13–11	12–6	17–2	14–10	13–7	12–1
2×12	20–5	17–9	16–2	14–6	19–11	17–3	15–9	14–1
Rafter Nominal Size	Southern Pine #2				Spruce-Pine-Fir #2			
	Rafter Spacing (in. o.c.)				Rafter Spacing (in. o.c.)			
	12	16	19.2	24	12	16	19.2	24
	ft.–in.	ft.–in.	ft.–in.	ft.–in.	ft.–in.	ft.–in.	ft.–in.	ft.–in.
2×4	6–11	6–1	5–7	5–0	6–11	6–4	5–11	5–5
2×6	10–6	9–2	8–4	7–5	10–11	9–9	8–11	7–11
2×8	13–4	11–7	10–7	9–5	14–3	12–4	11–3	10–1
2×10	15–10	13–9	12–6	11–3	17–5	15–1	13–9	12–4
2×12	18–8	16–2	14–9	13–2	20–2	17–6	15–11	14–3

A. Multiply by **T59** adjustment factor if joists or rafter ties do not create a tie at the bottom of attic space.

TABLE 61L — RAFTER SPANS[A] ◆ T802.4.1(6) — 50 PSF GROUND SNOW LOAD 20 PSF DEAD LOAD — CEILING ATTACHED TO RAFTERS, L/Δ=240

Rafter Nominal Size	Douglas Fir-Larch #2				Hem-Fir #2			
	Rafter Spacing (in. o.c.)				Rafter Spacing (in. o.c.)			
	12	16	19.2	24	12	16	19.2	24
	ft.–in.	ft.–in.	ft.–in.	ft.–in.	ft.–in.	ft.–in.	ft.–in.	ft.–in.
2×4	7–3	6–3	5–8	5–1	6–9	6–1	5–7	4–11
2×6	10–7	9–2	8–4	7–6	10–3	8–11	8–1	7–3
2×8	13–4	11–7	10–7	9–5	13–0	11–3	10–3	9–2
2×10	16–4	14–2	12–11	11–7	15–10	13–9	12–7	11–3
2×12	18–11	16–5	15–0	13–5	18–5	15–11	14–7	13–0
Rafter Nominal Size	Southern Pine #2				Spruce-Pine-Fir #2			
	Rafter Spacing (in. o.c.)				Rafter Spacing (in. o.c.)			
	12	16	19.2	24	12	16	19.2	24
	ft.–in.	ft.–in.	ft.–in.	ft.–in.	ft.–in.	ft.–in.	ft.–in.	ft.–in.
2×4	6–6	5–8	5–2	4–7	6–11	6–2	5–7	5–0
2×6	9–9	8–5	7–9	6–11	10–5	9–0	8–3	7–4
2×8	12–4	10–9	9–9	8–9	13–2	11–5	10–5	9–4
2×10	14–8	12–9	11–7	10–5	16–1	13–11	12–9	11–5
2×12	17–3	15–0	13–8	12–3	18–8	16–2	14–9	13–2

A. Multiply by **T59** adjustment factor if joists or rafter ties do not create a tie at the bottom of attic space.

IRC Rafter Span Tables: *The IRC provides 8 tables for rafter spans using common lumber species. Spans are measured as the horizontal distance between supports, including purlins. Each IRC table has separate sections for 10 psf and 20 psf dead load. Most roofing materials (including 2 layers of asphalt shingle) have a weight less than 10 psf, and the tables on the left side of these pages are used. Framing for tile or slate roofs weighing more than 10 psf should be sized using the 20 psf dead load columns on the right side of the page. The tables below are based on #2 grade lumber because it is the most common choice; the full IRC tables include other grades, including SS (select structural), #1, and #3. There are separate tables for 20 psf live loads, and for 30, 50, and 70 psf snow loads (see **T2**). There are also separate tables based on whether or not the ceiling is directly attached to the rafters. **T3** limits ceiling deflection to 1/240th the span, and the allowable spans in those tables are less than the tables that allow 1/180th deflection. If there is no tie at the bottom to connect the rafters, adjustment in accord with **T59** must be applied.*

TABLE 61M — RAFTER SPANS[A] ◆ T802.4.1(7) — 70 PSF GROUND SNOW LOAD 10 PSF DEAD LOAD — CEILING NOT ATTACHED TO RAFTERS, $L/\Delta = 180$

Rafter Nominal Size	Douglas Fir-Larch #2				Hem-Fir #2			
	Rafter Spacing (in. o.c.)				Rafter Spacing (in. o.c.)			
	12	16	19.2	24	12	16	19.2	24
	ft.–in.	ft.–in.	ft.–in.	ft.–in.	ft.–in.	ft.–in.	ft.–in.	ft.–in.
2×4	6–9	5–10	5–4	4–9	6–7	5–8	5–2	4–8
2×6	9–10	8–7	7–10	7–0	9–7	8–4	7–7	6–9
2×8	12–6	10–10	9–11	8–10	12–2	10–6	9–7	8–7
2×10	15–3	13–3	12–1	10–10	14–10	12–10	11–9	10–6
2×12	17–9	15–4	14–0	12–6	17–3	14–11	13–7	12–2

Rafter Nominal Size	Southern Pine #2				Spruce-Pine-Fir #2			
	Rafter Spacing (in. o.c.)				Rafter Spacing (in. o.c.)			
	12	16	19.2	24	12	16	19.2	24
	ft.–in.	ft.–in.	ft.–in.	ft.–in.	ft.–in.	ft.–in.	ft.–in.	ft.–in.
2×4	6–1	5–3	4–10	4–4	6–8	5–9	5–3	4–8
2×6	9–2	7–11	7–3	6–5	9–9	8–5	7–8	6–11
2×8	11–7	10–0	9–2	8–2	12–4	10–8	9–9	8–9
2×10	13–9	11–11	10–10	9–9	15–1	13–1	11–11	10–8
2×12	16–2	14–0	12–9	11–5	17–6	15–2	13–10	12–4

A. Multiply by **T59** adjustment factor if joists or rafter ties do not create a tie at the bottom of attic space.

TABLE 61N — RAFTER SPANS[A] ◆ T802.4.1(7) — 70 PSF GROUND SNOW LOAD 20 PSF DEAD LOAD — CEILING NOT ATTACHED TO RAFTERS, $L/\Delta = 180$

Rafter Nominal Size	Douglas Fir-Larch #2				Hem-Fir #2			
	Rafter Spacing (in. o.c.)				Rafter Spacing (in. o.c.)			
	12	16	19.2	24	12	16	19.2	24
	ft.–in.	ft.–in.	ft.–in.	ft.–in.	ft.–in.	ft.–in.	ft.–in.	ft.–in.
2×4	6–4	5–6	5–0	4–6	6–2	5–4	4–11	4–4
2×6	9–4	8–1	7–4	6–7	9–1	7–10	7–2	6–5
2×8	11–9	10–3	9–4	8–4	11–5	9–11	9–1	8–1
2×10	14–5	12–6	11–5	10–2	14–0	12–1	11–1	9–11
2×12	16–8	14–6	13–2	11–10	16–3	14–1	12–10	11–6

Rafter Nominal Size	Southern Pine #2				Spruce-Pine-Fir #2			
	Rafter Spacing (in. o.c.)				Rafter Spacing (in. o.c.)			
	12	16	19.2	24	12	16	19.2	24
	ft.–in.	ft.–in.	ft.–in.	ft.–in.	ft.–in.	ft.–in.	ft.–in.	ft.–in.
2×4	5–9	5–0	4–6	4–1	6–3	5–5	5–0	4–5
2×6	8–7	7–5	6–10	6–1	9–2	7–11	7–3	6–6
2×8	10–11	9–5	8–8	7–9	11–8	10–1	9–2	8–3
2×10	12–11	11–3	10–3	9–2	14–2	12–4	11–3	10–0
2×12	15–3	13–2	12–1	10–9	16–6	14–3	13–0	11–8

A. Multiply by **T59** adjustment factor if joists or rafter ties do not create a tie at the bottom of attic space.

*IRC Rafter Span Tables: The IRC provides 8 tables for rafter spans using common lumber species. Spans are measured as the horizontal distance between supports, including purlins. Each IRC table has separate sections for 10 psf and 20 psf dead load. Most roofing materials (including 2 layers of asphalt shingle) have a weight less than 10 psf, and the tables on the left side of these pages are used. Framing for tile or slate roofs weighing more than 10 psf should be sized using the 20 psf dead load columns on the right side of the page. The tables below are based on #2 grade lumber because it is the most common choice; the full IRC tables include other grades, including SS (select structural), #1, and #3. There are separate tables for 20 psf live loads, and for 30, 50, and 70 psf snow loads (see **T2**). There are also separate tables based on whether or not the ceiling is directly attached to the rafters. **T3** limits ceiling deflection to 1/240th the span, and the allowable spans in those tables are less than the tables that allow 1/180th deflection. If there is no tie at the bottom to connect the rafters, adjustment in accord with **T59** must be applied.*

TABLE 61O — RAFTER SPANS[A] ◆ T802.4.1(8)
70 PSF GROUND SNOW LOAD 10 PSF DEAD LOAD
CEILING ATTACHED TO RAFTERS, L/Δ=240

Rafter Nominal Size	Douglas Fir-Larch #2				Hem-Fir #2			
	Rafter Spacing (in. o.c.)				Rafter Spacing (in. o.c.)			
	12	16	19.2	24	12	16	19.2	24
	ft.–in.	ft.–in.	ft.–in.	ft.–in.	ft.–in.	ft.–in.	ft.–in.	ft.–in.
2×4	6–6	5–10	5–4	4–9	6–1	5–6	5–2	4–8
2×6	9–10	8–7	7–10	7–0	9–6	8–4	7–7	6–9
2×8	12–6	10–10	9–11	8–10	12–2	10–6	9–7	8–7
2×10	15–3	13–3	12–1	10–10	14–10	12–10	11–9	10–6
2×12	17–9	15–4	14–0	12–6	17–3	14–11	13–7	12–2
Rafter Nominal Size	Southern Pine #2				Spruce-Pine-Fir #2			
	Rafter Spacing (in. o.c.)				Rafter Spacing (in. o.c.)			
	12	16	19.2	24	12	16	19.2	24
	ft.–in.	ft.–in.	ft.–in.	ft.–in.	ft.–in.	ft.–in.	ft.–in.	ft.–in.
2×4	6–1	5–3	4–10	4–4	6–2	5–8	5–3	4–8
2×6	9–2	7–11	7–3	6–5	9–9	8–5	7–8	6–11
2×8	11–7	10–0	9–2	8–2	12–4	10–8	9–9	8–9
2×10	13–9	11–11	10–10	9–9	15–1	13–1	11–11	10–8
2×12	16–2	14–0	12–9	11–5	17–6	15–2	13–10	12–4

A. Multiply by **T59** adjustment factor if joists or rafter ties do not create a tie at the bottom of attic space.

TABLE 61P — RAFTER SPANS[A] ◆ T802.4.1(8)
70 PSF GROUND SNOW LOAD 20 PSF DEAD LOAD
CEILING ATTACHED TO RAFTERS, L/Δ=240

Rafter Nominal Size	Douglas Fir-Larch #2				Hem-Fir #2			
	Rafter Spacing (in. o.c.)				Rafter Spacing (in. o.c.)			
	12	16	19.2	24	12	16	19.2	24
	ft.–in.	ft.–in.	ft.–in.	ft.–in.	ft.–in.	ft.–in.	ft.–in.	ft.–in.
2×4	6–4	5–6	5–0	4–6	6–1	5–4	4–11	4–4
2×6	9–4	8–1	7–4	6–7	9–1	7–10	7–2	6–5
2×8	11–9	10–3	9–4	8–4	11–5	9–11	9–1	8–1
2×10	14–5	12–6	11–5	10–2	14–0	12–1	11–1	9–11
2×12	16–8	14–6	13–2	11–10	16–3	14–1	12–10	11–6
Rafter Nominal Size	Southern Pine #2				Spruce-Pine-Fir #2			
	Rafter Spacing (in. o.c.)				Rafter Spacing (in. o.c.)			
	12	16	19.2	24	12	16	19.2	24
	ft.–in.	ft.–in.	ft.–in.	ft.–in.	ft.–in.	ft.–in.	ft.–in.	ft.–in.
2×4	5–9	5–0	4–6	4–1	6–2	5–5	5–0	4–5
2×6	8–7	7–5	6–10	6–1	9–2	7–11	7–3	6–6
2×8	10–11	9–5	8–8	7–9	11–8	10–1	9–2	8–3
2×10	12–11	11–3	10–3	9–2	14–2	12–4	11–3	10–0
2×12	15–3	13–2	12–1	10–9	16–6	14–3	13–0	11–8

A. Multiply by **T59** adjustment factor if joists or rafter ties do not create a tie at the bottom of attic space.

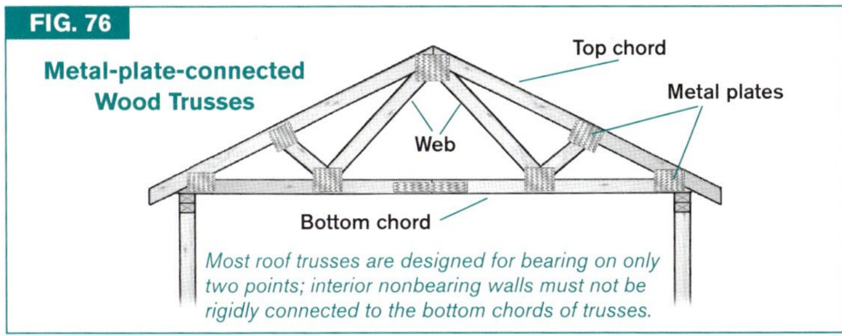

Most roof trusses are designed for bearing on only two points; interior nonbearing walls must not be rigidly connected to the bottom chords of trusses.

WOOD TRUSSES

Trusses are engineered systems and cannot be altered in the field without approval of a registered design professional, including the addition of loads such as HVAC equipment that exceeds the design load of the truss. Trusses are shipped with a booklet showing their placement and design criteria. Most trusses have two bearing points and do not bear weight on interior walls. The outside members are chords, and the interior members are the web (**F76**). Because of possible seasonal truss movement, connections to nonbearing interior walls are made with hardware that allows vertical movement (**F77**). Bracing must be installed in accordance with the plans or *BCSI—2018 Building Component Safety Information Guide to Good Practice for Handling, Installing, Restraining & Bracing of Metal Plate Connected Wood Trusses.* **T1**

Design & Drawings — 21 IRC

- ☐ Design drawings must be approved by BO prior to installation ____ 802.10.1
- ☐ Design drawings must be included w/ truss shipment at job site ____ 802.10.1
- ☐ Design in accordance w/ accepted engineering practice ____ 802.10.2
- ☐ Design per ANSI/TPI 1 ____ 802.10.2
- ☐ Drawings prepared by licensed design professional per AHJ ____ 802.10.2
- ☐ Where not otherwise specified, bracing per BCSI ____ 802.10.3
- ☐ Consult BCSI for handling procedures & temporary bracing ____ 802.10.3
- ☐ No alterations w/o approval of registered design professional ____ 802.10.4
- ☐ No added loads (such as HVAC) w/o verification of capacity ____ 802.10.4

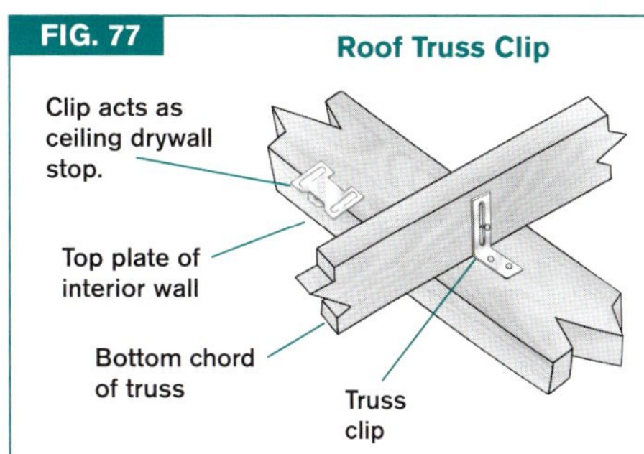

Trusses typically bear on points at their ends, and should not be rigidly attached to interior nonbearing walls. Seasonal movement of the trusses may occur with changes of humidity. The nail through the truss clip to the truss is not fully driven. Ceiling drywall should not be nailed closer than 12 in. from the wall (16 in. for ⅝ drywall) unless acting as a diaphragm.

Roof Tie Uplift Resistance — 21 IRC

- ☐ Roof assembly attachment to walls reqs uplift resistance **F78** in accordance w/ T802.11 EXC ____ 802.11
  - **T57** fastening sufficient if wind uplift ≤200 lb. or if located in Exposure Category B, basic wind speed ≤115 mph, roof pitch ≥ 5:12, roof span ≤32 ft. & rafter/truss spacing ≤24 in. o.c. ____ 802.11X
- ☐ Individual trusses req resistance to wind uplift based on truss design drawings for UDWS **T2** or as shown in plans or per T802.11 ____ 802.11.1
- ☐ Individual rafters req resistance to wind uplift based on T802.11 or per accepted engineering practice ____ 802.11.2

FIG. 78 — Roof Tie Uplift Resistance

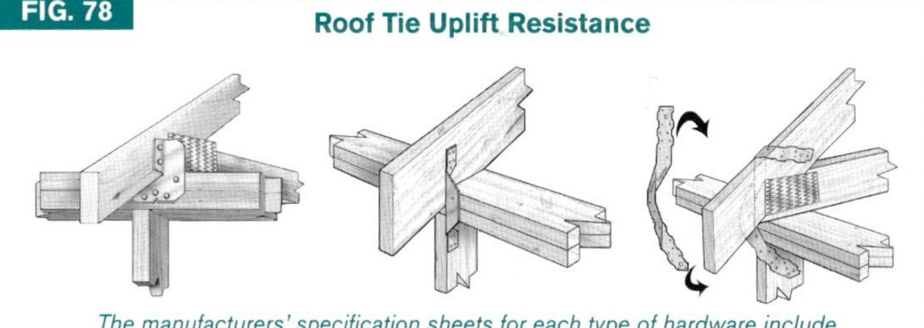

The manufacturers' specification sheets for each type of hardware include the uplift load in pounds. These products require an evaluation report from an approved agency such as the ICC Evaluation Service.

ATTICS

Effective attic ventilation methods vary considerably by the climate zone of the property. The IRC includes a detailed list by county of climate zones throughout the country. Attic insulation and ventilation must be coordinated with overall energy conservation design. Attic access is required for wood-framed attics when the vertical height and open area are as described below.

Access — 21 IRC

- ☐ Access reqd to combustible ceiling or roof construction if attic area is both ≥30 sq. ft. & ≥30 in. for that area ____ 807.1
- ☐ Height measured from top of ceiling frame to underside of roof frame ____ 807.1
- ☐ Rough-framed opening min. 22 × 30 in. in readily accessible area ____ 807.1
- ☐ Attic opening in wall min. 22 in. wide × 30 in. high ____ 807.1
- ☐ Attic opening in ceiling min. 30 in. headroom at some point above the opening as measured from bottom of ceiling framing ____ 807.1
- ☐ Opening must be large enough to remove mechanical equipment ____ 1305.1.2
- ☐ Access not reqd in noncombustible construction (steel frame & roof) ____ 807.1

FIG. 79

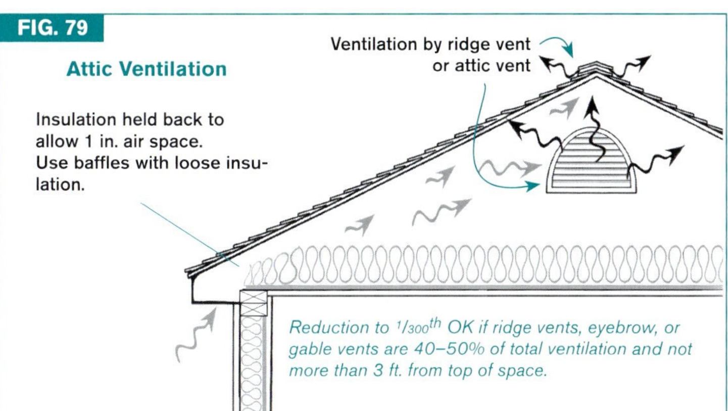

Ventilation — 21 IRC

- ☐ Vent each enclosed attic & enclosed rafter bay ____ 806.1
- ☐ Openings least dimension 1/16 in., max. dimension 1/4 in. ____ 806.1
- ☐ Openings >1/4 in. protected w/ screening 1/16 – 1/4 in. ____ 806.1
- ☐ Min 1-in. clearance between insulation & roof sheathing ____ 806.3
- ☐ Min 1-in. clearance between insulation and vent opening ____ 806.3
- ☐ Total area of ventilation 1/150th of vented space EXC ____ 806.2
  - Reduction to 1/300th OK if the following conditions are met:
    - (1) 40–50% of venting provided by openings in upper portion of space min. 3 ft. below highest point & balance from eave or cornice vents &
    - (2) Class I or II vapor retarder on warm-in-winter side of ceiling in climate zones 6, 7 & 8 ____ 806.2

Unvented Attic & Enclosed Rafter Assemblies — 21 IRC

- ☐ Unvented attics & unvented rafter assemblies (ceiling applied directly to underside of roof framing members) permitted if all the following: ____ 806.5
  1. Unvented attic space completely within building thermal envelope
  2. No Class I vapor retarders on ceiling side (attic floor) of unvented attic assembly or ceiling side of enclosed roof assembly
  3. Min 1/4-in. air space between sheathing & wood roofing if used
  4. In climate zones 5, 6, 7 & 8, any air-impermeable insulation shall be a Class II vapor retarder or be coated w/ same on underside
  5. Each sheet of air impermeable preformed insulation sealed at each individual sheet to form a continuous layer
- ☐ One of the following also reqd: ____ 806.5#5
  1. Air-impermeable insulation below roof sheathing w/ or without air permeable insulation below it, or air-permeable below sheathing & rigid board above per T806.5, or sufficient rigid board to maintain temp of 45° F
  2. In climate zones 1, 2 & 3, air-permeable insulation w/ vapor diffusion port, roof slope ≥3:12 & air supply by ductwork or supply fan—see full text of code for combinations of permeable/impermeable insulations

DECKS & BALCONIES

Deck failures occur most commonly at the ledger attachment to the building and at guards. Extensive changes and upgrades were made to deck codes in the 2021 IRC. The tables have expanded to include ground snow loads, which also allows the prescriptive tables to be applied when a local jurisdiction requires a live load capacity greater than the 40 psf in **T4**. A new section on guards was added. ICC also updated their publication, *Deck Construction Based on the 2021 IRC,* and we recommend it for a complete guide to deck building, including all relevant tables.

Balconies — 21 IRC

- ☐ Floor cantilevers for exterior balconies permitted to be per **T62** ____ 502.3.3
- ☐ Protect non-PT wood or non-NDW w/ impervious moisture barrier ____ 317.1
- ☐ Construct impervious balconies to prevent water entry & allow accumulated moisture to drain to exterior ____ 703.1.1

Note: Ventilation of enclosed joist spaces may be reqd by local AHJ.

TABLE 62 — CANTILEVER SPANS[A] FOR JOISTS SUPPORTING EXTERIOR BALCONY ◆ T502.3.3(2) JOISTS NOT DIRECTLY EXPOSED TO WEATHER

Member Size	Spacing	Max. Cantilever Span (Uplift Force at Backspan in lb.[B,C]) Ground Snow LoadD[D] ≤30 psf	50 psf	70 psf
2×8	12 in.	42 in. (139)	39 in. (156)	34 in. (165)
2×8	16 in.	36 in. (151)	34 in. (171)	29 in. (180)
2×10	12 in.	61 in. (164)	57 in. (189)	49 in. (201)
2×10	16 in.	53 in. (180)	49 in. (208)	42 in. (220)
2×10	24 in.	43 in. (212)	40 in. (241)	34 in. (255)
2×12	16 in.	72 in. (228)	67 in. (260)	57 in. (268)
2×12	24 in.	58 in. (279)	54 in. (319)	47 in. (330)

A. Based on #2 grade lumber for 3 or more repetitive members. Lengths do not include an incising factor. This table appears intended for enclosed cantilevers, not for joists reqd to be PT or NDW.
B. Backspan to cantilever ratio min. 2:1. Uplift values allowed reduction by factor equal to actual ratio/2.
C. Full-depth rim joist to be provided at end. Blocking reqd at support end (if cantilever >24 in. SDC A–C).
D. Linear interpolation permitted for ground snow loads other than shown.

Decks: General — 21 IRC

- ☐ Decks to be designed for greater of live load or snow load ____ 507.1[56]

Deck Materials

- ☐ Wood #2 grade or better, PT or approved NDW ____ 507.2.1
- ☐ Cuts, holes & notches in PT wood req field treatment ____ 507.2.1
- ☐ Wood in ground contact reqs label (PPT) for such use ____ 507.2.1
- ☐ Plastic composites per ASTM D7032 ____ 507.2.2
- ☐ Composite materials req labeling of allowable loads & max. spans _ 507.2.2.1
- ☐ Install composite materials AMI ____ 507.2.2.5
- ☐ Alternate materials (glass & metals) permitted ____ 507.2.5
- ☐ Fasteners & connectors for decks per **T63** ____ 507.2.3
- ☐ Flashing corrosion-resistant metal min. 0.019 in. ____ 507.2.4
- ☐ Approved nonmetallic flashing if compatible w/ decking materials ____ 507.2.4

TABLE 63 — FASTENER & CONNECTOR SPECIFICATIONS FOR DECKS[A] ◆ T507.2.3

Item	Material Standard	Minimum Finish/Coating	Alternate Finish/Coating
Nails & glulam rivets	ASTM F1667	Hot-dipped galvanized per ASTM A153, Class D for ≤⅜ in. diameter	Stainless steel, silicon bronze, or copper
Bolts[B]	ASTM A307	Hot-dipped galvanized per ASTM A153, Class C (Class D for ≤⅜ in. diameter) or mechanically galvanized per ASTM B695, Class 55 or 410 stainless steel	Stainless steel, silicon bronze, or copper
Lag screws[C] nuts & wash-ers	ASTM A563 ASTM F844		
Metal connectors	Per MFR spec	ASTM A653 type G185 zinc-coated galvanized steel or post hot-dipped galvanized per ASTM A123 providing min. average coating weight 2.0 oz/ft.^{2} (total both sides)	Stainless steel

A. Stainless-steel fasteners and connectors reqd if < 300 ft. from salt water shoreline.
B. Holes for bolts min. 1/32 in. max. 1/16 in. larger than bolt. (NDS 12.1.3.2)
C. Lag screws predrilled to avoid splitting. (NDS 12.1.4.2)

56. Snow load must now be considered and may be greater than the min. live load. In areas where the min. live load is locally amended (e.g., California – 60 psf), the 70 psf table could be used prescriptively. A 60 psf snow load would not apply since it assumes a different duration factor (CD).

Deck Footings & Posts — 21 IRC

- ☐ Concrete footing or other approved structural system reqd EXC ______ 507.3
  - Freestanding decks of joists directly supported on grade ______ 507.3X1
  - Freestanding decks of joists bearing directly on concrete pier blocks, max. area 200 sq. ft., max. 20 in. above grade within 36 in. ______ 507.3X2[57]
- ☐ Footings min. 12 in. below undisturbed ground surface ______ 507.3.2
- ☐ Min. footing size per T507.3.1 ______ 507.3.1[58]
- ☐ Post min. size per T507.4 ______ 507.4[59]
- ☐ Posts bearing on footings req lateral restraint from manufactured connectors or min. embedment of 12 in. in soils or concrete EXC ______ 507.4.1
  - Expansive or other questionable soils not OK for lateral support ______ 507.4.1X

Deck Beams

- ☐ Beam plies fastened w/ 2 rows 10d nails 16 in. o.c each edge ______ 507.5
- ☐ Beam spans per T507.5 ______ 507.5[60]
- ☐ Beams permitted to cantilever at each end to ¼ of beam span ______ 507.5
- ☐ Ends of beams req min. 1½ in. bearing on wood or metal ______ 507.5.1
- ☐ Multiple-span beams bearing on intermediate post must have each ply bearing on the post ______ 507.5.1
- ☐ Deck beam connections must resist horizontal displacement ______ 507.5.2
- ☐ MFR connectors AMI, bolts req washers under head & nut ______ 507.5.2

57. New inclusion of decks-on-grade, similar to reqs for permits for such decks.
58. The table now includes smaller tributary areas, resulting in allowances for smaller footings than the previous lower limit of 12 in. × 12 in. In some cases, 8-in.-round footings or 7-in.-square footings are now allowed. The column for 2,500 psf soil bearing was eliminated. Since interpolation is allowed, eliminating that column is not significant.
59. The new table for post heights is significantly expanded from the simple version that was in the 2018 code, and now includes adjustments for the tributary area supported by each post and for ground snow loads. Posts w/ small tributary areas are now allowed taller heights than in 2018.
60. The beam span table was expanded for ground snow loads and the lines for NDW are now separate from those that are PT. The "effective joist span" supported by beams includes a factor based on the amount of joist cantilever. Previous table was a half page; new table is 4 pages.

Deck Joists — 21 IRC

- ☐ Joist spans, cantilevers & spacing per T507.6 & **T64** ______ 507.6[61]
- ☐ Ends of joists req min. 1½ in. bearing on wood or metal ______ 507.6.1
- ☐ Joists bearing on top of multiple-ply beam or ledger can be nailed ______ 507.6.1
- ☐ Bearing on top of single-ply beam or ledger reqs mechanical connection ______ 507.6.1
- ☐ Joists bearing into side of beam or ledger req joist hangers ______ 507.6.1
- ☐ Ends & bearing locations req lateral restraint ______ 507.6.2
- ☐ Blocking & joist hangers min. 60% of joist depth ______ 507.6.2
- ☐ Rim joist secured to each joist w/ min. 3 10d nails or 3-in. screws ______ 507.6.2

Decking

- ☐ Max. joist spacing **T64** ______ 507.7
- ☐ Min. 2 8d threaded nails or screws attachment to joists ______ 507.7
- ☐ Max. spacing for joists for plastic composite decking AMI ______ 507.7

TABLE 64 — MAX. O.C. JOIST SPACING IN INCHES[62] ◆ T507.7

Wood Size	Decking Perpendicular to Joist		Decking Diagonal to Joist[A]	
	Single Span[B]	Multiple Span[B]	Single Span[B]	Multiple Span[B]
1¼ in. thick	12	16	8	12
2 in. thick	24	24	18	24

A. Max. angle 45° from perpendicular.
B. Support by 2 joists considered single span. Support by ≥ 3 joists considered multiple span.

Deck Guards — 21 IRC

- ☐ Guards must transfer loads w/ continuous path to deck joists ______ 507.10.1[63]
- ☐ Where guard is connected to side of joist or beam, connection to adjacent joist or beam reqd to prevent rotation ______ 507.10.1.1[63]
- ☐ Connections relying on fasteners in end-grain prohibited ______ 507.10.1.1[63]
- ☐ 4 in. × 4 in. posts supporting guard loads not to be notched at connection to supporting structure ______ 507.10.2[63]

61. The joist span table was expanded for ground snow loads. Cantilevers are now based upon the actual back span.
62. The joist spacing table was expanded to include both single-span and multiple-span conditions.
63. Entire section on deck guards is new in 2021.

Ledgers

- ☐ Attachment to exterior wall reqs positive anchoring for vertical & lateral loads—no toenails or nails subject to withdrawal ______ 311.5 & 507.8
- ☐ If positive attachment cannot be verified, deck must be self-supporting 507.8
- ☐ Ledgers min. 2-in. × 8-in. nominal PPT or NDW #2 grade ________ 507.9.1.1
- ☐ Flashing reqd to prevent water entry ______________________________ 703.4
- ☐ Ledgers not OK to support loads from beams or girders _________ 507.9.1.1
- ☐ Ledgers cannot be supported on stone/masonry veneer_ 507.9.1.1 & 703.8.3
- ☐ Band joists supporting ledger min. 2 in. nominal (or engineered wood) 507.9.1.2
- ☐ Band joists must fully bear on primary structure (no cantilever) ____ 507.9.1.2
- ☐ Ledger attachment per **T65**, **F80,81** or approved equivalent _____ 507.9.1.3[64]
- ☐ Lateral loads must transfer to ground or through structure to ground _507.9.2
- ☐ If hold-down tension devices transmit lateral loads per F507.9.2(1), install within 24 in. of each end of deck. Each hold-down min. 1,500-lb. capacity (can be used when floor joists parallel to deck joists) ______507.9.2
- ☐ If hold-down tension devices transmit lateral loads per F507.9.2(2), install at 4 evenly distributed locations. Each hold-down min. 750-lb. capacity (can be used when floor joists perpendicular to deck joists) 507.9.2

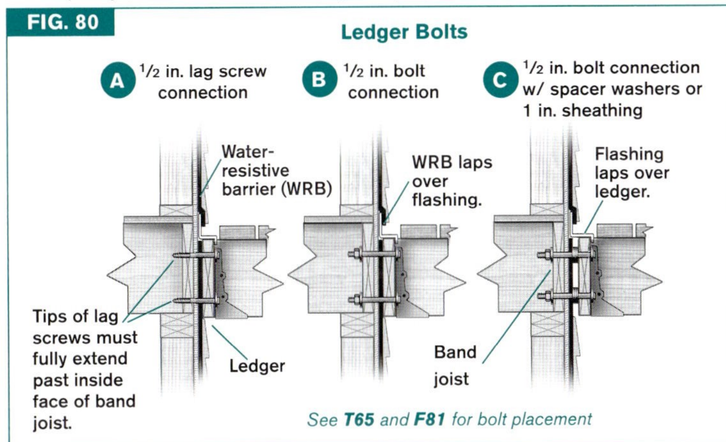

FIG. 80 Ledger Bolts

*See **T65** and **F81** for bolt placement*

64. The table was expanded for ground snow loads.

TABLE 65 DECK LEDGER CONNECTIONS TO BAND JOIST ◆ T507.9.1.3(1)

Load	Joist Span (ft.)	6	8	10	12	14	16	18
	Connection Details	On-center Fastener Spacing (in.)						
40 psf live load	½-in. lag screw w/ ½-in. max. sheathing[A] F80 (A)	30	23	18	15	13	11	10
	½-in. bolt w/ ½-in. max. sheathing[A] F80 (B)	36	36	34	29	24	21	19
	½ -in. bolt w/ 1-in. max. sheathing[B] F80 (C)	36	36	29	24	21	18	16
50 psf ground snow load	½-in. lag screw w/ ½-in. max. sheathing[A] F80 (A)	29	22	17	14	12	11	9
	½-in. bolt w/ ½-in. max. sheathing[A] F80 (B)	36	36	33	27	23	20	18
	½-in. bolt w/ 1-in. max. sheathing[B] F80 (C)	36	35	28	23	20	17	15
60 psf ground snow load	½-in. lag screw w/ ½-in. max. sheathing[A] F80 (A)	25	18	15	12	10	9	8
	½-in. bolt w/ ½-in. max. sheathing[A] F80 (B)	36	35	28	23	20	17	15
	½-in. bolt w/ 1-in. max. sheathing[B] F80 (C)	36	30	24	20	17	15	13
70 psf ground snow load	½-in. lag screw w/ ½-in. max. sheathing[A] F80 (A)	22	16	13	11	9	8	7
	½-in. bolt w/ ½-in. max. sheathing[A] F80 (B)	36	31	25	20	17	15	13
	½-in. bolt w/ 1-in. max. sheathing[B] F80 (C)	35	26	21	17	15	13	11

A. WSP sheathing or solid-sawn lumber.
B. WSP, SFB, GB, lumber, foam. Up to ½-in. thickness of stacked washers permitted w/ WSP or lumber.

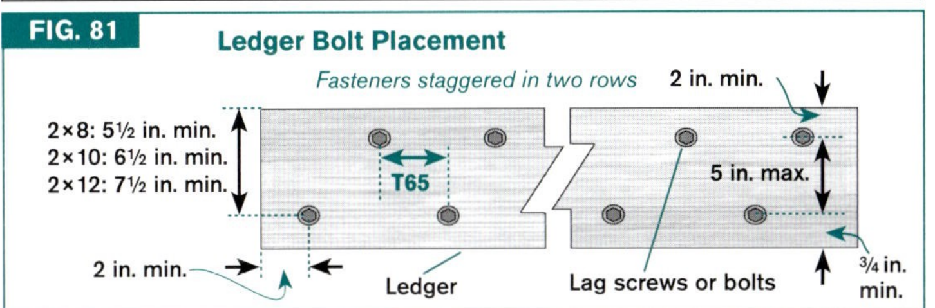

FIG. 81 Ledger Bolt Placement

ROOF ASSEMBLIES

General — 21 IRC

- ☐ Roof materials must be installed AMI ______ 903.1 & 904.1
- ☐ Materials req conformity to recognized standards ______ 904.3
- ☐ Materials req identification & test agency labels ______ 904.4
- ☐ Materials must resist design wind loads per **T2** ______ 905.1

Fire Classifications

- ☐ Class A, B, or C reqd per local laws or if <3 ft. of LL ______ 902.1
- ☐ Building-integrated photovoltaic (BIPV) shingles or roof-mounted PV panels req fire classification listing if <3 ft. from LL or in area where classified roofing reqd ______ 902.3&4
- ☐ Class A, B, or C listed & tested per UL 790 or ASTM E 108 EXC ___ 902.1
  - Roofs automatically considered Class A: ______ 902.1X
    1. Coverings of brick, masonry, or exposed concrete
    2. Metal, tile, or slate installed over noncombustible decks
    3. 16 oz. per sq. ft. copper sheets over combustible decks
    4. Slate over underlayment over combustible decks
- ☐ FRT wood reqs test label w/ class, company & QC agency each bundle 902.2

Flashing & Drainage

- ☐ Flashing reqd to prevent moisture from entering the roof & walls ______ 903.2
- ☐ Flashing reqd at wall & roof intersections, changes of roof slope or direction & around roof openings ______ 903.2.1
- ☐ Kickout flashing **F82** reqd to divert water away from where eave of roof intersects a vertical sidewall ______ 903.2.1
- ☐ Crickets reqd on ridge side of penetrations > 30 in. wide EXC ______ 903.2.2
  - Unit skylights installed & flashed AMI ______ 903.2.2X
- ☐ Metal flashing corrosion-resistant min. 26-ga galvanized steel ______ 903.2.1
- ☐ Parapet walls req noncombustible coping ≥ thickness of parapet ______ 903.3
- ☐ Drains at each low point of roof unless designed to run over edges ___ 903.4
- ☐ If roof traps water, overflow drains inlets reqd 2 in. above low points 903.4.1
- ☐ Overflow can be min. 4-in.-high scupper 3× drain size in parapet wall 903.4.1
- ☐ Overflow drains must discharge separately from main roof drains ___ 903.4.1
- ☐ Size of roof drains & leaders to comply w/ plumbing code ______ 903.4.1

FIG. 82

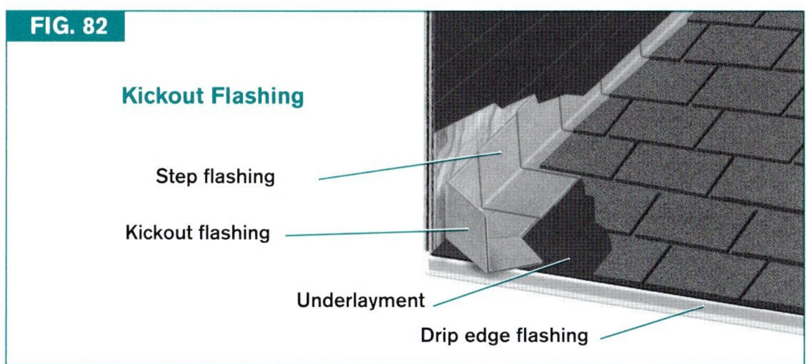

Ice Barriers — 21 IRC

Ice dams form when attic heat melts snow contacting upper portions of the roof, causing water to run under the snow until it reaches a lower, colder area and re-freezes into an ice dam. Ice dams then trap water, which seeps between layers of roofing underlayment and leaks into the building. The best solution is to prevent heat loss to the attic or to install a ventilated layer between the roof deck and attic. The code addresses barriers to prevent water trapped by the ice dam from reaching the building interior.

- ☐ In areas where ice barrier reqd by **T2**, install for asphalt shingles, metal roof shingles, mineral-surfaced roll roofing, slate & slate-type shingles, wood shingles & wood shakes EXC ______ 905.1.2
  - Not reqd for detached accessory structures w/o conditioned area 905.1.2X
- ☐ Ice barrier = 2 layers underlayment cemented together or self-adhering polymer modified bitumen sheet in place of normal underlayment ___ 905.1.2
- ☐ Extend from lowest edges of roof to a point at least 24 in. inside exterior wall line ______ 905.1.2
- ☐ If roof slope ≥8:12, barrier also min. 36 in. measured along roof slope 905.1.2

Underlayment

- ☐ Reqd for asphalt shingles, mineral-surfaced roll roofing, slate shingles, tile, wood shingles/shakes, metal roof panels/shingles & PV shingles EXC _ 905.1.1
  - Self-adhering modified bitumen underlayment or self-adhering strips AMI & underlayment per **T66** areas where wind design not reqd ______ 905.1.1X
- ☐ Apply & attach per **T66** ______ 905.1.1

<table>
<tr><th colspan="3">TABLE 66 — ROOF UNDERLAYMENT APPLICATION & FASTENING ◆ T905.1.1(2) & T905.1.1(3)</th></tr>
<tr><th>Roof Covering Type</th><th>Areas Where Wind Design not Required</th><th>Areas Where Wind Design is Required</th></tr>
<tr><td>Asphalt shingles & photovoltaic shingles</td><td>• For roof slopes ≥2:12 & < 4:12, min. 2 layers applied shingle fashion. Apply 19 in. starting strip parallel to eaves. 36 in. sheets then applied w/ 19-in. overlap.
• For roof slopes ≥4:12, underlayment starting at eaves & applied shingle fashion w/ 2-in. overlap.
• End laps 4 in. & offset min. 6 ft.
• Distortions in underlayment not to interfere w/ ability of shingles to seal.
• Fasten sufficiently to hold in place. Install AMI.</td><td rowspan="3">• 2 layers applied shingle fashion. Apply 19 in. starting strip parallel to eaves. 36 in. sheets then applied w/ 19-in. overlap.
• End laps 4 in. & offset min. 6 ft.
• Distortions in underlayment not to interfere w/ ability of shingles to seal.
• Attach w/ corrosion-resistant fasteners in a grid pattern of 12 in. between side laps, a 6 in. spacing at side and end laps.
• Attach underlayment using annular ring or deformed shank nails w/ 1-in.-diameter metal or plastic caps. Metal caps min. thickness 32-ga sheet metal. Power-driven metal caps min. thickness 0.010 in. Min. thickness of the outside edge of plastic caps 0.035 in. Cap nail shank min. 0.083 in. Cap nail shank length sufficient to penetrate through roof sheathing or min. ¾ in. into roof sheathing.</td></tr>
<tr><td>Clay & concrete tile</td><td>• Same as above except that 2 layers reqd if ≥2½ & <4:12 slope.
• Note: MFR installation instructions are often more restrictive.</td></tr>
<tr><td>Other roof types that req underlayment</td><td>Apply AMI</td></tr>
</table>

Concrete & Clay Tile — 21 IRC

The Tile Roofing Institute publishes several installation guides, including one for Florida high-wind areas and one for cold and snow regions. These can be downloaded from: tileroofing.org/industry/installation-guides/.

- ☐ Install only over solid sheathing EXC ____ 905.3.1
  - Spaced lumber sheathing permitted in SDC A, B & C if AMI ____ 905.3.1X
- ☐ Min. roof slope 2½:12, double underlayment if ≥2½ & <4:12 ____ 905.3.2
- ☐ Roof-to-wall flashings AMI, if metal min. 26-ga corrosion-resistant ____ 905.3.8
- ☐ Valley flashing min. 11 in. each way from centerline **F83** ____ 905.3.8

Concrete & Clay Tile Attachment

- ☐ Application AMI based on climate, slope, underlayment & tile type ____ 905.3.7
- ☐ Nails min. 11-ga corrosion-resistant, wire attachment min. 0.083 in. ____ 905.3.6
- ☐ Nails min. ¾-in. penetration into or through roof deck ____ 905.3.6
- ☐ Perimeter fastening min. 3 tile courses & min. 3 ft. from either side of hips & ridges & edges of eaves & rakes ____ 905.3.6
- ☐ Field tile fasteners not reqd if battens & slope <5:12 ____ T905.3.7
- ☐ Min. 1 fastener per tile if no battens ____ T905.3.7
- ☐ Min. 1 fastener per tile if weight <9 psf regardless of roof slope ____ 905.3.7
- ☐ Min. 1 fastener per tile if spaced sheathing ≥12:12 slope ____ T905.3.7
- ☐ Fasteners every other row if spaced sheathing ≥5:12 & <12:12 ____ T905.3.7
- ☐ Install AMI if UDWS >130 mph or if >40 ft. above grade ____ 905.3.7

FIG. 83

Tile Valley Flashing

Asphalt Shingles — 21 IRC

- ☐ Must be fastened to solidly sheathed decks ____ 905.2.1
- ☐ Min. roof slope 2:12, double underlayment if < 4:12 **T66** ____ 905.2.2
- ☐ Underlayment per **T66** ____ 905.2.3
- ☐ Shingles req labeling on packaging for wind speed classification ____ 905.2.4.1

Asphalt Shingle Fasteners

- ☐ Min. 12-ga w/ min. 3/8-in.-diameter head **F85** ____ 905.2.5
- ☐ Min. 3/4-in. penetration into or through roof deck **F85** ____ 905.2.5
- ☐ Min. number AMI & min. 4 per strip shingle **F84**, 2 per individual ____ 905.2.6

FIG. 84

Asphalt Shingle Nail Locations

Edge distance AMI – Typical 1/2 – 1 1/2 in.

Keyway

Self-sealing strip

Follow manufacturer instructions for nail locations in strip shingles. These may vary depending on the type and size of shingle.

FIG. 85

Shingle Nailing

Correct:

Min. 3/8-in. nail head

Asphalt shingles

Underlayment

Decking

Incorrect:

Crooked

Overdriven

Underdriven

Nails must penetrate through the roof deck or at least 3/4 in. into decking that is > 3/4 in.

Asphalt Shingle Flashings — 21 IRC

- ☐ Base flashings corrosion-resistant metal or mineral-surface roofing ____ 905.2.8.1
- ☐ Cap (counter) flashings min. 26-ga corrosion-resistant metal ____ 905.2.8.1
- ☐ Open valleys corrosion-resistant metal or 2 plies of mineral-surface roll roofing, bottom ply 18 in. wide top ply 36 in. wide ____ 905.2.8.2
- ☐ Closed valleys 1 ply 36 in. mineral-surface roll roofing or self-adhering modified bitumen underlayment ____ 905.2.8.2
- ☐ Sidewall flashing continuous or stepped, min. 4 in. high & wide ____ 905.2.8.3
- ☐ Vertical leg of flashing must be continuous under siding ____ 905.2.8.3
- ☐ Counterflashing reqd if sidewall is anchored masonry veneer **F100** ____ 905.2.8.3
- ☐ Sidewall flashings must terminate in kickout flashing **F82** ____ 903.2.1
- ☐ Wall & pipe jack flashings AMI ____ 905.2.8.4
- ☐ Drip edge flashing reqd at rake & eaves **F86** ____ 905.2.8.5
- ☐ Drip edge flashing fastening max. 12 in. o.c. **F86** ____ 905.2.8.5
- ☐ Underlayment over drip edge at eaves, under drip edge at rake **F86** 905.2.8.5

FIG. 86

Edge Flashing

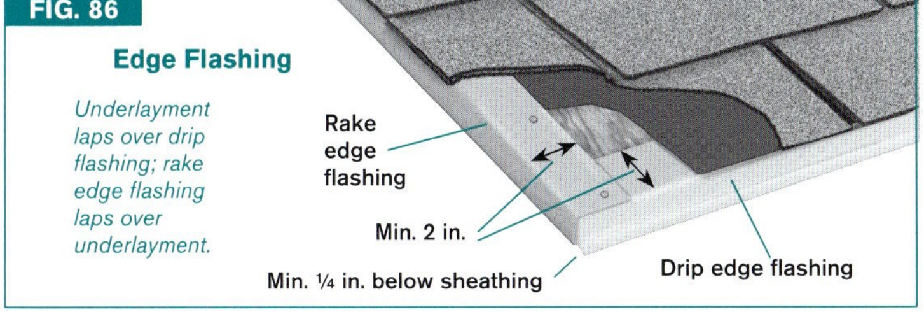

Underlayment laps over drip flashing; rake edge flashing laps over underlayment.

Slate Shingles — 21 IRC

- ☐ Must be fastened to solidly sheathed decks ____ 905.6.1
- ☐ Roof slope min. 4:12 ____ 905.6.2
- ☐ Underlayment reqd **T66** ____ 905.6.3
- ☐ Materials to comply w/ ASTM C406 ____ 905.6.4
- ☐ Headlap 4 in. if <8:12 slope, 3 in. if <20:12, 2 in. if ≥20:12 ____ T905.6.5
- ☐ Flashing must be sheet metal Zi-coated min. G90 ____ 905.6.6
- ☐ Valley flashing min. 15 in. wide ____ 905.6.6

Wood Shingles & Shakes — 21 IRC

- ☐ Each bundle reqs label from approved agency ________ 905.7.7 & 905.8.5&9
- ☐ Solid or min. 1-in. × 4-in. nominal spaced sheathing ______ 905.7.1 & 905.8.1
- ☐ Sheathing o.c. spacing to match weather exposure ______ 905.7.1 & 905.8.1
- ☐ Solid sheathing reqd where ice barriers reqd ________ 905.7.1.1 & 905.8.1.1
- ☐ Min. deck slope 3:12 ________ 905.7.2 & 905.8.2
- ☐ Valley flashing min. 26-ga corrosion-resistant metal ______ 905.7.6 & 905.8.8

Wood Shingles

- ☐ Spacing (keyways) 1/4–3/8 in., sidelap min. 1 1/2 in. **F87** ________ 905.7.5
- ☐ No keyways in direct alignment in any 3 adjacent courses **F87** ______ 905.7.5
- ☐ Valley flashing min. 10 in. from centerline each way, laps min. 4 in. ___ 905.7.6

TABLE 67 — WOOD SHINGLE & SHAKE NAILING[A–F] ◆ T905.7.5(2)

Material		Type & Min. Length	Min. Diameter
Shingles	16 & 18 in.	3d box 1 1/4 in.	0.076 in.
	24 in.	4d box 1 1/2 in.	0.076 in.
Shakes	18 in. straight split	5d box 1 1/4 in.	0.080 in.
	18 & 24 in. handsplit & resawn	6d box 2 in.	0.099 in.
	24 in. taper-split	5d box 1 3/4 in.	0.080 in.
	18 & 24 in. tapersawn	6d box 2 in.	0.099 in.

A. Nails hot-dipped galvanized or stainless steel Type 304 or Type 316.
B. Stainless 16-ga staples OK w/ crown with min. 7/16 in., max. 3/4 in.
C. Stainless Type 316 fasteners reqd in FRT or PT roofs or ≤15 miles of salt water coastal areas.
D. Fastener packaging label must indicate grade material or coating weight.
E. Min penetration into sheathing 3/4 in. or through.
F. 2 fasteners per shingle or shake.

Wood Shakes — 21 IRC

- ☐ If 1 × 4 sheathing used w/ 10 in. o.c. spacing, infill w/ 1 × 4s ______ 905.8.1
- ☐ Spacing (keyways) 3/8–5/8 in., sidelap min. 1 1/2 in. **F88** ________ 905.8.6
- ☐ 18 in. No. 30 felt interlayment installed over each layer in such a manner that no felt is exposed to sunlight. **F88** ________ 905.8.7
- ☐ Valley flashing min. 11 in. from centerline each way, laps min. 4 in. __ 905.8.8

FIG. 87

Wood Shingles

*The allowed exposure in **T68** of #1 grade wood shingles results in 4 layers of material for slopes < 4:12 and 3 layers of material for steeper slopes.*

Keyways cannot be aligned through any 3 successive courses.

2 fasteners **T67** per shingle

Exposure per **T68**

Keyways 1/4 – 3/8 in.

Sidelap between keyways min. 1 1/2 in.

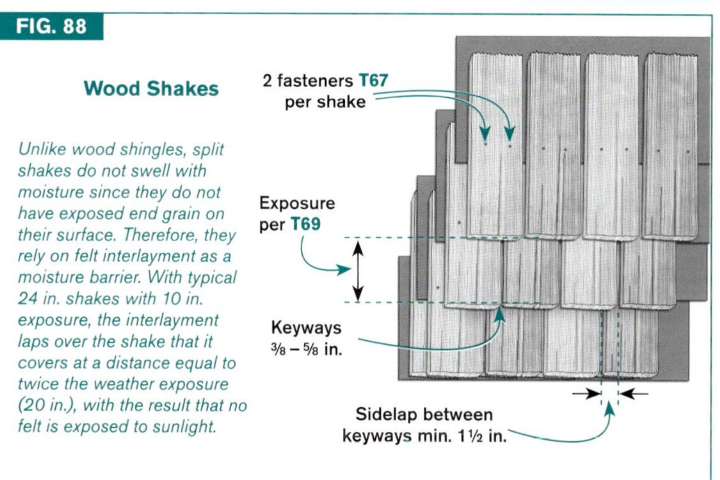

Unlike wood shingles, split shakes do not swell with moisture since they do not have exposed end grain on their surface. Therefore, they rely on felt interlayment as a moisture barrier. With typical 24 in. shakes with 10 in. exposure, the interlayment laps over the shake that it covers at a distance equal to twice the weather exposure (20 in.), with the result that no felt is exposed to sunlight.

TABLE 68 WOOD SHINGLE WEATHER EXPOSURE ◆ T905.7.5(1)

Shingle Length (in.)	Grade & Label Color	Exposure (in.)	
		3:12 slope to <4:12	4:12 slope or steeper
16	No. 1 – blue	3¾	5
	No. 2 – red	3½	4
	No. 3 – black[A]	3	3½
18	No. 1 – blue	4¼	5½
	No. 2 – red	4	4½
	No. 3 – black[A]	3½	4
24	No. 1 – blue	5¾	7½
	No. 2 – red	5½	6½
	No. 3 – black[A]	5	5½

A. The Cedar Shake & Shingle Bureau does not recommend #3 on primary buildings.

TABLE 69 WOOD SHAKE WEATHER EXPOSURE ◆ T905.8.6

Material	Length (in.)	Grade	Exposure[A] (in.)
Naturally durable wood (cedar)	18	No. 1	7½
	24	No. 1	10
PT taper-sawn Southern Pine	18	No. 1	7½
	24	No. 1	10
	18	No. 2	5½
	24	No. 2	7½
Taper-sawn naturally durable wood (cedar)	18	No. 1	7½
	24	No. 1	10
	18	No. 2	5½
	24	No. 2	7½

A. Assumes a 4:12 or greater slope.

Installation guidelines and other useful information for wood roofs can be obtained at https://www.cedarbureau.org.

Metal Roof Shingles — 21 IRC

- ☐ Apply to solid or closely fitted deck except where specifically designed to be applied to spaced sheathing ______ 905.4.1
- ☐ Materials corrosion-resistant, installation AMI ______ 905.4.4&5
- ☐ Shingle packaging to bear label indicating classification of wind resistance per ASTM D3161 ______ 905.4.4.1[65]
- ☐ Valley flashing same corrosion-resistant material as shingles ______ 905.4.6
- ☐ Valley flashing min. 8 in. from centerline, splash diverter reqd, laps min. 4 in., min. 36 in. underlayment below valley ______ 905.4.6

Metal Roof Panels

- ☐ Apply to solid or spaced sheathing or spaced supports ______ 905.10.1
- ☐ Min. 3:12 slope for lapped non-soldered seam w/o lap sealant ______ 905.10.2
- ☐ Min. ½:12 slope (4%) for lapped non-soldered seam w/ lap sealant ______ 905.10.2
- ☐ Min. ¼:12 slope (2%) for standing-seam systems ______ 905.10.2
- ☐ Roofs that include structural supporting members per IBC ______ 905.10.3

Modified Bitumen Roofing

- ☐ Min. ¼:12 slope (2%) ______ 905.11.1
- ☐ Base sheet per IBC 1507.11.2 or ASTM D1970 or D4601 ______ 905.11.2.1

Thermoset Single Ply (EPDM)

- ☐ Min. ¼:12 slope (2%) ______ 905.12.1
- ☐ Comply w/ ASTM D4637 or D5019 ______ 905.12.2

Thermoplastic Single-Ply Roofing (TPO)

- ☐ Min. ¼:12 slope (2%) ______ 905.13.1
- ☐ Comply w/ ASTM D4434, D6754, or D6878 ______ 905.13.2

Sprayed Polyurethane Foam Roofing

- ☐ Min. ¼:12 slope (2%) ______ 905.14.1
- ☐ Comply w/ ASTM C1029 Type III or IV or D7425 ______ 905.14.2
- ☐ Liquid-applied coating reqd min. 2 hrs. max. 72 hrs. after application 905.14.2

PV Shingles

- ☐ Min. 2:12 slope ______ 905.16.2
- ☐ Must be L&L to UL 7103 or both UL 61730-1&2 ______ 905.16.4

65. New req for wind-resistance labeling of metal shingles.

Built-Up Roofs (BUR) F89

- ☐ Min. 1/4:12 slope (2%) EXC ________ 905.9.1
  - Coal tar BUR min. 1/8:12 ________ 905.9.1
- ☐ Install per applicable standards & AMI ________ 905.9.2&3
- ☐ Not OK to reuse aggregate materials on reroof ________ 908.5

NRCA Recommendations & ASTM Requirements for BUR

- Store rolls on ends, not sides, to prevent deformation.
- Protect water-based materials from freezing prior to installation.
- Protect insulation from moisture.
- Do not install roofing while ice, rain, or snow is present.
- Use cant strips to limit bends to 45° at horizontal-to-vertical intersections.
- Sample temperature (typical 350°F to 425°F for Type I asphalt).
- Aggregate must be clean & dry to adhere to hot bitumen.

FIG. 89

3-Ply Built-Up Roof (BUR)

Inter-ply bitumen must be continuously bonded with no voids between the plies of material. Approximately 25 lb. of asphalt per square are required. The temperature must be maintained at the proper range for the specific type of asphalt.

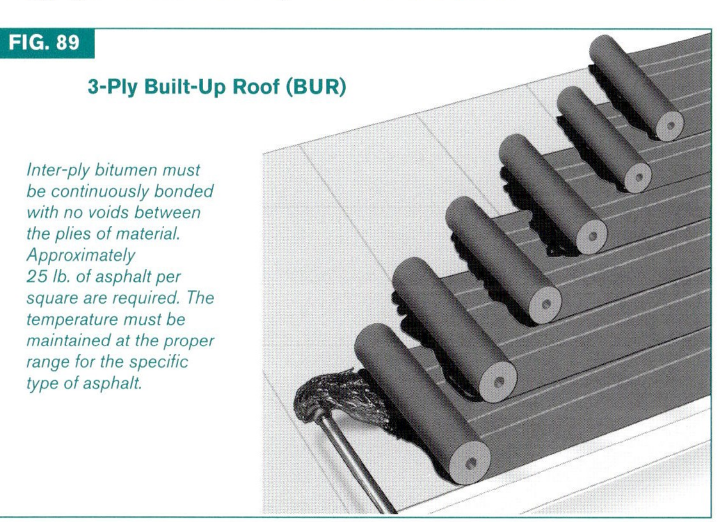

Building-Integrated PV Panels 21 IRC

- ☐ Apply to solid or closely fitted deck except where specifically designed to be applied to spaced sheathing ________ 905.17.1
- ☐ Min. 2:12 slope ________ 905.17.2
- ☐ Comply w/ NFPA 70 (National Electrical Code) ________ 905.17
- ☐ Fire classification ≥ reqd roof classification ________ 324.5.2
- ☐ Must be L&L to UL 7103 or both UL 61730-1&2 ________ 905.17.5

Reroofing

- ☐ Same requirements as for new roofs EXC ________ 908.1
  - Low slope <2% OK if providing *positive roof drainage** ________ 908.1X1
  - Adding secondary drains not reqd for roof w/ positive drainage ________ 908.1X2
- ☐ *Replacement* roof is considered the same as new roof, w/ old material removed to the roof deck EXC ________ 908.3
  - Existing ice-barrier membrane can remain if covered w/ new ________ 908.3X
- ☐ *Roof recover* refers to new roof covering over existing roof ________ 202
- ☐ Structural components must be rated for added weight of overlays & weight of equipment during installation of new roofing ________ 908.2
- ☐ Remove all existing layers of old roofing if existing roof is: ________ 908.3.1.1
  - waterlogged or deteriorated beyond forming adequate base
  - slate, clay, cement, or asbestos-cement tile
  - 2 or more layers of any type of roofing
- ☐ New protective coat OK over old foam, does not req tearoff ________ 908.3.1
- ☐ Where new covering over wood shingle or shake roof creates combustible concealed space, existing surface must first be covered w/ GB, mineral fiber, or glass fiber (fireblocking) ________ 908.4
- ☐ Replace rusted or damaged flashings ________ 908.5
- ☐ Prime flashings prior to application of bituminous materials ________ 908.6

**"Positive roof drainage" on an existing roof is confirmed by the absence of standing water 48 hours after the last precipitation. It also considers deflection due to loading conditions of the roof deck.*

Check with the local jurisdiction to determine its policy on required permits and inspections for reroofing. When removing roofs such as shakes or shingles over skip sheathing and recovering with asphalt shingles, solid underlayment or lumber infill is required, and the jurisdiction may require a nailing inspection.

EXTERIOR WALL COVERINGS

All cladding systems must include a water-resistive barrier to prevent moisture from entering exterior walls unless over masonry or concrete.

General — 21 IRC

- ☐ Exterior sheathing must be dry before installing exterior cover ________ 701.2
- ☐ Construct to prevent water entry & allow drainage to exterior________703.1.1
- ☐ Wall coverings must resist wind loads **T2** ________________________703.1.2
- ☐ Attachment of wall coverings must resist wind loads **T2** ____________703.3.2

Fasteners

- ☐ Fasteners for exterior wall coverings & soffits corrosion-resistant ____703.3.3
- ☐ Fasteners for wood, steel, fiber-cement, or aluminum siding materials min. 1½-in. penetration into studs ____________________703.3.4
- ☐ Fasteners for vinyl siding min. 1¼-in. penetration into combined thickness of studs & wood structural sheathing EXC ___________ 703.3.4#3
  - • Fastening through sheathing alone if per MFR instructions _____ 703.3.4#3
- ☐ Fasteners for vinyl siding over gypsum or fiberboard sheathing min. 1¼-in. penetration into framing_______________ 703.3.4#3
- ☐ Nail types & thickness per T703.3(1)___________________________ 703.3
- ☐ Screw substitutions for steel studs per T703.3(2)________________ 703.3

Water-Resistive Barriers (WRBs)

- ☐ WRB & means of draining to exterior reqd at all exterior walls EXC___703.1.1
  - • Masonry or concrete walls w/ proper flashings at penetrations__ 703.1.1X1
  - • Tested exterior wall envelopes per ASTM E331 ______703.1.1X2 & 703.2[66]
- ☐ WRB reqd over studs or sheathing at all exterior walls ____________ 703.2
- ☐ WRB must be continuous behind exterior wall veneer _____________ 703.2
- ☐ WRB = min. 1 layer No. 15 asphalt felt complying w/ ASTM D226 Type 1 or other barriers complying w/ ASTM E2568 Type 1 or 2, ASTM E331, or other approved materials installed AMI ___________ 703.2[67]
- ☐ Install shingle fashion (upper over lower) to prevent water entry into wall 703.2
- ☐ Min. 2 in. horizontal lap, 6 in. lap at vertical joints_________________ 703.2

66. Tested assemblies proven to resist wind-driven rain accepted in lieu of prescriptive WRB.
67. Code now lists ASTM standards other than D226 and clarifies that 1 layer is min.

Flashing — 21 IRC

- ☐ Flashing reqd shingle fashion to prevent water entry to wall or frame __ 703.4
- ☐ Self-adhered flashing must comply w/ AAMA 711 (note: caulking must be compatible w/ the self-adhered flashing) _____ 703.4
- ☐ Liquid flashings must comply with AAMA 714 ___________________ 703.4
- ☐ Reqd locations of flashing: ________________________________ 703.4
  - • Exterior door & window openings **F90**
  - • Intersections of chimneys w/ frame or stucco walls
  - • Under & at ends of masonry, wood, or metal copings & sills
  - • Continuously above all projecting wood trim
  - • Porch, deck, or stair attachment to a wood-framed wall or floor **F80**
  - • At wall & roof intersections **F82**
  - • At built-in gutters
- ☐ Window/door flashings must extend to WRB or to exterior **F90** _____703.4.1
- ☐ Air sealing reqd around window & door openings on interior side of rough opening gap ______________ 703.4.1[68]
- ☐ Follow door & window MFR instructions ______________________703.4.1
- ☐ If flashing details not provided, install pan flashing sealed & sloped to drain to exterior, install at head & sides **F90**_____________703.4.1

FIG. 90

Window Flashing

The flange on typical residential windows is incorporated in shingle fashion to the WRB.

Typical flashing and WRB sequence shown. Manufacturer's installation instructions must be followed.

68. Air sealing req is new in 2021 code.

Wood, Hardboard & Wood Panel Siding — 21 IRC

- ☐ Vertical wood siding reqs nailing to horizontal nailing strips or blocking at max. 24 in. o.c. ______ 703.5.1
- ☐ Spacing for 3/8-in. WSP siding applied direct to studs max. 16 in. o.c. 703.5.2
- ☐ Vertical joints in wood, hardboard, or WSP siding must be over framing members & shiplapped or covered w/ batten ______ 703.5.2
- ☐ Horizontal joints of panel siding lapped min. 1 in. or shiplapped, or flashed w/ Z-bar over solid blocking, wood, or WSP ______ 703.5.2
- ☐ Horizontal wood lap siding AMI ______ 703.5.3
- ☐ If no MFR instruction for horizontal wood siding, lap 1 in. or 1/2 in. if rabbeted, ends caulked, covered by batten, or sealed & over flashing ______ 703.5.3

Wood Shingle or Shake Siding

- ☐ Single or double course OK, bottom courses must be doubled ______ 703.6.1&4
- ☐ Must be over nominal 1/2-in. wood sheathing or over furring strips over 1/2-in. nominal non-wood sheathing ______ 703.6.1
- ☐ WRB reqd over all sheathing ______ 703.6.1
- ☐ Spacing between adjacent shingles 1/8 – 1/4 in., shakes 3/8 – 1/2 in. ______ 703.6.1
- ☐ Sidelaps min. 1 1/2 in. ______ 703.6.1
- ☐ Max. weather exposure per **T70** ______ 703.6.2

TABLE 70 — SHINGLE/SHAKE SIDING EXPOSURES[A] ◆ T703.6.1

Length	Single Course Exposure	Double Course Exposure
Shingles		
16 in.	7 in.	12 in.
18 in.	8 in.	14 in.
24 in.	10 1/2 in.	16 in.
Shakes		
18 in.	8 in.	14 in.
24 in.	10 1/2 in.	18 in.

A. Assumes No. 1 grade.

Exterior Insulation Finish Systems (EIFS) — 21 IRC

The earliest EIFS systems had several problem issues, especially those systems that did not have a drainage plane. Certification programs have since been created for designers, installers, and inspectors. Systems without a drainage plane are now allowed only over substrates of concrete or masonry wall assemblies. For further information, see the EIFS Industry Members Association at www.eima.com.

Exterior Insulation Finish Systems (EIFS) — 21 IRC

- ☐ All EIFS systems to comply w/ ASTM E2568 ______ 703.9.1&2
- ☐ Drainage plane-type EIFS reqd over all wall assemblies EXC ______ 703.9.2
  - Over concrete or masonry walls when EIFS installed AMI ______ 703.9.1
- ☐ WRB reqd between EIFS & wall sheathing ______ 703.9.2
- ☐ EIFS shall be installed AMI ______ 703.9.1&2
- ☐ Provide flashing per 703.4 ______ 703.9.1&2
- ☐ Terminate min. 6 in. above finished ground level ______ 703.9.1&2
- ☐ Decorative trim (plant-ons) not to be face-nailed through EIFS ______ 703.9.1&2
- ☐ Drainage plane-type EIFS min. drainage efficiency 90% ______ 703.9.2

Fiber Cement Siding

- ☐ Vertical & horizontal joints over framing & protected w/ caulk, flashing, battens, shiplap design, or other means AMI ______ 703.10.1
- ☐ Lap siding min. 1 1/4-in. lap, install AMI ______ 703.10.2
- ☐ Lap siding end joints caulked, protected w/ H-clips or flashing ______ 703.10.2

Vinyl Siding

- ☐ Must be labeled by approved agency to ASTM D3679 ______ 703.11
- ☐ Insulated vinyl siding labeled for conformity to ASTM D7793 ______ 703.13
- ☐ Install AMI ______ 703.11.1 & 703.13.1
- ☐ Max. fastener spacing for horizontal siding 16 in. or AMI ______ 703.11.1.3
- ☐ Vinyl siding over foam plastic sheathing reqs wind load design pressure rating in accordance w/ T703.11.2 ______ 703.11.2[69]

Adhered Masonry or Stone Veneer

- ☐ Install as per stucco or per TMS 602 section 3.3C or AMI ______ 703.12
- ☐ Flashing/veneer reqd 4 in. above earth, 2 in. above hardscape, or 1/2 in. above walking surfaces supported by same foundation as wall ______ 703.12.2
- ☐ WRB reqd to lap over flashing, flashing flange min. 3 1/2 in. vertical 703.12.2&3

69. Reqd wind load design pressures in T703.11.2 adjusted downward by factor of 0.72.

Portland cement exterior plaster (stucco) is required to comply with the standards in ASTM C926 and C1063, which are more extensive than the material covered in the code. Stucco by itself is not a water-resistive barrier. The requirements for the WRB behind stucco were expanded to ensure that it acts as a drainage plane.

Stucco (Portland Cement Plaster) — 21 IRC

- ☐ Must comply w/ ASTM C926 & ASTM C1063 **T72,73** ____ 703.7
- ☐ Min. 3-coat system over metal or wire lath **F91**, 2-coat over masonry, concrete, PPT, NDW, or gypsum backing ____ 703.7.2
- ☐ Proportions per T702.1(3) **T71** ____ 703.7.2
- ☐ Intervals between coats **T71** ____ 703.7.5
- ☐ Maintain moist min. 48 hrs before subsequent coats EXC ____ 703.7.4
  - Applications in accordance w/ ASTM C926 **T72** (X1.5.2.1) ____ 703.7.4X

Stucco Lath

- ☐ Expanded metal, welded wire, or woven wire lath can attach to wood framing members or to furring ____ 703.7.1[70]
- ☐ If plaster counts as wall bracing, lath must attach to framing ____ 703.7.1[71]
- ☐ Lath fastener spacing max. 7 in. o.c. on framing members ____ 703.7.1[72]
- ☐ Furring min. 1 × 2 in. wood, ¾ in. metal channels, or self-furring lath 703.7.1.1[73]
- ☐ Furring over wood or steel framing fastened into framing ____ 703.7.1.1[73]

Water-Resistive Barrier

- ☐ In dry climate zones, one of the following: ____ 703.7.3.1[74]
  1. 2 layers 10-minute Grade D paper installed independently w/ flashings between layers, or barrier ≥ 2 layers of ASTM E2556 compliant WRB
  2. 60-minute Grade D paper or barrier ≥ 1 layer ASTM E2556 WRB + foam insulating sheathing or other non-absorbing layer or designed drainage space between the paper and the stucco
- ☐ In moist or marine climate zones, one of the following: ____ 703.7.3.2[74]
  1. Item 1 or 2 above + $3/16$ in. space or drain material on exterior of WRB
  2. Item 2 above w/ WRB 90% efficiency per ASTM E2273 or E2925

70. Prior code did not specify method of attachment.
71. Prior code did not restrict bracing value based on attachment.
72. Prior code reqd 6-in.-o.c. spacing, which contradicted ASTM C1063.
73. Prior code did not address furring other than by reference to ASTM C1063.
74. Previous rule for WRB did not include the specific requirements for foam or other non-absorbing layer or air space and did not reference ASTM E2273 or E2925.

TABLE 71 — PORTLAND CEMENT PLASTER PROPORTIONS BY VOLUME ◆ T702.1(3)

Coat	Thickness[A]	Lime-to-Cement Volume Ratio	Sand-to-Cement Volume Ratio[B]	Interval after Previous Coat[C]
Scratch	⅜ in.	¾ to 1½[D]	2½ to 4	n/a
Brown	⅜ in.	¾ to 1½[D]	3 to 5[E]	Min 48 hrs
Finish	⅛ in.	1½ to 2	1½ to 3	Min 7 days

A. Based on vertical surfaces. Horizontal would be ¼, ¼, ⅛ per ASTM C926.
B. Ratio of sand to combined volume of cement and lime.
C. ASTM C 926 allows lesser curing times depending on climate.
D. Max. ¾ over low-absorption surfaces such as clay tile or brick.
E. Same or greater proportion of sand in 2nd coat as used in 1st coat.

Weep Screed F91 — 21 IRC

- ☐ Weep screed w/ min. 3½-in. vertical flange reqd ____ 703.7.2.1
- ☐ WRB & lath must lap over weep screed vertical flange ____ 703.7.2.1
- ☐ Placement min. 4 in. above earth or 2 in. above hardscape ____ 703.7.2.1
- ☐ Install weep screed in accordance w/ ASTM C926 (A2.2.1) ____ 703.7.2.1

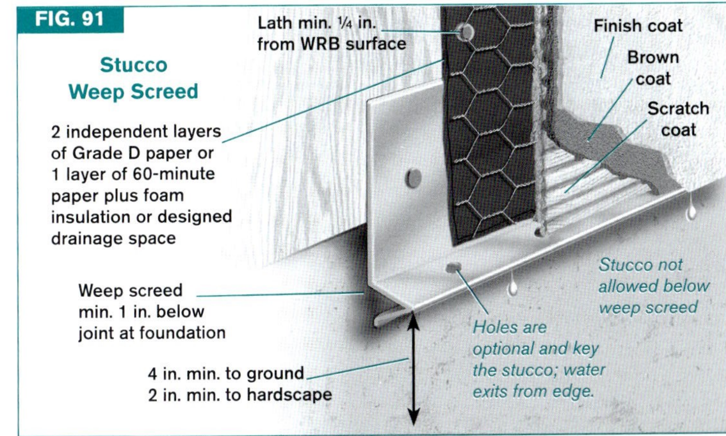

TABLE 72 ASTM C926 STUCCO APPLICATION SPECIFICATIONS

C 926	Summary of Requirement
7.2.1	All plaster to be mixed in mechanical mixer.
7.2.2	Base-coat plasters permitted one-time tempering.
7.2.2	Discard any plaster not used within 1½ hours of initial mixing.
7.2.3	Finish-coat plaster shall not be tempered.
7.3.5	Install each coat without interruption or cold joints.
7.8.1 & X1.5.2.1	Time between coats depends on climatic & job conditions. Moist curing can be fog coats of water or plastic film over surface. In some cases, the second coat should be applied as soon as first coat sufficiently rigid to resist cracking.
7.9.3.2	Ambient temperature must be at least 40°F to apply plaster.
7.3.9	Each coat must be permitted to set before next coat applied.
A1.5.2 & A2.3.1.2	Control joints to be included in contract documents, plans & specifications.
A2.1.2	Contract documents to describe flashing requirements.
A2.1.2	No aluminum flashings.
A2.2.1	Weep screed at bottom of all exterior drainage walls.
A2.2.2	Vertical-to-horizontal intersections req casing beads both surfaces, with vertical ¼ in. below horizontal to provide drip edge. Horizontal casing bead held back min. ¼ in. **F92**
A2.3.1.3	Grooves or cuts not considered to be control joints.
A2.6.5	Foam-core ornamental features adhesively attach to brown coat.

FIG. 92

Stucco Soffit

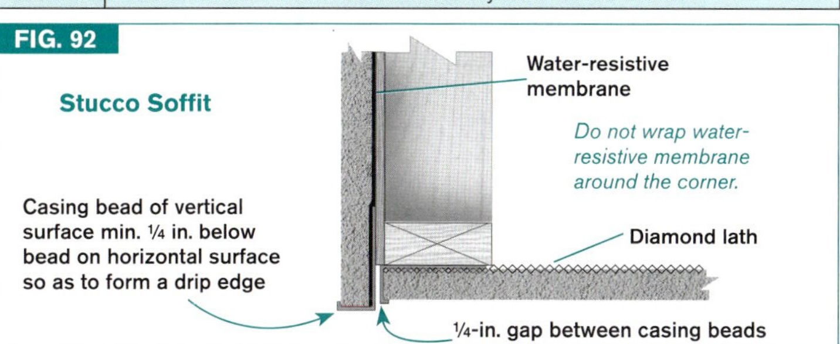

TABLE 73 ASTM C1063 STUCCO LATH SPECIFICATIONS

C 1063	Summary of Requirement
6.1.1	Framing member deflection max. *L*/360 (⅓ in. in 10 ft.)
6.1.2	Substrates straight & true to within ¼ in. in 10 ft.
6.1.3	Plywood & OSB ⅛-in. gaps, edges offset min. 4 in. from reentrant corners, such as corners of window & door openings.
6.1.5	Wood framing, plywood & OSB max. 19% moisture prior to plastering.
7.3.1.1	Plaster base (lath) furred away from surfaces ¼ in. **F91**
7.3.1.4	Ends of plaster base staggered.
7.3.1.5	Lath stopped & tied each side of control joints.
7.3.1.6	Ceilings req casing bead at intersections to walls, columns, or beams to maintain min. ⅜-in. clearance to other element. No internal corner reinforcement.
7.3.1.7	Load-bearing walls req casing bead or similar (no cornerite) at wall ends abutting structural walls or columns.
7.10.2.1	Wire lath lapped min. one mesh at sides & ends.
7.3.2.3	Lath w/ factory-attached WRB must be lapped WRB/WRB & wire/wire, NOT WRB/wire/WRB/wire.
7.3.3.1	Diamond-mesh lath to horizontal framing w/ min. 1½-in. nails.
7.4.2.1	Flanges of accessories secured at max. 7-in. intervals.
7.4.4	Bottom of weep screed ≥ 1 in. below joint between foundation & framing. **F91**
7.4.6	Install casing beads to separate plaster from dissimilar materials & penetrating elements. Install casing bead at windows that do not have a flange designed for stucco.
7.4.7	Install corner reinforcement at internal corner unless lathing continuous through corner or prohibited by conditions in 7.3.1.6 & 7.3.1.7.
7.4.8	Install corner reinforcement at external corners, or wrap lath around corners for min. distance of 1 framing member beyond corner.
7.4.10.1	Wall or partition height door frames considered control joints.
7.4.10.1	Control joints prefabricated or back-to-back casing beads w/ key attachment flanges & separation spacing min. ⅛ in.
7.4.10.2	Control joints to delineate areas not > 144 sq. ft.
7.4.10.3	Max 18 ft. between control joints or max. length-to-width ratio 2½ to 1.
7.4.10.4	Install control joints where ceiling framing or furring changes direction.

Anchored Masonry Veneer — 21 IRC

- ☐ Anchored veneer on wood or steel stud frame limited to 1st story above grade plane unless above a noncombustible foundation ______ T703.8
- ☐ SDC A, B, C max. thickness 5 in., max. 50 psf ______ T703.8(1)
- ☐ SDC D_0 & D_1 max. thickness 4 in., max. 40 psf ______ T703.8(2)
- ☐ SDC D_2 max. thickness 3 in., max. 30 psf, 1 & 2 story only ______ T703.8(2)
- ☐ SDC A, B, C & D_0 max. height 30 ft. + 8 ft. at gable walls ______ T703.8(1)
- ☐ Max. height 20 ft. in SDC D + 8 ft. at gable walls ______ T703.8(2)
- ☐ No additional loads on masonry veneer other than its own weight ______ 703.8.3

Anchored Veneer Support

- ☐ Veneer in SDC A, B, C w/ installed weight ≤40 psf allowed to be supported on wood or steel stud frame ______ 703.8.2
- ☐ Max. deflection of such support 1/600 of span ______ 703.8.2
- ☐ Steel angle support min. 6-in. × 4-in. × 5/16 in. to doubled studs ______ 703.8.2.1
- ☐ Steel angle support to tripled rafters per F703.8.2.2 ______ 703.8.2.2
- ☐ Lintels above openings min. bearing 4 in. ______ 703.8.3
- ☐ Lintels above openings size & span per T703.8.3.1 ______ 703.8.3.1&2
- ☐ Max. lintel span 18 ft. 3 in. (such as garage door header) ______ 703.8.3.2
- ☐ Min. 18 in. of veneer each side of max. openings ______ 703.8.3.2
- ☐ Height of veneer above max. openings T703.8.3.2 ______ 703.8.3.2

Anchorage

- ☐ Corrosion-resistant metal ties embedded min. 1½ in. in veneer mortar ______ 703.8.4
- ☐ Min. 5/8-in. mortar cover over ties from face of veneer ______ 703.8.4
- ☐ If over foam insulation to WSP, ties not reqd into studs ______ 703.8.4[75]
- ☐ Air space reqd behind veneer EXC ______ T703.8.4(1)[76]
  - Grout fill OK over WRB over studs ______ 703.8.4.2
- ☐ Air space nominal 1 in. for ties, per **T74** for metal strand tie wire ______ T703.8.4(1)
- ☐ Ties max. 24 in. o.c. vertical & 32 in. o.c. horizontal ______ 703.8.4.1
- ☐ Max. supported wall area of each tie 2.67 sq. ft. EXC ______ 703.8.4.1
  - Max. 2 sq. ft. SDC D (Townhouse C), or wind pressure >30 psf ______ 703.8.4.1X

75. The 2018 IRC introduced T703.8.4(2) that provides spacing guidelines when ties penetrate up to 2 in. of insulating sheathing and tie into WSP sheathing. The table considers UDWS and Exposure Zones. The 2021 IRC clarifies that the use of the table allows attachment to the WSP and not necessarily into studs.
76. Table formerly allowed max. space of 4½ in. New provisions for larger wire-tied spaces allow for installation over thicker foam insulation.

Weeps & Flashings — 21 IRC

- ☐ Flashing reqd beneath first course above ground **F93** ______ 703.8.5
- ☐ Flashing reqd at other points of support such as lintels ______ 703.8.5
- ☐ Min. 3/16-in. weep holes immediately above flashing **F93** ______ 703.8.6
- ☐ Weep holes max. 33 in. o.c. **F93** ______ 703.8.6

FIG. 93 Masonry Veneer

TABLE 74 — VENEER TIE ATTACHMENT & AIRSPACE ◆ T703.8.4(1)

Ties	Stud	Tie Fastener[A]	Airspace	
22 ga × 7/8 in.	Wood	8d common[B]	1 in. between sheathing & veneer	
W1.7 adjustable metal strand wire w/ hook embedded in mortar joint	Wood	8d common[B]	≥1 in. between sheathing & veneer	Max. 4⅝ in. between backing & veneer
	Steel	No. 10 screw		
W2.8 adjustable metal strand wire w/ hook embedded in mortar joint	Wood	8d common[B]	> 4⅝ in. between backing & veneer	Max. 6⅝ in. between backing & veneer
	Steel	No. 10 screw		

A. All fasteners req rust-inhibiting coating.
B. Fasteners in SDC D req 8d ring-shank nails.

INTERIOR WALL COVERINGS

Gypsum board should not be stored or installed in a building until the weather shell is complete, including roofing and water-resistive barriers on exterior walls. To reduce the possibility of mold growth or other moisture-related problems, interior walls should not be covered if moisture content of framing is over 19%. The Gypsum Association (gypsum.org) publishes several guides, including *GA-600 The Fire Resistance & Sound Control Manual*. Their website also has a page of Frequently Asked Questions. Types of gypsum board in residential construction also include water-resistant gypsum board, Type X (used in fire-rated assemblies and some prescriptive applications), and glass-mat board for exterior applications.

Gypsum Board (GB) — 21 IRC

- ☐ Protect from adverse weather during construction ______ 701.2
- ☐ Do not install interior GB where exposed to weather or water ______ 702.3.5
- ☐ Install only after all rough inspections & insulation complete ______ 109.1.2
- ☐ Edges & ends over framing unless perpendicular to framing ______ 702.3.5
- ☐ Fastening per **T75** ______ 702.3.5
- ☐ Min. screw penetration into wood ⅝ in., steel stud ⅜ in. ______ 702.3.5.1
- ☐ GB screws must be Type W or S per ASTM C1002 ______ 702.3.5.1

Water-Resistant Gypsum Backing Board (Purple or Green Board)

- ☐ OK on ceilings ______ 702.3.7
- ☐ OK as tile backer in areas w/ limited water exposure such as toilet or sink areas or ceilings above showers ______ 702.3.7
- ☐ Not OK with direct exposure to water or continuous high humidity, such as showers, saunas, steam rooms ______ 702.3.7.1
- ☐ Not OK over vapor retarder in tub or shower compartment ______ 702.3.7

Wood Veneer Paneling & Hardboard Paneling

- ☐ Framing for wood veneer & hardboard paneling max. 16 in. o.c. ______ 702.5
- ☐ Wood veneer & hardboard paneling < ¼-in. nominal thickness reqs min. ⅜-in.-thick GB backer ______ 702.5
- ☐ Wood veneer paneling to conform to ANSI/HPVA HP-1 ______ 702.5
- ☐ Hardboard paneling to conform to CPA/ANSI A135.5 ______ 702.5
- ☐ Wall & ceiling finishes max. flame spread index 200, max. smoke-developed index 450 in accordance with ASTM E84 / UL 723 EXC ______ 302.9.1–3

TABLE 75 — GYPSUM BOARD FASTENING SCHEDULE ◆ T702.3.5

Thickness (inches)	Location	Orientation to Framing	Max. Frame Spacing	Fastener Spacing	
				Nails[A]	Screws
⅜	Ceiling[B]	Perpendicular	16	7	12
⅜	Wall	Either direction	16	8	16
½	Ceiling	Either direction	16	7	12
½	Ceiling	Perpendicular	24	7	12
½	Wall	Either direction	24	8	12
½	Wall	Either direction	16	8	16
⅝	Ceiling	Either direction	16	7	12
⅝	Ceiling	Perpendicular	24	7	12
⅝	Garage ceiling[C]	Perpendicular	24	6	6
⅝	Wall	Either direction	24	8	12
⅝	Wall	Either direction	16	8	16

A. Min. nail length for ⅜-in. GB 1¼ in., ½-in. GB 1⅜ in., and ⅝-in. GB 1⅝ in.
B. ⅜-in. GB is not allowed on ceilings supporting insulation or where water-based texture to be applied.
C. Applies beneath habitable rooms: Type X GB and min. 1⅞ in. nails or equivalent drywall screws.

Ceramic Tile — 21 IRC

- ☐ Install per ANSI A108: *Standard for the Installation of Ceramic Tile* ______ 702.4.1
- ☐ Backer = fiber-cement board, fiber-mat reinforced cement board, glass-mat gypsum, fiber-reinforced gypsum backers ______ 702.4.2
- ☐ Backer must meet ASTM C1178, C1278, C1288, or C1325 ______ T702.4.2
- ☐ Lippage (elevation differences between adjacent tiles) per **T76** ______ 702.4.1

TABLE 76 — RECOMMENDED MAX. TILE LIPPAGE ◆ ANSI A108.02

Tile Type	Tile Size (in.)	Joint Width	Allowable Lippage[A]
Glazed wall/Mosaics	1 × 1 to 6 × 6	⅛ in. or less	1/32 in.
Quarry	6 × 6 to 8 × 8	¼ in. or greater	1/16 in.
Paver	All	⅛ to ¼ in.	1/32 in.
Paver	All	¼ in. or greater	1/16 in.

A. In addition to inherent warpage of tile manufactured in accordance w/ ANSI A137.1.

*IRC Chapter 11 lists all U.S. counties and their respective climate zones. States with their own energy code may have different numbering systems for their climate zones than the ones in the IRC. The vapor retarder requirements of Chapter 7 contribute to, but do not supersede, the insulation requirements of Chapter 11. The overall energy-conservation design can utilize the table on this page to assist in prescriptive design to prevent accumulation of moisture and condensation in exterior walls. "Vented cladding" systems include vinyl siding, brick veneer with an airspace **F93**, or other approved vented claddings.*

Vapor Retarders — 21 IRC

- ☐ Vapor retarders classified per **T77** ____ 702.7
- ☐ Provide on interior side of frame walls per **T77** EXC ____ 702.7
  - Approved alternate design using accepted engineering practice for hygrothermal analysis ____ 702.7[77]
  - Basement walls or below-grade portion of any wall ____ 702.7.X1&2
  - Construction that will not be damaged by condensation or freezing 702.7.X3
  - Climate Zones 1, 2 & 3 ____ 702.7.X4[78]
- ☐ Spray foam w/ max. 1.5 perms considered sufficient continuous insulation moisture control if R-value ≥ than specified in T702.7(3&4) ____ 702.7.1[79]
- ☐ Class I vapor retarders not permitted Zones 1-4 (Marine 4 OK) ____ T702.7(2)[80]
- ☐ Class II vapor retarders not permitted Zones 1-2 ____ T702.7(2)[80]
- ☐ Vapor retarders w/ permeance >1 perm OK interior side all zones T702.7(2)[80]
- ☐ Class III vapor retarders & continuous insulation w/ Class II retarders per T702.7(3&4) ____ 702.7

TABLE 77 — VAPOR RETARDER MATERIALS ◆ T702.7(1)

Class	Materials	Perm Rating
I	Sheet polyethylene, non-perforated aluminum foil, or other approved materials	≤ 0.1
II	Kraft-faced fiberglass batts, vapor retarder paint, or other approved materials applied AMI	> 0.1 & ≤ 1.0
III	Latex or enamel paint or other approved materials applied AMI	> 1.0 & ≤ 10.0

77. New recognition of alternate engineered systems in lieu of prescriptive vapor retarders.
78. Previous code also exempted Climate Zone Marine 4.
79. New section recognizing vapor retardance of spray foams.
80. T702.7(2) is a new table that assists in design.

SKYLIGHTS

Compliance with the AAMA standard referenced below helps ensure that a skylight will resist air leakage, water infiltration, and the design load pressures. A common problem with unit skylights is failure to properly secure the unit to the framing.

Skylights — 21 IRC

- ☐ Skylight = glazing at ≥15° from vertical ____ 308.6.1
- ☐ Unit skylight = factory-assembled glazed unit in roof assembly ____ 308.6.1
- ☐ Unit skylights & tubular daylighting devices req labeling from approved independent laboratory indicating performance grade rating & compliance w/ AAMA/WDMA/CSA 101/I.S.2/A440 ____ 308.6.9
- ☐ May be laminated, fully tempered, heat-strengthened, wired glass, or approved rigid plastics ____ 308.6.2
- ☐ Unit skylights min. 4-in. curb in roof w/ <3:12 slope unless AMI **F94** 308.6.8
- ☐ Cricket or saddle reqd if >30-in.-wide opening unless allowed AMI ____ 903.2.2
- ☐ Screens reqd below tempered or heat-strengthened glass EXC ____ 308.6.3
  - Glass ≤3/16 in., area ≤16 sq. ft., highest point ≤12 ft. ____ 308.6.5
  - Glass ≤30° from vertical, area >16 sq. ft., highest point ≤10 ft. ____ 308.6.5
- ☐ Any glass OK in greenhouses w/o screens if ≤20 ft. above grade ____ 308.6.6

FIG. 94 — Unit Skylight

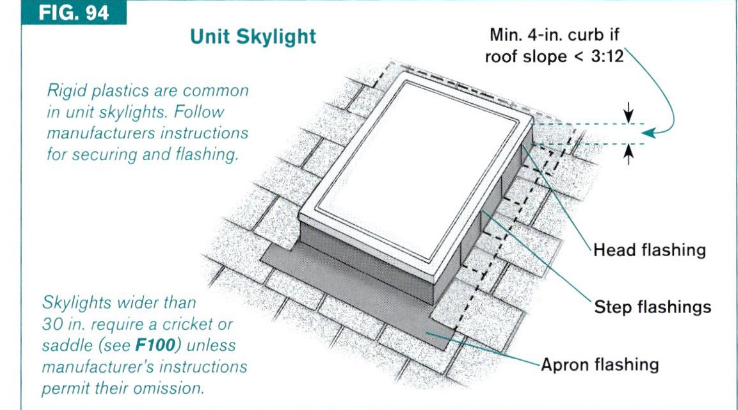

Rigid plastics are common in unit skylights. Follow manufacturers instructions for securing and flashing.

*Skylights wider than 30 in. require a cricket or saddle (see **F100**) unless manufacturer's instructions permit their omission.*

WINDOWS & EXTERIOR DOORS

The American Architectural Manufacturer's Association (AAMA) provides standards for performance and installation of new and retrofit windows. There are different standards for each siding and climate type and for special wind regions. Always follow the installation instructions.

Performance, Installation & Labeling — 21 IRC

- ☐ Written installation instructions reqd for each window & door ________ 609.1
- ☐ Install windows & doors AMI ________ 609.1
- ☐ Window & door openings req flashing per 703.4 ________ 609.1
- ☐ Windows & doors must be capable of resisting design wind loads ____ 609.2
- ☐ Windows, sliding doors & exterior side-hinged doors req labeling from approved agency to indicate compliance w/ AAMA standards EXC ___ 609.3
  - Decorative glazed openings ________ 609.3X
- ☐ Window & glass door assemblies must be anchored AMI ________ 609.7.1

Child Fall Prevention

- ☐ Openable windows w/ bottom of clear <24 in. above floor & >72 in. above finished grade or surface below req protection as follows: ____312.2.1
  - Will not allow passage of 4 in. sphere in fully open position ____ 312.2.1#1
  - Window fall-prevention devices per ASTM F2090 ________ 312.2.1#2
- ☐ Window-opening control devices in released position may not reduce net clear area reqd for escape & rescue **T7,8** ________312.2.2

FIG. 95 Tempered Glass Identification

SAFETY GLASS

Safety glazing is required in locations deemed to be hazardous, and includes tempered or laminated glass and approved plastics. In addition to building codes, safety glazing is regulated by federal standards. CPSC 16 CFR 1201 establishes standards for impact resistance for safety glazing. Category I glazing must comply with standards for a 150 lb. impact test, and Category II glazing a 400 lb. impact test. The standards in ANSI Z97.1 are similar as shown in **T78**. Wire-reinforced glass is not safety glass unless it also has one of the required markings.

Identification & Classification — 21 IRC

- ☐ Safety glass reqs permanent etched label that is visible after final installation **F95** EXC ________ 308.1
  - Non-tempered safety glazing OK to provide certificate to BO_____308.1X1
  - Tempered spandrel glass may have removable paper label ________308.1X2
- ☐ Glass panes ≤1 sq. ft. in multipane assemblies 1 label per above, others can state only CPSC 16 CFR 1201 or ANSI Z97.1 ________ 308.1.1
- ☐ Glazing to comply w/ CPSC 16 CFR 1201 Category II **T78** EXC___ 308.3.1
  - Glazing not associated w/ doors or enclosures for hot tubs, whirlpools, saunas, steam rooms, bathtubs or showers OK to have ANSI Z97.1 Category A label w/o a CPSC label ________ 308.3.1X

TABLE 78 CATEGORY CLASSIFICATION OF GLAZING ◆ T308.3.1

Area or Condition	Classification per 16 CFR 1201		Classification per ANSI Z97.1	
	≤9 sq. ft.[A]	> 9 sq. ft.[A]	≤9 sq. ft.[A]	> 9 sq. ft.[A]
Storm doors	I	II	n/a	n/a
Glazing indoors	I	II	n/a	n/a
Windows	NR[B]	II	NR[B]	A
Sidelites	I	II	B	A
Wet areas	II	II	A[C]	A[C]
Sliding doors	II	II	n/a	n/a

A. Exposed surface area of one side of one lite.
B. NR = no requirement.
C. ANSI-only labeling not allowed in areas covered by exception to 308.3.1 – see text above.

SAFETY GLASS

Hazardous Locations That Require Safety Glazing 21 IRC

- ☐ Glazing in swinging, sliding, or bifold doors **F96** EXC ______ 308.4.1
  - Glazing through which 3-in.-diameter sphere could not pass **F96** 308.4.1X1
  - Decorative glazing ______ 308.4.1X2
- ☐ Sidelites (glazing adjacent to doors) within 24 in. horizontal of door in the closed position **F96,97** EXC ______ 308.4.2#1
  - Glazing not in same plane (< 180°) as door other than on hinge side toward which the door swings **F97** ______ 308.4.2#2
  - Decorative glazing ______ 308.4.2X1
  - Where separated by intervening wall or permanent barrier ______ 308.4.2X2
  - Where door accesses closet or storeroom <3 ft. deep ______ 308.4.2X3
  - Glazing adjacent to fixed pane of sliding patio doors ______ 308.4.2X4
- ☐ Glazing in windows meeting all 4 **F96** conditions ______ 308.4.3
- ☐ Exceptions to the rule above apply to: ______ 308.4.3X
  1. Decorative glazing
  2. Protection by horizontal rail 34 – 38 in. AFF, min. 1½-in. cross-sectional rail height, capable of horizontal load of 50 psf w/o contacting glass
  3. Outboard panes of insulating glass ≥25 ft. above grade
- ☐ Guards & railings ______ 308.4.4
- ☐ Structural glass baluster panels req top rail or handrail supported by min. 3 panels so that if one panel fails the rail remains in place EXC 308.4.4.1
  - Laminated glass balusters do not req top rail ______ 308.4.4.1X
- ☐ Wet surface areas, including glazing in walls, enclosures, or fences adjacent to hot tubs, spas, whirlpools, saunas, steam rooms, bathtubs, showers & indoor or outdoor swimming pools where bottom edge of glazing < 60 in. above standing or walking surface **F97** EXC ______ 308.4.5
  - Glazing > 60 in. horizontally from water's edge or the edge of a shower, sauna, or steam room **F97** ______ 308.4.5X
- ☐ Glazing adjacent to stairs & ramps where bottom exposed edge <36 in. above plane of walking surface of stairs, landings & ramps EXC ______ 308.4.6
  - If protected by horizontal rail as in 308.4.3X2 above ______ 308.4.6X1
  - Glazing >36 in. horizontally from walking surface ______ 308.4.6X2
- ☐ Glazing <36 in. above bottom stair landing & within 60 in. horizontal arc of bottom tread <180° of bottom tread nosing EXC ______ 308.4.7
  - If protected by intervening guard min. 18 in. from glazing ______ 308.4.7X

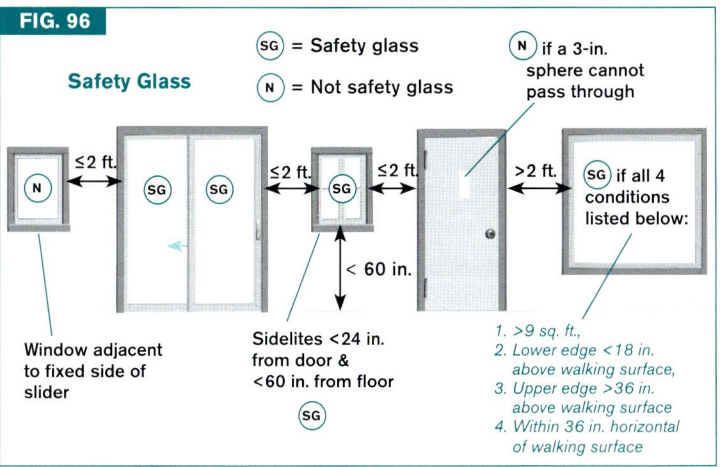

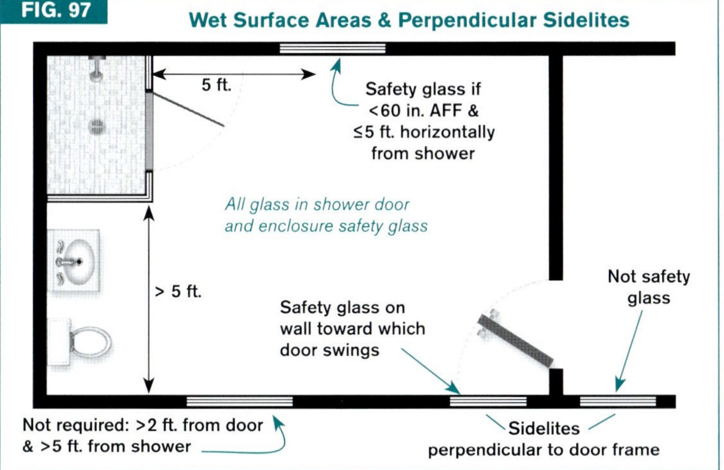

FIREPLACES & CHIMNEYS

Masonry fireplaces are becoming less common in new construction due to mandates for reduction of air pollution and for increased energy efficiency. Chimneys in earthquake country require reinforcement. Freestanding fireplace stoves, gas fireplaces, and decorative gas appliances are covered in *Code Check Mechanical.*

Masonry Fireplace & Chimney Construction — 21 IRC

- ☐ Footing min. 12 in. thick & 6 in. beyond all sides ________ 1001.2 & 1003.2
- ☐ Framing or other combustible material min. 4 in. from back of fireplace & min. 2 in. from chimneys & front & side faces of fireplaces EXC 1001.11 & 1003.18
  - Where fireplaces are part of masonry or concrete walls, combustible materials min. 12 in. from firebox or flue lining ____ 1001.11X2 & 1003.18X2
  - Combustible material can abut if 12 in. from inside surface of firebox lining or 8 in. from flue lining **F98** ________ 1001.11X3 & 1003.18X3
- ☐ Clear air space not filled except for fireblocking **F11** 1001.11 & 1003.18 & 19
- ☐ Fireblocking self-supporting or on strips of metal lath **F11** ________ 1003.19
- ☐ Combustible clearance AMI for lined chimneys L&L per UL 1777 _1003.18X1
- ☐ Corbeling max. ½ chimney's wall thickness from wall or foundation___ 1003.5
- ☐ Projection of single course lesser of ½ unit height or ⅓ bed depth __ 1003.5
- ☐ Chimneys to support no other loads unless engineer-designed______ 1003.8
- ☐ Chimney cap reqd w/ drip edge & caulked bond break at flue liner __1003.9.1

SDC D Reinforcement

- ☐ Min. 4 #4 vertical bars **F98** ________________ 1001.3.1 & 1003.3.1
- ☐ If >40 in. wide, add 2 bars each 40 in. or fraction thereof 1001.3.1 & 1003.3.1
- ☐ Min. ¼-in. horizontal ties 18 in. o.c. around vertical bars _ 1001.3.2 & 1003.3.2
- ☐ Horizontal ties reqd at each bend in vertical bars_______ 1001.3.2 & 1003.3.2
- ☐ Grout must enclose rebar & not bond w/ flue liner______ 1001.3.1 & 1003.3.1
- ☐ Anchor at each floor, ceiling, or roof > 6 ft. above grade EXC_ 1001.4 & 1003.4
  - Chimneys completely inside exterior walls ____________ 1001.4 & 1003.4
- ☐ Anchor straps hooked around outer bars **F98** _________ 1001.4.1 & 1003.4.1
- ☐ Fasten each strap to min. 4 joists w/ two ½ in. bolts **F98** 1001.4.1 & 1003.4.1
- ☐ For steel stud framing, reinforce location of bolts w/ min. 3 × 3 in. steel plate fastened w/ min. seven #6 screws _____ 1001.4.1.1 & 1003.4.1.1

FIG. 98 Chimney Clearances & Reinforcement

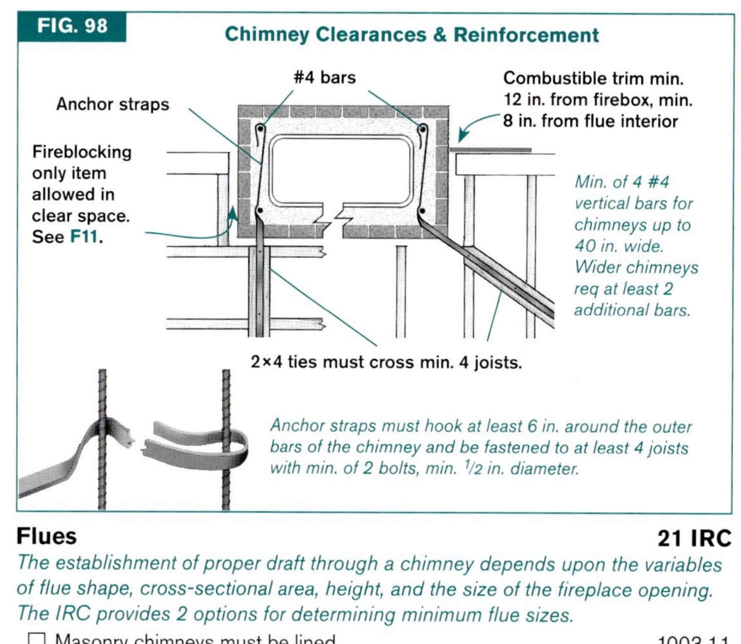

Flues — 21 IRC

The establishment of proper draft through a chimney depends upon the variables of flue shape, cross-sectional area, height, and the size of the fireplace opening. The IRC provides 2 options for determining minimum flue sizes.

- ☐ Masonry chimneys must be lined ____________________ 1003.11
- ☐ Lining can be clay to ASTM C315, lining systems listed to UL 1777, or other systems listed or approved for temps to 1,800°F_______ 1003.11.1
- ☐ Clay liner joints smooth on flue interior _______________ 1003.12
- ☐ Clay liners req either air space or insulation between liner & masonry 1003.12
- ☐ Space between liner & masonry not OK to vent other appliances _ 1003.12.2
- ☐ Multiple flues in same chimney req min. 4-in. masonry wythe between 1003.13
- ☐ Round flue cross-sectional area min. 1/12 area of fireplace opening 1003.15.1
- ☐ Rectangular flues w/ aspect ratio <2:1 1/10 area of opening _____ 1003.15.1
- ☐ Rectangular flues w/ aspect ratio ≥2:1 ⅛ area of opening______ 1003.15.1
- ☐ Option 2: Determine flue area per F1003.15.2_____________ 1003.15.2

Masonry Fireplaces 21 IRC

- ☐ Firebox walls min. 8 in. thick including liner if lined w/ min. 2-in. firebrick 1001.5
- ☐ Width of joints between firebrick max. ¼ in. ________ 1001.5
- ☐ If unlined, min. 10-in. solid masonry at sides & back________ 1001.5
- ☐ Min. firebox depth 20 in. EXC________ 1001.6
  - • Rumford fireplaces depth min. ⅓ width of opening & min. 12 in.___ 1001.6X
- ☐ Throat min. 8 in. above fireplace opening & min. 4 in. deep________ 1001.6
- ☐ Masonry over opening reqs lintel w/ min. 4-in. bearing each side_____ 1001.7
- ☐ Ferrous metal damper reqd min. 8 in. above fireplace opening______ 1001.7.1
- ☐ Damper must be operable from room containing fireplace ________ 1001.7.1
- ☐ Smoke chamber parged smooth w/ refractory mortar ________ 1001.8
- ☐ Corbelled smoke chamber max. 30° from vertical________ 1001.8.1
- ☐ Pre-fab (form damper) smoke chamber max. 45° from vertical ______ 1001.8.1
- ☐ If ash dump provided, cleanouts req metal door or frame ________ 1001.2.1
- ☐ Ash dump door to remain tightly closed except when in use________ 1001.2.1
- ☐ Locate so ash removal will not create hazard w/ combustible materials 1001.2.1

FIG. 99

Masonry Fireplace Clearances

Trim min. clearance 6 in. from fireplace opening. Trim <12 in. from opening max. projection ⅛ in. for each 1-in. distance from opening.

Extension min. 16 in. deep if opening < 6 sq. ft., 20 in. if opening ≥ 6 sq. ft.

Extension min. 8 in. to side of opening if < 6 sq. ft., 12 in. if ≥ 6 sq. ft.

Steel Fireplace Units 21 IRC

- ☐ Steel fireplaces w/ steel firebox lining min. ¼ in. thick ________ 1001.5.1
- ☐ Must have air-circulating chamber ducted to interior of building_____ 1001.5.1
- ☐ Firebox lining must be encased in solid masonry; total thickness 8 in. at back & sides, of which min. 4 in. solid masonry or concrete __ 1001.5.1
- ☐ Circulating air ducts shall be metal or masonry ________ 1001.5.1

Hearth & Hearth Extension

- ☐ Hearth & extension construction concrete or masonry________ 1001.9
- ☐ Hearth & extension reinforced to carry their weight & imposed loads__ 1001.9
- ☐ Remove all combustible material from under hearth & extension _____ 1001.9
- ☐ Min. hearth thickness 4 in., min. extension thickness 2 in. EXC __ 1001.9.1&2
  - • ⅜-in.-thick noncombustible extension OK if bottom of fireplace opening ≥8 in. above extension ________ 1001.9.2X
- ☐ Extension min. 16 in. front, 8 in. side, if opening <6 sq. ft **F99**_____ 1001.10
- ☐ Extension min. 20 in. front, 12 in. side, if opening ≥6 sq. ft. **F99** ____ 1001.10
- ☐ No combustible material within 6 in. of opening ________ 1001.11X4
- ☐ Combustible material ≤12 in. from opening limited to projection of ⅛ in. for each inch distance from opening **F99** ________ 1001.11X4

Exterior Air Supply (Masonry or Factory-Built)

- ☐ Exterior air supply reqd unless room mechanically ventilated & controlled to ensure neutral or positive indoor air pressure________ 1006.1
- ☐ Exterior air ducts of factory-built fireplace must be listed component of fireplace & be installed AMI ________ 1006.1.1
- ☐ Exterior air ducts for masonry fireplace must be listed & AMI ______ 1006.1.2
- ☐ Air source must be from exterior or space vented to exterior ________ 1006.2
- ☐ Air source not from garage or basement ________ 1006.2
- ☐ Unlisted air ducts min. 1 in. from combustibles for all parts of duct within 5 ft. of duct outlet________ 1006.3
- ☐ Combustion air passageway min. 6 sq. in. max. 55 sq. in. or per listing 1006.4
- ☐ Outlet closable & located in back or side of firebox or outside firebox at level of hearth & within 24 in. of firebox opening____ 1006.5

Fireplaces without an exterior air supply can negatively impact energy efficiency due to the large volume of conditioned air necessary for combustion. The exterior air supply helps maintain proper air pressure and aids proper drafting.

Chimney & Flue Termination 21 IRC

- ☐ Terminate min. 3 ft. above roof & 2 ft. above building within 10 ft. **F100** 1003.9
- ☐ Concrete, metal, or stone cap sloped to shed water **F100** ________ 1003.9.1
- ☐ Spark arrester screen net free area min. 4× flue opening size **F100** _ 1003.9.2
- ☐ Screening mesh must permit passage of ⅜-in. sphere & block passage of ½-in. sphere ________ 1003.9.2
- ☐ Screen or rain-cap assembly removable for cleaning of flue **F100** ___ 1003.9.2
- ☐ Net free area under metal or masonry rain cap 4× flue opening size _ 1003.9.3
- ☐ Cricket reqd if chimney width parallel to ridge >30 in. **F100** ______ 1003.20
- ☐ Cricket reqs flashing & counterflashing same as other roof-chimney intersections (step flashing covered by counterflashing in reglet)____ 1003.20
- ☐ Cricket height per **T79** ________ 1003.20

TABLE 79	CRICKET DIMENSIONS ◆ T1003.20		
Roof Slope	Cricket Height	Roof Slope	Cricket Height
12:12	½ of width	4:12	⅙ of width
8:12	⅓ of width	3:12	⅛ of width
6:12	¼ of width		

FIG. 100 Chimney Height

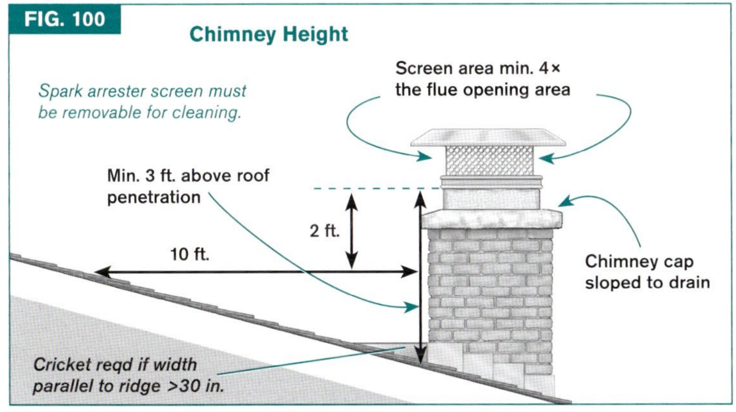

Masonry Heaters 21 IRC

- ☐ A masonry heater is constructed of concrete or solid masonry designed to absorb heat & provide a heat source as a result of its large thermal mass. The flue passage typically includes horizontal or down-flow sections _ 1002.1
- ☐ Comply w/ ASTM E1602 or L&L to UL 1482 AMI ________ 1002.2

Factory-Built Fireplaces & Chimneys

- ☐ Must be listed to & in compliance w/ UL 127 ________ 1004.1 & 1005.4
- ☐ Hearth extensions AMI & distinguishable from surrounding floor _____ 1004.2
- ☐ Decorative shrouds req L&L for specific system AMI _______ 1004.3 & 1005.2
- ☐ Gasketed fireplace doors req L&L for specific system AMI ________ 1004.5
- ☐ Factory-built chimneys must comply w/ UL 103 ________ 1005.3
- ☐ Factory-built chimneys must be marked "Type HT" & "Residential Type & Building Heating Appliance Chimney" ________ 1005.3
- ☐ Firestop spacer AMI where passing through ceilings________ 1005.4
- ☐ Offsets max. 30° from vertical ________ 1005.7
- ☐ Insulation shield per UL 127 if passing through loose-fill in attic _____ 1005.8
- ☐ Insulation shield min. 2 in. above insulation materials________ 1005.8
- ☐ Replacement parts per MFR (refractory panels, caps, doors, etc.)____ 1004.1
- ☐ Inserts only OK if tested per UL 127 for specific installed fireplace___ 1004.1

Recommended Inspections of Existing Chimneys NFPA 211

NFPA 211 – Standard for Chimneys, Fireplaces, Vents & Solid Fuel-Burning Appliances is an industry standard that includes recommendations for maintenance, retroactivity, and inspections of existing fireplaces & chimneys. The current 2019 edition includes the following recommendations in section 15.2.1.

Level 1: Visual inspection of all readily accessible areas (not including attic area) of chimney, flue, and structure for deposits or obstructions. To be performed annually, during routine cleaning, and when replacing w/ a similar appliance.

Level 2: Level 1 + areas within accessible attics & crawlspaces + video scan of flue. Verify flue connections, clearances, size and suitability of flues. To be performed upon resale or transfer of property. To be performed when adding, removing, or replacing appliances, or after an operating malfunction.

Level 3: Level 1 & 2 + removal of components or finishes as necessary to gain access to concealed areas of the building or chimney. To be performed when Level 1 or Level 2 cannot identify conditions deemed critical to renewed or continued use; also performed as part of fire or damage investigations.

ENERGY EFFICIENCY

The energy rules in chapter 11 of the IRC are derived from the International Energy Conservation Code—Residential Provisions. Several states and local jurisdictions have their own energy codes and standards. Depending upon the scope of the project, separate energy consultants, designers, and inspectors may be involved, and compliance is confirmed through the use of software that weighs different factors to determine an overall performance level. The prescriptive items shown here are only a beginning piece of the steps necessary to achieve compliance.

The first step is to determine the climate zone of the property, for which the IRC has a listing by county for all of the United States. Other IRC chapters also reference these climate zones. IRC chapter 11 also has its own section of definitions.

Intent & Scope — 21 IRC

- ☐ Intended to ensure effective energy use & allow for innovation ______ 1101.2
- ☐ Software can be approved to demonstrate compliance ______ 1101.3
- ☐ Information to be included in construction documents: ______ 1101.5
  1. Energy compliance path
  2. Insulation materials & their R-values
  3. Fenestration U-factors & SHGC
  4. Area-weighted U-factor and SHGC calculations
  5. Mechanical system design criteria
  6. Mechanical & water heating equipment types, sizes & efficiencies
  7. Equipment & system controls
  8. Duct sealing, duct & pipe insulation & location
  9. Air sealing details

Compliance Options

- ☐ Prescriptive Compliance option per sections 1101–1104 ______ 1101.13.1
- ☐ Total Building Performance option per section 1105 ______ 1101.13.2
- ☐ Energy Rating Index option per section 1106 ______ 1101.13.3
- ☐ Tropical Climate Region option per section 1107 ______ 1101.13.4
- ☐ Additional Energy Efficiency (options) posted on certificate ______ 1101.13.5

Certification

- ☐ Certificate of compliance with component performance values and test results posted at furnace, utility room, or other approved area __ 1101.14
- ☐ Maintenance instructions reqd where equipment reqs same ______ 1101.12

Additions & Alterations — 21 IRC

- ☐ Additions must comply w/ same rules as new construction ______ 1110.1
- ☐ Existing unaltered portion of building need not be upgraded ______ 1110.1
- ☐ Alterations same as new construction EXC ______ 1109.1
  - Reroofs, storm windows, window film to reduce solar heat gain __ 1111.1.1X

Building Thermal Envelope

- ☐ Class I or II vapor retarder reqd interior of frame walls in zones 5, 6, 7, 8 & Marine 4 ______ 1102.1.1 & 702.7
- ☐ Walls, floors & ceilings insulated per climate zone & T1102.1.3 ______ 1102.1.2
- ☐ Insulation & weatherstripping reqd attic hatches & doors ______ 1102.2.4
- ☐ Insulate attic hatches & doors equivalent to adjacent area ______ 1102.2.4
- ☐ Area-weighted average of U-factors & SHGC of fenestration allowed to be used for compliance w/ 1102 ______ 1102.3
- ☐ Air barriers, air sealing & insulation installation per T1102.4.1.1 ______ 1102.4
- ☐ Air leakage testing reqd per RESNET/ICC 380, ASTM E779, or E1827, ≤5 ACH in climate zones 1–2 & ≤ 3 ACH in zones 3–8 ______ 1102.4

Systems

- ☐ Solid-fuel burning fireplaces req damper or tight-fitting door ______ 1102.4.2
- ☐ HVAC systems sized per ACCA Manual S & J ______ 1103.7
- ☐ Programmable thermostat reqd for primary heating/cooling system ______ 1103.1.1
- ☐ Ducts ≥3 in. diameter outside conditioned space min. R-8 insulation _ 1103.3.1
- ☐ Insulation not reqd if completely inside building thermal envelope 1103.3.2&3
- ☐ Duct leakage test mandatory ______ 1103.3.5
- ☐ Heated water systems req circulation pump ______ 1103.5.1.1
- ☐ Hot water pipe insulation min. R-3 insulation ______ 1103.5.2
- ☐ Mechanical ventilation per 1505 (see *p. 216*) ______ 1103.6
- ☐ All permanently installed lighting must be high-efficacy ______ 1104.1
- ☐ Permanently installed lighting reqs dimmer, occupant sensor, or other control (overall lighting control system) EXC ______ 1104.2
  - Bathrooms, hallways, exterior lights, safety or security lights ______ 1104.2X
- ☐ All recessed luminaires type IC, airtight & gasketed trim ______ 1102.4.5

Changes to the energy code have not been highlighted on this page. There have been extensive changes, and local jurisdictions also make extensive modifications. A brief summary of the changes would not be adequate and could be misleading. Contact the local jurisdiction for specific requirements in your area.

Code ✓Check® Plumbing Sixth Edition

Part 2 of Code ✓Check Complete Third Edition

By DOUGLAS HANSEN, REDWOOD KARDON & SKIP WALKER

Illustrations by Paddy Morrissey, Douglas Hansen & Kaia Mathewson

Code Check Plumbing 6th edition is an illustrated reference guide to code requirements and common code violations in residential plumbing systems. The main codes referenced in this book are the *2021 International Residential Code®*, published by the International Code Council, and the *2021 Uniform Plumbing Code®*, published by the International Association of Plumbing and Mechanical Officials (IAPMO). For most topics, these codes are in agreement. These are the most widely used plumbing codes throughout the United States. NFPA 54, the *National Fuel Gas Code*, is the basis for the fuel gas provisions of the IRC, UPC, and UMC. Other referenced codes used in the book are listed in Table 1 (**T1**).

Model codes are updated on a 3-year cycle. In most areas, the 2021 code cycle will remain in effect for 3 to 6 years after the cover date. Significant changes from the previous code editions are highlighted in the text, and this book can be used for areas still using older editions of the codes. Minor changes and those that only affected numbering (not substance) are not highlighted.

Energy codes vary greatly from one area to another and may modify or overrule the requirements shown in this book. Before beginning any project, check with your local building department to determine the codes and editions that apply in your area. Some jurisdictions modify the model codes. The codes also reference standards, many of which are maintained by the organizations in Table 2 (**T2**).

For further information, updates, and more, contact us at www.codecheck.com

TABLE 1 — CODES USED IN THIS BOOK

Organization	Edition	Code
ICC	2021	International Residential Code
ICC	2021	IPSDC—International Private Sewage Disposal Code
IAPMO	2021	Uniform Plumbing Code
NFPA	2021	NFPA 54 National Fuel Gas Code
NFPA	2020	NFPA 58 Liquefied Petroleum Gas Code
NFPA	2020	NFPA 70 National Electrical Code

The information in this document is believed to be accurate; however, it is provided for informational purposes only and is not intended as a substitute for the full text of the referenced codes. Publication by The Taunton Press, ICC, and the authors should not be considered by the user to be a substitute for the advice of a registered design professional or the enforceable interpretation of the local building department.

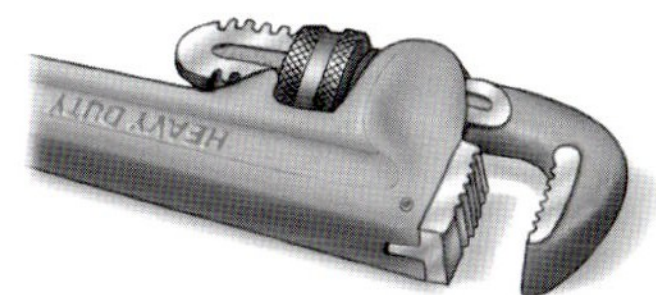

TABLE OF CONTENTS

AAV = air admittance valve
ABS = acrylonitrile-butadiene-styrene drain (black plastic pipe)
AHJ = authority having jurisdiction
AL = aluminum
AMI = in accordance with MFR's instructions
AMM = alternative materials, design, or method
AVB = atmospheric vacuum breaker
BO = building official
BT = bathtub
Btu = British thermal unit(s)
C = centigrade
cfm = cubic feet per minute
CI = cast iron
CO = cleanout
CPVC = chlorinated PVC pipe
CSST = corrugated stainless-steel (gas) tubing
cu. = cubic, as in cu. ft.
Cu = copper
CW = clothes washer
CW&V = combination waste & vent
DFU = drainage fixture unit
DW = dishwasher
DWV = drain, waste & vent
EGC = equipment grounding conductor
e.g. = for example (exempli gratia)
ex: = example
EXC = exception to rule follows in the next line
exc = except
F = Fahrenheit
FAU = forced-air unit
FLR = flood level rim
ft. = foot/feet
FVIR = flammable vapor ignition-resistant
gal = gallon(s)
GPF = gallons per flush
gpm = gallons per minute
HDPE = high-density polyethylene
hr. = hour(s)
IAPMO = International Association of Plumbing & Mechanical Officials
ICC = International Code Council
IFGC = International Fuel Gas Code
in. = inch(es)
IPC = International Plumbing Code
IRC = International Residential Code
k = 1,000 (1kBtu = 1,000Btu)
KS = kitchen sink
lav = lavatory sink
L&L = listed & labeled
LL = lot line
LP = liquefied petroleum (LP gas)
LT = laundry tray
max. = maximum
MFR = manufacturer
min. = minimum
MP = medium pressure
n/a = not applicable
NEC = National Electrical Code
NFPA = National Fire Protection Association
o.c. = on center
O.D. = outside diameter
PB = polybutylene (water tubing)
PE = polyethylene (water or gas tubing)
PE-RT = polyethylene (raised temperature)
PEX = crossed-link polyethylene tubing
PP = polypropylene plastic tubing
PRV = pressure relief valve
psf = pounds per square foot
psi = pounds per square inch
psig = pounds per square inch gauge
PVC = polyvinyl chloride pipe
req = require, requirement
reqd, reqs = required, requires
RP = reduced-pressure principle backflow preventer
SDC = Seismic Design Category
SFD = single-family dwelling
sq. = square, as in sq. ft.
SS = stainless steel
TPRV = temperature & pressure relief valve
UL = UL (formerly Underwriters Laboratory)
UMC = Uniform Mechanical Code
UPC = Uniform Plumbing Code
w/ = with
w/o = without
WC = water closet (toilet)
WH = water heater
WSFU = water supply fixture unit
Zi = zinc, galvanized

PLUMBING GLOSSARY

Note: The definitions below do not include the complete text that is found in the codes. Refer to IRC sections 202 and 2403 and UPC Chapter 2 and the referenced standards in Table 1 for complete definitions of these and other terms used throughout this book.

Access (to) That which enables a device, appliance, or equipment to be reached. The necessity to first remove a door, panel, or similar obstruction is allowed, unlike equipment which has ***ready access to***, for which no obstructions are allowed.

Air admittance valve (AAV): F44,45 A normally closed valve that substitutes for a vent and allows air into the drainage system under negative pressure, thereby protecting traps from siphonage.

Air break (drainage): An arrangement where discharge from a fixture, appliance, or device drains indirectly into a receptor and enters below the FLR and above the trap of a receptor, such as a clothes washer standpipe. **F59**

Air gap, drainage: The unobstructed vertical distance **F52** through free atmosphere between a waste pipe outlet and the FLR of the fixture or receptor into which it discharges. Air gap devices **F63** are used for dishwasher drains, reverse osmosis filters, and water softener brine drains.

Air gap, water distribution: F52 The unobstructed vertical distance through free atmosphere between the lowest opening of water supply discharge to the FLR of a plumbing fixture.

Approved: Acceptable to the building official (AHJ). UL and other testing laboratories do not *approve* materials; they test products and determine their conformity to published standards. Only the BO/AHJ can approve them.

Authority Having Jurisdiction (AHJ): An organization responsible for enforcing the code, typically the building department and its authorized representatives.

Backflow: A flow of water or other liquids, mixtures, or substances into the distributing pipes of a potable supply of water from any source other than its intended source.

Backwater valve: F22,23 A device to prevent reverse flow in a drainage system.

Bathroom: In the UPC, a bathroom is a room containing a bathtub, shower, or combination tub and shower. A room containing only a water closet and lavatory is considered a half bathroom.

Branch: Any part of the piping system other than a riser, main, or stack.

Branch interval: A vertical measure of distance, 8 ft. or more, between connections of horizontal branches to a drainage stack. Measurements are taken down the stack from the highest horizontal branch connection.

Branch vent: A vent connecting 2 or more individual vents with a vent stack or stack vent. **F32**

Btu (British thermal unit): The quantity of heat necessary to raise the temperature of 1 lb. of water 1°F (roughly equal to what is given off by one stick match).

Btu/hr.: The maximum capacity of a gas-burning appliance expressed in Btu/hr.

Building drain: The lowest piping that collects discharge from all other drainage piping inside the house. It extends for 30 in. beyond the exterior walls and conveys the drainage to the building sewer.

Building official: The AHJ; an officer or other designated authority charged with administration and enforcement of the code, and its authorized representatives.

Building sewer: The part of the drainage system that extends from the end of the building drain to convey its discharge to a public or private sewer or individual sewage disposal system.

Check valve: A device used to prevent the flow of liquids in a direction not intended in the design of the system. Check valves are not backflow preventers. They are often used in solar water systems and hot water circulation loops.

Cleanout: An access opening in the drainage system utilized for removing obstructions.

Combination waste & vent: A specially designed system of waste piping using the horizontal wet venting of one or more sinks, lavatories, or floor drains by means of a common waste and vent pipe sized to provide free movement of air above the flow line of the drain. **F42**

Common vent (plumbing): A single pipe venting two trap arms within the same branch interval, either back-to-back or one above the other. **F35,36**

Concealed: Rendered inaccessible by the structure or finish of the building.

Continuous waste: A drain from two or more adjacent similar fixtures connected to a single trap. **F25**

Fixture drain: The drain from a trap of a fixture to the connection w/ any other drain pipe. Note: this is not the same as **Trap arm**.

Flood level rim: The top edge of a receptor from which water overflows.

Full-open valve: A valve which in the open position does not restrict the component's flow-through area. **F48,49**

Graywater: Water discharged from lavatories, bathtubs, showers, clothes washers, and laundry trays. Discharge from kitchen sinks is not considered graywater.

Horizontal: Any pipe or fitting that is less than 45° from horizontal.

Horizontal branch, drainage: A drain pipe extending laterally from a soil or waste stack or building drain that receives the discharge from one or more fixture drains.

Joint: Connection between two pipes:

- **Brazed joint:** Joint obtained by joining metal parts with alloys that melt at temperatures > 840°F (449°C) but lower than the melting temperature of the parts to be joined.
- **Expansion joint:** Loop, return bend, or return offset that accommodates pipe expansion and contraction.
- **Flexible joint:** Joint that allows movement of one pipe without deflecting the other pipe.
- **Mechanical joint:** Joint that uses a positive holding mechanism such as flanged, screwed, clamped, or flared connections.
- **Press-connect joint:** Permanent mechanical joint incorporating an elastomeric seal and made with a crimping tool and ring approved by the MFR.
- **Slip joint:** Joint that creates a seal by compressing a washer against the pipe by the tightening of a slip nut.
- **Soldered joint:** Joint obtained by joining of metal parts with metallic mixtures or alloys that melt at a temperature < 800°F (427°C) and > 300°F (149°C).
- **Welded joint or seam:** Joint or seam obtained by the joining of metal parts in the plastic molten state.

Label: An identification applied on a product by the manufacturer that contains the name of the manufacturer, the function and performance characteristics of the product or material, and the name and identification of an approved agency and that indicates that the representative sample of the product or material has been tested and evaluated by an approved agency.

Labeled: Equipment, materials, or products to which have been affixed a label, seal, symbol, or other identifying mark of a nationally recognized testing laboratory, approved agency, or other organization concerned with product evaluation that maintains periodic inspection of the production of such labeled items and whose labeling indicates either that the equipment, material, or product meets identified standards or has been tested and found suitable for a specified purpose.

Liquefied petroleum (LP) gas: LP or propane gas is composed primarily of propane, propylene, butanes, or butylenes or mixtures thereof that are gaseous under normal atmospheric conditions but capable of being liquefied under moderate pressure at normal temperatures. LP gas is typically stored in tanks on site. Unlike natural gas (CH_4), LP gas (C_3H_8) is heavier than air.

Listed: Equipment, materials, products, or services included in a list published by an organization acceptable to the code official and concerned with evaluation of products or services that maintains periodic inspection of production of listed equipment or materials or periodic evaluation of services and whose listing states either that the equipment, material, product, or service meets identified standards or has been tested and found suitable for a specified purpose.

Nationally Recognized Testing Laboratory (NRTL): A testing facility recognized by OSHA as qualified to provide testing and certification of products and services. Examples of NRTLs are CSA, IAPMO, and UL.

Offset: A combination of elbows or bends in a line of piping that brings a section of pipe or a vent out of line, but into a line parallel with the other section.

PEX tubing: Water-supply or hydronic heat tubing made of cross-linked polyethylene. PEX-AL-PEX has a layer of aluminum sandwiched between layers of PEX.

Potable water: Water free from impurities in quantities sufficient to harm people and acceptable to the public health authority having jurisdiction.

Pressure-relief valve (PRV): A device designed to protect against high pressure and to function as a relief mechanism. F75

Ready access to: Access that does not require removing a panel or door. For electrical equipment, this also means not having to resort to use of a ladder.

Slope: The fall (pitch) of a line of pipe in reference to a horizontal plane. In drainage, the slope is expressed as the fall in units vertical per units horizontal (percent) for a length of pipe.

Supports: Devices used to support or secure pipes, fixtures, or equipment.

Trap arm: That portion of a fixture drain between a trap weir and the vent fitting. F26

Vertical: Any pipe or fitting that makes an angle of 45° or more with the horizontal.

Wet vent: A vent that also receives discharge of waste from other fixtures. F37–39

KEY TO USING THIS BOOK

Code Check Plumbing condenses large amounts of code information by using several "shorthand" conventions that are explained here. Each rule described in Code Check begins with a checkbox and ends with code citations. Where there are 2 columns of citations, the first one is from the IRC and the second one from the UPC, as in this example from ***p. 130***:

Inspections **21 IRC** **21 UPC**

☐ All piping tested before casting concrete ____________ 109.1.2 105.1

This section tells us that piping must be tested before being covered by concrete. The IRC code reference is 109.1.2 & the UPC reference 105.1.

References to figures and tables are preceded by an **F** or a **T** as in the following example from ***p. 140***:

☐ Trap seal min. 2 in., max. 4 in. **F24** ________________ 3201.2 1005.1

Figure 24 illustrates an example of this code rule.

Also from ***p. 140***:

☐ Size trap for fixture per **T9** ________________ 3201.7 1003.3

This line directs us to Table 9 for the required size of fixture traps.

If one of the codes prohibits a practice that is allowed by the other code, the prohibition is shown by the universal "no" symbol, as in this example from ***p. 131***:

☐ Min. pipe slope 1/4 in./ft. EXC ________________ 3005.3 708.1

• 1/8 in./ft. OK for 3-in. or larger pipe ____________ 3005.3 Ø

These lines tell us that both codes require drains to slope 1/4 in./ft. and that the IRC allows 1/8 in./ft. for 3-in. & larger pipes. The UPC does not allow this shallower slope for 3-in. pipes.

Code changes are highlighted by showing the code citation in a different color, and by the superscript character that references a further explanation at the bottom of the page, as in this example from ***p. 132***.

☐ Max. 5 WCs on 3-in. horizontal or vertical drain **T10** ________ n/a T703.2[2]

The UPC changed the maximum allowed number of WCs on a 3-in. drain, as explained in the following note that appears at the bottom of that page:

2. Previous UPC edition limited 3-in. pipe to 4 WCs on vertical drain & 3 on horizontal drain.

In situations where there is a commonly accepted practice but no specific rule in one of the model codes, the code citation may simply be "local," as in the following example from ***p. 152***:

☐ Female threaded CPVC fittings w/ male plastic only ______ local 605.2.3

The UPC has a specific rule against using female plastic CPVC fittings with anything other than a male CPVC fitting. While there is no specific IRC rule against doing this, the IRC does provide other recommended means for making such joints, and the item here would likely be enforced locally.

When a code line ends with the letters EXC, it means that an exception follows in the next line, as in this example from ***p. 140***:

☐ Fixture tailpiece max. 24-in. vertical distance EXC **F25** __ 3201.6 1001.2

• CW standpipes 18–42 in. (UPC: 18–30 in.) **F59** ____ 2706.1.2 804.1

This line tells us that the maximum height of a fixture tailpiece (the vertical distance between the fixture outlet and its trap) is 24 inches in both codes. There is an exception for a clothes washer standpipe. Notice also that the maximum height of the standpipe is not the same in the two codes, and the UPC size is shown in parentheses.

An "X" in a code reference stands for the word "exception," as in this example from ***p. 144:***

☐ Increase 1 pipe size if >1/3 of vent is horizontal ____________ n/a 904.2X

This line tells us that the UPC reference is 904.2 Exception.

In a few cases, there are code rules in one of the codes, and the other code has not taken a position on the issue. In these cases, we enter the code reference as "n/a"—meaning not "applicable," as in this example from ***p. 127***:

☐ Min. hanger rod size 3/8 in. ____________________ n/a 313.6

The UPC has specific requirements for the size of piping support rods. While the IRC does not have this rule, an IRC jurisdiction might still consider it to be the minimum size, or they might accept other methods.

Note*: The code numbers in the IRC begin with a letter. In the building section, numbers start with an R. Energy starts with an N, Mechanical an M, Fuel Gas a G, Plumbing a P, and Electrical an E. We omit those letters to save space.*

MATERIALS STANDARDS & PERMITS

Materials or systems that do not conform to the standards (T2) or codes adopted by the local jurisdiction can be considered for approval on a case-by-case basis using the provisions for alternative materials, designs, and methods of construction (AMM). The permit applicant must provide documentation showing the proposed method to be equivalent to the intent of the code. If accepted by the BO, the approval would be limited to the property covered under the application; it does not mean the code is different than written for other properties in that jurisdiction.

Required Permits — 21 IRC — 21 UPC

- ☐ Permits reqd for installation, alteration, repair, replacement, or remodeling of a plumbing system EXC ___ 105.1 — 104.1
  - • Stopping of leaks or clearing of stoppages___________ 105.2 — 104.2
- ☐ If work so exempted results in necessity to replace or rearrange pipes, valves, or fixtures, a permit must be obtained ______ 105.1 — 104.1
- ☐ Exempt work must still be done in accordance with code _ 105.2 — 103.1

Materials

- ☐ Plumbing materials must be listed (3rd party certified) ___ 2609.4 — 301.2
- ☐ Install components in accordance w/ listing and AMI ____ 2609.2 — 309.4
- ☐ Each pipe, fitting, trap, fixture, material & device reqs MFR identification & any markings reqd by applicable standards EXC______ 2609.1 — 301.2.1
  - • Field-cut nipples______________________________ 2609.1 — 301.2.1X
  - • Identification may be on packaging for small fittings _ 2609.1X — n/a
- ☐ Locate so as to prevent contamination in flood zones___ 2601.3 — 301.4

Alternative Materials, Designs & Methods

- ☐ BO has authority to approve AMM if design satisfactory & meets intent of the code & is equivalent in terms of fire resistance, strength, effectiveness, durability, quality & safety _______ 104.11 — 301.3
- ☐ Approved AMM is specific only to project in its scope ___ 104.11 — 301.3
- ☐ When BO does not approve AMM, response must be written & state reason why it was not approved________ 104.11 — n/a

TABLE 2	STANDARDS ORGANIZATIONS
Acronym	**Name**
ANSI	American National Standards Institute
ASME	American Society of Mechanical Engineers
ASSE	American Society of Sanitary Engineering
ASTM	ASTM International (formerly American Society for Testing & Materials)
CSA	CSA Group (Canadian Standards Association)
IAPMO	International Association of Plumbing & Mechanical Officials
NFPA	National Fire Protection Association
ICC	International Code Council
NSF	National Sanitation Foundation
UL	UL (formerly Underwriters Laboratories)

Existing Buildings — 21 IRC — 21 UPC

- ☐ Existing installations that met code of the time of construction allowed to remain if posing no hazard_______ 102.7 — 102.2
- ☐ Additions, alterations & repairs to comply w/ rules for new construction w/o req existing areas to be brought to current code ____ 102.7.1 — 102.4
- ☐ Not OK for additions, alterations & repairs to make existing building less compliant, unsafe, unsanitary, or overloaded _______ 102.7.1 — 102.4
- ☐ Rehabilitation of existing pressure piping systems (epoxy lining) per ASTM F2831 _________________________ n/a — 320.1

INSPECTIONS & TESTING

General

General	21 IRC	21 UPC
☐ No covering or concealing work prior to inspection	109.1.2	105.1
☐ Underground inspection before backfill	109.1.2	105.2
☐ Rough-in prior to covering or concealment	109.1.2	105.2
☐ Final inspection upon completion	109.1.6	105.2

Water Supply

Water Supply	21 IRC	21 UPC
☐ Test all piping before cover, concealment, or use	2503.2	105.2.1.1&2
☐ Water pipe test under working pressure 15 minutes EXC	2503.7	609.4
• 50 psi air for other than plastic pipe	2503.7	609.4
• Air for PEX where specifically AMI & approved	2503.7X	609.4X
☐ Water for testing must be from potable water source	2503.7	609.4
☐ RP devices tested at installation & annually	2503.8.2	603.4.2

DWV Systems

DWV Systems	21 IRC	21 UPC
☐ Rough-in piping to be tested by one of the following:		
• Water test: 10-ft. head for 15 minutes OR	2503.5.1	712.2
• Air test: 5 psi (10 in. mercury column) for 15 minutes (IRC: no pressurized air testing of plastic piping systems)	2503.5.1	712.3
• Vacuum test: Hold negative 5 psi for 15 minutes	2503.5.1[1]	n/a
☐ Building sewer: insert test plug at point of connection w/ public sewer; 10-ft. head for 15 minutes (UPC: or air test)	2503.4	723.1
☐ UPC: No air testing of plastic sewer pipe	n/a	723.1
☐ Finished plumbing: Fill each drain, inspect traps	2503.5.2(1)	712.1

Fixtures

Fixtures	21 IRC	21 UPC
☐ After fixtures set, fill traps & prove gastight or watertight	2503.2	712.1
☐ Water test: Fill each fixture, drain & visually inspect	2503.2(1)	712.1
☐ Gas test w/ smoke: Introduce pungent smoke into system, cap vent terminals after smoke appears, pressurize system 1-in. water column for 15 minutes	2503.2(2.1)	local
☐ Gas test w/ peppermint oil: Introduce 2 oz. oil, 10 quarts hot water, seal vent terminals, check for odor at traps	2503.2(2.2)	local

1. Vacuum test is new in this edition.

Shower Liner

Shower Liner	21 IRC	21 UPC
☐ Fill receptor area min. 2 in. measured at threshold UPC: Fill to top of threshold	2503.6	408.7.5
☐ If no threshold (curbless), build temporary threshold	2503.6	local
☐ Plug pipe w/ test balloon below weep holes	2503.6	408.7.5
☐ Must hold water min. 15 minutes w/ no leakage	2503.6	local

Water Test Gauges

Water Test Gauges	21 IRC	21 UPC
☐ Test gauges reqd to have increments of:	2503.9	318.1
• 0.1 psi up to test pressure of 10 psi	2503.9	318.2
• 1 psi up to test pressure of 100 psi	2503.9	318.3
• 2 psi where test pressure is greater than 100 psi	2503.9	318.4
• UPC: Gauge range max. 2× applied test pressure	n/a	318.5

Gas

Gas	21 IRC	21 UPC
☐ All piping installations to be pressure tested EXC	2417.1	1213.1
• Minor repairs & additions & new branches can be tested w/ non-corrosive leak-detecting fluid or other methods	2417.1.2&3	1213.1.2
☐ Test medium air, nitrogen, or CO2 (not oxygen)	2417.2	1213.3
☐ Leave all joints exposed until tested	2417.3	1213.2.1
☐ IRC: Test min. 1½ × working pressure, min. 3 psig	2417.4.1	n/a
☐ IRC: Test duration min. 10 minutes	2417.4.2	n/a
☐ UPC: Test pressure min. 10 psig (MP CSST: min. 30 psig)	n/a	1213.3
☐ UPC: Test time min. 15 minutes (MP CSST: min. 30 min.)	n/a	1213.3
☐ Range of test gauge scale ≤ 5× (UPC: ≤ 2×) test pressure	2417.4	318.5
☐ If existing appliances not rated for test pressure, isolate by disconnecting & capping their outlets	2417.3.3	1213.2.4
☐ If existing appliances rated for test pressure, isolation by closing their valves OK	2417.3.4	1213.2.5
☐ Use approved non-corrosive leak-detecting fluid or gas detector for locating leaks	2417.5.1	1213.4.1
☐ Matches, open flames not OK for locating leaks	2417.5.1	1213.4.1
☐ Inspect for open fittings or valves before turning on gas	2417.6.2	1213.5.1
☐ Check for leakage immediately after turning on gas	2417.6.3	1213.5.2

PIPE SUPPORT & PROTECTION

Pipe Support

	21 IRC	21 UPC
☐ Hangers must ensure alignment, prevent sagging & allow for expansion (no wires or metal straps contacting plastic pipe) **F1**	2605.1	313.2&4
☐ Isolate dissimilar materials, e.g., Zi hangers & Cu pipe	2605.1	313.2
☐ Max. support intervals for water & DWV piping **T3,4**	2605.1	313.3
☐ Min. hanger rod size ⅜ in.	n/a	313.6
☐ Gas pipe support per **T36**	2424.1	313.7

Freezing Protection

☐ Pipes subject to freezing req protection (insulation or heat), e.g., outside buildings, attics, crawlspaces, or exterior walls	2603.5	312.6
☐ Applies to water, soil & waste pipes	2603.5 & 3001.2	312.6

TABLE 3 UPC WATER PIPE HANGER MAX. SPACING ◆ T313.3

Material	Horizontal	Vertical
Schedule 40 PVC & ABS DWV	4 ft.[A]; allow for expansion every 30 ft.	Base & each floor[B]; allow for expansion every 30 ft.
Zi steel	10 ft. if ≤¾ in. diameter, 12 ft. if ≥1 in.	Every other floor, max. 25 ft.
CI lead & oakum	5 ft. (10 ft. if 10-ft. lengths used)[A,C,D]	Base & each floor, max. 15 ft.
CI hubless	Every other joint. If joints > 4 ft. apart, support each joint[A,C,D]	Base & each floor, max. 15 ft.
Cu tubing	6 ft. if ≤1½ in. diameter, 10 ft. if ≥2 in.	Each floor, max. 10 ft.
PVC water distribution[E]	4 ft.[A]; allow for expansion every 30 ft.	Base & each floor[B]; allow for expansion every 30 ft.
CPVC	3 ft. for ≤ 1 in. diameter, 4 ft. if ≥1¼ in.	Base & each floor[B]
PEX	32 in. if ≤1in. diameter, 4 ft. if ≥1¼ in.	Base & each floor[B]
PEX-AL-PEX	98 in.[F]	Base & each floor[B]

A. Support at each horizontal branch connection.
B. Provide mid-story guides.
C. Supports to be within 18 in. of joint. Hangers not to be placed directly on couplings.
D. Brace at max. 40-ft. intervals to prevent horizontal movement.
E. Not allowed for water distribution pipe downstream of water service; OK for condensate drain.
F. MFRs req closer support spacing.

FIG. 1 ABS/PVC Support & Spacing

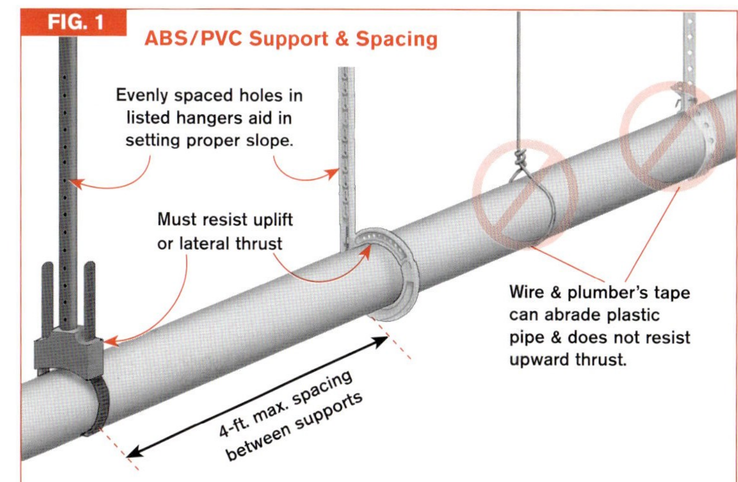

TABLE 4 IRC WATER PIPE HANGER MAX. SPACING ◆ T2605.1

Pipe Material	Horizontal	Vertical
ABS/PVC DWV	4 ft.	10 ft.[A]
Zi steel	12 ft.	15 ft.
CI	5 ft. (10 ft. OK for 10-ft. lengths of pipe)	15 ft.
Cu tubing	6 ft. if ≤ 1¼ in. diameter, 10 ft. if ≥1½ in.	10 ft.
PB	32 in.	4 ft.
PVC[B]	4 ft.	10 ft.[A]
CPVC	3 ft. for ≤1 in. diameter, 4 ft. if ≥1¼ in.	10 ft.[A]
PEX	32 in. if ≤1in. diameter, 4 ft. if ≥1¼ in.	10 ft.[A]
PEX-AL-PEX	32 in.	4 ft.[A]

A. Provide mid-story guides for pipes ≤ 2 in. diameter.
B. Not allowed for water distribution pipe downstream of water service; OK for condensate drain.

Framing & Pipe Protection	21 IRC	21 UPC
☐ Walls, ceilings, etc., to be left in safe structural condition	2603.1	312.11
☐ Drilling & notching per **F2,3** & **T5,6**	2603.2	312.11
☐ Steel-plate protection for other than CI or Zi steel in notches or holes < 1¼ in. to face of framing (UPC: ≤ 1 in.) **F4**	2603.2.1	312.9
☐ Extend plates min. 2 in. above & below sole & top plates	2603.2.1	n/a
☐ Protection min. 1½ in. beyond outside diameter of pipe **F4**	n/a	312.9
☐ Protective plates min. 16 gauge (UPC: 18 gauge)	2603.2.1	312.9

FIG. 2

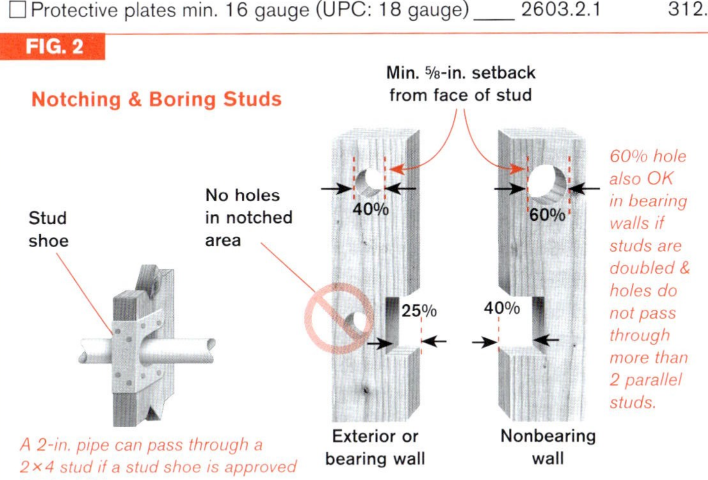

A 2-in. pipe can pass through a 2×4 stud if a stud shoe is approved by the AHJ.

TABLE 5 — MAX. NOTCHES & BORED HOLES IN STUDS ◆ 602.6

Wall Type	Exterior or Bearing Wall		Nonbearing Walls		
	2×4[A]	2×6[A]	2×3[A]	2×4[A]	2×6[A]
Notches	⅞ in.	1⅜ in.	1 in.	1⅜ in.	2³⁄₁₆ in.
Holes[B]	1⅜ in.	2³⁄₁₆ in.	1½ in.	2⅛ in.	3¼ in.

A. Nominal sizes: table numbers based on actual dimensions actual sizes (½ in. less each dimension).
B. Holes min. ⅝ in. from edge of stud.

FIG. 3

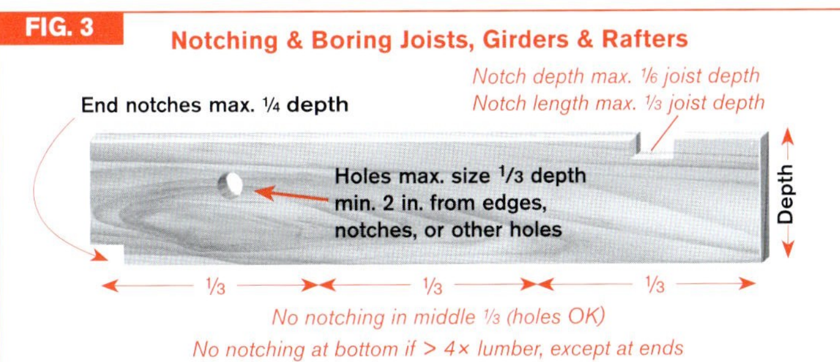

TABLE 6 — NOTCHING & BORING JOISTS ◆ 502.8.1

Nominal[A] Dimension Joist or Girder	Max. Diameter Bored Hole	Max. Notch Length	Max. Notch Depth Outer ⅓	Max. Depth End Notch
6	1½ in.	1¹³⁄₁₆ in.	⅞ in.	1⅜ in.
8	2⅜ in.	2⅜ in.	1³⁄₁₆ in.	1¹³⁄₁₆ in.
10	3¹⁄₁₆ in.	3¹⁄₁₆ in.	1½ in.	2⁵⁄₁₆ in.
12	3¾ in.	3¾ in.	1⅞ in.	2¹³⁄₁₆ in.

A. Table numbers based on actual dimensions: typically 5½, 7¼, 9¼ & 11¼.

FIG. 4

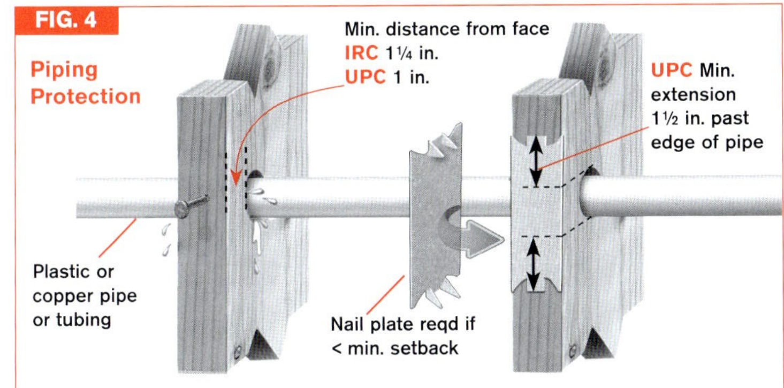

UNDERGROUND INSTALLATION

Pipes in soil must be supported for their entire length. This is especially important for drain and sewer piping to prevent sags that could cause effluent to be trapped and lead to blockage. Smooth, self-compacting backfill such as sand or pea gravel is typically used to achieve this. Pipes must be protected from sharp rocks or other debris in both the bedding and backfill. Piping encased in or passing through concrete requires protection and must not be subjected to structural loads.

Trenching & Backfilling	21 IRC	21 UPC
☐ Pipes in trench req smooth continuous bearing support	2604.1	313.5
☐ Pipe supported on firm bed, no contact w/sharp objects	2604.1	314.4
☐ No rocks or debris in first 12 in. of backfill over pipe	2604.3	314.4
☐ Backfill in thin layers (max. 6 in.) & tamp in place	2604.3	314.4
☐ No backhoe or grader until 12 in. of tamped earth **F5**	2604.3	314.4
☐ Parallel trenches not under footings (within 45°) **F6**	2604.4	314.1
☐ Water service min. 12 in. below finished grade **F9**	2603.5	609.1
☐ Plastic underground water service req #14 blue-insulated tracer wire terminating above ground at each end	n/a	604.10.1
☐ Water pipe min. 6 in. (UPC: 12 in.) below frost line	2603.5	609.1
☐ Building sewer depth per BO & utility (UPC: min. 1 ft.)	2603.5.1	718.3
☐ Plastic drain pipe trench width = pipe O.D. + 16 in. **F5**	n/a	314.4.1

FIG. 5 Plastic Pipes in Trench

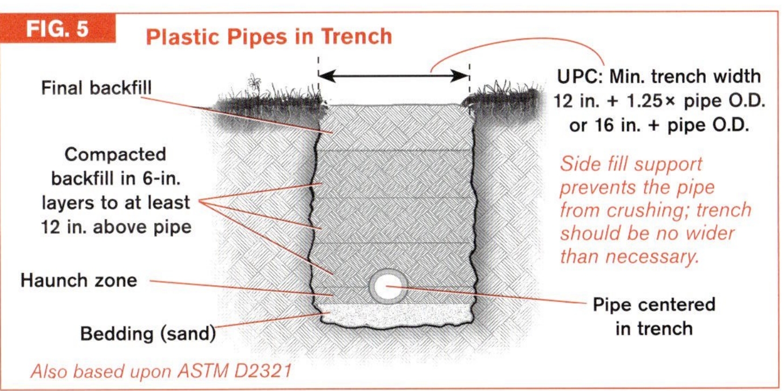

Also based upon ASTM D2321

FIG. 6 Pipes Parallel to Footings

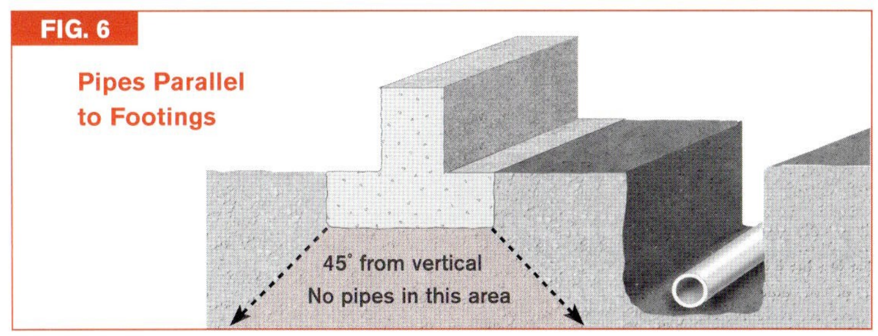

Piping in Concrete or Masonry	21 IRC	21 UPC
☐ No piping directly embedded in concrete or masonry	n/a	312.2
☐ Piping embedded in corrosive soil reqs protective sheath	2603.3	n/a
☐ Sheath min. 8-mil plastic & allow for movement	2603.3	n/a
☐ Sleeve reqd to prevent structural load on pipes through foundation walls or under footings EXC **F7**	2603.4	312.10.1
• Not reqd for bored or drilled openings	n/a	312.10X
☐ Sleeve min. 2 sizes > pipe through foundation **F7**	2603.4	n/a
☐ Seal annular spaces between pipes & sleeves **F7**	2606.1	312.10.2

FIG. 7 Pipes through Foundation Wall

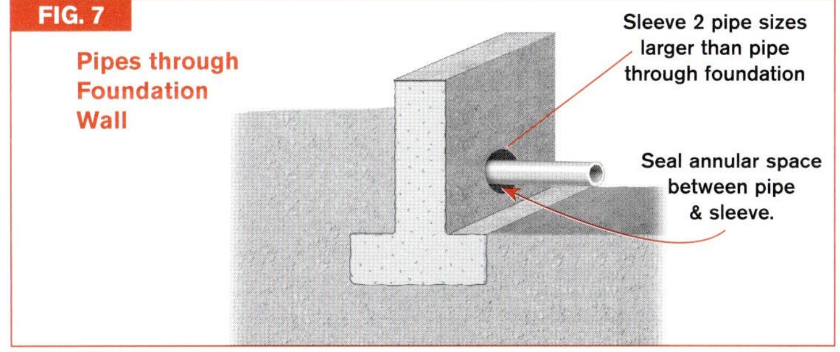

Piping in Common Trench	21 IRC	21 UPC
☐ Water & sewer OK in same trench if sewer material is a type approved for use inside the building **F8** ________	2906.4.1	609.2
☐ Water & sewer pipes separated min. 5 ft. if sewer materials not approved for use within the building **F8** EXC ________	2906.4.1	local
• Water pipe min. 12 in. above perpendicular sewer _	2906.4.1	609.2
• Water pipe <12 in. above perpendicular sewer & sleeved min. 5 ft. each direction over sewer pipe crossing __	2906.4.1	local
• Water min. 12 in. above parallel sewer pipe **F9** ____	2906.4.1	609.2
• UPC: On shelf providing 12-in. horizontal separation _____	n/a	609.2

FIG. 8 Separate & Common Trenches

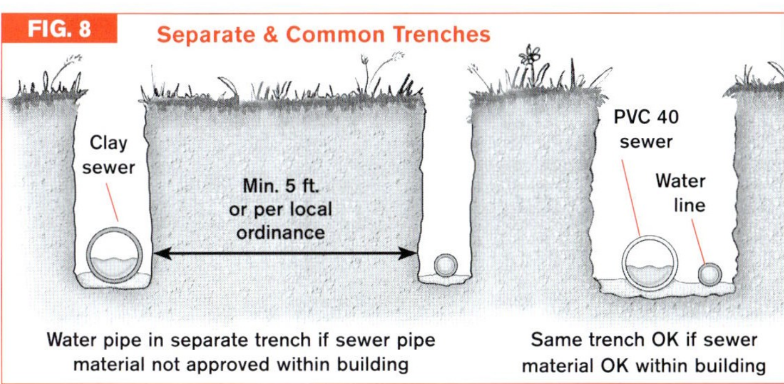

FIG. 9 Water & Sewer Separation

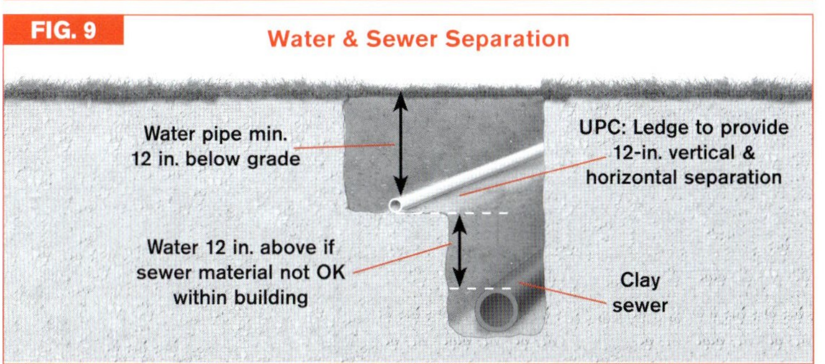

Building Drain & Building Sewer	21 IRC	21 UPC
☐ Building drain = lowest piping carrying all drains in building to the building sewer ____________________	202	204.0
☐ IRC: Building sewer begins min. 30 in. beyond exterior walls	202	n/a
☐ UPC: Building sewer begins min. 2 ft. outside building wall _	n/a	204.0
☐ CO reqd at junction of building drain/sewer or in building drain upstream of junction (IRC: within 10 ft.) EXC **F10** ____	3005.2.3	719.1
• Not reqd if sewer <10 ft. & straight line from building drain	n/a	719.2
☐ Additional building drain COs at max. 100-ft. intervals _	3005.2.1	707.4
☐ Additional sewer cleanouts at max. 100-ft. intervals ________	n/a	719.1

FIG. 10 2-Way Cleanout

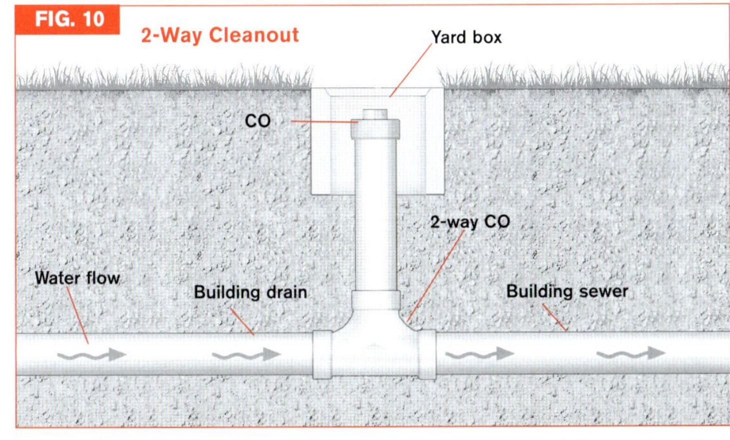

Piping Under Concrete Slabs	21 IRC	21 UPC
☐ Galvanized piping not permitted ____________________	3002.1	609.3(1)
☐ Cu pipe to be installed w/o joints where possible __________	n/a	609.3(2)
☐ Cu pipe joints brazed not soldered ____________________	n/a	609.3(2)
☐ All piping tested before casting concrete ______________	109.1.2	105.1

DRAINAGE

Older DWV systems were typically made with galvanized or cast-iron (CI) pipe. Galvanized pipe (only above ground) threaded into iron "Durham" fittings with expanded hubs to maintain a smooth interior water flow. Cast-iron to cast-iron fittings had expanded hubs, which were joined with oakum and lead. Plastic & no-hub cast iron are now more common. Because of the sound-dampening properties of cast iron, it is sometimes referred to as quiet pipe.

General

	21 IRC	21 UPC
☐ Materials per **T7** & applicable standards	3002.1&2	T701.2
☐ Min. pipe slope ¼ in./ft. EXC	3005.3	708.1
• ⅛ in./ft. OK for 3-in. or larger pipe	3005.3	Ø
• ⅛ in./ft. OK for ≥4-in. pipe where necessary if OK by AHJ	n/a	708.1
☐ No drilled or tapped connections (e.g., saddle fitting)	3003.2	310.2
☐ Joints between different materials req mechanical joints either compression or self-sealing type installed AMI	3003.13	705.1&2
☐ CI couplings req metallic shield & center stop **F12**	3003.4.3	705.2.2
☐ ABS & PVC not directly glued together EXC	3003.2 #5	705.1&5
• Transition of building drain to building sewer OK w/ listed transition solvent cement per ASTM D3138	3003.13.4	705.9.4
☐ No reduction in direction of flow EXC **F11,13**	3002.3.1	315.2
• 4-in. × 3-in. water closet bend OK **F11**	3005.1.6	310.5
☐ ABS & PVC prohibited in residential >2 stories	n/a	California

FIG. 11 Closet Bend Reductions

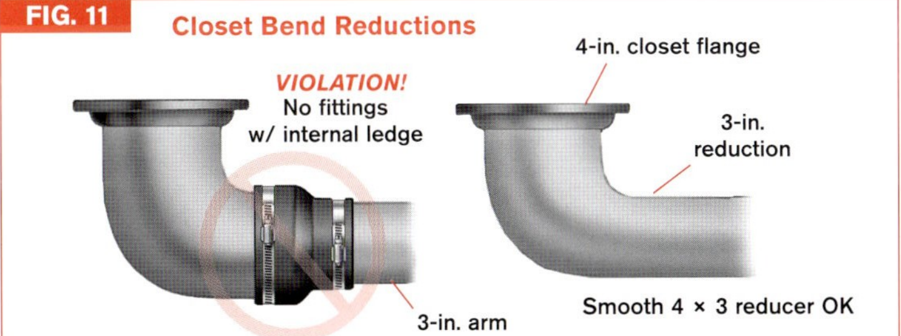

TABLE 7 DWV MATERIALS ◆ IRC T3002.1 & 2 & UPC T701.2

Material	IRC Above Ground	IRC Below Ground	IRC Building Sewer	UPC Above Ground	UPC Below Ground	UPC Building Sewer
ABS schedule 40	✔	✔	✔	✔	✔	✔
ABS DR 22 & DR 24	✔	✔	✔	Ø	Ø	Ø
ABS/PVC SDR 35[A] (UPC: PVC Sewer & Drain)	Ø	Ø	✔	Ø	Ø	✔
Cast iron	✔	✔	✔	✔	✔	✔
Cu tubing DWV	✔	✔	Ø	✔	✔	✔
Cu tubing K or L	✔	✔	✔	✔[B]	✔[B]	✔[B]
Cu tubing M	✔	✔	Ø	✔[B]	✔[B]	✔[B]
Galvanized steel[C]	✔	Ø	Ø	✔	Ø	Ø
PVC schedule 40	✔	✔	✔	✔	✔	✔
PVC DR 22 & DR 24	✔	✔	✔	Ø	Ø	Ø
PVC 3.25 in. O.D.	✔	✔	✔	Ø	Ø	Ø
Vitrified clay	Ø	Ø	✔	Ø	Ø	✔

A. The IRC also accepts ABS SDR 42 & PVC SDR 26 & 41 for building sewers.
B. UPC 701.2(4) allows Cu alloy tubing thicker than type DWV, even though not stated in T701.2.
C. Min. 6 in. above soil (UPC).

FIG. 12 No-Hub Cast Iron

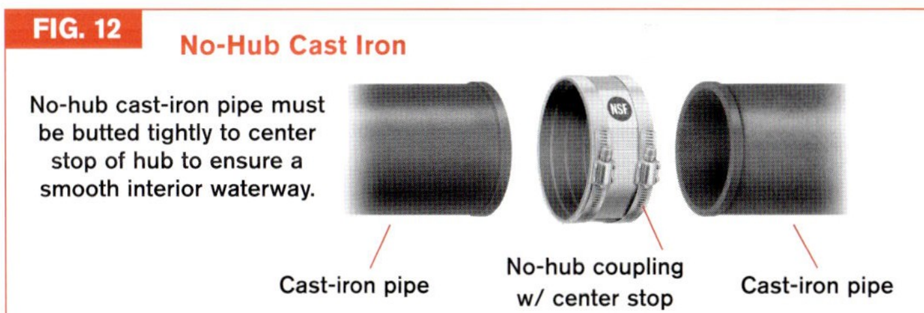

*Drain, waste, and vent (DWV) pipe sizes are determined by the number of drainage fixture units (DFUs) that each pipe carries. Begin by drawing an isometric diagram of all the fixtures and assign each the appropriate number of drainage fixture units from **T9**. Starting at the highest point of the system and working down to the building drain, size each pipe per **T10** or **T11** for the number of DFUs. In the IRC, kitchen, bath, and laundry groups can be sized using **T8**, which allows a smaller number of DFUs than would be calculated if each individual fixture drain were assigned values from **T9**. UPC Appendix C (Alternate Plumbing Systems) provides a similar system. This appendix is not a regular part of the code and its use requires approval by the AHJ. It is most commonly used in multifamily dwellings.*

Drain Pipe Size

	21 IRC	21 UPC
☐ Size traps & arms per DFU loads **T9** ______	T3004.1 & T3201.7	T702.1
☐ Kitchen, bath & laundry group DFUs can be per **T8** ____	T3004.1	Appendix C
☐ Stacks & horizontal branches per DFU loads **T10** _____	3005.4.1	703.1&2
☐ Building drain & horizontal branches directly connected to building drain allowed to be sized per **T11** _________	3005.4.2	n/a
☐ Max. 5 WCs on 3-in. horizontal or vertical drain **T10** ________	n/a	T703.2[2]
☐ Horizontal branches not to connect within 10 pipe diameters downstream of stack base or horizontal offset __________	3005.5	n/a

TABLE 8 — KITCHEN, LAUNDRY & BATH GROUP DFUs IRC T3004.1 & UPC APPENDIX C T303.3

Group	Description	IRC	UPC[A]
Kitchen	Separate DW & sink	2	n/a
Laundry	CW standpipe + laundry tray	3	n/a
Half bath	1.6 GPF WC + lav	4[B]	3
Full bath	≤1.6 GPF WC, lav, tub w/ or w/o shower	5	5
Full bath	>1.6 GPF WC, lav, tub w/ or w/o shower	6	5½[C]
Multiple bath groups	1 full bath + 1 half bath	7[D]	6[D]

A. Reqs adoption of Appendix C or permission of AHJ.
B. Add 1 DFU if WC is >1.6 gal. per flush.
C. Number entered for UPC is for 1.6 GPF pressure-tank WCs.
D. For each additional bath beyond 1½ baths, add 1 DFU per half bath, 2 DFUs per full bath.

2. Previous UPC edition limited 3-in. pipe to 4 WCs on vertical drain & 3 on horizontal drain.

TABLE 9 — DFUs & TRAP SIZE ◆ IRC T3004.1 & T3201.7 UPC T702.1

Fixture	IRC		UPC	
	DFUs	Trap & trap arm size (in.)	DFUs	Trap & trap arm size (in.)
Bar sink	1	1¼	1	1½
Bathtub (w/ or w/o shower)	2	1½	2	1½
Bidet	1	1¼	1	1¼
Bidet (1½-in. outlet)	1	1½	2	1½
Clothes washer (CW standpipe)	2	2	3	2
Dishwasher (independent drain)	2	1½	2	1½[A]
Floor drain	0	2	0	2
Drinking fountain			0.5	1¼
Kitchen sink (KS)	2[B]	1½	2	1½[A]
(Laundry tray) LT	2	1½	2	1½
Lavatory	1	1¼	1	1¼
Lavatories in sets[C]	2	1½	2	1½
Shower stall	2	1½[D]	2	2[E]
Water closet (toilet) ≤ 1.6 GPF	3	n/a	3	3
Water closet (toilet) > 1.6 GPF	4	n/a	4	3

A. UPC: Min. 2-in. drain.
B. W/ or w/o DW or food waste grinder.
C. Example would be 2 lavs on one trap.
D. Up to 5.7 gpm; larger traps reqd for greater flow rates.
E. For a bathtub to shower retrofit, 1½-in. trap & arm permitted for showers ≤ 36 × 60 in.[3]

3. New in this code edition: allows for simpler process in retrofits of tubs to showers & contradicts the requirement that the shower waste outlet be a min. 2-in. diameter. See *p. 162*

TABLE 10	BRANCH DRAINS & STACKS MAX. DFUS IRC T3005.4.1 & UPC T703.2						
Pipe Size		1¼ in.	1½ in.	2 in.	2½ in.	3 in.	4 in.
IRC DFUs	Vertical	1	4	10	20	48	240
	Horizontal	1[A]	3	6	12	20	160
UPC DFUs	Vertical	1	2	16	–	48[B]	256
	Horizontal	1	1	8	–	35[B]	216[C]

A. Limited to a single fixture drain.
B. Max. 5 WCs on 3-in. vertical or horizontal drain.[2]
C. Based on ¼-in./ft. slope. If ⅛-in./ft. slope, multiply allowable DFUs by a factor of 0.8.

In the IRC, building drain branches are the horizontal pipes that connect directly to the building drain. They can carry drainage from multiple branch drains that are less likely to all be used at the same time. Therefore, the IRC allows such drains, and the building drain and building sewer, a larger number of DFUs than for the upstream branch drains of the same pipe size. The UPC does not have such a rule. Pipe size reductions would require an engineered design approved by the AHJ.

TABLE 11	IRC MAX. DFUs ON BUILDING DRAIN, BUILDING DRAIN BRANCHES & BUILDING SEWER ◆ IRC T3005.4.2		
Pipe Size (in.)	Slope (in. per ft.)		
	⅛	¼	½
1½[A,B]	n/a	Note A	Note A
2[B]	n/a	21	27
2½[B]	n/a	24	31
3	36	42	50
4	180	216	250

A. 1½-in. horizontal branches to building drains limited to 1 pumped fixture (included food waste grinder) or 2 nonpumped fixtures.
B. Drains <3 in. may not receive discharge from water closets.

2. Previous UPC edition limited 3-in. pipe to 4 WCs on vertical drain & 3 on horizontal drain.

FIG. 13 Durham Systems

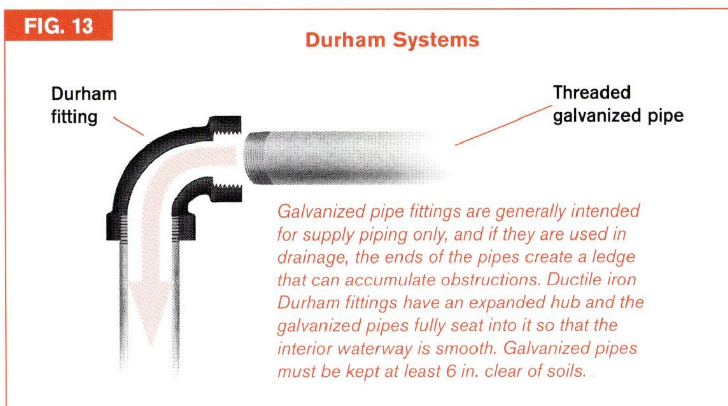

Galvanized pipe fittings are generally intended for supply piping only, and if they are used in drainage, the ends of the pipes create a ledge that can accumulate obstructions. Ductile iron Durham fittings have an expanded hub and the galvanized pipes fully seat into it so that the interior waterway is smooth. Galvanized pipes must be kept at least 6 in. clear of soils.

Durham systems were common in the days before plastic piping. They included threaded cast-iron fittings with expanded hubs and sections of galvanized pipe. Durham systems have a smooth interior waterway, whereas threaded water supply fittings have an internal ledge and are not suitable for drainage. Durham systems are seldomly used in new construction, having been replaced by no-hub cast-iron, which has the advantage of being quieter than plastics.

Older plumbing systems used lead, cast-iron, and galvanized steel for potable water delivery, and terra-cotta or asbestos-cement for building sewers. In some parts of the country, bituminous fiber pipe was used for building sewers. Cast-iron piping, though somewhat protected by surface coatings, is vulnerable to corrosion on both interior and exterior surfaces. Hydrogen sulfide in sewer gas can also deteriorate the pipe. Iron pipe today (since the 1980s) is a superior ductile iron with protective coatings.

Plastic pipes for drain, waste, and vent (DWV) provide a smooth impervious interior waterway and resistance to corrosion, providing a longer expected life than older iron and steel systems. One concern with plastics is flame spread and smoke development when exposed to a building fire. In certain types of construction, the use of plastic pipe requires flame spread and smoke development testing to meet recognized test methods. Fire-stopping requirements also apply. Certain jurisdictions restrict the use of plastic piping to buildings of a certain type or height. Check with your local building department to learn which rules apply in your area.

Flow in vertical piping is faster than flow in horizontal piping. The type of fitting for each change of direction relies on that principle. The transition from vertical to horizontal is from fast-moving to slow-moving, and therefore fittings with greater sweep are required. Horizontal-to-vertical transitions are from slow-moving to fast-moving and do not require as gradual a bend, so sanitary tees are allowed. The transition from horizontal to horizontal tends to decrease velocity and requires sweep similar to that for vertical to horizontal.

Fittings & Changes of Direction — 21 IRC — 21 UPC

*See **page 142** for fittings used with fixture drains.*

	21 IRC	21 UPC
☐ Changes in direction req appropriate fittings **F14–17,T12**	3005.1	706.1
☐ Sanitary tee horizontal to vertical only, not on "back" **F15**	3005.1	706.2
☐ Heel-inlet quarter bends not to serve WC **F14**	3005.1.2	n/a
☐ Heel-inlets OK as dry vents when in vertical position **F14**	3005.1.3	706.2

FIG. 14 DWV Fittings

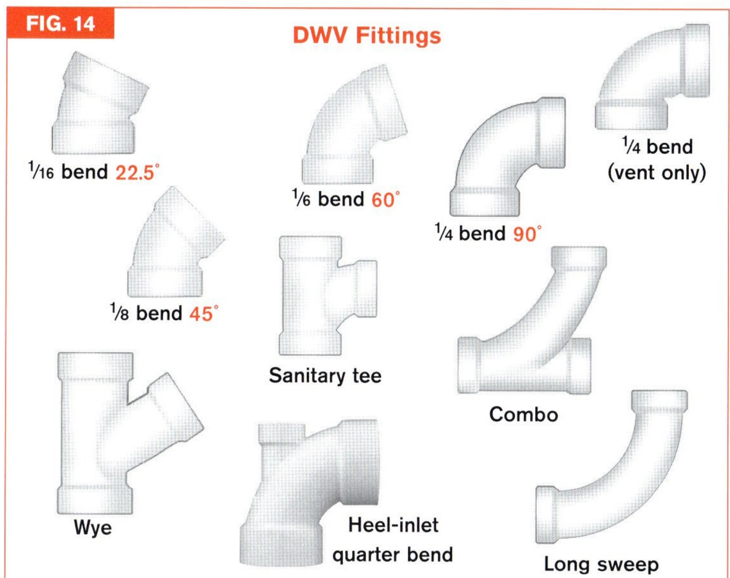

TABLE 12 APPLICATION OF FITTINGS ◆ IRC T3005.1 & UPC 706

Fitting	Horizontal to Vertical	Vertical to Horizontal	Horizontal to Horizontal
1/16 bend (22.5°)	✔	✔	✔
1/8 bend (45°)	✔	✔	✔
1/6 bend (60°)	✔	IRC ✔ UPC[A]	IRC ✔ • UPC Ø
1/4 bend	✔	IRC[B]	IRC[B] • UPC Ø
Short sweep (hubless CI)	✔	✔[B,C]	IRC[B] • UPC ✔
Long sweep	✔	✔	✔
Sanitary tee[D]	✔	Ø	Ø
Wye	✔	✔	✔
Combo wye & 1/8 bend	✔	✔	✔

A. Branches or offsets permitted if installed in a true vertical position.
B. Allowed for IRC fixture drain ≤2 in. diameter. **F17**
C. 3 in. & larger diameter.
D. See **F15** & comments.

FIG. 15 Sanitary Tees

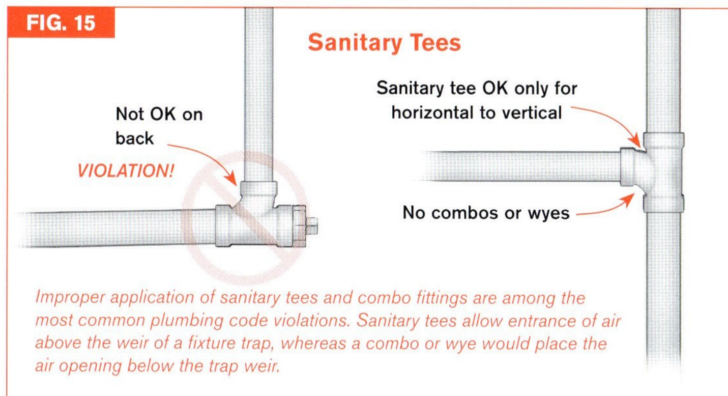

Improper application of sanitary tees and combo fittings are among the most common plumbing code violations. Sanitary tees allow entrance of air above the weir of a fixture trap, whereas a combo or wye would place the air opening below the trap weir.

Back-to-Back Horizontal-to-Vertical Fittings	**21 IRC**	**21 UPC**
☐ Permitted if constructed so one inlet does not readily discharge into opposing inlet **F16** ___________	3005.1.1	706.2
☐ Permitted only if opposing connections same size & from similar fixtures or fixture groups _________	3005.1.1	n/a
☐ Double sanitary tee barrel min. 2 sizes larger than inlets **F16**	n/a	706.2
☐ Double sanitary tee may not receive discharge of back-to-back WCs or pumped fixtures EXC ________	3005.1.1	n/a
• Horizontal developed length of fixture drains ≥18 in.	3005.1.1X	n/a

FIG. 16

Drains Entering at Same Level

Back-to-back fitting

Double san tee

A back-to-back fixture fitting should be used for fixture drains or trap arms entering at the same level. The IRC allows a double sanitary tee to be used for this purpose where the inlets serve similar fixtures and both drains are the same size. The UPC allows it only for drains entering at the same level and into a barrel that is a min.. of two pipe sizes larger than the inlets, thereby reducing the chance that horizontal flow from one fixture would cross over to the inlet of the opposing fixture.

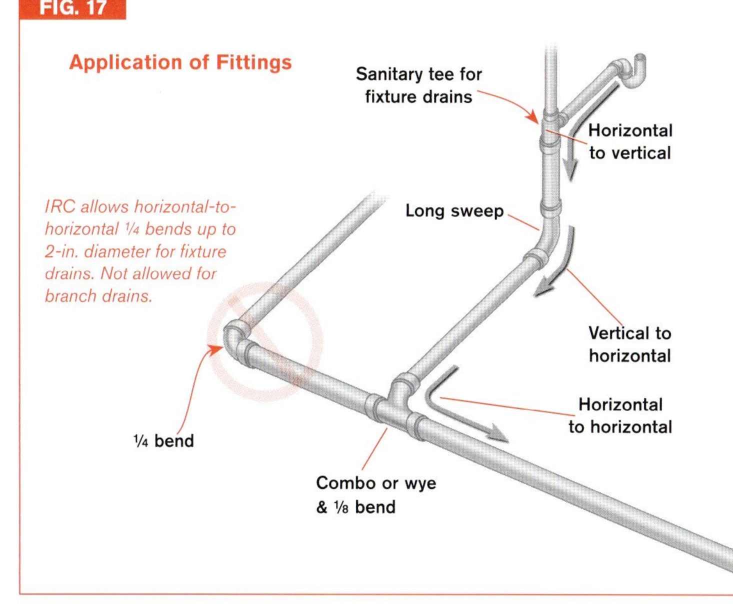

FIG. 17

Application of Fittings

IRC allows horizontal-to-horizontal ¼ bends up to 2-in. diameter for fixture drains. Not allowed for branch drains.

CLEANOUTS

Cleanouts are necessary for clearing drain obstructions and for inspecting the building sewer with a sewer camera. Cleanouts must be accessible, and each code places restrictions and limitations on their location in crawlspaces.

IRC Cleanout Requirements — 21 IRC

- ☐ Reqd in horizontal drains each change of direction >45° **F19** EXC ___ 3005.2.4
  - First CO may serve first 40 ft. downstream w/ other changes **F19** 3005.2.4
  - Not reqd for horizontal fixture drain w/ nonremovable trap for the section of piping between trap & its vent connection ___ 3005.2.1X
- ☐ Horizontal drains & building drains max. cleanout interval 100 ft. ___ 3005.2.1
- ☐ Building sewers <8-in. max. cleanout interval 100 ft. ___ 3005.2.2
- ☐ CO reqd at (or within 10 ft. developed length upstream of) junction of building drain & building sewer. **F10** ___ 3005.2.3
- ☐ CO plugs req raised or countersunk sq. head or countersunk slot _ 3005.2.6
- ☐ CO same size same as drain pipes EXC ___ 3005.2.5
  - 4-in. CO OK for piping >4 in. ___ 3005.2.5X
  - Removable trap OK 1 size smaller than drain (e.g., kitchen) ___ 3005.2.5X1
  - CO in stacks OK 1 size smaller than stack ___ 3005.2.5X2
- ☐ CO in crawlspace reqs travel path min. 24 in. high ___ 3005.2.10
- ☐ COs below grade must be extended to grade level **F10** ___ 3005.2.10
- ☐ Install COs to allow cleaning in direction of flow ___ 3005.2.8
- ☐ Removal of WC or a fixture trap OK as reqd CO EXC ___ 3005.2.10.1[4]
  - CO for building sewer not to depend on removal of WC ___ 3005.2.3
- ☐ Pipes ≤6 in. diameter req 18-in. clearance opposite CO ___ 3005.2.9
- ☐ Not OK to obstruct CO w/ permanent finishes, etc. ___ 3005.2.9
- ☐ CO openings not OK for new fixtures w/o new CO installed **F20** _ 3005.2.11

4. Explicitly allows something that has long been part of standard plumbing practice.

UPC Cleanout Requirements — 21 UPC

- ☐ COs reqd to be watertight & gastight ___ 707.3
- ☐ COs & plugs per approved standards ___ 707.2
- ☐ CO plugs req raised square heads or countersunk rectangular slots ___ 707.1
- ☐ CO plug sizes per **T13** ___ 707.1
- ☐ Reqd at upper terminal of all horizontal runs **F18** EXC ___ 707.4
  - Horizontal runs <5 ft. (unless serving sinks or urinals) ___ 707.4X1
  - Horizontal pipes ≤72° from vertical (1/5 bend) ___ 707.4X2
  - Pipes (other than building drain) above lowest floor of building ___ 707.4X3
  - No upper terminal CO reqd if 2-way CO at junction of building drain and building sewer **F10,18** ___ 707.4X4
- ☐ Reqd every 100-ft. length or fraction of developed length ___ 707.4
- ☐ Reqd for runs w/ aggregate change of direction >135° **F19** ___ 707.4
- ☐ Trap arm bends <90° do not req CO ___ 707.14
- ☐ Takeoff above flow line unless wye branch or end of line **F20** ___ 707.5
- ☐ Clearance in front of CO min. 24 in. exc ≤ 2-in. pipe 18 in. OK ___ 707.9
- ☐ Underfloor CO must extend above finished floor or outside building if >5 ft. from crawlspace access door or if <18-in. vertical clearance or if passageway to CO <30 in. wide ___ 707.9
- ☐ COs must terminate above grade & be readily accessible or under approved cover plate ___ 707.8

TABLE 13 — UPC CLEANOUT PLUGS ◆ T707.1

Pipe Size (in.)	Cleanout Size (in.)	Pipe Size (in.)	Cleanout Size (in.)
1½	1½	3	2½
2	1½	4	3½
2½	2½	>4	3½

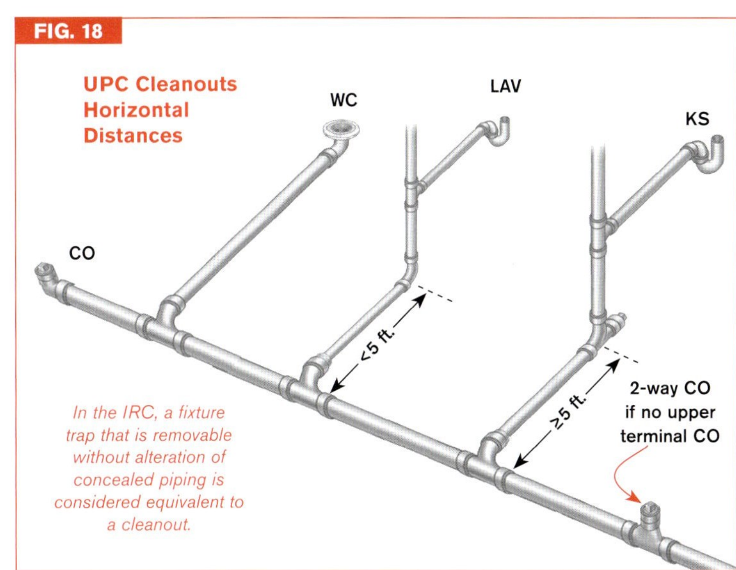
FIG. 18
UPC Cleanouts Horizontal Distances
WC
LAV
KS
CO
<5 ft.
≥5 ft.
2-way CO if no upper terminal CO
In the IRC, a fixture trap that is removable without alteration of concealed piping is considered equivalent to a cleanout.

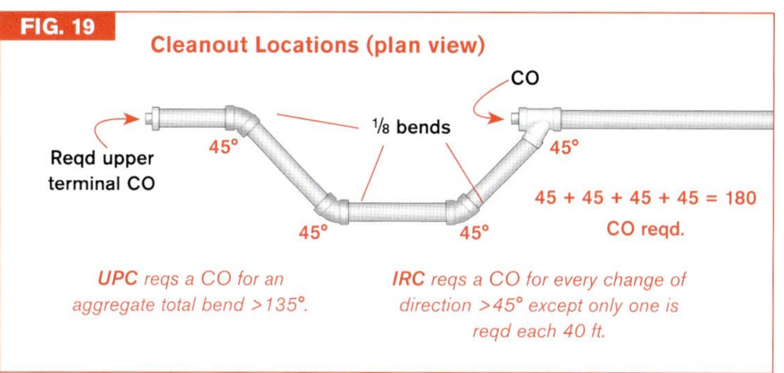
FIG. 19
Cleanout Locations (plan view)
CO
1/8 bends
Reqd upper terminal CO
45°
45°
45°
45°
45 + 45 + 45 + 45 = 180
CO reqd.
UPC reqs a CO for an aggregate total bend >135°.
IRC reqs a CO for every change of direction >45° except only one is reqd each 40 ft.

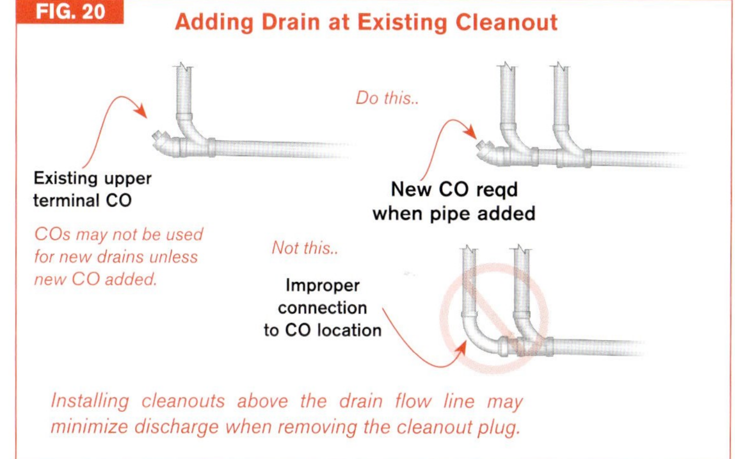
FIG. 20
Adding Drain at Existing Cleanout
Do this..
Existing upper terminal CO
New CO reqd when pipe added
COs may not be used for new drains unless new CO added.
Not this..
Improper connection to CO location
Installing cleanouts above the drain flow line may minimize discharge when removing the cleanout plug.

FIXTURES BELOW SEWER OR MANHOLE

Fixtures above the sewer drain toward it by gravity. Where fixtures or their drains are located below the upstream manhole cover, a sewage backup at the street may result in effluent discharge into the lower fixtures. Backups can be prevented by installing backwater valves on the drain lines that are below the manhole cover. Backwater valves must be accessible for maintenance. Cleanouts that could lead to a backwater valve should be labeled to warn against potential damage to the backwater valve from attempting to run a snake through it.

Fixtures below Sewer	21 IRC	21 UPC
☐ Fixtures must drain to sewer by gravity where possible	3007.1	709.1
☐ Sewer ejector pumps must operate automatically	3007.4	710.9
☐ Sump discharge must be lifted above gravity drain **F21**	3007.1	710.4
☐ Sump min. 18 in. diameter 24 in. deep **F22**	3007.3.2	n/a
☐ Sump concrete, metal, or other approved materials (IRC: Also tile or plastic; UPC: Metal reqs corrosion protection)	3007.3.2	710.8
☐ Sump reqs gastight removable cover **F22**	3007.3.2	710.10
☐ Sump pit vented as reqd for gravity systems	3007.3.2	710.10
☐ Sump vent min. 1¼ in. (UPC: 1½ in.)	T3113.4.1	710.10
☐ Sump effluent level adjustment min. 2 in. below inlet	3007.3.4	710.9
☐ Connect to wye in top of horizontal gravity drain **F21**	3007.3.5	710.4
☐ Discharge pipe materials must be pressure rated	3007.3.3.1	710.4
☐ Discharge pipe materials Cu, CPVC, CI, PE, or PVC	3007.3.3.2	n/a
☐ Accessible backwater or swing check valve reqd on ejector discharge pipe **F21,22**	3007.2	710.4
☐ Full-open valve reqd at check valve discharge side **F20,21**	3007.2	710.4
☐ Valve bodies corrosion-resistant metal (no plastic valves)	n/a	710.4
☐ Min. pump capacity 21 gpm (UPC: 20 gpm)	3007.6	710.3 #1
☐ Min. 2-in. discharge piping **T14** EXC	3007.6	710.3 #2
• Grinder pumps min. 1¼-in. discharge	3007.6X1	710.12.1
• Macerating toilets min. ¾-in. discharge	3007.6X2	710.13.2
☐ Gravity drains receiving discharge from ejector sized at 1.5 DFU for each gpm of pump (UPC: 2 DFU)	T3004.1	710.5

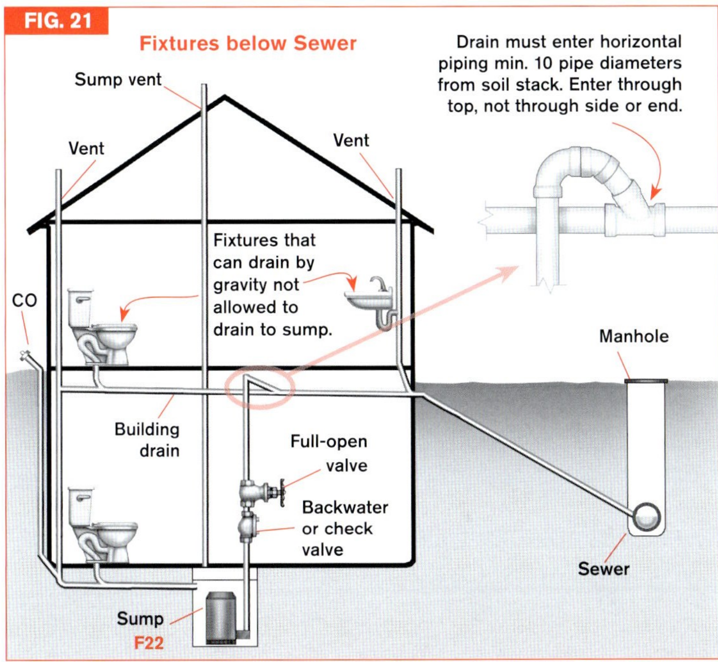

TABLE 14 IRC MINIMUM EJECTOR PUMP CAPACITY ◆ T3007.6

Discharge Pipe Diameter	Pump Capacity
2 in.	21 gpm
2½ in.	30 gpm
3 in.	46 gpm

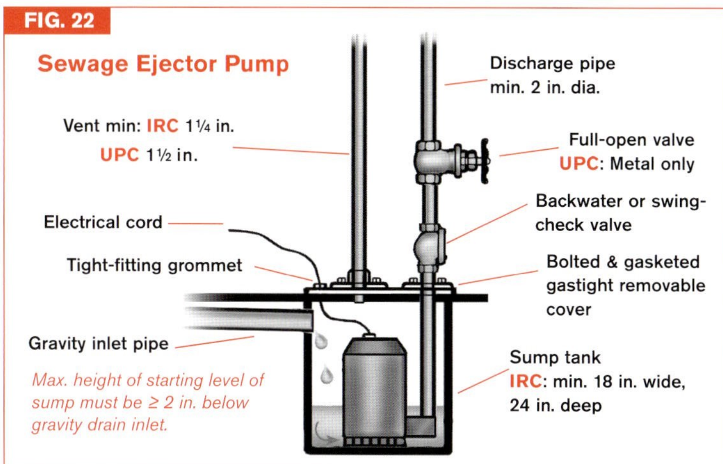

Fixtures below Upstream Manhole Cover F23

	21 IRC	21 UPC
☐ Fixtures below next upstream manhole req backwater valve (measured from FLR in IRC, from floor level in UPC)	3008.1	710.1
☐ Fixtures above elevation of manhole not allowed to discharge through backwater valve EXC	3008.1	710.1
• OK if backwater valve normally open type	3008.2	Ø
• Normally closed type OK in existing buildings	3008.2X	Ø
☐ Backwater valves reqd to be accessible for service	3008.4	710.6
☐ COs for drains through backwater valve req label	n/a	710.1

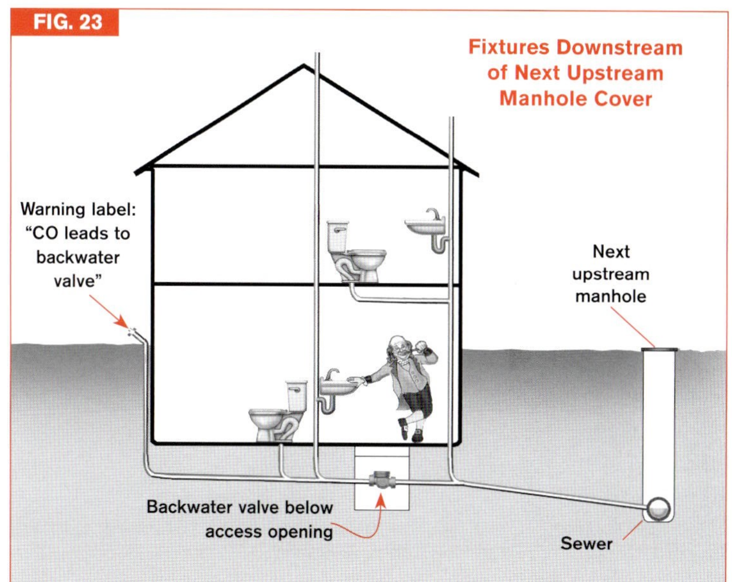

*Fixtures above the sewer but below the next upstream manhole are reqd to be protected by an accessible backwater valve (a type of check valve) as shown here. The valve protects the building from sewer contamination in the event of a street main backup. The **UPC** also requires a backwater valve for fixtures below the manhole cover of a private sewer system.*

TRAPS, FIXTURE TAILPIECES & TRAP ARMS

Traps provide an air barrier between the contaminated atmosphere of the sewer and the indoor air we breathe. Without a proper trap seal, sewer gases, airborne bacteria, vermin, and other contaminants can enter the living area. If the seal is too shallow, the seal could be lost due to evaporation. If too deep, drainage could be blocked with sludge. Trap arms (fixture drains) must be vented, otherwise the negative pressure created by water moving down the pipe will cause water to be sucked out of the trap and the seal to be lost. Maintaining a proper trap seal is the underlying principle behind the code rules for drainage, traps, and venting.

Traps & Fixture Tailpieces	21 IRC	21 UPC
☐ Each fixture reqs separate trap EXC	3201.6	1001.2
• Fixtures w/ integral traps (toilets)	3201.6X1	1001.2
• 2 or 3 like fixtures (sinks, laundry tubs, or lavs) in same room allowed on single trap at center fixture if fixture outlets ≤30 in. apart **F25**	3201.6X2	1001.2
• Laundry tray (sink) may drain to CW standpipe **F60**	3201.6X3	n/a
☐ Trap seal min. 2 in., max. 4 in. **F24**	3201.2	1005.1
☐ Set traps level & protect from freezing	3201.3	1005.1
☐ Vent opening must be at or above trap weir **F26**	3201.3	1002.4
☐ No “S” traps, bell traps, drum traps, crown-vented traps, or traps w/ moving parts or interior partitions EXC **F27**	3105.3 & 3201.5	1004.1&2
• Lav traps w/ plastic or stainless partitions	3201.5(2)	1004.1
☐ Drum & bottle traps allowed for special conditions	104.11	1004.1
☐ Size trap for fixture per **T9**	3201.7	1003.3
☐ Trap size ≥ fixture tailpiece (UPC: max. one size larger)	3201.7	1003.3
☐ One trap per trap arm, no double traps (in series)	3201.6	1004.1
☐ No corrugated or flexible traps	3201.1	1003.1
☐ Fixture tailpiece max. 24-in. vertical distance EXC **F25**	3201.6	1001.2
• CW standpipes 18–42 in. (UPC: 18–30 in.) **F59**	2706.1.2	804.1
☐ UPC: Tailpiece max. 24-in. total developed length except for the common fixtures joined by continuous waste **F25**	n/a	1001.2
☐ Directional fittings reqd for continuous wastes from disposer (i.e., wyes, combos, or tees w/baffles) **F25,30**	2707.1	419.2
☐ Building traps prohibited (UPC: unless reqd by AHJ)	3201.4	1008.1

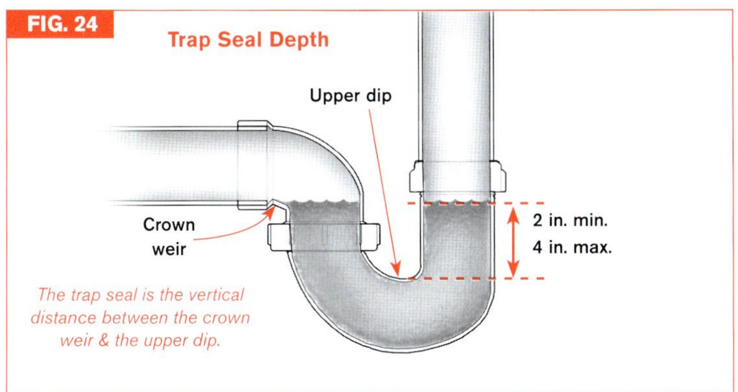

FIG. 24 Trap Seal Depth

The trap seal is the vertical distance between the crown weir & the upper dip.

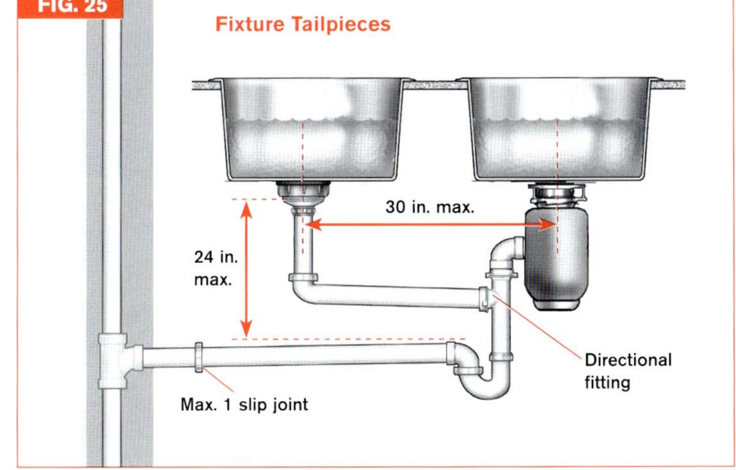

FIG. 25 Fixture Tailpieces

Trap Arms

	21 IRC	21 UPC
☐ Trap same size as trap arm	3201.7	1003.3
☐ No crown venting—min. length 2× trap arm diameter **F29**	3105.3	1002.2
☐ Length & slope per table EXC **T9**	3105.1	1002.2
• Trap arm length from WC unlimited (UPC: 6 ft.)	3105.1X	T1002.2
☐ Min. slope 1/4 in./ft. (IRC 1/8 in. ft. OK for ≥3-in. pipe)	T3105.1	T1002.2
☐ Total fall of trap arm max. 1 pipe diameter **F26,T15**	3105.2	n/a
☐ Vent connection not below weir of trap (except WCs)	3105.2	1002.4
☐ Only 1 trap permitted on trap arm EXC	n/a	1001.2
• 2 trap arms on same level allowed to join through double-wye fitting to common vent **F35**	3107.2	Ø
☐ Tubing traps req trap adapter **F31**	n/a	1003.2
☐ Max. 1 slip joint allowed on outlet side of trap **F25**	n/a	1003.2
☐ Horizontal direction changes in trap arms per **T7**	n/a	1002.3
☐ CO reqd if direction change >45° (UPC 90°)	3005.2.4	1002.3
☐ Slip joints connections reqd to be accessible	2704.1	402.10
☐ Access openings min. 12 in. × 12 in. **F28**	2704.1, 3201.1	402.10

TABLE 15 — TRAP ARM DISTANCE TO VENT — IRC T3105.1 & UPC T1002.2

Trap Arm Diameter	Min. Arm Length	IRC Max. Arm Length	UPC Max. Arm Length
1¼ in.	2½ in.	5 ft. (60 in.)	2½ ft. (30 in.)
1½ in.	3 in.	6 ft. (72 in.)	3½ ft. (42 in.)
2 in.	4 in.	8 ft. (96 in.)	5 ft. (60 in.)
3 in.[A]	6 in.	12 ft. (144 in.)	6 ft. (72in.)
4 in. or larger[A]	8 in.	16 ft. (192 in.)	10 ft. (120 in.)[B]

A. In the IRC, these arms can have 1/8-in./ft. slope. In the UPC, all arms must slope 1/4 in./ft.
B. Max. developed length from a water closet to the vent is 6 ft. in the UPC & unlimited in the IRC.

FIG. 26

Trap Arms & Vents

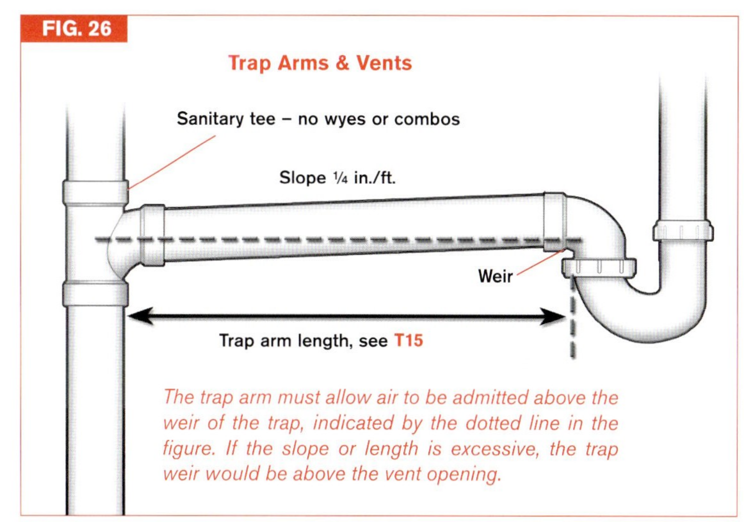

The trap arm must allow air to be admitted above the weir of the trap, indicated by the dotted line in the figure. If the slope or length is excessive, the trap weir would be above the vent opening.

FIG. 27

S Trap

For water to drain in the vertical pipe downstream of the trap, it must have air to prevent a vacuum behind it. If that air comes from the fixture tailpiece, rather than from a vent, the water in the trap also gets siphoned into the drain pipe. That can leave the trap with no water seal to keep out sewer odors & vermin.

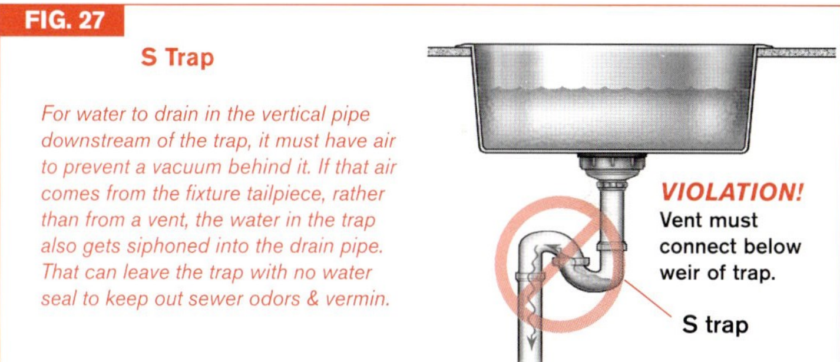

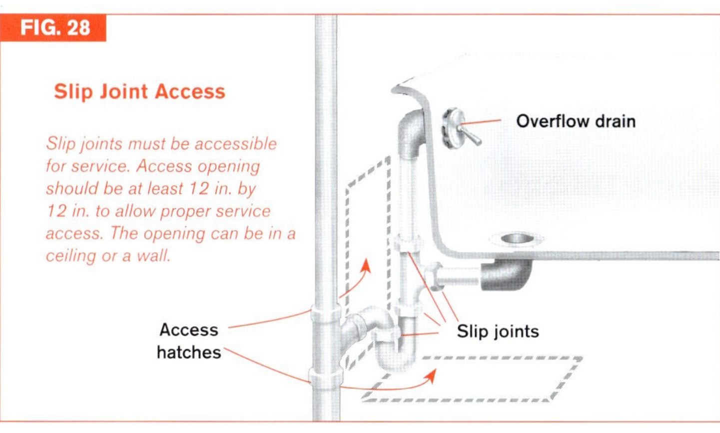
FIG. 28
Slip Joint Access
Slip joints must be accessible for service. Access opening should be at least 12 in. by 12 in. to allow proper service access. The opening can be in a ceiling or a wall.
Overflow drain
Access hatches
Slip joints

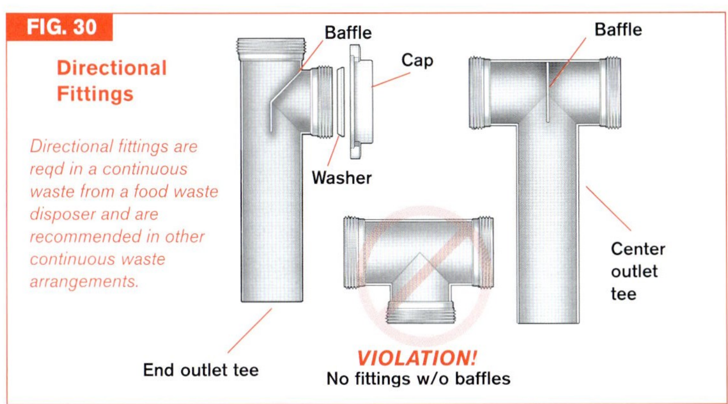
FIG. 30
Directional Fittings
Directional fittings are reqd in a continuous waste from a food waste disposer and are recommended in other continuous waste arrangements.
Baffle
Cap
Baffle
Washer
Center outlet tee
End outlet tee
VIOLATION!
No fittings w/o baffles

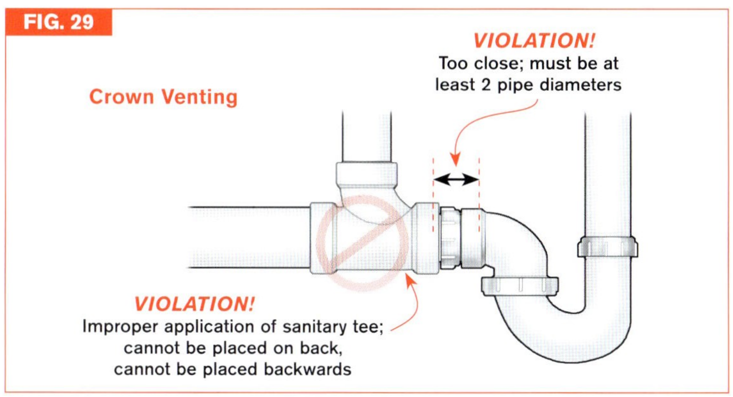
FIG. 29
Crown Venting
VIOLATION!
Too close; must be at least 2 pipe diameters
VIOLATION!
Improper application of sanitary tee; cannot be placed on back, cannot be placed backwards

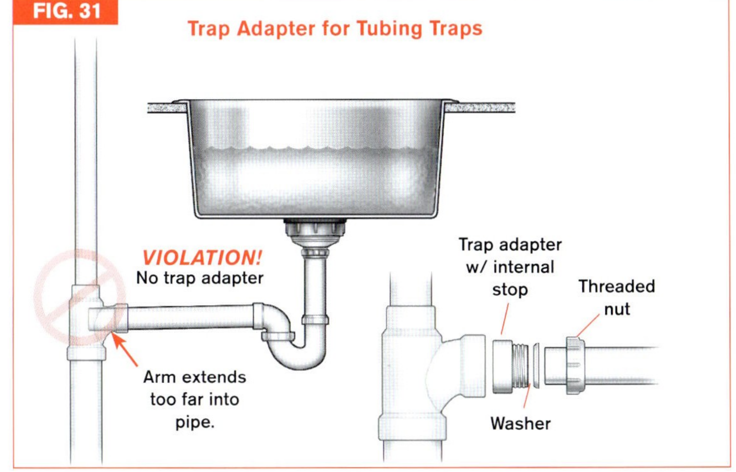
FIG. 31
Trap Adapter for Tubing Traps
VIOLATION!
No trap adapter
Trap adapter w/ internal stop
Threaded nut
Arm extends too far into pipe.
Washer

VENTS

Vents prevent atmospheric pressure differences across traps and are essential to maintaining the trap seal. Without vents, the water in the seal could be sucked out, leaving the occupants unprotected from contaminants downstream of the trap. The IRC and UPC have very different approaches to venting.

General	21 IRC	21 UPC
☐ All traps req venting	3101.2.1	901.2
☐ Vents must limit trap pressure to max. 1-in. water column	3101.2	901.3
☐ Vent system not to be used for any other purposes	3101.3	local
☐ Vents to horizontal drains must take off above centerline **F34**	3104.3	905.2
☐ Grade & support vents to drain to soil or waste piping	3104.2	905.1
☐ Change direction w/ appropriate fittings **F14,32**	3005.1	903.3
☐ No vent opening below trap weir except toilets **F26**	3105.2	905.5
☐ No crown vents: min. 2 pipe diameters from trap **F29**	3105.3	1002.2
☐ Connection to vent stack min. 6 in. above FLR of trapped fixture served by vent	3104.4&5	905.3
☐ Vents not horizontal until min. 6 in. above FLR **F33**	3005.1	905.3
☐ Piping <6 in. above flood rim reqs drainage-type fittings	3104.5	905.3

FIG. 32

Branch Vents

Two or more individual vents may combine to form a branch vent, thereby reducing the number of penetrations through the roof. Horizontal vent piping must be graded to drain by gravity to the drain served.

*In the IRC, vents must be at least half the size of the drain they are venting. In the UPC, all vents are sized per **T16** based on their DFUs.*

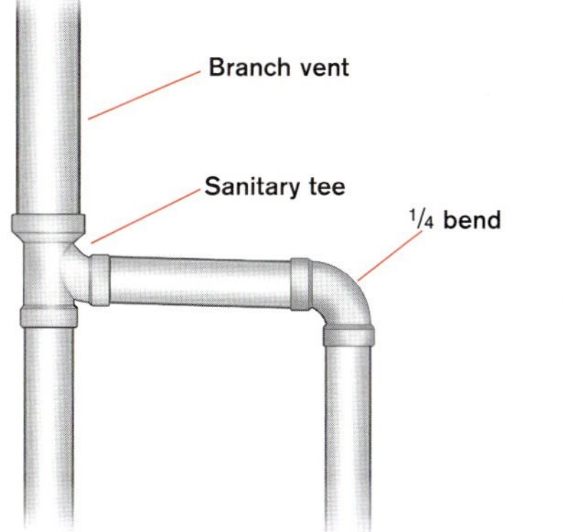

FIG. 33

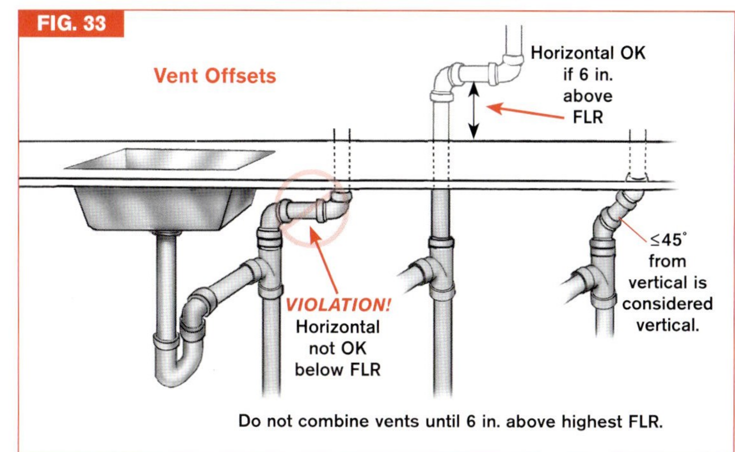

FIG. 34

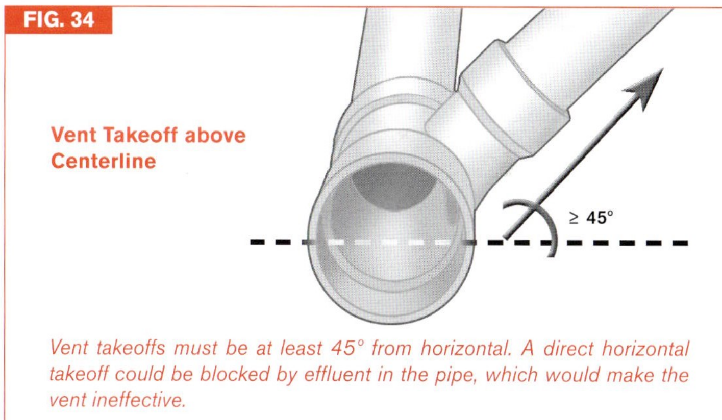

Vent takeoffs must be at least 45° from horizontal. A direct horizontal takeoff could be blocked by effluent in the pipe, which would make the vent ineffective.

Vent Size

	21 IRC	21 UPC
☐ Min. size 1¼ in.	3113.1	904.1
☐ Vents min. ½ size of drain served	3113.1	904.1
☐ Size per # of DFUs served & length of vent (UPC: **T16**)	3102.3	904.1
☐ Increase 1 pipe size if developed vent length >40 ft.	3113.1	n/a
☐ Increase 1 pipe size if >⅓ of vent is horizontal	n/a	904.2X
☐ Waste stack vent same size as waste stack **F43**	3109.3	n/a
☐ Total area of vents ≥ size of building sewer **T20**	n/a	904.1
☐ Vents for fixtures discharging through pumps, ejectors, or backwater valves do not count towards min. vent requirement	n/a	904.1

TABLE 16 UPC VENT SIZE AND LENGTH ◆ T703.2

Pipe Size (in.)	1¼	1½	2	3	4
Max. DFUs	1	8[A]	24	84	256
Max. Length (ft.)[B]	45	60	120	212	300

A. Not applicable to water closets, which must have a min. 2-in. vent.
B. Max. horizontal length is ⅓ of total length. If a minimum-sized vent is increased one size, the length limitations of this table do not apply.

Common Vent

	21 IRC	21 UPC
☐ Common vent only OK for fixtures on same floor level	3107.1	905.6
☐ Max. 2 traps or trapped fixtures to vertical common vent	3107.1	905.6
☐ Vent connection OK downstream of fixture drains **F35,36**	3107.2	Ø
☐ Size common vent per DFUs of upper drain **F36,T17**	3107.3	n/a
☐ Upper fixture cannot be WC	3107.3	n/a
☐ UPC: Only allowed to double-inlet fitting **F16**	n/a	905.6

TABLE 17 IRC COMMON VENT SIZES ◆ T3107.3

Pipe Size (in.)	Max. Discharge from Upper Fixture Drain (Fixture Units)[A]
1½	1
2	4
2½ to 3	6

A. In the UPC, the vertical wet vent is one size larger than the reqd size of the drain for the upper fixture drain, as well as a min. of 2 in.

FIG. 35

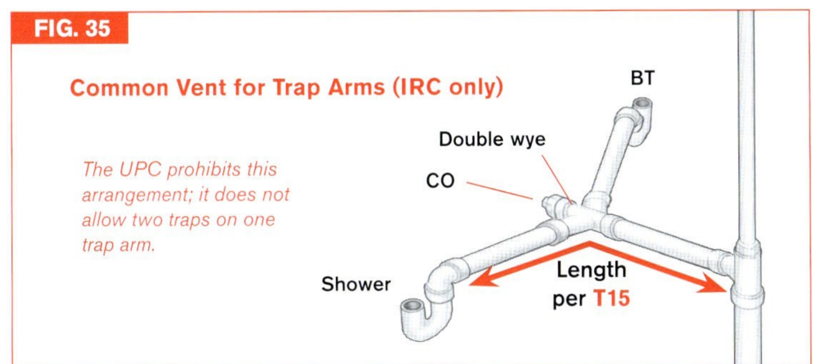

Vertical Wet Venting

	21 IRC	21 UPC
☐ All wet vented fixtures to be on same story	3108.4	908.1
☐ IRC: Size to # of DFUs discharging to wet vent **T18**	3108.3	n/a
☐ UPC: Min. 2 in. & 1 pipe size larger than reqd waste **F37**	n/a	908.1.1
☐ WC fixture drains must connect at same elevation	3108.4	908.1
☐ Each fixture drain connects independently to wet vent	3108.4	n/a
☐ UPC: Limited to trap arms of 1-DFU & 2-DFU fixtures	n/a	908.1
☐ Max. 4 fixtures, max. 6 ft. developed length of wet vent **F37**	n/a	908.1

FIG. 36 **FIG. 37**

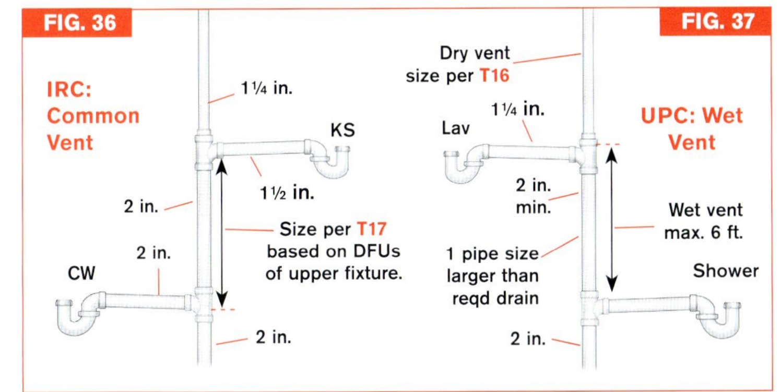

Horizontal Wet Venting

	21 IRC	21 UPC
☐ Horizontal wet venting OK for combinations of fixtures within 2 bath groups (UPC: 1 group) on same floor **F38,39** ___	3108.1	908.2
☐ Fixtures within the bathroom group(s) only ones allowed on horizontal wet vent (no other upstream fixtures) ______	3108.1	908.2.5
☐ Other vented fixtures OK downstream of wet vent ______	3108.1	908.2.5
☐ UPC: WC must be downstream of other drain connections _	n/a	908.2.4
☐ Dry vent connection not from floor drain vent ________	3108.2.1	908.2.1
☐ Dry vent from individual or common vent from any other bath group fixture, if WC drain must connect horizontal ____	3108.2.1	Ø
☐ Dry vent only individual vent from shower, tub, lav, or bidet __	n/a	908.2.1
☐ Max. 1 wet-vented fixture upstream of dry vent connection	3108.2.1	908.2.1
☐ Max. trap arm length from trap weir to wet vent **T15** _____	3108.5	908.2.3
☐ Size based on DFUs into wet vent **T18** ______________	3108.3	908.2.2

FIG. 38

IRC Horizontal Wet Venting

The IRC allows 2 bathroom groups to be horizontally wet-vented.

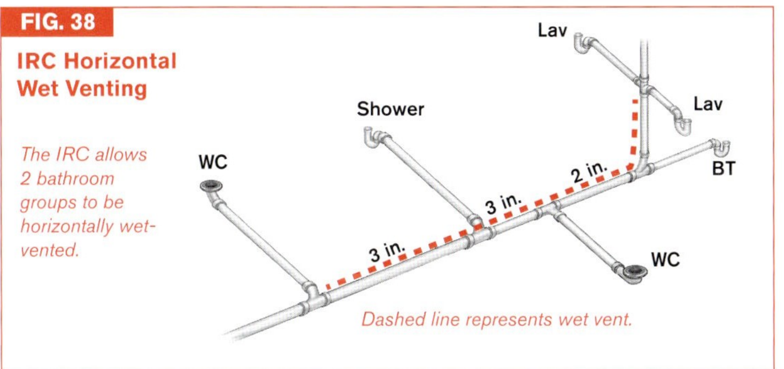

Dashed line represents wet vent.

FIG. 39

UPC Horizontal Wet Venting

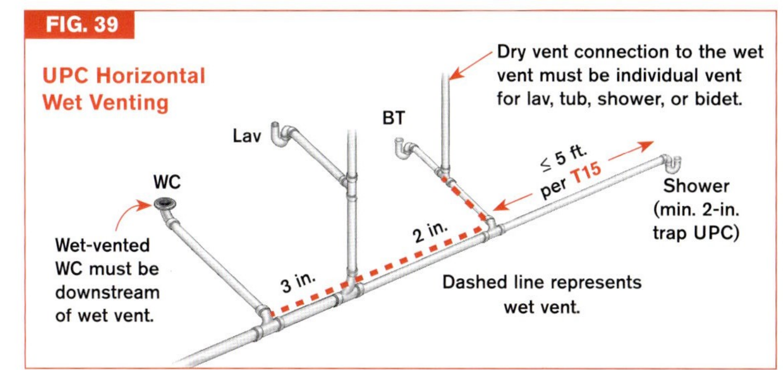

Dashed line represents wet vent.

TABLE 18 — WET VENT MIN. SIZE ◆ IRC T3108.3 & UPC 908.2.2

IRC		UPC	
# of DFUs	Min. Pipe Size	# of DFUs	Min. Pipe Size
1	1½ in.	1 – 4	2 in.
2 – 4	2 in.	≥ 5	3 in.
5 – 6	2½ in.	Above sizes are for horizontal wet vents. Vertical wet vents are sized one size larger than the reqd drain for the fixtures above. The dry vent to wet vent size is per **T16**.	
7 – 12	3 in.		
13 – 32	4 in.		

SPECIAL VENTING SYSTEMS

The IRC offers a number of options for island sinks, including air admittance valves, combination waste and vent (CW&V), and the loop vents shown in **F40** and **F41**. The UPC allows only the method in **F40**. In the UPC, a sink in a kitchen peninsula could have a horizontal vent under the countertop and connecting to a vertical vent in the wall if drainage type fittings are used.

Island Sinks	21 IRC	21 UPC
☐ Island venting limited to sinks (disposer OK) & lavs	3112.1	909.1
☐ Island vented w/ drain-type fittings only **F40,41**	3112.3	909.1
☐ Island vent above fixture drain outlet **F41** (UPC: as high as possible **F40**) before returning downward	3112.2	909.1
☐ Lowest part of island vent shall connect full size to a vertical drain or top half of a horizontal drain **F41**	3112.3	n/a
☐ Air admittance valves OK (see AAV section)	3114.3	Ø
☐ COs required in island vents & drains **F40,41**	3112.3	909.1
☐ Connect island vent downstream of fixture drain **F40**	n/a	909.1
☐ Foot vent reqd through wye branch off below-floor vent **F40**	n/a	909.1
☐ CO reqd in vertical section of foot vent **F40**	n/a	909.1
☐ No upstream fixtures on drain serving island	n/a	909.1

IRC: Combination Waste & Vent (CW&V)	IRC
☐ Only allowed for sinks, lavs, floor drains & drinking fountains	3111.1
☐ One vertical pipe (max. 8-ft. length) allowed between fixture drain & horizontal CW&V pipe **F42**	3111.2
☐ Max. slope of CW&V piping ½ in./ft., min. slope ¼ in./ft. **F42**	3111.2.1
☐ CW&V must connect to dry vent or to vented horizontal drain **F42**	3111.2.2
☐ Vent connected to CW&V pipe must rise 6 in. min. above fixture flood level rim before horizontal offsets	3111.2.2

UPC: Combination Waste & Vent (CW&V)	UPC
☐ Only allowed where structural conditions prevent conventional system & reqs specific advance approval by AHJ	910.1&2
☐ Waste pipe & trap min. 2 pipe sizes larger than otherwise reqd	910.4
☐ No vertical waste pipe exc 1 45° offset allowed in branch lines	910.5
☐ 1, 2 & 3 DFU fixtures only, no WCs or urinals	910.7

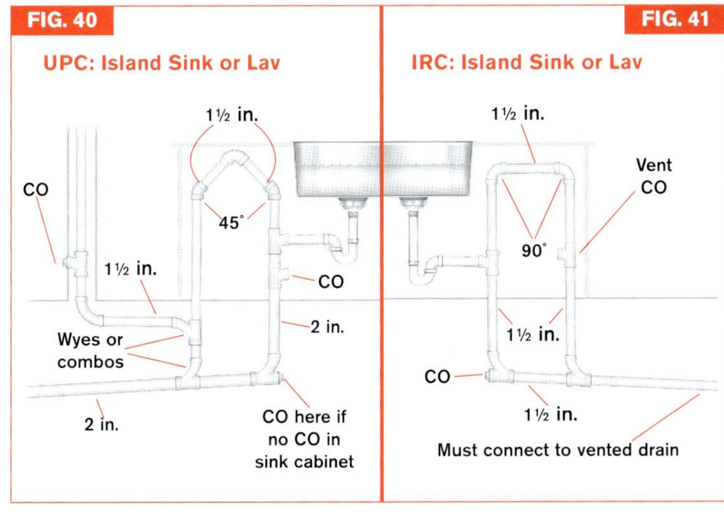

FIG. 42

IRC: Combination Waste & Vent

The concept of a CW&V is that the larger pipes will always have air & prevent siphoning of the trap. Limiting the slope of the horizontal connection also prevents siphoning.

The IRC allows them for sinks, drinking fountains, floor drains, and lavatories. Prior approval by the AHJ is required in the UPC.

1½ in. (typical)

Length per **T15**

CW&V pipes 2 in. (typical)

2-in. × 1½-in. quarter bend

Length unlimited; max. slope ½ in./ft., min. slope ¼ in./ft.

IRC Waste Stack Vents 21 IRC

- ☐ No toilet or urinal discharge allowed into waste stack ____________ 3109.2
- ☐ No branch drains into waste stack—only fixture drains ____________ 3109.2
- ☐ Stack must be vertical w/ no offsets between fixture drains **F43** _____ 3109.3
- ☐ Offsets OK min. 6 in. above FLR of highest fixture **F43** ____________ 3109.3
- ☐ OK for stack vent to combine w/ other stack vents or vent stacks ____ 3109.3
- ☐ Waste stack & stack vent same size for entire length **F43** __________ 3109.3&4
- ☐ Size waste stack per total DFUs discharging into it **T19** ____________ 3109.4

TABLE 19 IRC WASTE STACK VENT SIZE ◆ T3109.4

Stack Size (in.)	Total Discharge into 1 Branch Interval (DFUs)	Total Discharge for Stack (DFUs)
1½	1	2
2	2	4
2½	no limit	8
3	no limit	24
4	no limit	50

FIG. 43

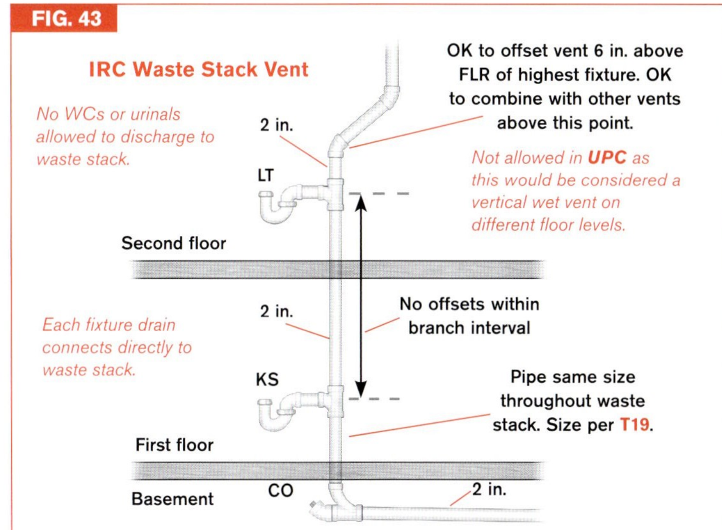

A waste stack provides a way to connect fixtures on different floor levels using a simpler pipe arrangement. Toilets and urinals may not discharge into the waste stack. The waste stack must be undiminished in size to its vent, and offsets are only allowed 6 in. above the highest fixture draining to the stack. Without the size limitations of ***T19****, excessive flow above the lower inlets could push air ahead of liquids draining from upper fixtures & cause a loss of trap seal in the lower fixture. UPC Appendix C, Alternate Plumbing Systems, requires single-stack venting to be designed by a registered design professional (section C 601.1). Prior approval by the AHJ is also required in UPC jurisdictions.*

FIG. 44 Air Admittance Valve Operation

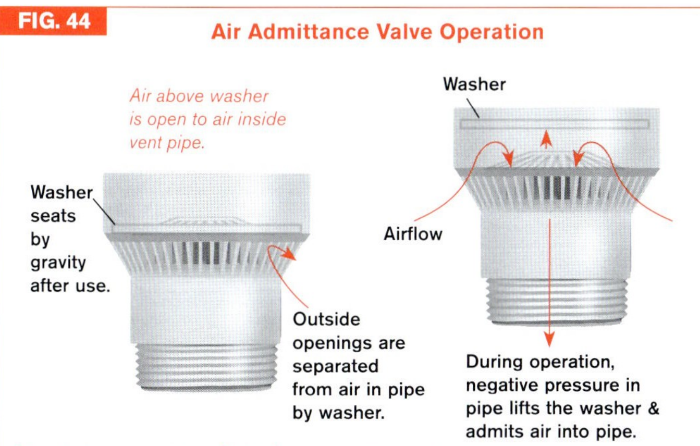

Air admittance valves (AAVs) operate by gravity and have no metal or rubber parts that could corrode or deform. In the IRC they can be used for individual fixtures or for branches. The UPC does not allow AAVs. UPC jurisdictions sometimes accept them on a case-by-case basis under the provisions for Alternate Materials and Methods found in 301.3. If the UPC is the code in your area, be sure to check with your local building department (AHJ) before installing AAVs.

Air Admittance Valves F44 — 21 IRC

- ☐ Install after DWV leak test ____ 3114.2
- ☐ OK at individual, branch, circuit & stack vents ____ 3114.3
- ☐ Individual & branch type AAV to vent only fixtures on same floor level & that connect to a horizontal branch drain ____ 3114.3
- ☐ Individual fixture & branch AAV ≥4 in. above branch or fixture drain **F45** 3114.4
- ☐ Stack-type AAV min. 6 in. above FLR of highest fixture ____ 3114.4
- ☐ Trap arms same min. & max. length as conventional vent **T45,T15** ____ 3114.4
- ☐ AAVs terminating in attic min. 6 in. above insulation ____ 3114.4
- ☐ AAVs must be accessible for service & inspection **F45** ____ 3114.5
- ☐ Space containing air admittance valve must be ventilated ____ 3114.5
- ☐ Min. 1 vent to outdoors (UPC: all vents to exterior) ____ 3102.1 & 3114.7
- ☐ Not OK for sewer ejector pump or tanks ____ 3114.8
- ☐ Not OK solely to reduce reqd clearances in **F46** ____ 3114.8

FIG. 45 Air Admittance Valve Locations

An AAV cannot be located inside a stud cavity or other area where not accessible & open to free air.

When AAVs are placed in attics, they must be at least 6 in. above insulation.

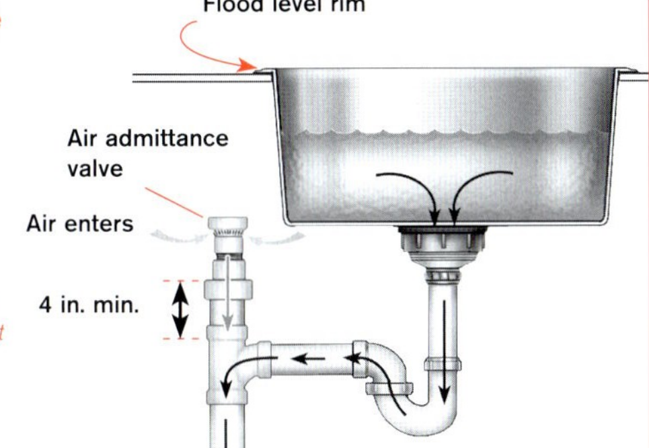

VENT TERMINATION

Vents facilitate drainage flow and protect the seal of traps, thereby preventing sewer odors from entering the living area.

Vent Termination	**21 IRC**	**21 UPC**
☐ IRC: sidewall vents allowed; UPC: all vents through roof	3103.1	905.4
☐ IRC: Min. 1 vent must extend outdoors; UPC: all vents __	3102.1	906.1
☐ IRC sole vent to exterior not an island fixture vent **F40** __	3102.2	n/a
☐ IRC exterior vent min. ½ size of building drain __	3102.3 & 3113.1	n/a
☐ Reqd sum of UPC vents ≥ size of building sewer **T20** ______	n/a	904.1
☐ Vents through roof min. 6 in. above roof EXC ________	3103.1.1	906.1&3
• 2 in. OK if vent terminates under solar panel _______	3103.1.3	Ø
☐ Protect exposed plastic pipe above roof w/ latex paint _____	MFR	906.1
☐ Min. 7 ft. above roof decks (UPC: or if within 10 ft.) ____	3103.1.2	906.3
☐ Flagpoling of vents prohibited except where roof is used for parking or assembly purposes _________________	n/a	906.3
☐ Min. 12 in. horizontal from adjacent vertical surfaces _______	n/a	906.1
☐ Min. 3 ft. above openings within 10 ft. EXC **F46** ________	3103.5	906.2
• OK if ≥4 ft. below building openings **F46** ____________	3103.5	n/a
☐ Roof termination min. 3-ft. distance from LL other than street	n/a	906.2
☐ IRC sidewall terminations min. 10 ft. from LL, min. 10 ft. from grade within 10 ft., not under vented eaves or soffits __	3103.1.4	Ø
☐ Sidewall terminations req bird & rodent protection ____	3103.1.4	Ø
☐ Vent termination not to be used for any other purpose ___	3103.4	n/a
☐ Provide flashing for roof penetrations _________	2607.1 & 3103.3	906.5
☐ If flashing tucked into vent, max. reduction 1 pipe size ___	2607.1	n/a

Snow or Frost Closure (Design Temperature <0°F)

☐ Min. 3-in.-diameter termination (UPC: min. 2 in.)________	3103.2	906.7
☐ Increase vent diameter min. 1 ft. inside thermal envelope _	3103.2	906.7
☐ Terminate min. 6 in. above snow line (UPC: 10 in. above roof or per AHJ)_______________	3103.1.1	906.7

FIG. 46

Vent Termination Clearances to Building Openings

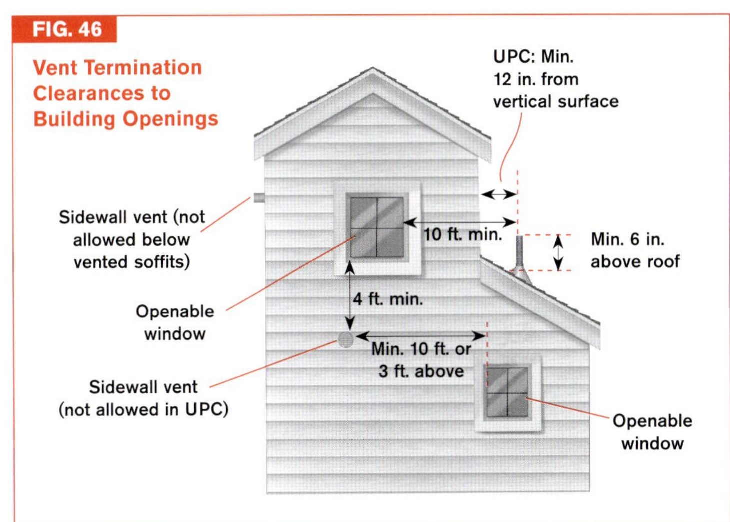

TABLE 20 — UPC VENT AREA WORKSHEET ◆ UPC 904.1

Vent Size (in.)	Area (sq. in.)	# Vents	Net Vent Area
1¼	1.23		
1½	1.77		
2	3.14		
3	7.07		
4	12.57		
TOTAL			

Use the fill-in area to the left to determine if the vents through the roof meet the required min. area.

Example:
Reqd 4-in. bldg. drain = 12.57 sq. in.
One 1¼-in. vent = 1.23 sq. in.
Three 2-in. vents = 9.42 sq. in.
1.23 + 9.42 = 10.65 sq. in.
Thus, more venting reqd through roof.

*The UPC requirement for the aggregate area of vents being no less than the size of the building drain can be met by having more vents through the roof, or by upsizing where vents are joined as branch vents as in **F32**.*

ON-SITE DISPOSAL SYSTEMS

On-site sewage disposal systems are generally regulated by local environmental health services agencies. Septic systems must be sized and located so as not to impact potable water supply. The areas shown in **T22** are a general planning guide only; local regulations must be followed. Soil percolation testing and the type of construction will determine the actual size. In the IRC, users are directed to use the International Private Sewage Disposal Code (IPSDC). In the UPC, on-site systems are found in Appendix H and are subject to local adoption.

Septic Tanks	21 IPSDC	21 UPC
☐ Locate system on same parcel as building served EXC	101.2	H101.8
• Common systems to comply w/ regs for public systems	101.2	Ø
☐ Tank min. 5 ft. from building	802.8	H101.8
☐ Tank & disposal field min. 5 ft. from lot line	T406.1	T H101.8
☐ Tank min. 25 ft. (50 ft. UPC) from water wells	T802.8	T H101.8
☐ Disposal field min. 50 ft. (UPC: 100 ft.) from water wells	T406.1	T H101.8
☐ Min. tank capacity per **T21**	802.7.1	H201.1
☐ Design to minimize inundation in flood hazard area	303.2	H101.5X

TABLE 21 SEPTIC TANK CAPACITY ◆ IPSDC T802.7.1 UPC H201.1(1)

Bedrooms	Min. Tank Size IPSDC	Min. Tank Size UPC	Max. UPC DFUs
1-2	750	750	15
3	1,000	1,000	20
4	1,200	1,200	25
5	1,425	1,500	33
6	1,650	1,500	33

TABLE 22 1 & 2 FAMILY – MIN. ABSORPTION AREA ◆ IPSCD T603.1

Percolation Class	Percolation Rate[A]	Seepage Trenches[B]	Seepage Beds[B]
1	0 to <10	165	205
2	10 to <30	250	315
3	30 to <45	300	375
4	45 to 60	330	415

A. Minutes reqd for water to fall 1 in.
B. Sq. ft. per bedroom.

NONPOTABLE WATER SUPPLY

Water conservation measures include the reuse of water collected from rainwater catchment systems, gray water drains, and recycled water for applications where drinking water standards are not required. Nonpotable water from these sources requires separate piping systems and other measures to ensure against contamination of the potable water supply. "Black water" from toilets, kitchen sinks, and dishwashers must always be directed to the sewer or on-site disposal system. Gray water can be obtained from other plumbing fixtures and be reused for landscape irrigation and for refilling toilet tanks.

Nonpotable Water Supply: General	21 IRC	21 UPC
☐ Permits reqd for nonpotable water systems	2910.4	1501.3
☐ Operation & maintenance manual to be provided	2911.13	1501.6
☐ Diverter valves reqd for gray water systems	2911.8.1	1503.2.2
☐ Gray water storage (surge) tanks req backwater valve (on piping from overflow to sewer)	2911.8.2	1503.9.7
☐ Plot plan reqd for gray water systems	local	1503.5

System Identification		
☐ Outlets (e.g., hose bibbs) req signage per **F47**	2901.2.1 & 2910.3	601.3.5
☐ Distribution piping reqd to be purple	2901.2.2	601.3.3
☐ Piping reqs label stating "CAUTION: NONPOTABLE WATER, DO NOT DRINK." (UPC: Fill in blank w/ type, such as GRAY WATER, RECLAIMED WATER, RAINWATER)	2901.2.2	601.3.3
☐ Label every 25 ft. (UPC: 20 ft.) & min. once each room	2901.2.2	601.3.2
☐ Lettering min. ½ in. high (¾-in. pipes 1½ in.–2 in.)	2901.2.2.2	601.3.2
☐ Labels to indicate direction of flow	2901.2.2	601.3.2

FIG. 47 Nonpotable Water Supply Outlets

IRC Pictograph

Hose bibbs or other outlets of nonpotable water systems require a warning sign stating **"CAUTION: NONPOTABLE WATER. DO NOT DRINK"** *in letters min. ½ in. high and the accompanying pictograph.*

UPC Pictograph

WATER SUPPLY & DISTRIBUTION

Plumbing systems must be designed and maintained to prevent contamination of potable water from cross-connections to drains or other contaminated sources. Piping must be protected against movement and damage during construction. Plastics typically can tolerate exposure to sunlight for only limited periods, and some types of plastics require flushing procedures to remove solvents prior to use.

Materials — 21 IRC | 21 UPC

- ☐ All materials must meet NSF 61 & be approved T23 _ 2906.4&5 | 604.1
- ☐ Water supply system pipe & fittings max. 8% lead content for non-drinking water applications ____ 2906.2 | 604.2.1
- ☐ Drinking water pipe, fittings, joints, valves & fixtures weighted average lead content of max. 0.25% ____ 2906.2.1 | 604.2
- ☐ Cu alloy fittings & valves >15% Zi by weight & used w/ plastic piping systems req resistance to dezincification per NSF 14 ___ 2609.3 | 604.1
- ☐ Cu pipe markings: K = green, L = blue, M = red ____ n/a | 604.4
- ☐ Piping or tubing previously used for any purpose other than potable water may not be used for potable water ____ local | 604.4

Hot Water Piping: UPC — 21 UPC

- ☐ Hot water piping reqs insulation w thickness ≥ pipe diameter for pipes up to 2 in., 2 in. thick for larger pipes. ___ n/a 609.12.1&2

Hot Water Piping: IRC — 21 IRC

- ☐ Hot water piping max. developed length 100 ft. from source of hot water to fixtures ____ 2905.3[5]
- ☐ Heated water circulation systems req circulation pump ____ 1103.5.1.1
- ☐ Circulation system returns dedicated or to cold water pipe ____ 1103.5.1.1
- ☐ Returns to cold water pipe req controls to limit to 104°F ____ 1103.5.1.1
- ☐ Min. R-3 insulation reqd for the following: ____ 1103.5.2
  - Piping ≥¾ in. inside conditioned space
  - Piping serving ≥1 dwelling unit
  - Piping outside the conditioned space
  - Piping from the water heater to a distribution manifold
  - Piping located under a floor slab
  - Buried piping
  - Supply & return piping in circulation systems (other than cold water return)

Pipe Installation: General — 21 IRC | 21 UPC

- ☐ PVC not to be exposed to direct sunlight unless max. 24 in. & protected by 0.04-in.-thick tape or other UV protection. ____ n/a | 605.12
- ☐ Mechanical ASSE 1010 water hammer arrestors (not air chambers) reqd near quick-close valves (DW or CW) ___ 2903.5 | 609.11
- ☐ Dead legs must have method of flushing ____ n/a | 309.6[6]
- ☐ Flex connectors accessible (UPC: readily accessible) __ 2906.7 | 604.5
- ☐ Burred ends to be reamed to full bore of pipe or tubing __ 2608.1 | 609.1

TABLE 23 WATER PIPE MATERIALS ◆ IRC T2906.4&5 & UPC T604.1

Material	IRC		UPC	
	Service	Distribution	Service	Distribution
ABS	✔	∅	∅	∅
Cu alloy pipe (brass)	✔	✔	✔	✔
CPVC	✔	✔	✔	✔
CPVC-AL-CPVC	✔	✔	✔	✔
Cu tubing	✔	✔	✔	✔
Ductile iron	✔	∅	✔	✔
Galvanized steel	✔	✔	✔	✔
PE pipe or tubing	✔	∅	✔	∅
PE-AL-PE	✔	✔	✔	✔
PE-RT	✔	✔	✔	✔
PEX	✔	✔	✔	✔
PEX-AL-PEX	✔	✔	✔	✔
PEX-AL-HDPE	✔	✔	∅	∅
PP	✔	✔	✔	✔
PVC	✔	∅	✔	∅

5. New restriction on length of hot water piping regardless of insulation.
6. This new rule would also prohibit "air chamber" water hammer arrestors.

Joints & Connections

	21 IRC	21 UPC
☐ Solder joints ASTM B828; solder & flux max. 0.2% lead	2906.15	605.1.4
☐ Flux per ASTM B813 & rated for potable water	2906.15	605.1.4
☐ Joints between dissimilar materials AMI	2906.18	605.16
☐ Cu to Fe reqs brass (UPC: min. 6 in.) or dielectric fitting	2906.18.1	605.16.1
☐ PVC service to CPVC distribution mechanical fittings or solvent-cement joint per ASTM F493	2906.18.2	605.2.2
☐ CPVC joints AMI, primer must be orange EXC	2906.9.1.2	605.2.2
• One-step cements AMI yellow (IRC: or red)	2906.9.1.2	605.2.2
☐ Plastic to other piping w/ approved adapter fittings	2906.18.3	605.16.2
☐ Female threaded CPVC fittings w/ male plastic only	local	605.2.3
☐ PVC threaded fittings min. schedule 80	local	605.12.3
☐ Female PVC threaded fittings only OK w/ male plastic	local	605.12.3
☐ Press-connect joints on Cu tubing AMI w/ MFR's tool	2906.19	605.1.3.2
☐ Push-fitting joints OK on CPVC, PEX, PE-RT & Cu tubing that is outside-dimensioned on Cu tubing size, AMI & per ASSE 1061	2906.21	605.9.3
☐ Cu joints in or under concrete slab on grade within building req brazed wrought-copper fittings	local	609.3(2)
☐ Slip joints only on exposed fixture supply	local	605.14
☐ Unions reqd within 12 in. of WHs, softeners, filters, regulators & similar equipment that may req removal for servicing	local	609.5
☐ Except for necessary valves, intermixing of dissimilar metals only at exposed or accessible locations	local	310.6

Valves

	21 IRC	21 UPC
☐ Accessible main valve reqd near water entrance	2903.9.1	606.2
☐ Main valve must have bleed orifice or separate drain	2903.9.1	n/a
☐ Additional valve at curb, meter, or lot line per local req	2903.9.1	n/a
☐ Main valve must be on discharge side of water meter	local	606.2
☐ Main valve reqd for each separate building EXC	local	606.2
• SFD & accessory building OK to have only 1 valve	local	606.2
☐ In multiple dwelling units, shutoff valves reqd each unit	local	606.3

Valves (Continued)

	21 IRC	21 UPC
☐ Main & WH valve must be full-open type **F48,49**	2903.9.1&2	606.2
☐ Throttling valves not OK for main & WH **F50**	2903.9.1&2	606.2
☐ Valve reqd on cold water supply to WHs	2903.9.2	606.2
☐ Reqd shutoffs must be accessible	2903.9.3	606.6
☐ Hose bibbs subject to freezing req accessible stop & waste valve inside building EXC	2903.10	local
• Frostproof hose bibbs w/ stem into heated space	2903.10X	603.5.7
☐ Valves reqd on each appliance or fixture supply EXC	2903.9.3	606.5
• Tubs & showers (UPC: fixtures w/o slip joints)	2903.9.3	606.5
☐ Valves OK at accessible manifold **F51** if labeled EXC	2903.8.4	606.5
▪ If manifold in attic, crawlspace, or otherwise not readily accessible, separate shutoff reqd at each individual fixture	n/a	606.5

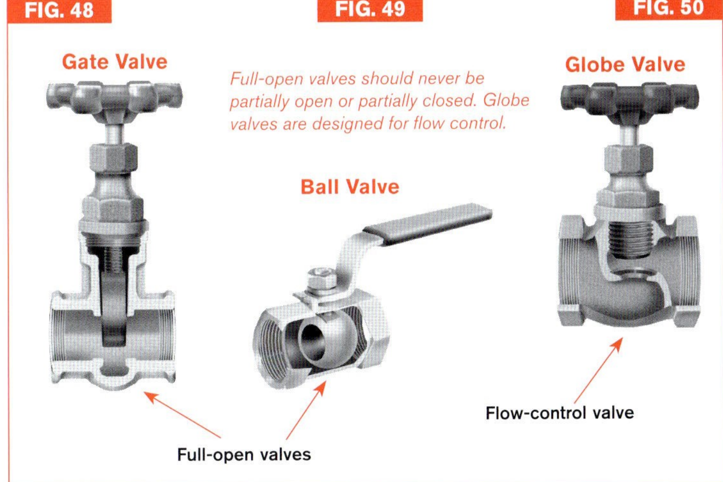

PEX Tubing — 21 IRC — 21 UPC

	21 IRC	21 UPC
☐ Secure AMI & support per **T3,4**	2903.8.3	313.3
☐ Wrap or sleeve bundles at change of direction ≥45°	2903.8.3	MFR
☐ Bend radius AMI **T24**	MFR	MFR
☐ No PEX within first 18 in. of tank-type WH	MFR	604.13

The Plastic Pipe and Fittings Association and the Plastic Piping Educational Foundation publish helpful design guides and training materials for PEX users. These include the following recommendations:

- Do not store unprotected PEX tubing outdoors and exposed to sunlight.
- Keep tubing & fittings in original packaging until time of installation.
- Minimize sunlight exposure as recommended by MFR.
- Maintain adequate distance between tubing and heat sources, such as light fixtures, flue vents, and heating appliances so that the pipe surface temperature does not exceed 180°F.
- Supports should allow free tubing movement for thermal expansion.
- Tubing should not be pulled tight; allow slack for expansion/contraction.
- Provide for expansion/contraction using offsets & expansion loops
- Min. bend radius 8× tubing diameter in direction of coil bend. **T24**
- Do not use supports that pinch or cut the tubing.
- Provide support near bends to prevent stress on fittings.
- Do not install within first 18 in. of connections to WH.

TABLE 24 RECOMMENDED[A] MIN. BEND RADIUS FOR PEX

Tubing Size (in. nominal)	Tubing Outer Diameter (in.)	Bend Radius (in.)
3/8	1/2	4
1/2	5/8	5
3/4	7/8	7
1	1 1/8	9

A: If bending the piping in the opposite direction from which it came off the coil, bending radius should be 3× the value shown in the table.

WATER SUPPLY SIZING

Water supply systems can be a "trunk and branch" system or a parallel system. Trunk and branch systems start with a large supply pipe and progressively smaller pipes toward each fixture outlet. Parallel systems have a manifold **F51** supplying "home runs" to each fixture, or there could be remote manifolds near clusters of fixtures. Each system has its advantages. A trunk and branch system will use less pipe but more fittings. Systems with manifolds generally use PEX tubing. The IRC supply size rules are based on parallel systems, while the UPC methods are based on the trunk and branch system. Each code requires a design that meets minimum required flow rates at the fixture outlets. Both methods start with assigning values of water supply fixture units (WSFUs) to determine the required capacity.

TABLE 25 WSFU FILL-IN TABLE ◆ IRC T2903.6 & UPC T610.3

Fixture	IRC			UPC	#	Extension
	Hot	Cold	Comb.	Comb.[A]		
Bathtub	1.0	1.0	1.4	4.0		
CW	1.0	1.0	1.4	4.0		
DW	1.4	—	1.4	1.5		
Hose bibb	—	2.5	2.5	2.5[B]		
KS	1.0	1.0	1.4	1.5		
Lav	0.5	0.5	0.7	1.0		
LT	1.0	1.0	1.4	1.5		
Shower (per head)	1.0	1.0	1.4	2.0		
Water closet	—	2.2	2.2	2.5		
Laundry group[C]	1.8	1.8	2.5	—		
Kitchen group[D]	1.9	1.0	2.5	—		
Half-bath group[E]	0.5	2.5	2.6	—		
Full-bath group[F]	1.5	2.7	3.6	—		
Total Demand						

A. UPC fixtures that have both hot & cold connections permitted to use 75% of listed total value of fixture.
B. First hose bibb counts as 2.5 WSFU. Additional hose bibbs add 1.0 WSFU.
C. Laundry group = CW standpipe and LT.
D. Kitchen group = DW and sink w/ or w/o garbage grinder.
E. Half-bath group = water closet and lavatory.
F. Full-bath group = water closet and lavatory and tub (w/ or w/o shower) or shower stall.

WATER SUPPLY SIZE

*WSFU values for individual fixtures take into account the fact that not all fixtures are used at the same time. The size of system and branch supplies in **T25** has a graduated scale for determining the size of a manifold based on this principle. The next step after determining the total WSFUs is to convert to gpm using **T26**. The manifold can then be sized using **T27**. Refer to the MFR instructions for other considerations of pipe length, pressure, and elevation changes.*

TABLE 26 CONVERTING WSFUs to GPM ◆ IRC T2903.6(1)

Load (WSFUs)	Demand (gpm) (flush tanks)[A]	Demand (gpm) (flushometer)[A]	Load (WSFUs)	Demand (gpm) (flush tanks)[A]	Demand (gpm) (flushometer)[A]
1	3.0	–	14	17.0	30.2
2	5.0	–	15	17.5	31.0
3	6.5	–	16	18.0	31.8
4	8.0	–	17	18.4	32.6
5	9.4	15.0	18	18.8	33.4
6	10.7	17.4	19	19.2	34.2
7	11.8	19.8	20	19.6	35.0
8	12.8	22.2	25	21.5	38.0
9	13.7	24.6	30	23.3	42.0
10	14.6	27.0	35	24.9	44.0
11	15.4	27.8	40	26.3	46.0
12	16.0	28.6	45	27.7	48.0
13	16.5	29.4	50	29.1	50.0

A. Choose demand from appropriate column based on whether predominately flush tanks or flushometer.

TABLE 27 MANIFOLD SIZING ◆ IRC T2903.8.1

Inlet Pipe Size (in.)	Max. GPM Plastic[A]	Max. GPM Metal[B]
¾	17	11
1	29	20
1¼	46	31
1½	66	44

A. Based on velocity limitation of 12 ft./second.
B. Based on velocity limitation of 8 ft./second.

FIG. 51

PEX Manifold

Hot water from WH
Cold water to WH
Hot-water lines out to fixtures
Cold-water lines out to fixtures
KITCHEN SINK HOT
KITCHEN SINK COLD
MASTER LAV HOT
MASTER LAV COLD
MASTER SH HOT
MASTER SH COLD
DISHWASHER HOT
1BR TOILET COLD
Shutoff valves
Manifold
Water inlet (size per **T27** & 1 size larger than WH feed)

Pipe & Tubing Size — 21 IRC

- ☐ Min. water service ¾ in. ____ 2903.7
- ☐ Mains, branches & risers size determined by demand gpm, available pressure & friction losses from water meter & developed length of pipe including equivalent length of fittings ____ 2903.7
- ☐ Size parallel system per **T25–27** ____ 2903.8.1
- ☐ Size system to provide required flow at peak demand **T28** ____ 2903.1
- ☐ If WH fed from end of cold-water manifold, **P51** manifold one size larger than WH feed ____ 2903.8.2
- ☐ Distribution lines ≤ 60 ft. can be ⅜ in. if meter pressure ≥40 psi ____ 2903.8.2
- ☐ Lines >⅜ in. reqd AMI for fixtures such as tubs & showers ____ 2903.8.2

TABLE 28 MIN. CAPACITIES AT FIXTURE OUTLETS ◆ IRC T2903.1

Fixture Outlet	Flow Rate (gpm)	Flow Pressure (psi)
Bathtub (BT)	4	20
Bidet	2	20
Dishwasher (DW)	2.75	8
Laundry tray (LT)	4	8
Lavatory/Lav (Sink)	0.8	8
Shower (pressure-balancing or thermostatic mixing)[A]	2.5	20
Hose bibb	5	8
Sink	1.75	8
Water closet (WC) (tank type)	3	20
WC (flushometer)	1.6	20
WC (one piece)	6	20

A. Where valve MFR indicates lower flow, use lower value.

The procedure for sizing in the UPC is based on the number of fixture units served by each section of piping, including mains and branches. A tree diagram showing the WSFUs on each section of piping can then be filled in with the appropriate sizes from ***T30****. A similar method is also included in IRC Appendix AP.*

TABLE 29 METER & PIPE SIZING WORKSHEET ◆ UPC 610.4

1. Determine fixture unit demand (total from **T30**).	
2. Determine min. daily static pressure at meter or source.	
3. Subtract (add) ½ lb. pressure per ft. of rise (fall).	
4. Deduct pressure losses for filters, regulators, etc.	
5. Find pressure range group in **T30.**	
6. Find column for developed length to most remote fixture.	
7. Find row meeting fixture unit demand (total from **T30**).	
8. Find reqd meter & pipe size in left column of **T30**.	

NOTE: The same procedure can be used for branches.

TABLE 30 WATER SUPPLY SIZING ◆ UPC T610.4

Meter (in.)	Supply (in.)	Max. Fixture Units Allowed Per Length of Pipe					
30-45 PSI		**40 FT.**	**60 ft.**	**80 ft.**	**100 ft.**	**150 ft.**	**200 ft.**
¾	½[A]	6	5	4	3	2	1
¾	¾	16	16	14	12	9	6
¾	1	29	25	23	21	17	15
1	1	36	31	27	25	20	17
¾	1¼	36	33	31	28	24	23
1	1¼	54	47	42	38	32	28
1½	1¼	78	68	57	48	38	32
1	1½	85	84	79	65	56	48
1½	1½	150	124	105	91	70	57
2	1½	151	129	129	110	80	64
46-60 PSI		**40 ft.**	**60 ft.**	**80 ft.**	**100 ft.**	**150 ft.**	**200 ft.**
¾	½[A]	7	7	6	5	4	3
¾	¾	20	20	19	17	14	11
¾	1	39	39	36	33	28	23
1	1	39	39	39	36	30	25
¾	1¼	39	39	39	39	39	39
1	1¼	78	78	76	67	52	44
1½	1¼	78	78	78	78	66	52
1	1½	85	85	85	85	85	85
1½	1½	151	151	151	151	128	105
2	1 ½	151	151	151	151	150	117
Over 60 PSI		**40 ft.**	**60 ft.**	**80 ft.**	**100 ft.**	**150 ft.**	**200 ft.**
¾	½[A]	7	7	7	6	5	4
¾	¾	20	20	20	20	17	13
¾	1	39	39	39	39	35	30
1	1	39	39	39	39	38	32
¾	1¼	39	39	39	39	39	39
1	1¼	78	78	78	78	74	62
1½	1¼	78	78	78	78	78	74
1	1½	85	85	85	85	85	85
1½	1½	151	151	151	151	151	151
2	1½	151	151	151	151	151	151

A: Min. building supply is ¾ in.

CROSS-CONNECTION CONTROL

Backflow prevention devices protect water systems from backup and contamination. An air gap is a physical separation and is used to protect waste receptors, such as sinks. Atmospheric vacuum breakers (AVBs) **F55** prevent contaminants from entering through systems such as lawn sprinklers and must be in locations above the elevation of the potential contaminant. A reduced-pressure principal backflow protection assembly (RP) **F54** consists of two independently acting check valves, a differential pressure relief valve, test cocks, and isolation valves. These afford the greatest degree of protection, Municipalities sometimes require them to protect the public system from contamination by a customer. They require testing upon installation and must be at least 12 inches above grade or floor.

Protection of Potable Water — 21 IRC — 21 UPC

- ☐ Prevent contamination of potable water supply ________ 2902.1 — 602.1
- ☐ Connections from private to public water supply prohibited 2902.1 — 602.2
- ☐ Fixture outlet receptor air gaps:
  - Min. 2× diameter of outlet and per table **F52,T31** ___ 2902.3.1 — 603.3.1

TABLE 31 MINIMUM AIR GAPS ◆ IRC T2902.3.1 & UPC T603.3.1

Max. Opening Diameter & Typical Fixtures (in.)	Not Affected by Side Walls (in.)		Affected by Side Walls[A] (in.)	
	IRC	UPC	IRC	UPC
≤½ (lav)	1	1	1½	1½
≤¾ (LT)	1½	1½	2½	2¼
≤1(BT)	2	2	3	3
>1 (pool)	2× diameter	2× diameter	3× diameter	3× diameter

A. Affected by side walls = any time the distance from the spout to the wall is <3× the diameter of the effective opening, or <4× the diameter for 2 intersecting walls.

Backflow Prevention Devices — 21 IRC — 21 UPC

- ☐ RP reqd **F54** for:
  - Boilers w/ conditioning chemicals ________ 2902.5.1 — 603.5.10
  - Fire-sprinkler systems w/ additives ________ 2902.5.4.1 — 603.5.14.2
  - Lawn irrigation systems w/ chemical injectors ______ 2902.5.3 — 603.5.6.3
  - Solar heating piping w/ additives ________ 2902.5.5.3 — 603.5.6.3
  - Pool/spa makeup water—RP or air gap reqd ________ 2902.4 — 603.5.20
- ☐ AVB reqd for:
  - Hose bibbs exc tank drains or CW valves **F53** ______ 2902.4.3 — 603.5.7
  - Pool/spa inlets min. 6 in. above critical level ________ 2902.3.2 — 603.5.5
  - Irrigation system, 6 in. above highest head ________ 2902.3.2 — 603.5.6
  - Pressure-type AVBs min. 12 in. above highest head **F55** 2902.3.4 — 603.5.6
  - Flushometer valves, 6 in. above fixture FLR________ 2902.3.2 — 603.5.1
- ☐ Integral air gaps in fixtures to recognized standards OK for:
  - Reverse osmosis drinking water treatment units________ 2909.2 — 603.4.6
  - DWs (UPC: comply w/ UL 749 section SA 3.4) ______ 2717.1 — 414.2

*(Air gaps on the supply are not the same as drainage air gap devices **F62**).*

  - Pullout spouts and sprayers w/ integral AVB AMI ____ 2902.4.2 — 603.4.6
  - Pullout or separate shower spray wands__________ 2902.4.2 — 603.4.6
  - Flush tank w/ antisiphon fill valves (ballcock valves) critical level min. 1 in. above opening of overflow pipe______ 2902.4.1 — 603.5.2

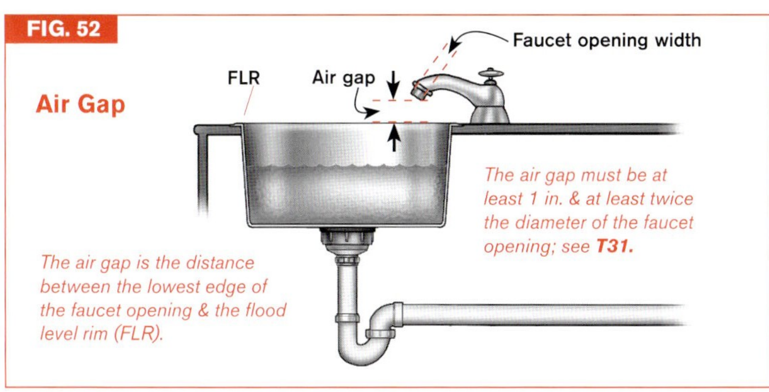
FIG. 52
Air Gap
FLR
Air gap
Faucet opening width
The air gap must be at least 1 in. & at least twice the diameter of the faucet opening; see T31.
The air gap is the distance between the lowest edge of the faucet opening & the flood level rim (FLR).

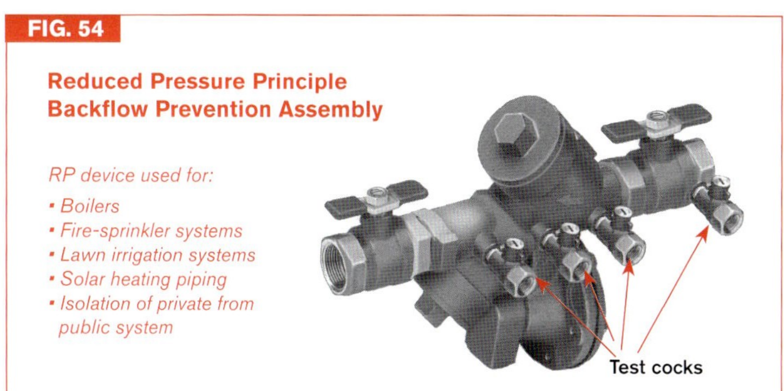
FIG. 54
Reduced Pressure Principle Backflow Prevention Assembly
RP device used for:
• Boilers
• Fire-sprinkler systems
• Lawn irrigation systems
• Solar heating piping
• Isolation of private from public system
Test cocks

FIG. 53
Hose Bibb Backflow Protection
Hose bibb vacuum breaker
Backflow prevention device
Built-in backflow preventer
Hose bibbs (including laundry sinks) require backflow protection devices, except for clothes washers & tank drains (such as water heaters).

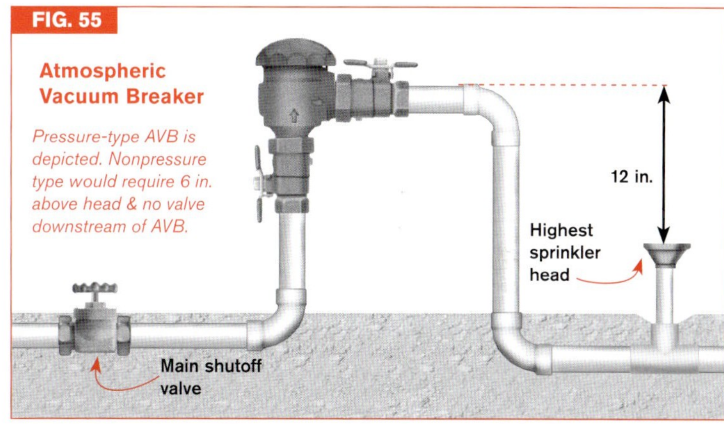
FIG. 55
Atmospheric Vacuum Breaker
Pressure-type AVB is depicted. Nonpressure type would require 6 in. above head & no valve downstream of AVB.
12 in.
Highest sprinkler head
Main shutoff valve

WATER PRESSURE

Excessive water pressure is controlled by installation of a pressure-reducing regulator on the incoming line. These regulators must conform to the ASSE 1003 standard, which includes a requirement for a screen that may require periodic cleaning. A "closed system" is created when a one-way valve is installed on the main water supply. Filters, backflow preventers, and regulators have such valves.

As water in a storage tank water heater is replaced by cold water, pressure in the tank is reduced. As the temperature recovers in the tank, pressure increases and is normally equalized with the municipal water system pressure. Closed systems prevent this pressure equalization, resulting in excessive pressure in the piping downstream from the regulator. The solution is an expansion tank installed on the cold water line at the water heater. The IRC calls for a "device for controlling pressure" in these situations, whereas the UPC explicitly requires that the device be an expansion tank. IRC jurisdictions might allow a pressure-relief valve rather than an expansion tank.

General	**21 IRC**	**21 UPC**
☐ Public water main or individual water supply pressure must provide reqd flow at fixtures **T28**	2903.3	608.1
☐ If pressure insufficient, install booster pump, tanks, etc.	2903.3	608.1
☐ UPC min. 15 psi after allowing for all pressure losses	n/a	608.1
☐ Max. building water pressure 80 psi	2903.3.2	608.2
☐ Pressure-reducing regulator **F56** reqd when > 80 psi	2903.3.2	608.2
☐ Strainer **F56** reqd ahead of regulator EXC	2903.3.2	608.2
• Regulators for piping >1½ in.	n/a	608.2
☐ Regulator & strainer accessible w/o removing piping	MFR	608.2
☐ Pipe sizing based on 80% of regulated pressure	n/a	608.2
☐ Device for controlling pressure (UPC: expansion tank) reqd on systems w/ regulators that prevent pressure dissipation **F57**	2903.4.1	608.3
Note: older regulators w/ "integral bypass feature" are no longer recognized by codes & should also be considered as creating a closed system.		
☐ Device for controlling pressure (UPC: expansion tank) reqd if backflow device prevents pressure dissipation	2903.4.2	608.3

FIG. 56

Pressure Regulator

Pressure-reducing valves must conform to ASSE 1003 or CSA B356.

Pressure is increased by turning the bolt further *into* the regulator.

Strainer must remain accessible.

Strainer

FIG. 57

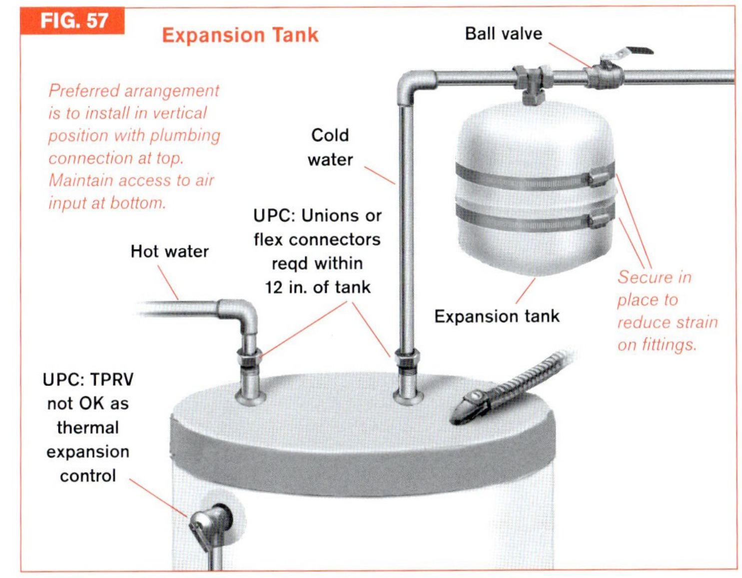

FIXTURES

Fixtures include faucets, showers, sinks, toilets, hose bibbs, and similar equipment. Fixtures must meet recognized standards. Faucets, toilets, and showers must conform to federal water conservation regulations. Many states and local jurisdictions have stricter conservation standards.

General	21 IRC	21 UPC
☐ Max. water consumption of fixtures per **T32**	2903.2	See **T32**
☐ Fixtures reqd to be smooth, impervious & free from concealed fouling areas **F58**	2701.1	401.2
☐ Watertight seal reqd between fixtures & walls or floors (e.g.; caulk base of toilet)	2705.1(3)	402.2
☐ Rigidly secure fixtures to walls/floors	2705.1(1&2)	402.3&4
☐ Valves reqd on each fixture supply EXC	2903.9.3	606.5
• Tubs & showers (UPC: fixtures w/o slip joints)	2903.9.3	606.5
• Shutoff may be at manifold (***see p. 36***) **F51**	2903.8.4	606.5
☐ Hot on left, cold on right when facing outlet EXC	2722.2	417.5
• Single-handle controls—orientation per control labels	2722.2X	417.5
☐ Sinks & lavs req drain strainer (UPC: stopper in lav OK)	2702.1	407.5&420.4
☐ Tailpiece min. 1¼ in. for lavs & bidets	2703.1	T702.1
☐ Tailpiece min. 1½ in. for other residential fixtures	2703.1	420.4
☐ Floor drains req removable strainers	2719.1	418.2

FIG. 58

Concealed Fouling Areas

No part of a fixture should be concealed such that it cannot be cleaned. Sinks secured to the underside of a drainboard often harbor a neglected fouling surface.

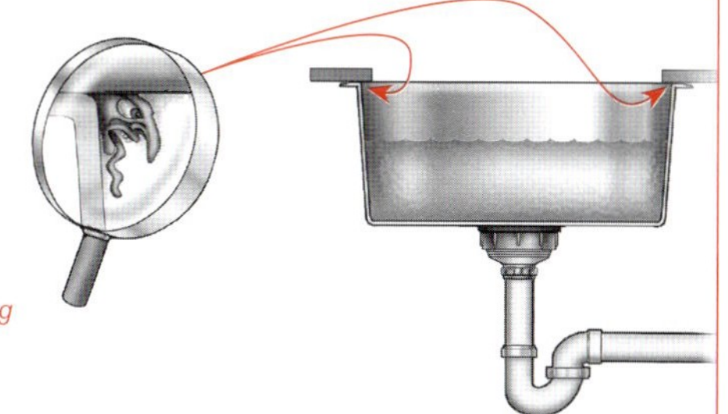

TABLE 32 MAX. FLOW RATES FOR PLUMBING FIXTURES IRC T2903.2 & UPC 407.2, 408.2, 411.2, 420.2

Plumbing Fixture or Fixture Fitting	Max. Flow Rate
Lavatory faucet	2.2 gpm at 60 psi[A]
Shower head[B]	2.5 gpm at 80 psi
Sink faucet	2.2 gpm at 60 psi
Water closet	1.6 gal. per flush

A. Private only; max. flow rate for public lav faucet is 0.5 gpm in the IPC & UPC.
B. Handheld shower sprays are also considered shower heads.

Clothes Washers & Laundry Sinks (Trays)	21 IRC	21 UPC
☐ Standpipe ≥18 in. & ≤42 in. (30 in. UPC) above trap **F59**	2706.1.2	804.1
☐ Must drain through air break (no pressurized waste)	2718.1	805.1
☐ No trap below floor	n/a	804.1
☐ Trap ≥6 in. & ≤18 in. above floor **F59**	n/a	804.1
☐ LT may drain into washer standpipe within 30 in. if standpipe min. 30 in. above trap weir & above FLR of LT **F60**	2706.1.2.1	local

FIG. 59

Laundry Standpipe

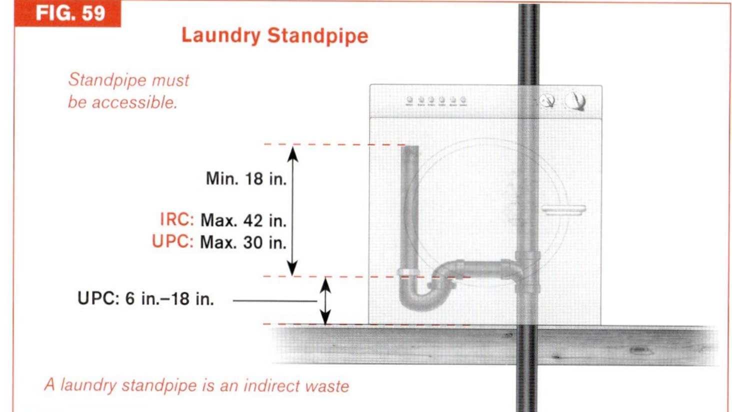

A laundry standpipe is an indirect waste

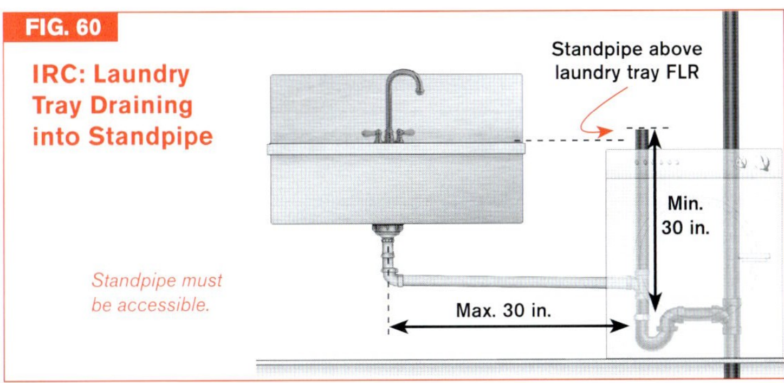

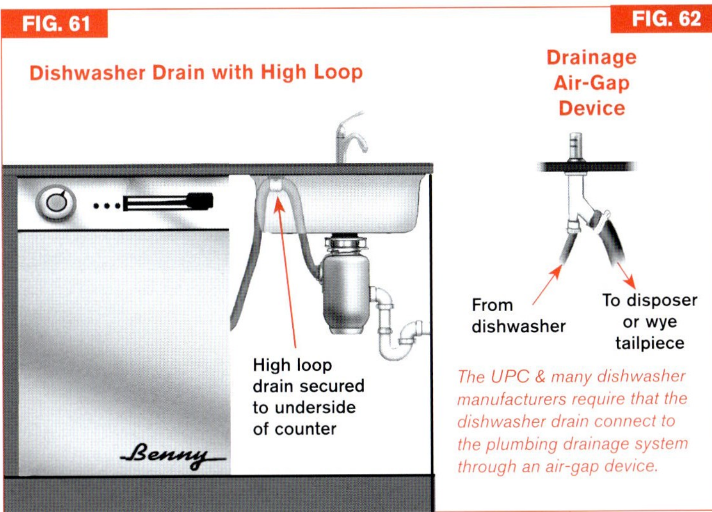

The supply to a dishwasher is required to have backflow protection in the form of an air gap complying with ASME A112.1.3 or A112.1.2. That air gap is often confused with the requirement for a drainage air gap fitting. The supply air gap protects the potable water supply from being contaminated by what is in the dishwasher. The drainage air gap protects the clean dishes from being contaminated by a drain line backup. Dishwasher manufacturers may require them regardless of whether the applicable code also requires them.

Kitchen Sinks & Fixtures	21 IRC	21 UPC
☐ Sink min. outlet 1½ in. diameter	2714.1	T702.1
☐ OK for sink, DW & disposer on same 1½-in. trap	2717.2	T702.1
☐ 2-in. drain reqd for sink downstream of trap	n/a	T702.1
☐ DW supply reqs air gap or integral backflow device	2717.1	602.3
☐ DW may discharge (UPC: through air gap fitting) directly to a branch wye tailpiece on KS or to head of food waste disposer **F61,62**	2717.2	414.3
☐ Secure DW drain hose to underside of counter **F62**	2717.2	n/a
☐ Air gap fitting reqd for DW drain **F61**	n/a	807.3
☐ Air gap fitting critical level above FLR of sink	n/a	807.3
☐ No DW connection to discharge side of disposer	MFR	414.3
☐ Reverse osmosis systems to recognized standards	2909.2	611.1
☐ Reverse osmosis system discharge reqs air gap **F63**	2909.2	611.2
☐ No saddle fittings or tapping/drilling of drain line	3003.2	310.2

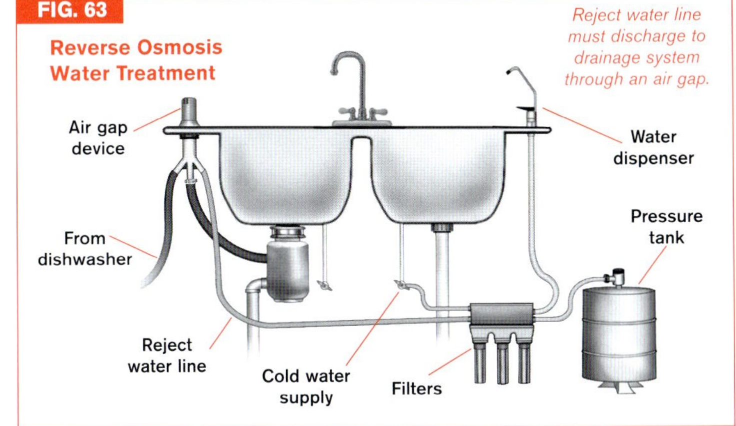

Toilets & Bidets

	21 IRC	21 UPC
☐ Secure floor flange to drainage connection & to floor w/ corrosion-resistant fasteners	2705.1(1)	402.6.2
☐ Install flanges AMI w/ no concealed fouling area **F66**	2701.1	402.6.1
☐ No offset closet flanges for floor-mounted back outlet WCs	n/a	402.6.3[7]
☐ 15-in. min. clearance from center toilet (WC) or bidet to side wall, vanity, or outer rim of adjacent fixtures **F65**	2705.1(5)	402.5
☐ 21 in. min. (UPC : 24 in.) clear in front of lav or toilet **F65**	2705.1(5)	402.5
☐ Toilet or bidet min. 30-in. separation center to center	2705.1(5)	402.5
☐ Offset flanges must be listed & approved for same	3005.1.6(3)	310.5
☐ UPC: closet flange to vent max. 6 ft. (IRC: unlimited)	3105.1X	T1002.2
☐ Ballcock critical level ≥1 in. above overflow pipe **F64**	2902.4.1	603.5.2
☐ Joint between fixture & floor or wall to be watertight	2705.1(3)	402.2
☐ Bidet supply reqs air gap vacuum breaker fixture supply	2721.1	410.2
☐ Max. discharge temp at bidet 110°F	2721.2	410.3
☐ Bidet temperature limiting device per ASSE 1070/ASME A112.1070/CSA B125.70	2721.2	410.3

FIG. 64 Flush Tank Fill Valves

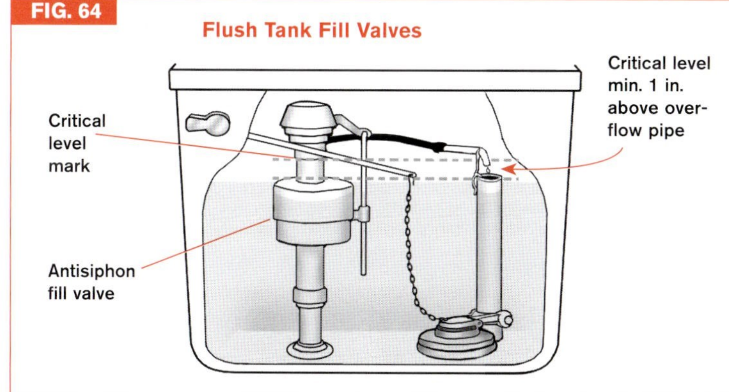

7. Previous code specifically prohibited offsets for floor flanges. The wording changed to "closet flanges" and is part of a paragraph about back-outlet WCs. Offset floor flanges that are listed and labeled (such as with an IAPMO shield) & approved & that do not pose an obstruction are allowed by the UPC.

FIG. 65 Fixture Layout

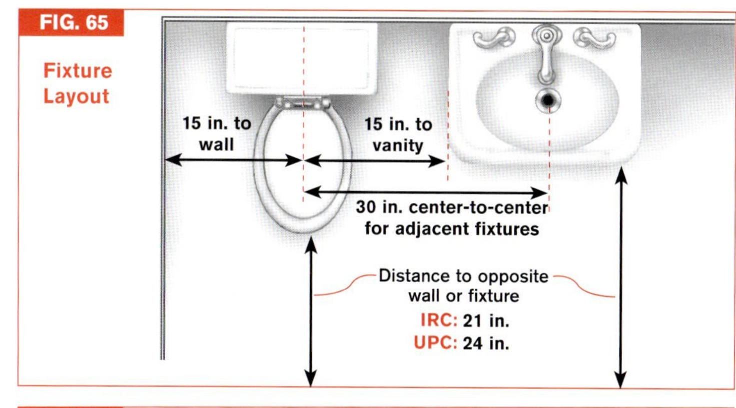

FIG. 66 Toilet Flanges (Closet Rings)

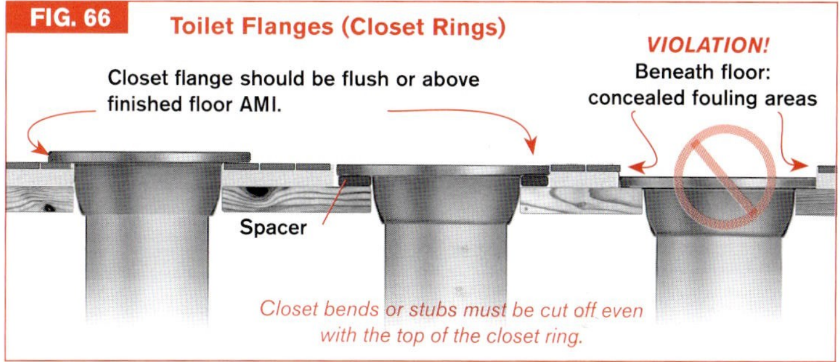

Tubs & Whirlpools *(also see Code Check Electrical)*

	21 IRC	21 UPC
☐ Slip joints accessible, min. 12-in. × 12-in. access **F28**	2704.1	402.10
☐ Tub waste opening to crawlspace reqs rodent screen	n/a	312.12.3
☐ Over-rim spigot min. vertical air gap 2× outlet diameter	T2902.3.1	T603.3.1
☐ Tubs, whirlpools req temp-limiting device at max. 120°F, water heater thermostat is not acceptable method	2713.3	409.4
☐ Whirlpool pump accessible & above trap crown weir	2720.2	409.6
☐ Pump access ≥12 × 12 in., 18 × 18 in. if >2 ft. from access	2720.1	n/a

Showers

Showers	21 IRC	21 UPC
☐ Min. area 900 sq. in. (UPC: 1,024 sq. in.) **F67** EXC	2708.1	408.6
• Fold-down seats protruding into space must allow the min. 900-sq.-in. area w/ seat in folded-up position	2708.1X1	n/a
☐ Must be able to encompass 30-in.-diameter circle from top of threshold to point 70 in. above drain outlet EXC	2708.1	408.6
• Shower heads, valves, grab bars & soap dishes allowed to protrude into reqd min. space	2708.1	408.6
• 25-in. cross section OK if area ≥1300 sq. in.	2708.1X2	n/a
• Area & dimensions not reqd if min. 30-in. × 60-in. enclosure	n/a	408.6X2
☐ Shower walls nonabsorbent to min. 72 in. above drain	307.2	local
☐ If threshold provided, height min. 1 in. below top of shower receptor membrane & min. 2 in. max. 9 in. above top of drain **F68**	2709.1	408.5
☐ If no threshold, adjacent floor considered a wet location	local	408.5
☐ Door min. 22-in.-wide clear egress opening **F67**	2708.1.1	408.5
☐ Door must open outward **F67**	2708.1	local
☐ Finished floor slope min. 1/4 in./ft. (UPC 1/8 in.) max. 1/2 in./ft.	2709.1	408.5
☐ Secure shower valve, head/riser to permanent structure	2708.3	408.10
☐ Shower head cannot discharge directly at entrance	local	408.9
☐ Listed anti-scald/pressure balance valve reqd 120° max.	2708.4	408.3
☐ Min. 2-in. drain outlet (IRC 1 1/2-in.), strainer of equivalent area	2708.2	408.4

Shower Pan & Liner

Shower Pan & Liner	21 IRC	21 UPC
☐ Site-built liner materials conform to approved standards	2709.2	408.7
☐ Slope underlayment 1/4 in./ft. to weep holes **F68**	2709.3	408.7
• Liner min. 2 in. above dam or threshold (UPC: 3 in.) **F68**	2709.2	408.7
☐ Pan liner plastic AMI or 3 layers hot mop type 15 felt	2709.2	408.7
☐ Special attention to hot mop corner installation; extend 4 in. all directions from corner	2709.2.3	408.7
☐ PVC & CPE sheet lining cemented AMI	2709.2.1&2	408.7.1&2
☐ Weep holes at drain reqd & must remain clear **F68**	2709.4	408.7
☐ No fasteners in liner <1 in. above finished threshold	2709. 3	408.7
☐ Roll over top of rough threshold (no penetrations through top) & fasten to outside edge **F68**	2709.3	408.7
☐ Watertight connection between liner and drain flange	2709.4	408.7

Testing

Testing	21 IRC	21 UPC
☐ Pan leak test min. 2 in. water measured at threshold, min. 15 minutes (UPC: water level ≥ rough threshold height)	2503.6	408.7.5
☐ Pan leak test reqs plug (balloon) in pipe below flange	2503.6	408.7.5

FIG. 67

Shower Receptor

Overall net area
***IRC**: 900 sq. in.*
***UPC:** 1024 sq. in*

Soap dishes, grab bars, shower heads & valves allowed in 30-in.-wide space.

Min. 30 in.
Min. 30 in.

Min. 30 in. cross-section area; circle is measured from center of threshold.

Min. 22-in. clear opening

Door swings outward in direction of egress from shower.

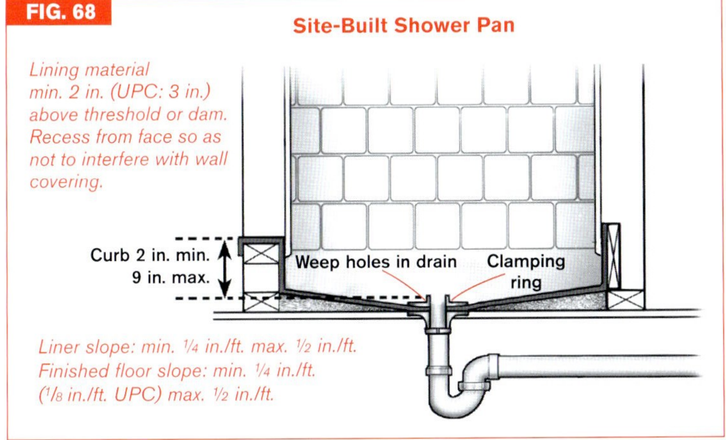

WATER HEATERS

Water heaters should be maintained at the lowest temperature needed to minimize scalding risk, but high enough to reduce the possibility of unwanted biologic growth in the system. An undersized water heater is more likely to be turned to a dangerously high setting. Protection against scalding can also be provided by tempering valves at the water heater or at individual fixtures. Tankless water heaters are becoming more popular, including hybrid systems that contain a small storage tank and circulating line. Heat pump water heaters may be mandated or encouraged by local energy codes and require a location with adequate air volume for the extraction of heat from ambient air. Indirect water heaters are discussed in *Code Check Mechanical* on ***p. 213***.

General

	21 IRC	21 UPC
☐ Replacement water heaters req permits	105.1	502.1
☐ Installation & maintenance instructions to be left w/ WH	1307.1	507.24
☐ Size to meet demand **T33**	2448.1.1	501.1
☐ Installation AMI & all instructions in L&L	2005.1 & 2801.3	501.1
☐ WH also used for space heating must be L&L for both	2448.2	501.1
☐ Electric WH reqs in-sight or lockable disconnect **F76**	T4101.5	NEC
☐ Fuel-fired WH combustion air; see ***pp. 188–189***	2407.1	506.1
☐ Fuel-fired WH venting; see ***pp. 190–198***	1801.1 & 2427.1	509.0

Valves & Connections

	21 IRC	21 UPC
☐ Full-open type valve reqd on supply at WH **F48,49,70**	2903.9.2	606.2
☐ Systems also used for space heating req temperature-actuated mixing valve to temper domestic water to 140°F or less	2803.2	n/a
☐ Unions reqd (UPC: within 12 in.) to allow removal **F70,76**	MFR	609.5
☐ Cu, brass, or stainless steel flexible connectors max. 24 in.	n/a	604.12
☐ Where water heater tank located at elevation above fixture outlets (e.g., attic), vacuum relief valve reqd on water heater	n/a	608.7
☐ PEX, PEX-AL-PEX, PE-AL-PE, or PE-RT tubing not within first 18 in. of piping connected to WH	MFR	604.13

TABLE 33 UPC WATER HEATER MIN. CAPACITY[A] ◆ T501.1(2)

Number of Bathrooms	Number of Bedrooms	1st-hr. Rating[B]
1 to 1½	1	38
	2	49
	3	49
2 to 2½	2	49
	3	62
	4	62
	5	74
3 to 3½	3	62
	4	74
	5	74
	6	74

A. Based upon the first-hour rating found on the "Energy Guide" label. This number is approximately equal to the storage size plus hourly recovery rate.
B. This table can also be used to size tankless water heaters.

FIG. 69

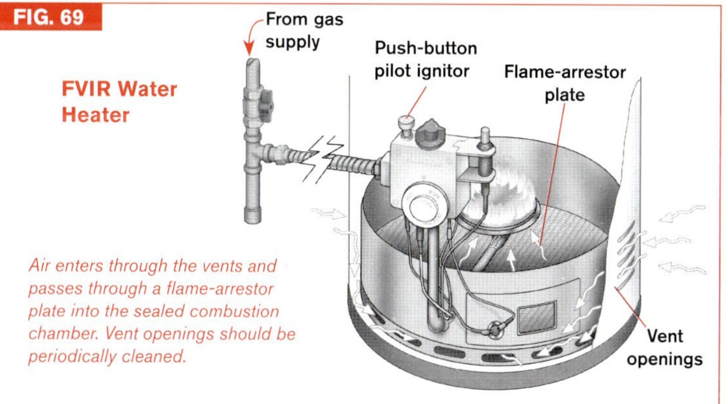

Air enters through the vents and passes through a flame-arrestor plate into the sealed combustion chamber. Vent openings should be periodically cleaned.

Special Locations	21 IRC	21 UPC
☐ Fuel-fired WH prohibited in storage closets __	2005.2 & 2406.2	local
☐ Not in bedrooms or bathrooms EXC________	2005.2 & 2406.2	504.1
• Direct-vent WH OK w/o enclosure ________	2005.2 & 2406.2	504.1(1)
• In dedicated enclosure w/ solid, weatherstripped, self-close door & all combustion air from exterior ______	2005.2 & 2406.2	504.1(2)
☐ Ignition source ≥18 in. above garage floor EXC **F70** ____	2801.7	507.13
• Flammable Vapor Ignition-Resistant (FVIR) WH **F69**__	2801.7X	507.13
• WH in separate enclosure accessible only from outside the garage & no combustion air from garage __	1307.3	507.13.2
☐ Not to be installed where flammables are stored__________	MFR	507.12
☐ Seismic bracing reqd upper & lower ⅓ of tank in SDC D & townhomes SDC C (UPC: all occupancies SDC C–F) **F70**_	1307.2 & 2801.8	507.2
☐ Barrier or elevation reqd in vehicle path (garages, etc.) **F70**_	1307.3.1	507.13.1
☐ Min. 3-in. concrete pad reqd if supported on ground	1305.1.3.1	507.4

Access & Working Space		
☐ Clearances to combustibles per L&L and AMI_	1306.1 & 2801.4	504.3.1
☐ Remain accessible for service, inspection & removal ____	1305.1	504.3.1
☐ Attic hatch or door min. 22 in. wide × 30 in. high ___	1305.1.2&3	508.4
☐ Largest appliance fits through access (crawl, attic)____	1305.1.2&3	508.4
☐ Attic min. 24-in. passageway, solid floor to WH ______	1305.1.2	508.4.2
☐ Max. 20 ft. from access opening if ceiling <6 ft. ______	1305.1.2	508.4.1
☐ Min. 30-in. × 30-in. level working platform reqd EXC __	1305.1.2	508.4.3
• Platform not reqd if service possible from opening___	1305.1.2	local
☐ Light & receptacle near WH in attic _____________	1305.1.2.1	508.4.4
☐ Light switch reqd at passageway entrance ____________	3903.4	508.4.4

FIG. 70

FVIR Water Heater in Garage

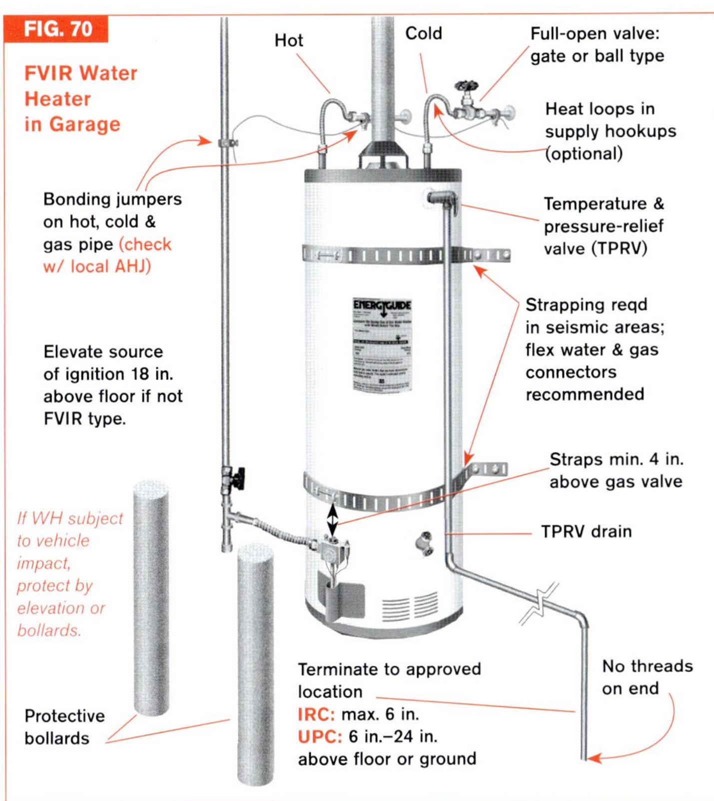

Tankless (On Demand) Water Heaters F71

	21 IRC	21 UPC
☐ Size AMI to meet demand	2005.1	501.1
☐ Size gas line to max. Btu input rating	2413.1	1215.2
☐ Vent AMI, Category III or IV typically reqd	2005.1	509.1.1
☐ PRV AMI, PRV size at appliance input rating or above	2804.2&3	504.6
☐ No venting in common unless AMI	2427.10.4	509.10.3.2
☐ Direct-vent water heater vent clearances per F72,T34	2427.8[8]	T509.8.2

TABLE 34 THROUGH-WALL DIRECT VENT TERMINAL CLEARANCES ◆ IRC T2427.8 UPC T509.8.2

Location of Vent Terminal	Min. Clearance
Clearance above finished grade, porch, deck, or balcony	12 in.
Clearance to openable window or door	6 in. for appliances ≤10kBtu/hr. 9 in. if > 10kBtu/hr. ≤50kBtu/hr. 12 in. if > 50kBtu/hr. ≤150kBtu/hr. 4 ft. below or to side or 1 ft. above if >150kBtu/hr.
Clearance to non-openable window	None
Vertical clearance to ventilated or unventilated soffit above terminal	None unless AMI
Clearance to inside or outside corner	None unless AMI
Clearance to vertical centerline of gas meter regulator vent outlet	3 ft. up to height of 15 ft. above outlet or per utility
Clearance in any direction from gas meter regulator vent outlet	3 ft. for pressures ≤2 psi, 10 ft. if >2 psi, or per utility
Clearance to air supply inlet or to combustion air inlet of appliances	Same as clearance to openable window
Clearance to mechanical air supply inlet	10 ft. horizontal or 3 ft. above
Clearance above paved sidewalk or driveway on public property	7 ft. & not located where condensate or vapor could cause nuisance or hazard
Clearance to underside of porch deck or balcony	12 in. where porch deck or balcony open on at least 2 sides. Not allowed if only one side is open.

8. Table is new in this code edition. Most items were already part of previous code in various places & have been collected into a table format.

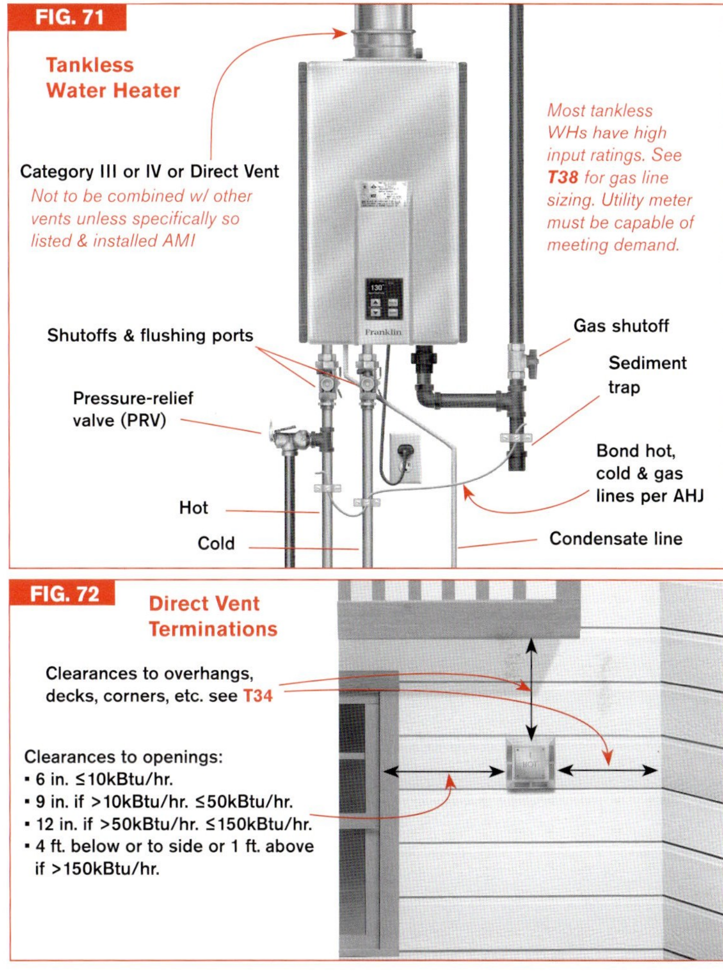

Temperature & Pressure Relief Valves (TPRVs)	21 IRC	21 UPC
☐ All WHs req pressure relief device **F70,71,75,76**	2804.1	504.4
☐ All WHs req temperature-limiting device **F70,71,74,76**	2804.1	504.5
☐ IRC: devices may be combination TPRV (UPC: mandatory for storage-tank water heaters) **F70,76**	2804.1(2)	608.3
☐ Temp probe in top 6 in. of tank (UPC: AMI) **F70,74,76**	2804.4	504.5
☐ Device must open at 150 psi OR 210°F	2804.3&4	608.4
☐ Watts 210 also reqs PRV **F74,75**	2804.1	504.6
TPRV Drain Piping		
☐ No shutoff or check valves before or after TPRV	2804.6	504.6
☐ Must discharge through air gap in same room as WH	2804.6(2)	n/a
☐ Drain min. 3/4 in. & ≥ valve outlet EXC	2804.6.1(3)	608.5(1)
• PEX or PE-RT min. 1 size larger if insert fittings used	2804.6.1(14)	n/a
• Secure end of PEX or PE-RT	2804.6.1(14)	n/a
☐ Material rated for temperature & in accord w/ ASME A112.4.1 (typically any material allowed for water distribution)	2804.6.1(13)	608.5(2)
☐ Drain must end outdoors or to indirect waste	2804.6.1(5)	608.5(3)
☐ May not drain to crawlspace	2803.6.1(6&7)	608.5(3)
☐ Terminate min. 2× pipe diameter max. 6 in. from ground or receptor (UPC: 6 in. min., 24 in. max.)	2804.6.1(10)	608.5(3)
☐ Must not discharge in a manner that could cause injury	2804.6.1(6)	608.5(4)
☐ Drain by gravity; cannot run uphill or be trapped	2804.6.1(8&9)	608.5(3&5)
☐ No threads on end of pipe	2804.6.1(11)	608.5(6)
☐ Each TPRV piped independently, may not be shared w/ condensate drain or relief valves of other systems	2804.6.1(4)	608.5(7)
☐ IRC: May discharge into pan (UPC: prohibited) **F76**	2804.5.1	Ø 608.5(7)
☐ No kinks or restrictions in pipe	2804.6.1(3)	608.5(1)
☐ Terminate in readily observable location	2804.6.1(7)	608.5(8)[9]
☐ End of pipe must be pointing down	n/a	608.5(1)
☐ Protect from freezing (terminate through air gap to indirect receptor located in a heated space)	2804.6.1(2)	608.5(5)

9. New to the UPC in this code edition.

FIG. 73 Combination Temperature & Pressure-Relief Valve

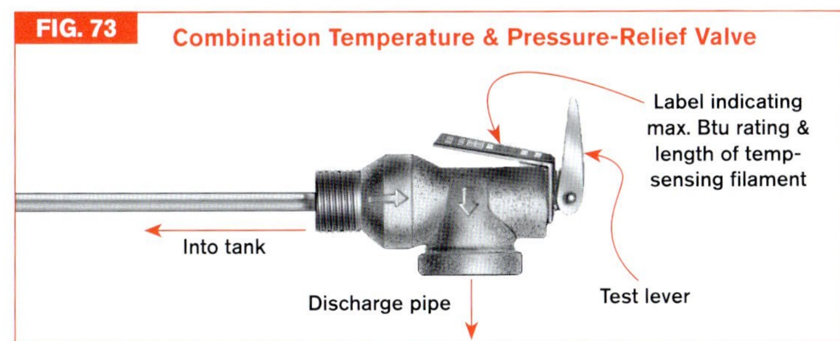

FIG. 74 Watts 210 Gas Shutoff Valve

FIG. 75 Pressure-Relief Valve

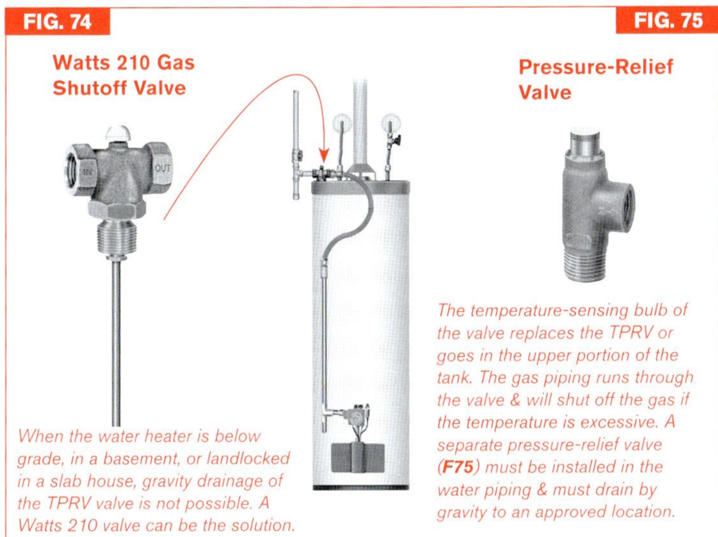

When the water heater is below grade, in a basement, or landlocked in a slab house, gravity drainage of the TPRV valve is not possible. A Watts 210 valve can be the solution.

*The temperature-sensing bulb of the valve replaces the TPRV or goes in the upper portion of the tank. The gas piping runs through the valve & will shut off the gas if the temperature is excessive. A separate pressure-relief valve (**F75**) must be installed in the water piping & must drain by gravity to an approved location.*

Required Pans & Drain

	21 IRC	21 UPC
☐ Watertight corrosion-resistant pan reqd for WHs located where leakage could cause damage (UPC: to framing) **F76**	2801.6	507.5
☐ Pan min. 1½ in. deep **F76**	2801.6.1	507.5
☐ Pan not reqd under tankless water heater	2801.6	local
☐ Plastic pans under gas water heaters req flame spread index ≤25 & smoke-developed index ≤450	2801.6	n/a
☐ Min. ¾-in.-diameter drain reqd EXC **F76**	2801.6.1	507.5
• Not reqd for replacement WH if none at existing pan	2801.6.1	n/a
☐ PVC not OK for pan drain piping	2801.6.1	n/a
☐ Pan drain reqd to end in indirect waste or outdoors 6 in. to 24 in. above grade (UPC: to any approved location)	2801.6.2	507.5

FIG. 76 Drain Pan & TPRV Discharge

TPRV discharge pipe:
- No threads on end
- Not trapped (not uphill)
- No smaller than TPRV outlet
- No valves or tee fittings
- IRC: Max. 6 in. above receptor
- UPC: Not to terminate in pan; discharge 6-24 in. above ground
- Discharge to readily observable location

TPRV & discharge pipe

Disconnect within sight, or breaker w/ locking hasp

Min. 1½ in. deep

TPRV drain materials approved for interior water pipe (no PVC)

IRC: Pan drain only w/ materials approved for interior water pipe (no PVC)

GAS PIPING

The model code upon which others are based is the *NFPA 54, The National Fuel Gas Code, ANSI Z223.1*. There are few differences between it and the fuel gas provisions of the IRC, IFGC, UPC, and UMC. This conformity allows appliance manufacturers and installers to have uniform nationwide standards and practices.

General

	21 IRC	21 UPC
☐ Nonsteel pipe reqs yellow label marked “gas” in black letters at ≤5-ft. intervals EXC	2412.5	n/a
• When located in same room as appliance served	2412.5	n/a
☐ If >1 meter, mark each meter as to the premise served	2412.7	1208.7.4
☐ LPG storage & piping per NFPA 58 (***page 175***)	2412.2	1212.11
☐ No piping in circulating air duct, chimney or gas vent, ventilating duct, or elevator shaft	2415.3	1210.3.4
☐ No concealed piping in solid partitions (concrete or CMU walls) except in chase	2415.4	1210.4.2

Metallic Pipe Joints & Fittings

	21 IRC	21 UPC
☐ ≥Schedule 40 threaded, flanged, brazed, or press-connected fittings, <schedule 40 press-connect, flanges, brazing, or welding	2414.9.1	1208.6.10.1
☐ Clear fittings of burrs; brush & blow out chips & scales	2414.6	1208.6.8
☐ Concealed locations (see glossary) req threaded elbows, tees & couplings, brazed or welded fittings, or fittings listed for the purpose: no unions, bushings, or compression couplings	2415.5	1210.4.1

Materials

	21 IRC	21 UPC
☐ Steel & wrought iron min. schedule 10 (UPC 40)	2414.3.2[10]	1208.6.3.1
☐ Cu tubing type K or L	2414.4.3	1208.6.4.3
☐ No Cu or brass if >0.3 grains H_2S per 100 cu. ft. gas	2414.4.3	1208.6.4.3
☐ No pipe repair—pipe w/ defects must be replaced	2414.6	1208.6.8
☐ Plastic pipe only OK outdoors & underground EXC	2415.17.1	1210.1.7
• Anodeless risers or wall head adapters	2415.17.1X	1210.1.7X
☐ Provide yellow insulated tracer wire min. #18 (UPC: #14) along plastic pipe & terminating above ground	2415.17.3	1210.1.7.2
☐ CSST per approvals, listing & AMI	2415.2	1208.6.4.5

10. Previous code editions limited the size to schedule 40 for steel pipe & black pipe. That would still be the case for threaded pipe. Schedule 10 can be connected w/ press fittings.

TABLE 35	TYPICAL GAS APPLIANCE DEMAND[A] ◆ UPC T1208.4.1			
Appliance	Typical kBtu/hr.	Actual kBtu/hr.	Typical cu.ft./hr.[B]	Actual cu.ft./hr.
FAU or hydronic boiler SFD	100		97	
FAU or hydronic boiler multifamily dwelling, per unit	60		58	
Space & water heating units	120		116	
Instantaneous WH 2 gpm	143		138	
Instantaneous WH 4 gpm	285		275	
Storage tank WH 30–40 gal.	35		34	
Storage tank WH 50 gal.	50		48	
Built-in oven	25		24	
Built-in cooktop	40		39	
Freestanding range	65		63	
Barbecue	40		39	
Clothes dryer	35		34	
Direct-vent fireplace	40		39	
Gas log	80		78	
Total cu. ft./hr. max. gas demand				

A. Typical appliance demands; fill in w/ actual nameplate values.
B. Based on the U.S. average of 1,037 Btu/cu. ft.; consult local provider for actual values. For simplicity, many designers simply choose a value of 1kBtu/cu.ft., which gives a slightly conservative result.

Protection & Installation

	21 IRC	21 UPC
☐ Outdoor piping min. 3½ in. above ground or roof surface	2415.9	n/a
☐ Piping in light-frame construction reqs shield plates to protect against fastener penetration if < 1½ from face of framing EXC	2415.7.1&2	1210.4.3
• Black or galvanized steel piping	2415.7X	1210.4.3
☐ Shield plates min. 16 ga or per MFR	2415.7.3	1210.4.3
☐ Extend shield plates 4 in. horizontally past pipe/tubing	2415.7.1	1210.4.3
☐ Extend plates 4 in. vertically above bottom plate & 4 in. down from top plate	2415.7.1	n/a

Piping Support

☐ Max. support intervals for gas pipe & smooth tubing **T36**	2424.1	1210.3.5.1
☐ CSST support AMI	2424.1	1210.3.5.1
☐ Hangers to prevent stress & dampen excessive vibration	2418.2	1210.3.5
☐ Hangers must allow for pipe expansion & contraction	2418.2	1210.3.5.2
☐ Piping outdoors or on roofs elevated (IRC: min. 3½ in.)	2415.9	1210.3.5.3

TABLE 36	GAS PIPING & TUBING SUPPORT[A] IRC T2424.1 & UPC T1210.3.5.1		
Steel Pipe Nominal Size (in.)	Max. Support Spacing (ft.)	Smooth-Wall Tubing Nominal Size (in.)	Max. Support Spacing (ft.)
½	6	½	4
¾ or 1	8	⅝ or ¾	6
≥1¼ (horizontal)	10	⅞ or 1 (horizontal)	8
≥1¼ (vertical)	every floor level	⅞ or 1 (vertical)	every floor level

A. CSST support AMI, not to this table.

Underground

	21 IRC	21 UPC
☐ Protect metallic piping from corrosion	2415.11	1210.1.3
☐ Zi coatings not sufficient as corrosion protection	2415.11.1	1210.1.3.1
☐ Factory-applied electrically insulating coatings AMI	2415.11.2	1210.1.3.2
• Field application of nipples & fittings OK if AMI	2415.11.2	1210.1.3.2
(Note: The AHJ may req observation of field wrapping after pressure testing.)		
☐ Cathodic protection reqs monitoring & maintenance	2415.11.2	1210.1.3.3
☐ Steel risers from plastic pipe req cathodic protection EXC	2415.11.4	1210.1.3.9
• Anodeless risers	2415.5.1 & 2415.11.4	1210.1.3.9
☐ Min. cover depth 12 in. (UPC: 18 in. if damage likely)	2415.12	1210.1.1
☐ If <12 in. provide conduit or bridge	n/a	1210.1.1
☐ 8-in. cover OK for single appliance if damage not likely	2415.12.1	n/a
☐ Pipe trenches to have firm continuous bearing	2415.13	1210.1.2
☐ Piping not to penetrate foundation below grade (UPC: OK if sleeved & sealed)	2415.6	1210.1.5

Gas Piping Underground Beneath Buildings

☐ Piping in slab reqs protected channel or conduit	2415.8	n/a
☐ Piping underground beneath buildings reqs protective conduit **F77**	2415.14	1210.1.6
☐ Conduit w/ one end on exterior & one on interior: Pipe sealed gastight to conduit at interior, exterior pipe terminated min. 4 in. outside building & conduit vented above grade and configured to prevent water & insect entry **F77**	2415.8.1 & 2415.14.1	1210.1.6.1
☐ Conduit w/ both ends terminating inside building should not have ends sealed & both must be accessible	2415.8.2 & 2415.14.2	1210.1.6.2

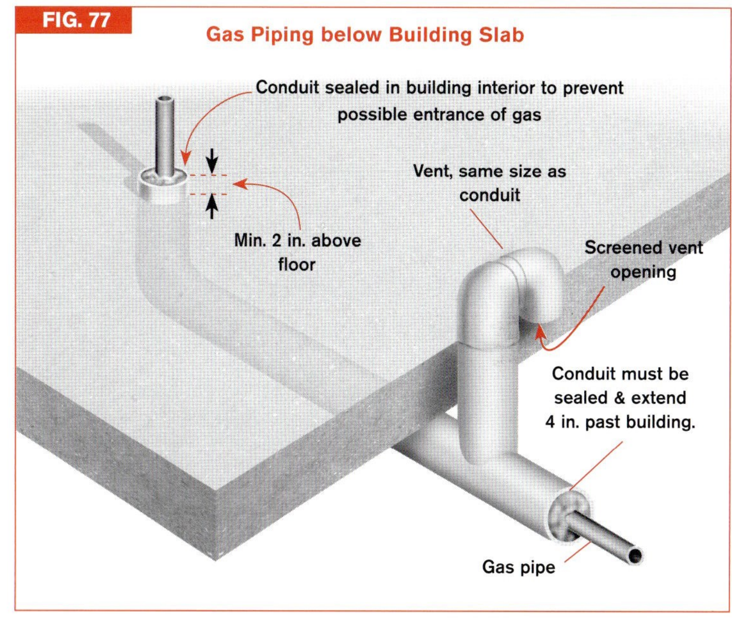

Electrical Bonding other than CSST

	21 IRC	21 UPC
☐ Electrical bond reqd for above-ground gas piping	3609.7	1211.1
☐ EGC of circuit supplying equipment OK as bond	3609.7	1211.1
☐ Gas piping not OK as grounding electrode in earth	2410.1	1211.4

Valves

	21 IRC	21 UPC
☐ All valves accessible & protected from damage	2420.1.3	1212.6
☐ Valve within 6 ft. of appliance & in same room EXC	2420.5.1	1212.6
• Valve at manifold within 50 ft. & permanently marked	2420.5.3	Ø
☐ Valve upstream from union or connector at appliance	2420.5.1	1212.6
☐ Shutoff valves in tubing systems rigidly supported independently of the tubing	2420.6	MFR
☐ Shutoff valves reqd outdoors at each building	2420.3	1210.9.2
☐ Each appliance reqs its own shutoff valve	2420.5	1212.6
☐ Valve reqd ahead of gas connector	2422.1.2.4	1212.6
☐ Listed valve reqd ahead of each MP regulator **F80**	2420.4	1210.9
☐ Valve for decorative appliances in fireplace install AMI (UPC: must be listed for such use)	2420.5.1	1212.6X1
☐ Valve in fireplace must be removed & pipe capped if fireplace to be used with solid fuels	n/a	1210.8.2
☐ Cap any unused outlets (valve alone not OK)	2417.6.2	1210.8.1

Drips & Sediment Traps

	21 IRC	21 UPC
☐ Slope piping min. 1/4 in./15 ft. unless dry gas	2419.1	1210.3.3
☐ If non-dry gas, install drips to prevent moisture from reaching meter	2419.2	1210.7
☐ Sediment traps reqd as close as practical to appliance inlets **F78** EXC	2419.4	1212.9[11]
• Ranges, dryers, gas lights, fireplaces & outdoor grills	2419.4	1212.9

FIG. 78

Sediment Trap

Place sediment traps as close as practical to appliance inlets. The sediment trap must cause a 90° turn in the direction of the gas.

11. Previous edition also required that the sediment trap be upstream of any flex connector.

Appliance Connections

	21 IRC	21 UPC
☐ Connectors rigid pipe, L&L flexible connectors, CSST AMI to appliance fixed in place, or listed outdoor gas hose connectors	2422.1	1212.1
☐ Connector max. 6-ft. length EXC	2422.1.2.1	1212.6
• Rigid piping w/ valve ≤6 ft. of appliance served & sized as piping rather than as connector	2422.1.2.1X	n/a
☐ Flexible connectors max. one per appliance	2422.1.2.1	1212.1(3)
☐ Flex connectors in same room as appliance	2422.1(3)	1212.1(3)
☐ Flex connectors not to pass through walls, walls, partitions, ceilings, or floors EXC	2422.1.2.3	1212.5.3
• Semi-rigid tubing & listed connectors OK to pass through opening in appliance housing if protected against damage	2422.1.2.3X4	1212.1(3)
☐ Connectors capacity ≥ appliance demand **T37**	2422.1.2.2	1212.1(3)
☐ Flex connectors one-time use only—do not reuse	2422.1(3)	1212.1(3)
☐ Flex connectors rated for max. 0.5 psig or AMI	2422.1.2	1212.1(3)

TABLE 37 TYPICAL[A] FLEXIBLE GAS CONNECTOR CAPACITY

Nom. O.D.[B]	Nom. I.D.[B]	Lengths (in.) & Capacity (Btu/hr.)							
		12	18	24	30	36	48	60	72
3/8	1/4	48,000	43,800	40,000	36,400	33,400	28,300	24,900	23,100
1/2	3/8	102,000	93,100	85,000	77,100	71,100	60,500	53,200	49,100
5/8	1/2	180,000	164,200	150,000	136,000	125,000	106,000	93,200	86,000
7/8	3/4	290,900	290,900	290,900	270,500	255,900	215,000	197,400	173,900

A. Based on typical MFR instructions for standard (not high-capacity) connectors, gas at 1K/Btu/cu. ft., gas at 0.5 in water column pressure drop.
B. O.D. = outside diameter in., I.D. = inside diameter in.

Corrugated Stainless-Steel Tubing: CSST

	21 IRC	21 UPC
☐ Follow MFR instructions—install AMI:	2415.2	1210.2
• Size, support & bend radius AMI per MFR tables		
• Route below grade using conduit unless specifically allowed AMI		
• Proprietary shield plates per MFR **F79**		
• Avoid kinking, twisting, or contact w/ sharp objects		

Electrical Bonding for CSST

	21 IRC	21 UPC
☐ Arc-resistant CSST must be electrically continuous & connected to effective ground-fault current path	2411.3	1211.3[12]
☐ Arc-resistant CSST considered bonded when connected to appliances w/ equipment grounding conductor	2411.3	1211.3[12]
☐ If any CSST component lacks arc-resistant jacket or coating, bonding is reqd same as for other CSST	2411.3	1211.3[12]
☐ Piping systems containing 1 or more segments of CSST req bond to electrical service grounding electrode system or to lightning protection system	2411.2	1211.2
☐ Connect bonding jumper to metal pipe, metal pipe fitting, or CSST fitting	2411.2.1	1211.2.1
☐ Bonding jumper min. #6 Cu wire	2411.2.2	1211.2.2
☐ Bonding jumper max. 75 ft. length	2411.2.3	1211.2.3
☐ Bonding jumper clamps listed for the purpose	2411.2.5	1211.2.4&5

Medium Pressure (MP) Regulators F80

	21 IRC	21 UPC
☐ Regulators reqd when line pressure exceeds allowed inlet pressure of appliances served	2421.1	1208.8
☐ Regulators req listing to ANSI Z21.80	2421.1	1208.8.1
☐ MP regulators must be accessible	2421.1&2	1208.8.2
☐ Capped or plugged tee fitting reqd between regulator & its upstream shutoff valve	2421.2	MFR
☐ Capped tee fitting reqd downstream of regulator	2421.2	MFR
☐ Vented regulators must be vented to outdoors EXC	2421.3	1208.8.4(1)
• If equipped w/ approved vent-limiting device	2421.3X	1208.8.4(1)X

12. Previous code edition recognized CSST installed AMI in accord w/ its listing. This added section provides additional clarity regarding arc-resistant jacketed & coated systems.

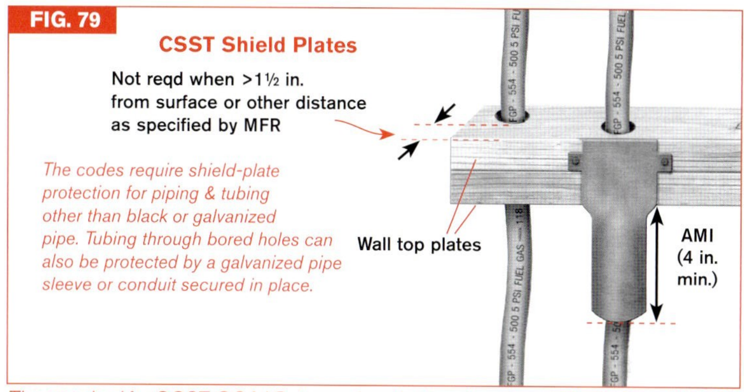

The codes require shield-plate protection for piping & tubing other than black or galvanized pipe. Tubing through bored holes can also be protected by a galvanized pipe sleeve or conduit secured in place.

*The standard for CSST, CSA LC-1, requires that workers be certified to install CSST. The manufacturers offer training & certification courses. Installers should carry their certification card and present it to inspectors upon request. Min. 16-gauge shield plates **F79** are required. Concern over damage from indirect lightning strikes has resulted in requirements for bonding beyond the NEC requirements.*

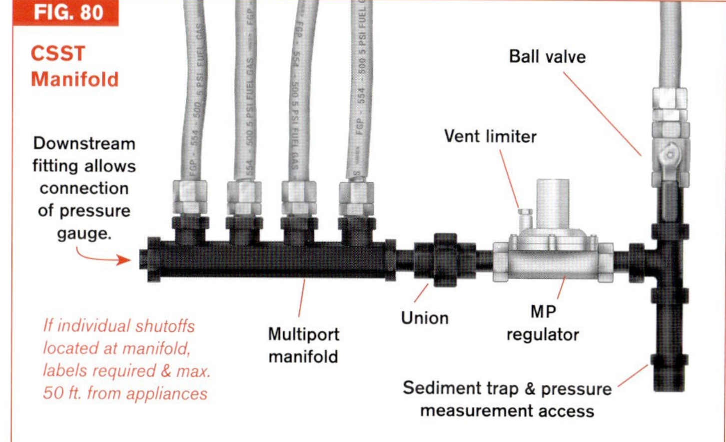

If individual shutoffs located at manifold, labels required & max. 50 ft. from appliances

GAS PIPE SIZE

Gas pipe sizing is a function of aggregate appliance demand, gas pressure, BTUs per cubic foot of gas, and the pipe run length. Corrugated stainless-steel tubing systems (CSST) can be run at medium pressure (approximately 2 psig) to a central manifold F80 where the pressure is reduced to the operating pressure of appliances, typically not more than 0.5 psig. This method allows smaller main runs and uses less tubing than a system where all piping is operated at utilization pressure.

Gas piping systems in series F81 can be sized using either the longest length or the branch length method. Systems with MP regulators are sized using the hybrid pressure method. There are separate tables for steel pipe and CSST tubing. The corrugations of CSST reduce its effective interior diameter, and its size is converted to "equivalent hydraulic diameter." In general, it must be 1 size larger than the corresponding size of steel pipe to have the same capacity.

Pipe Size	21 IRC	21 UPC
☐ Size per max. demand based on appliance input ratings	2413.2	1208.4.1
☐ Assume all appliances operating simultaneously EXC	2413.2	1208.4.1
• Where diversity of load can be established	2413.2	1208.4.1X
☐ Size AMI or per tables T38,T40,42,43	2413.3	1208.4.2
☐ Adjust volumetric flow rate for altitudes > 2,000 ft.	2413.2	1208.4.1

TABLE 38 GAS PIPE SIZING PROCEDURE ◆ IRC 2413.3 & UPC 1215.1
1. Determine Btu/cu.ft. from local gas provider.
2. Determine cu.ft./hr. demand for each appliance.
3. Sketch layout w/ piping lengths to each appliance F81.
4. Determine total cu.ft./hr. demand on each pipe section.
5. Determine length to most remote appliance.
6A. (longest length method) Use row of T39 for that length for all appliances.
6B. (branch length method) Use same row for all sections in series w/ most remote appliance. For other branches, use actual length of each branch.
The "longest length" method is more conservative and compensates for pressure losses throughout the system. The "branch length method" has less leeway, and consideration should be given to the lengths of pipe fittings. The codes accept both methods. Systems w/ MP regulators use the "hybrid pressure" method, where the pipe sizes before the regulator are determined separately, each by the longest length method.

FIG. 81 Gas Pipe Size Example

TABLE 39 GAS PIPE SIZE EXAMPLE

Pipe Section	Total cu. ft./hr.[A]	Longest Length	Longest Length Method	Actual Length	Branch Length Method
A	363	90 ft.	1¼ in.	90 ft.	1¼ in.
B	272	90 ft.	1¼ in.	90 ft.	1¼ in.
C	213	90 ft.	1¼ in.	90 ft.	1¼ in.
D	181	90 ft.	1 in.	90 ft.	1 in.
E	91	90 ft.	¾ in.	30 ft.	½ in.
F	59	90 ft.	¾ in.	40 ft.	½ in.
G	32	90 ft.	½ in.	80 ft.	½ in.

A. Ex based on 1,100 Btu/cu. ft.—contact local provider for actual values.

TABLE 40	CUBIC FEET CAPACITY OF SCHEDULE 40 METALLIC GAS PIPE[A] ◆ IRC T2413.4(1) & UPC T1215.2(1)								
Pipe Length (in ft.)	Nominal Pipe Size (in.)								
	½	¾	1	1¼	1½	2	2½	3	4
	Demand Capacity (in cu.ft./hr.)								
10	172	360	678	1,390	2,090	4,020	6,400	11,300	23,100
20	118	247	466	957	1,430	2,760	4,400	7,780	15,900
30	95	199	374	768	1,150	2,220	3,530	6,250	12,700
40	81	170	320	657	985	1,900	3,020	5,350	10,900
50	72	151	284	583	873	1,680	2,680	4,740	9,660
60	65	137	257	528	791	1,520	2,430	4,290	8,760
70	60	126	237	486	728	1,400	2,230	3,950	8,050
80	56	117	220	452	677	1,300	2,080	3,670	7,490
90	52	110	207	424	635	1,220	1,950	3,450	7,030
100	50	104	195	400	600	1,160	1,840	3,260	6,640
125	44	92	173	355	532	1,020	1,630	2,890	5,890
150	40	83	157	322	482	928	1,480	2,610	5,330
175	37	77	144	296	443	854	1,360	2,410	4,910
200	34	71	134	275	412	794	1,270	2,240	4,560
250	30	63	119	244	366	704	1,120	1,980	4,050
300	27	57	108	221	331	638	1,020	1,800	3,670
350	25	53	99	203	305	587	935	1,650	3,370
400	23	49	92	189	283	546	870	1,540	3,140
450	22	46	86	177	266	512	816	1,440	2,940
500	21	43	82	168	251	484	771	1,360	2,780

A. Based on inlet pressure <2 psi, pressure drop 0.5-in. water column, specific gravity 0.60.

*To use the fill-in table below, first create a diagram such as the example in **F81**. If the Btu per cubic foot capacity of the gas is not known, use a 1:1 ratio, which also simplifies the equations and in most cases yields a more conservative result. Next, assign the cubic foot values for each appliance and the cubic foot for each section of piping. Working from the most remote appliance back toward the meter, assign pipe sizes to each section of the diagram.*

*If the system is CSST, the same methods can be used for individual branches for appliances. If the system has a manifold and pressure regulators, as in **F80**, **T42** would be used downstream of the regulator and **T43** upstream of the regulator. If the CSST MFR provides their own size tables, they would take precedence over the ones in this book.*

TABLE 41	GAS PIPE SIZE EXAMPLE FILL-IN				
Pipe Section	Total cu. ft./hr.[A]	Longest Length	Longest Length Method	Actual Length	Branch Length Method
A					
B					
C					
D					
E					
F					
G					

A. Btu/cu.ft. (from gas supplier).

TABLE 42 CUBIC FEET CAPACITY OF CSST[A] – LOW PRESSURE IRC T2413.4(5) & UPC T1215.2(14)

Pipe Length (ft.)	Effective Hydraulic Diameter[B] (EHD) and Corresponding Approximate Nominal Pipe Size (in.)[C]									
	13	18	19	23	25	31	37	39	46	62
	3/8	1/2	1/2	3/4	3/4	1	1 1/4	1 1/4	1 1/2	2
	Demand Capacity (in cu.ft./hr.)									
5	46	115	134	225	270	546	895	1037	1790	4,140
10	32	82	95	161	192	383	639	746	1260	2,530
15	25	66	77	132	157	310	524	615	1030	2,400
20	22	58	67	116	137	269	456	536	888	2,080
25	19	52	60	104	122	240	409	482	793	1,860
30	18	47	55	96	112	218	374	442	723	1,700
40	15	41	47	83	97	188	325	386	625	1,470
50	13	37	42	75	87	168	292	347	559	1,320
60	12	34	38	68	80	153	267	318	509	1,200
70	11	31	36	63	74	141	248	295	471	1,110
80	10	29	33	60	69	132	232	277	440	1,040
90	10	28	32	57	65	125	219	262	415	983
100	9	26	30	54	62	118	208	249	393	933
150	7	20	23	42	48	91	171	205	320	762
200	6	18	21	38	44	82	148	179	277	661
250	5	16	19	34	39	74	133	161	247	591
300	5	15	17	32	36	67	95	148	226	540

A. Based on inlet pressure < 2 psi, pressure drop 0.5-in. water column, specific gravity 0.60.
B. EHD is a measure of relative efficiency. These values vary from one manufacturer to another. The tables are given here to determine approximate pipe sizes. These tables include 4 90° bends and 2 end fittings. Additional bends req adjustment in accordance w/ the manufacturer's instructions.
C. EHD values for pipe sizes vary from one MFR to another, hence there are multiple columns for identical pipe sizes. If MFR values do not align w/ this table, follow the tables provided by the MFR.

TABLE 43 CUBIC FEET CAPACITY OF CSST[A] – MEDIUM PRESSURE ◆ IRC T2413.4(6) & UPC T1215.2(17)

Pipe Length (ft.)	Effective Hydraulic Diameter[B] (EHD) and Corresponding Approximate Nominal Pipe Size (in.)[C]									
	15	18	19	23	25	31	37	39	46	62
	3/8	1/2	1/2	3/4	3/4	1	1 1/4	1 1/4	1 1/2	2
	Demand Capacity (in cu.ft./hr.)									
10	353	587	700	1,100	1,370	2,990	4,510	5,037	9,600	21,600
25	220	374	444	709	876	1,870	2,890	3,258	6,040	13,700
30	200	342	405	650	801	1,700	2,640	2,987	5,510	12,500
40	172	297	351	567	696	1,470	2,300	2,605	4,760	10,900
50	154	266	314	510	624	1,310	2,060	2,343	4,260	9,720
75	124	218	257	420	512	1,070	1,690	1,932	3,470	7,940
80	120	211	249	407	496	1,030	1,640	1,874	3,360	7,690
100	107	189	222	366	445	920	1,470	1,685	3,000	6,880
150	87	155	182	302	364	748	1,210	1,389	2,440	5,620
200	75	135	157	263	317	645	1,050	1,212	2,110	4,870
250	67	121	141	236	284	576	941	1,090	1,890	4,360
300	61	110	129	217	260	525	862	999	1,720	3,980

A. Based on inlet pressure 2.0 psi, pressure drop 0.5-in. water column, specific gravity 0.60. This table does not include effect of pressure drop across the line regulator. Where regulator losses exceed 3/4 psi, do not use this table; refer to MFR.
B. EHD is a measure of relative efficiency. These values vary from one manufacturer to another. The tables are given here to determine approximate pipe sizes. These tables include 4 90° bends and 2 end fittings. Additional bends req adjustment in accordance w/ the manufacturer's instructions.
C. EHD values for pipe sizes vary from one MFR to another, hence there are multiple columns for identical pipe sizes. If MFR values do not align w/ this table, follow the tables provided by the MFR.

PROPANE (LP GAS)

NFPA 58, the Liquefied Petroleum Gas Code, is the reference standard for LP gas systems. LP liquefies under moderate pressure and vaporizes upon release of the pressure. Horizontal storage tanks are manufactured to standards from the American Society of Mechanical Engineers (ASME), and portable cylinders are manufactured to U.S. Department of Transportation (DOT) standards. As a liquid or gas, propane is heavier than air, and when gas leakage occurs in a pit or basement, an invisible pool of combustible material can accumulate until it rises to the level of an ignition source, such as the pilot or igniter on an appliance. One method of protection against this hazard is an interlock that would shut off the gas flow. Another method is to install a pan drain below the equipment with a duct sloped to the exterior.

Horizontal ASME Tanks — 20 NFPA 58

- ☐ Tank clearances **F82** ____ T6.4.1.1 T6.4.4.3 & Annex I
- ☐ Tank not allowed indoors ____ 6.2.1
- ☐ Protect tanks from damage (bollards) where ≤10 ft. of vehicle path ____ 6.8.1.2
- ☐ Masonry or concrete foundation reqd under tanks ____ 6.8.3.1
- ☐ Supports & saddles must be corrosion resistant & noncombustible ____ 6.8.3.4
- ☐ Secure tank against flotation in flood hazard areas ____ 6.8.1.6
- ☐ Secure tanks in seismic areas per ASCE SEI 7 as approved by AHJ ____ 5.2.4.4D
- ☐ Min. 10 ft. from easily ignitable material (firewood) ____ 6.5.3.3
- ☐ Replace containers w/ excessive dents or corrosion ____ 5.2.1.4

Piping & Tubing Systems

- ☐ Material black pipe, galvanized, brass, PE, SS, Cu, or polyamide AMI 5.11.3.1
- ☐ Tubing brass, Cu L or K, CSST, PE, or polyamide AMI ____ 5.11.3.2
- ☐ Plastic tubing and fittings only outdoors & underground ____ 6.11.4.1
- ☐ Min. #14 tracer wire reqd to be run w/ plastic pipe ____ 6.11.4.6
- ☐ No cast-iron pipe fittings ____ 5.11.4.2
- ☐ Buried metal pipe min. 12-in. cover (18 in. if damage likely) ____ 6.11.3.13
- ☐ Conduit or shielding OK when 12-in. cover not possible ____ 6.11.3.13B
- ☐ Underground metal piping reqs corrosion protection ____ 6.11.3.15
- ☐ LP gas piping not OK as grounding electrode ____ 6.11.3.16
- ☐ Grounding & bonding for static electricity protection not reqd ____ A6.25.1.3
- ☐ Dielectric fitting reqd between above- & below-ground pipe ____ 6.11.3.17
- ☐ Dielectric fitting to be above ground and outdoors ____ 6.11.3.17

Tank Valves & Regulators — 20 NFPA 58

- ☐ Vapor & liquid shutoff w/ internal excess flow valve reqd ____ T5.9.4.1
- ☐ Shutoff valve reqd to be readily accessible ____ 5.9.8.1G
- ☐ PRV reqd ____ 5.9.2.5 & 5.9.4.1
- ☐ Rain cap reqd over PRV ____ 6.9.2.4
- ☐ No shutoff valve between tank & PRV or on outlet of PRV ____ 6.9.2.7&9
- ☐ First-stage or high-pressure regulator must be installed outdoors ____ 6.10.1.3
- ☐ Regulator must be designed to resist elements (freezing) ____ 6.10.1.4

FIG. 82 Propane Tank Container Spacing

Clearances are for tanks that are filled on site.

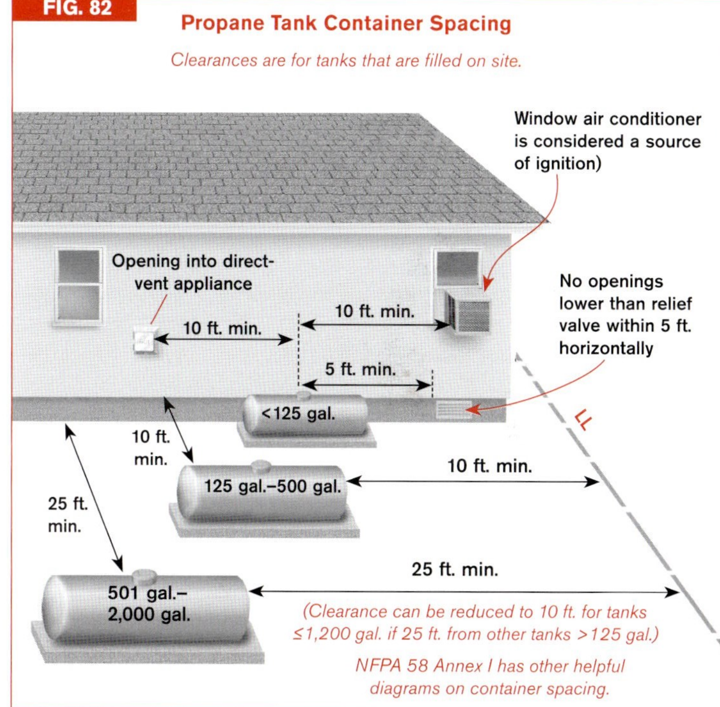

NFPA 58 Annex I has other helpful diagrams on container spacing.

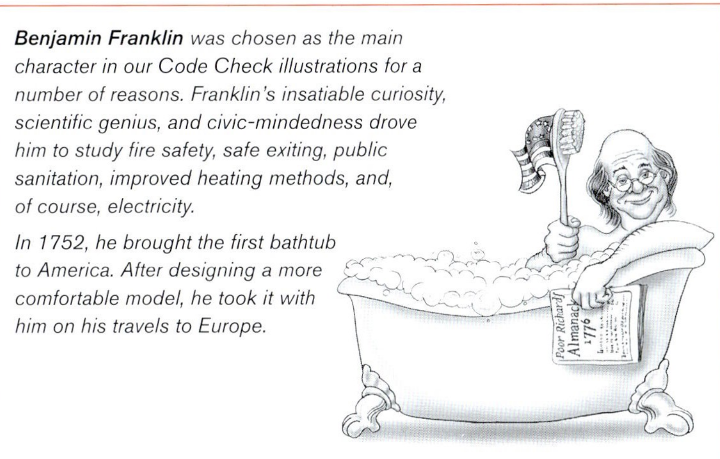

Benjamin Franklin *was chosen as the main character in our Code Check illustrations for a number of reasons. Franklin's insatiable curiosity, scientific genius, and civic-mindedness drove him to study fire safety, safe exiting, public sanitation, improved heating methods, and, of course, electricity.*

In 1752, he brought the first bathtub to America. After designing a more comfortable model, he took it with him on his travels to Europe.

Code ✓Check® Mechanical Sixth Edition

Part 3 of Code ✓Check Complete Third Edition

By DOUGLAS HANSEN, REDWOOD KARDON & SKIP WALKER

Code Check Mechanical 6th edition is an illustrated reference guide to code requirements and common code violations in residential mechanical systems. The main code referenced in this book is the *2021 International Residential Code® (IRC)*. The mechanical & fuel gas provisions of the IRC are derived from the *2021 International Mechanical Code® and the 2021 International Fuel Gas Code®*. The other main code referenced here is the *2021 Uniform Mechanical Code®*, adopted as a model code by California & several other jurisdictions throughout the United States. For most topics, these codes are in agreement. NFPA 54, the *National Fuel Gas Code®*, is the basis for the fuel-gas provisions of the IRC, UPC, and UMC. Other codes and standards used in the book are listed in Table 1 (**T1**).

Model codes are updated on a 3-year cycle. In most areas, the 2021 code cycle will remain in effect for 3 to 6 years after the cover date. Significant changes from the previous code editions are highlighted in the text, so that this book can be used for areas still using older editions of the codes. If a line in Code Check is not highlighted, that line also applied in the 2018 code editions. Minor changes and those that only affected numbering (not substance) are not highlighted.

Energy codes vary greatly from one area to another and may modify or overrule the requirements shown in this book. Before beginning any project, check with your local building department to determine the codes, editions, and local modifications or amendments that apply in your area.

TABLE 1 — CODES USED IN THIS BOOK

Organization	Edition	Code
ASHRAE	2019	ASHRAE 62.2 Ventilation and Acceptable Indoor Air Quality in Residential Buildings
ICC	2021	International Residential Code
IAPMO	2021	Uniform Mechanical Code
IAPMO	2021	Uniform Plumbing Code
NFPA	2020	NFPA 31 Standard for the Installation of Oil-Burning Equipment
NFPA	2021	NFPA 54 National Fuel Gas Code
NFPA	2020	NFPA 70 National Electrical Code
NFPA	2019	NFPA 211 Standard for Chimneys, Fireplaces, Vents, and Solid Fuel–Burning Appliances

The information in this book is believed to be accurate; however, it is provided for informational purposes only and is not intended as a substitute for the full text of the referenced codes. It should not be considered by the user to be a substitute for the enforceable interpretation of the local building department.

TABLE OF CONTENTS

KEY TO USING THIS BOOK

Code Check Mechanical 6th edition is a condensed guide to codes used for mechanical systems in residential construction. The primary references are the *2021 International Residential Code (IRC)* and the *2021 Uniform Mechanical Code (UMC), and standards in* ***Table 1***.

Each line that starts with a checkbox ends with a code reference. The code being referenced is shown in the top of the column at the right side, as in this example from ***p. 182***:

Appliance Access	**21 IRC**	**21 UMC**
☐ Maintain accessibility for service of appliances________	1305.1	304.1

This line tells us that access to appliances must be maintained. In the IRC, this reference is found in section 1305.1, and in the UMC in section 304.1.

Note*: The code numbers in the IRC begin with a letter. In the building section, numbers start with an R. Energy starts with an N, Mechanical an M, Fuel Gas a G, Plumbing a P, and Electrical with an E. We omit those letters to save space. The full IRC section name for the above line would be M1305.1*

There are 53 illustrations and 13 tables in this book. They are referenced in the text as in this example from ***p. 188*** on the topic of combustion air:

☐ Volume includes rooms directly communicating w/ appliance space through openings w/o doors or openings per **T2**,**F11** ___	2407.5	701.4

This line tells us to reference Table 2 for the size of openings to rooms with appliances, and that Figure 11 depicts an example of this rule.

Changes from the prior code edition are highlighted by use of a different color for the code reference, followed by a superscript number. At the bottom of the page, there is a further explanation of the code change, as in this example from ***p. 200***:

☐ GFCI-protected receptacle within 25 ft. of equipment ___	3901.12[4]	301.4

The code line in the IRC column ends with a different color and the superscript "4", indicating it is code change #4, and that change is further explained at the bottom of the page (see below). Note that this change does not occur in the UMC, which requires the receptacle within 25 ft. but does not specify GFCI protection. The rule at the bottom of the page helps us to understand that the change is not about the requirement for a receptacle, it is about the GFCI protection:

4. GFCI protection now reqd for such receptacle outlets.

Code Check uses abbreviations to save space, as in this example from ***p. 182:***

☐ Install listed appliances AMI _____________	1307.1 & 1401.1	303.1

This line tells us to install listed appliances "in accordance with manufacturer's instructions" (AMI). A full list of abbreviations is on the following page. Specialized terms such as "listed" are explained in the glossary beginning on p. 220.

When a line ends with the letters EXC, it means that an exception to the code rule follows in the next line, as in this example from ***p. 182*** regarding work that does not require a building permit:

☐ New installations, alterations & repairs req permits EXC	105.1	104.1
• Portable equipment & minor replacement parts________	105.2	104.2

This line tells us that the basic rule is to require permits for new work, alterations, and repairs, but not for portable equipment or minor replacement parts.

The letter "X" in a code citation refers to a code exception, as in this example from ***p. 198***:

☐ Direct-vent combustion air intakes **F27** not subject to **T7**	2427.8X	802.8.X1

This line tells us that the combustion air intake of a direct-vent appliance, as depicted in figure 27, is not subject to the through-wall vent clearance requirements found in Table 7. The code reference is the exception that follows IRC section 2427.8 or the first exception that follows UMC section 802.8.

A reference of "local" is given rather than a code number in certain instances where the issue is beyond the specific scope of a code, yet likely to be enforced, as in this example from ***p. 183***:

☐ Ducts & penetrations min. 26-gauge steel __________	302.5.2	local

The subheading above this line is ***Appliances in Garages****. In the UMC column, the reference given is "local" because the issue is really a building code issue, not a mechanical code issue. The IRC reference is from the building section of the IRC. Despite the lack of a specific UMC section, a building code with this provision is likely to be enforced locally in UMC jurisdictions.*

A reference of "n/a" may be used when a given code does not cover a specific item. It does not mean that the code either requires or permits the item in that line, but simply that it does not have specific rules for it, as in this example from ***p. 217***:

☐ Duct min. diameter per **T12**______________________	T5.3[9]	n/a

This line tells us that the UMC does not have a table like that of ASHRAE for sizing a kitchen or bath exhaust duct. The ASHRAE table could be used as a guide, but is not mandatory if the only governing code is the UMC.

1&2FD = 1- & 2-family dwellings
AC = air conditioning
ACCA = Air Conditioning Contractors of America
ACH = air changes per hour
AFF = above finished floor
AHJ = Authority Having Jurisdiction (usually building official)
AMI = in accordance with manufacturer's instructions
AMM = alternative materials, design & methods
ANSI = American National Standards Institute, Inc.
ASHRAE = American Society of Heating, Refrigerating & AC Engineers
ASME = American Society of Mechanical Engineering
ASTM = ASTM International (formerly American Society for Testing & Materials)
BFE = base flood elevation
BO = building official
C.A. = combustion air
Cat. = Category (appliance vent category: Cat. I, Cat. II, Cat. III, or Cat. IV)
cfm = cubic feet per minute
CMU = concrete masonry unit
CPSC = Consumer Product Safety Commission
Cu = copper
DFE = design flood elevation
DWV = drain, waste & vent
EMT = electrical metallic tubing
EXC = exception (in following line)
F = Fahrenheit
ft. = foot, feet
ga = gauge
gal = gallon, gallons
GB = gypsum board
hr., hrs. = hour, hours
IAPMO = International Association of Plumbing & Mechanical Officials
IBC = International Building Code
ICC = International Code Council
IMC = International Mechanical Code
in. = inch(es)
L&L = listed & labeled
lb. = pound(s)
max. = maximum
MEP = mechanical, electrical & plumbing
MFR = manufacturer
min. = minimum
mph = miles per hour
NEC = NFPA 70 National Electrical Code
NFPA = National Fire Protection Association
NP = not permitted, not allowed
NRTL = Nationally Recognized Testing Laboratory
O.D. = outside diameter
p. = page, as in "***see p. 5***"
PRV = pressure-relief valve
psf = pounds per square foot
psi = pounds per square inch
req, reqs, reqd = require, requires, requirements, required
RP = reduced pressure principle backflow preventer ***(p. 157)***
SDC = Seismic Design Category
SDC D = Seismic Design Categories D_0, D_1 & D_2 inclusive
SMACNA = Sheet Metal & Air Conditioning Contractors National Association
spec = specification
sq. = square, as in sq. ft.
SS = stainless steel
temp = temperature
TPRV = combination temperature & pressure-relief valve
UL = UL (Underwriters Laboratories)
VRF = variable refrigerant flow
w/ = with
w/o = without
WC = water closet (toilet)
WH = water heater
Zi = zinc, galvanized

GENERAL MECHANICAL SYSTEM REQUIREMENTS

Permits & Interpretations	21 IRC	21 UMC
☐ New installations, alterations & repairs req permits EXC__	105.1	104.1
• Portable equipment & minor replacement parts________	105.2	104.2
☐ BO may accept AMM that is equivalent in strength, quality, effectiveness, fire resistance, durability & safety _______	104.11	302.2
☐ Written response reqd for rejected AMM applications___	104.11	local

Conflicts Between Codes		
☐ Installations not addressed by IRC to comply w/ IMC___	1301.1	n/a
☐ If general & specific rules in conflict, specific rule prevails	102.1	102.1
☐ When codes in conflict, the more stringent prevails______	102.1	102.1
☐ Plumbing code prevails if conflicting w/ mechanical code___	n/a	102.1

Listing & Labeling		
☐ Appliances req L&L (UMC: L&L or approval by AHJ)____	1302.1	301.2
☐ Install per conditions of listing & AMI ________	1307.1 & 1401.1	303.1
☐ Attach installation & operating instructions to appliance _	1307.1	303.1
☐ Fuel-burning factory-applied nameplates must include:__	1303.1	307.1–3
• MFR name, model, serial number & listing mark of testing agency		
• Electrical rating (where applicable) in volts, amps & phase		
• Type of fuel and hourly Btu rating		
• Reqd clearances from combustibles		

Electrical Requirements	21 IRC	20 NEC
☐ Receptacle within 25 ft. of appliance_______________	3901.12	210.63
☐ Receptacle on same level as appliance_____________	3901.12	210.63A
☐ Crawlspace furnace reqs light w/switch at access _	1305.1.3.3	210.70C
☐ Attic furnace reqs light w/switch at access________	1305.1.2.1	210.70C
☐ Individual circuit reqd for central heating_____________	3703.1	422.12
☐ No other equipment on central heating circuit EXC_____	3703.1	422.12
• Associated pumps, humidifiers, air cleaners & AC ____	3703.1	422.12X1&2

Existing Installations	21 IRC	21 UMC
☐ Continued use of existing installations OK if safe & compliant w/ code in effect at time of construction ____________	1202.2	102.2
☐ Owner responsible to maintain existing installations in safe condition & compliant w/ code in effect at time of construction ___	1202.2	102.3
☐ BO may order reinspections to determine compliance __	1202.3	102.3

(IRC Appendix AD is a recommended procedure for safety inspection of existing appliances. The UMC covers procedures for placing gas-fired equipment into operation, and UMC Appendix E addresses sustainable practices.)

APPLIANCE ACCESS & ANCHORAGE

Appliances must remain accessible for inspection, service, repair, and replacement without the need to remove permanent construction. Appliances must be located where they are not subject to flooding or damage and with adequate clearances from combustible surfaces. Listed appliances typically are marked with the required clearance from combustible surfaces.

Appliance Access	21 IRC	21 UMC
☐ Maintain access to service appliances_______________	1305.1	304.1
☐ Min. 30-in. × 30-in. level work space on control side EXC	1305.1–3	304.1
• Unit heaters & room heaters_______________________	n/a	304.1X
• Attic installations w/ access from opening **F1** ____	1305.1.2X1	304.4.3X
☐ Door & unobstructed passageway min. 24 in. wide to access appliances in rooms _______________	1305.1.1	n/a
☐ Openings in attics or crawlspaces must be large enough to remove the largest appliance (*see p. 184*) _	1305.1.2&3	304.4

Appliance Anchorage		
☐ Fixed appliances req anchorage in an approved manner (UMC: AMI) _______________	1307.2	303.4
☐ WHs in SDC D 1&2FD & SDC C townhouses req strapping at upper & lower ⅓ of vertical dimension _____	1307.2	UPC 507.2
☐ Locate WH straps 4 in. above controls _____________	1307.2	UPC 507.2I

APPLIANCE LOCATIONS

Flood Elevation

	21 IRC	21 UMC
☐ Locate above design flood elevation EXC	1301.1.1 & 1401.5	305.3
• If designed to prevent water entry & resist buoyancy	322.1.6X	305.3X
☐ If equipment replaced as part of substantial improvement, compliance w/ current standards mandatory	322.1.6	local
☐ No equipment mounted on breakaway flood walls	322.3.5(1)	305.3.1

Clearance to Combustibles

	21 IRC	21 UMC
☐ Clearance to combustibles AMI	1306.1, 1402.2 & 2409.3.1	303.1
☐ Clearance reduction allowed per **T10** (*p. 215*) EXC	1306.2	303.10.1
• No reductions for appliances listed for closet or alcoves	n/a	303.2
☐ Appliances not listed for closet or alcoves req room min. 12× volume of furnace, 16× volume of boiler	n/a	303.2

The concept of the room being required to be "large in relation to the size of the appliance" was removed from the IRC after the 2009 edition.

Appliances in Bedrooms & Bathrooms

	21 IRC	21 UMC
☐ Fuel-burning appliances prohibited in bedrooms, bathrooms, toilet rooms, or (IRC only: storage closets) EXC	2406.2	904.1*
• Direct-vent type installed AMI	2406.2#1	904.1(2)
• Room heaters (*p. 185*)	2406.2#2–4	916.2
• Bedroom or bathroom enclosure used for no other purpose, separated by weatherstripped self-closing door & all combustion air taken from exterior	2406.2#5	904.1(1)

* Also see UMC 911.1, 912.1, 914.2, 915.2 & 916.2.1.1

Appliances in Garages

	21 IRC	21 UMC
☐ Protect appliance from impact *(p. 164)*	1307.3.1 & 2408.3X	305.1.1
☐ Ignition source min. 18 in. above floor EXC	1307.3 & 2408.2	305.1
• Flammable vapor ignition resistant (FVIR)	1307.3X & 2408.2X	305.1
☐ Gas-fired appliance OK on garage floor if in separate space w/ access only from outside & exterior combustion air	2408.2.1	305.1.2
☐ Ducts & penetrations min. 26-gauge steel	302.5.2	local
☐ No duct openings into garage	302.5.2	local
☐ Openings around duct penetrations through house/garage separation wall sealed w/ approved materials	302.5.3	local

Rooftop Installations

	21 IRC	21 UMC
☐ Buildings > 15 ft. high must have inside means of access to roof or other means acceptable to AHJ	n/a	304.3.1
☐ Min. 30-in. × 30-in. level work space reqd on service side of appliance if roof slope ≥3:12 (UMC: if ≥4:12)	1305.1	304.2
☐ Guard reqd if <10 ft. (<6 ft. UMC) from roof edge	1301.1	304.3.1.1
☐ Guard min. 42 in. high	1301.1	304.3.1.1

The IRC does not directly address rooftop installations. Section 1301.1 directs users to the IMC in the absence of a specific IRC rule. The IMC (& IBC) require a 42-in. guard when appliances are less than 10 ft. from a roof edge.

Appliances in Attics F1

	21 IRC	21 UMC
☐ Appliance must fit through access opening	1305.1.2	304.4
☐ Opening & passageway min. 22 in. wide × 30 in. high	1305.1.2	304.4
☐ Max. 20 ft. from access opening to appliance EXC	1305.1.2	304.4.1
• If passageway ≥6 ft. high, 50-ft. length (UMC: no limit)	1305.1.2X2	304.4.1
☐ Solid floor min. 24 in. wide to equipment	1305.1.2	304.4.2
☐ Min. 30-in. × 30-in. platform at service area EXC	1305.1.2	304.4.3
• Not reqd if equipment can be serviced from opening	1305.1.2X1	304.4.3X
• UMC: max. 1-ft. setback if serviced from opening	n/a	304.4.3X
☐ Floor under furnace noncombustible construction EXC	2449.4	904.3
• Not reqd if appliance L&L for combustible floor	2449.4	904.3X1
• Not reqd if floor protected in approved manner	2449.4	904.3X2

FIG. 1

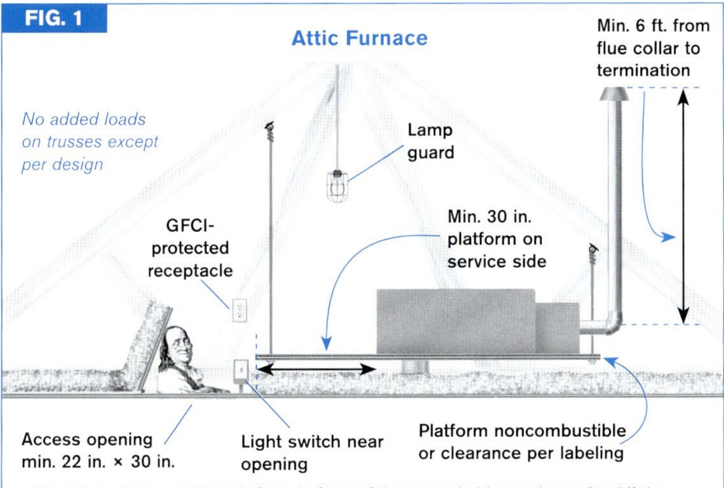

The 30-in.-deep working platform in front of the control side can be omitted if the furnace can be serviced from the opening. In the UMC, the max. setback from the opening for this exception is 12 in.

Appliances under Floors

	21 IRC	21 UMC
☐ Access opening min. size 22 in. × 30 in.	1305.1.3	304.4
☐ Appliance must fit through opening	1305.1.3	304.4
☐ Passageway min. 22 in. wide (UMC: min. 24 in.)	1305.1.3	304.4.2
☐ Passageway max. 20 ft. long EXC	1305.1.3	304.4.1
• Passageway ≥6 ft. high OK for unlimited length	1305.1.3X2	304.4.1
☐ Min. 30-in. × 30-in. level space on service side F2	1305.1.3	304.4.3
☐ Support on concrete slab min. 3 in. above adjoining ground or suspend from floor AMI & min. 6 in. above ground F2	1305.1.3.1	904.3.1
☐ Excavations min. 3 in. (UMC: 6 in.) below appliance, 12 in. on sides, 30 in. on control side F2	1305.1.3.2	305.2
☐ If excavation >12 in. below adjacent grade, line w/ concrete extending 4 in. above adjacent grade F2	1305.1.3	305.2
☐ Luminaire & receptacle outlet near appliance F2	1305.1.3.3	304.4.4
☐ Switch for luminaire at passageway entrance	1305.1.3.3	304.4.4
☐ Protect exposed lamps by location or guards F2	1305.1.3.3	n/a
☐ Crawlspace lighting & receptacles req GFCI protection	3902.4	NEC 210.8

FIG. 2

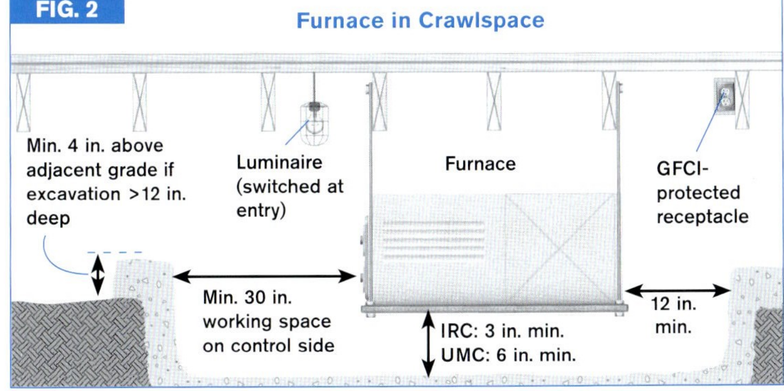

ROOM HEATERS

Room heaters other than direct-vent types must be supplied with combustion air from the interior and are typically found only in older buildings with high air-infiltration rates. They must be secured to prevent displacement of their vent. Though unvented heaters are recognized in the model codes, many jurisdictions (including California) prohibit their use. They must be provided with a nontamperable oxygen depletion sensor. Carbon monoxide alarms must also be present.

Vented Room Heaters	21 IRC	21 UMC
☐ Listing in accordance w/ ANSI Z21.86/CSA 2.32	2446.1	n/a
☐ Secure in place AMI	1307.2	303.4
☐ Install AMI & leave manuals w/ unit	2446.1	303.1
☐ Flame safeguard (pilot safety) reqd	2446.1	306.1
☐ Room must meet reqd indoor air volume (*p. 188*)	2406.2(2)	701.1
☐ Locate to avoid hazard to walls, curtains, free movement	MFR	916.2.3
☐ Circulating-type w/ outer jacket around combustion chamber min. 12-in. clearance sides & rear	MFR	916.2.3
☐ Radiating noncirculating-type min. 18 in. sides, 36 in. front, 12 in. at back OK if double back of metal or ceramic	MFR	916.2.3

Unvented Room Heaters		
☐ Must be listed in accordance w/ ANSI Z21.11.2	2445.1	n/a
☐ Install AMI & leave manuals w/ unit	2445.1	303.1
☐ Unvented heater may NOT be sole heat source	2445.2	916.2.1
☐ Heater ≤6k Btu OK in bath w/reqd volume	2406.2(3)	916.2.1.1X
☐ Heater ≤10k Btu OK in bedroom w/ reqd volume	2406.2(4)	916.2.1.1X
☐ Max. size 40k Btu	2445.3	n/a
☐ Max. input ratings ≤ 20 Btu/cu. ft. of room or space	2445.5	n/a
☐ Adjacent spaces w/ permanent large openings (doorway or archway) considered part of room volume	2445.5	701.4
☐ Unvented heater reqs oxygen-depletion sensor that shuts off when oxygen level below set point (IRC: or 18%)	2445.6	916.2.1.1

DIRECT-VENT HEATING APPLIANCES

Direct-vent appliances draw their source of combustion air from the same area where they vent combustion gases. This arrangement equalizes pressure on the inlet and outlet of the firebox, which is sealed and has no open flame on the building interior. Because these appliances do not require interior combustion air, they can be located in rooms that are considered confined spaces.

Direct-Vent Gas Wall Heaters F3	21 IRC	21 UMC
☐ Install listed direct-vent appliances AMI	2427.2.1	303.1
☐ Combustion air reqd to be from outdoors AMI	2407.1	907.1.3

*See **T7** for locations & clearances of through-wall terminations of direct-vent appliances.*

FIG. 3

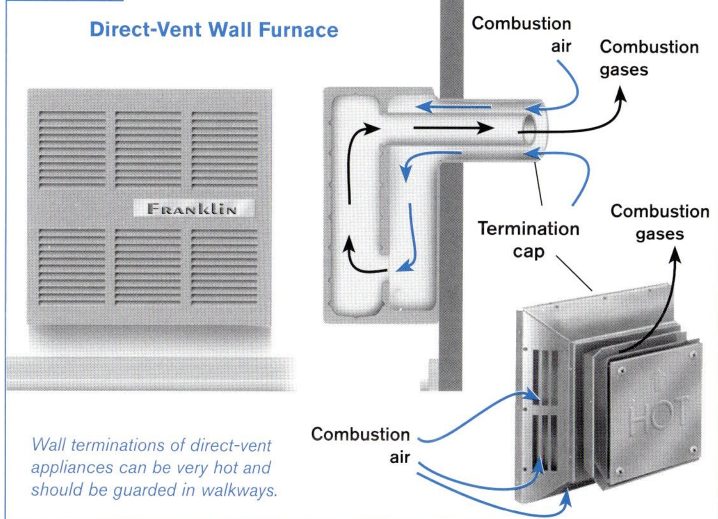

Wall terminations of direct-vent appliances can be very hot and should be guarded in walkways.

GAS WALL FURNACES

Gas-fired wall furnaces that are not direct-vent can only be located in rooms or spaces large enough to meet the combustion air requirements of the appliance. Because they use indoor air for combustion, they are typically found only in older buildings with high air-infiltration rates. Vent installation on wall furnaces is especially important. The clearances for type BW vent in a wall are less than the minimums for type B vent. When a wall furnace is replaced in an existing building, one side of the wall above the furnace should be opened for inspection of vent clearances and proper installation of the header plate (base plate) that connects the furnace to its vent.

Furnace Clearances	21 IRC	21 UMC
☐ From sidewall—install AMI F4	2436.1&3	907.2
☐ From door swing 12 in. IRC (UMC: AMI) F4	2436.4	907.1
☐ Do not rely on doorstops to maintain clearance	2436.4	n/a
☐ Clearance below structural projections AMI	2436.3	907.1

FIG. 4

Wall Furnace Clearances

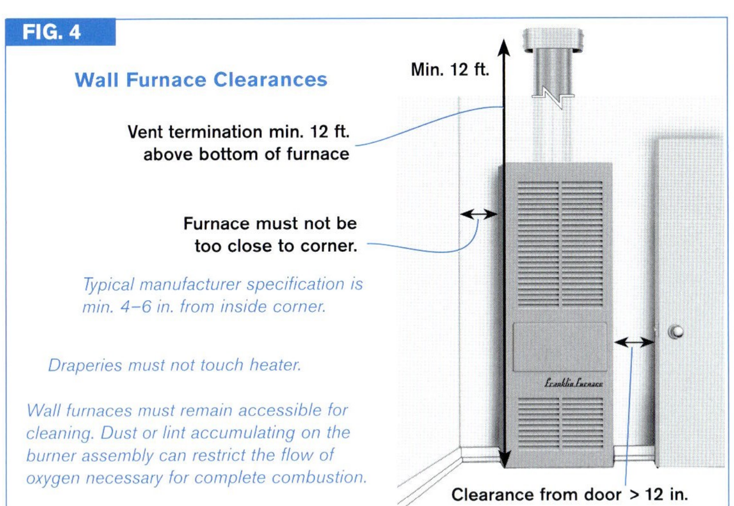

Vent Installation	21 IRC	21 UMC
☐ BW vent capacity ≥ appliance input rating	2427.6.3	802.6(2)
☐ Cut top & floor plates flush to stud F5	2436.2	907.1.2
☐ Ceiling plate spacers ventilate first stud space F5	2436.2	907.1.2
☐ Subsequent ceiling stud plates firestopped AMI F5	2436.2	907.1.2
☐ Single-story vent systems only single story or top floor	2436.2	907.1.2
☐ Multistory systems OK in single story or multistory	2436.2	907.1.2
☐ Approved sleeve min. 2 in. above attic insulation F6	2426.4	802.6.1.1
☐ Vent min. 12 ft. above bottom of furnace F4	2427.6.5	802.6.1(3)

FIG. 5

Wall Furnace Vent

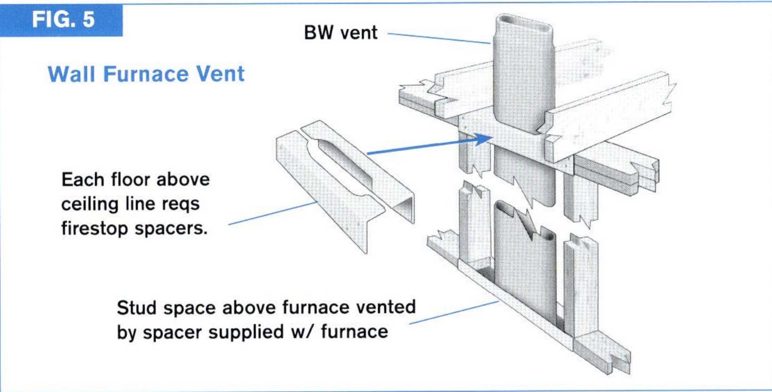

FIG. 6

BW Vent Insulation Sleeve

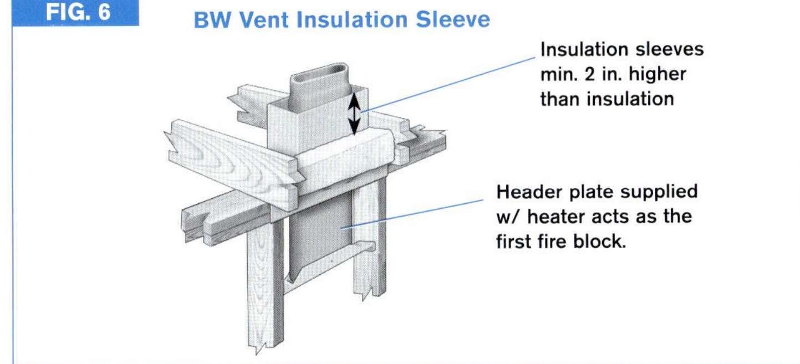

Wall Furnace Installation

	21 IRC	21 UMC
☐ Must be listed (IRC: ANSI Z21.86/CSA 2.32)	2436.1	907.1
☐ Install AMI	2436.1	907.1
☐ OK in bedroom or bath if adequate combustion air	2406.2(2)	902.2
☐ Fan assist only if L&L & AMI	2436.1	907.1
☐ No ducts attached to wall furnaces	2436.5	907.1
☐ Panels, grills & access doors not attached to building	2436.6	907.1.4
☐ Header plate at top of furnace AMI	2436.1	907.1
☐ Stud bay depth AMI	2436.1	907.1
☐ Unlisted furnaces not OK in combustible construction	2404.3	907.1.1

GAS FLOOR FURNACES

See *p. 184* for rules governing underfloor access & passageways to a floor furnace. Grills for these furnaces can become dangerously hot; child-protective measures may be necessary. The furnace must be located such that a person can walk around the floor register without stepping on it directly.

Underfloor Area

	21 IRC	21 UMC
☐ Must be listed (IRC: ANSI Z21.86/CSA 2.32)	2437.1	906.1(1)
☐ Install AMI	2437.1	906.1(1)
☐ Temp limit control reqd	2437.1	906.2(1)
☐ Unlisted furnaces allowed only in noncombustible floors & must be equipped w/ temp limit control	∅	906.2(2)
☐ Framing around opening properly braced & headed	2437.3	906.5

Excavation Clearances

☐ 6-in. clearance to ground (2-in. if factory sealed) **F7**	2437.4	906.7
☐ 12-in. side clearance; 18-in. on control side **F7**	2437.4	906.7

Upper Floor Installations

☐ May not project into habitable space below	2437.5&6	906.11
☐ Projection into nonhabitable space OK if supplied w/ combustion air & enclosed w/ noncombustible materials	2437.6	906.11
☐ Projection into nonhabitable basement space OK	2437.5	906.12

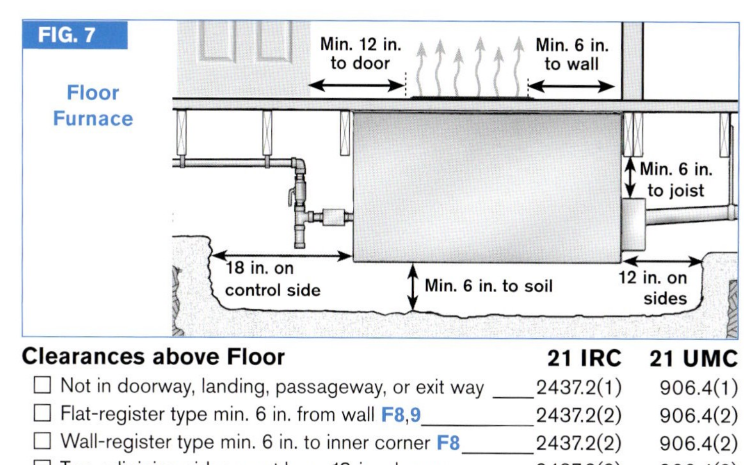

Clearances above Floor

	21 IRC	21 UMC
☐ Not in doorway, landing, passageway, or exit way	2437.2(1)	906.4(1)
☐ Flat-register type min. 6 in. from wall **F8,9**	2437.2(2)	906.4(2)
☐ Wall-register type min. 6 in. to inner corner **F8**	2437.2(2)	906.4(2)
☐ Two adjoining sides must have 18-in. clearance	2437.2(2)	906.4(2)
☐ Min. 12 in. from door swing or draperies **F8**	2437.2(3)	906.4(3)
☐ Thermostat in same area as register; no intervening doors	2437.2(5)	906.1(3)

FIG. 8

Wall-Register Floor Furnace Clearances

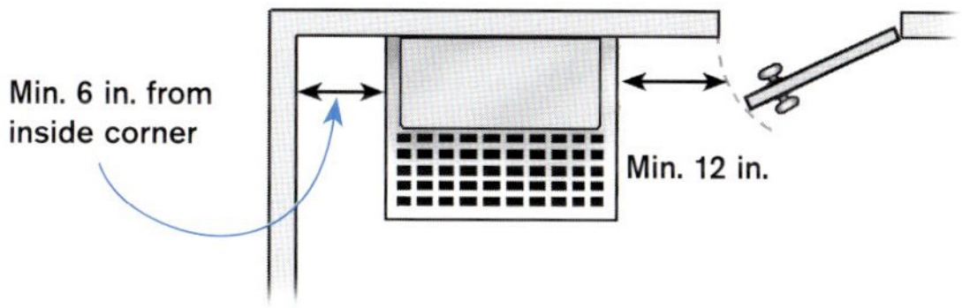

Min. 6 in. from inside corner

Min. 12 in.

FIG. 9

Improper Floor Register Clearances

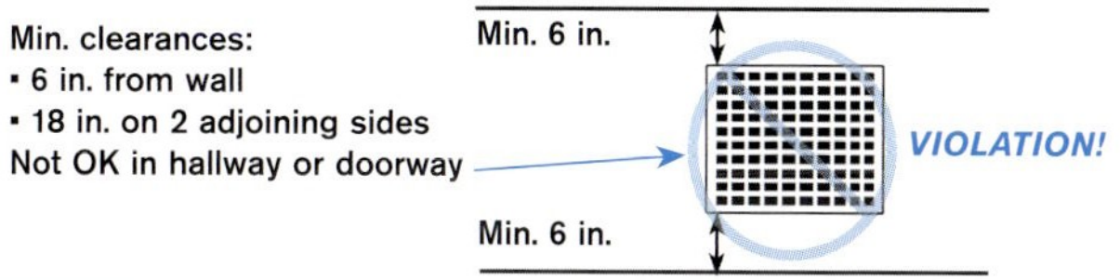

Min. clearances:
- 6 in. from wall
- 18 in. on 2 adjoining sides

Not OK in hallway or doorway

Min. 6 in.

Min. 6 in.

VIOLATION!

GAS APPLIANCE COMBUSTION AIR (C.A.)

As buildings have become tighter, the necessary air for combustion, ventilation, and dilution of flue gases inside a building must typically be supplied directly to the appliance space. Modern furnaces are often direct-vent and do not use the space at the appliance location as the source of combustion air. Local energy codes may have more restrictive requirements limiting the use of interior air for combustion.

General	21 IRC	21 UMC
☐ Spaces containing natural-draft (Cat. I) appliances req C.A.	2407.1	701.1
☐ Other appliances (not Cat. I) req C.A. AMI	2407.1	701.1.1
☐ Draft hood must be in same space as appliance	2407.3	701.2
☐ Provide makeup air to offset effect of exhaust fans, such as kitchen & bath fans, dryers, etc.	2407.4	701.3
☐ Makeup air reqd if kitchen exhaust >400 cfm	1503.6	local
☐ Engineered installations using approved methods allowed	2407.8	701.8

Mechanically Supplied Combustion Air

☐ Mechanical C.A. supply min. 0.35 cu.ft./minute/kBtu	2407.9	701.9
☐ Appliance interlock reqd if mechanically supplied C.A.	2407.9.2	701.9.2

Indoor Air Source

☐ Indoor air source alone only OK if infiltration ≥0.40 ACH	2407.5	701.4
☐ Min. volume of space 50 cu. ft./1kBtu/hr. **F10**	2407.5.1	701.4.1
☐ Volume includes rooms directly communicating w/ appliance space through openings w/o doors or openings per **T2,F11**	2407.5	701.4
☐ Openings connecting indoor spaces reqd to be located in upper & lower 12 in. of appliance space **F11**	2407.5.3.1	701.5(1)
☐ Openings connecting indoor spaces on same story min. 100 sq.in. each & min. 1 sq.in./kBtu of appliances **T2**	2407.5.3.1	701.5(1)
☐ If on different levels, min. 2 sq.in./kBtu of appliances	2407.5.3.2	701.5(2)
☐ If ACH <0.40, min. volumes for known air-infiltration method:		
• Non fan-assisted appliance (21cu. ft./ACH) per kBtu	2407.5.2	701.4.2
• Fan-assisted appliance (15 cu. ft./ACH) per kBtu	2407.5.2	701.4.2
☐ Combined indoor + outdoor air calculated by ratio of communicating spaces divided by reqd volume. Reduction factor of 1 minus that ratio is applied to the values in **T2**	2407.7	701.7

FIG. 10 All Air from Indoors

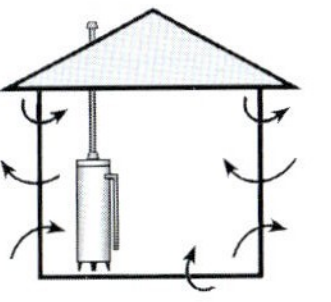

Space w/ > 0.40 ACH sufficient if volume ≥ 50 cu.ft./kBtu.

Indoor air cannot be the sole source of combustion air in tightly constructed homes. The air-infiltration rate must be > 0.40 ACH.

FIG. 11 Openings into Enclosed Indoor Space

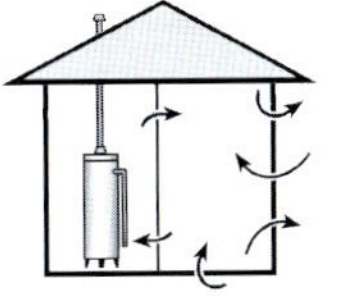

Openings from enclosed space in upper 12 in. & in lower 12 in.

TABLE 2 MIN. COMBUSTION AIR OPENING SIZES

	Indoor Air[A]		Outdoor Air Openings		
Btu	Opening size[B]	cu.ft. (sq. ft.[C])	1 in./2kBtu/hr.[D]	1 in./3kBtu/hr.[E]	1 in./4kBtu/hr.[F]
30k	100 sq.in.	1,500 (188)	15 sq.in.	10 sq.in.	7.5 sq.in.
40k	100 sq.in.	2,000 (250)	20 sq.in.	13.3 sq.in.	10 sq.in.
50k	100 sq.in.	2,500 (313)	25 sq.in.	16.7 sq.in.	12.5 sq.in.
60k	100 sq.in.	3,000 (375)	30 sq.in.	20 sq.in.	15 sq.in.
80k	100 sq.in.	4,000 (500)	40 sq.in.	26.7 sq.in.	20 sq.in.
100k	100 sq.in.	5,000 (625)	50 sq.in.	33.3 sq.in.	25 sq.in.
125k	125 sq.in.	6,250 (781)	62.5 sq.in.	41.7 sq.in.	31.3 sq.in.
150k	150 sq.in.	7,500 (938)	75 sq.in.	50 sq.in.	37.5 sq.in.
200k	200 sq.in.	10,000 (1250)	100 sq.in.	67 sq.in.	50 sq.in.

A. For construction w/ known air-infiltration rate >0.40/hr.
B. Reqd opening between confined space (<50 cu.ft. per kBtus) & unconfined space. Refer to **F11**.
C. Example sq. ft. based on 8-ft. ceiling—use actual room volume.
D. Applies to horizontal ducts **F15**.
E. Applies to single opening method **F12**.
F. Applies to direct exterior openings (2 opening method) or to vertical ducts **F13,14,16,18**.

The basic infiltration rate of 0.40 ACH is not directly comparable to the required ACH from energy codes, and most homes have a lower rate than 0.40 ACH under passive conditions. Outdoor openings are typically needed for combustion air.

Single Permanent Opening Method F12

	21 IRC	21 UMC
☐ Single direct exterior opening OK in upper 12 in. of enclosure min. 1 sq.in./3kBtu & ≥ sum of vent connectors	2407.6.2	701.6.2
☐ Appliance min. 1 in. clearance sides & back, 6-in. front	2407.6.2	701.6.2
☐ Can be ducted to exterior or spaces communicating w/ exterior (crawlspaces, attics)	2407.6.2	701.6.2

Two Permanent Openings Method

	21 IRC	21 UMC
☐ 2 openings—locate in upper & lower 12 in. F13	2407.6.1	701.6.1
☐ 2 direct exterior openings min. 1 sq.in./4kBtu T2,F13	2407.6.1	701.6.1
☐ 2 vertical ducts min. 1 sq.in./4kBtu T2,F14,18	2407.6.1	701.6.1
☐ 2 horizontal ducts min. 1 sq.in./2kBtu T2,F15	2407.6.1	701.6.1

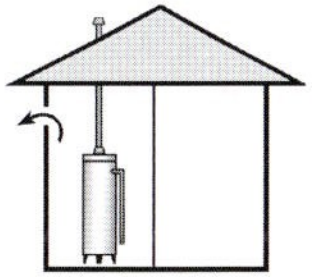

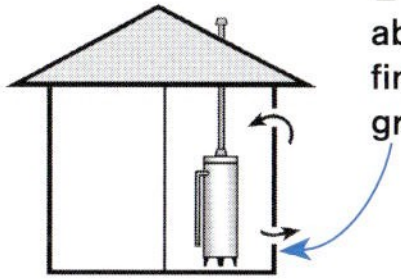

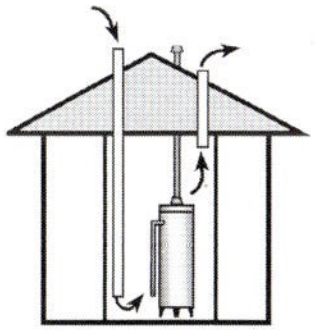

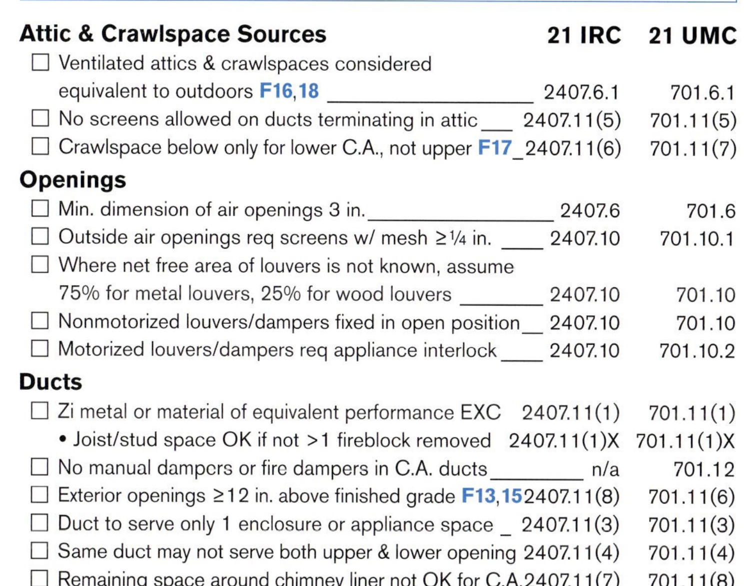

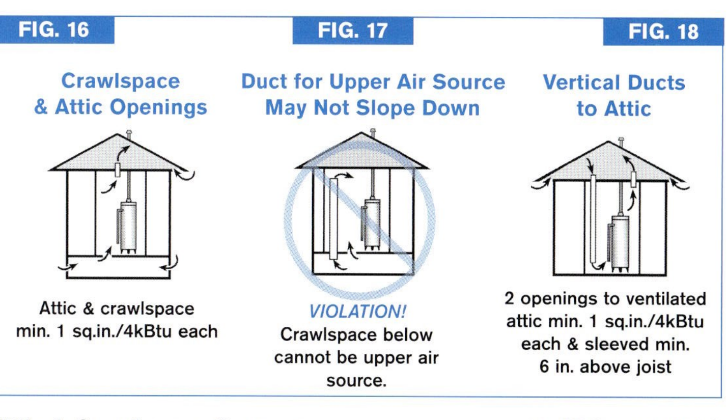

Attic & Crawlspace Sources

	21 IRC	21 UMC
☐ Ventilated attics & crawlspaces considered equivalent to outdoors F16,18	2407.6.1	701.6.1
☐ No screens allowed on ducts terminating in attic	2407.11(5)	701.11(5)
☐ Crawlspace below only for lower C.A., not upper F17	2407.11(6)	701.11(7)

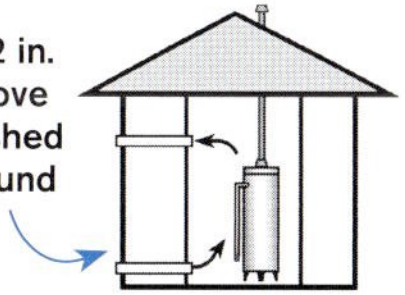

Openings

	21 IRC	21 UMC
☐ Min. dimension of air openings 3 in.	2407.6	701.6
☐ Outside air openings req screens w/ mesh ≥¼ in.	2407.10	701.10.1
☐ Where net free area of louvers is not known, assume 75% for metal louvers, 25% for wood louvers	2407.10	701.10
☐ Nonmotorized louvers/dampers fixed in open position	2407.10	701.10
☐ Motorized louvers/dampers req appliance interlock	2407.10	701.10.2

Ducts

	21 IRC	21 UMC
☐ Zi metal or material of equivalent performance EXC	2407.11(1)	701.11(1)
• Joist/stud space OK if not >1 fireblock removed	2407.11(1)X	701.11(1)X
☐ No manual dampers or fire dampers in C.A. ducts	n/a	701.12
☐ Exterior openings ≥12 in. above finished grade F13,15	2407.11(8)	701.11(6)
☐ Duct to serve only 1 enclosure or appliance space	2407.11(3)	701.11(3)
☐ Same duct may not serve both upper & lower opening	2407.11(4)	701.11(4)
☐ Remaining space around chimney liner not OK for C.A.	2407.11(7)	701.11(8)

GAS APPLIANCE CHIMNEYS & VENTS

Gas appliances at one time were almost exclusively a "gravity" vent design, where combustion gases lighter than the surrounding air rose by convection through a flue or chimney to the outdoors. As appliances became more efficient, other types of venting systems were developed, including fan-assisted appliances that induced the flow of combustion gases through a heat exchanger while still delivering these gases in a condition that is lighter than the air outside the flue. These fan-assisted appliances are still considered as "Category I" in T3 even though they do not have draft hoods. Category IV appliances with greater efficiency extract so much heat that their vent gases are cooled to the dew point and are at positive pressure relative to the outside air. The vent system must match the appliance category and manufacturer's recommendations.

General — 21 IRC — 21 UMC

- ☐ System must convey all flue & vent gases to outdoors___ 2427.3 — 802.3
- ☐ Choose type of vent system per T4 ____ 2427.4 — 802.4
- ☐ Induced-draft furnaces are "fan-assisted" Category I ___ 2428.1 — 803.1
- ☐ B & B-W vents L&L per UL 441, Type L per UL 641 ___ 2426.1 — 802.1
- ☐ Vents must be L&L EXC ____ 2426.1 — 802.1
  - Single-wall metal vents ____ 2426.1 — 802.7
  - Plastic for Cat. IV as specified by MFR & installed AMI 2426.1 — 802.4.1
- ☐ Install all vents AMI ____ 2426.5 — 802.6
- ☐ Appliances not reqd to be vented include ranges, built-in cooking units L&L for optional venting, clothes dryers (exhaust reqd), refrigerators, counter appliances, listed unvented room heaters *(p. 185)* _2425.8 — 802.2.1
- ☐ Aggregate total of unvented appliances max. 20 Btu/hr/cu. ft. of space containing such appliances ____ 2425.8 — 802.2.2

Locations & Protection

- ☐ Sheet metal shield to 2 in. above attic insulation ____ 2426.4 — 802.6.1.1
- ☐ No screw into inner wall of double-wall vent EXC ___ 2427.6.12 — 802.6(4)
  - At draft-hood outlet or to single-wall connector ___ 2427.6.12 — 802.6(4)
- ☐ Protect concealed vents <1½ in. from face of members such as studs, joists & rafters w/ min. 16-ga steel shield plates extending min. 4 in. beyond framing inside wall___ 2426.7 — n/a
- ☐ Vents not to pass through fabricated ducts or plenums 2427.3.4 — 802.3.5

TABLE 3 APPLIANCE VENTING CATEGORIES ◆ NFPA 54 3.3.4.10[A]

Category	Condensation	Static Pressure	Typical Vent
I	No	Nonpositive	B Vent
II	Yes	Nonpositive	AMI
III	No	Positive	Stainless or plastic
IV	Yes	Positive	Plastic

A. See glossary for complete definitions. These definitions are also in IRC 2403 & UMC 224.0.

TABLE 4 TYPE OF VENTING SYSTEM ◆ IRC T2427.4 & UMC T802.4

Appliances	Type of Vent	IRC	UMC
Listed Cat. 1, listed appliances w/ draft hoods, appliances listed for B vent	Type B gas vent	2427.6	802.6
	Chimney	2427.5	802.5
	Single-wall metal pipe[A]	2427.7	Ø 802.7.3
	Listed chimney lining for gas	2427.5.2	802.5.3
	Special vent listed for appliance (e.g.; pellet stove)	2427.4.2	802.4.3
Listed vented wall furnaces	Type B-W gas vent	2427.6	802.6 907.0
Cat. II, III & IV appliances	As specified by MFR (typically plastic or SS)	2427.4.1 2427.4.2	802.4.1 802.4.3
Unlisted appliances	Chimney	2427.5	802.5
Decorative appliances in vented fireplaces	Chimney	2427.5	911.2
Direct-vent appliances	As specified by MFR	2427.2.1	802.2.6
Appliances w/ integral vent	As specified by MFR	2427.2.2	802.2.7

A. Prohibited for residential applications in UMC per section 802.7.3.

Chimneys

	21 IRC	21 UMC
☐ Inspection reqd before connecting to existing chimney	2427.5.5	802.5.7
☐ Must be lined per NFPA 211 (w/ clay or metal) ____	2427.5.5.1[1]	802.5.7.1
• Like-for-like appliance OK to chimney passing inspection __	Ø[1]	802.5.7.1X
☐ Gas appliances shall not share a chimney flue w/ a separate solid-fuel appliance ____________	2427.5.6.1	802.5.8
☐ Vent connectors shall not be connected to a fireplace chimney flue unless fireplace flue opening permanently sealed ____	2427.10.13	802.10.11
☐ Chimney cross-sectional area ≥ appliance flue collar & ≤7× area of draft-hood outlet ____________	2427.5.4(2)	802.5.5(2)
☐ Chimneys min. 3 ft. above roof *(p. 118)* ____________	2427.5.3	802.5.4
☐ Min. 2 ft. higher than part of building within 10 ft. *(p. 118)*	2427.5.3	802.5.4
☐ No decorative shrouds unless L&L & AMI ____________	2427.5.3	802.5.4.3
☐ Secure connector to prevent blocking chimney ____	2427.10.11	802.10.9
☐ Connector must enter chimney above extreme bottom to avoid stoppage ____________	2427.10.11	802.10.9
☐ Connector must be secured & have thimble or stop to prevent entering so far as to restrict space to opposite wall __	2427.10.11	802.10.9

1. Exception to rule for unlined chimneys that have passed inspection was removed.

NFPA 54 and the UMC do not allow single-wall vents for dwellings. Single-wall vents require greater clearances and lose their heat more readily than B vents. Their flue gases may cool before reaching outdoors, resulting in a weak draft. Single-wall vents are not required to be a listed product.

Single-Wall Vents

	21 IRC	21 UMC
☐ Not allowed in dwellings & residential occupancies ________	n/a	802.7.3
☐ Galvanized sheet steel min. 0.0304 in. (22 gauge) thick	2427.7.1	802.7
☐ Not allowed outdoors in cold (freezing) climates ______	2427.7.2	802.7.1
☐ Only for runs from appliance space directly to outside _	2427.7.4	802.7.3.1
☐ Termination min. 5 ft. above flue collar or draft hood ___	2427.7.3	802.7.2(1)
☐ Termination min. 2 ft. above roof ____________	2427.7.3	802.7.2(2)
☐ Termination min. 2 ft. higher than building within 10 ft.__	2427.7.3	802.7.2(2)
☐ Approved cap or roof assembly reqd at termination____	2427.7.3	802.7.2(3)
☐ May not originate in attic or pass through inside wall___	2427.7.6	802.7.3.2
☐ Min. 6 in. clear to combustibles for single-wall pipe____	2427.7.8	802.7.3.3
☐ Passage through combustible exterior wall reqs thimble	2427.7.7	802.7.3.4
☐ Passage through combustible roof reqs thimble_______	2427.7.5	802.7.3.5
☐ Roof thimble min. 18 in. above & 6 in. below roof______	2427.7.5	802.7.3.5

CATEGORY I APPLIANCE VENT CONNECTORS

Appliances can be directly connected to their vent, or by a vent connector. Connectors for draft hood–equipped appliances and other Category I appliances are not required to be listed. The use of single-wall connectors in cold spaces is restricted as they are likely to produce condensation under such conditions. Listed flexible vent connectors that have clearance ratings as B vents can more easily resolve difficult structural arrangements. Listed connectors that are supplied with collars to connect to B vents should not be cut or altered in the field.

General	21 IRC	21 UMC
☐ Connector reqd unless vent directly attached	2427.10.1	802.10
☐ Must be as straight as practical—no dips or sags	2427.10.8	802.10.6
☐ Min. 1/4-in./ft. slope upwards to vent connection **F19,20**	2427.10.8	802.10.6
☐ Joints between sections & connections to draft hoods req sheet-metal screws or listed materials installed AMI	2427.10.6	802.10.5
☐ Provide adequate support	2427.10.10	802.10.8
☐ Entire connector reqd to have ready access	2427.10.12	802.10.10
☐ Necessary size increases reqd to be made only at appliance outlet connection	2427.10.3.5	802.10.2.4
☐ Connectors not to be smaller than draft-hood outlet	2428.3.17	803.2.21
☐ Connectors not >2 sizes > than flue collar diameter	2428.3.17	803.2.21
Single-Wall Connectors for Category I Appliances		
☐ Not in attics or crawlspaces EXC	2427.10.2.2	802.10.1.1
• OK in other unconditioned space within exterior walls if local 99% winter design temp ≥ 5°F	2427.10.2.2X	802.10.1.1X
☐ Horizontal connector length ≤ 75% of vertical vent for draft hood–equipped appliance **F19**	2427.10.9	802.10.7.1
☐ Min. 6-in. clearance to combustibles **T6** EXC	2427.10.5	802.10.4
• Lesser clearances w/ system per **F48,T10**	2427.10.5X	802.10.4X
☐ May not pass through interior wall, floor, or ceiling	2427.10.14	802.10.12
☐ May not be covered w/ insulation	2427.10.2.3	802.10.1.2
Type B Double-Wall Vent Connectors		
☐ Clearance to combustibles per L&L (1 in. typical) **T6**	2427.10.5	802.10.4
☐ Horizontal connector length ≤ 100% of vertical vent for draft hood–equipped appliance **F19**	2427.10.9	802.10.7.2

FIG. 19

Connector Length (draft-hood appliances)

L

H

B vent

Connector min. 1/4 in./ft. slope

Single-wall connector sections secured to each other & to draft hood, 3 screws typical

Max. length L for single-wall is 75% of H. When the connector is double-wall, the max. length of L is 100% of H.

The lengths shown in these 2 illustrations are only applicable to draft hood–equipped appliances and are not used for other Category I appliances. The vent size tables are used for those and can also be used for draft hood–equipped appliances instead of these examples.

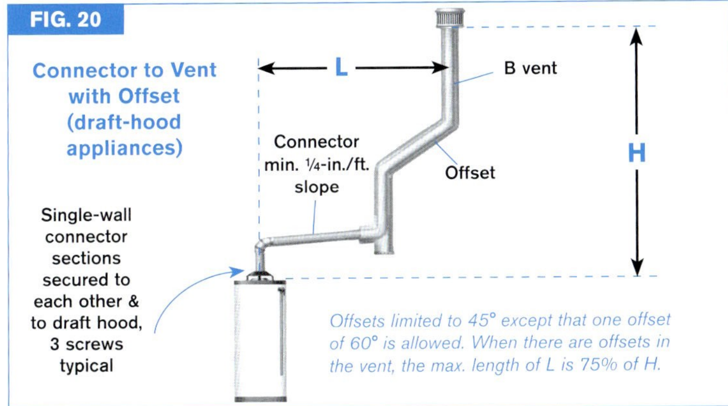

FIG. 20

Connector to Vent with Offset (draft-hood appliances)

Offsets limited to 45° except that one offset of 60° is allowed. When there are offsets in the vent, the max. length of L is 75% of H.

Category I appliances may use separate connectors to a common vent. When the appliances all have draft hoods, the vent and connector sizes are allowed to be determined by the size of the draft hood outlets, or by the vent tables that are supplied with the appliance. These tables are also in the codes. If one or more appliances are fan-assisted, sizes must be determined by the tables.

Appliances Vented in Common: General — 21 IRC — 21 UMC

- ☐ Join common vent connectors as high as possible per available headroom & clearance ______ 2427.10.3.4 — 802.10.2.3
- ☐ Two or more connectors to common vent must enter at different levels EXC **F21** ______ 2427.10.4.1 — 802.10.3
  - • OK at same level if max. 45° from vertical **F21** ___ 2427.10.4.1 — 802.10.3
- ☐ Smaller connector to enter above larger ______ 2427.10.4 — 802.10.3.1
- ☐ Junctions w/ tee or wye must be MFR for purpose __ 2427.10.7[2] — n/a
- ☐ If both appliances have draft hoods, vent allowed to be sized at 100% of larger draft hood outlet + 50% of smaller & ≤7× area of smaller draft hood outlet ______ 2427.6.9.1(3) — 802.6.2.1

Common Connector Size & Length per Tables

- ☐ Tables mandatory for fan-assisted Category I ______ 2427.6.9.1 — 802.6.2.1
- ☐ Route connectors using shortest possible length ______ 2428.3.2 — 803.2.2
- ☐ Max. horizontal length of vent connector 18 in. per in. of connector diameter **T5** EXC ______ 2428.3.2 — 803.2.1
  - • Longer lengths allowed by subtracting 10% of max. table capacity for each added multiplier of allowed length in **T5** & connector capacity based on corresponding single-appliance table as if other appliances were not present ______ 2428.3.3 — 803.2.2

Example: If a 4 in. connector, normally allowed to be 6 ft., is between 6 ft. & 12 ft. in length (one multiplier of 6), reduce the allowed BTU capacity in the tables by 10%. Use the "single appliance" table for minimum capacity of each vent connector.

- ☐ If a single draft hood & fan-assisted appliance are vented in common, size connectors using supplied tables ___ 2427.10.3.1 — 802.10.2.2
- ☐ Connector capacity in tables allows 2 90° elbows; subtract 5% additional elbows ≤45° & 10% for each elbow >45° & ≤90° ___ 2428.3.7 — 803.2.6
- ☐ Max. size of vertical vent not >7× smallest flue collar 2428.3.13 — 803.2.17
- ☐ Common vent height measured from highest draft hood 2428.3.12 — 803.2.12

2. New IRC req that fitting manufactured for the purpose be used to join connectors.

TABLE 5 — MAX. HORIZONTAL LENGTH VENT CONNECTOR FOR COMMON VENTING ◆ IRC T2428.3.2 & UMC T803.2.1

Diameter (in.)	Max. Horizontal Length (ft.)	Diameter (in.)	Max. Horizontal Length (ft.)
3	4½	7	10½
4	6	8	12
5	7½	9	13½
6	9	10	15

FIG. 21

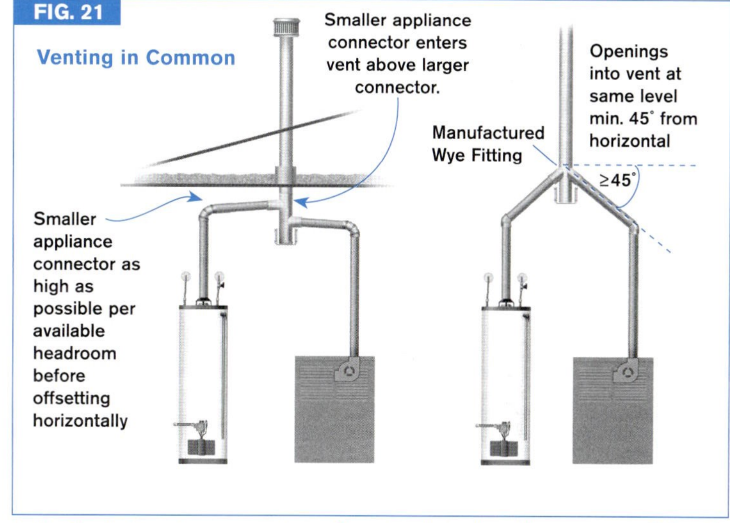

In the illustration above, assuming a B vent and single-wall connectors, IRC table 2428.3(2) or UMC table 803.2(2) or NFPA 54 table 13.2(b) would be used. Based on the Btu rating of each appliance, the tables determine the diameters of the connectors and vent for different vent heights and connector rise. The tables include allowance for up to 2 90° elbows.

TABLE 6	CONNECTOR CLEARANCES FROM COMBUSTIBLE MATERIAL ◆ IRC T2427.10.5 UMC T802.7.3.3		
Appliance	**Listed Type B**	**Listed Type L**	**Single-Wall Metal Pipe**
Listed appliances w/ draft hoods & appliances listed for Type B gas vents	As listed	As Listed	6 in.
Residential boilers & furnaces w/ listed gas conversion & with draft hood	6 in.	6 in.	9 in.
Residential appliances listed for Type L	NP	As listed	9 in.
Unlisted appliances w/ draft hood	NP	6 in.	9 in.
Other residential & low heat appliances	NP	9 in.	18 in.
Medium heat appliances	NP	NP	36 in.

TABLE 7	THROUGH-WALL VENT TERMINAL CLEARANCES ◆ IRC T2427.8 UMC 808.8.1&2
Type & Location of Vent Terminal	**Min. Clearance**
Clearance above finished grade, porch, deck, or balcony	12 in.
Direct-vent clearance from any opening into building	≤10kBtu/hr. – 6 in. for appliances >10kBtu/hr. & ≤50kBtu/hr. – 9 in. >50kBtu/hr. & ≤150kBtu/hr. – 12 in. >150kBtu/hr. – 4 ft. below or to side, 1 ft. above
Vertical clearance to ventilated or unventilated soffit above terminal	None unless AMI
Clearance to inside or outside corner	None unless AMI
Clearance to building openings or to combustion air inlet of appliances	4 ft. below or to side of opening or 1 ft. above
Clearance to mechanical supply inlet	10 ft. horizontal or 3 ft. above
Clearance above paved sidewalk or driveway on public property	7 ft. & not located where condensate or vapor could cause nuisance or hazard
Clearance to underside of porch deck or balcony	12 in. where porch deck or balcony open on at least 2 sides. Not allowed if only one side is open.
Clearance perpendicular to wall openings in adjacent buildings	10 ft. unless 2 ft. above or 25 ft. below opening

CATEGORY I APPLIANCE VENT SIZES

Category I appliances ship with tables for sizing the vent system. These supplied tables were developed by GAMA (the Gas Appliance Manufacturers Association). They are repeated in the model codes and downloadable from many websites. IRC Appendix AB and UMC Appendix G contain instructions and examples on how to use the tables. The tables distinguish between fan-assisted and "natural" draft appliances. Fan-assisted appliances, including those vented in common with an appliance that has a draft hood, must be sized using the tables.

Vent Size (Appliances w/ Draft Hoods) — 21 IRC / 21 UMC

- ☐ Min. size same as flue collar ________ 2427.6.9.1(2) 802.6.2.1(3)
- ☐ Max. size 7× area of smallest flue collar ________ 2427.6.9.1(2) 802.6.2.1(3)
- ☐ If 2 appliances, 100% of larger + 50% of smaller 2427.6.9.1(3) 802.6.2.1(4)
- ☐ Offsets 45° max. except one of 60° OK ________ 2427.6.9.2 802.6.3.2
- ☐ Total horizontal distance of vent + connector ≤ 75% of vertical height of vent if offsets in vent **F20** ________ 2427.6.9.2 802.6.2.2

Vent Size Using Vent Tables

- ☐ Tables can be used for all Category I appliances _ 2427.6.9.1(1) 802.6.2.1(1)
- ☐ Tables mandatory for fan-assisted Category I ____ 2427.6.9.1(1) 802.6.2.1(2)
- ☐ If vertical vent diameter > than connector, vent diameter determines min. vent capacity & connector determines max. capacity __ 2428.2.8 803.1.8
- ☐ Flow area of vertical vent max. 7× appliance flue collar 2428.2.8 803.1.8
- ☐ Tables for single appliance to Type B double-wall only for vents not exposed to outdoors below the roof line ____ 2428.2.9 803.1.10
- ☐ Type B vent in unvented chase insulated to R-8 or in unused masonry chimney flue not considered outdoors **F26** __ 2428.2.9 803.1.10
- ☐ Zero lateral values in tables only OK if straight vertical vent connects directly to a top outlet draft hood or flue collar ________ 2428.2.4 803.1.3
- ☐ No elbows if using "zero lateral length" table column __ 2428.2.3 803.1.2
- ☐ Tables w/ lateral length allow for 2 90° elbows **F22** ___ 2428.2.3 803.1.2
- ☐ Reduce table capacity 5% for each additional elbow up to 45° & 10% for each additional elbow >45° up to 90° _ 2428.2.3 803.1.2
- ☐ Reductions for elbows in common vents same as above 2428.3.6 803.2.5
- ☐ Common vent cross-sectional area ≥ largest connector 2428.3.8 803.2.7
- ☐ Wye/tee fitting vent connection size = common vent size 2428.3.9 803.2.9

Vent Table Example 1:

The first step is to select the correct table based on the type of vent or chimney, the connector type, and the number of appliances.

In **F22**, an 80kBtu fan-assisted furnace is directly connected to a double-wall B vent with 2 90° elbows. The lateral distance **L** of the offset is 5 ft., and the overall height **H** of the vent is 10 ft.

Question: What size B vent is needed?

Solution: IRC Section 2428.2.3 & UMC section 803.1.2 allow 2 90° elbows without requiring a further reduction in table values. The tables have different columns for natural and fan-assisted appliances. Use IRC table 2428.2(1) or UMC table 803.1.2(1) for Type B Double-Wall Gas Vent, Single Appliance, Connected Directly to Vent. Go down the "height" column at the left of the table to the line with 10 ft. Go to the row for lateral length of 5 ft. Go across that row to the first number that is large than 80 in the "FAN" "Max" column. That is under the column for 4 in. diameter.

FIG. 22

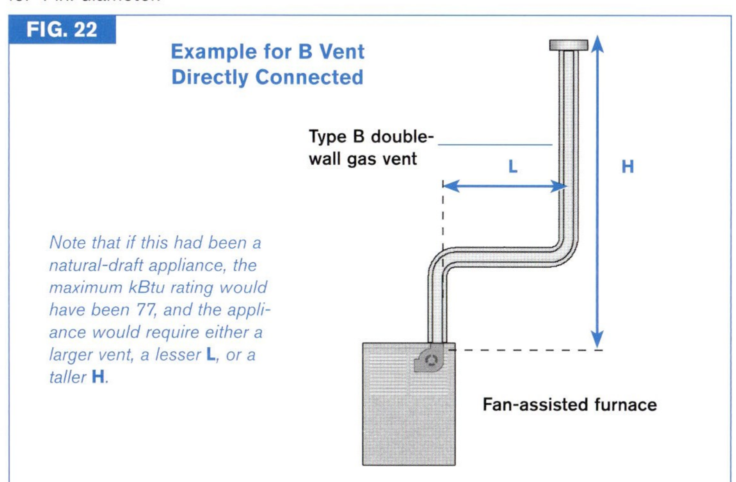

Vent Table Example 2:

In **F23** a 100kBtu draft-hood-equipped furnace w/ a 5-in. draft hood outlet is connected to a B vent with an overall height **H** of 10 ft. above the appliance draft hood and a single-wall connector with a lateral length **L** of 5 ft.

Question: What size B vent and single-wall connector are needed?

Solution: Use IRC table 2428.2(2) or UMC table 803.1.2(1) for Type B Double-Wall Gas Vent, Single Appliance, Single-Wall Vent Connector. As with the first example, go down the height column to the row for 5-ft. lateral, and go across to the first entry in the "NAT" column that is greater than 100. That is in the 5-in. column. The vent connector should also be 5 in, since it cannot be smaller than the flue collar at the draft hood.

FIG. 23

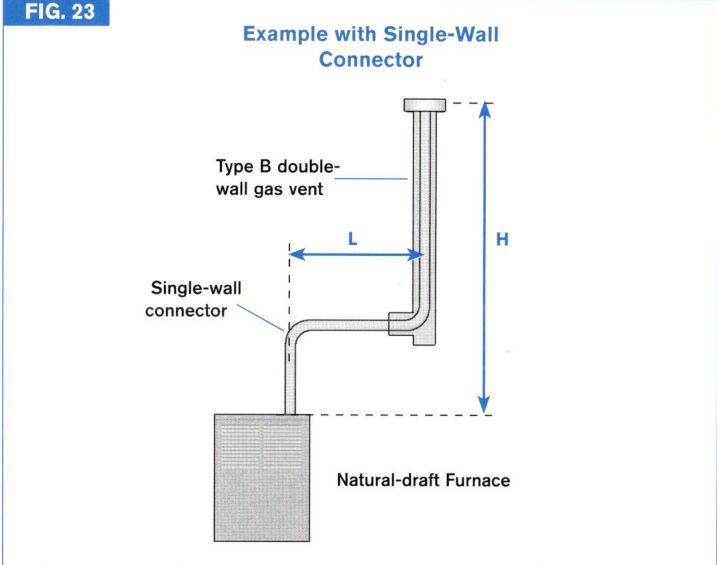

Example of Vent Tables for Common Venting

F24 depicts an 80kBTU fan-assisted furnace vented in common with a 35kBtu water heater. The combined inputs are 115kBtus. Each appliance has a 4 in. flue collar, and the connectors joint at a type B common vent. The overall height of the common vent (measured from the taller appliance outlet to the top of the common vent) is 20 ft. The horizontal length of the water heater vent connector is 3 ft., the vertical rise of the water heater connector is 2 ft., and the rise of the furnace connector is 3 ft. The common vent is offset in the attic space with 2 60° elbows, and the horizontal offset distance is 3 ft.

Question: What diameter connectors and Type B common vent should be used?

Solution: IRC table 2428.3(2) or UMC table 803.2(2) is based on 2 or more appliances with single-wall connectors to a common Type B double-wall vent.

Start with the water heater. Go to the table row for 20-ft. vent height. Go across to the row for connector height of 2 ft. Go across to that row to find the first number in the "NAT" column that is greater than 35. That is in the 3-in. column. However, a 3-in connector would be smaller than the flue collar, so a 4-in connector is needed.

Next compute the size for the furnace. Using the same steps, go down the vent height column to the row for 20 ft. and go across to 3-ft. connector rise. Move across that row to the first column with a "FAN" "Max" rating exceeding 80. That is in the 4-in. column. However, the "FAN" "Min" rating is 87. Therefore, either a 5-in. single-wall connector is needed, or we could go to table 2428.3(1) for double-wall connectors, where the "Min" rating for a 4-in connector is 35 and the max. rating is 110. Using a listed type B flexible connector, a 4-in connector is acceptable.

Next compute the size for the common vent. The second part of the table is common vent capacity. In the 20-ft. row, go across to the first number in the "FAN+NAT" column that exceeds 115. That is 118 in the 4-inch column. However, due to the offset in the common vent, section 2428.3.6 tells us to subtract 10% for each offset greater than 45°. Therefore, we must subtract 20%, and a 4-in. common vent is too small. In the 5-in. column, the "FAN+NAT" entry is 177. Subtracting 20% from 177 gives us 141, which is greater than our combined input rating. Therefore, a min. 5-in common vent is required. That also complies with 2428.3.5, which limits the horizontal distance of the offset to 1½ ft. for each in. of diameter.

FIG. 24 Common Venting Example

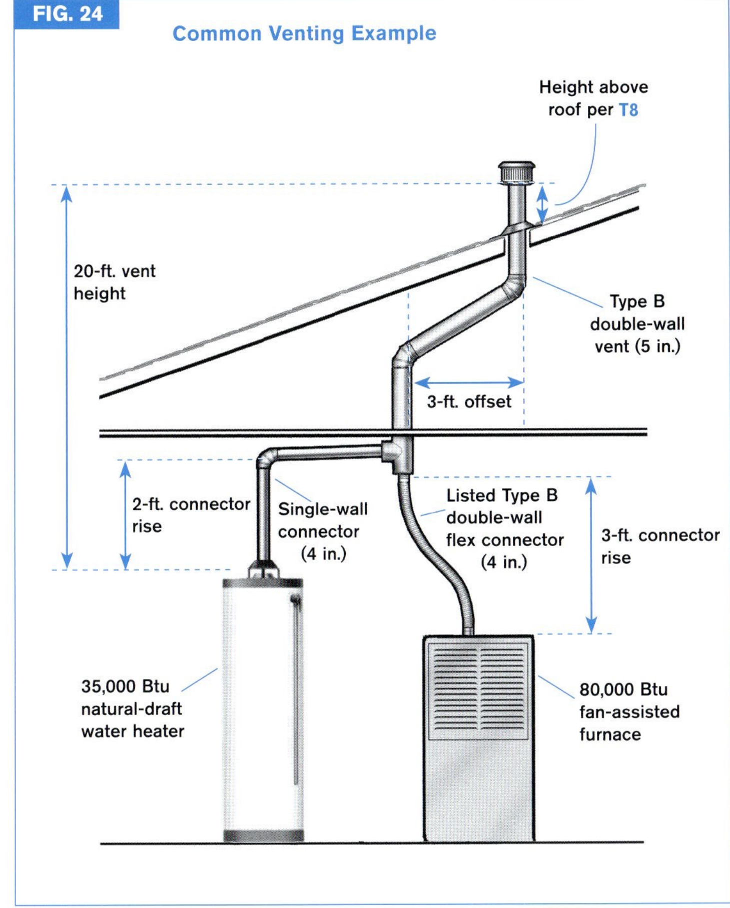

GAS VENT TERMINATIONS

General	21 IRC	21 UMC
☐ Gas vents must extend above roof EXC	2427.6.4(1&2)	802.6.2(1)
• Direct-vent appliances **F3,29,37**	2427.6.4(3)	802.6.1(1d)
• Appliances w/ integral vents	2427.6.4(4)	802.6.2(1e)
• Mechanical draft appliances AMI ***(p. 198)***	2427.6.4(5)	802.6.2(f)
☐ Roof penetration reqs flashing	2427.6.6	802.6.1(6)
☐ Must have listed cap or listed roof assembly	2427.6.6	802.6.1(6)
☐ Decorative shrouds only if L&L & AMI	2427.6.4.1	802.6.1(5)
☐ Type B or L vent termination min. 5 ft. vertical above draft hood or flue collar EXC	2427.6.5	802.6.1(2)
• Type B-W vent min. 12 ft. from bottom of wall furnace	2427.6.5	802.6.1(3)
☐ Min. 6 ft. when sized per vent tables	2428.2	803.0
☐ Vents ≤12 in. per **F25**, **T8** if > 8 ft. from wall	2427.6.4(1)	802.6.2(1a)
☐ Vents >12 in. diameter min. 2 ft. above roof	2427.6.4(2)	802.6.2(1b)
☐ Terminate min. 3 ft. above forced-air inlet within 10 ft.	2427.6.7	802.6.1(7)

FIG. 25

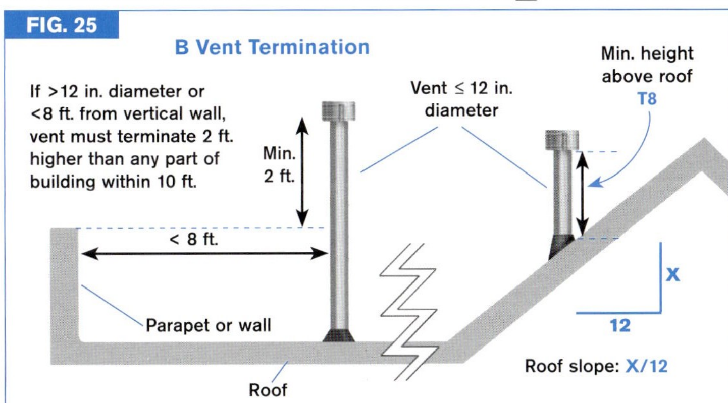

TABLE 8 B VENT TERMINATION ◆ IRC 2427.6.4 & UMC 802.6.1

Roof Slope	Min. Height	Roof Slope	Min. Height
Flat to 6/12	1 ft.	>11/12 to 12/12	4 ft.
>6/12 to 7/12	1 ft. 3 in.	>12/12 to 14/12	5 ft.
>7/12 to 8/12	1 ft. 6 in.	>14/12 to 16/12	6 ft.
>8/12 to 9/12	2 ft.	>16/12 to 18/12	7 ft.
>9/12 to 10/12	2 ft. 6 in.	>18/12 to 20/12	7 ft. ½
>10/12 to 11/12	3 ft. 3 in.	>20/12 to 21/12	8 ft.

FIG. 26

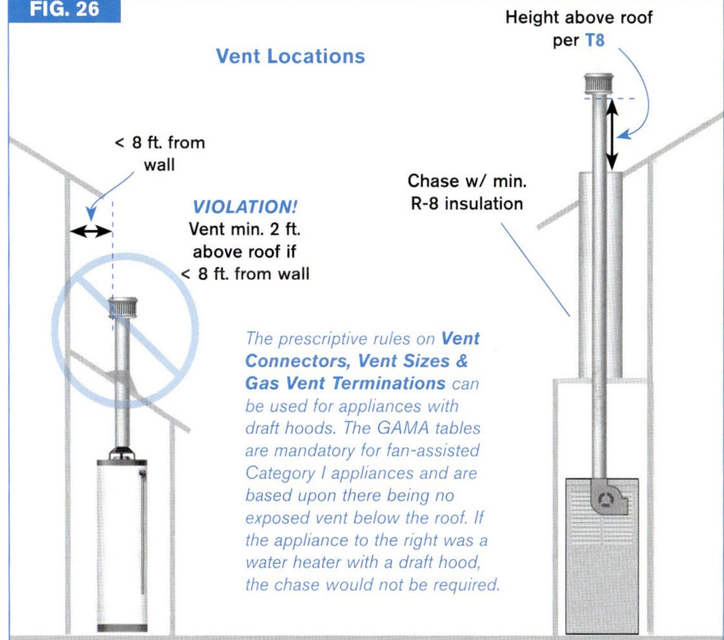

The prescriptive rules on ***Vent Connectors, Vent Sizes & Gas Vent Terminations*** *can be used for appliances with draft hoods. The GAMA tables are mandatory for fan-assisted Category I appliances and are based upon there being no exposed vent below the roof. If the appliance to the right was a water heater with a draft hood, the chase would not be required.*

Cat. IV Appliance Vents	21 IRC	21 UMC
☐ Mechanical draft systems L&L to UL 378; install AMI	2427.3.3(1)	802.3.3
☐ Positive-pressure systems reqd to be gastight ____	2427.3.3(3)	802.3.3.2
☐ No mixing natural & forced-draft connectors or vents	2427.3.3(4)	802.3.3.3
☐ Burner interlock reqd to forced-vent fan ________	2427.3.3(5)	802.3.3.4
☐ Installation & support of vent AMI ______________	2426.5	802.6.4
☐ Size Category II, III & IV appliance vents AMI ______	2427.6.9.3	802.6.2.3
☐ Plastic piping reqs labeling for product standard specified by appliance MFR or listing in accordance w/ UL 1738 __	2427.4.1	802.4.1
☐ Install plastic piping AMI per vent MFR instructions _	2427.4.1.1	802.4.2
☐ Plastic vent joint primer must be contrasting color __	2427.4.1.1	802.4.2

FIG. 27 Direct-Vent Terminations

Exhaust
Intake air
Intake air

Intake
Exhaust

Sidewall Vents

Rooftop Vents

Exhaust
Intake air

Intake vent terminal 90°
Exhaust vent terminal
Distance AMI
Screen
Min. 12 in. to grade or snow level
Screen

For clearances to building openings, see ***T7.***

Cat. IV Vent Terminations (not Direct Vent)	21 IRC	21 UMC
☐ Termination through wall OK **F27,28** clearances **T7** ___	2427.8	802.8
☐ Terminate min. 3 ft. above forced-air inlets within 10 ft. _	2427.6.7	802.6.1(7)
☐ Terminate min. 4 ft. to side or below or 1 ft. above building openings, min. 1 ft. above ground level **F28,T7** ____________	T2427.8	802.8.1
☐ Through-wall vents of condensate-producing appliances not to terminate over public way or where creating nuisance _	T2427.8	802.8.3
☐ Min. 7 ft. above ground if adjacent to public walkway _	T2427.8	802.3.3.5
☐ Through-wall vent min. 10 ft. horizontally from openings in (facing) buildings if ≤ 2 ft. above or ≤ 25 ft. below openings __	T2427.8	802.8.5
☐ Collect & dispose of condensate from vent *(pp. 203–204)* ______________________	2427.9	802.9
☐ Condensate drains AMI for appliance & vent MFR ____	2427.9	802.8.3

Cat. IV Vent Terminations (Direct Vent)	21 IRC	21 UMC
☐ Termination through wall OK **F28**, clearances **T7** ______	2427.8	802.8X1
☐ Furnaces w/ combustion air piping terminating AMI in same location as vent considered direct vent (MFR) **F37** ___	2427.8X	802.8X1
☐ Direct-vent combustion air intakes **F27** not subject to **T7**	2427.8X	802.8X1

FIG. 28 Forced-Vent Terminations

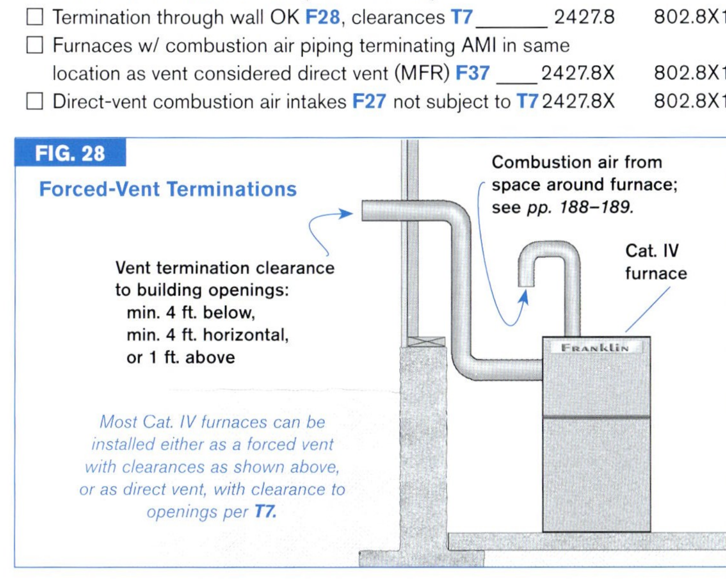

Most Cat. IV furnaces can be installed either as a forced vent with clearances as shown above, or as direct vent, with clearance to openings per ***T7.***

GAS APPLIANCES IN FIREPLACES

Gas can be brought to fireplaces for log lighters to assist a solid-fuel fire, or for decorative appliances, where the primary function is the aesthetic effect of the flames. Artificial log sets inside a fireplace are decorative appliances. They do not provide heat, since the flue must be open and the heated air goes up the chimney. Direct-vent gas fireplaces, such as shown in F29, are now popular since they do not cause smoke pollution and they are a functional heat source.

Decorative Appliances (Log Sets) in Fireplaces	21 IRC	21 UMC
☐ Not in bath or bedroom if confined space *(p. 188)*	2432.3	911.1
☐ Maintain open vent (block damper in open position*)	MFR	911.2
☐ Thermostatic control not allowed	MFR	911.2
☐ Must be listed to ANSI Z21.60/CSA 6.26	2432.1	n/a
☐ Install AMI & per L&L	2432.1	911.2.1
☐ Fireplace screen reqd	MFR	911.3
☐ Appliance w/pilot or ignition system reqs pilot safety	2432.2	306.1
☐ Shutoff inside firepit only if shutoff listed for same	2420.5.1	1312.6X1
☐ Shutoff in same room & within 6 ft. EXC	2420.5.1	1312.6
• Where provided w/ ready access & connector ≤6 ft.	2420.5.2	Ø
• Remote shutoffs may not serve other appliances	2420.5.2	Ø

Vented Decorative Gas Fireplaces

☐ Not in bath or bedroom if confined space EXC	2432.3	912.1
• OK if direct vent	2406.2(1)	912.1X
☐ Must be L&L to w/ ANSI Z21.50 & be installed AMI	2434.1	912.2(1)
☐ Appliance w/pilot or ignition system reqs pilot safety	2432.2	306.1
☐ Service access panels not attached to building	2434.2	912.2(3)

Vented Gas Fireplace Heaters

☐ Comply w/ same rules as above for decorative fireplaces	2435.1	912.0
☐ Must be L&L to ANSI Z21.88 & install AMI	2435.1	912.2(1)

Log Lighters

☐ Install log lighters AMI	2433.1	MFR
☐ Shutoff in same room & within 6 ft.	2420.5.1	1312.6
☐ No flexible connectors in firepit	2422.1.1	1312.1

**Damper stops are not required for log lighters as they are assistive devices. They are only intended to start combustion of the solid fuel and then be turned off.*

Direct-Vent Gas Fireplaces F29	21 IRC	21 UMC
☐ OK in bedroom or bath if L&L & installed AMI	2406.2(1)	912.1&2
☐ Vent intake air terminal must be outdoors	2427.2.1	912.2(1&4)
☐ CSST or flex reqs grommet through appliance wall	2422.1.2.3X4	1312.1
☐ Termination clearances from building openings T7	2427.8	802.8.2

FIG. 29

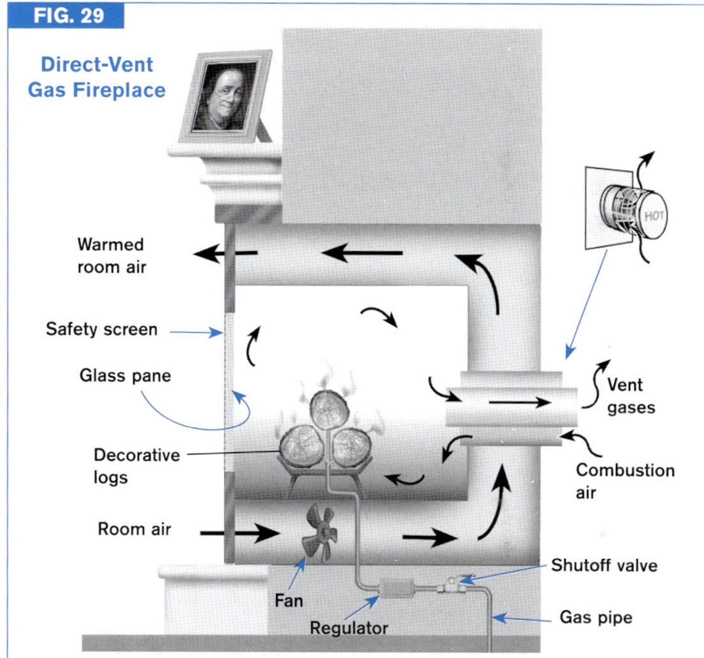

A direct-vent fireplace can vent horizontally out a sidewall or vertically to the roof. With a completely enclosed chamber, it draws in outside air for combustion and expels flue gases to the outside. The front glass enclosure allows radiant heat to pass into the room, and ducts around the firebox provide warmed air. It heats a room without consuming oxygen or heated air from the room. The glass fronts are dangerously hot and require protective screening to avoid contact. Manufacturers offer retrofit kits for older systems that lack this safety feature.

AIR CONDITIONING & HEAT PUMPS

Air-conditioning and heat-pump efficiency is measured in SEER (Seasonal Energy Efficiency Rating) or in HSPF (Heating Seasonal Performance Factor). The numbers are higher as efficiency is increased. The minimum standards for equipment sold in the United States are set by the U.S. Department of Energy and will increase slightly in 2023.

Required heating and cooling loads are determined by a calculation using ACCA Manual J. The proper sizes of equipment to meet that load are then determined by ACCA Manual S. Bigger is not better. Systems need only be sized to make up for the temperature gains or losses that occur through the building envelope; proper insulation and vapor retarders reduce the need for larger equipment. Oversized systems can lead to short-cycling, condensation, and less comfort.

Heat Pumps (HPs) & Air Conditioning (AC)	21 IRC	21 UMC
☐ Size system per ACCA Manual J & S	1103.7	1105.1
☐ Appliances must be anchored in place	1307.2	303.4
☐ Unit supported from ground on min. 3-in. raised pad F30	1401.4	1105.2
☐ Furnace w/ cooling coil must have blower capable of overcoming resistance of cooling coil + duct system	1411.2	904.7(1)
☐ Cooling coil downstream from heat exchangers unless L&L for upstream (e.g., SS heat exchanger)	1411.2	904.7(2&3)
☐ Central AC reqs air filter	AD 106	311.2
☐ Condenser not near clothes dryer vent (California 5 ft.)	MFR	MFR
☐ Refrigerant vapor (suction) lines insulation & vapor retarder (IRC min. R3 & max. 0.05 perm) F30	1411.6	1109.9
☐ Protect refrigerant piping < 1½ in. from underside of roof deck from nails/fasteners (UMC: no specific distance)	1411.7	1109.7
☐ Secure refrigerant tubing within 6 ft. of condensing unit	1411.8[3]	1109.6
☐ Secure refrigerant tubing at max. 15-ft. intervals	n/a	1109.6
☐ Tamper-resistant caps outdoor refrigerant ports F30 EXC	1411.9	1105.11
• Where protected by walls/fencing w/ key access	1411.9	1105.11X
☐ Disconnecting means reqd within sight of condenser	4101.5	301.4
☐ GFCI-protected receptacle within 25 ft. of equipment	3901.12[4]	301.4

3. Rule for securing within 6 ft. new to this IRC edition.
4. GFCI protection now reqd for such receptacle outlets.

FIG. 30 Air-Conditioning Condenser

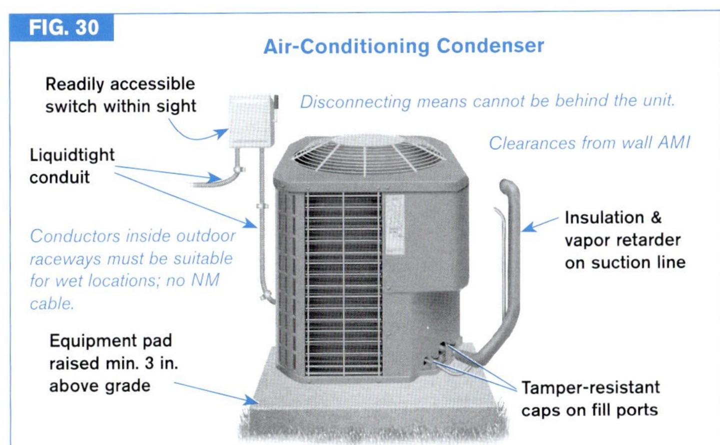

FIG. 31 Multizoned Mini-Split System

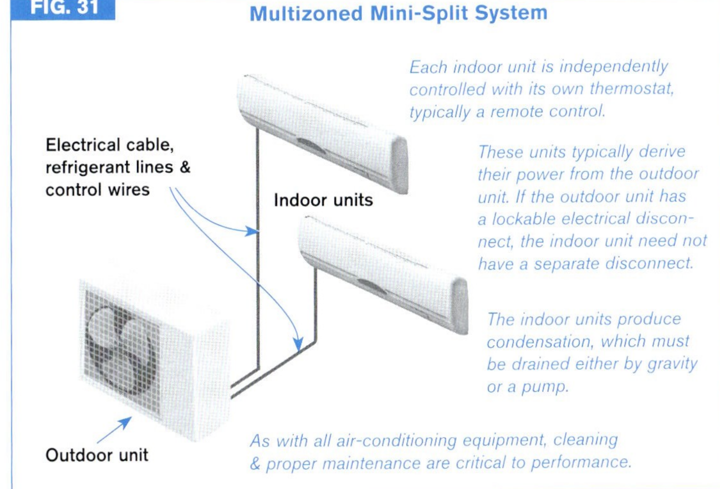

FIG. 32

Heat Pump Operating in Cooling Mode

INDOOR UNIT

Plenum

Supplemental electric strip heaters

Indoor air handler

Indoor coil

Filter

Check valve

Liquid line

Condensate

Overflow drain pan

Suction line

Insulation & vapor retarder

OUTDOOR UNIT

Reversing valve

Accumulator

Outdoor coil

Outdoor fan

Compressor

Filter/dryer

Check valve

Min. 3-in. raised pad

Reversing Valve in Heating Mode

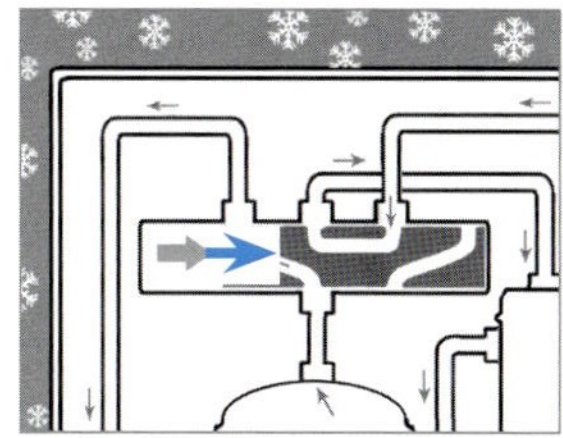

Heat pumps can be used for both heating and cooling.

*A **reversing valve** determines the direction of refrigerant flow.*

*In **cooling mode**, the system operates as in the figure at left.*

*In **heating mode**, the outdoor coil extracts heat from the atmosphere and the indoor coil gives up that heat to the interior space.*

In heating mode, if the outdoor temperature is below the balance point, supplemental electric strip heaters are activated in the indoor air handler.

An interlocked leak detector or a secondary drain or pan is reqd when the indoor unit is located over furred space. Secondary drains must discharge to a conspicuous location.

*Because heat pumps are a very efficient form of heating without the direct consumption of fossil fuels, they are becoming more popular. In addition to the ducted system shown here, mini-split units **F31** are becoming more popular, especially for smaller dwellings or accessory buildings. Mini-splits have the advantage of being able to supply heat to a specific room.*

Window & Through-Wall AC Units

	21 IRC	20 NEC
☐ Must have equipment grounding conductor; no adapters to existing 2-slot receptacles	3908.1	440.61
☐ Max. cord length 10 ft. if 120V, 6 ft. if 240V	MFR	440.64
☐ Cord plug OK as disconnect if controls ≤6 ft. of floor	MFR	440.63
☐ AFCI (arc fault circuit interrupter) or LCDI (leakage current detection interrupter) or HDCI (heat-detecting circuit interrupter) reqd in attachment plug F33	MFR	440.65
☐ Max. load rating 80% of individual circuit	3702.12.1	440.62B
☐ Max. load rating 50% of shared circuit	3702.12.2	440.62C
☐ Condensate not to drain over public way	1411.3	UMC 310.1

FIG. 33 **Room Air-Conditioner Plug**

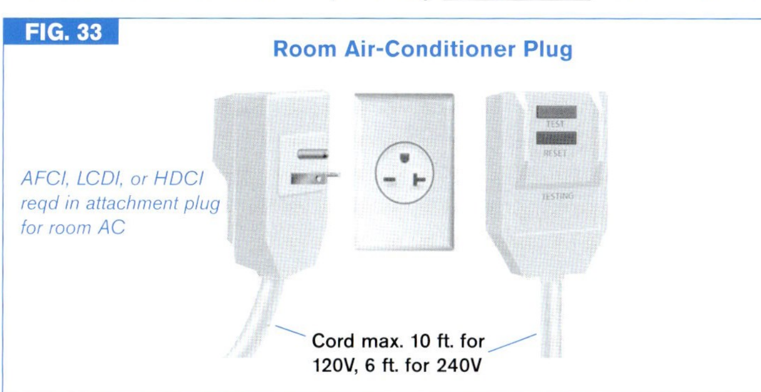

EVAPORATIVE (SWAMP) COOLERS

Evaporative Coolers F34

	21 IRC	21 UMC
☐ Install AMI & on level platform	1413.1(1&2)	933.4
☐ Locate so as to minimize probability of damage	1413.1	933.2
☐ Ground-mounted min. 3 in. above adjoining ground	1413.1	933.4.2
☐ Platform-mounted min. 6 in. above adjoining ground	n/a	933.4.3
☐ Provide flashing at openings into building	1413.1(3)	933.4.1
☐ OFF switch or disconnect in sight if motor >1/8 hp	4101.5	301.4
☐ Backflow protection on supply (internal air gap OK)	1413.1(4)	local
☐ Min. 10-ft. horizontal clearance to plumbing or gas vents	303.5.1	311.3(1)
☐ UMC: electrical receptacle ≤25 ft. (IRC: not reqd)	3901.12X	301.4

FIG. 34 **Evaporative (Swamp) Coolers**

Hot outside air is pulled through moist pads where it is cooled by evaporation and circulated through the house or building by a large blower, leaving the air cooler & slightly more humid than when it entered the cooler. These systems are suited for climates where the air is hot and humidity is low, and they are also used for makeup air in commercial kitchens.

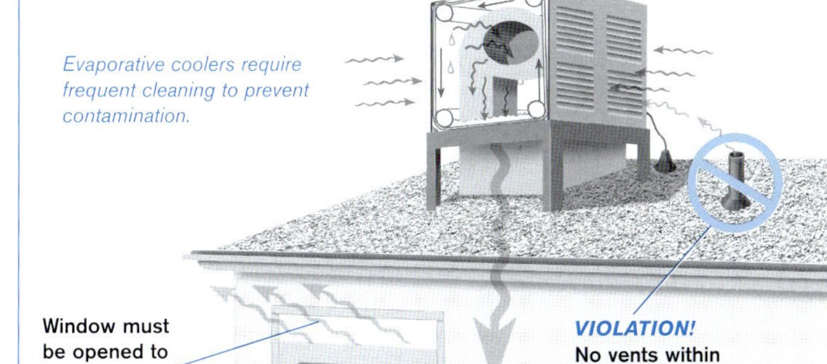

CONDENSATE DISPOSAL

Air conditioners, Category IV high-efficiency furnaces, and tankless water heaters produce condensate, which must be disposed of to an approved location. Drains are typically connected as an indirect waste to the sanitary sewer system, though in some areas condensate is allowed to go to landscape or storm drains. Individual jurisdictions sometimes have specific directives for appliances that produce a large amount of condensate as compared to a minor amount. Condensate from high-efficiency furnaces may need to be neutralized before connecting to a sewer system. Building conditions may require use of a pump to reach an approved discharge location. Equipment located over a space where leakage would cause damage requires a secondary means to control condensate leakage.

Drain Piping	**21 IRC**	**21 UMC**
☐ Drain pipe min. ¾ in. w/ min. ⅛-in./ft. slope **F35**	1411.3	310.1
☐ If drains from >1 unit joined together, upsize in accordance w/ approved method (UMC: 1-in. pipe if > 20 tons cooling)	1411.3.2	310.3
☐ Drain trap (in primary drain) reqd AMI	1401.1	310.5
☐ AC discharge to approved location (UMC: indirectly to drywell, pit, plumbing fixture, or trapped & vented receptor)	1411.3	310.5
☐ No direct connection to waste or vent pipe	1411.3	310.1
☐ Indirect waste connection OK (lavatory tailpiece) **F35**	1411.3	310.1
☐ Not OK to drain over walkway, street, or public way	1411.3	310.1
☐ Cleanouts reqd to allow clearing of blockages **F36**	1411.3.3	310.3.1
☐ No threaded metal fittings into female plastic fittings	2609.2	310.7
☐ No drilling (saddle fittings) of DWV pipes to accept condensate drain (use wye tailpiece)	3003.2	UPC 310.2
Condensate Pumps		
☐ Install AMI	1411.4	310.1.1
☐ Discharge to rise vertically to gravity condensate drain	n/a	310.1.1
☐ Each appliance to have separate pump w/ interlock to prevent operation during pump failure	1411.4 & 2404.11	310.1.1
☐ Separate pumps OK to connect to single gravity indirect waste if equipped w/ check valves & approved	n/a	310.1.1

FIG. 35

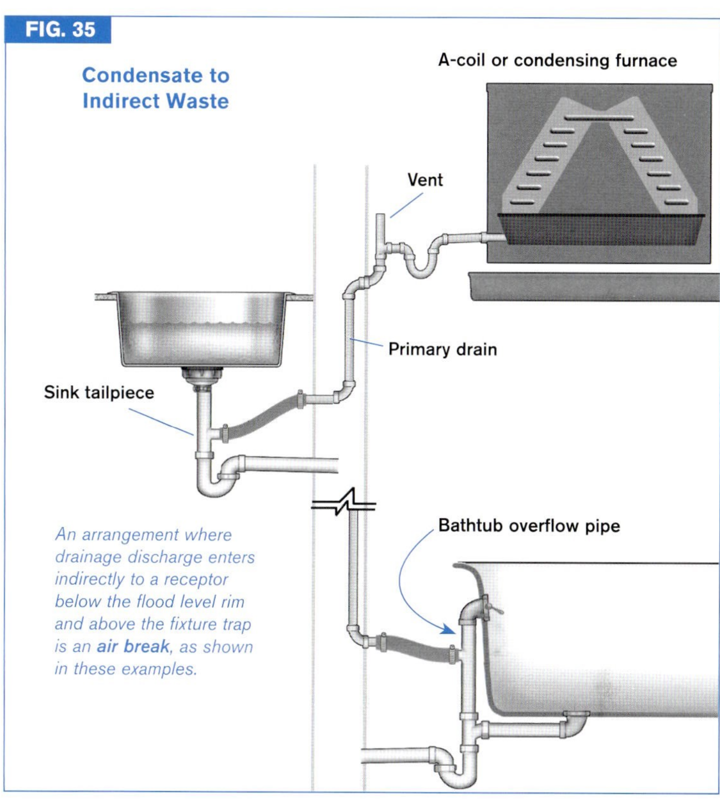

Secondary Containment F36

	21 IRC	21 UMC
☐ If condensate stoppage would damage any building components, install one of the following methods:	1411.3.1	310.2
• Water level detection in primary w/ interlocked cutout	1411.3.1(4)	310.2(1)
• Auxiliary pan w/ separate drain to readily observed location, such as over a window	1411.3.1(1)	310.2(2)
• Secondary drain piped to readily observed location	1411.3.1(2)	310.2(3)
• Auxiliary drain pan w/ leak detector & drain fitting	1411.3.1(3)	310.2(4)
☐ Equipment over drain pans above FLR of drain pan	1411.3.4	310.2.1
☐ Down-flow units w/ no secondary & no way to install auxiliary drain pan req internal blockage detector w/ interlocked cutout	1411.3.1.1	n/a

FIG. 36 Condensate Control

A-coil or condensing furnace

(1) Secondary drain from A-coil (at higher elevation than primary)

Trap depth per MFR *(sufficient to maintain trap seal against pressure of air over coil)*

Vent down-stream of trap

All condensate drains req ⅛-in./ft. slope

(2&3) Pan with drain or interlocked leak detector

(4) Interlocked leak detector in one of these locations

Cleanout

Primary drain

*When located over a space where blockage could damage building components, provide one of these 4 options to control secondary drainage: **(1)** pipe from secondary drain connection at A-coil, **(2)** pan with drain, **(3)** pan w/ water detection, or **(4)** blockage detection device in primary drain. The water detection device is interlocked to the controls for the unit.*

Secondary drains must discharge to a readily observable location, such as above a window.

High-Efficiency Appliances (Category IV)

	21 IRC	21 UMC
☐ Provide means to collect & dispose of condensate F35	2427.9	802.9
☐ Condensate drain also reqd for Category I or III if local experience shows need (reqd for some tankless WH) *(p. 165)*	2427.9	802.9.1
☐ Condensate drains AMI	2427.9	802.8.3
☐ Auxiliary drain pan F36 reqd if condensate stoppage could damage any building component EXC	1411.5 & 2404.10	n/a
• Automatic cutout installed in drain system	1411.5X & 2404.10X	n/a

FIG. 37 See *F27* for terminations

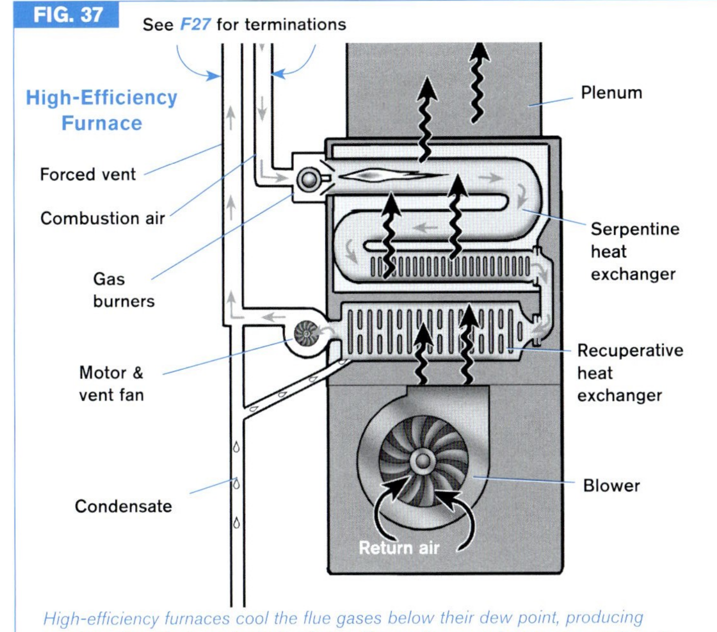

High-efficiency furnaces cool the flue gases below their dew point, producing condensation. Vents are typically plastic. The appliance and vents req condensate drain piping to an approved point of disposal. Joints in the plastic piping req primers & must be installed AMI.

DUCTS

ACCA Manual D is the design standard for sizing residential duct systems and helps to ensure a balanced air flow throughout a building. Factory-made ducts and closure systems (tape) must comply with UL standards. SMACNA provides fabrication and support standards for sheet-metal ducting and installation standards for factory-made duct systems. The Air Duct Council (formerly the Air Diffusion Council) also provides standards for installation & support of factory-made flexible ducts. Manufacturer's installation instructions typically follow their standard. The code's standards for insulation and duct leakage testing are typically superseded by local or state energy codes.

General

General	21 IRC	21 UMC
☐ Duct sizes per ACCA Manual D or other approved methods	1601.1	601.2X
☐ Factory-made ducts L&L per UL 181	1601.1.1(2)	603.4
☐ Max. 2 stories for vertical riser on factory-made duct	n/a	603.1.4
☐ Fireblock openings around ducts between floors	302.11(4)	local
☐ Vibration isolators max. 10 in. length	1601.2	602.5
☐ Garage ducts min. 26-ga sheet steel; no flex	302.5.2& 1601.4.9	local
☐ No duct openings into garage	302.5.2	local

Underground Ducts

Underground Ducts	21 IRC	21 UMC
☐ Metal ducts protected from corrosion in approved manner or completely encased in ≥2 in. of concrete	1601.1.2	603.11
☐ Ducts sealed, secured & tested prior to encasement	1601.1.2	603.11
☐ Ducts must be sloped to drain to drainage point (UMC: min. 1/8 in./ft. back to main riser)	1601.1.2	603.11
☐ Factory-made ducts not allowed underground	1601.4.7	603.11

SMACNA Rigid Duct Support

SMACNA Rigid Duct Support	ANSI/SMACNA 006
☐ Rigid horizontal ducts req support within 2 ft. each elbow	5.1.1
☐ Rigid horizontal ducts req support within 4 ft. each branch intersection	5.1.1
☐ Rigid round duct max. support spacing 12 ft.	T5-2
☐ Round duct up to 24 in. diameter: support straps 1 in. × 22 gauge	T5-2
☐ Round 10-in.-diameter duct support wires 1 @ 12 gauge	T5-2
☐ Two 12-ga or one 8-ga wire for round ducts 11 – 18 in. diameter	T5-2
☐ Round 19 in.–24-in.-diameter duct support wires 2 @ 10 gauge	T5-2

UMC Rigid Duct Support

UMC Rigid Duct Support	21 UMC
☐ Support at each change of direction	603.7.1
☐ Riser ducts req support by metal straps or angles to the structure	603.7.1
☐ Rectangular ducts req support on 2 opposite sides of each duct attached by rivets, bolts, or screws at intervals in SMACNA T5-1	603.7.1.1
☐ Horizontal round ducts ≤40 in. diameter 1 hanger per 12-ft. interval	603.7.1.2
☐ Horizontal round ducts req tight-fitting circular bands around entire perimeter of duct at each support interval EXC	603.7.1.3
• Round ducts ≤10 in. diameter 18-ga Zi steel wire OK as support	603.7.1.4X
☐ Circular bands around ducts min. 1 in. wide	603.7.1.4

Joints & Seams

Joints & Seams	21 IRC	21 UMC
☐ Joints, seams & connections per SMACNA standards	1601.4.1	603.9
☐ Mechanically fasten ducts to plenums & flanges	1601.4.1	603.9
☐ Crimp joints contact lap min. 1 in. (UMC: 1½ in.)	1601.4.1	603.9
☐ Crimp joints fasten w/ min. 3 sheet metal screws	1601.4.1	603.9
☐ Male end into adjoining duct in direction of flow	1601.4.2	603.9
☐ Flex duct fasteners must be per UL 181 B	1601.4.1	603.9.1
☐ Tapes for flex ducts req marking of UL 181 B-FX **F38**	1601.4.1	603.9.1
☐ Mastic for flex ducts reqs marking of UL 181 B-M	1601.4.1	603.9.1
☐ Closure systems to seal ducts must be installed AMI	1601.4.1	603.9.1

Flex Duct Installation

	21 IRC	21 UMC
☐ Install & support all ducts per SMACNA standards	1601.1.1(4)	603.3&4
☐ Flexible ducts must comply w/ UL 181 & be installed AMI	1601.4.4	603.4
☐ Ground clearance min. 4 in.	1601.4.8	603.1.3
☐ 18-in. vertical clearance where needed under duct to prevent cutting off access to crawlspace	n/a	603.2
☐ Flexible ducts in nonresidential occupancies max. 5-ft. length	n/a	603.4.1
☐ Use min. reqd length to make connection **F40**	1601.4.4	603.4(1)
☐ Support horizontal ducts at max. 4-ft. intervals **F39**	1601.4.4	603.4(2)
☐ Support vertical risers at max. 6-ft. intervals	1601.4.4	603.4(3)
☐ Sag max. ½ in. per foot of support spacing **F39**	1601.4.4	603.4(4)
☐ Band supports must be rigid & min. 1½ in. wide **F39**	1601.4.4	603.4(5)
☐ Duct bend radius min. 1 duct diameter **F40**	1601.4.4	603.4(6)
☐ Screws not to penetrate inner liner unless AMI	1601.4.4	603.4(7)
☐ Attachment fitting collar must be beaded & min. 2 in. each side; metal worm-gear clamps must be used **F38**	1601.4.4	603.4(8)
☐ Inner liners 1 in. past bead prior to fastener **F38**	1601.4.4	603.4(9)
☐ Outer vapor barrier min. 2 wraps UL 181B tape **F38**	1601.4.4	603.4(10)

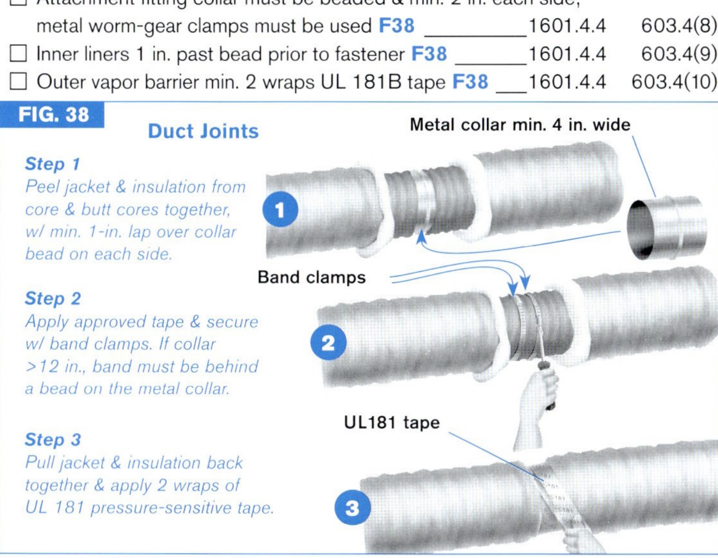

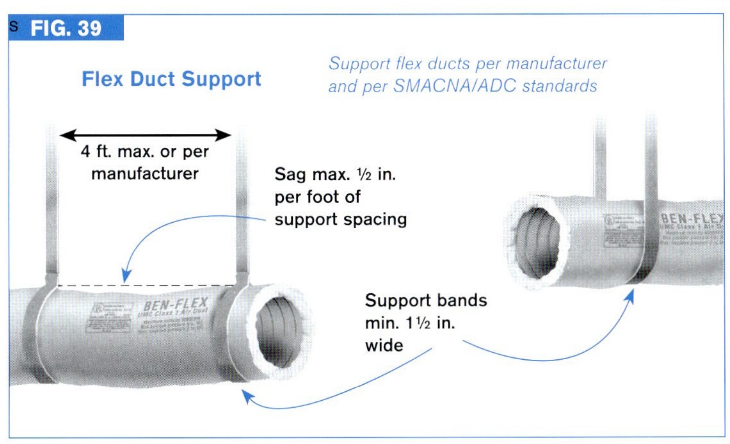

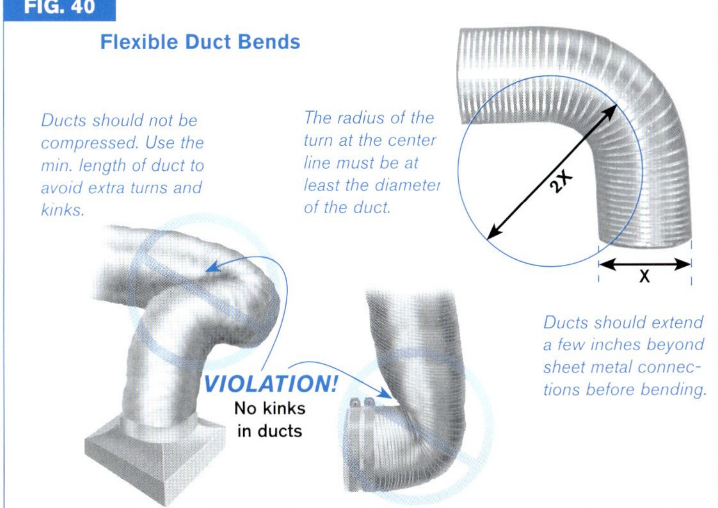

Return Air Sources

	21 IRC	21 UMC
☐ Not from bathroom, toilet room, kitchen, mechanical room, closet, garage (IRC: crawlspace or attic)	1602.2(4&6) & 2442.3	311.3
☐ Amount of return air from any space ≤ supply air	1602.2(2)	n/a
☐ System must be balanced by an approved method	1602.2(3)	314.1
☐ No return air from one dwelling to another dwelling unit	1602.2(7) & 2442.5	311.4
☐ Must be open to min. 25% area served	2442.3	311.3(4)
☐ Min. 10 ft. from burners or draft hoods **F41**	1602.2(1) & 2442.3	311.3(1)
☐ Return OK from room w/ fuel-burning equipment if supply air provided to replace return air, return min. 10 ft. from draft hood & room volume min. 100 cu. ft. per 1,000Btu of equipment	2442.3(5)X	311.3(6)X3
☐ Air filters reqd	AD106	311.2

FIG. 41

Closet Furnace above Return Air Opening

Separation of combustion and circulating air is essential for safe and complete combustion of fuel gas. The basic rule is that return air must be at least 10 ft. from the appliance draft hood and burners.

In this common arrangement, the closet door is used to separate the space with the return air and the space requiring combustion air. If the door is open or inadequately sealed, the return air competes w/ the combustion air ducts, resulting in incomplete combustion and the potential for carbon monoxide in the living area.

Use of Stud Cavities as Ducts

Energy codes may prohibit use of building cavities as ducts—check with local AHJ.

	21 IRC	21 UMC
☐ Stud cavities prohibited as supply air plenum	1601.1.1(7)	602.1&4.2
☐ Exposed GB in return air stud cavity limited to 50–125°F & moisture-controlled to prevent condensation	1601.1.1(5)	602.4.2
☐ Exposed GB reqs mold/mildew-resistant surface	n/a	602.4.2
☐ Cavities must be fireblocked & sealed	1601.1.1(7)	n/a
☐ Stud cavity return not to convey from >1 floor	1601.1.1(7)	n/a
☐ Not permitted in outside walls of building envelope	1601.1.1(7)	n/a

Insulation

	21 IRC	21 UMC
☐ Insulation value reqd to be marked on factory-made ducts	1601.3	605.1
☐ Duct coverings & linings max. flame spread index 25, max. smoke-developed index 50	1601.3	605.1.2
☐ Duct coverings not to penetrate fireblocked wall or floor (UMC: not to penetrate fire-resistance rated assembly)	1601.4.6	605.1.2
☐ Min. insulation in unconditioned space R-8 for ducts >3 in. diameter, R-6 if ≤3 in. diameter	1103.3.1	local
☐ Insulation not reqd in conditioned space completely within building thermal envelope & within the continuous air barrier	1103.3.2	605.1(X2)
☐ Space can be considered within thermal envelope in floor cavities, exterior walls & ceiling when air barriers & insulation separate the ducts from the unconditioned spaces	1103.3.2	local

Max. Allowable Duct Leakage

	21 IRC
☐ Rough-in test: Leakage ≤4.0 cu. ft./minute per 100 sq. ft. of conditioned floor area if air handler installed, 3.0 cu. ft./minute if not installed	1103.3.6
☐ Post-construction test: Leakage ≤4.0 cu. ft./minute per 100 sq. ft. of conditioned floor area, 8.0 cu. ft./minute if all ducts & air handlers located entirely within building thermal envelope	1103.3.6

The UMC uses a formula based upon the SMACNA HVAC Air Duct Leakage Test Manual. However, areas using the UMC are more likely to regulate duct leakage in accordance with the locally adopted energy code. Properly sealed duct work is one of the most impactful energy conservation measures available. Legacy ducts may leak an average of 40-60% of conditioned air.

OIL TANKS & PIPING

The IRC provides specific rules for oil systems and oil-burning appliances in chapters 14, 18 & 22. The UMC defers to NFPA 31 for oil systems and appliances. Jurisdictions using the UMC should use the NFPA 31 columns. While the IRC and NFPA 31 provide rules for buried tanks, many jurisdictions do not allow them due to the risk of groundwater contamination should they leak. Storage tanks may also be under the jurisdiction of the state or local environmental agency and the local fire protection district. There are special considerations with tanks in flood-prone areas or those with high seismic risk.

Tanks: General	21 IRC	NFPA 31
☐ Tanks L&L (IRC: indoor UL 80, underground UL 58)	2201.1	7.2.1
☐ Install above design flood elevation or anchor per NFPA 30	2201.6	7.2.8.1
☐ Restrain against earthquake movement per local codes	1307.2	7.2.8.2
☐ Tanks & supports req solid concrete foundations	n/a	7.3.1
☐ Design foundation to minimize settling & corrosion	2201.2	7.3.2
☐ Max. 660 gal above ground or inside building	2201.2	7.5.5 & 7.8.2
Abandoned Tanks		
☐ Temporarily unused tanks emptied, cleaned & tank opening capped or fill pipe filled w/concrete	2201.7	7.12.1
☐ Remove permanently abandoned tanks including outside fill piping & any appliance piping	2201.7	7.13.1
Fill & Vent Piping		
☐ Each tank system reqs separate fill & vent **F42**	2203.3&4	7.5.9
☐ Fill & vent pipes must terminate outside building **F42**	2203.3&5	8.4.7
☐ Tank fill & vent piping min. schedule 40 steel or brass	2202.1	8.2.1.1
☐ No cast-iron fittings	2202.2	8.3.4
☐ Fill pipe min. 1¼ in. & pitched toward tank **F42**	MFR	8.5.1
☐ Vent pipe min. 1¼ in. & pitched toward tank **F42**	2203.4	8.6.1
☐ Fill piping min. 2 ft. from building openings	2203.3	8.5.2
☐ Each tank reqs fill gauge (IRC: tanks inside buildings)	2201.5	7.5.10
☐ No glass gauges or gauges subject to breakage	2201.5	8.10.4
☐ Vent termination min. 2 ft. from building openings	2203.5	8.6.2
☐ Vent terminal screened & w/weatherproof cap	2203.5	8.6.3&4
☐ Vent terminal above snow level & visible from fill	2203.5	8.6.2.1&2

Outside Tanks	21 IRC	NFPA 31
☐ Outside tank supports firmly anchored to foundation	2201.2	7.3.3
☐ Tanks ≤275 gal (IRC: ≤660 gal) min. 5 ft. from PL	2201.2.2	7.8.2(1)
☐ Tanks >275 gal & ≤660 gal min. 10 ft. from PL	n/a	7.8.2(2)
☐ Protect external tanks from corrosion & damage	2201.2.2	7.8.4
Inside Tanks		
☐ Inside tanks >60 gal only on lowest floor EXC	local	7.5.4
• Spill containment & no floor or open space below	local	7.5.5
☐ Tanks >10 gal min. 5 ft. from any fire or open flame	2201.2.1	7.5.7

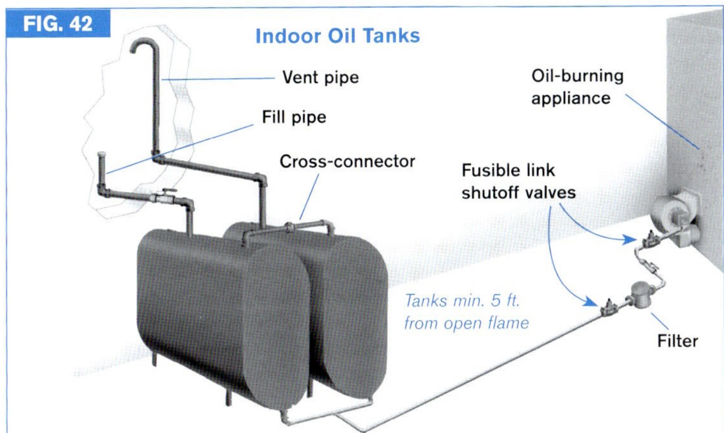

Compared to other fuels, heating oil has the greatest number of Btus per gallon (approximately 139k). It can be safely stored indoors as it is less readily ignitable than gasoline or propane. It is a commonly used fuel in the Northeast and relatively rare in western states or areas where natural gas is readily available. It displaced coal as the primary fuel source in many areas of the country. Heating oil typically has a red dye added to distinguish it from diesel oil. In areas with outdoor tanks subject to freezing, special fuel oil mixtures are supplied, and they contain a mixture of kerosene and #2 oil.

Oil-fired appliances require regular maintenance. Filters need to be inspected and cleaned, and other routine adjustments will be necessary. Systems should be serviced by a qualified heating professional at least once a year. Black stains or soot in any part of the vent or chimney system are an indicator of improper combustion and should prompt an immediate service call.

OIL-FIRED APPLIANCES

General

	21 IRC	NFPA 31
☐ Appliances must be listed	1302.1 & 1402.1	13.2
☐ Install appliance AMI	1401.1	4.3.2
☐ Readily accessible oil shutoff valve reqd **F42**	2204.2	10.5.1
☐ Electrical disconnect switch reqd in sight of burner		10.5.2
☐ Clearance reductions **T10** not allowed in alcoves **F43**		10.6.2

Piping & Tubing to Appliances

☐ Above-ground fuel supply schedule 40 steel or brass or seamless Cu, brass, or steel tubing	2202.1	8.2.2.1
☐ Tubing reqs corrosion-resistant coating or protective conduit to within 12 in. of tank or appliance	n/a	8.2.2.2.1
☐ Min. tubing size 3/8 in. O.D., Cu min. Type L	2203.2	8.7.1
☐ Readily accessible manual shutoff reqd at tank outlet	2204.2	8.7.1
☐ Shutoff reqd at building entrance if tank outdoors	n/a	8.7.1(4)
☐ Filter or strainer reqd on appliance supply	local	7.5.8(4)
☐ Cross-connected tanks max. 660 gal total **F42**	2203.6	8.9.1
☐ Fusible link safety shutoffs reqd as close as practical to filter on tank side & on inlet connection to burner EXC **F42**	n/a	8.10.6.1[5]
• Where the filter & inlet connection to burner ≤18 in. apart only 1 fusible link valve reqd on tank side of the filter	n/a	8.10.6.2[5]

5. Previous edition specified within 6 in. of filter on tank side and within 12 in. of inlet to burner.

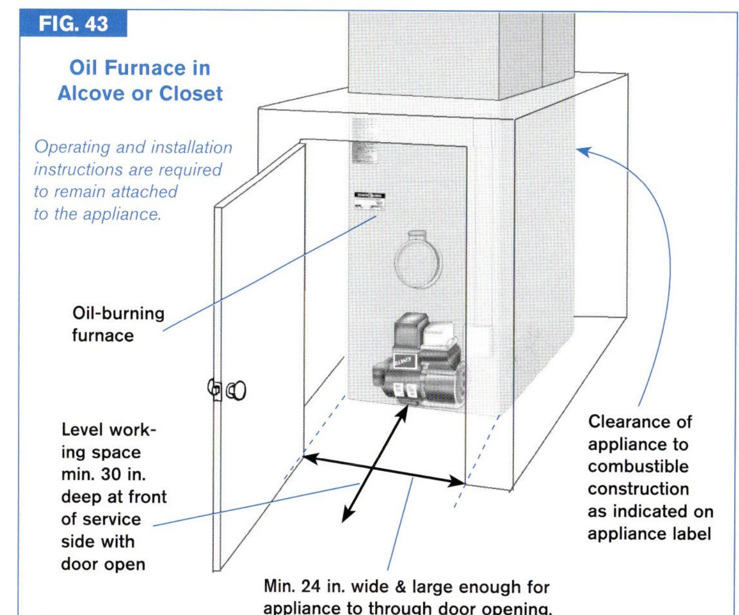

Oil-Fired Floor Furnaces F7

	21 IRC	NFPA 31
☐ Must be L&L for combustible construction	1408.1	10.9.1
☐ Framing to be properly braced & headed	502.10	10.9.2
☐ Install AMI	1408.1	4.3.2
☐ Floor register types min. 6 in. from wall	1408.3	10.9.4
☐ Wall register type min. 6 in. from inside corners	1408.3	10.9.5
☐ Min. 12 in. from door swing arc, draperies, or combustibles	1408.3	10.9.4
☐ Min. 5-ft. clearance above furnace to combustible materials	1408.3	10.9.6
☐ Not OK to project into habitable space below	1408.3	10.9.9
☐ Support furnace independent of grill	1408.5	10.9.3
☐ Not OK to support from ground	1408.5	MFR
☐ Furnace must be accessible (not OK in slab)	1408.3&4	10.9.7
☐ Access to underfloor area min. 18 in. × 24 in.	1408.4	10.9.7.1
• IRC: If floor access, min. 22 in. × 30 in.	1408.4	Ø
☐ Min. 6-in. clearance to ground	1408.5	10.9.6
☐ Min. 6-in. clearance on all sides below floor	n/a	10.9.9.2
☐ Provide adequate combustion air	1701.1	10.9.8
☐ Chimney connector clearance min. 9 in. EXC	1803.3.4	10.9.11
• Lesser clearances w/ clearance reduction system T10	1803.3.4	10.9.11
☐ Thermostat in same room as floor register	1408.5	MFR

Oil-Fired Recessed Wall Furnaces

	21 IRC	NFPA 31
☐ Must be L&L for combustible construction	1409.1	10.13.1
☐ Install AMI	1409.1	10.13.3
☐ Locate so no fire hazard to walls, floors, or furnishings	1409.2	10.13.4
☐ Door's swing arc not within 12 in. of face of furnace	1409.2	MFR
☐ Doorstop cannot be used to maintain reqd clearance	1409.2	MFR
☐ Min. 3 ft. from wall opposite register	MFR	10.13.5
☐ Panels, grills & access doors not attached to walls	MFR	10.13.6
☐ Provide adequate combustion air	1701.1	10.13.7

COMBUSTION AIR FOR OIL-FIRED APPLIANCES

The IRC no longer includes a separate set of rules for combustion air for oil-burning appliances. Section 1701.1 refers to NFPA 31 for oil appliance combustion air.

Oil-fired Appliance Combustion Air: General

	NFPA 31
☐ Source from outside if building is unusually tight construction	5.2.3
☐ Consider effect from exhaust fans (kitchen, bath, laundry)	5.2.3
☐ Screen reqd on outside openings, mesh openings ≥¼ in.	5.6.2
☐ Consider restrictive effect of louvers on openings:	5.6.3
• Net free area 75% for metal louvers	
• Net free area 25% for wood louvers	

Indoor Air Source

☐ Only OK for buildings of ordinary tightness	5.3.1
☐ Infiltration sufficient for unconfined space	5.3.1
☐ Unconfined space = ≥50 cu. ft./kBtu/hr. of all appliances in space F10	3.3.60
☐ Confined area reqs openings to unconfined space of adequate volume	5.4.1.3
☐ Openings to unconfined space min. 1sq.in./kBtu/hr. T2	5.4.1.2
☐ Openings located near top & bottom of confined space F11	5.4.1.1

Outside Air Source

☐ Openings located near top & bottom of confined space F13	5.4.2.1
☐ Openings to vented attic or crawlspace equivalent to outdoors F16	5.4.2.2
☐ Direct exterior openings each sized at 1sq.in./4kBtu/hr. F13	5.4.2.3
☐ Vertical ducts each sized at 1sq.in./4kBtu/hr. F14,18	5.4.2.3
☐ Horizontal ducts each sized at 1sq.in./2kBtu/hr. F15	5.4.2.4

OIL-FIRED APPLIANCE CHIMNEYS & VENTS

Oil-fired appliances can be vented to listed L vents or into masonry or listed chimneys. IRC chapter 18 deals with this subject. The UMC defers to NFPA 211 for oil-fired appliances, though NFPA 31 also contains similar rules. NFPA 211 does not address as many topics on oil-fired vents as NFPA 31, and for consistency with the rest of the codes in this section we are providing the NFPA 31 rules below.

General

	21 IRC	NFPA 31
☐ Fuel-burning appliances req venting to outdoors	1801.1	6.2.1
☐ Vent system AMI of connected appliance	1801.2	6.3.1
☐ Draft regulator reqd if connected to chimney EXC	1802.3	6.4.1
• Arrangements that prevent excessive chimney draft	n/a	6.4.1
• Appliances L&L for use w/o draft regulator	n/a	6.4.1
☐ No manually operated dampers	1802.2.1	6.4.2
☐ Automatic dampers AMI per L&L, burner interlock reqd	1802.2.2	6.4.3
☐ Unused openings not OK in vent system	1801.10	n/a
☐ Draft fan reqs burner interlock	n/a	6.3.2

Chimney Connectors

	21 IRC	NFPA 31
☐ Connectors as short & straight as practical	1803.3	6.5.1
☐ Min. rise ¼ in./ft.	1803.3	6.5.10
☐ Secure support, screw, or rivet joints (NFPA 31: min. 3)	1803.3	6.5.13&14
☐ Single-wall clearance 18 in., 9 in. if appliance listed type L	1803.3.4	T10.6.1
☐ Reduced clearances per **T10**	1803.3.4	6.5.15
☐ Diameter ≥ flue collar size of appliance unless AMI	1803.3.3	6.5.7
☐ Entire length accessible for cleaning & replacement	1803.3.5	6.5.16
☐ Unlisted connector horizontal run max. 75% of vertical	1803.3.2	6.5.1.2
☐ Horizontal distance max. 10 ft. w/o draft fan	n/a	6.5.1.1
☐ Connector must enter past inner liner of chimney flue	n/a	6.5.5
☐ Cement connector in place at chimney flue	n/a	6.5.5
☐ Connector thimble in chimney OK if cemented in place	n/a	6.5.5.1

Chimneys & Type L Vents

	21 IRC	NFPA 31
☐ Verify existing chimney OK if installing new appliance	1801.3	6.6.7
☐ Installer verify chimney size OK or resize per NFPA 31	1801.3.1	6.6.7
☐ If deterioration visible, inspect per NFPA 211 (Chapter 14)	n/a	6.6.7.2
☐ Type L vents must be L&L & installed AMI	1804.1&3	6.7.1.2
☐ Type L vent termination min. 2 ft. above roof	1804.2.4	6.7.1.4
☐ Chimney termination min. 3 ft. above roof ***(see p. 118)***	1805.1	6.6.6
☐ Vent or chimney termination min. 2 ft. above any portion of building within 10 ft. ***(see p. 118)***	1804.2.4 & 1805.1	6.7.1.4
☐ Type L termination caps L&L, AMI	1804.2.4	6.7.1.2
☐ Masonry chimneys req liner	1805.1	6.6.8

FIG. 44

BOILERS & HYDRONICS

Modern high-efficiency boilers can be used for both hydronic heating systems and indirect-fired water heaters. Distribution can be through radiators, baseboard convectors, radiant in-floor tubing, or duct heaters. Valves, backflow preventers, drain piping, pipe support, and other items are also governed by plumbing codes.

Boilers	21 IRC	21 UMC
☐ Install AMI & per ASME standards	2001.1	1002.1
☐ Oil-burning boilers req L&L to UL 726	2001.1.1	1002.2.1
☐ Installer to supply control diagram & operating manual	2001.1	1012.1
☐ Must be securely anchored to structure	1307.2	1001.5
☐ Clearance per L&L	2001.2	MFR
☐ Hot water boilers req pressure & temperature gauges **F46**	2002.2	1003.3
☐ Steam boilers req sight-glass & pressure gauge	2002.3	1003.3
☐ Shutoff valves reqd in supply & return piping **F46**	2001.3	1212.3
☐ Low-water cutoff control reqd EXC	2002.5	1008.1
• Coil-type or forced-circulation boiler w/ flow sensor	2002.5X	1008.1
☐ PRV reqd **F46**	2002.4	1005.1
☐ PRV drain piped to within 18 in. of floor or receptor	2002.4	Ø
☐ Discharge piping—see rules for WH (*p. 166*)	n/a	1005.2

Dual-Purpose Water Heaters		
☐ Water heaters used for space heating & domestic HW L&L for the purpose & installed AMI **F45**	2004.1 & 2448.2	1203.2
☐ Tempering valve must limit potable water to 140°F **F45**	2803.2	1207.3.1

Expansion Tanks		
☐ Expansion tank reqd for every hydronic system **F46**	2003.1	1209.1
☐ Expansion tank can be open or closed type	2003.1	1209.1
☐ Expansion tank must be rated for system pressure	2003.1.1	1209.1
☐ Tank test pressure 2½× allowable working pressure	2003.1.1	1004.3
☐ Nonpressurized tanks (UMC: all tanks) securely fastened to structure w/ supports rated twice weight of full tank	2003.1	1209.2
☐ Min. tank capacity per **T9**	2003.2	1004.4

Hydronic Piping: General	21 IRC	21 UMC
☐ Support piping to avoid strain (*p. 127*)	2101.9	1210.3
☐ Allow for expansion & contraction	2101.8	1210.2
☐ Install piping, valves, fittings & connections AMI (UMC: per applicable standards)	2101.24[6]	1210.1
☐ PEX & PE-RT tubing in closed systems req oxygen barrier	n/a	1210.4
☐ Pressure test min. 1.5×design pressure min. 100 psi	2101.10	1205.2
☐ Maintain backflow protection to potable water	2101.3	1202.1
☐ RP reqd to protect potable water if additives used	2101.3	1202.2
☐ Pipe bends min. 6× pipe diameter or AMI	MFR	1211.1
☐ If potable & nonpotable piping installed, provide identification on each piping system (*p. 150*)	2901.2	1204.1-5
☐ Indicate flow directions on system **F46**	n/a	1204.6

TABLE 9 — MIN. EXPANSION TANK CAPACITY[A] IRC T2003.2[B] & UMC T1004.4(2)[C]

System Volume (gal)	Diaphragm Tanks	Non-Diaphragm Tanks	System Volume (gal)	Diaphragm Tanks	Non-Diaphragm Tanks
10	1.0	1.5	90	7.5	13.5
20	1.5	3.0	100	8.0[D]	15.0
30	2.5	4.5	200	17	30
40	3.0	6.0	300	25	45
50	4.0	7.5	400	33	60
60	5.0	9.0	500	42	75
70	6.0	10.5	1000	83	150
80	6.5	12.0	2000	165	300

A. Based on average water temperature of 195°F, fill pressure 12 PSIG, max. operating pressure 30 PSIG.
B. Volumes ≤100 gal based on IRC T2003.2.
C. Volumes ≥100 gal. based on UMC T1004.4(2).
D. UMC table 1004.(2) gives this value at 9.0 gal. Both codes agree on 15.0 for non-diaphragm tanks.

6. Section 2101 (hydronic piping systems) was greatly expanded and now includes many specific requirements for joints and connections for different types of pipe and tubing.

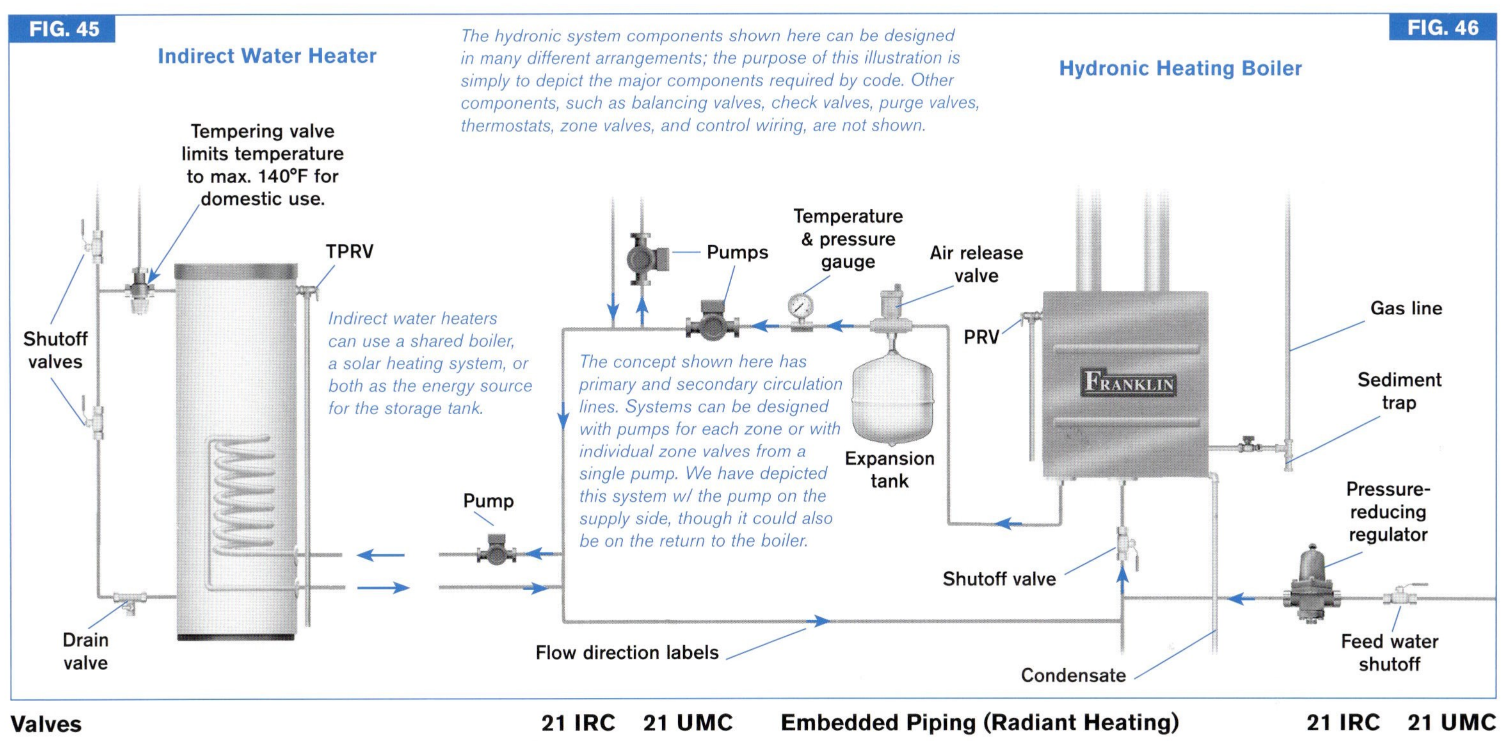

Valves	21 IRC	21 UMC
☐ Pressure-reducing valve reqd on makeup water feed **F46**	MFR	1214.4
☐ PRV reqd on low-pressure side	2101.23	1214.4
☐ Shutoff valve reqd both sides of PRVs	2101.22.4[7]	1212.5
☐ Air separation device reqd in hydronic systems	MFR	1214.7
☐ Isolation valves reqd at air-removal devices or vents	MFR	1212.11

7. This rule had formerly only applied in the IRC to ground-source heat pump systems.

Embedded Piping (Radiant Heating)	21 IRC	21 UMC
☐ Plastic pipe rated min. 80 psi at 180°F	2103.1	1221.2
☐ Cu tubing joints brazed not soldered	2103.3(2)	1221.2.2
☐ Tubing embedded in concrete min. 2 in. below surface	n/a	1217.5
☐ Min. R-5 insulation under poured concrete radiant system in soil contact & R-5 on vertical slab edges on grade	2103.2	1217.5.2

FREESTANDING FIREPLACE STOVES (SOLID FUEL)

The IRC (section 1414.1) requires fireplace stoves to be listed, labeled & tested in accord with UL 737, which in turn references the current edition of NFPA 211. UMC section 902.10 refers to NFPA 211 for solid fuel–burning appliances. The rules for clearance, protection, and clearance reductions are virtually identical among the IRC, UMC, and NFPA 211.

Fireplace Stoves & Solid-Fuel Room Heaters — NFPA 211

- ☐ Equipment must be listed & installed per L&L or be approved by AHJ___ 13.1
- ☐ Unlisted equipment must be approved & installed AMI ______________ 13.1.1
- ☐ No unlisted equipment in mobile homes ____________________________ 13.1.2
- ☐ Not in alcove or enclosed space <512 cu. ft. unless listed for same___ 13.2.2
- ☐ Not OK in garages or where flammable vapors or liquids present __ 13.2.3&4
- ☐ Listed appliances OK on combustible floors if per L&L & AMI _____ 13.5.1.1
- ☐ Noncombustible floor material 18 in. beyond stove on all sides EXC_ 13.5.1.4
  - L&L floor protection assemblies OK AMI ______________________ 13.5.1.5
- ☐ Unlisted appliance floor protection 18 in. beyond on all sides, plus: _ 13.5.1.2
  - If legs provide ≥6 in. of ventilated clearance under stove, 2-in.-thick masonry covered w/ min. 24-ga metal F47 ___________ 13.5.2.1
  - If legs provide ≥2 in. to <6 in. of ventilated clearance, min. 4-in.-thick hollow masonry + metal, cores open to allow airflow F47 ________ 13.5.2.2
- ☐ If legs provide <2 in. clearance, floor reqd to be noncombustible ___ 13.5.2.3
- ☐ Fuel storage (firewood) min. 36 in. from appliance___________T13.6.1 note a
- ☐ 36-in. side, top & front clearance from appliance to combustibles EXC 13.6.1
  - Listed appliance clearance to combustibles AMI ______________ 13.6.1.1
  - Reduced clearances OK per T10,F49 _______________________ 13.6.2.1

Connectors

- ☐ Must be accessible for inspection, cleaning & replacement __________ 9.7.10
- ☐ Single-wall min. 18-in. clearance to combustibles EXC F47 ________ T9.5.1.1
  - Lesser clearance w/ approved clearance reduction system T10 ___9.5.1.2.1
- ☐ Not to pass through wall EXC ____________________________________ 9.7.4
  - Listed pass-through system______________________________________ 9.7.4
  - Pass-through system constructed per NFPA 211 figure 9.7.4________ 9.7.4
- ☐ Maintain min. 1/4-in./ft. rise from appliance collar to chimney ____________ 9.7.6

FIG. 47

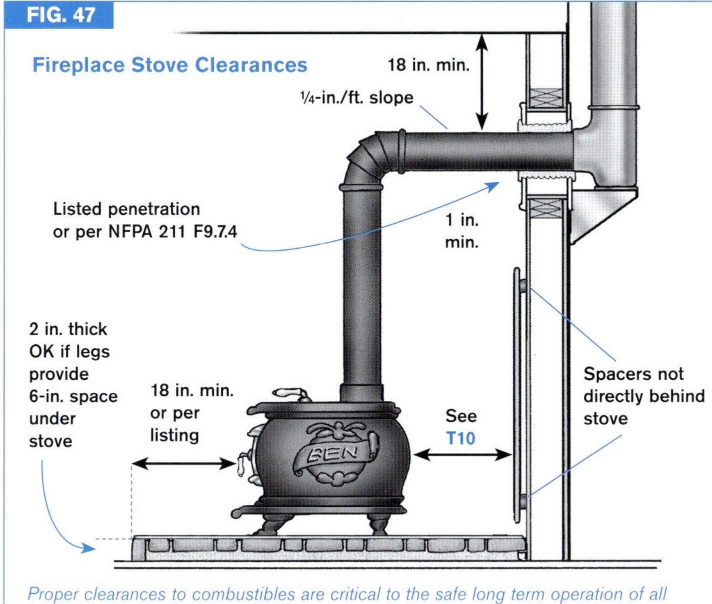

Proper clearances to combustibles are critical to the safe long term operation of all fuel burning systems. Improper clearances can allow heat transfer to adjacent combustible materials. Over time, heat degrades wood and lowers its ignition temperature. This process—pyrolysis—can eventually result in a fire.

Stoves & Fireplace Inserts to Masonry Fireplaces — NFPA 211

- ☐ Connector must extend to flue liner—not just to firebox____________ 13.4.5.1
- ☐ If connector enters direct through chimney wall above smoke chamber, noncombustible seal reqd below entry ______________________ 13.4.5.1
- ☐ No dilution of combustion products in flue w/ habitable space air ___ 13.4.5.1
- ☐ Flue not less than size of appliance collar ____________________ 13.4.5.1
- ☐ Flue diameter max. 2× appliance collar if chimney walls exposed to exterior below roof, 3× if no part exposed below roof____________ 13.4.5.1
- ☐ Installation must allow for chimney inspection & cleaning __________ 13.4.5.1

CLEARANCE REDUCTION SYSTEMS

Clearance reduction systems are used with solid fuel, oil-burning, and gas-burning appliances. While the basic rule is that appliances be installed with their required clearances to combustible materials, practical considerations must be taken into effect. The codes therefore provide a means to reduce the required clearances by the use of intermediary systems that protect the combustible construction. **T10** has the same values as T9.5.1.2 & 13.6.2.1 in NFPA 211 and 10.2.3 in NFPA 54. Though gypsum as a material is noncombustible, gypsum board is considered a combustible material. Prolonged heat exposure will cause it to decompose, and its paper backing is considered combustible.

Clearance Reduction Systems — 21 IRC

- ☐ Clearance reductions allowed per **T10** EXC ______ 1306.2, 1803.3.4, 2409.2
  - Clearance allowed based on assembly L&L to UL 1618 1306.2.1 & 2409.2
- ☐ Gas appliance & vent connector reductions per **F48**,**T10** ______ 2409.2
- ☐ Solid fuel appliances cannot be reduced to <12 in. EXC ______ 1306.2.3
  - Appliances listed for <12 in. & installed AMI ______ 1306.2.3
- ☐ No spacers directly behind appliance or connector **F47**,**49** ______ F1306.2
- ☐ Spaces noncombustible (stacked washers, conduit, etc.) ______ F1306.2
- ☐ Ventilated air space min. 1 in. & open at edges **F47–49**,**T10** ______ 1306.2
- ☐ Air space in corner open top & bottom **F49**,**T10** ______ 1306.2
- ☐ Air space on flat wall open top & bottom or side & top **F48**,**T10** ______ 1306.2

FIG. 48 Clearance Reduction for Gas Equipment or Gas Vent Connectors

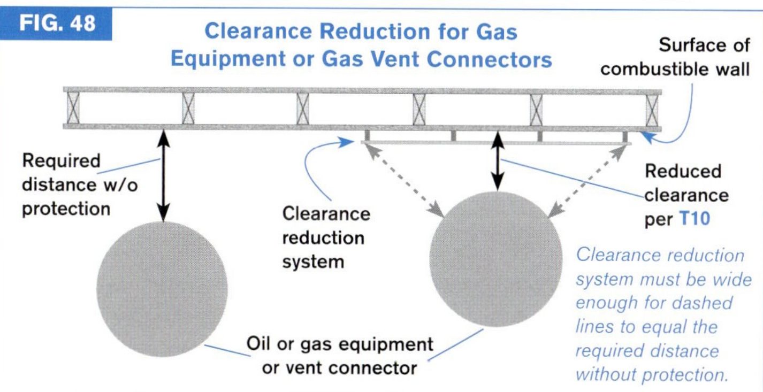

TABLE 10 CLEARANCE REDUCTION ◆ IRC T1306.2 UMC T303.10.1

Unprotected Clearance	36	18	12	9	6	36	18	12	9	6
Protection Method	Protected Wall Clearance (in.)[A]					Protected Ceiling Clearance (in.)[A]				
3½-in. masonry w/o air space[B]	24	12	9	6	5	n/a	n/a	n/a	n/a	n/a
½-in. insulation board over 1-in. fiber or mineral wool batts[C]	18	9	6	5	3	24	12	9	6	4
24-ga Zi steel over reinforced batts w/ air space[B]	12	6	4	3	3	18	9	6	5	3
3½-in. masonry w/ air space[B]	12	6	6	6	6	n/a	n/a	n/a	n/a	n/a
24-ga Zi steel w/ air space[B]	12	6	4	3	2	18	9	6	5	3
½-in. insulation board w/ air space[B]	12	6	4	3	3	18	9	6	5	3
24-ga Zi steel w/ air space over 24-ga Zi steel w/ air space[B]	12	6	4	3	3	18	9	6	5	3
1-in. insulating batts[C] between 2 24-ga Zi steel w/ air space[B]	12	6	4	3	3	18	9	6	5	3

A. Clearances are measured in closest stretched-string distance. In no case can a solid fuel–burning appliance clearance be reduced to <12 in.
B. Air spaces must be a min. of 1 in. and be ventilated by being open at the bottom & top edges or sides & top edges. Spacers must be noncombustible & cannot be mounted directly opposite the appliance or connector.
C. Insulation fiber or mineral wool must have thermal conductivity ≤1.0 Btu/sq. ft. Mineral wool blankets or board min. density 8 lb./cu. ft. & min. melting point 1,500°F.

FIG. 49 Clearance Reduction System for Fireplace Stove

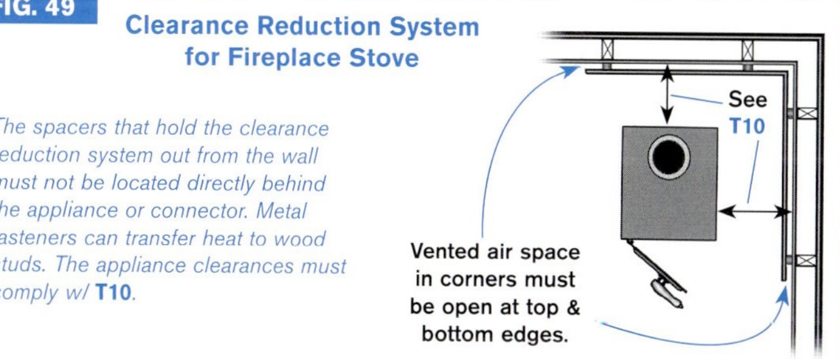

VENTILATION & EXHAUST SYSTEMS

In general, building codes tell us ***when*** to provide ventilation for interior spaces, while mechanical and energy codes tell us ***how*** to provide it. Proper ventilation is necessary to maintain a healthy indoor environment. ASHRAE 62.2, Ventilation and Acceptable Indoor Air Quality in Low-Rise Residential Buildings, is the standard referenced by many energy codes, and the same material appears in abbreviated form in IRC section 1103.6 and 1505. Check with your local jurisdiction to determine the standards in your area. One purpose of whole-house ventilation is to dilute contaminants from materials such as volatile organic compounds (VOCs) found in furnishings and building products. Localized exhaust removes contaminants from specific sources, such as kitchens and baths.

Whole Building Ventilation — ASHRAE 62.2

- ☐ Mechanical exhaust, supply, or combination system reqd ______ 4.1
- ☐ Min. ventilation rate must comply w/ **T11** EXC ______ 4.1.1
  - In Climate Zone 1 or 2, local AHJ determines that window operation provides sufficient ventilation, no mechanical cooling is present & thermally conditioned for human occupancy < 876 hr. per year ______ 4.1.1X
- ☐ Measured infiltration rate can be used as credit to reqd ventilation ______ 4.1.2
- ☐ **T11** assumes 2 persons in studio or 1-bedroom unit & 1 person per each additional bedroom. Add 7.5 cfm per person for higher densities ______ 4.1.3
- ☐ 20% reduction to **T11** allowed w/ improved air filtration ______ 4.1.4
- ☐ Local exhaust fans can count to reqd whole-house continuous ventilation 4.2
- ☐ Outdoor air duct to return of air handler can supply ventilation if return air temp per MFR ______ 4.2
- ☐ Quantity of air can be based on equipment MFR install instructions ______ 4.3
- ☐ ON-OFF control reqd w/ ready access & text indicating its purpose EXC ______ 4.4
  - Not reqd to be readily accessible in multifamily dwelling units ______ 4.4X

Sound Levels

- ☐ Whole building or continuous ventilation fans max. 1.0 sone ______ 7.2.1
- ☐ Bath exhaust fans max. 3 sones ______ 7.2.2
- ☐ Kitchen exhaust max. 3 sones at 1 or more settings ≥100 CFM EXC ______ 7.2.2
  - Kitchen exhaust >400 CFM ______ 7.2.2

TABLE 11 MIN. VENTILATION RATES IN CFM ◆ ASHRAE 62.2 T4.1A

Floor Area (sq. ft.)	Number of Bedrooms				
	1	2	3	4	5
< 500	30	38	45	53	60
501–1000	45	53	60	68	75
1001–1500	60	68	75	83	90
1501–2000	75	83	90	98	105
2001–2500	90	98	105	113	120
2501–3000	105	113	120	128	135
3001–3500	120	128	135	143	150
3501–4000	135	143	150	158	165
4001–4500	150	158	165	173	180
4501–5000	165	173	180	188	195

Energy-Recovery Ventilators — 21 IMC — 21 UMC

- ☐ Non-ducted to comply w/ UL 1815, ducted to UL 1812 ______ 514.1 — 504.5
- ☐ Install per L&L & AMI ______ 304.1 — 504.5
- ☐ Air conveyed not considered as recirculated if cross-leakage between air streams <10% of design capacity ______ 514.4 — n/a

FIG. 50 Energy-Recovery Ventilator

Required in climate zones 7 & 8

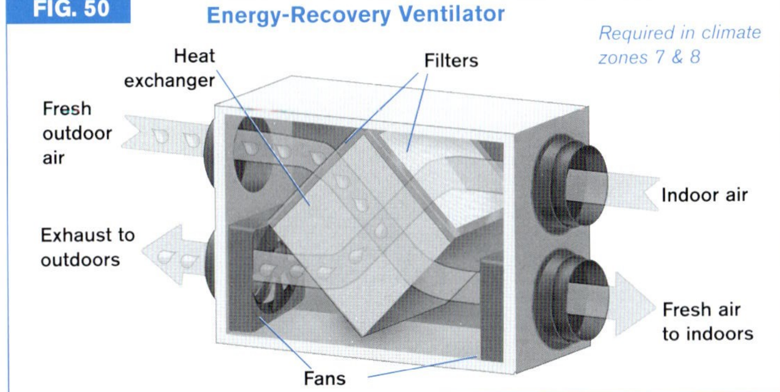

Kitchen & Bath Exhaust*

	ASHRAE 62.2	21 UMC
☐ Mechanical exhaust reqd each kitchen	5.1	405.4[8]
☐ Kitchen min. 100 cfm intermittent, min. 300 cfm if downdraft	T5.1	405.4.1[8]
☐ Kitchen min. 5 ACH if continuous	T5.2	405.4.1[8]
☐ Mechanical exhaust reqd each bath w/ tub or shower	5.1	405.3[8]
☐ Bathroom 50 cfm intermittent or 20 cfm continuous	T5.1 & T5.2	405.3.1[8]
☐ Controls manual or automatic w/ ON override	5.2.1	405.3[8]
☐ Duct min. diameter per T12	T5.3[9]	n/a

TABLE 12 PRESCRIPTIVE DUCT SIZES (IN.) ◆ ASHRAE 62.2 T5-3

Fan cfm	50	80	100	125	150	175	200	250	350	400	450	700	800
Rigid duct	4	5	5	6	6	7	7	8	9	10	10	12	12
Flex duct[A]	4	5	6	6	7	7	8	8	9	10	NP	NP	NP

A. Flex duct must be fully extended. Elbows to have min. bend radius of one duct diameter.

Additional ASHRAE Requirements

	ASHRAE 62.2
☐ Label controls as to function unless obvious by location	6.2
☐ Door from attached garage to house weatherstripped	6.5.1
☐ Space conditioning duct leakage outside pressure boundary max. 6%	6.5.2
☐ Habitable spaces req ventilation ≥4% (min. 5 sq. ft.) of floor area	6.6.1
☐ Utility/WC rooms req ventilation ≥4% (min. 1½ sq. ft.) of floor area EXC	6.6.2
• Utility rooms w/ dryer exhaust duct	6.6.2X
☐ Central furnace or AC system filter min. efficiency MERV 6	6.7
☐ Air inlets min. 10 ft. from contaminants such as plumbing vents	6.8

Exhaust Openings

	21 IRC	21 UMC
☐ Exhaust air not to be directed to walkways	303.5.2	502.2.1
☐ Exhaust & intake openings req screens	303.6	502.1
☐ Screen opening min. ¼ in. max. ½ in.	303.6	502.1
☐ Exhaust ducts req backdraft dampers	1103.6	504.1.1

* May be superseded by local energy codes.

8. UMC section 405 is new in the 2021 edition. In addition to the reqs shown here, it also reqs whole house ventilation & natural ventilation similar to the previous page & to the building code.

9. The 2016 edition of this table also included maximum lengths.

FIG. 51

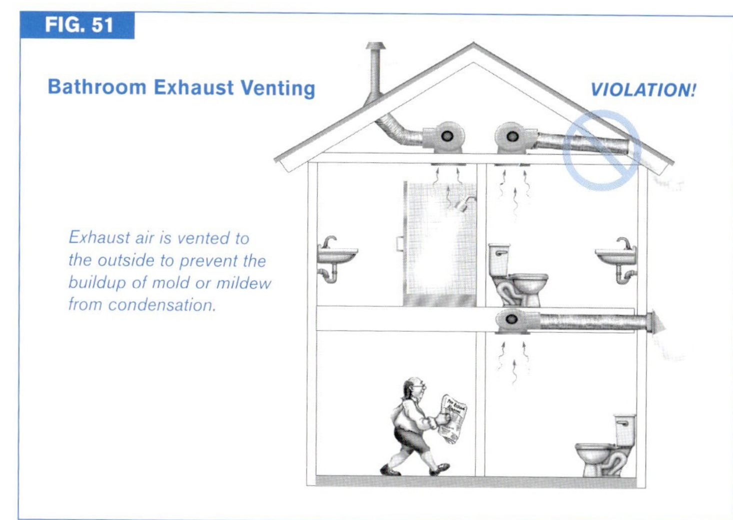

IRC Bathroom Exhaust & Ventilation

	21 IRC
☐ Bathrooms & WC rooms req min. 3-sq.-ft. glazed openings w/ min. 50% openable for ventilation EXC	303.3
• Not reqd if fan direct to exterior F51	303.3X
☐ Fan 50 cfm intermittent or 20 cfm continuous	T1505.4.4
☐ Air may not be exhausted into attic F51	1501.1

RANGES & RANGE HOODS

Freestanding Ranges	21 IRC	21 UMC
☐ L&L as household type—not commercial	1901.2 & 2447.2&3[10]	902.1,MFR
☐ Anti-tip bracket reqd AMI	MFR	MFR
☐ Vertical clearance to combustibles min. 30 in. F52 EXC	1901.1	920.3.2
• Clearances per L&L of range hoods or ovens F52	1901.1	920.3.2(3)
• 24 in. OK w/ metal hood or metal over 1/4-in. millboard	n/a	920.3.2(1)
☐ Side clearance to combustibles AMI EXC	1901.2	920.3.1(1)
• 6 in. min. sides & rear for unlisted appliances	Ø	920.3.1(4)
Built-in Ranges		
☐ Install AMI	1901.1 & 2447.1	920.4.1
☐ Vertical clearance to combustibles min. 30 in. EXC F52	1901.1	920.4.2
• Lesser clearances per L&L and AMI F52	1901.1	920.4.2(3)
• 24 in. OK w/ metal hood or metal over 1/4-in. millboard	n/a	920.4.2(1)
☐ Must be level	MFR	920.4.3
☐ Must be ducted to outdoors & have backdraft damper	1503.3	504.1.1
Range Hoods & Exhaust Ducts		
☐ Terminate min. 3 ft. from building openings	1504.3*	502.2.1*
☐ Gas ranges do not req vent to outdoors	2425.8(1)	802.2.1(1)
☐ Ducts smooth interior surface (not corrugated)	1503.3	504.3
☐ Ducts must be Zi steel, SS, or Cu EXC	1503.4	504.3
• Downdraft duct, PVC OK for portion under slab	1503.4X	504.3X
☐ Terminate outdoors—not in attic or crawlspace EXC	1503.3	504.1.1
• L&L ductless range hoods installed AMI	1503.3X	504.1X(1)
Hoods for Open-Top Broilers		
☐ Hood reqd & must extend as wide as broiler unit EXC	1503.2.1	922.3
• Hood not reqd for L&L units w/ integral exhaust	1503.2.1X	922.3
☐ Min. 1/4-in. clearance between hood & underside of combustible or metal cabinets	1503.2.1	922.3
☐ Min. 24 in. from cooking surface to combustible materials	1503.2.1	922.3

10. Commercial ranges were allowed under direction of licensed professional engineer. This rule has been removed, as commercial ranges have very different clearance requirements. Many manufacturers supply "commercial style" ranges listed as household type.

* ASHRAE 62.2 specifically allows a bathroom/kitchen fan to terminate outdoors less than 3 ft. from an openable window to the bathroom/kitchen.

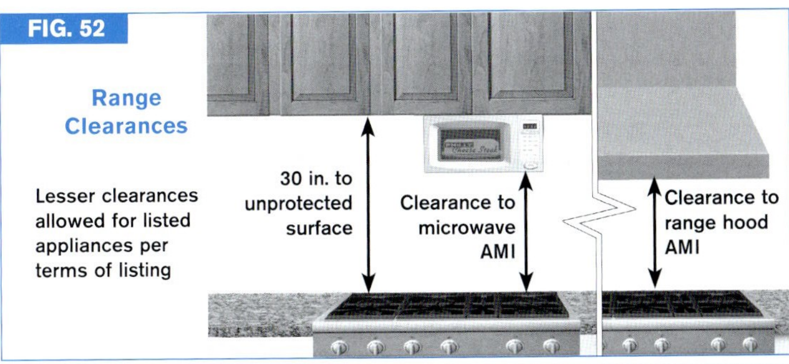

CLOTHES DRYERS

Houses built prior to adoption of the 1996 NEC often have 3-hole 240-volt dryer receptacles, where the dryer neutral is also its equipment ground. Dryers installed in such receptacles should have their internal bonding jumper connected. In newer installations with 4-wire cords the bonding jumper should be removed. See *Code Check Electrical* ***p. 295*** for further information.

UMC Clothes Dryer Exhaust	21 UMC
☐ Exhaust must be independent of other systems	504.4
☐ Duct must be rigid metal 4 in. nominal diameter	504.4 & 504.4.2
☐ Male end at joints must point in direction of flow	504.4
☐ Screws & fasteners not to project into duct	504.4
☐ Terminate outside w/ backdraft damper, no screens F53	504.4
☐ Exhaust must terminate outside building min. 3 ft. from any opening into building (5 ft. recommended to AC coils)	504.4 & 502.2.1
☐ Transition ducts (connectors) L&L to UL 2158A	504.4
☐ Transition ducts (connectors) max. 6 ft., AMI & not concealed	504.4.2.2
☐ Closet locations reqs min. 100-sq.-in. makeup air opening	504.4.1
☐ Duct length total combined vertical & horizontal length 14 ft. EXC	504.4.2.1
• AMI & approved by AHJ	504.4.2.1
• AMI per duct power ventilator	504.4.2.1X
☐ Deduct 2 ft. from allowed length for each elbow in excess of 2	504.4.2.1
☐ Power ventilators req L&L to UL 705, installation AMI	504.4.2.3

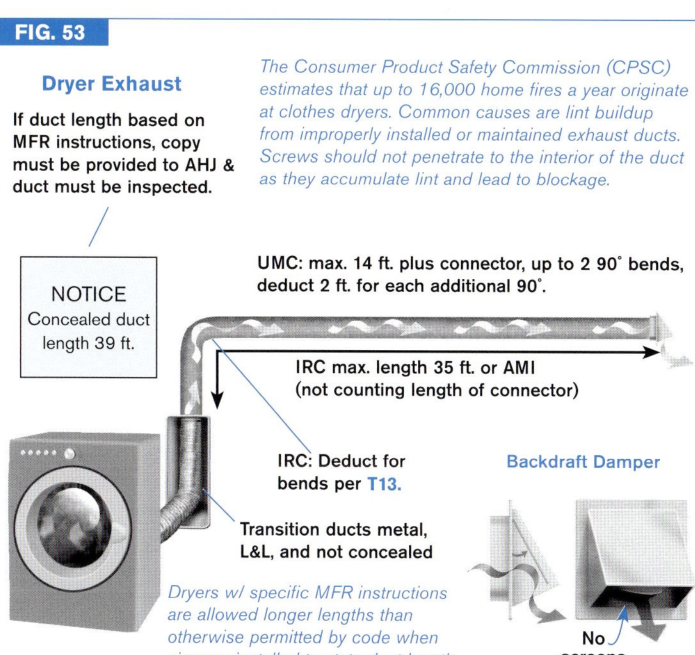

TABLE 13	DRYER FITTING EQUIVALENT LENGTH IRC T1502.4.6.1 & T2439.7.4.1	
Fitting Radius	Equivalent Length	
	45° Elbow	90° Elbow
4 in. mitered	2 ft. 6 in.	5 ft.
6 in. smooth	1 ft.	1 ft. 9 in.
8 in. smooth	1 ft.	1 ft. 7 in.
10 in. smooth	9 in.	1 ft. 6 in.

21 IRC Dryer Exhaust: General	Electric	Gas
☐ Exhaust AMI w/ dryer MFR	1502.1	2439.1
☐ Exhaust must be independent of other systems	1502.2	2439.1
☐ Exhaust must convey moisture to outdoors EXC	1502.2	2439.1
• L&L condensing (ductless) dryers	1502.2X	2439.7.6X
☐ Must convey combustion products to outdoors	n/a	2439.1
☐ Exhaust must terminate outside building min. 3 ft. from any opening into building (5 ft. recommended to AC coils)	1502.3	1502.3
☐ Termination reqs backdraft damper, no screens **F53**	1502.3	2439.3
☐ Closet location reqs min. 100-sq.-in. makeup air opening	n/a	2439.5.1

21 IRC Exhaust Ducts		
☐ If dryer space provided, exhaust duct reqd EXC	1502.4.8	2439.7.6
• Listed condensing dryer installed prior to occupancy	1502.4.8X	2439.7.6X
☐ Duct must be smooth metal 4 in. nominal diameter	1502.4.1	2439.7.1
☐ Duct reqs support at max. 12-ft. (4-ft. gas) intervals	1502.4.2	2439.7.2
☐ Male end at joints must point in direction of flow	1502.4.2	2439.7.2
☐ Ducts concealed in cavities shall not be deformed	1502.4.2	2439.7.2
☐ Screws & fasteners not to project > 1/8 in. into duct	1502.4.2	24397.2
☐ Transition ducts (connectors) L&L to UL 2158A	1502.4.3	2439.7.3
☐ Transition ducts (connectors) max. 8 ft., not concealed	1502.4.3	2439.7.3
☐ Shield plates reqd if duct <1¼ in. from framing surface	1502.5	2439.6

21 IRC Duct Length		
☐ Option 1: Max. 35 ft. minus bends per **T13,F53**	1502.4.6.1	2439.7.4.1
☐ Option 2: AMI—provide installation instructions to BO	1502.4.6.2	2439.7.4.2
☐ Option 3: Lengths >35 ft. AMI of power ventilator	1502.4.6.3	2439.7.4.3
☐ Lengths >35 ft. req sign within 6 ft. of connection stating equivalent length of exhaust duct	1502.4.7	2439.7.5
☐ Power ventilators req L&L to UL 705, installation AMI	1502.4.4	2439.4
☐ Booster fans (not listed to UL 705) prohibited	1502.4.5	2439.4

GLOSSARY

ABS (acrylonitrile-butadiene-styrene): Black plastic pipe, typically with a foam core, used for DWV. Some types of ABS are also used for vent piping of high-efficiency condensing appliances specifically listed for such pipe.

Access (to): Capable of being exposed without damage to the building or component structure or finishes, and that may req removal of access doors or fasteners.

AHJ (Authority Having Jurisdiction): An organization responsible for enforcing the code, typically the building department & its authorized representatives.

Air break: F35 A physical separation in which discharge (such as condensate) from a fixture, appliance, or device drains indirectly into a receptor & enters below the flood level rim of a receptor and above the trap seal, such as a sink tailpiece or clothes washer standpipe.

Air conditioning: The process of heating, cooling, humidifying, dehumidifying, filtering, or otherwise treating air in a building. The most common usage of this term is to refer to cooling.

Air handler: A blower or fan enclosed in a metal box used for the purpose of distributing supply air to a room, space, or area.

Alcove: Aside from the common meaning of this term, it is also used to define a space such as a closet that is not "large" in relationship to the appliances within it. In the UMC, appliances in alcoves must be listed for same, and their clearances cannot be reduced. In the IRC and NFPA 54, this rule went away in the 2012 code cycle, and appliance clearances are only per the listing of the appliance. Also see "Room large in comparison to size of equipment."

Approved: Accepted by the Authority Having Jurisdiction (AHJ). UL & other testing laboratories do not approve materials; they test products & determine their conformity to published standards. Only the AHJ can approve them.

Backflow: A flow of water or other liquids, mixtures, or substances into the distributing pipes of a potable supply of water from any source other than its intended source.

Bathroom: In ASHRAE & the UPC, a bathroom is a room containing a bathtub, shower, or combination tub and shower. A half bath containing only a water closet & lavatory is a toilet room and is not considered a bathroom. In the NEC, a bathroom is a room containing a basin & another plumbing fixture such as a tub or toilet or shower. The IRC defines a bathroom *group* as a group of fixtures, including or excluding a bidet, consisting of a water closet, lavatory, and bathtub or shower. In a bathroom group, such fixtures are located together on the same floor level.

Btu (British thermal unit): The quantity of heat necessary to raise the temperature of 1 lb. of water 1°F (roughly equal to what is given off by one stick match).

Building thermal envelope: The basement walls, exterior walls, floor, roof & any other building element that encloses conditioned spaces.

Central-fan-integrated supply system: A method of supplying whole-house ventilation through a makeup air duct connected to a forced-air system & a timer on the furnace fan control.

Check valve: A device used to prevent the flow of liquids in a direction not intended in the design of the system. Check valves are not backflow preventers. They are often used in solar systems.

Chimney: A primarily vertical structure containing one or more flues for the purpose of carrying gaseous products of combustion & air from an appliance to the outside atmosphere. Factory-built chimneys must be listed & labeled. Masonry chimneys are field-constructed of solid masonry units, bricks, stones, or concrete.

Chimney connector: A pipe connecting a fuel-burning appliance to a chimney flue.

Clothes dryer, Type 1: Primarily used in family living environment. May or may not be coin-operated for public use, such as in a multifamily dwelling.

Clothes dryer, Type 2: Used in business with direct interaction with public. Usually coin-operated.

Combustible material: Any material not defined as noncombustible. The extent of combustibility of surface materials is measured in flame spread index & smoke-developed index. Many HVAC components req specified clearances from combustible material, including gypsum board.

Combustion air: Air reqd for combustion of a fuel. It includes (1) air that is burned with the fuel, (2) air for dilution of the flue gases and that is introduced into draft hoods, and (3) ventilation air that cools appliances.

Common vent (gas appliances): A vent carrying the discharge of 2 or more gas appliances to outdoors.

Concealed: Not exposed to view without removal of building surfaces or finishes.

Confined space: A room or space having a volume less than 50 cu. ft. for each 1,000 Btu input rating of all fuel-burning appliances in the room or space.

Decorative appliance for installation in fireplaces: An assembly with artificial logs & with gas burners to simulate a solid-fuel fire, installed inside a fireplace otherwise capable of burning solid fuel. They can be either manually or automatically operated. If automatic, they must include a flame safeguard device.

Decorative shroud: A partial enclosure for aesthetic purposes that surrounds or conceals the termination of a chimney or vent. Decorative shrouds for prefabricated fireplaces must be specifically listed for the chimney or vent assembly & are often installed incorrectly.

Dilution air: Air that combines with flue gases at the draft hood of an appliance. *See "Combustion air."*

Direct-vent appliances: F3,29,37 Appliances that are constructed and installed so that combustion air and flue gases are conveyed directly from and to the outside atmosphere. These have a dual pipe system or a coaxial flue pipe inside the combustion air pipe.

Draft: The flow of gases or air through a chimney or flue caused by pressure differences. Induced draft appliances have a fan to overcome the resistance of the combustion chamber while still delivering flue gas to the vent at lower pressure relative to the atmosphere. Natural, or "gravity," draft is created by the hot flue gases being lighter than outside atmosphere. A forced-draft appliance delivers flue gas under positive pressure.

Draft hood: A nonadjustable device integral to an appliance or made part of the appliance connector. It provides for the escape of flue gases from the appliance in the event of flue blockage, allows dilution air to be introduced into the flue, prevents backdraft from entering the appliance & neutralizes the stack effect on the operation of the appliance.

Draft regulator: A device that functions to maintain a desired draft in the appliance by automatically reducing the draft to the desired value. These are usually adjustable, such as the barometric damper on an oil-burning appliance flue. A double-acting barometric draft regulator is free to move in either direction & protect against both excessive draft (that could allow the flame to lift) & backdraft.

Duct: A continuous passageway for the transmission of air (usually forced) made of factory-built components.

Energy-recovery ventilator (ERV): F50 Same as heat-recovery ventilator, with a heat-exchanger core that controls the humidity of the air being transferred.

Evaporative cooler: F34 A device used for reducing the sensible heat of air for cooling by evaporation of water into an airstream. Also known as a "swamp cooler." Evaporative coolers are used in hot, dry climates & for makeup air in commercial kitchens.

Factory-built fireplace: A fireplace composed of listed factory-built components assembled in accordance with the terms of the listing to form the completed fireplace. The appliance must be suitable for solid fuel & be equipped with a listed & properly installed chimney.

Fan-assisted appliance: An appliance equipped with an integral mechanical means to either draw or force products of combustion through the combustion chamber &/or heat exchanger.

Fireblock: Building materials installed to resist the free passage of flame to other areas through small concealed spaces of the building.

Fireplace stove: F47 A freestanding solid fuel–burning device designed to be operated with the firebox door either open or closed.

Firestop: Until the early 1990s, this term was used for what today is called fireblocking. A penetration firestop assembly is a group of materials installed to resist free passage of flame through an assembly, typically around a duct, vent, or chimney passing through a rated ceiling, floor, or wall.

Flame safeguard: A device that will automatically shut off the fuel supply to a main burner or group of burners when the means of ignition of those burners becomes disabled & when flame failure occurs.

Flue: A passageway intended to carry hot gases through a chimney. The term is also used as a substitute for "vent."

Flue collar: The outlet of an appliance designed for the attachment of a draft hood, vent connector, or venting system.

Flue gases: Products of combustion & air in appliance flues or heat exchangers.

Forced draft: F37 A vent system using a fan or other mechanical means to expel flue gases under positive static vent pressure.

Furnace: A device that is completely self-contained & designed to supply heated air to spaces remote from or adjacent to the furnace location. A central furnace uses ducts to supply heat to spaces.

Gas connector: Tubing or piping that connects the gas supply piping to the appliance.

Habitable room: A room used for living, sleeping, eating, or cooking. Bathrooms, closets, halls, storage spaces & laundry rooms are not considered habitable rooms.

Hangers: *See "Supports."*

Heat pump: F32 A system that uses the change of state of a refrigerant to extract heat from one substance & transfer it to another area of the same or a different substance. Heat pumps can provide both heating & cooling.

Heat-recovery ventilator (HRV): A combination ventilation system that replaces indoor air with outdoor air that passes through a heat exchanger. The heat exchanger tempers the outdoor air to minimize energy losses.

Horizontal: Any pipe or vent that is less than 45° from horizontal.

H.S.P.F. (Heating seasonal-performance factor): The measure of a system's efficiency in heating mode. The higher the number, the more efficient the system.

In sight: *See "Within sight."*

Indirect-fired WH: F45 A water heater with a storage tank equipped with a heat exchanger used to transfer heat from an external source to heat potable water. The storage tank could derive its heat source from an external source, such as solar or a boiler, or an internal source.

Induced draft appliance: F22,24 An appliance that utilizes a fan to overcome resistance of a heat exchanger & to assist in the delivery of flue gases to the appliance outlet (flue collar). Induced draft appliances typically deliver the flue gases to the flue collar at nonpositive pressure due to the temperature of those gases relative to outside atmosphere. Usually referred to in code as fan assisted. Also see Vented gas appliance categories.

Induced draft burner: A burner that depends upon a draft that is induced by a fan that is integral to the appliance & is downstream from the burner.

Joint: Connection between two pipes:

- **Brazed joint:** Joint obtained by joining metal parts with alloys that melt at temperatures > 840°F (449°C) but lower than the melting temperature of the parts to be joined.
- **Expansion joint:** Loop, return bend, or return offset that accommodates pipe expansion & contraction.
- **Flexible joint:** Joint allowing movement of one pipe without deflecting other pipe.
- **Mechanical joint:** Joint that uses compression to seal the joint.
- **Slip joint:** Joint that incorporates a washer or special packing to create a seal.
- **Soldered joint:** Joint obtained by joining of metal parts with metallic mixtures or alloys that melt at a temperature < 800°F (427°C) & > 300°F (149°C).
- **Welded joint or seam:** Joint or seam obtained by the joining of metal parts in the plastic molten state.

Label: An identifying mark applied to a product by the manufacturer indicating that a sample of the product has met appropriate standards for the product to be listed by an approved agency or organization. Manufacturer's instructions are by default a part of the listing of products that are listed and labeled.

Labeled: Equipment, materials, or products affixed with a label or other identifying mark to attest that the product complies with identified standards or has been found suitable for a specific purpose. *See "Listed."*

Listed: Equipment or materials on a list published by an approved organization that is concerned with product evaluation and that maintains periodic inspection of production of listed equipment or materials. The listing will state that the product meets specified standards or has been found suitable for a specific purpose.

Log lighter, gas-fired: A manually operated solid-fuel ignition device for installation in a vented solid fuel-burning fireplace. These devices are intended to help initiate a fire in a solid fuel–burning fireplace, as compared to a decorative appliance for installation in a fireplace.

Low-pressure hot-water heating boiler: F46 A boiler furnishing hot water at pressures not exceeding 160 psi or temperatures not exceeding 250°F.

Low-pressure steam-heating boiler: A steam boiler that operates at pressures not exceeding 15 psi.

Makeup air: Air provided to replace air being exhausted.

Nationally Recognized Testing Laboratory (NRTL): A testing facility recognized by OSHA as qualified to provide testing & certification of products & services. Examples of NRTLs are CSA, IAPMO & UL.

Natural-draft burner: A burner in which proper combustion depends on establishing a draft of flue gases that will rise by the pressure difference between the flue gases & outside atmosphere.

Noncombustible material: Material that passes a test procedure as set forth in ASTM E136 for defining noncombustibility of materials. This includes materials that will not ignite & burn when subjected to fire, or material having a structural base of noncombustible material with a surfacing material not >⅛ in. thick & a flame-spread index not higher than 50. This does not apply to surface-finish materials, the entire material of which must be noncombustible from the standpoint of clearances to heating appliances.

Offset: A combination of elbows or bends in a line of piping that brings a section of pipe or a vent out of line but into a line parallel with the other section.

PEX tubing: Water supply or hydronic heat tubing made of cross-linked polyethylene. PEX-AL-PEX has a layer of aluminum sandwiched between layers of PEX.

Plenum: A chamber, other than the occupied space being conditioned, that forms part of the air circulation system.

Power vent: *See "Forced draft."*

Pressure boundary: The boundary separating indoor from outdoor air. A ventilated crawlspace or attic would be outside the pressure boundary.

Pressure-relief valve (PRV): A device designed to automatically relieve pressure at the pressure at which it is set.

Ready access to: Access that does not req removing a panel or door. For electrical equipment, this also means not having to resort to use of a ladder.

Room heater, circulating: A room heater with an outer jacket surrounding the heat exchanger & with openings at the top & bottom designed to circulate air between the heat exchanger & outer jacket.

Room heater (liquid or gas fuel): A room heater installed in the space to be heated & not connected to duct.

Room heater, radiant: A room heater designed to transfer heat primarily by direct radiation.

Room heater (solid fuel): A solid fuel–burning appliance designed to be operated with the fire chamber door closed. *See "Fireplace stove."*

Room large in comparison to size of equipment: (pre-2012 code cycle or UMC) A room having at least 12 times the volume of a furnace or other air-handling device, or 16 times the volume of a boiler. When the ceiling is greater than 8 ft., the volume is calculated based on an 8 ft. height. *See "Alcove."*

Slope: Fall or pitch along a line of a pipe or vent.

Supports: Devices used to support or secure pipes, fixtures, or equipment.

Ton (cooling): The amount of heat energy reqd to melt 1 ton of ice (288,000 Btus). Air conditioners & heat pumps are typically sized in terms of tonnage, based on melting 1 ton of ice in 1 day. Therefore 1 ton of AC = 288,000 Btus/24hr. = 12,000 Btus. The tonnage of a unit is usually encoded in the model number as a multiplier of 12, i.e., the number 36 would equal a 3-ton unit, the number 30 would be for a 2½-ton unit.

Unconfined space: F10 A room or space having at least 50 cu. ft. for each 1,000 Btu of the fuel-burning appliances contained in the room or space.

Unlisted: An appliance not shown to comply with nationally recognized standards by an approved testing agency. An unlisted appliance might still have nameplate instructions. The IRC does not accept unlisted appliances. The UMC leaves their acceptance to the AHJ.

Vent (fuel-burning appliances): A passageway for conveying flue gases from an appliance to the outside atmosphere.

Vent, Type B: A vent listed & labeled for use with appliances with draft hoods & other Category I appliances

Vent, Type BW: A vent listed & labeled for use with wall furnaces.

Vent, Type L: A vent listed & labeled for appliances requiring either type L (oil-fired appliance) vents or Type B vents.

Vent connector: A device that connects an appliance to a vent.

Vented decorative gas appliance: A vented appliance that does not provide significant heat & whose primary function is the aesthetic effect of the gas flames.

Vented gas appliance categories:

Category I: An appliance that operates with nonpositive vent static pressure & with a gas vent temperature that avoids excessive condensate production in the vent.

Category II: An appliance that operates with a nonpositive vent static pressure and with a vent gas temperature that can cause excessive condensate production in the vent.

Category III: An appliance that operates with a positive vent static pressure and with a vent gas temperature that avoids excessive condensate production in the vent.

Category IV: An appliance that operates with a positive vent static pressure and with a vent gas temperature that can cause excessive condensate production in the vent.

Vertical: Any pipe or vent that is 45° or more from horizontal.

Within sight: Visible, unobstructed & not more than 50 ft. away.

Wood stove: *See "Fireplace stove" or "Room heater (solid fuel)."*

In colonial America, most homes were warmed by building a fire in a fireplace. This method resulted in sending most of the heat up the chimney, using a lot of wood and causing many house fires. In 1742, Ben Franklin invented an iron furnace stove, equipped with loosely fitting iron plates through which air circulated & warmed before passing into the room. It warmed homes more efficiently, less dangerously & with less wood—resulting in less air pollution. Throughout his life, he continued to tinker with it, and in 1771 he came up with the freestanding bulbous design that is known today as the "Franklin Stove."

Code ✓ Check® Electrical Ninth Edition

Based on the 2020 NEC®

Including Commentary on Changes from the 2017 NEC

Part 4 of Code ✓ Check Complete Third Edition

Code Check Electrical 9th Edition is a field guide to common electrical code issues. It is based on the ***2020 National Electrical Code® (NEC)*** and the ***2021 International Residential Code® (IRC)***. Significant changes are highlighted throughout the text. If an item is not shown as a change, then the code line is also valid for the 2017 NEC. Therefore this book can be used in areas using either the 2017 NEC or the 2020 NEC. Before beginning any electrical project, check with your local building department to determine the code edition used in your area. In addition to a model code, energy codes and utility regulations also apply to electrical installations. Smoke and carbon-monoxide alarm information is in Part 1 (Building) of this book. This publication also contains information on multifamily and light commercial electrical installations that is not found in the separately printed 9th edition of *Code Check Electrical.*

The electrical portion of the IRC is produced and copyrighted by the National Fire Protection Association (NFPA®) using material extracted from the NEC. It only includes portions of the NEC that are relevant to 1- & 2-Family Dwellings and does not include some of the specific topics that might still apply to such dwellings. Examples are rules for temporary wiring, energy storage systems, and photovoltaics. Where both codes do cover a specific item, we provide both code citations. This book includes information on multifamily and commercial installations. For such subjects there is no IRC reference. Because the IRC is derived from the NEC, there are no conflicts between the two codes. In sections of this book, the omission of an IRC column or reference does not imply that an IRC jurisdiction would not adopt the rule in question. As an example, the scope of electrical services in the IRC is limited to those not greater than 400 amps. Even some single-family homes have services larger than 400 amps, and this book includes such equipment. The IRC is essentially for new construction and does not include information for old wiring systems or methods that are included here.

The information in this book is believed to be accurate; however, it is provided for informational purposes only and is not intended as a substitute for the full text of the referenced codes. Users of this book should rely upon their own independent judgment and the services of qualified competent professionals. Publication by The Taunton Press, ICC, and the authors should not be considered by the user to be a substitute for the interpretation of the local Authority Having Jurisdiction. Contact the building department in your area to learn what codes apply as well as any local amendments and procedures.

TABLE OF CONTENTS

KEY & EXAMPLES FOR USING THIS BOOK

Each line that begins with a checkbox is a code rule, and the specific code sections are at the right end of the line as in the following example from *p. 236*:

Service Equipment	**21 IRC**	**20 NEC**
☐ Only 1 service per building ____________	3601.2	230.2

IRC section 3601.1 & NEC section 230.2 each allow only one service per building.

Code Check abbreviates the punctuation in code references. For example, the NEC has code section 110.14(C)(1)(a). We eliminate the parentheses and write this simply as 110.14C1a. In order to fit material into this book, we use several common abbreviations and also abbreviate many other terms, as shown on *p. 229*.

When a code rule has exceptions, the line ends with EXC and exceptions follow in a bulleted item or list of items below that line, as in the following example from *p. 255:*

☐ Backfed breakers secured in place EXC ____________	3706.5	408.36D
• Output circuits from listed utility interactive inverters _____	n/a	705.12E

The basic rule is that a backfed breaker (where the source of power is the conductor, not the breaker bus bar) must have a device to secure it in place. The exception is for output circuits of utility interactive inverters (because when they are disconnected from the utility their power output ceases). Note also that the IRC reference for this exception is "n/a" (not applicable). The IRC does not include photovoltaic systems. If an item is not covered by the IRC, the IRC tells us to follow the rules of the NEC.

When a code citation includes the letter "X," as in the following example from *p. 235*, the "X" stands for the word "exception":

☐ Conductors other than service conductors not allowed in same raceway w/ service conductors EXC __________	3601.4	230.7
• GECs or supply-side bonding jumpers __________	3601.4X1	230.7X1
• OCPD-protected load management control conductors	3601.4X2	230.7X2

The code citations here are exceptions 1 & 2 to 3601.4 & 230.7.

This book contains 101 figures and 57 tables. They are referenced throughout the text as in this example from *p. 237*:

Working Space (General & Residential)	**21 IRC**	**20 NEC**
☐ Front working clearance min. 36 in. deep **F4,T2** ____	305.4.2(4)	110.26A1

The rules for working clearance in front of equipment are shown graphically in Figure 4 and also in Table 2, which shows required clearances depending upon voltage.

Significant changes from the previous editions of the IRC and NEC are highlighted by using a different color for the code citation and by summarizing the change at the bottom of the page where it occurs, as in this example from *p. 236*:

☐ All services supplying dwelling units req SPD _______	3606.5[10]	230.67A[10]

This line tells us that a new rule requires surge-protective devices on the services supplying dwelling units and that it is code change #10 in this book. The summary at the bottom of the page has a color background and provides additional information about this change:

10. SPD reqd at service must be Type 1 or 2. Additional SPDs are allowed.

After proving lightning and electricity are the same thing, Ben invented the lightning rod. He believed it was his most important invention.

Benjamin Franklin *was chosen as the main character in our Code Check illustrations for a number of reasons. The "First American's" insatiable curiosity, scientific genius, and civic-mindedness drove him to promote fire safety, safe exiting, public sanitation, improved heating methods to reduce air pollution, and, of course, electricity. Franklin contributed to each of the four main disciplines of building inspection: Building, Plumbing, Mechanical, and Electrical.*

To find out more, visit: ***codecheck.com/why-ben/***

Snatched lightning from the sky and the scepter from tyrants

For further information, articles, videos and all things Code Check visit: ***www.codecheck.com***

ABBREVIATIONS

Ω = ohms (unit of electrical resistance)
1FD = single family dwelling
1&2FD = 1- & 2-family dwellings
A = amp(s), amperage, amps
AC = alternating current
AC = armored cable, a.k.a. "BX"
AFC = available fault current
AFCI = arc-fault circuit interrupter
AFF = above finished floor or grade
AHJ = Authority Having Jurisdiction
AIC = ampere interrupting capacity (see IR)
AL = aluminum
AMI = in accordance w/ manufacturer's instructions
ASCC = available short circuit current
ASCE = American Society of Civil Engineers
AWG = American Wire Gauge, commonly stated as "number" (#8 = 8 AWG)
CSA = cross-sectional area
cu. = cubic, as in cu. in.
Cu = copper
DC = direct current
DW = dishwasher
e.g. = for example (*exempli gratia*)
EGC = equipment grounding conductor
EMT = electrical metallic tubing
ENT = electrical nonmetallic tubing
ESS = energy storage system
EV = electric vehicle
EVSE = electric vehicle supply equipment
EXC = exception(s) (in following line)
Fe = ferrous
FLA = full load amperage
FLC = full load current
FMC = flexible metal conduit
ft. = foot, feet
GEC = grounding electrode conductor
GES = grounding electrode system
GFCI = ground-fault circuit interrupter
GFPE = ground-fault protection of equipment
hp = horsepower
IBC = 2021 International Building Code®
IBT = intersystem bonding termination
IFC = 2021 International Fire Code®
IMC = intermediate metal conduit
IR = interrupting rating (see AIC)
IRC = 2021 International Residential Code®
in. = inch(es)
j-box = junction box
kcmil = 1,000 circular mil units (wire size)
KO = knockout
kVA = kilovolt-amperes (1,000's of VAs)
kW = kilowatts (1,000s of Watts)
L&L = listed & labeled, listing & labeling
LED = light-emitting diode
lb. = pound(s)
LFMC = liquidtight flexible metal conduit
LFNC = liquidtight flexible nonmetallic conduit
max. = maximum
MBJ = main bonding jumper
MC = metal-clad cable
MFD = multifamily dwelling
MFR = manufacturer(s)
min. = minimum
MWBC = multiwire branch circuit
n/a = not applicable
NEC = National Electrical Code
NEMA® = National Electrical Manufacturers Association
NFPA® = National Fire Protection Association
NM = nonmetallic-sheathed cable
OBC AFCI = outlet branch circuit AFCI
OCPD = overcurrent protection device
p. = page (as in see ***p. 229***)
PCS = power control system
PPE = electrical personal protective equipment
PV = photovoltaic
req, reqs, reqd = require, requires, required
RMC = rigid metal conduit
RNC = rigid nonmetallic conduit (PVC)
RS = rapid shutdown (photovoltaics)
RTRC = reinforced thermosetting resin conduit
SBJ = system bonding jumper
SCCR = short circuit current rating
SDC = Seismic Design Category
SDS = separately derived system
SE = service entrance (cable)
SPD = surge-protective device
SSBJ = supply-side bonding jumper
sq. = square, as in sq. in.
temp = temperature
TR = tamper-resistant
UF = underground feeder cable
UL® = Underwriters Laboratories
USE = underground service-entrance cable
util = utility
V = volt(s), such as a 120V circuit
VA = volt-ampere(s), units of apparent power
VD = voltage drop
VFD = variable frequency drive (adjustable speed drive)
W = watt(s), units of true (useful) power
w/ = with
w/o = without
WR = weather-resistant
XFMR = transformer
Z = impedance (of a transformer)

GLOSSARY

Note: The definitions below do not include the complete text that is found in the codes. Refer to IRC sections 202 and 3501, NEC article 100, and to the UL standards for complete definitions of these and other terms used throughout this book.

Accessible: Not permanently concealed or enclosed by building construction. A piece of equipment can be considered accessible even if tools must be used or other equipment must be removed to gain access to it. A piece of equipment is not accessible if building finishes would need to be removed to gain access.

Accessible, readily: Capable of being reached quickly for operation or inspection without the use of tools, portable ladders, or the need to remove obstacles. For purposes of this rule, a key is not considered a tool.

Appliance: Utilization equipment normally built in standardized sizes and types, such as clothes washers, air conditioners, water heaters, etc.

Approved: Acceptable to the Authority Having Jurisdiction (AHJ). The AHJ will usually approve materials that are listed and labeled.

Arc-fault circuit interrupter (AFCI): A device intended to mitigate the effects of arcing faults by de-energizing the circuit when an arc fault occurs.

- **Branch feeder AFCI:** A device installed at the origin of a branch circuit that protects the wiring and provides a limited degree of protection to equipment extending from the branch circuit. These were the first generation of AFCIs.
- **Combination AFCI:** A device that complies with both the standard for branch feeder AFCIs and for outlet circuit AFCIs. The term "combination" does not imply that they also provide GFCI protection. See *Dual-Function AFCI/GFCI.*
- **Outlet circuit AFCI:** A device installed at a branch circuit outlet, such as a box. It provides protection to cord sets and feed-through protection to downstream receptacles. It detects a wider range of arcing types than a branch feeder.

Arcing: A luminous discharge (spark) across an insulating medium, such as air.

Authority Having Jurisdiction (AHJ): The building official or persons authorized to act on his or her behalf.

Bonded, bonding: Connected to establish continuity and conductivity.

Branch circuit: The circuit conductors located between the last OCPD (breaker or fuse) and the outlet or outlets that utilize electrical energy.

- **Branch circuit, general purpose:** Branch circuit that supplies 2 or more receptacles or outlets for lighting and appliances.
- **Branch circuit, individual:** Branch circuit supplying only 1 piece of equipment.
- **Branch circuit, multiwire, residential:** Branch circuit consisting of 2 ungrounded "hot" conductors having 208V or 240V potential between them and a grounded neutral having 120V potential to each hot conductor. **F19,20**
- **Branch circuit, small appliance:** Branch circuit supplying portable household appliances in kitchens and related rooms.

Continuous load: A load where the maximum current is expected to continue for 3 hours or more.

Controller: A device that governs the power to an apparatus to which it is connected. The most common use of the term is for equipment that starts and stops a motor and which may include overload protection for the motor.

Cross-sectional area (CSA): The net interior area of an imaginary slice through a conduit, wireway, box, or cabinet for purposes of determining conductor and device fill.

Dead front: Without live parts exposed to a person on the operating side of the equipment. A panelboard door is not a dead front.

Dedicated: Installed for a specific purpose, such as a circuit dedicated to laundry equipment. This is not necessarily the same as an individual circuit.

Device: A piece of equipment that carries or controls electrical energy as its primary function, such as a switch, receptacle, or circuit breaker. **F37**

Double insulated: Equipment meeting the UL 2097 standard for double insulation, whereby a fault on one of the components will not cause an accessible part to become a live part. It is marked with the words "double insulation—when servicing use only identical replacement parts" or with the symbol for double insulation—a square within a square, and an explanation of the symbol in the instructions.

Dual-function AFCI/GFCI: A device providing both AFCI protection and Class A GFCI protection.

Effective ground-fault current path: A low-impedance electrically conductive path that will carry high enough current to open an overcurrent protection device in the event of a ground fault. Earth is not an effective ground-fault current path.

Equipment grounding conductor (EGC): A wire or conductive path that limits voltage on metal surfaces and provides a path for fault currents. **F16**

Exothermic welding: An irreversible joining of metallic parts, such as a grounding electrode conductor and a ground rod, by means of tools designed to weld them together.

Fault current: The current delivered at a point on the system during a short-circuit condition. See ***p. 261***.

Feeders: Conductors between the source of supply and the final overcurrent device, such as the conductors between a service and subpanel.

Ground, grounded: The earth, connected to earth.

Ground fault: An unintentional connection of a current-carrying conductor to equipment, earth, or conductors that are not normally intended to carry current.

Ground-fault circuit interrupter (GFCI): A device to protect people against shock hazards by de-energizing a circuit when a ground fault occurs. Class A GFCIs must open the circuit when an imbalance of 6 milliamps or more is detected. **F63,64**

Ground-fault protection of equipment (GFPE): A system intended to protect equipment from damage from line to ground faults by de-energizing the circuit. This protection is provided at a level less than that of the OCPD that protects conductors and at a higher level than would be required to provide personnel protection.

Grounded conductor: A current-carrying conductor intentionally connected to earth at the source of the system (typically a utility transformer). In residential systems, the neutral is a grounded conductor.

Grounding electrode conductor (GEC): A conductor that connects the service neutral or the service equipment to a grounding electrode or a point on the grounding electrode system. **F7**

Grounding electrode system (GES): The conductive metallic elements installed in the earth and bonded together to form a grounding electrode system. **F7**

Identified for the purpose: As applied to equipment, the term means recognized as suitable for a specific function, use, environment, or application. The term is not synonymous with labeled.

Impedance: The total opposition to current flow in a conductor. Impedance(Z) is the result of calculating 3 factors; the resistance(R), inductive reactance(X_L) and capacitive reactance(X_C) of a circuit.

In sight, within sight: Visible and within 50 ft.

Interrupting rating: The highest current at rated voltage that a device (such as a fuse or circuit breaker) is identified to open (interrupt current) under standard test conditions. See *p. 261*.

Labeled: Equipment bearing an identifying mark of an organization acceptable to the AHJ and that conducts product evaluations and maintains periodic inspection of production of labeled equipment or materials. A label indicates compliance by the manufacturer with appropriate standards or performance.

Listed: Included in a list published by a Nationally Recognized Testing Laboratory (NRTL) acceptable to the AHJ and concerned with evaluation of products or services. The listing must state the appropriate designated standards or specific purpose for which the product has been found suitable. Listing requirements may also prescribe labeling requirements.

Low voltage: The definition of this term depends upon the context in which it is used. In utilities, low voltage refers to systems operating at ≤1,000V. In the NEC, the general usage of the term is for systems where the protection is primarily for fire protection rather than shock hazard, such as doorbell or thermostat wiring.

Low voltage contact limit: In most NEC articles, low-voltage systems are ≤30V, and in Article 680 (pools and similar) the *low-voltage contact limit* is defined as 15V for AC and 30V for DC.

Luminaire (formerly lighting fixture): A complete lighting unit including parts to connect it to the power supply and possibly parts to protect or distribute the light source. A lampholder, such as a porcelain socket, is not itself a luminaire.

Location, damp: A location protected from weather but subject to moderate degrees of moisture, such as the area under an open porch.

Location, dry: A location not normally subject to dampness or wetness. It may be subject to dampness or wetness for a short time, such as a building under construction.

Location, wet: Installation underground or in concrete or masonry in direct contact w/ the earth, or location subject to saturation or unprotected exposed to weather.

Microgrid system: A premises' wiring system that has generation (such as a photovoltaic system), energy storage, and loads, or any combination thereof, and that can operate independently or in parallel with the utility.

Neutral conductor: The grounded conductor connected to the neutral point of a system and that is intended to carry current under normal operating conditions. **F20**

Outlet: The point on a wiring system at which current is taken to supply equipment. A box for a receptacle, luminaire (fixture), or smoke alarm is an outlet.

Overcurrent: Any current in excess of the rating of equipment, device, or conductor ampacity. Overcurrents are produced by overloads, ground faults, or short circuits.

Power distribution block: A device that is secured in place for the termination of conductors, typically within a wireway, box, or cabinet.

Raceway: A channel for enclosing wires, cables, or bus bars and used solely for this purpose. Examples are conduit, tubing, wireways, auxiliary gutters, and wiremold.

Service: The conductors and equipment providing a connection to the utility. **F3,17**

Service drop: The overhead conductors supplied by the utility **F3**.

Service equipment: The equipment at which power conductors from the utility can be switched off to disconnect the premises' wiring from the utility power source. **F17,18**

Service-entrance head (weatherhead): Equipment placed on the end of a conduit or cable and containing separately bushed insulated holes for entry of conductors.

Service lateral: Underground conductors from the utility to the service point.

Weatherproof: Constructed so that exposure to the weather will not interfere with successful operation.

GENERAL RULES

The IRC requires all electrical materials to be listed & labeled by an approved agency. The NEC does not require all materials to be listed and labeled, though it does require listed materials in approximately 300 individual sections within the code. The internal components of listed and labeled materials do not need to be re-evaluated in the field. Listed materials must always be installed in accordance with any instructions that are included in their listing & labeling.

Permits & Inspections — 21 IRC

- ☐ Construction, alteration, relocation, or repair of electrical equipment reqs permit EXC ______ 105.1
  - Listed cord-&-plug-connected temporary holiday lighting ______ 105.2
  - Re-installation of receptacles, but not the outlets (boxes) therefor ___ 105.2
  - Replacement of branch circuit OCPDs in same location ______ 105.2
  - Wiring, devices & appliances <25V & <50W ______ 105.2
  - Minor repairs (lamp replacement) or connection of portable equipment 105.2

IRC Scope

- ☐ NEC wiring methods also allowed ______ 3401.1
- ☐ Services limited to 120/240V single phase ≤400A ______ 3401.2

Items not in Scope — 20 NEC

- ☐ Installations under exclusive control of communications utilities ______ 90.2B
- ☐ Installations under exclusive control of electric utilities including service drops, service laterals & metering ______ 90.2B
- ☐ By special permission, installations not under exclusive control of electric utilities & used to connect the utility to the premises' service conductors ___ 90.2C

Inspection & Approval

	21 IRC	20 NEC
☐ Code is intended for enforcement by local AHJ	104.1	90.4
☐ Materials, components & equipment must be approved	3403.2	110.2
☐ AHJ may approve alternative means, materials & methods	104.11	90.4
☐ Intent is enforcement by local AHJ	104.1	90.4

Listing & Labeling of Equipment

☐ Listed, labeled, or L&L materials, components, devices, fixtures & equipment must be installed & used in accordance w/ instructions in the L&L	104.1	110.3B

Nationally Recognized Testing Laboratories (NRTLs)

Listing & labeling is performed by qualified Nationally Recognized Testing Laboratories (NRTLs). The Occupational Safety and Health Administration (OSHA) establishes qualifications for NRTLs and maintains a list of them on the OSHA website. Standards for electrical equipment are developed and maintained by organizations such as NEMA, NFPA, UL, and the Institute of Electrical and Electronics Engineers, Inc. (IEEE). The evaluation of specific products can be performed by NRTLs other than the ones that developed the standard. The most widely recognized NRTL is UL. Their standards are available in read-only mode at shopulstandards.com. Registration is required for viewing.

FIG. 1 NRTL Labels

Marking for a UL listed product:

A UL listing mark consists of 4 elements: The agency logo, the word "listed," a product identifier, and a control number.

Marking for a product that is classified for a specific application:

An example of a classified product could be a circuit breaker suitable for another manufacturer's panel.

Marking of a component within a listed product:

An example of a registered component could be a pump motor within a listed spa. The individual component is not listed other than as part of the listed spa.

Equipment that is altered, reconditioned, or field-assembled may have a field evaluation performed by an independent agency approved by the local jurisdiction.

Other NRTL logos:

Based on data from the Occupational Safety and Health Administration August 22, 2022. To verify current status, visit the OSHA website.

TEMPORARY POWER

Rules for permanent wiring also apply to temporary installations unless specifically modified in the rules listed here. Temporary service and distribution equipment is often reused, and should be carefully inspected for wear or damage before being energized. Reconditioned equipment requires markings identifying it as such. The equipment must be rated for the available fault current supplied by the utility, an especially important consideration in commercial construction.

General — 20 NEC

- ☐ Rules for permanent wiring apply except as specifically stated below 590.2A
- ☐ Allowed only during period of construction—remove at completion 590.3A&D
- ☐ Holiday decorative lighting & similar allowed for 90 days max. ________ 590.3B

Services

- ☐ Service height, grounding, clearance, etc., same as permanent **F3** ______ 590.4A
- ☐ Temporary pole size, depth & bracing typically per utility **F2** ____________ 90.2C
- ☐ AIC rating of OCPDs & equipment ≥ AFC from utility ____________ 110.9&10
- ☐ Reused OCPDs req examination for proper installation & maintenance or indications of impending failure (***see p. 260***) ________ 590.8A[1]
- ☐ Systems over >150V to ground req current limiting OCPD ________ 590.8B[2]

Feeders

- ☐ NM & SE cables OK in any type or height building w/o concealment in walls, floors, or ceilings __________________________ 590.4B
- ☐ SE cable OK in underground raceway __________________________ 590.4C
- ☐ Single insulated conductors permitted for emergencies & tests where accessible only to qualified personnel ______________ 590.4BX

Lighting

- ☐ Lampholders req guards ______________________________________ 590.4F
- ☐ Single insulated conductors for holiday/decorative lighting OK if voltage to ground <150V, not subject to damage & max. support interval 10 ft. 590.4CX
- ☐ No receptacles on branch circuits supplying temporary lighting ____ 590.4D1
- ☐ Holiday decorative lighting & similar req L&L on the product _________ 590.5

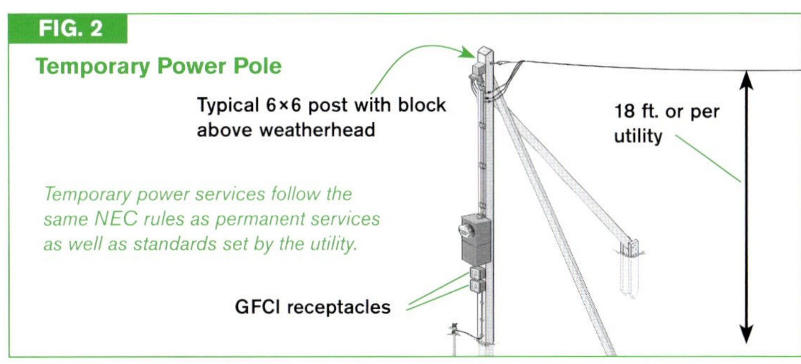

Wiring Methods — 20 NEC

- ☐ Box or other enclosure w/ cover reqd for all splices EXC __________ 590.4G
  - Nonmetallic cable assemblies OK w/o splice box if continuity of EGC maintained ________________ 590.4GX1(1)
  - Metallic cable assemblies OK w/o splice box if terminating in listed metal cable fittings that maintain continuity __________ 590.4GX1(2)
  - Permanent branch circuit w/ GFCI protection in framed walls & ceilings OK w/o box cover if splice inside box w/ plaster ring or pigtail-type lampholders from ceiling box w/ plaster ring _______ 590.4GX2[3]
- ☐ Protect cords & cables from damage, guard at pinch points _________ 590.4H
- ☐ Cords & cables not OK on floor or ground except extension cords ___ 590.4J
- ☐ Cords & cables not OK supported on vegetation EXC ____________ 590.4J
  - Holiday lighting w/ means to accommodate vegetation movement _ 590.4JX

Receptacles

- ☐ Receptacles in wet locations req extra-duty in-use covers **F68** ____ 590.4D2
- ☐ GFCI reqd on all 125V 15, 20 & 30A temporary receptacles ______ 590.6A1
- ☐ Listed cord-set GFCI can be used in addition to other GFCIs ______ 590.6A1
- ☐ Existing permanently wired outlets OK if GFCI protected or if using listed cord set into non-GFCI-protected receptacle ________ 590.6A2
- ☐ Other receptacles GFCI or compliance w/ assured EGC program _____ 590.6B[4]
- ☐ Assured EGC documentation to be available to the AHJ ____________ 590.6B2[5]

1. New requirement for evaluating reused equipment in accordance w/ NEMA & IEEE standards.
2. New requirement for current-limiting service OCPDs.
3. Temporary splices OK from permanent wiring where protected as noted.
4. Previous alternative for "special purpose GFCIs" has been deleted.
5. Assured EGC program documentation must now be available to the AHJ.

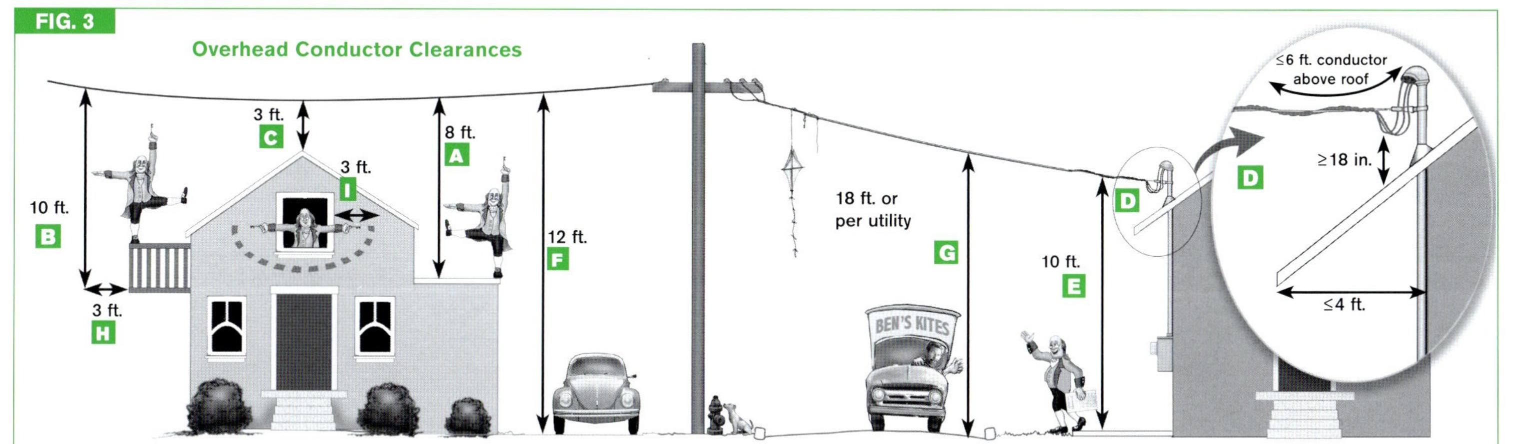

OVERHEAD SERVICE DROP CLEARANCES

The splice between the utility service drop and permanent building wiring is the service point—the handoff from the utility to the customer. In an underground system, the service point may be at the service panel or some other agreed-upon location. The utility may share jurisdiction with the building department for conductors up to the meter. The utility typically determines the rules for meter heights and clearance.

Vertical Clearances above Roofs F3

	21 IRC	20 NEC
☐ Min. 8 ft. if slope <4:12 EXC A	3604.2.1	230.24A
• Min. 10 ft. vertical above walkable roof deck B	3604.2.1X1	230.24AX1
☐ Min. 3 ft. if slope ≥ 4:12 EXC C	3604.2.1X2	230.24AX2
• 18 in. above roof OK ≤4-ft. overhanging eave D	3604.2.1X3	230.24AX3
☐ Maintain reqd clearance for 3 ft. past roof edge EXC	3604.2.1	230.24A
• When attached to side of building	3604.2.1X4	230.24AX4
☐ 3-ft. clearance OK for guarded/isolated roof areas	3604.2.1X5	230.24AX5
☐ Metal support structures for conductors passing over roofs req bonding to neutral of service drop	3604.6	230.29

Vertical Clearances from Grade F3

	21 IRC	20 NEC
☐ Service conductors (including drip loop) 10 ft. min. above areas accessible only to pedestrians E	3604.2.2	230.24.B1
☐ 12 ft. above residential property & driveways F	3604.2.2	230.24.B2
☐ 18 ft. above public streets & tractor trailer parking G	3604.2.2	230.24.B4

Clearances from Openings F3

	21 IRC	20 NEC
☐ Vertical above decks & balconies: 10 ft. B	3604.2.1X1	230.9B
☐ Overhead clearance 3 ft. past deck edge B, H	3604.2.1	230.9A&B
☐ 3 ft. to sides of doors/windows & below openable windows I EXC		230.9A
• Not reqd for raceway or cable w/ overall outer jacket	3604.1	230.9A
☐ Distance above window per utility or local AHJ	3604.1	230.9AX

Clearance for Communications Wires & Cables

	20 NEC
☐ If from same pole, locate below power conductors where practical	800.44A1
☐ Min. 1-ft. separation from parallel insulated ungrounded power wires	800.44A4
☐ Above-roof clearances same as for power conductors	800.44B
☐ May terminate on separate mast, not on power mast	230.28 & 800.44C

SERVICES

The term ***electrical service*** refers to the conductors and equipment that connect a wiring system to the utility. ***Service equipment*** is where the main control and disconnect are located and consists of a breaker, switch, or fuse that can isolate the premises from the utility power. The conductors on the utility side of the main disconnect are always "live" and do not have overcurrent protection. A short circuit or ground fault to these conductors can unleash all the potential energy from the utility transformer and cause extensive property damage. Special precautions are taken to protect these conductors from damage and to protect people from contacting them. In **F3**, we see examples of protecting these by isolation. In equipment, we protect them by insulation and barriers. The rules regarding those barriers have changed significantly in the last 2 code cycles.

Service Risers — 21 IRC | 20 NEC

Item	21 IRC	20 NEC
☐ Raceway size, material & bracing also per utility	3401.3	90.2C
☐ Riser reqd to have adequate strength & bracing	3604.5.1	230.28A
☐ Conduit hubs to be identified for use w/ service	3604.5.1	230.28A
☐ Only service conductors on riser (no CATV or phone)	3604.5	230.28
☐ No couplings between last structural support of mast & the service head	3604.5.1	230.28B
☐ Attach service drop below service head EXC	3605.9.3	230.54C
• OK ≤24 in. above when necessary (sidewall)	3605.9.3X	230.54CX
☐ Arrange to drain where exposed to weather	3605.9.6	230.53
☐ Service head must be listed for wet locations	3605.9.1	230.54A
☐ Secure conduit within 3 ft. of service box	T3802.1	344.30A
☐ Conductor fill in raceway 40% **T32–40**	T3904.6(1-10)	Ch 9-T1&T4
☐ Not OK to pass through interior of another building	3601.3	230.3
☐ Arrange conductors of different potential through separately bushed holes in weatherhead, length per utility specs	3605.9.4	230.54E
☐ Arrange conductors to prevent water entry into riser	3605.9.6	230.54G
☐ Form each conductor w/ drip loops **F3**	3605.9.5	230.54F
☐ Identify (white tape OK) insulated neutral at each end	3407.1	200.6B
☐ Exposed wire either listed or L&L sunlight-resistant or covered w/ tape or sleeving that is listed or L&L as sunlight-resistant	3605.6	310.10D

Service-Entrance Conductors — 21 IRC | 20 NEC

Item	21 IRC	20 NEC
☐ Conductors other than service conductors not allowed in same raceway w/ service conductors EXC	3601.4	230.7
• GECs or supply-side bonding jumpers	3601.4X1	230.7X1
• OCPD-protected load management control conductors	3601.4X2	230.7X2
☐ Splices w/ listed means & within enclosures or listed underground splice kits	3605.3	230.46
☐ Power distribution blocks on supply side req marking as "suitable for use on the line side of the service equipment"	3605.3[6]	230.46[6]
☐ Pressure connectors & splicing/tapping devices req marking as "suitable for use on the line side of the service equipment"	3605.3[6]	230.46[6]
☐ Size service conductors to meet load of **T9,11** EXC	3602.1	230.42
• 83% of **T23** allowed for 1FD & for feeders supplying total load of individual dwelling units **T1**	3603.1.1	310.12A
☐ Sum of rating of 2 to 6 mains may exceed service conductor ampacity if conductors adequate for calculated load	3603.3.1X	230.90AX3

TABLE 1 — DWELLING UNIT SERVICE CONDUCTOR SIZE[A,B]
IRC T3601.1.1 ◆ NEC T310.12

Rating (Amps)	Cu Wire Size (AWG)	AL Wire Size (AWG)	Rating (Amps)	Cu Wire Size (AWG)	AL Wire Size (AWG)
100	4	2	225	3/0	250
110	3	1	250	4/0	300
125	2	1/0	300	250	350
150	1	2/0	350	350	500
175	1/0	3/0	400	400	600
200	2/0	4/0			

A. Based on 83% of ampacity in **T23** per 310.12.
B. This table is allowed for service conductors or main power feeders that carry the entire load of an individual dwelling using conductors rated ≥75°C.

6. Requirement for listing of pressure connectors and devices on supply side to become effective January 1, 2023.

SE Cables F56 as Service Entrance

	21 IRC	20 NEC
☐ Secure SE cable max. 30-in. intervals	3605.7	230.51A
☐ Secure within 12 in. of termination of box & weatherhead	3605.7	230.51A
☐ Where subject to damage, protect SE cables w/ RMC, IMC, PVC-80, EMT, RTRC, or other approved means	3605.5	230.50B
☐ Overhead cable reqs service head listed for wet locations EXC	3605.9.2	230.54A&B
• SE cable OK w/ gooseneck & taped connections	3605.9.2	230.54BX
☐ Use waterproof gland or equivalent to prevent water entry into service equipment	3605.9.6	230.54G

Service Equipment

	21 IRC	20 NEC
☐ Only 1 service per building	3601.2	230.2
☐ Verify meter height, location, fees w/ utility	3401.3	90.2C
☐ Service equipment reqs listing or field labeling as such	3606.4	230.66A
☐ Equipment reqs marking as suitable for service F17,18	3606.4	230.66A
☐ Meter socket alone not considered service equipment	3606.4	230.66B
☐ Meter sockets req listing & rating for service EXC	3606.4	230.66B
• If supplied by & under exclusive control of utility	3606.4X	230.66B
☐ Barriers reqd over supply terminals & buses in services F17	n/a	230.62C[7]
☐ Neutral bar bonded in service equipment F17,18	3607.5	250.24B

Emergency Disconnects in 1&2FD

	21 IRC	20 NEC
☐ Emergency disconnect must be outdoors	3601.8[8]	230.85[8]
☐ Service disconnects req marking as follows: EMERGENCY DISCONNECT, SERVICE DISCONNECT	3601.8[8]	230.85[8]
☐ Meter disconnects & other listed disconnect switches upstream of service also allowed as emergency disconnects & req marking as such	3601.8[8]	230.85[8]

7. Moved from article 408 & deleted exception for services w/ >1 main; if the main is open, no uninsulated component within its enclosure can have voltage.
8. Purpose of exterior emergency disconnect is for first responders.

Service Disconnects

	21 IRC	20 NEC
☐ Service disconnect readily accessible & nearest to the point of entrance of service conductors	3601.6.2	230.70A1
☐ Max. 1 disconnecting means per service EXC	3601.7[9]	230.71[9]
• 2 to 6 disconnects if each in separate enclosure w/ single main disconnect in each enclosure	3601.7.1[9]	230.71B1[9]
• 2 to 6 panelboards each w/ single main disconnect	3601.7.2[9]	230.71B2[9]
• 2 to 6 disconnects in switchboards w/ separate disconnects in each vertical section & w/ barriers separating each vertical section	n/a	230.71B[9]
• 2 to 6 disconnects in meter centers or switchboards w/ separate compartment for each disconnect	3601.7.3[9]	230.71B[9]
☐ Where 2 to 6 disconnects allowed, they must be grouped in one location EXC	3601.7	230.72A
• Fire pump disconnect remote from service; post plaque at service disconnects denoting the location of the fire pump disconnect	n/a	230.72AX
☐ Each service disconnect permanently marked as such	3601.6.1	230.70B

2-Family Dwellings

	21 IRC	20 NEC
☐ Only 1 service per building	3601.2	230.2
☐ Branch circuits for equipment such as lighting common areas not to be supplied by individual unit	3702.14	210.25B

Surge Protection

	21 IRC	20 NEC
☐ All services supplying dwelling units req SPD	3606.5[10]	230.67A[10]
☐ SPD integral w/ or immediately adjacent to service EXC	3606.5.1[10]	230.67B[10]
• Type 2 SPD each next-level distribution equipment	3606.5.1X[10]	230.67BX[10]
☐ SPD to be Type 1 or Type 2	3606.5.2[10]	230.67C[10]
☐ Applicable to replacement service equipment	3606.5.3[10]	230.67D[10]

9. Each service enclosure allowed only 1 disconnecting means (formerly ≤6). This change is also reflected in the UL standards (UL67 & UL 489). The purpose of the change is to limit exposure to live components once the main OCPD has been opened (turned off).
10. SPD reqd at service must be Type 1 or 2. Additional SPDs are allowed.

Multifamily Dwellings (MFDs) & Commercial — 20 NEC

- ☐ Only 1 service per building EXC ____ 230.2
  - Special conditions (fire pumps, standby systems, cogeneration) ____ 230.2A
  - Special occupancies ____ 230.2B
  - Capacity >2,000A or per util or by special permission ____ 230.2C
  - Different characteristics (e.g., wye & high-leg delta) ____ 230.2D
- ☐ If >1 service, identifying plaque or directory @ each service location denoting other services & area served by each ____ 230.2E
- ☐ Adjoining units considered separate buildings if separated by firewalls ____ 100
- ☐ Service conductors may not pass through another building ____ 230.3
- ☐ Each occupant of multifamily to have access to their disconnect EXC ____ 230.72C
  - Where under continuous building management supervision ____ 230.72CX
- ☐ MFD common areas not to be supplied by individual unit ____ 210.25B

EQUIPMENT SPACES & CLEARANCES

Working space is essential for worker safety. These requirements apply to panels and all electrical equipment that requires examination, adjustment, servicing, or maintenance while energized. Working space should not be used for storage.

Working Space (General & Residential) — 21 IRC — 20 NEC

Item	21 IRC	20 NEC
☐ Front working clearance min. 36 in. deep **F4,F22,T2**	3405.2	110.26A1
☐ Measure distance from exposed live parts or enclosure face	3405.2	110.26A1
☐ Min. headroom 6½ ft. AFF or equipment height EXC	3405.2	110.26A3
• Existing dwelling service ≤200A OK < 6½ ft.	3405.2X1	110.26A3X2
☐ Working space extends from floor to reqd height EXC	3405.2	110.26A3
• Related equipment OK 6 in. into working space **F41**	3405.2	110.26A3
• Meter may extend into working space	3405.2X2	110.26A3X3
☐ Clear width greater of 30 in. or width of equipment	3405.2	110.26A2
☐ Equipment doors or hinged panels must be openable at least 90°	3405.2	110.26A2
☐ Working space not to be used for storage	3405.5	110.26B
☐ Illumination reqd for working space at all indoor panels	3405.7	110.26D

FIG. 4

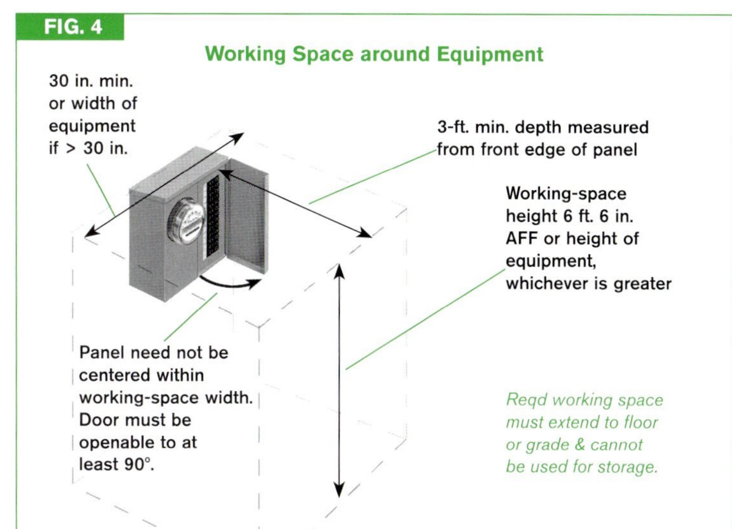

TABLE 2 — MIN. WORKING-SPACE DEPTH ◆ T110.26A1 & T110.34A

Nominal Voltage to Ground	Condition 1	Condition 2	Condition 3
0–150	3 ft.	3 ft.	3 ft.
151–600	3 ft.	3 ft. 6 in.	4 ft.
601–2500	3 ft.	4 ft.	5 ft.
2501–9000	4 ft.	5 ft.	6 ft.
9001–25000	6 ft.	8 ft.	9 ft.

Condition 1 = Exposed live parts on 1 side of space, no grounded or live parts opposite.
Condition 2 = Grounded parts or surfaces on opposite side of space from live parts.
Condition 3 = Exposed live parts on both sides of working space.

SEPARATE BUILDINGS

Separate structures provided with more than 1 branch circuit req their own GES, to which piping and other systems are bonded. Like all panels after the service disconnect, panels in separate buildings are subpanels. The feeder EGC bonds to the GES, and not the neutral. Prior to the 2008 NEC, feeders were allowed with no EGC and their neutral was the fault return path. This condition is allowed to continue only when no parallel conductive paths existed, such as metal piping.

The IRC does not have a separate section for overhead feeders. The NEC rules for feeder heights are identical to those for services, with the exception of the clearance above low slope roofs.

Outside Feeders — 20 NEC

- ☐ Trees may not support overhead conductors ______ 225.26
- ☐ Overhead feeder mast: same rules as services **F3** EXC ______ 225.15—19
  - Height above roofs <4:12 slope min. 8 ft. 6 in. ______ 225.19A
- ☐ All raceways entering building from outside must be sealed ______ 225.27
- ☐ Sealants must be identified for use w/ cable insulation ______ 225.27
- ☐ Max. 1 feeder or branch circuit between each building EXC ______ 225.30
  - EV chargers L&L for more than single branch circuit or feeder __ 225.30A7
  - Up to 6 feeders from common supply to grouped disconnects __ 225.30B[11]
- ☐ Disconnect reqd at each building **F17** ______ 225.31
- ☐ Disconnect at readily accessible location nearest entry of conductors 225.32
- ☐ Max. 6 switches or breakers as disconnecting means ______ 225.33A
- ☐ MWBC counts as 1 circuit for purpose of above rules ___ 225.30 & 225.33B
- ☐ Disconnects must be grouped & marked to indicate load served ___ 225.34A

11. Allows multiple feeders from a pedestal service if disconnects grouped at destination.

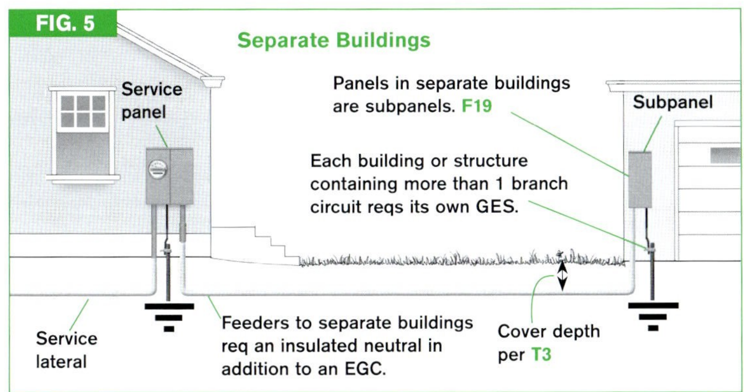

Grounding in Separate Buildings

	21 IRC	20 NEC
☐ Each building or structure reqs GES **F5,F7** EXC ______	3607.3	250.32A
• Building or structure w/ only 1 branch circuit (can be a MWBC) & that includes an EGC ______	3607.3X	250.32AX
☐ Feeder to panel in separate building reqs separate EGC bonded to GES & disconnecting means, not to neutral EXC ___	3607.3.1	250.32B
• Existing installations w/ no EGC may bond neutral to GES & to disconnecting means if no continuous metal paths exist between GES of either building, e.g., no metal water pipe, etc.	3607.3.2	250.32BX1
• Separate building disconnect reqs rating as service equipment when using above exception ______	n/a	225.36
• For exception, grounded conductor must be larger of min. reqd size as EGC or min. size as feeder grounded conductor _	3607.3.2	250.32BX1

UNDERGROUND WIRING

Anticipate that water will enter underground conduits, and when there are significant elevation differences from one end to the other, drain boxes may be needed. Joint trenches typically include communication cables, and separation of these from power conductors is typically per agreement of the parties (utilities).

General	21 IRC	20 NEC
☐ Cover to finish grade per **T3, F6** ________________	3803.1	300.5A
☐ Measure cover from top of cable or conduit **T3, F6** ____	T3803.1	T300.5A
☐ Backfill w/ smooth granular material, no rocks, cinders, or paving materials **F6** ____________	3803.5	300.5F
☐ Provide running boards if subject to damage from backfill	3803.5	300.5F
☐ Direct-buried splices & taps OK w/out boxes if splicing means listed for the purpose (e.g., resin kits) ______________	3803.4	300.5E

Underground Raceways

☐ Provide for earth movement (settlement or frost) using "S" loops, flexible connections, expansion fittings, etc. ___	3803.9	300.5J
☐ Cables & raceways installed w/ directional boring req approval for the purpose (specialized fittings typically reqd)_________	n/a	300.5K
☐ Interior of underground raceways considered wet location	3803.10	300.5B
☐ Conductors underground must be L&L for wet locations	3803.10	310.10C
☐ Seal underground raceway entries at either or both ends	3803.6	300.5G
☐ Sealants must be identified for use w/ cable insulation __	3803.6	300.5G
☐ Spare or unused raceways also to be sealed __________	3803.6	300.5G

Parallel Raceways

☐ All conductors of circuit in same trench or raceway EXC _	3803.8	300.5(I)
• Parallel raceways each containing all conductors & EGC of circuit_____________________	3803.8X	300.5(I)X1
☐ Maintain spacing between raceways ________________	n/a	310.15C2

NEC Informative Annex B contains examples of spacing for duct banks, as well as information on performance of Neher/McGrath calculations to determine the necessary spacing between raceways.

FIG. 6 Conductors in Trench

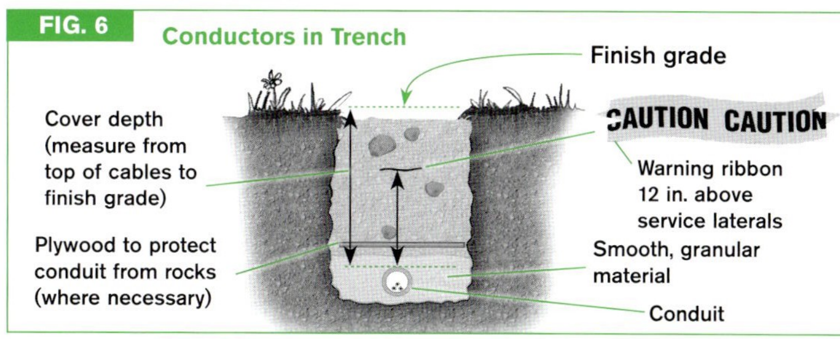

TABLE 3 MIN. COVER REQUIREMENTS ◆ IRC T3803.1 NEC 300.5

Cover	UF Cable	RMC or IMC	PVC	GFCI ≤20A Circuit	≤30V[A]
Other than below	24 in.	6 in.	18 in.	12 in.	6 in.
≥2 in. concrete	18 in.	6 in.	12 in.	6 in.	6 in.
Under building	0[B]	0[B]	0[B]	0[B]	0[B]
≥4-in. slab, no vehicles	18 in.	4 in.	4 in.	6 in. 4-in. raceway	6 in. 4 -in. raceway
Street	24 in.	24 in.	24 in.	24 in.	24 in.
1&2FD Driveway	18 in.	18 in.	18 in.	12 in.	18 in.

A. Applies to central irrigation or landscape lighting in UF cable or a raceway. Listed low-voltage lighting OK per installation instructions at lesser depths. Listed pool, spa, or fountain lighting ≤30V OK in raceway w/ 6-in. cover.
B. Applies to raceways & MC cable identified for direct burial or concrete encasement.

Service Laterals	21 IRC	20 NEC
☐ Size, depth, material & testing (mandrel) per utility_________	util	util
☐ Sewer not in joint trench _____________________________	util	util
☐ Warning ribbon reqd min. 12 in. above service conductors that are ≥18 in. below grade unless encased in concrete **F6** ___	3803.2	300.5D3
☐ Seal underground raceways (see left column) _________	3601.6	230.8

MINIMUM SERVICE SIZE

Many jurisdictions mandate larger 1FD services than the code minimum 100A. Larger services may be necessary to support EV charging. For purposes of load calculations, EV charging is considered a continuous load.

Services	21 IRC	20 NEC
☐ Service equipment for 1FD reqs min. 100A rating	3602.3	230.79C
☐ Service conductor ampacity ≥ max. load served	3602.1	230.42A2
☐ Conductor ampacity ≥ rating of service disconnect EXC	n/a	230.42B
• Services or feeders to single-phase dwelling unit 100A – 400A allowed to be 83% of service rating **T1**	3603.1.1&2	310.12A&B
☐ Service conductor size min. 100% of noncontinuous load + 125% of continuous load EXC	n/a	230.42A1
• 100% OK if terminating in OCPD & enclosure rated (listed) at 100%	n/a	230.42A1X1
☐ Services supplying only a single circuit min. 15A	3603.2X1	230.79A
☐ Services supplying ≤2 circuits min. 30A	3603.2X1	230.79B
☐ Services supplying >2 circuits min. 60A	3603.2	230.79D
☐ Grounded (neutral) conductor ≥ reqd size of MBJ	3603.1.4	230.23C

NON-DWELLING LOAD CALCULATIONS

See *pp. 243-246* for dwelling load calculations. See *p. 241* for demand factors on the loads below. Loads are expressed in Volt-Amps (VA) rather than in Watts.

General Lighting Loads	20 NEC
☐ Calculate lighting load per **T4** for non-dwelling occupancies	220.12
☐ Areas are calculated from outside dimensions of building	220.11
☐ Motors <⅛hp connected to general lighting circuits are considered part of general lighting load	220.12A[12]
☐ Local energy code values OK as substitute for **T4** if:	220.12B[13]
• Power-monitoring system provides continuous usage data	
• System provides notification if usage exceeds energy code allowance	
• No demand factors applied to general lighting load	
• 125% multiplier for continuous loads is applied	

Other Loads: All Occupancies	
☐ Specific appliance loads based on their ampere rating	220.14A
☐ Dryers or electric cooking in instructional programs – see dwellings	220.14B
☐ Motors—see *p. 310*	220.14C & 220.50
☐ Luminaire ratings based on max. lamping rating of luminaire	220.14D
☐ Heavy-duty lampholders basis min. 600VA	220.14E
☐ Sign & outline lighting basis min. 1200VA per branch circuit	220.14F
☐ Multi-outlet assemblies w/ nonsimultaneous load 180VA per 5 ft.	220.14H1
☐ Multi-outlet assemblies w/ simultaneous load 180VA per 1 ft.	220.14H2
☐ Receptacle outlets 180 VA per each single or multiple receptacle EXC	220.14I
• Optional method for office building receptacles 1VA per sq. ft.	220.14K
☐ Multiple receptacle w/ ≥4 receptacles counts as 90VA each	220.14I
☐ Dwelling units—see *pp. 243-246*	220.14J
☐ Hotels & motels general lighting load in **T4** includes all general use receptacles & all bath, garage & balcony receptacles	220.14M[14]
☐ Calculated load ≥ sum of branch circuit loads after application of demand factors	220.40

12. Small motors do not need to be considered in addition to lighting load.
13. Code now allows greater coordination w/ local energy codes.
14. Clarification on hotel/motel occupancies not reqd to count receptacles separately.

Show Windows & Track Lighting — 20 NEC

- ☐ Show windows min. 200VA/lineal ft. measured horizontally EXC ___ 220.43A
  - Use unit load per outlet if >200VA/lineal foot ___ 220.14G
- ☐ Track lighting min. 150VA per 2 ft. or fraction thereof EXC ___ 220.43B
  - May be based on rating of device limiting current to the track ___ 220.43BX

DEMAND FACTORS

General — 20 NEC

- ☐ Where ≥2 loads are unlikely to be used simultaneously, only the larger load need be included in the load calculation EXC ___ 220.60
  - When the smaller of the 2 loads includes the largest motor in the load calculation, the motor must be calculated at 125% ___ 220.60[15]
- ☐ Calculated load ≥ sum of branch circuit loads after application of demand factors **T5** ___ 220.40
- ☐ Do not use demand factors to determine # of lighting branch circuits ___ 220.42

Non-Dwelling Occupancies

- ☐ Receptacle loads allowed demand factors in **T5** ___ 220.44
- ☐ Demand factors for commercial kitchen equipment (electric cooking, dishwashers, water heaters, etc.) allowed per **T7** EXC ___ 220.56
  - May not be used for space heating, ventilating, or air conditioning ___ 220.56
  - Calculated load can never be less than sum of 2 largest loads ___ 220.56
- ☐ New restaurants permitted to use **T8** in lieu of all other load calcs ___ 220.88

Feeder or Service Neutral Load

- ☐ Load = max. unbalanced load (neutral to ungrounded conductor) ___ 220.61A
- ☐ 70% demand factor allowed for feeder or service as follows: ___ 220.61B
  - Unbalanced load determined by **T12**,**13** for ranges & dryers ___ 220.61B1
  - Unbalanced load > 200A in 4-wire 3-phase system ___ 220.61B2
- ☐ Service or feeder supplying entire load to new restaurants **T8** OK ___ 220.88

15. Clarification that the largest motor load is always 125% even when a noncoincident load.

TABLE 4 — NON-DWELLING LIGHTING LOADS[A] ◆ T220.12

Occupancy	VA per sq. ft.	Occupancy	VA per sq. ft.
Automotive	1.5	Parking Garages	0.3
Convention Center	1.4	Penitentiary	1.2
Courthouse	1.4	Performing Arts Theater	1.5
Dormitory	1.5	Police Station	1.3
Exercise Center	1.4	Post Office	1.6
Fire Station	1.3	Religious Facility	2.2
Gymnasium	1.7	Restaurants & Clubs	1.5
Health Care Clinic	1.6	Retail	1.9
Hospital	1.6	School/University	3.0
Hotels & Motels[B]	1.7	Sports Arena	3.0
Library	1.5	Town Hall	1.4
MFR facility	2.2	Transportation	1.2
Motion Picture Theater	1.6	Warehouse	1.2
Museum	1.6	Workshop	1.7
Offices & Banks	1.6		

A. A multiplier of 125% for continuous loads is added to the values shown here.
B. Includes apartment houses without permanent facilities for cooking.

TABLE 5 — DEMAND FACTORS FOR NON-DWELLING RECEPTACLE LOADS ◆ T220.44

Portion of Load	Demand Factor (%)
1st 10 kVA	100
Amount >10 kVA	50

TABLE 6	LIGHTING LOAD DEMAND FACTORS ◆ T220.42	
Occupancy	Portion of Load (VA)	Demand Factor (%)
Hotels & Motels[A]	1st 20,000	60%
	20,001 – 100,000	50%
	>100,000	35%
Warehouses	First 12,500	100%
	Remainder >12,500	50%
All others	All	100%

A. Does not apply to feeders or services supplying areas such as ballrooms or dining rooms where the entire lighting load is likely to be used at one time.

DETERMINING EXISTING LOADS (COMMERCIAL)

The method shown below can be used to determine if an existing service is capable of supporting additional loads and is often used for large commercial applications.

Determining Existing Loads — 20 NEC

- ☐ Actual max. demand OK in lieu of calculations if all of the following: __ 220.87
  - Max. demand data available for a 1-year period______________220.87(1)
  - Max. demand @125% plus new load ≤ feeder or service ampacity 220.87(2)
  - Feeder OCPD in compliance w/ 240.4 & 230.90 ____________220.87(1)
- ☐ If maximum data for 1-year period not available, calculated load permitted to be based on peak 15-minute demand continuously recorded over 30-day occupied time period & inclusive of larger of heating or cooling load 220.87(1)X
- ☐ These methods not permitted if feeder or service has any renewable energy source (e.g., solar) or employs peak load shaving ________220.87X[16]

TABLE 7	DEMAND FACTORS FOR COMMERCIAL KITCHEN EQUIPMENT ◆ T220.56		
# of Equipment Units	Demand Factor (%)	# of Equipment Units	Demand Factor (%)
1 – 2	100	5	70
3	90	6 & over	65
4	80		

TABLE 8	OPTIONAL CALCULATION FOR NEW RESTAURANT SERVICES & FEEDERS	
Total Connected Load (kVA)	All-Electric Restaurant Calculated Loads (kVA)	Not All-Electric Restaurant Calculated Loads (kVA)
0 – 200	80%	100%
201 – 325	160 + 10% amount >200	200 + 50% amount >200
326 – 800	172.5 + 50% amount >325	262.5+ 45% amount >325
> 800	410+ 50% amount >800	476.3+ 20% amount >800

A. Add all loads, including both heating & cooling, to calculate connected load. Apply demand factor from this table and no other demand factors other than for neutral.

16. New restriction on application of this alternative to calculation of load.

RESIDENTIAL LOAD CALCULATIONS

The "long form," in **T9**, is the most common calculation method for residential services and feeders. Because all potential electrical loads are not used at the same time, the calculation method allows the use of demand factors. In the IRC, this form is used for feeder calculations and **T11** is used for services.

Load Calculation Steps (Long Form) T9 — 20 NEC

1. Determine the sq. ft. area of the residence & multiply by 3VA (exclude garage & covered patios) ________ 220.14J
2. Min. of 2 small-appliance circuits at 1,500VA each ________ 220.52A
3. Each additional small-appliance circuit at 1,500VA ________ 220.52A
4. Minimum 1 laundry circuit at 1,500VA ________ 220.52B
5. Enter total of appliance circuits & general lighting (lines 1–4) ________ 220.42
6. First 3,000VA counted at 100% (carries to right column) ________ T220.42
7. Subtract 3,000 from amount in line 5 & enter difference in middle column. Multiply the middle column amount by 35% & enter in right column ________ T220.42
8. Range loads are calculated at nameplate rating. If a single range is >8,000VA & <12,000VA, it still counts as 8,000VA (8kW); if >12,000VA, add 5% of each additional 1,000VA of nameplate load. Nameplates of a counter-mounted range & up to 2 wall ovens can be added together & computed as if they were 1 range; see **T12**. Enter in right column ________ 220.55
9. Enter dryer circuit at 5,000VA (or nameplate rating if greater) ________ 220.54
10. Enter larger of fixed space heating or AC load ________ 220.60
11. Level II electric vehicle charger (also check MFR specs) ________ MFR

12–17. Enter nameplate ratings of appliances ≥¼ hp that are fixed in place. For appliances rated in amps, multiply amps times voltage to determine watts. If nameplate ratings unknown, use estimates in **T4** ________ 220.53

18. Enter total load of fixed appliances ________ 220.53
19. If there are <4 fixed appliances, enter number from line 19 in right column ________ 220.53
20. If there are ≥4 fixed appliances, multiply line 19 by 75% & enter in right column ________ 220.53
21. Add 25% of the largest motor load. Skip this step if a nameplate-rated AC is largest load; it is already factored into min. conductor ampacity ________ 220.18A
22. Add numbers in third column ________ 220.40
23. Divide line 22 by 240 to find reqd min. amperage ________ 220.40

TABLE 9	RESIDENTIAL LOAD CALCULATIONS IRC T3704.2(1) ◆ NEC 220.14(J)		
General Lighting & Receptacle Loads			
1	Sq. ft. × 3VA		
Small Appliance & Laundry Loads			
2	2 small-appliance circuit	3,000	
3	Additional small appliance		
4	Laundry circuit	1,500	
5	Subtotal		
6	First 3,000VA @ 100%	3,000	3,000
7	Balance @ 35%	× .35	=
Special Appliance Loads			
8	Range	8,000 up to 12kW nameplate	
9	Dryer	5,000 (or nameplate if >)	
10	Heating or AC @ 100%		
11	Level II electric vehicle	9,600	9,600
Appliances Fastened in Place			
12	Water heater		
13	Microwave		
14	Dishwasher		
15	Compactor		
16	Disposer		
17	Other		
18	Subtotal		
19	If <4 appliances, enter line 19 subtotal @100% *or*		
20	If ≥4 appliances, enter line 19 subtotal × 75%		
21	Largest motor (if not AC compressor) × 25%		
22	Total load		
23	Total load ÷ 240V = SERVICE AMPS		

Optional Method T11 (Short Form) — 20 NEC

1. 3VA per ft. (exclude garage & covered patios) ________ 220.82B1
2. Min. 2 small-appliance circuits at 1,500VA each, each additional small-appliance circuit at 1,500VA ________ 220.82B2
3. Min. 1 laundry circuit at 1,500VA ________ 220.82B2
4. Nameplate ratings of fixed appliances (see T10 if ratings not known); these include full nameplate rating of ranges & ovens w/o applying reductions allowed in the "long form" method ________ 220.82B3
5. Enter sum of items 1–4 ________ 220.82B
6. 100% of first 10,000VA ________ 220.82B
7. Subtract line 6 from line 5, multiply by 40% ________ 220.82B
8. Determine largest of the heating or cooling load. When using nameplate rating of heat pumps or AC, multiply "minimum circuit ampacity" times the voltage (240). If only size (tonnage) is known, refer to T10 ____ 220.82C
9. Add numbers in right column & enter total ________ 220.82A
10. Divide by 240 = amperage

TABLE 10 — TYPICAL APPLIANCE LOADS

Use actual nameplate ratings when known. This table is for estimating purposes when appliances are not yet specified.

Appliance	Typical Load (VA)	Appliance	Typical Load (VA)
Central AC	1,500/ton[A]	Electric clothes dryer	5,000
Dishwasher	1,200	Water heater	4,500
Food waste disposer	900	Electric cooktop	3,600
Trash compactor	1,200	Single wall oven	4,800
Microwave	1,500	Double wall oven	8,000
Central furnace	1,000	Pool pump	2,000
Central vacuum	1,500	Well pump	2,000

A. This approximation varies depending on the efficiency of the unit.

TABLE 11 — OPTIONAL DWELLING UNIT CALCULATION — IRC T3602.2 ◆ NEC 220.82

1.	Indoor sq. ft. × 3VA/ft.		
2.	Min. 2 small-appliance circuits @ 1,500VA each	3,000	
3.	Laundry circuit @ 1,500VA	1,500	
4.	Nameplate VA of fixed appliances:		
	Dryer @ 5,000VA		
	Oven(s)		
	Cooktop		
	Water heater		
	Dishwasher		
	Disposer		
	Other		
5.	Subtotal of fixed appliances		
6.	First 10,000VA @ 100%	10,000	10,000
7.	Balance @ 40% (subtract line 6 from line 5)	× .40	=
8.	Largest of heating or cooling load		
8a.	Nameplate rating(s) of air-conditioning & cooling equipment OR		
8b.	Heat pump nameplate if no supplemental electric heat OR		
8c.	Continuous electric thermal storage @ nameplate rating OR		
8d.	100% of heat pump nameplate rating plus 65% of supplemental electric heat or central electric heat OR		
8e.	Space heaters @ 65% of nameplate rating if < 4 units OR		
8f.	Space heaters @ 40% of nameplate rating if ≥ 4 units		
9.	Total load in VA		
10.	Divide by 240 = minimum service rating		

Adding Loads to an Existing Dwelling — 20 NEC

- ☐ If no new heating or AC equipment to be installed, add the following and count the first 8,000W @ 100% & the remainder @ 40%: _____ 220.83A
  - 3W per ft. (exclude garage & covered patios)
  - 1500W for each small-appliance & laundry branch circuit
  - Nameplate rating of all appliances fastened in place, on specific circuits, or permanently connected + nameplate of WH & range/oven + clothes dryer
- ☐ If new heating or AC equipment to be installed, add 100% of the larger of the heating or air conditioning to the above calculation_________ 220.83B

Demand Factors for Household Cooking Equipment

- ☐ Load calculations of cooking appliances rated > 1.75kW permitted to be calculated per **T12** ______________ 220.55
- ☐ Column C used in all cases EXC ______________ T220.55
  - Columns A & B allowable as alternate where applicable _________ T220.55
- ☐ kVA considered equivalent to kW for loads under this section ______ 220.55
- ☐ Where ≥2 single-phase ranges are supplied from a 3-phase 4-wire system, calculate load based on twice the max. number connected between any 2 phases______________ 220.55

T12 Examples:

1. 3 ranges each rated 15kW:
   The column C rating for 3 appliances is 14kW. The appliances are >12kW.
   Add 5% for each kW over 12. 15kW–12kW=3kW. 5% × 3 = 15%.
   Add 15% to the demand kW in Column C for 3 ranges.
   *14kW × 115% = **16.1kW***
2. 4 ranges rated 8kW, 10kW, 14kW & 14kW:
   Add the ratings using 12kW as the min. number. 12+12+14+14=52kW.
   Divide by number of appliances. 52÷4 = 13kW.
   Add 5% for each kW over 12kW.
   Column C for 4 12kW appliances = 17kW.
   *Add 5%: 17kW × 105% = **17.85kW**.*
3. 8kW counter-mounted cooktop + 7kW wall oven:
   *Using column C, load for 2 appliances is **11kW**.*
   Using column B, add these together. 8kW + 7kW = 15kW.
   Apply 65% demand factor.
   *65% × 15kW = **9.75kW**.*

***T12** provides demand factors for electric cooking appliances because the maximum loads are unlikely to be used simultaneously. It is used for both a single dwelling unit and for multifamily dwellings. Column C provides allowable kW ratings, whereas Columns A and B provide percentages of demand factor that can be applied to the nameplate rating of the appliances. Column C is used in most cases. This table can be used for feeder loads and also for loads of individual branch circuits. Note that section 210.19A3 requires branch circuits supplying these appliances to have a rating not less than the load and at least 40A for ranges ≥8¾kW. The table is not used if also applying demand factors of 220.84 (**T14**).*

TABLE 12 — DEMAND FACTORS[A,D] FOR HOUSEHOLD COOKING APPLIANCES RATED >1¾KW ◆ T220.55

Number of Appliances[E]	Demand Factor (%)[C]		Column C Max. Demand kW[B] (not >12kW rating)
	Column A <3.5kW	Column B 3.5kW – 8.75kW	
1	80	80	8
2	75	65	11
3	70	55	14
4	66	50	17
5	62	45	20
6	59	43	21
7	56	40	22
8	53	36	23
9	51	35	24
10	49	34	25

A. Column C to be used in all cases except as otherwise permitted in note C.
B. If multiple ranges have the same rating and are less than 12kW each, use the kW for the number of ranges in Column C. If the ranges are larger than 12kW, increase the demand by 5% for each kW above 12kW. For ranges that are different sizes and are >8¾kW & <27kW, add together their kW ratings (using 12kW as the value for ranges <12kW) and divide by the number of ranges, i.e., base the number on their average kW. If that average is >12kW, add 5% for each kW above 12.
C. For appliances >1¾kW and ≤8¾kW, the nameplate ratings can be added and the demand factor for the number of appliances within each range (Column A or B) can be used.
D. The branch circuit load for a single appliance is permitted to be calculated using this table. If the branch circuit supplies a counter-mounted cooking unit and ≤2 wall ovens, the load is determined by adding the nameplate ratings and treating this total as 1 range. ***See p. 267** regarding taps.*
E. NEC table continues to over 61 appliances. The IRC version of this table only considers 2 appliances.

Multifamily Dwellings 20 NEC

- ☐ Feeder or service load supplying ≥3 dwelling units may be sized w/ demand factors of **T14** provided all the following are met: __ 220.84A
  - No dwelling unit supplied by more than 1 feeder
  - Each unit equipped w/ electric cooking equipment; if not so equipped, then add 8kW of load for each unit
  - Each unit supplied w/ electric heating or air conditioning or both
- ☐ Feeder or service neutral OK sized per max. unbalanced load 220.61 & 220.84A
- ☐ House loads not part of **T14** demand factors ________ 220.84B
- ☐ Calculated load to include: ________ 220.84C
  - 3VA/sq. ft. general lighting & receptacles
  - 15,000VA each small-appliance branch circuit & laundry circuit
  - Nameplate rating of all appliances fastened in place, permanently connected, or located on specific circuit, plus ranges, ovens, cooking units, plus clothes dryers not connected to laundry branch circuit, plus water heaters
  - Larger of air-conditioning or fixed electric space heating load

TABLE 13	DEMAND FACTORS FOR ELECTRIC CLOTHES DRYERS IN DWELLING UNITS ◆ T220.54		
# of Dryers	Demand Factor (%)	# of Dryers	Demand Factor (%)
1–4	100	10	50
5	85	11	47
6	75	12–23	47% minus 1% each dryer over 11
7	65	24–42	35% minus 0.5% each dryer over 23
8	60	43 & over	25
9	55		

Clothes Dryers 20 NEC

- ☐ Load = the larger of 5,000VA or nameplate rating ________ 220.54
- ☐ Demand factors permitted for electric clothes dryers per **T13** ________ 220.54
- ☐ When ≥ 2 single-phase dryers supplied by 3-phase 4-wire system, total load calculated on basis of 2× max. # connected between any 2 phases __ 220.54

2-Family Dwellings

- ☐ If calculated load for 2 dwelling units supplied by single feeder exceeds calculated load per **T14** for 3 such units, lesser of 2 loads permitted _ 220.85
- ☐ Common area branch circuits not OK to supply from individual dwelling unit; loads are counted separately for units & common areas ________ 210.25B

TABLE 14	MULTIFAMILY DWELLING DEMAND FACTORS ◆ T220.84		
Number of Dwelling Units	Demand Factor (%)	Number of Dwelling Units	Demand Factor (%)
3–5	45	28–30	33
6–7	44	31	32
8–10	43	32–33	31
11	42	34–36	30
12–13	41	37–38	29
14–15	40	39–42	28
16–17	39	43–45	27
18–20	38	46–50	26
21	37	51–55	25
22–23	36	56–61	24
24–25	35	≥62	23
26–27	34		

GROUNDING ELECTRODES

Proper grounding & bonding of electrical systems is essential for safety. These two different but related subjects are commonly misunderstood, even by veteran electricians. Connecting the system to earth helps to limit the voltage imposed by lightning, line surges, or accidental contact with higher voltage lines. It stabilizes a system and reduces electrical "noise" on communications systems. Grounding electrodes are the metallic components within the earth to which we connect electrical systems, including one of the current-carrying conductors of the system. Common grounding electrodes in residential construction are metal underground water piping, ground rods, and concrete-encased electrodes. Other types include ground rings, metal plates, metal well casings, listed grounding electrode systems, underground tanks, and the steel frame of a building connected to earth as shown below. Gas piping is not an acceptable grounding electrode.

Grounding Electrode System (GES) F7

	21 IRC	20 NEC
☐ Use all electrodes that are available on premises EXC	3608.1	250.50
• Concrete-encased electrode of existing building need not be included if not accessible w/o disturbing concrete	36081.X	250.50X
☐ Bond all electrodes together to form the GES	3608.1	250.50
☐ Metal underground gas piping systems, aluminum electrodes & pool or spa shell bonding grids not permitted as grounding electrodes	3608.5–7	250.52B

Water Pipe Electrodes

	21 IRC	20 NEC
☐ Use metal water pipe if ≥10 ft. in contact w/ soil F7	3608.1.1	250.52A1
☐ Bond around water meters, filters, pressure regulators & similar equipment	3608.1.1.2	250.53D1
☐ Water pipe cannot be the sole electrode—it must be supplemented by another type of electrode	3608.1.1.2	250.53D2
☐ Metal well casing electrodes req bonding around insulating joints or pipes	3608.1.1	250.52A8

Rod & Plate Electrodes

	21 IRC	20 NEC
☐ Copper-clad rods min. 5/8 in. diameter unless listed	3608.1.4	250.52A5b
☐ Rods min. 8 ft. in contact w/ soil F7	3608.1.4.1	250.53A4
☐ Drive rods vertically & fully below grade EXC	3608.1.4.1	250.53A4
• If bedrock encountered, rod may be buried horizontally 2½ ft. deep or driven at max. 45° angle from vertical	3608.1.4.1	250.53A4
• Rod end & clamps above ground req protection against physical damage	3608.1.4.1	250.53A4
☐ Ferrous plates min. 1/4 in. thick, min. 2 sq. ft. in contact w/ soil	3608.1.5	250.52A7
☐ Plate electrodes min. 30 in. below surface of earth	3608.1.5	250.53A5

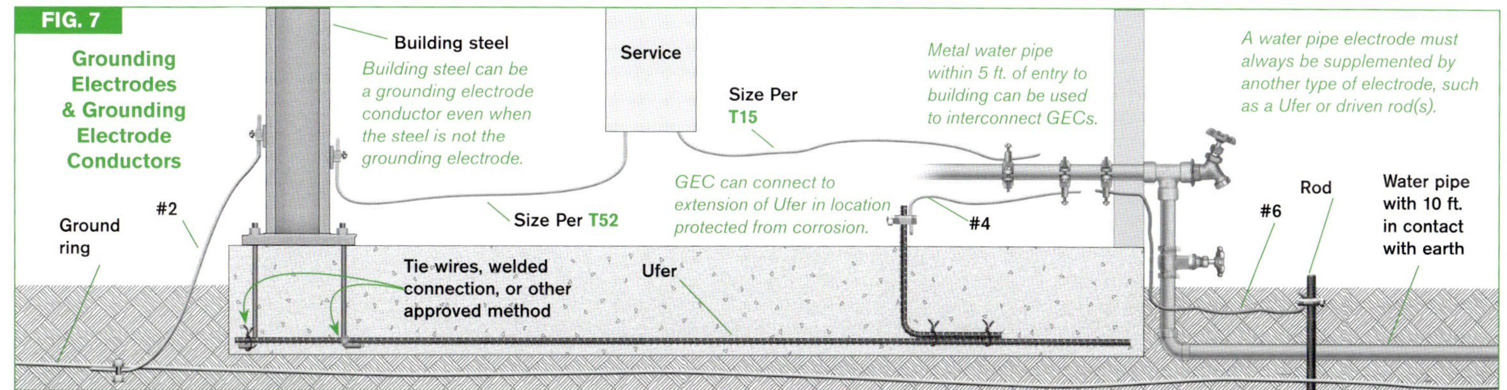

FIG. 7 Grounding Electrodes & Grounding Electrode Conductors

Concrete-Encased Electrode (Ufer) — 21 IRC — 20 NEC

- ☐ Ufer = 20-ft. uncoated rebar or bare Cu wire w/ min. 2-in. encasement in footings or piers in direct earth contact — 3608.1.2 — 250.52A3
- ☐ Min. size rebar #4 or Cu wire #4 — 3608.1.2 — 250.52A3
- ☐ Ufer must be used if present during construction EXC — 3608.1 — 250.50
  - Not reqd to demo concrete in existing building — 3608.1X — 250.50X
- ☐ Shorter sections of rebar can be connected w/ steel tie wires or welding to obtain 20-ft. continuous length **F7** — 3608.1.2 — 250.52A3
- ☐ Where multiple concrete-encased electrodes present, only 1 reqd to be bonded to GES — 3608.1.2 — 250.52A3

Metal In-ground Support Structures

- ☐ Metal support structures w/ ≥10 ft. vertically in direct contact w/ earth & w/ or w/o concrete encasement — n/a — 250.52A4

Ground Ring

- ☐ Min. #2 Cu encircling building or structure w/ min. 20-ft. length in direct contact w/ earth **F7** — 3608.1.3 — 250.52A4
- ☐ Min. 30 in. below surface of earth — 3608.1.3 — 250.53F

Supplemental Electrodes

- ☐ Supplemental rod or plate electrode reqs another supplemental electrode other than water piping EXC — 3608.4 — 250.53A2
  Single rod or plate w/ <25Ω resistance to earth — 3608.4X — 250.53A2X
- ☐ Min. 6-ft. spacing (16-ft. preferred for rods) for multiple rods/plates installed to meet above req — 3608.3 — 250.53A3
- ☐ Supplemental electrode bond to one of the following: — 3608.3 — 250.53A3
  1. A rod, pipe, or plate electrode
  2. A grounding electrode conductor
  3. A grounded service conductor
  4. A nonflexible grounded service raceway
  5. A grounded service enclosure

Other Electrodes

- ☐ Local metal underground systems, such as tanks — n/a — 250.52A8
- ☐ Listed grounding electrode systems — 3608.1.6 — 250.52A6

An example of this last item would be an electrolyte-filled rod installed in a drilled hole with a specified type of backfill in accordance with the listing of the system.

GROUNDING ELECTRODE CONDUCTORS (GECs)

The GEC connecting the grounding electrodes to the electrical system must have adequate size and protection. Individual GECs can be run to each electrode of the GES, or a single GEC can be run to one of them provided it is of adequate size and the other GECs are connected to it by bonding conductors that form the GES.

Size — 21 IRC — 20 NEC

- ☐ Size GEC per service conductor size **T15** EXC — 3603.4 — 250.66
  - #6 Cu or #4 AL is largest size needed if connecting only to single or multiple rod or plate electrodes — T3603.4 — 250.66A
  - #4 Cu largest size needed if ending at Ufer — T3603.4 — 250.66B
  - #2 Cu largest size needed if ending at ground ring — n/a — 250.66C
- ☐ Size GEC per largest reqd size among all electrodes in the GES — T3603.4 — 250.64F
- ☐ Size bonding conductors of GES per GEC above rules — 250.53C

TABLE 15 — GEC SIZING[A,B] ◆ IRC T3603.4 NEC 250.66

Service-Entrance Conductor (AWG)		GEC (AWG)	
Cu	AL	Cu	AL
≤#2	≤1/0	8	6
#1 or 1/0	2/0 or 3/0	6	4
2/0 or 3/0	4/0 or 250kcmil	4	2
4/0 to 350kcmil	>250kcmil to 500kcmil	2	1/0
>350kcmil to 600kcmil	>500kcmil to 900kcmil	1/0	3/0
> 600 to 1100kcmil	>900kcmil to 1,750kcmil	2/0	4/0
>1100kcmil	>1750kcmil	3/0[C]	250kcmil[C]

A. If multiple (paralleled) sets of service-entrance conductors, equivalent size of largest service-entrance conductor is determined by the largest sum of the areas of each set.
B. Where there are no service-entrance conductors yet installed, size is determined by the equivalent size of the largest service-entrance conductor required for the load served.
C. Largest required GEC regardless of service. See **T52** for sizes of main bonding jumpers.

GEC Connection Locations: General

	21 IRC	20 NEC
☐ GEC connects EGCs, service equipment, & service neutral to the grounding electrodes	3607.4	250.24D
☐ Connect GEC to service neutral at any accessible point from load end of service drop to neutral bus in service disconnect	3607.2	250.24A1
☐ No splices between service & GES EXC	3610.1	250.64C
• Listed irreversible compression connectors or exothermic welding	3610.1	250.64C
☐ No bare or covered AL or Cu-clad AL GECs w/o polymeric covering where subject to corrosion or in direct contact w/ concrete	3610.2[17]	250.64A[17]
☐ AL or Cu-clad AL GECs not to be terminated ≤18 in. above earth outdoors EXC	3610.2	250.64A
• Within listed outdoor enclosures	3610.2[18]	250.64A[18]
☐ Connections must be accessible EXC	3611.2	250.68A
• Buried or encased connections	3611.2	250.68AX1

GEC Connections to Electrodes

	21 IRC	20 NEC
☐ GEC can connect to any GES electrode when other electrodes interconnected by bonding jumpers to form the GES	3610.1	250.64F1
☐ Individual GECs can connect to electrodes in GES	3610.1	250.64F2
☐ GECs can connect at common bus that is securely fastened, accessible & min. ¼ in. thick & min. 2 in. wide	n/a	250.64F3
☐ Interior metal water pipe OK as means to extend the GES connection or to interconnect other electrodes only within 1st 5 ft. from entrance into building **F7**	3611.4	250.68C1
☐ Metal structural building frame OK to interconnect GECs	n/a	250.68C2
☐ Hold-down bolts of metal structural columns can be connection to Ufer w/ tie wires, welding, or other means **F7**	n/a	250.68C2
☐ Ufer bar extended through foundation OK as connection point for GEC if accessible & not subject to corrosion **F7**	3611.5	250.68C3
☐ Ufer not OK for interconnection of GECs	3611.5[19]	250.68C3[19]

17. Previous edition prohibited such conductors when bare and in contact w/ earth or corrosive conditions.
18. Previous edition prohibited any termination of AL GEC within 18 in. of earth, including within enclosures.
19. New limitation preventing the use of Ufer as bonding conductor to interconnect electrodes.

Connection Methods

	21 IRC	20 NEC
☐ Buried clamps L&L for direct burial (marked "DB")	3611.1	250.70
☐ Cu water tubing clamps L&L for Cu tubing	3611.1	250.70
☐ Ufer clamps L&L for rebar & encasement	3611.1	250.70
☐ Listed sheet-metal strap-type clamps suitable only for indoor telecommunications	3611.1	250.70
☐ Max. 1 conductor per clamp unless listed for more	3611.1	250.70
☐ Connections dependent on solder not allowed	3611.1	250.8B
☐ Remove nonconductive coatings (e.g., paint, enamel & lacquer) from contact surfaces to ensure electrical continuity	3611.7	250.12

Protection F8,9,13,14

	21 IRC	20 NEC
☐ #8 GEC reqs protection by raceway or armor	T3603.4	250.64B3
☐ >#8 GECs not exposed to damage do not req protection	T3603.4	250.64B1
☐ GECs subject to physical damage req protection w/ RMC IMC, PVC 80, RTRC, EMT, or cable armor	T3603.4[20]	250.64B2[20]
☐ Bond each end of ferrous raceways enclosing GECs to the enclosure or electrode or to the GEC	3610.3	250.64E1
☐ Bonding methods same as supply-side bonding	3610.3	250.64E2
☐ Bonding jumper same size as enclosed GEC **F12**	3610.3	250.64E2
☐ Clamps & other fittings protected from physical damage by location or enclosures if not approved for applications w/o protection	3611.6	250.10

FIG. 8

Armor-clad GEC

#8 GEC

Clamp bonds metal sheath to GEC.

#8 requires protection from physical damage.

FIG. 9

#6 GEC

"Acorn" clamp

Unprotected GEC

Securely fastened conductors ≥#6 permitted on building surfaces without additional protection.

20. PVC protective conduit must now be Schedule 80.

BONDING

Bonding ensures electrical continuity to limit voltage potential between conductive components. On the *supply side* (ahead of the main disconnect **F17**), it provides a path back to the utility transformer for faults on service conductors and also limits voltage potential to other systems, such as telephones or cable TV. On the *load side* (after the main overcurrent protection), bonding and equipment grounding provide a path to clear faults and protect against shocks.

Bonding & Equipment Grounding Methods

Bonding & Equipment Grounding Methods	21 IRC	20 NEC
☐ Permitted connection methods for GECs, EGCs & bonding jumpers include listed pressure connectors, terminal bars, exothermic welding, machine screws engaging at least 2 threads or secured w/ nut **F10**, thread-forming machine screws w/ at least 2 threads in the enclosure **F10**, connections that are part of a listed assembly & other listed means	3406.14.1	250.8A
☐ No sheet-metal or drywall screws **F10**	3406.14.1	250.8A
☐ Connections may not depend solely on solder	3406.14.2	250.8B
☐ Clean nonconductive coatings from contact surfaces **F10**	3908.18	250.12

FIG. 10 Grounding & Bonding Methods

Machine screws engaging min. 2 threads OK; sheet-metal screws and drywall screws NOT OK

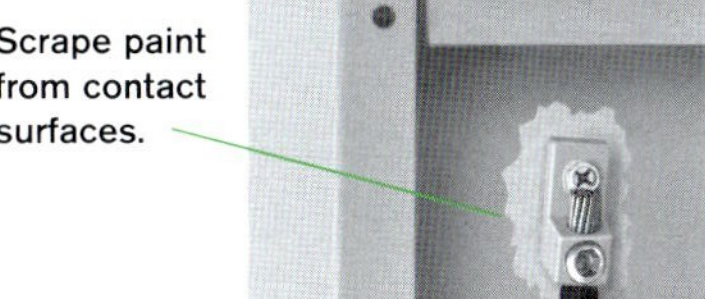

Scrape paint from contact surfaces.

Bonding for over 250 Volts

Bonding for over 250 Volts	20 NEC
☐ Circuits over 250V to ground req bonding of raceways & metal-sheathed cables by same methods **F11,12** as supply-side bonding (but not connection to grounded conductor) EXC	250.97
• Boxes w/ concentric or eccentric KOs listed for bonding	250.97X
• Threadless couplings & connectors for metal-sheathed cables	250.97X
• 2 locknuts on RMC (1 inside & 1 outside) on metal boxes/cabinets	250.97X
• Fittings w/ firmly seated shoulders & locknuts inside box	250.97X
• Listed fittings	250.97X

Supply-Side Bonding F11,12

Supply-Side Bonding **F11,12**	21 IRC	20 NEC
☐ Bond all service equipment, raceways, cable armor & enclosures that contain service conductors	3609.2	250.92A
☐ Threaded couplings or listed threaded hubs made wrenchtight OK for bonding service conduit	3609.4.3	250.92B2
☐ Standard locknuts not OK on supply side of service	3609.4.3	250.92B
☐ Bonding locknuts OK if no remaining concentric KOs **F11**	3609.4.4	250.92B4
☐ Jumpers reqd around impaired connections (concentric KOs or reducing washers) on supply side of service **F12**	3609.4.4	250.92B
☐ Service neutral can bond supply-side equipment	n/a	250.142A
☐ Size supply-side bonding jumpers per **T15**	3609.5	250.102C
☐ Service enclosure main bonding jumper must connect enclosure, service neutral & equipment grounds **F17,19**	3607.5	250.24B
☐ Bond lightning protection systems to the GES	n/a	250.106

FIG. 11 Bonding Fittings when no Concentric Knockouts Remain

FIG. 12 Bonding at Impaired Connections

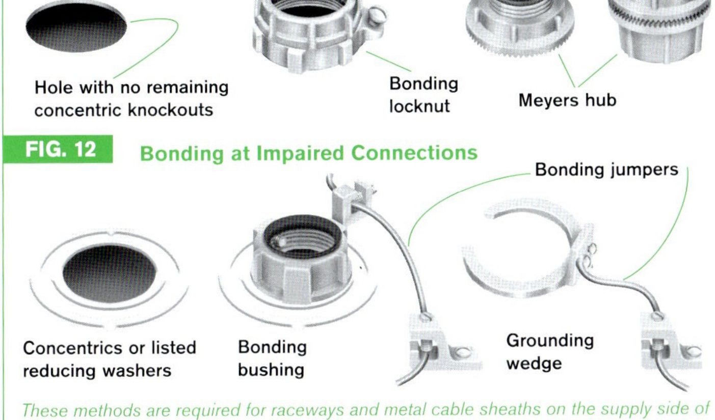

These methods are required for raceways and metal cable sheaths on the supply side of services at all voltages and on the load side of services for systems over 250V to ground. Threaded couplings or hubs, or threadless couplings made up tight, are also suitable.

Bonding Other Enclosures

	21 IRC	20 NEC
☐ Bond metal enclosures of conductors, devices & equipment to the EGC EXC	3908.1	250.86
• Short sections of protective metal raceways	3908.1X1	250.86X2
• Metallic components in run of underground nonmetallic conduit where isolated by 18 in. of cover or by 2 in. of concrete	3908.1X1	250.86X2
☐ Bond metal raceways, cable armor, cable sheath, enclosures, frames & fittings that serve as EGCs	3908.19	250.96A
☐ Remove nonconductive coatings before adding bonding jumpers or use fittings that make such removal unnecessary	3908.19	250.96A
☐ Structural metal building frame reqs bonding sized to **T52** to service enclosure, grounded service conductor, GEC of sufficient size, or disconnecting means for building supplied by feeder	n/a	250.104C

Bonding of Piping Systems

	21 IRC	20 NEC
☐ Size water pipe bonding per **T15** EXC	3609.6	250.104A1
• Metal systems of individual units of multifamily that are isolated by plastic from other units can be bonded to EGC of panel for that unit	n/a	250.104A2
☐ Bond any metal piping system capable of becoming energized, including gas, metal ducts, etc.	3609.7	250.104
☐ Size gas pipe bonding per **T16**	3609.7	250.104B
☐ Gas may be bonded by EGC of circuit that is capable of energizing the piping	3609.7	250.104B
☐ Bond metal well casings to EGC of pump motor	3908.3(2)	250.112M

Intersystem Bonding F15

	21 IRC	20 NEC
☐ If separate electrodes installed for phone/CATV, min. #6 bond reqd to power GES	n/a	800.100D
☐ IBT device reqd external to service equipment & at disconnecting means of separate buildings EXC	3609.3.1	250.94A
• If communications systems unlikely to be used	3609.3.1X	250.94X
☐ IBT must be accessible for connection & inspection	3609.3.1(1)	250.94A1
☐ Min. 3 terminals for intersystem bond conductors	3609.3.1(2)	250.94A2
☐ IBT not to interfere w/ opening the enclosure cover	3609.3.1(3)	250.94A3
☐ Mount IBT to meter or service enclosure or nonflexible metal service raceway, or connect w/ #6 Cu from IBT to one of those enclosures	3609.3.(4)	250.94A4
☐ Mount IBT to disconnecting means for other buildings or connect w/ #6 Cu from IBT to disconnecting means	3609.3.(5)	250.94A5
☐ IBT reqs listing as grounding & bonding equipment	3609.3.(6)	250.94A6
☐ IBT not reqd in existing buildings if other system GECs can be bonded to a nonflexible raceway or exposed GEC	n/a	250.94AX
☐ IBT can be AL or Cu busbar min. ¼ in. thick × 2 in. × sufficient length for ≥3 terminations for communications systems **F22**	3609.3.2	250.94B

FIG. 15

Intersystem Bonding Termination (IBT)

The IBT can be attached directly to the service enclosure or connect with a #6 copper bond wire to a terminal inside the service enclosure or a tap on the grounding electrode conductor.

Electrical service
Telephone
Bond wires min. #14 Cu
Cable TV
Grounding electrode system
Min. #6 Cu bond
Intersystem bonding termination with at least 3 IBT terminals

EQUIPMENT GROUNDING CONDUCTORS (EGCs)

Equipment grounding provides a low-impedance path so the overcurrent device will open the circuit in a fault. The purpose of equipment grounding is completely different than that of earth grounding; earth plays no part in helping clear faults.

Purpose & Routing — 21 IRC — 20 NEC

- ☐ Effective ground-fault current path must be established _3908.4 250.4A5
- ☐ Earth is not an effective ground-fault current path ______3908.5 250.4A5
- ☐ GEC not to be used as an EGC EXC ____________________ n/a 250.121A
  - Where meeting reqs for both & no objectionable current__ n/a 250.121AX
- ☐ Metal building frame or structure not allowed as EGC _____ n/a 250.121B[21]
- ☐ EGCs must run w/ other conductors of circuit EXC____3908.10 250.134
  - Replacement of nongrounding receptacles (*see* ***p. 298***) _____ 250.130C

Types & Identification of EGCs

- ☐ Wire EGCs can be Cu, AL, Cu-clad AL, solid or stranded, bare, covered, or insulated, ____________________ 3908.9(1) 250.118
- ☐ Conductors ≤#6 must be bare or factory insulated w/ green (or green w/ yellow stripes)________________ 3407.2 250.119
- ☐ Conductors ≥#4 OK bare for entire exposed length, or use green tape or labels encircling the conductor at each end and at every point where the conductor is accessible ___ 3407.2 250.119A
- ☐ Green never OK for neutral or ungrounded conductors _ 3407.2 250.119
- ☐ RMC, IMC, EMT, AC cable armor, electrically continuous raceways & surface metal raceways OK as EGC EXC __3908.9 250.118
  - Wire EGC reqd in outdoor raceways w/ compression-type fittings when supplying rooftop air conditioning __________ n/a 440.9
- ☐ Raceways & cable armor as EGC must approved fittings; all joints, fittings & connections to be made tight _____ 3908.12 250.120A
- ☐ FMC as EGC w/ listed fittings, max. 20A OCPD, max. length of FMC & LFMC in same fault-current path ≤6 ft., max. trade size 1 1/4 in. & no vibration or flexibility after installation **F45**_ 3908.9.1 250.118
- ☐ LFMC same as FMC & 60A OCPD allowable in trade sizes 3/4–1 1/4 **F44** ______________________ 3908.9.2 250.118

21. Reorganization of material that had been in 250.136. Building can be used as a GEC but not as an EGC.

Size — 21 IRC — 20 NEC

- ☐ Size EGCs per **T16** __________________________ 3908.13 250.122A
- ☐ When multiple circuits in same raceway, single EGC OK based on largest OCPD of conductors in raceway ________3908.13.1 250.122C
- ☐ If ungrounded conductors increased in size for other than derating, EGCs must be increased in size proportionately __________ n/a 250.122B[22]

TABLE 16 — MIN. EQUIPMENT GROUNDING CONDUCTOR (EGC) SIZE
IRC T3908.13 ◆ NEC T250.122

Max. Rating of OCPD (Amps)	Size of Cu EGC (AWG)	Size of AL EGC (AWG)
15	14	12
20	12	10
25–60	10	8
70–100	8	6
110–200	6	4
225–300	4	2
400	3	1
500	2	1/0
600	1	2/0
800	1/0	3/0
1000	2/0	4/0
1200	3/0	250 kcmil
1600	4/0	350 kcmil

22. Clarification that increases in size of EGC not needed for increased conductor sizes as a result of ambient temperature or conductor proximity. It still must be increased in size if the ungrounded conductors are upsized for voltage drop.

EGCs in Boxes

	21 IRC	20 NEC
☐ Splices req devices listed for the purpose **F16** ______	3406.11	110.14B
☐ Spliced conductors in box do not req insulation ______	3908.14	250.148A
☐ EGCs of spliced conductors must all be connected within the box or to the box **F16** EXC ______	3908.14	250.148
• Isolated ground receptacles ______	(n/a)	250.148X
☐ Removal of device in box cannot interrupt EGC continuity (use pigtails to devices) **F16** ______	3908.14	250.148B
☐ Connection used for no other purpose reqd for connection of EGCs to metal box **F16** ______	3908.16[23]	250.148C[23]

EGCs to Receptacles in Boxes

	21 IRC	20 NEC
☐ Equipment bonding jumper sized to **T16** reqd for connecting receptacle to metal box EXC ______	3908.15	250.146
• Direct metal contact between device yoke & surface-mounted metal box permitted if ≥1 insulating washer removed	3908.15	250.146A
• Listed exposed-work covers where device secured by ≥2 thread-locking or screw-&-nut locking means or by rivets __	3908.15	250.146A
• Self-grounding yoke & supporting screws (captive metal screw w/o insulating washer) OK for flush-mounted boxes _	3908.15	250.146B
• Floor boxes listed as providing continuity to box ____	3908.15	250.146C

Use of Grounded Conductor for Equipment Grounding

	21 IRC	20 NEC
☐ May connect to noncurrent-carrying metal parts of equipment on the supply side or within the service disconnecting means __	3908.6	250.142A
☐ Allowed in main disconnect of separate existing buildings using exception to the requirement for separate EGC in feeder (*p. 238*) _	3908.6	250.142A
☐ Not OK for grounding load-side equipment EXC ____	3908.7&8	250.142B
• Existing ranges & dryers w/ min. #10 Cu or #8 AL if neutral insulated or part of SE cable & originates at service equipment _____	n/a	250.142BX1

FIG. 16

Box Grounding Methods

Listed splicing devices (barrel crimps, push-in connectors, twist-on connectors) must also be listed for bonding.

Connect all equipment grounding connectors inside box.

A machine screw used for no other purpose connects the EGCs to the box. Sheet-metal screws or box attachment screws or nails NOT OK.

Continuity must be maintained if device is removed.

Isolated Ground Receptacles

	20 NEC
☐ Insulated EGC from isolated ground receptacles permitted to not be bonded to box ______	250.146D
☐ Insulated EGC allowed to pass through panelboards w/o connections to equipment ground bus ______	250.146D
☐ Metal boxes & raceways of isolated ground receptacle circuit reqd to be connected to an EGC ______	250.146D
☐ Orange triangle identification reqd on receptacle face ______	406.3D
☐ Identified isolated ground receptacles not allowed for nonisolated ground installations ______	406.3D
☐ Isolated ground receptacles in nonmetallic boxes req nonmetallic faceplate or metal faceplate that connects to an EGC ______	406.3D

23. Prior code specified that the connection was a grounding screw.

PANELBOARDS & CABINETS

What we commonly call an "electrical panel" is referred to as a panelboard (NEC 408) inside a cabinet (NEC 312) See *p. 237* for working-space requirements. Panels that distribute power to branch circuits are often referred to as load centers.

Clearances & Location	**21 IRC**	**20 NEC**
☐ OCPDs readily accessible	3705.7	240.24A
☐ Max. height of operating handle of breaker 6 ft. 7 in. AFF	3705.7	240.24A
☐ Not allowed where subject to physical damage	3705.7	240.24C
☐ Not near easily ignitable material such as clothes closet	3705.7	240.24D
☐ Not in bathrooms of dwellings, dormitories, or guest rooms	3705.7	240.24E
☐ Not allowed over steps of a stairway	3705.7	240.24F
Dry, Damp & Wet Locations		
☐ Wet or damp location enclosures weatherproof **T17**	3907.2	312.2
☐ Surface-mounted metal enclosures in wet or damp locations req min. ¼-in. airspace between enclosure & wall	3907.2	312.2
☐ In wet locations, raceways & cables entering above level of uninsulated live parts req fittings listed for wet locations	3907.2	312.2
☐ Equipment rated for dry or damp locations must be protected against damage from weather during construction	3404.5	110.11
☐ Enclosures req marking with enclosure type **T17**	3404.4	110.28
☐ Equipment rated for dry or damp locations or "indoor use only" or enclosure types 1, 2, 5, 12, 12K & 13 must be protected against damage from weather during construction	3404.5	110.11
Enclosures (Cabinets)		
☐ Max. setback in noncombustible wall (e.g., steel studs) ¼ in.	3907.3	312.3
☐ Flush to finish surface in combustible (wood-frame) wall	3907.3	312.3
☐ Max. plaster gap at side of flush-mount panel ⅛ in.	3907.4	312.4
☐ Enclosures for OCPDs to be in vertical position	n/a	240.33
☐ Panelboards may not be installed in face-up position	n/a	408.43[24]
☐ Open KOs durably filled EXC	3404.6	110.12A
• MFR holes such as those for mounting do not req fill	3907.5	110.12A

24. Panels cannot be installed in a face-up position; in the 2023 NEC, face-down orientation also prohibited.

TABLE 17 — ENCLOSURE SELECTION ◆ IRC T3404.4 NEC T110.28

Provides a Degree of Protection Against the Following Environmental Conditions	Outdoor Use Enclosure Types and Numbers[A]									
	3	3R	3S	3X	3RX	3SX	4	4X	6	6P
Incidental contact with the enclosed equipment	✓	✓	✓	✓	✓	✓	✓	✓	✓	✓
Rain, snow, and sleet	✓	✓	✓	✓	✓	✓	✓	✓	✓	✓
Sleet	–	–	✓	–	–	✓	–	–	–	–
Windblown dust	✓	–	✓	✓	–	✓	✓	✓	✓	✓
Hosedown	–	–	–	–	–	–	✓	✓	✓	✓
Corrosive agents	–	–	–	✓	✓	✓	–	✓	–	✓
Provides a Degree of Protection Against the Following Environmental Conditions	**Indoor Use Enclosure Types and Numbers[A]**									
	1	2	4	4X	5	6	6P	12	12K	13
Incidental contact with the enclosed equipment	✓	✓	✓	✓	✓	✓	✓	✓	✓	✓
Falling dirt	✓	✓	✓	✓	✓	✓	✓	✓	✓	✓
Falling liquids and light splashing	–	✓	✓	✓	✓	✓	✓	✓	✓	✓
Circulating dust, lint, fibers, and flyings	–	✓	✓	✓	–	✓	✓	✓	✓	✓
Settling airborne dust, lint, fibers, and flyings	–	–	✓	✓	✓	✓	✓	✓	✓	✓
Hosedown	–	–	✓	✓	–	✓	✓	–	–	–

A. The term "raintight" is used with types 3, 3S, 3SX, 3X 4, 4X, 6, and 6P. The term "rainproof" is used with types 3R and 3X. The term "watertight" is used with types 4, 4X, 6, and 6P. The term "driptight" is used with types 2, 5, 12, 12K, and 13. The term "dusttight" is used with enclosure types 3, 3S, 3SX, 3X, 5, 12, 12K &13. Enclosure type ratings are derived from NEMA standards. See codes for full table.

Overcurrent Protection Devices (OCPDs)	21 IRC	20 NEC
☐ Breakers must be listed or classified AMI for panel _____	3403.3	110.3B
☐ Backfed breakers secured in place EXC _____________	3706.5	408.36D
• Output circuits from listed utility interactive inverters _____	n/a	705.12E
☐ Breakers must indicate whether off or on _____________	n/a	240.81
☐ If breaker operates vertically, up must = "ON" ___________	n/a	240.81
☐ 2-pole breaker or 2 single-pole breakers w/ approved handle ties reqd for receptacles on shared yoke or mounting strap __	n/a	210.7

*(see **pp. 265–266** for conductor ampacity)*

FIG. 17

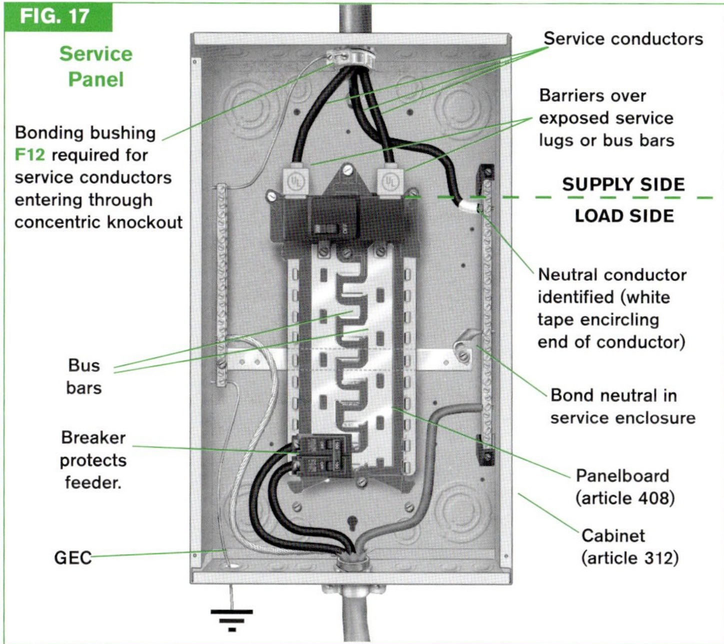

Conductors on the utility side of the service are referred to as being on the "supply side" (sometimes referred to as the "line side"), and the conductors after the service are on the "load side." In most cases (and all residential services), one of the conductors being brought to the service equipment is a grounded conductor that carries current. After the service, this grounded (neutral) conductor should not be re-grounded or bonded to enclosures as objectionable current will also take the paths of that grounding and bonding.

FIG. 18

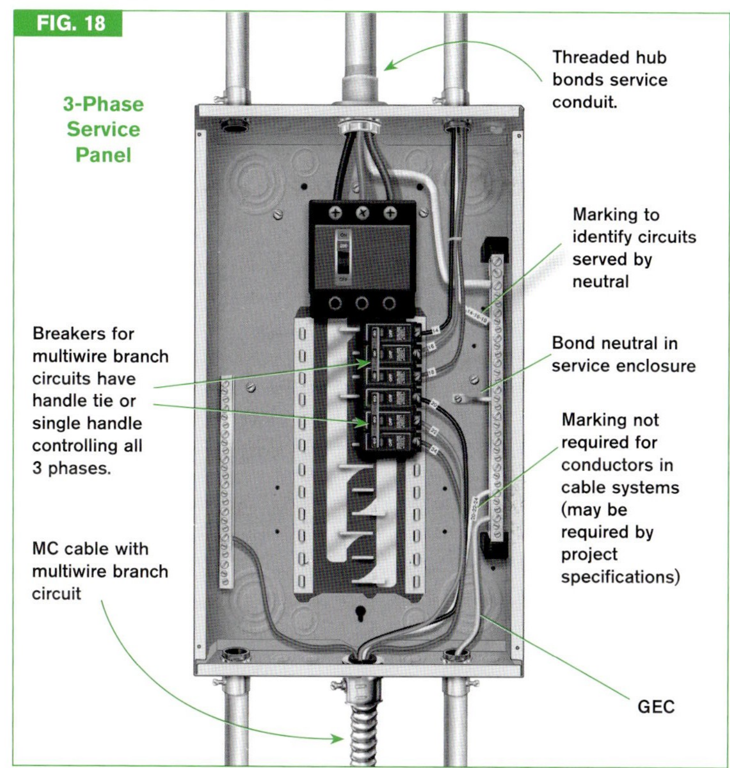

FIG. 19

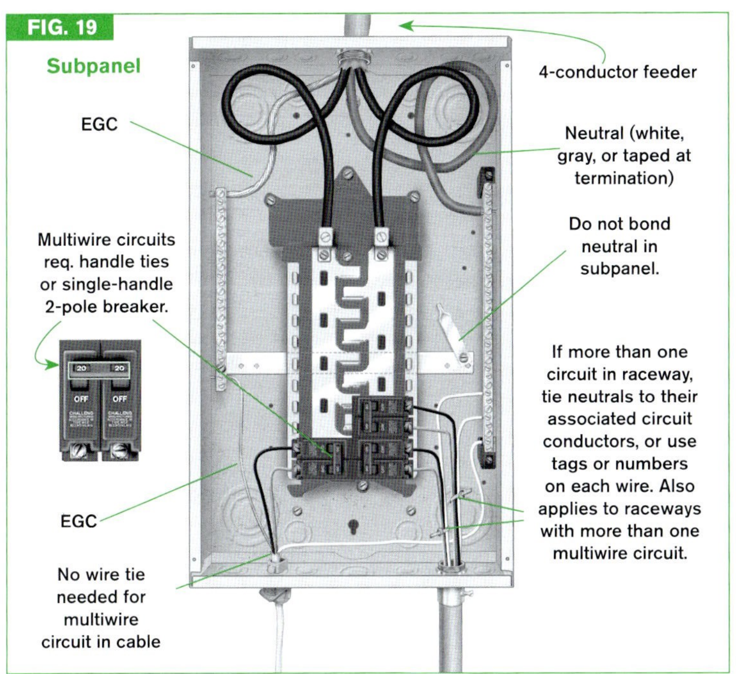

If the subpanel above were located in a separate building, one more conductor type would be present—a grounding electrode conductor (GEC).

Bus Bars

	21 IRC	20 NEC
☐ Protect bus bars & other internal parts from contamination (paint or plaster) during construction	3404.7	110.12B
☐ Bus reqs overcurrent protection on supply side EXC **F19**	3706.3	408.36
• Existing services for individual residential occupancy	n/a	408.36X2[25]

Covers & Circuit Directories

	21 IRC	20 NEC
☐ In other than 1&2FD, each panel supplied by a feeder reqs durable label (not hand-written) w/ origin where power originates	n/a	408.4B
☐ Dead-front cover reqd	n/a	408.38
☐ Breaker handle does not have to be behind a door	3705.9	240.40B
☐ Circuit directories to distinguish each circuit from all others	3706.2	408.4A
☐ Circuit description not dependent on transient conditions	3706.2	408.4A
☐ Label spare positions containing unused OCPDs	3706.2	408.4A
☐ Install fill plates in missing twist-outs that have no breakers	3907.5	110.12A
☐ No empty Edison-base fuse sockets	3907.5	110.12A

Panel Wiring

	21 IRC	20 NEC
☐ Only 1 wire per terminal unless identified for >1	3406.10	110.14A
(panel instructions may allow 2 or 3 EGCs per terminal)		
☐ Each neutral reqs its own individual terminal EXC	3706.4	408.41
• Paralleled conductors on terminal identified for >1	3706.4	408.41
☐ EGCs & neutrals may not share same terminal, even in service equipment where they are allowed on same terminal bar	3706.4	408.41
☐ Torque all breakers & terminals AMI	3403.3	110.3B
☐ Use approved means to achieve indicated torque	3406.12[26]	110.14D[26]
☐ Antioxidant on AL conductors AMI	3403.3	110.14
☐ Secure each cable to cabinet or enclosure **F17–19**	3907.8	312.5C

High-Leg Delta Systems

	20 NEC
☐ On 4-wire Delta-connected system w/ midpoint of one phase grounded, phase conductor w/ higher voltage to ground **F89** marked orange at each point where a connection is made if grounded conductor also present	110.15
☐ Panel phase arrangement A, B, C from left to right, B phase to be the phase w/ higher voltage to ground EXC	408.3E1
• OK to have same arrangement as metering within same panelboard or switchboard section as metering equipment (typically on C)	408.3E1X
☐ Each switchboard or panel to have permanent label stating "Caution _____ Phase has _____ Volts to Ground"	408.3E2
☐ "Slash rated" breakers, such as 120/240, not to be used if lower rating is less than the highest voltage to ground in the panel	240.85

25. Removed exemption for new services w/ >1 main.

26. Clarification that means other than calibrated torque tool can be approved.

Neutral Conductors & EGCs

Neutral Conductors & EGCs	21 IRC	20 NEC
☐ Bond neutral, EGCs & enclosure in service panels **F17**	3607.5	250.24B
☐ Do not bond neutrals in subpanels **F19**	3908.7	250.24A5
☐ Continuity of neutrals not to depend on enclosures	3406.13	200.2B
☐ Each neutral conductor reqs individual terminal EXC	3706.4	408.41
• Paralleled conductors in terminal identified for >1	3706.4	408.41X
☐ Neutral cannot serve more than one circuit or MWBC circuit	n/a	200.4A
☐ Neutrals factory-applied white or grey EXC	3407.1	200.6A
• Conductors ≥#4 white or grey tape encircling ends	3407.1	200.6B
☐ White not OK on ungrounded conductors EXC	3407.3	200.7A
• White conductors of a cable assembly OK as ungrounded conductors w/ tape (not white, gray, or green) encircling ends	3407.3X	200.7C
☐ Grounding terminal bar reqd if wire EGCs present **F19**	n/a	408.40
☐ EGCs not on neutral bar in subpanels	3908.7	250.24A5
☐ >1 EGC per terminal OK if allowed by L&L of panel	3403.3	110.14A
☐ OCPDs not allowed in series w/ neutral EXC	3705.5	240.22
• When OCPD simultaneously opens all other conductors of circuit or where reqd for motor overload protection	n/a	240.22

Multiwire Branch Circuits (MWBC) F20

Multiwire Branch Circuits (MWBC)	21 IRC	20 NEC
☐ Ungrounded conductors must have voltage potential between them, i.e., not originate from same pole	3501	100
☐ All MWBC conductors must originate from same panel	3701.5	210.4A
☐ Identify **F18,19** or group each neutral w/ ungrounded conductors of the circuit EXC	3701.5.2	200.4B
• When grouping is obvious, such as a cable system	3701.5.2X	200.4BX1
• When passing through a box w/ no loop or splice	3701.5.2X	200.4BX2
☐ Continuity of neutral not to depend on connected device (Pigtail from neutral to devices in box; not feed-through. Connect neutral to device as in **F37** not as in **F16**)	3406.11.2	300.13B
☐ All MWBCs req handle ties or single handle breaker	3701.5.1	210.4B
☐ Individual single-pole breakers w/ approved handle tie OK for multiwire circuits that serve only line-to-neutral loads	n/a	240.15B1

FIG. 20 Multiwire Circuits

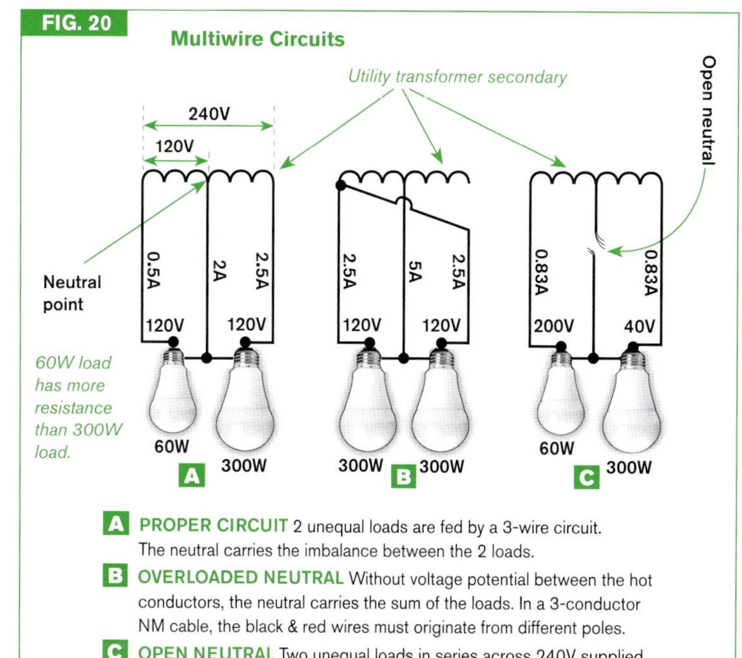

A PROPER CIRCUIT 2 unequal loads are fed by a 3-wire circuit. The neutral carries the imbalance between the 2 loads.

B OVERLOADED NEUTRAL Without voltage potential between the hot conductors, the neutral carries the sum of the loads. In a 3-conductor NM cable, the black & red wires must originate from different poles.

C OPEN NEUTRAL Two unequal loads in series across 240V supplied from the transformer. The highest resistance (the 60W load) sees the highest proportion of the voltage drop. Voltage at each load depends on other loads and is unstable.

In 120/208V systems, the neutral of a 120V circuit always carries current. The principles here still apply; the neutral stabilizes voltage and limits voltage to ground to 120V.

WIRING SPACE OPPOSITE TERMINALS

TABLE 18	MINIMUM WIRING SPACE OPPOSITE TERMINALS WIRE SIZES[A] & REQD DISTANCES (INCHES) ◆ 312.6				
L Bends—Wire not through wall opposite terminal (A)			(B) S Bends—Wire through wall opposite terminal		
Cu Wire	AL Wire[B]	Distance[3]	Cu Wire	AL Wire[B]	Distance[C]
14–10	12 –8	n/a	14 – 10	12 –8	n/a
8–6	6 –4	1½	8	6	1½
4–3	2 –1	2	6	4	2
2	1/0	2½	4	2	3
1	2/0	3	3	1	3
1/0–2/0	3/0–4/0	3½	2	1/0	3½
3/0–4/0	250–300	4	1	2/0	4½
250	350	4½	1/0	3/0	5½
300–350	400–500	5	2/0	4/0	6
400–500	600–750	6	3/0	250	6½
600–700	800–1000	8	4/0	300	7

A. Based on 1 wire per terminal or >1 wire for sizes up to #1 Cu or #2/0 AL.
B. Compact stranded aluminum conductors using AA-8000 series alloys.
C. The distance is measured in a straight line from the lug in a direction perpendicular to the panel wall.

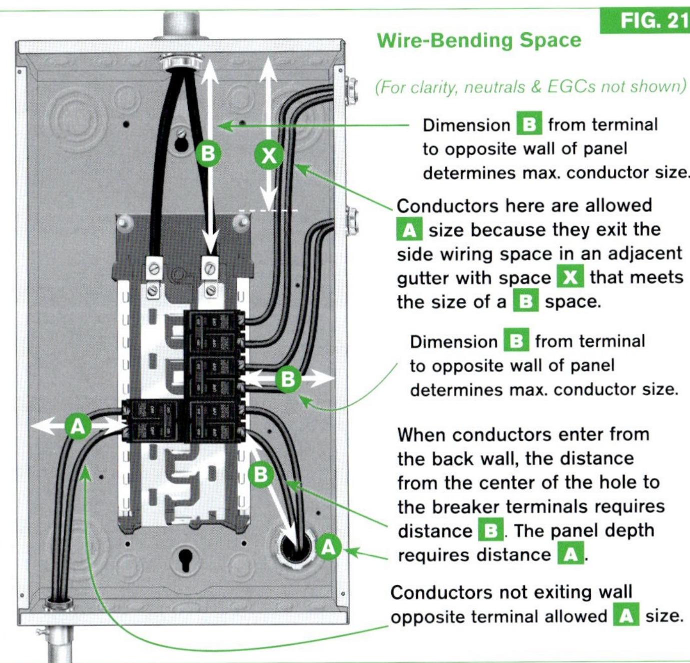

Wiring Space Inside Cabinets — 20 NEC

- ☐ Avoid crowding of conductors ____ 312.7
- ☐ Splices & taps max. 40% fill, max. 75% of CSA ____ 312.8
- ☐ Power-monitoring or energy-management equipment & conductors OK within enclosure if listed & meeting above fill reqs ____ 312.8B[27]
- ☐ Feed-through conductors OK to pass through panel if warning label applied that identifies power source is applied to enclosure ____ 312.8A3
- ☐ Wire-bending space in switchboards & panels per 312.6 ____ 408.3G

27. Small conductors for these devices rated 600V & either in raceway or secured at max. 10-in. intervals & protected from contact w/ current-carrying components.

Wiring Space Inside Cabinets (Cont.) — 20 NEC

- ☐ Min. bending space for conductors not entering or leaving wall opposite terminals ("L" bend) per **T18 A, F21** ____ 312.6B1
- ☐ Min. bending space for conductors entering or leaving wall opposite terminals ("S" bend) per **T18 B, F21** EXC ____ 312.6B2
  - If distance opposite terminal meets **T18 A** & **F21** distance **X** meets the reqd distance for condition **B**, conductors can be sized for **T18 A** ____ 312.6B2X1
- ☐ Conductors entering from back wall req **T18 A** distance to cover and **T18 B** distance from terminals **F21** ____ 408.55C

Dedicated Space F22 | 21 IRC | 20 NEC

Dedicated space is necessary to allow room for future re-entries to electrical equipment and to protect it from leaks or other contamination.

- ☐ Dedicated space is from the equipment footprint to the floor below it & for 6 ft. above it or to structural ceiling ________ 3405.3&4 110.26E1a
- ☐ No piping, ducts, or other systems foreign to the electrical system are allowed in dedicated space EXC ______ 3405.3&4 110.26E1a
  - Suspended ceilings w/ removable panels OK _____ 3405.3X 110.26E1aX
- ☐ Foreign systems allowed above dedicated space if leak protection supplied >6 ft. above equipment __________ 3405.3 110.26F1b
- ☐ Foreign systems allowed above dedicated space if leak protection supplied above dedicated space, i.e., at least 6 ft. above the equipment being protected __________ 3405.3 110.26F1b
- ☐ Sprinkler protection (but not sprinkler head & piping) allowed in dedicated space ________________________ n/a 110.26E1c

SWITCHGEAR & COMMERCIAL PANELS

Working Space (Commercial) | 20 NEC

- ☐ Large equipment = equipment >6 ft. wide & rated ≥1,200A (or if combined rating of service disconnects ≥1,200A) ________ 110.26C2
- ☐ Egress min. 24 in. wide & 78 in. high required at each end of working space of large equipment EXC ____________________ 110.26C1
  - Single egress OK if continuous & unobstructed path ________ 110.26C2a
  - Single egress OK if working-space distance T2 doubled _____ 110.26C2b
- ☐ Equipment doors in open position cannot impede egress________ 110.26C2[28]
- ☐ Egress doors ≤25 ft. from working space containing electrical equipment rated ≥800A req listed panic hardware ____________ 110.26C1
- ☐ Sole source of illumination reqd for working space at indoor panels cannot be controlled by automatic means (such as occupancy sensor)_____ 110.26D
- ☐ When rear access to nonelectrical portions of switchgear (e.g., air filters) is reqd, provide 30-in. working space ___________ 110.26A1a
- ☐ Receptacle reqd in room containing indoor service equipment EXC _ 210.63B1
  - 1&2FD ____ 210.63B

28. This new rule helps prevent a situation where a worker could be trapped in front of equipment because a switchboard door was in the fully open position.

FIG. 22

Working Space and Dedicated Space

Dedicated space extends 6 ft. above footprint of equipment.

6 ft.

Dedicated space

Working space

Sprinkler piping not allowed in dedicated space; protection of dedicated space (sprinkler coverage) is allowed.

Height of working space min. 6½ ft. & at least height of switchboard

IBT

Ventilating openings

Depth per T2

Width min. 30 in. or width of equipment

See p. 268 for Ground-Fault Protection of Equipment over 150V to ground.

Mounting & Cooling Equipment | 20 NEC

- ☐ Ventilating openings & area above must be kept clear F22 ________ 110.13B
- ☐ Equipment must be firmly secured to surface on which it is mounted 110.13A

Seismic Anchoring in SDC D, E & F | 21 IBC

- ☐ Nonstructural components must be designed & constructed to resist effects of earthquake motions in accordance w/ ASCE 7_____ 1613.1

Seismic Restraint of Electrical Equipment | ASCE 7

- ☐ Equipment & switchboards req seismic certification & anchoring AMI 13.6.4.5
- ☐ Expansion anchors or epoxy bolts may req special inspections ________ local
- ☐ Trapeze assemblies req bracing when supporting raceways ≥2½ in. 13.6.5.6
- ☐ Fittings designed for the purpose where crossing expansion joints ____ 13.6.3
- ☐ Battery racks req wraparound restraints, spacers between restraints & cells, racks to have sufficient lateral load capacity ________ 13.6.3

Reconditioned Equipment — 20 NEC

Reconditioned equipment, such as flood-damaged gear, is typically listed as a part of a field evaluation. Temporary switchgear & panels for use during construction are often reused and may require a field evaluation. *See **p. 233**.*

- ☐ Equipment markings to include date of reconditioning & name or mark of organization responsible for reconditioning ____ 110.21A2
- ☐ Original listing mark must be removed ____ 110.21A2[29]
- ☐ Approval not to be based solely on equipment's original listing ____ 110.21A2
- ☐ Equipment shall be listed as "reconditioned" ____ 240.88[30]
- ☐ Low-voltage (<1kV) fuseholders, nonrenewable fuses & molded case breakers cannot be reconditioned ____ 240.62 & 240.88A[31]
- ☐ Low- & medium-voltage & high-voltage circuit breakers permitted to be reconditioned ____ 240.88A&B[31]

Arc-Energy Reduction — 20 NEC

The "incident energy" of an electrical arc is expressed in calories per square centimeter. Arc flash is a critical safety hazard to electrical workers. The requirements for "arc-energy reduction" first appeared in the 2011 NEC to address breakers that could be adjusted to have no intentional delay, thereby reducing the clearing time and potential arc energy during the period when a properly protected worker is within the arc-flash boundary. In that scenario, once the work is completed the breaker is reset to normal. The scope of this section expanded in the 2014 edition and has been modified in each subsequent edition.

- ☐ Where highest-rated fuse or highest continuous current setting for breaker ≥1,200A, means to clear at < arcing current reqd: ____ 240.67 & 87
  - zone-selective interlocking, differential relaying, energy-reducing maintenance switching w/ local status indicator, energy-reducing arc-flash mitigation system, instantaneous trip setting (temporary adjustment not permitted), current-limiting electronically actuated fuses, instantaneous override, or approved equivalent means 240.67B & 87B
- ☐ Documentation must be provided to prove clearing time below available arcing current ____ 240.67A & 87A[32]
- ☐ Performance testing reqd by qualified person ____ 240.67C & 87C[32]
- ☐ Written record of testing must be made available to AHJ ____ 240.67C & 87C[32]

29. Requirement that original listing mark be removed is new.
30. The listing could be applied as a result of field evaluation.
31. Clarification on what is and is not allowed to be reconditioned.
32. New requirements for documentation, performance testing, and written record to AHJ.

Arc-Flash Hazard Warning — 20 NEC

- ☐ In other than dwelling units, switchboards, panelboards, etc., req marking of potential electrical arc-flash hazards **F23A** ____ 110.16A
- ☐ Service equipment ≥1,200A reqs label w/ nominal system voltage, ASCC, clearing time of OCPDs & date label applied **F23A** ____ 110.16B

*OSHA requires that employers implement and document an overall electrical safety program that directs activity appropriate to the risk associated with electrical hazards. This program must include training to qualify persons to perform electrical work. NFPA 70E: Standard for Electrical Safety in the Workplace is the standard for implementation of these programs and requires equipment labels **F23B** beyond the NEC 110.16 requirements. ANSI Z535.4 provides guidelines for suitable font sizes, words, colors, symbols, and location requirements.*

FIG. 23

Hazard-Warning Labels

The label to the right complies with NEC 110.16A&B & 110.24.

The label below complies with NFPA 70E.

A

WARNING

ARC FLASH AND SHOCK HAZARD
APPROPRIATE PPE REQUIRED

NOMINAL SYSTEM VOLTAGE	480/277 VOLTS
AVAILABLE FAULT CURRENT	22,000 AMPERES
SERVICE OCPD CLEARING TIME	0.03 SECONDS
DATE LABEL APPLIED	2022-10-31

B

WARNING

Arc Flash and Shock Hazard

ARC FLASH PROTECTION		SHOCK PROTECTION	
Working Distance	18 inches	Shock hazard when covers removed	480 VAC
Incident Energy	11 cal/cm²	Limited approach	42 inches
Arc Flash Boundary	50 inches	Restricted approach	12 inches
Refer to <company> safety program for PPE Requirements			

Location: MCC #1 Bldg SWGR 1
Equipment: Load side of FB1
Report # SGKD XXX-XX-XXX

Study provided by SGKD
Date: 2022-10-31
Label #: 3

Arc-Flash Boundary: *During an arc-flash event, the distance at which a person has a high probability of receiving a 2nd-degree burn is the Arc-Flash Boundary. When a worker crosses inside this boundary they risk exposure to 3rd- or 4th-degree burns, which can be lethal or disabling. Arc flash–rated PPE is required inside this boundary. The working distance and incident energy determine the arc-flash rating (AR) of PPE.*

Only properly protected hands and arms can extend within this working distance zone. Arc-flash boundaries do not have fixed values such as for shock-hazard boundaries.

Restricted-Approach Boundary: *An approach limit at a distance from an exposed energized electrical conductor or circuit part within which there is an increased risk of shock (due to electrical arc-over combined with inadvertent movement).*

Limited-Approach Boundary: *An approach limit at a distance from an exposed energized electrical conductor or circuit part within which a shock hazard exists, within which unqualified persons are not permitted to enter.*

INTERRUPTING RATINGS & WITHSTAND RATINGS

OCPDs must be capable of interrupting current flow (opening) when subjected to the maximum available short circuit current (ASCC), and their enclosures must be capable of withstanding the powerful magnetic fields of such a "worst case" fault. The ASCC supplied to the service can be obtained from the utility provider. Other contributions, such as large motors, solar, or batteries, must also be considered. In general, utilities will not supply more than 10,000 amps ASCC to residential services up to 400 amps. Modern residential equipment is rated for at least that much ASCC, whereas commercial installations typically require equipment with higher ratings. In commercial installations, equipment is either "fully rated" or "series rated." Series-rated systems can be a tested (listed) system or an engineered design. A series-rated system will have a fully rated OCPD at the origin of the circuit and lower-rated (less expensive) OCPDs downstream from it. In a listed system, the main and downstream device may open simultaneously from a downstream fault.

General — 20 NEC

- ☐ Each OCPD must have IR ≥ ASCC EXC ____ 110.9
  - • Series-rated system OCPDs after main OCPD ____ 240.86
- ☐ Breakers req marking of IR rating if >5,000A ____ 240.83C
- ☐ Fuses req marking of IR rating if >10,000A ____ 240.60C
- ☐ Select equipment SCCR to allow OCPD to clear fault w/o damage ____ 110.10
- ☐ Listed equipment installed per L&L meets above req ____ 110.10
- ☐ Equipment SCCR must exceed available fault current rating ____ 110.10

FIG. 24

Example Instruction for Securing Conductors

Switchboards may contain a label such as this one with instructions for "lashing" conductors to restrict their movement due to magnetic fields during a fault condition. Compliance with all instructions in the listing & labeling is required.

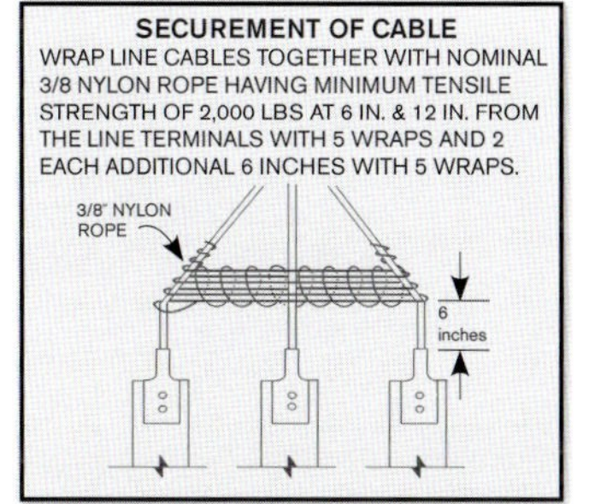

Service Equipment (Commercial) — 20 NEC

- ☐ Service equipment reqs durable field marking F23 of available fault current including date calculation was performed EXC ____ 110.24A
  - • Dwelling units ____ 110.24A
- ☐ Field marking reqs updating when alterations affecting available fault current are performed (e.g., utility XFMR upgraded, adding solar, wind, or large motors) ____ 110.24B

Series-Rated Systems

- ☐ Enclosures for OCPDs of series-rated system req field marking F25 to indicate equipment is applied w/ series-combination rating ____ 110.22B&C
- ☐ Systems selected under engineering supervision req signed stamped documentation available to the AHJ ____ 240.86A
- ☐ In engineered systems, downstream breakers to be passive during interruption period of line-side fully rated device ____ 240.86A
- ☐ Tested (listed) equipment reqs marking on end-use equipment F25 240.86B
- ☐ SRS not allowed if motors connected on line side of lower-rated OCPD & sum of motor FLCs >1% of IR of lower-rated breaker ____ 240.86C

FIG. 25

Series-Rated System Labels

Reqd wording for engineered system:	Reqd wording for listed system:
CAUTION–ENGINEERED SERIES COMBINATION SYSTEM RATED ___AMPERES IDENTIFIED REPLACEMENT COMPONENTS REQUIRED	CAUTION–SERIES COMBINATION SYSTEM RATED ___AMPERES IDENTIFIED REPLACEMENT COMPONENTS REQUIRED

A listed series-combination system will typically have a booklet showing the allowed downstream device model numbers. The booklet should be attached to the equipment. The labels will typically have a yellow background.

CONDUCTORS

Conductor Identification — 21 IRC — 20 NEC

- ☐ Grounded conductors <#4 white or gray or 3 continuous white or gray stripes on other than green insulation ________ 3407.1 — 200.6A
- ☐ Grounded conductors ≥#4 same as above or distinctive white or gray marking encircling conductor at terminations ____ 3407.1 — 200.6B
- ☐ Green never OK for neutral or ungrounded conductors _ 3407.2 — 250.119
- ☐ EGCs ≤#6 green, green w/ yellow stripes, or bare ____ 3407.2 — 250.119
- ☐ EGCs ≥#4 OK bare for entire exposed length or use green tape or labels encircling the conductor at each end and at every point where the conductor is accessible ___ 3407.2 — 250.119A
- ☐ Ungrounded conductors not white, gray, or green EXC _ 3407.3 — 310.6C
  - White or gray in cable where insulation re-identified by tape, paint, etc., at terminations & where visible. In switch loops, re-identified conductor is for supply to switch, not return to outlet **F75** ______ 3407.3X — 200.7C1

Marking

- ☐ Conductors & cables req marking of max. rated voltage, letter(s) for wire type **T19**, MFR name or trademark & AWG size 3407.1 — 310.8A
- ☐ Cable assemblies w/ neutral smaller than ungrounded conductors req marking as such ______________________ n/a — 310.8B1
- ☐ AWG size marked every 24 in., other markings 40 in. ______ n/a — 310.8B1
- ☐ Optional marking allowed on individual conductors of multiconductor cable types MC, tray cable, irrigation cable, power-limited tray cable or fire alarm cable & instrumentation tray cable ______ n/a — 310.8B4

This last rule allows the conductors of MC cable with individual conductor markings to be pulled into raceways without a splice at the point where the MC transitions to the raceway.

Buildings with More than One Nominal Voltage — 20 NEC

- ☐ If more than one nominal voltage (e.g. 480/277V & 208/120V) in building, each termination, connection & splice point reqs identification by color coding, tape, tagging, or other effective means ______ 210.5C1 & 215.12C1
- ☐ Identification method to be posted w/ durable label at each panel or other distribution equipment______________ 210.5C1 & 215.12C1

For buildings with more than one nominal voltage, an example is a posting that would say 208/120V Black, Red, Blue, White or 480/277V Brown, Orange, Yellow, Gray. Preprinted labels with the actual colors are commonly used.

TABLE 19 — INSULATION LETTER CODES ◆ T310.4A

Type[A]	Trade Name	Application	Temp
RHH[B]	Thermoset	Dry/Damp	90°C
RHW[B]	Moisture-resistant thermoset	Dry/Wet	75°C
RHW-2[B]	Moisture-resistant thermoset	Dry/Wet	90°C
TW	Thermoplastic moisture-resistant	Dry/Wet	60°C
THW	Thermoplastic heat- & moisture-resistant	Dry/Wet	75°C
THHW	Thermoplastic heat- & moisture-resistant	Dry/Wet	90°/75°C
THW-2	Thermoplastic heat- & moisture-resistant	Dry/Wet	90°C
THHN	Thermoplastic, heat-resistant, nylon-jacketed	Dry/Damp	90°C
THWN	Thermoplastic, heat- & moisture-resistant, nylon-jacketed	Dry/Wet	75°C
THWN-2	Thermoplastic, heat- & moisture-resistant, nylon-jacketed	Dry/Wet	90°C
UF	Underground feeder (single conductor)	Dry/Wet	60°C
USE	Underground service entrance (single conductor)	Dry/Wet[C]	75°C
USE-2	Underground service entrance (single conductor)	Dry/Wet[C]	90°C
XHHW	Cross-linked polyethylene, heat- & moisture-resistant, nylon-jacketed	Dry/Wet	90°/75°C
XHHW-2	Cross-linked polyethylene, heat- & moisture-resistant, nylon-jacketed	Dry/Wet	90°C

A. Conductors that are dual rated have a temperature rating based upon their location. For example, THHN/THWN conductors are rated 90° in a dry location, 75° in a wet location.
B. Prior to the 1993 NEC, the letter R designated rubber. The word *thermoset* first appeared in 1996.
C. Not allowed for interior wiring except where emerging from underground terminating into enclosure.

General

	21 IRC	20 NEC
☐ All conductors of a circuit, including grounded & EGC, to be run together in same raceway, cable, or cord EXC	3406.7	300.3B
• Conductors in parallel	3406.6	300.3B1
• EGCs for certain replacement devices *(p. 298)*	n/a	300.3B2
☐ Min. size for feeders or branch circuits #14Cu or #12AL	3406.3	310.3A

Copper & Aluminum

	21 IRC	20 NEC
☐ When material not spec'd, sizes apply to Cu conductors	3406.2	110.5
☐ Termination devices req rating for the conductor material	3406.8	110.14
☐ Terminals for AL must be identified for such use	3406.10	110.14A
☐ Dissimilar conductors in physical contact req devices identified for the purpose **F59**	3406.8[33]	110.14
☐ AL conductors must be AA-8000 series AL alloy material	n/a	310.3B
☐ If antioxidant used, apply AMI	3406.8	110.14

Parallel Conductors

	21 IRC	20 NEC
☐ Conductors min. 1/0 AWG EXC	3406.6	310.10G1
• #2 & #1 neutral of an existing system permitted in parallel under engineering supervision *(allows supplementing an existing feeder when nonlinear loads added)*	n/a	310.10G1X2
☐ Conductors of each phase, neutral or EGC must have the same length, material, size, insulation type & termination	3406.6	310.10G2
☐ Derate parallel conductors in common conduit ***p. 266***	3705.3	310.10G4
☐ In multiple conduits, each conduit reqs same number of conductors & same electrical characteristics	3406.6	310.10G3
☐ Each conduit to contain all phases, neutral & EGC	3406.7	300.3B1
• Conductors in nonmetallic raceways underground can be isolated phase & neutral installations when run in close proximity	n/a	300.3B1X
☐ Connections, taps, or extensions from paralleled conductors must connect to all conductors of the paralleled set	n/a	300.3B1[34]
☐ Each paralleled EGC fully sized per **T15**	n/a	250.122F

33. The 2017 NEC limited the examples of dissimilar contact to Cu-to-AL and Cu-clad-to-AL. It dropped the inclusion of Cu-clad-to-Cu. However, the IRC version of this section has not been updated. The NEC does not prohibit copper-clad aluminum in splicing devices and terminals rated only for Cu, since Cu is the surface material that is making the contact.

34. This new rule prevents imbalances in the paralleled sets that could occur if one isolated set served different loads than the rest of the set.

Minimum Circuit Sizes

	20 NEC
☐ Feeder conductor size min. 100% of noncontinuous load + 125% of continuous load EXC	215.2A1a
• 100% OK if feeder OCPD & enclosure rated at 100%	215.2A1aX1
• 100% of continuous & noncontinuous OK for portion of feeder between separately installed pressure connectors that are outside of the enclosure at each end of feeder **F26**	215.2A1aX2
• Neutrals OK 100% of continuous & noncontinuous	215.2A1aX3
☐ Branch circuit conductor size min. 100% of noncontinuous load + 125% of continuous load EXC	210.20A
• 100% OK if OCPD & enclosure rated at 100%	210.20A1X1
• 100% of continuous & noncontinuous OK for portion of feeder between separately installed pressure connectors that are outside of the enclosure at each end of circuit **F26**	210.19A1aX2
☐ Separately installed pressure connectors req listing & temp rating	110.14C2

FIG. 26 Separately Installed Pressure Connectors

OCPD 75° terminations
Supply-side segment
Intervening segment
Load-side segment
Load 75° terminations
Separately installed pressure connectors rated 90°C

*The feeder must be sized for 100% of the noncontinuous load plus 125% of the continuous load. The conductor size is based on the 75°C ratings so as not to exceed the temperature rating of the terminals (See **p. 265**). When listed 90°C pressure connectors are installed entirely outside the enclosures at each end of the feeder, the intervening segment can be based on the temperature rating of the pressure connectors.*

*In this example, a 400-amp load would require a 600kcmil copper feeder, the first size in the 75°C column of **T23** that is ≥400 amps. With 90°C pressure connectors, the intervening segment could be 500kcmil copper, based on the 90°C column of **T23**.*

ELECTRICAL CONNECTIONS

The rules for proper connections of electrical conductors apply to all parts of the electrical system, including panels, boxes, and devices. Manufacturer's instructions are to be followed for the tightening torque of terminals, including those in panels, breakers, and devices. In the absence of a specific marking or instruction, terminals are assumed to be rated for copper conductors and for only one conductor per terminal.

Terminals	**21 IRC**	**20 NEC**
☐ Tightening torque on terminals AMI	3406.12	110.14D
☐ Torque values of Annex I if no MFR instructions **T20**	n/a	110.14D
☐ Verify tightening torque by approved means	3406.12[35]	110.14D[35]
☐ Max. #10 wire for upturned lugs or screws	3406.10	110.14A
☐ Terminals for >1 conductor identified for such use **F27**	3406.10	110.14A
☐ Connectors & terminals for fine-stranded conductors reqd to be identified for specific conductor class or classes **F27**	3406.9	110.14

TABLE 20 — TIGHTENING TORQUE—RECESSED ALLEN DRIVES NEC ANNEX I TI.3 (UL486A-486B)[A]

Socket Width (in.)	N-m	lb./ft	lb./in.
1/8	5.1	3.75	45
5/32	11.3	8.33	100
3/16	13.5	10	120
7/32	16.9	12.5	150
1/4	22.5	16.66	200
5/16	31.1	29.9	275
3/8	42.4	31.25	375
1/2	56.5	41.66	500
9/16	67.8	50	600

1. Values stated on the device override this table, e.g., a breaker with a 5/16 drive & MFR instructions of 375 in./lb. should be set to 375 in./lb., not 275 in./lb.

TABLE 21 — CONDUCTOR STRANDING IRC T3406.9 ◆ NEC CHAPTER 9 T10[A]

Conductor Size AWG or kcmil	Number of Strands		
	Copper		Aluminum
	Class B	Class C	Class B
14 – 2	7	19	7[B]
1 – 4/0	19	37	19
250 – 500	37	61	37
600 – 1000	61	91	61

A. Derived from UL Standard 486A-486B copyrighted by UL.
B. #14 stranded is not available in aluminum.

Conductors more finely stranded than Class B or Class C have greater flexibility and may have thousands of strands. They are popular with photovoltaic installers, and in larger sizes they are often used with transfer switches, generators, and motor conductors where space limitations necessitate a conductor with greater flexibility. Specialized termination devices are needed. If placed under ordinary conical lugs, strands of conductors can be cut, and relaxation of the metal will cause a loss of torque on the connection. A common solution is to slip a conical ferrule over the ends of the conductor. UL 486F does not list or evaluate ferrules for conductors larger than 1/0. In such cases, crimp connections with pin connectors or other listed termination devices are required.

FIG. 27 — Connections & Terminations

Torque at terminals per marking on equipment

TORQUE
14-10 AWG 20 IN. LBS.
8 AWG 25 IN. LBS.
6-4 AWG 27 IN. LBS.
3-1/0 AWG 45 IN. LBS.

Breaker marking

Compression connector for transition of fine-strand to standard lug

Size, type & number of conductors must be in accordance with instructions in packaging of twist-on connectors & push-in connectors.

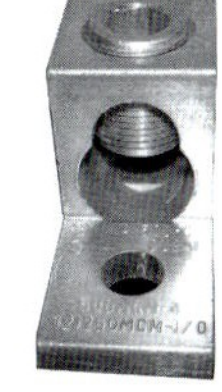

Lug rated for 2 conductors

35. Clarification that means other than calibrated torque tool can be approved, such as thermal imaging.

CONDUCTOR AMPACITY

General	21 IRC	20 NEC
☐ Protect ungrounded conductors w/ OCPDs at source	3705.5	240.4
☐ Protect conductors at their ampacity **T23** EXC	3705.5	240.4
• If ampacity is between standard sizes of **T22**, next higher standard OCPD allowed to be used provided it is not a branch circuit w/ >1 receptacle for cord/plug portable loads & next higher OCPD ≤800A (400A IRC)	3705.5.2	240.4B
• Small conductors (≤#10) per **T24**	3705.5.3	240.4D
• Tap conductors *p. 267*	n/a	240.4E
• Air-conditioning equipment **F82** per nameplate	3705.5.4	240.4G
• Motors per **T46,47** *pp. 310–311*	n/a	240.4G
☐ Circuits >800A req ampacity ≥ rating of OCPD	n/a	240.4C
☐ Temp rating of conductor not to exceed lowest rating of connected conductor, termination, or device	3705.4	110.14C
☐ Terminations for circuits ≤100A or marked for ≤#1 conductors only OK for:		
• 60° conductors	3705.4.1	110.14C1a
• >60° conductors OK if ampacity based on 60°	3705.4.1	110.14C1a
• >60° conductors OK if equipment L&L for same	3705.4.1	110.14C1a
• ≥75° conductors OK for motors w/ design letters B, C, or D provided ampacity ≤75°	3705.4.1	110.14C1a
☐ Terminations for circuits >100A or marked for >#1 conductors req conductors rated ≥75°	3705.4.2	110.14C1b
☐ 83% of **T23** ampacity OK for service or feeder that carries entire load of individual dwelling unit ≤400A **T1**	3603.1.1	310.12
☐ NM & AC cable 90°C for derating; final OCPD 60°C	3705.4.4	334.80

TABLE 22 STANDARD AMPERE RATING FOR FUSES & INVERSE TIME CIRCUIT BREAKERS ◆ IRC T3705.6 NEC T240.6A

15	20	25	30	35	40	45	50
60	70	80	90	100	110	125	150
175	200	225	250	300	350	400	450
500	600	700	800	1000	1200	1600	2000

TABLE 23 WIRE AMPACITIES ◆ IRC T3705.1 ◆ NEC T310.16

	60°C	75°C	90°C	60°C	75°C	90°C	
	INSULATION TYPES						
Cu Size (AWG)	TW UF	THHW THW THWN USE	THHN THHW THW-2 THWN-2 USE-2	TW UF	XHHW USE	USE-2, XHHW-2	AL Size (AWG)
14[A]	15	20	25	—	—	—	—
12[A]	20	25	30	15	20	25	12[A]
10[A]	30	35	40	25	30	35	10[A]
8	40	50	55	35	40	45	8
6	55	65	75	40	50	55	6
4	70	85	95	55	65	75	4
3	85	100	115	65	75	85	3
2	95	115	130	75	90	100	2
1	110	130	145	85	100	115	1
1/0	125	150	170	100	120	135	1/0
2/0	145	175	195	115	135	150	2/0
3/0	165	200	225	130	155	175	3/0
4/0	195	230	260	150	180	205	4/0
250	215	255	290	170	205	230	250
300	240	285	320	195	230	260	300
350	260	310	350	210	250	280	350
400	280	335	380	225	270	305	400
500	320	380	430	260	310	350	500
600	350	420	475	285	340	385	600
700	385	460	520	315	375	425	700
750	400	475	535	320	385	435	750
1000	455	545	615	375	445	500	1000

A. OCPD selection for small conductors limited to ampacities in **T24**.

Small Conductors

	21 IRC	20 NEC
☐ Max. overcurrent protection based on **T24** EXC	3705.5.3	240.4D
• IRC: Air conditioning per nameplate	3705.5.4	240.4G
• NEC: Special equipment (motors, air conditioning, etc.)	n/a	240.4G

TABLE 24	MIN. SIZE OF SMALL CONDUCTORS[A] IRC T3705.5.3 ◆ NEC 240.4D			
Fuse or breaker size	15	20	25	30
Cu conductor	14	12	10	10
AL or Cu-clad AL conductor	12	10	10	8

A. Restriction does not apply when all terminals rated >60°C and supplying tap conductors, and special loads in NEC T240.4G, such as motors (*p. 311*) and air conditioners, in accordance with their nameplate ratings.

TABLE 25	AMBIENT TEMPERATURE CORRECTION[A] ◆ T310.15B1			
Ambient Temp. °C	For ambient temp. >30°C (86°F), multiply the ampacity in **T23** by the following percentages:			Ambient Temp. °F
	60°C	75°C	90°C	
31–35	0.91	0.94	0.96	87–95
36–40	0.82	0.88	0.91	96–104
41–45	0.71	0.82	0.87	105–113
46–50	0.58	0.75	0.82	114–122
51–55	0.41	0.67	0.76	123–131
56–60	—	0.58	0.71	132–140
61–65	—	0.47	0.65	141–149
66–70	—	0.33	0.58	150–158
71–75	—	—	0.50	159–167
76–80	—	—	0.41	168–176
81–85	—	—	0.29	177-185

A. This table is important in remodels with older (pre-1984) 60°C wire, especially with hot attic spaces.

Derating

	21 IRC	20 NEC
☐ Apply temperature correction factor **T25**	3705.2	310.15B1
☐ Add 33°C to **T25** for conduits <⅞ in. above roofs EXC	n/a	310.15B2
• XHHW-2 insulated conductors	n/a	310.15B2X
☐ Derate for >3 current-carrying conductors in raceway or cables grouped w/o spacing > 24 in. in length **T26** EXC	3705.3	310.15C1
• Type AC or MC cables w/ #12 Cu conductors, w/o overall outer jacket & ≤3 current-carrying conductors in each cable allowed to have up to 20 current-carrying conductors w/o spacing, or 60% adjustment if >20 current-carrying conductors	3705.3X	310.15C1
☐ Neutrals are current-carrying conductors for **T26** EXC	3705.3	310.15E
• Neutral carrying only imbalanced load of other conductors in the same circuit **F20**	3705.3	310.15E1

The neutral is considered a current-carrying conductor in a 3-wire circuit with 2 phase conductors plus a neutral from a 4-wire 3-phase wye system (such as a 120/208V) and in 4-wire 3-phase wye circuits with nonlinear loads (harmonics).

	21 IRC	20 NEC
☐ Derate >2 cables in caulked (fireblocked) hole or installed w/o spacing in contact w/ thermal insulation **T26**	3705.4.4	3**.80[36]
☐ NM cable 90°C for derating; final OCPD selection 60°C	3705.4.4	334.80

TABLE 26	DERATING FOR BUNDLED CONDUCTORS[A] IRC T3705.3 ◆ T310.15C1
Number of Current-Carrying Conductors in Raceway or Cable	Ampacity Correction (Percentage of Values in **T23**)
4–6	0.80
7–9	0.70
10–20	0.50
21–30	0.45
31–40	0.40
≥41	0.35

A. Modern 90°C small conductors that do not req an ambient temperature correction can have as many as 9 current-carrying conductors and still be within the sizes in the simplified table **T28**.

36. This adjustment now applicable to AC, MC & SE, not just NM & UF.

Tap Conductors **20 NEC**

- ☐ Conductor ampacity no less than load served ______ 210.19A1
- ☐ Feeder taps ≤10 ft. OK w/o overcurrent protection at tap if ampacity ≥1/10 rating of OCPD protecting the tap, enclosed in raceway & equipment loads/OCPD(s) ≤ rating of tap conductors **F30** ______ 240.21B1
- ☐ Feeder taps ≤25 ft. OK w/o overcurrent protection at tap if ampacity ≥1/3 rating of OCPD protecting the tap, enclosed in raceway & terminating in single OCPD ≤ rating of tap conductors **F30** ______ 240.21B2
- ☐ Feeder taps may not "round up" to next standard size OCPD **F30** ___ 240.21
- ☐ Not OK to tap a tap conductor ______ 240.21
- ☐ 15A tap conductors allowed on 40A circuit, 20A taps on 50A circuit (typically in accessible ceilings) if supplying a luminaire ______ 240.19A4X1
- ☐ Tap conductors (whips) to luminaires min. 18 in. max. 6 ft. in length, must be AC or MC cable, outlet box min. 12 in. from luminaire **F28** ______ 410.117C
- ☐ Conductors tapped from 50A branch circuit to ranges, ovens, min. 20A ampacity & not longer than needed to reach appliance **F29** ______ 210.19A3

FIG. 28 Luminaire Tap

40A OCPD

#8 feeder

Outlet (box)

Min. 1-ft. separation

#12 or #14 AC or MC cable min. 18 in. max. 6 ft.

Ceiling-Suspended Luminaire

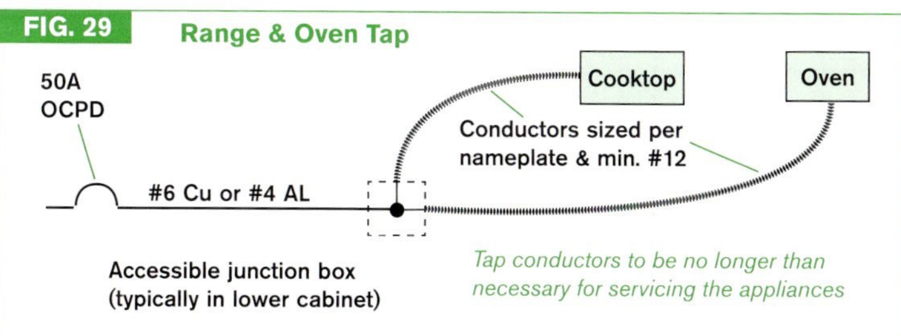

FIG. 29 Range & Oven Tap

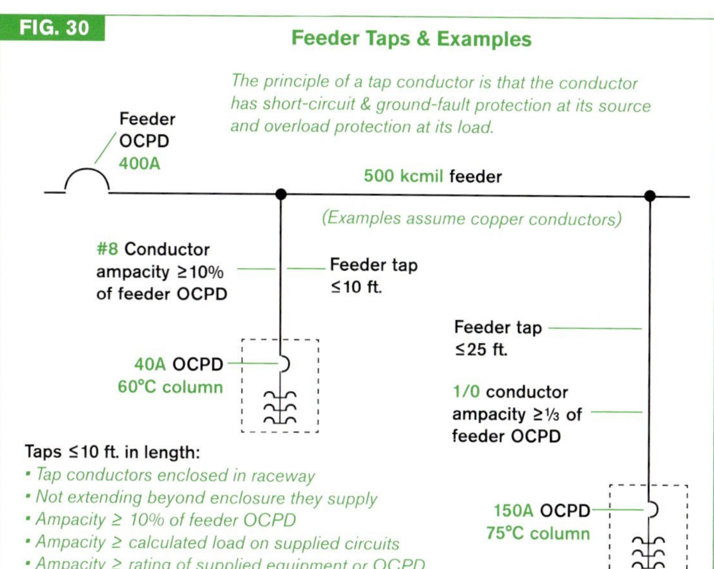

FIG. 30 Feeder Taps & Examples

Taps ≤25 ft. in length:

- *Ampacity ≥1/3 feeder OCPD*
- *Terminate in single OCPD*
- *Protected from physical damage (raceway)*

25-ft. tap rule example:

- *The ampacity of the 500 kcmil feeder @75°C is 380A (T310.16).*
- *A 400A OCPD (rounding up to next larger standard size) is allowed when the ampacity is between standard sizes and <800A (240.4B).*
- *The 25-ft. tap conductor ampacity must be ≥ 1/3 the feeder OCPD.*
- *1/3 × 400A = 133A. A #1 conductor is rated for130A.*
- *Rounding up to next larger standard size OCPD is NOT allowed.*
- *A 1/0 conductor (rated at 150A) is required.*
- *The OCPD at the termination of the tap must be rated at no more than the ampacity of this 1/0 conductor. A 150A breaker is allowed to protect this tap from overloads. Note that this is >1/3 the rating of the feeder OCPD.*

Voltage Drop

20 NEC

- ☐ For reasonable efficiency of operation, size conductors to prevent VD >3% at farthest outlet of loads or >5% total VD of feeders + branch circuits **T27** ______ Informational note to 210.19A & 215.2A

TABLE 27 — ONE-WAY CABLE LENGTHS TO LIMIT VOLTAGE DROP TO 2% FOR FEEDERS & 3% FOR BRANCH CIRCUITS

OCPD	Load[A]	Cu Wire Size	Max. Length Cu wire (ft.)	AL Wire Size	Max. Length AL wire (ft.)
		120V Branch circuits sized for 3% voltage drop[B]			
15	12	14	56	12	54
20	16	12	65	10	53
30	24	10	71	8	66
		240V Branch circuits sized for 3% voltage drop[C]			
40	32	8	163	6	158
50	40	6	203	6	126
60	48	6	170	4	164
		240V Feeders sized for 2% voltage drop[C]			
60	48	6	113	6	70
100	80	2	165	1/0	144
125	100	1	162	1/0	115
150	120	1/0	154	2/0	123
200	160	3/0	171	4/0	128

A. Based on 80% circuit loading for OCPD sized per **T23**.
B. For 240V circuits on these conductor sizes, the distances are twice what is shown in the table.
C. For 208V subtract approximately 15% from cable length.

Informational note #4 of 210.19 recommends a maximum voltage drop of 3% on branch circuits and 5% overall, including the feeders. Excessive voltage drop causes problems in connected equipment and adds to energy costs. Voltage drop problems are reduced by using larger wire than the minimum size and by tight connections that do not introduce additional impedance. Voltage drop increases proportionately to the load on the circuit. Adding more than the minimum number of circuits helps prevent individual circuits from overloading. The added cost of larger wiring and additional circuits may pay for itself over time in reduced utility costs and greater equipment efficiency. Local energy codes may mandate that conductors be sized to limit voltage drop.

TABLE 28 — BRANCH CIRCUIT & FEEDER SIZES (SIMPLIFIED)[A]

Fuse or Breaker	Wire Size (AWG) Cu	Wire Size (AWG) AL	Fuse or Breaker	Wire Size (AWG) Cu	Wire Size (AWG) AL
15	14	12	100	2	1/0
20	12	10	110	2	1/0
30	10	8	125	1	1/0
40	8	6	150	1/0	2/0
50	6	4	175	2/0	3/0
60	6	4	200	3/0	4/0
70	4	3	225	4/0	250 kcmil
90	3	1	400	500 kcmil	(2)250

A. Based on **T23** before application of derating or temperature correction. This simplified table is intended for field use for conditions that do not require ampacity adjustments of **T25** & **T26**.

GROUND-FAULT PROTECTION OF EQUIPMENT

Systems over 150V to ground, such as 480/277V wye systems, can sustain a ground fault through air, and GFPE protection limits the damage potential of such faults.

Services

20 NEC

- ☐ Ground-fault protection of equipment reqd for solidly grounded wye electrical services ≥1,000A & >150V to ground ______ 230.95
- ☐ GFPE must open all ungrounded conductors of faulted circuit ____ 230.95A
- ☐ Max. setting of GFPE device 1,200A ______ 230.95A
- ☐ GFPE must be performance-tested by primary current injection AMI 230.95C
- ☐ Written record of testing must be made available to AHJ ______ 230.95C

Feeders

- ☐ GFPE reqd for feeders of solidly grounded wye electrical system >150V to ground & ≥1,000A EXC ______ 215.10
  - Not reqd if GFPE provided on supply side of feeder & on load side of any XFMR supplying the feeder ______ 215.10X2

BOXES

Boxes must be large enough to prevent crushing & overheating of devices and wiring. Wires must be long enough so splices & connections can be worked on clear of the box opening. Luminaires supported from boxes are generally designed for connections inside the box, rather than inside the luminaire canopy. Device boxes are threaded for 6–32 screws used to mount switches and receptacles. Lighting outlet boxes provide 8–32 (for luminaires) or 10–24 screws (for listed paddle-fan boxes).

General

General	21 IRC	20 NEC
☐ Boxes reqd for each outlet, splice, or pull point EXC	3905.1	300.15
• Wiring methods w/ removable covers, e.g., wireway	n/a	300.15A
• Integral j-boxes in approved equipment	3905.1.1	300.15B
• Not reqd for conduit or tubing used to provide support or protection; bushing is reqd to prevent abrasion	3905.1.2	300.15C
• NM wiring device w/ integral enclosure & brackets	3905.1.3	300.15E
• Fitting (e.g., A-head) in lieu of box if no splices therein	3905.1.4	300.15F
• Listed underground splice kits	3905.1.5	300.15G
• Insulated wiring splice & tap devices listed for NM	n/a	300.15H
• In cabinets (electrical panels) & cutout boxes	n/a	300.15I
• Luminaires used as raceways	3905.1.6	300.15J
☐ Metal boxes must be grounded	3905.2	314.4
☐ Box & conduit body covers must remain accessible w/o removing any part of the structure	3905.10	314.29
☐ Boxes must be closed w/cover, faceplate, or luminaire	3906.9	314.25
☐ Cover screws must match thread gauge of box	3906.9	314.25
☐ Wet location boxes req listing for wet locations	3905.11	314.15
☐ Place wet location boxes so they do not retain water	3905.11	314.15
☐ OK to drill 1/8 –1/4-in. drainage holes in boxes	3905.11	314.15
☐ Unused KOs must be filled	3404.6	110.12A

Support

Support	21 IRC	20 NEC
☐ Boxes must be supported	3906.8	314.23
☐ Surface mounting must be securely fastened	3906.8.1	314.23A
☐ Screws that secure boxes to structural members not to pass unprotected through box	3906.8.2	314.23B

Raceway Supported Boxes & Enclosures

Raceway Supported Boxes & Enclosures	21 IRC	20 NEC
☐ Boxes max. 100 cu. in. **F31A** & min. 2 threaded entries supported by conduits secured wrenchtight **F31B**	3906.8.4&5	314.23E&F
☐ Conduits secured max. 3 ft. from enclosure, 18 in. if all entries on same side of enclosure **F31C**	3906.8.4	314.23E
☐ L&L integral box OK **F31D** w/o external j-box	3905.1.1	300.15B
☐ Single unbroken RMC or IMC OK to support luminaire if last point of conduit support max. 3 ft. from luminaire, min. 8 ft. above grade, max. supported weight 20 lb. **F31E**	3906.8.5X2	314.23FX2
☐ Box supported by flexible cord OK w/ strain relief	n/a	314.23H1
☐ RMC & IMC conduit stems OK for pendant boxes **F31F**	n/a	314.23H2
☐ Conduit-stem threaded joints secured w/set screws or 8 ft. above grade & 3 ft. from building openings and platforms **F31G**	n/a	314.23H2
☐ PVC, RMC, IMC & EMT OK to support conduit bodies	3906.8.4X	314.23E&FX
☐ PVC & EMT not OK for box support	3906.8.4X	314.23E&FX

FIG. 31 Raceway-Supported Boxes and Luminaires

Boxes Supporting Ceiling-Suspended Fans

	21 IRC	20 NEC
☐ Boxes & box systems supporting fans rated for >35 lb. req marking of max. weight to be supported **F32**	3905.8	314.27C
☐ Max. 70 lb. for fan supported by box or box system **F32**	3905.8	314.27C
☐ Independent support OK—reqd if fan >70 lb. **F32**	4101.6	422.18
☐ Listed locking support & mounting receptacle & compatible factory-installed attachment fitting allowed **F33**	4101.6	422.18
☐ Ceiling boxes in locations acceptable for paddle fans req listing as fan support or access to framing for pass-through box	3905.8[37]	314.27C[37]

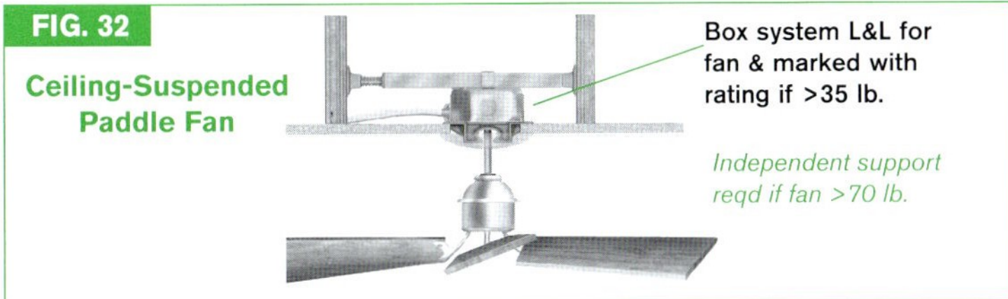

FIG. 32 Ceiling-Suspended Paddle Fan

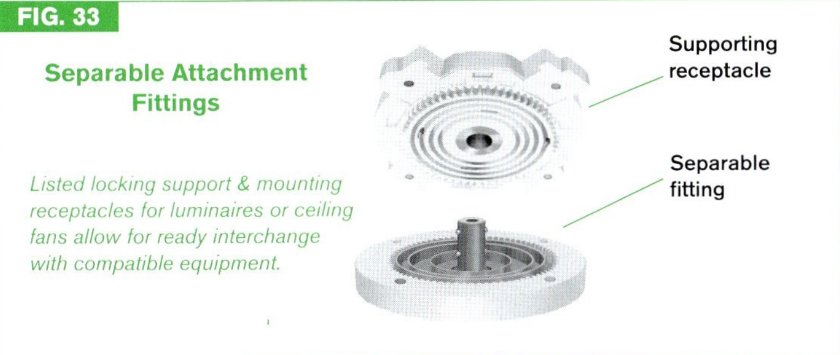

FIG. 33 Separable Attachment Fittings

Listed locking support & mounting receptacles for luminaires or ceiling fans allow for ready interchange with compatible equipment.

Boxes Supporting Luminaires

	21 IRC	20 NEC
☐ Boxes supporting luminaires must be rated for luminaire support (not device support) EXC	3905.6	314.27
• Equipment ≤6 lb. (smoke alarms, some sconces) allowed to be supported on device boxes **F37**	3905.9X	314.27DX
☐ Wall luminaire boxes rated other than 50 lb. must be marked to indicate max. weight of luminaire	3905.6.1	314.27A1
☐ Ceiling luminaire boxes req 50-lb. rating **F34**	3905.6.2	314.27A2
☐ Ceiling luminaires >50-lb. req independent support	3905.6.2	314.27A2

FIG. 34 Luminaire Support Boxes

Octagonal box with 8-32 mounting holes

Luminaire mud ring 8-32 mounting holes

Conduit Bodies

	21 IRC	20 NEC
☐ Conduit bodies not OK for splices or taps unless durably marked w/ their cu. in. capacity	3905.12.3.1	314.16C2
☐ No splices, taps, or devices in short-radius elbows enclosing conductors ≤#6	3905.12.3.2	314.16C3

37. Previous code only required this if spare separately switched conductors installed. With this new rule, all locations that are eligible for a future fan must be fan-ready.

Pull & Junction Boxes w/ Conductors ≥#4 — 20 NEC

- ☐ Conduit entries req smoothly rounded bushing or equivalent ______ 300.4G
- ☐ Box length for straight pull min. 8× raceway diameter **F35A** ______ 314.28A1
- ☐ Box length for splices or angle or U pulls min. 6× raceway size + sum of other raceways in same row on same wall **F35B&C** ______ 314.28A2
- ☐ The distance between raceway entries enclosing the same conductor must be at least 6× the trade size of the larger raceway **F35Z** ______ 314.28A2
- ☐ Conductors in large boxes (any dimension >6 ft.) must be racked ___ 314.28B

FIG. 35

Pull Boxes

Straight pull **A**: Distance **X** must be at least 8× conduit diameter

Angle pulls **B**, U pulls **C**, and splices: Distance **Y** must be at least 6× conduit diameter plus the diameter of all other raceways in the same row. If >1 row, calculated each row individually and the single row providing the longest distance is used.

Example: Suppose that the raceway entries are all 2-in. conduit. For the straight pull **A** *the minimum distance* **X** *between entries must be 8 × 2 in. = 16 in.*

For the angle pull **B** *the minimum distance* **Y** *to the opposite wall from the bottom entries must be 6 × 2 in. + 2 in. + 2 in. = 16 in. Looked at from the right wall of the box, the required distance* **X** *would be 6 × 2 in. + 2 in. = 14 in.*

The distance **Z** *between the two raceway entries for* **B** *must be 6 × 2 in. = 12 in. The distance between the entries for U pull is also 12 in.*

Position in Walls & Ceilings F36

	21 IRC	20 NEC
☐ Max. 1/4-in. setback from noncombustible wall surface	3906.5	314.20
☐ Flush w/ or projecting if combustible wall surface	3906.5	314.20
☐ Listed box extenders OK to correct excess setback	3906.5	314.20
☐ Repair plaster gaps >1/8 in. for flush cover boxes	3906.6	314.21
☐ Extension rings must be mounted & secured to box	3906.7	314.22

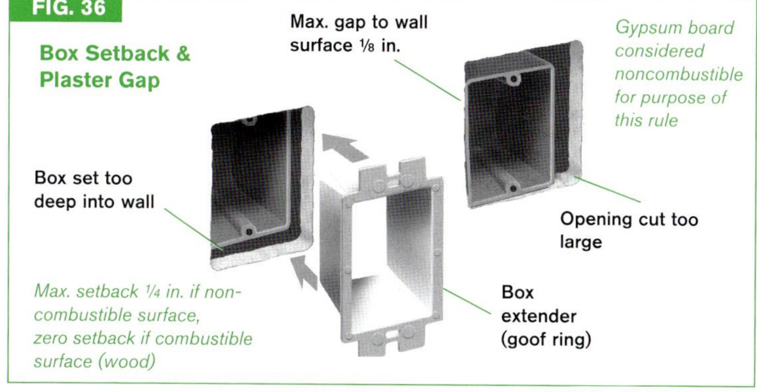

Power-Distribution Blocks — 20 NEC

- ☐ Power-distribution blocks must be listed ______ 314.28E1
- ☐ Min. box or wireway dimension per listing of power-distribution block 314.28E2
- ☐ Wire-bending space per **T18**, **F21** ______ 314.28E3
- ☐ No uninsulated live parts w/ box cover on or off ______ 314.28E4
- ☐ Other pull-through conductors not to obstruct distribution blocks __ 314.28E5
- ☐ Power-distribution blocks for service conductors must be L&L & marked "suitable for use on the line side of service equipment" ____ 230.46[38]
- ☐ Pressure connectors & splicing/tapping devices for service conductors req marking as "suitable for use on the line side of the service equipment" ______ 230.46[38]

38. Req for listing of pressure connectors and devices on supply side to become effective January 1, 2023.

TABLE 29A — METAL BOX STANDARD VOLUMES IRC T3905.12.1 NEC T314.16A

Box Trade Size	Shape or Type	Cu. in. volume	Size (AWG) and Number of Conductors				
			6	8	10	12	14
4 × 1¼	Round/octagonal[A]	12.5	2	5	5	5	6
4 × 1½	Round/octagonal[A]	15.5	3	5	6	6	7
4 × 2⅛	Round/octagonal[A]	21.5	4	7	8	9	10
4 × 1¼	Square[A]	18.0	3	6	7	8	9
4 × 1½	Square[A]	21.0	4	7	8	9	10
4 × 2⅛	Square[A]	30.3	6	10	12	13	15
4¹¹⁄₁₆ × 1¼	Square[A]	25.5	5	8	10	11	12
4¹¹⁄₁₆ × 1½	Square[A]	29.5	5	9	11	13	14
4¹¹⁄₁₆ × 2⅛	Square[A]	42.0	8	14	16	18	21
3 × 2 × 1½	Device[B]	7.5	1	2	3	3	3
3 × 2 × 2	Device[B]	10.0	2	3	4	4	5
3 × 2 × 2¼	Device[B]	10.5	2	3	4	4	5
3 × 2 × 2½	Device[B]	12.5	2	4	5	5	6
3 × 2 × 2¾	Device[B]	14.0	2	4	5	6	7
3 × 2 × 3½	Device[B]	18.0	3	6	7	8	9
4 × 2⅛ × 1½	Device[B]	10.3	2	3	4	4	5
4 × 2⅛ × 1⅞	Device[B]	13.0	2	4	5	5	6
4 × 2⅛ × 2⅛	Device[A]	14.5	2	4	5	6	7
3¾ × 2 × 2½	Masonry box/gang	14.0	2	4	5	6	7
3¾ × 2 × 3½	Masonry box/gang	21.0	4	7	8	9	10

A. Boxes accept 8–32 screws.
B. Boxes accept 6–32.

TABLE 29B — METAL BOX STANDARD VOLUMES (CONTINUED) NEC T314.16A

Box Trade Size	Shape or Type	Cu. in. volume	Size (AWG) and Number of Conductors				
			6	8	10	12	14
FS 1¾	Single cover	13.5	2	4	5	6	6
FD 2⅜	Single cover	18.0	3	6	7	8	9
FS 1¾	Multiple cover	18.0	3	6	7	8	9
FD 2⅜	Multiple cover	24.0	4	8	9	10	12

Box Volume

	21 IRC	20 NEC
☐ Size to provide free space for conductors **T30**	3905.12	314.16
☐ Standard metal boxes per **T29**	3905.12.1.1	314.16A1
☐ Plastic boxes reqd to be marked w/ their volume	3905.12.1.2	314.16A2
☐ Include volume of marked mud rings & extensions	3905.12.1	314.16A
☐ Spaces created by fixed barriers calculated separately	3905.12.1	314.16A
☐ Volume of barriers as marked	3905.12.1	314.16A
☐ Unmarked barriers ½-cu.-in. metal boxes, 1-cu.-in. plastic	3905.12.1	314.16A

TABLE 30 — VOLUME ALLOWANCE PER CONDUCTOR IRC T3905.12.2.1 NEC 314.16B

Conductor Size (AWG)	Free Space within Box (cu. in.)
18	1.50
16	1.75
14	2.00
12	2.25
10	2.50
8	3.00
6	5.00

Box Fill Factors T31

	21 IRC	20 NEC
☐ Count each conductor exiting box EXC	3905.12.2.1	314.16B1
• EGCs & up to 4 conductors <#14 from luminaires w/ domed canopies	3905.12.2.1X	314.16B1X
• Unbroken conductors passing through box count as only 1 conductor EXC	3905.12.2.1	314.16B1
• Looped unbroken conductors > 12 in. count as 2	3905.12.2.1	314.16B1
☐ Do not count pigtailed conductors to devices	3905.12.2.1	314.16B1
☐ Count only 1 internal clamp	3905.12.2.2	314.16B2
☐ Base internal clamp size on largest conductor in box	3905.12.2.2	314.16B2
☐ Count only 1 support fitting (studs or hickeys)	3905.12.2.3	314.16B3
☐ Base fitting size on largest conductor in box	3905.12.2.3	314.16B3
☐ Count each device on yoke as 2 conductors	3905.12.2.4	314.16B4
☐ Device volume based on connected wire size	3905.12.2.4	314.16B4
☐ Small fittings (locknuts & bushings) do not count	3905.12.2	314.16B
☐ First 4 EGCs count only as 1 based on largest	3905.12.2.5	314.16B5
☐ Add ¼ of largest conductor for each EGC >4	3905.12.2.5[39]	314.16B5[39]
☐ 4-in. (6-cu.-in.) pancake only at end of 14/2 run **F38**	3905.12	314.16B
☐ 18-cu.-in. box not OK for 3 12/2 Romex **F37**	3905.12	314.16B
☐ Spaces created by fixed barriers calculated separately	3905.12.1	314.16A

FIG. 37

Box Fill

Device box

Yoke

Device

*The 18-cu.-in. box in this example is allowable w/ 3 #14/2 cables exiting the box. It would be overfilled if the cables were #12. See **T31***

A min. of 3 in. of conductor must be able to extend outside the box in order to make splices and device connections.

3⁹⁄₃₂ in.

Device boxes have 6-32 mounting holes

39. New requirement that reqs a volume allowance for EGCs when >4 are present. Amount is ¼ of the reqd amount per conductor for each EGC in excess of 4, based on the largest size EGC in the box.

Conductors in Boxes

	21 IRC	20 NEC
☐ Continuity of EGC not dependent on devices supplied by wiring in box (use pigtails to devices) **F16**	3908.14	250.148B
☐ Min. 6-in. conductor brought into box **F37**	3406.11.3	300.14
☐ Min. 3-in. free conductor past face of box if any dimension of opening to box <8 in. **F37**	3406.11.3	300.14

TABLE 31 BOX FILL (CUBIC INCHES) WORKSHEET ◆ 314.16

Item	Size	#	Total
#14 conductors exiting box	2.00		
#12 conductors exiting box	2.25		
#10 conductors exiting box	2.50		
#8 conductors exiting box	3.00		
#6 conductors exiting box	5.00		
Up to 4 EGCs—count only largest one		1	
Each EGC >4—count ¼ of largest in box for each			
Devices: 2× connected conductor size			
Internal clamps—one based on largest wire present		1	
Fixture fittings—one for each type based on largest wire			
TOTAL			

FIG. 38

Pancake Boxes

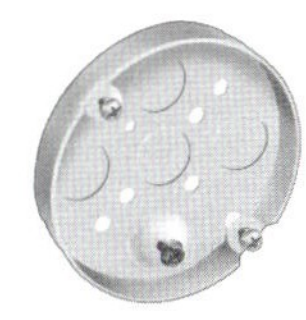

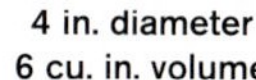

4 in. diameter
6 cu. in. volume

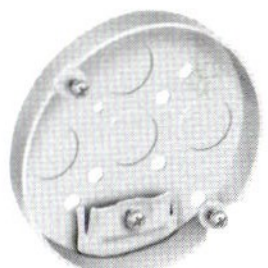

3 in. diameter
4 cu. in. volume

A 6-cu.-in. pancake box can be used at the end of a run of 14/2 NM cable if there is no internal clamp in the box. Otherwise, pancake boxes can only be used with luminaires having a raised canopy with sufficient volume marked on the luminaire.

RACEWAYS

Conduit, tubing & wireways are forms of electrical raceways. The NEC numbering system for raceways & cables starts with the 3 numbers of the code article, then a period. Numbers after the period are the same topic for each article. For example, the limitation on the number of bends for IMC is found in 342.26, for RMC in 344.26, for FMC in 348.26, for LFMC in 350.26, etc. In our text we abbreviate code citations by saying ***.26 to cover that rule for all raceway types, where *** represents the specific raceway article in the code.

General

General	21 IRC	20 NEC
☐ Join metal raceways into continuous electrical conductor mechanically secured to boxes, cabinets, etc. EXC	3904.1	300.18A
• Short sections of raceway for cable protection	3904.1X	300.18AX
☐ Raceway system complete before pulling wire EXC	3904.5	300.18A
• Where reqd to facilitate installing utilization equipment	n/a	300.18AX
☐ Interior of underground raceways is a wet location **F6**	3803.10	300.5B
☐ Interior of above-grade raceways in wet locations is a wet location & conductors must be rated for same	3802.8	300.9
☐ Box & conduit body covers must remain accessible	3905.10	314.29
☐ Raceways not OK to support other cables or boxes EXC	3904.4	300.11C
• Associated control wiring (e.g., thermostat to AC)	3904.4	300.11C2
• Boxes or conduit bodies (***see p. 269***)	3904.4	300.11C2
☐ Metal raceways not OK w/ plastic boxes EXC	3905.3	314.3
• Internal bonding means supplied between entries	3905.3X	314.3X1
☐ Bends reqd to have even radius—no kinks **F39**	3802.5	***.24
☐ Max. 360° bends between pull points **F39**	T3802.1	***.26
☐ Raceway must be reamed smooth after cutting	T3802.1	***.28
☐ Conduit bushings of insulated material not OK to secure raceway to box or cabinet	3906.1.1	300.4G
☐ Raceways exposed to different temperatures where condensation could result req seal to prevent circulation of air; sealants must be compatible w/ conductor insulation	3802.7	300.7A

Examples are conduits entering a walk-in refrigerator or conduits from the exterior of a building passing through to the interior of the building.

Conductors in Raceways

Conductors in Raceways	21 IRC	20 NEC
☐ Size & number of conductors to be selected so they can be inserted or withdrawn w/out conductor or insulation damage	3904.6	300.17
☐ Max. 40% fill if > 2 conductors **F41,T32** EXC	3904.6	9 T1
• Straight conduits ≤24 in. OK to have 60% fill **F41**	n/a	9 T1
☐ Derate conductors in accordance w/ **T25,26**	3705.3	310.15B&C
☐ Conductors ≥ #8 must be stranded EXC	3406.4	310.3C
• GECs & bonding conductors (***pp. 248–252***) solid OK	3406.4	250.62&118
☐ No splices or taps inside raceways EXC	3406.11.1	300.13A
• Raceways w/ removable covers, e.g., wireways	3406.11.1	300.13A
☐ Splicing in conduit bodies only if marked w/ volume & volume is sufficient **T30**	3905.12.3.1	314.16C2
☐ Wet-rated reqd in wet location raceways	3803.10	310.10C
☐ Raceways (including PVC) containing conductors ≥#4 req smoothly rounded bushing/liner where entering enclosures **F47**	3906.1.1	300.4G[40]

FIG. 39 Conduit Bends

Not more than the equivalent of 4 quarter bends (360°) is allowed between pull points.

Offsets are included in the calculation for maximum number of bends.

90° 90° 90° 45° 45° 90°

90+90+90+45+45+90 = 450°

VIOLATION!

A pull point, such as a box or conduit body, should have been inserted.

40. Smoothly rounded metal (uninsulated) fitting now OK in NEC; IRC still requires insulated fitting.

Metal Wireways & Auxiliary Gutters — 20 NEC

Auxiliary gutters supplement the wiring space of cabinets (panelboard enclosures), switchboards, and meter centers and may also contain bus bars. Wireways are essentially the same materials as auxiliary gutters and are re-enterable as a raceway system. The rules for auxiliary gutters are in NEC article 366.

- ☐ Wet-location wireways must be listed for wet locations **T17** ________ 376.10
- ☐ Where horizontal, support at each end & at max. 5-ft. intervals ______ 376.30A
- ☐ Where vertical, support at max. 15-ft. intervals ________ 376.30B
- ☐ Max. 1 joint between supports on vertical runs ________ 376.30B
- ☐ Group parallel conductors in sets w/ 1 of each phase & neutral ______ 376.20
- ☐ Max. conductor fill 20% of wireway CSA **F40** ________ 376.22A
- ☐ Splices & taps max. 75% CSA of wireway ________ 376.56A
- ☐ Derating applicable only where >30 conductors at CSA **F40** ______ 376.22B
- ☐ Deflected conductors req clearance as per **T18A,F21** ________ 376.23A
- ☐ Clearance for deflected conductors applies to wireways that are deflected >30° ________ 376.23A
- ☐ When used as pull boxes, same dimension reqs as **F35** ________ 376.23B

FIG. 40

Metal Wireways

Derating for conductor proximity (bundling) is not applicable for ≤30 current-carrying conductors at any one cross-sectional area.

Nonmetallic Wireways & Auxiliary Gutters — 20 NEC

- ☐ Nonmetallic wireways & auxiliary gutters must be listed ________ 378.6
- ☐ Horizontal support intervals max. 3 ft., vertical 4 ft. ________ 378.30A&B
- ☐ Expansion fittings reqd if length change anticipated to be >¼ in. ____ 378.44
- ☐ Derating per 310.15C1 is applicable to conductors ________ 378.22

Other than the four items above, the rules for metal wireways apply to nonmetallic wireways and auxiliary gutters.

FIG. 41

Raceway Fill

TABLE 32 — PERCENTAGE OF CROSS-SECTIONAL AREA OF CONDUIT OR TUBING FOR CONDUCTORS & CABLES ◆ CHAPTER 9 TABLE 1

Number of Conductors or Cables	Max. Cross-Sectional Area[A,B,C]
1	55
2	31
>2	40[D]

A. When pulling 3 conductors where the ratio of the raceway (inside diameter) to the conductor (outside diameter) is between 2.8 & 3.2, jamming can occur. A larger raceway should be chosen.
B. Multiconductor cables in raceways are considered a single conductor for purposes of fill. Use the major diameter of elliptical cables as a circle diameter for fill purposes.
C. This table only applies to complete conduit and tubing systems, not to short sections installed to protect exposed wiring from damage.
D. Conduit or tubing nipples ≤24 in. between boxes or cabinets are allowed 60% fill.

CONDUCTOR FILL-IN RACEWAYS

__T33__ & __T34__ are used to determine the minimum size raceway when conductors are not all the same size, as will often be necessary for a particular size circuit plus its equipment grounding conductors or for a combination of circuits in a raceway. When all conductors are the same size, NEC Annex C contains 85 pages of tables for which the 40% fill calculation is considered. We have included excerpts from 6 of the most commonly used wire and raceway types from these tables, __T35–40__. In addition to physical fill limitations, derating (__p. 266__) must be considered.

TABLE 33	CONDUCTOR AREA ◆ (CHAPTER 9 TABLES 5, 5A, 8)				
Size AWG or kcmil	Bare (Stranded)	TW, THW THHW, THW-2	THHN, THWN THWN-2	XHHW, XHHW-2	XHHW (Compact AL)
14	0.004	0.0139	0.0097	0.0139	—
12	0.006	0.0181	0.0133	0.0181	—
10	0.011	0.0243	0.0211	0.0243	—
8	0.017	0.0437	0.0366	0.0437	0.0394
6	0.027	0.0726	0.0507	0.0590	0.0530
4	0.042	0.0973	0.0824	0.0814	0.0730
3	0.053	0.1134	0.0973	0.0962	—
2	0.067	0.1333	0.1158	0.1146	0.1017
1	0.087	0.1901	0.1562	0.1534	0.1352
1/0	0.109	0.2223	0.1855	0.1825	0.1590
2/0	0.137	0.2624	0.2223	0.2190	0.1885
3/0	0.173	0.3117	0.2679	0.2642	0.2290
4/0	0.219	0.3718	0.3237	0.3197	0.2733
250	0.260	0.4596	0.3970	0.3904	0.3421
300	0.312	0.5281	0.4608	0.4536	0.4015
350	0.364	0.5958	0.5242	0.5166	0.4536
400	0.416	0.6619	0.5863	0.5782	0.5026
500	0.519	0.7901	0.7073	0.6984	0.6082
600	0.626	0.9729	0.8676	0.8709	0.7542
700	0.730	1.1010	0.9887	0.9923	0.8659
750	0.782	1.1652	1.0496	1.0532	0.9331
800	0.834	1.2272	1.1085	1.1122	—
900	0.940	1.3561	1.2311	1.2351	1.0733
1000	1.042	1.4784	1.3478	1.3519	1.1882

TABLE 34	40% AREA FOR RACEWAY FILL ◆ (CHAPTER 9 TABLE 4)								
Trade Size	Square-Inch Area for >2 Conductors (40% of CSA)								
	EMT	ENT	FMC	LFMC	LFNC(B)	IMC	RMC	PVC80	PVC40
⅜	—	—	0.046	0.077	0.077	—	—	—	—
½	0.122	0.114	0.127	0.125	0.125	0.137	0.125	0.087	0.114
¾	0.213	0.203	0.213	0.216	0.216	0.235	0.220	0.164	0.203
1	0.346	0.333	0.327	0.349	0.349	0.384	0.355	0.275	0.333
1¼	0.598	0.581	0.511	0.611	0.611	0.659	0.610	0.495	0.581
1½	0.814	0.794	0.743	0.792	0.792	0.890	0.829	0.684	0.794
2	1.342	1.316	1.307	1.298	1.298	1.452	1.363	1.150	1.316
2½	2.343	—	1.963	1.953	—	2.054	1.946	1.647	1.878
3	3.538	—	2.827	2.990	—	3.169	3.000	2.577	2.907
3½	4.618	—	3.848	3.893	—	4.234	4.004	3.475	3.895
4	5.901	—	5.027	5.077	—	5.452	5.153	4.503	5.022
5	—	—	—	—	—	—	8.085	7.142	7.904
6	—	—	—	—	—	—	11.663	10.239	11.427

Conduit Fill Example:

Chapter 9 table 1 states that 3 or more conductors cannot fill >40% of the raceway area.

Example: A circuit has 3 #2 current-carrying conductors & 1 #6 EGC, all with THHN insulation. What size PVC Schedule 40 is needed?

From **T33**, #2 THHN = 0.1158 sq. in.
From **T33**, #6 THHN = 0.0507 sq. in.

3 × 0.1158 = 0.3474 sq. in.
1 × 0.0507 = 0.0507 sq. in.

Total min. area = 0.3981 sq. in.

From **T34**, the next larger size PVC 40 is 0.581 sq. in. in the row for 1¼-in. conduit.

TABLE 35	EMT FILL—ALL CONDUCTORS SAME SIZE ◆ ANNEX TC.1									
Size	Maximum Number of Conductors in THHN, THWN, THWN-2									
▪	½	¾	1	1¼	1½	2	2½	3	3½	4
14	12	22	35	61	84	138	241	364	476	608
12	9	16	26	45	61	101	176	266	347	443
10	5	10	16	28	38	63	111	167	219	279
8	3	6	9	16	22	36	64	96	126	161
6	2	4	7	12	16	26	46	69	91	116
4	1	2	4	7	10	16	28	43	56	71
3	1	1	3	6	8	13	24	36	47	60
2	1	1	3	5	7	11	20	30	40	51
1	1	1	1	4	5	8	15	22	29	37
1/0	1	1	1	3	4	7	12	19	25	32
2/0	0	1	1	2	3	6	10	16	20	26
3/0	0	1	1	1	3	5	8	13	17	22
4/0	0	1	1	1	2	4	7	11	14	18
250	0	0	1	1	1	3	6	9	11	15
300	0	0	1	1	1	3	5	7	10	13
350	0	0	1	1	1	2	4	6	9	11
400	0	0	0	1	1	1	4	6	8	10
500	0	0	0	1	1	1	3	5	6	8
600	0	0	0	1	1	1	2	4	5	7
700	0	0	0	1	1	1	2	3	4	6
750	0	0	0	0	1	1	1	3	4	5
800	0	0	0	0	1	1	1	3	4	5
900	0	0	0	0	1	1	1	3	3	4
1000	0	0	0	0	1	1	1	2	3	4

TABLE 36	EMT FILL—ALL CONDUCTORS SAME SIZE ◆ ANNEX TC.1A									
Size	Maximum Number of Conductors in Compact Stranded XHHW, XHHW-2									
▪	½	¾	1	1¼	1½	2	2½	3	3½	4
14	–	–	–	–	–	–	–	–	–	–
12	–	–	–	–	–	–	–	–	–	–
10	–	–	–	–	–	–	–	–	–	–
8	3	5	8	15	20	34	59	90	117	149
6	1	4	6	11	15	25	44	66	87	111
4	1	3	4	8	11	18	32	48	63	81
3	–	–	–	–	–	–	–	–	–	–
2	1	1	3	6	8	13	23	34	45	58
1	1	1	2	4	6	10	17	26	34	43
1/0	1	1	1	3	5	8	14	22	29	37
2/0	1	1	1	3	4	7	12	18	24	31
3/0	0	1	1	2	3	6	10	15	20	25
4/0	0	1	1	1	3	5	8	13	17	21
250	0	1	1	1	2	4	7	10	13	17
300	0	0	1	1	1	3	6	9	11	14
350	0	0	1	1	1	3	5	8	10	13
400	0	0	1	1	1	2	4	7	9	11
500	0	0	0	1	1	1	4	6	7	9
600	0	0	0	1	1	1	3	4	6	8
700	0	0	0	1	1	1	2	4	5	7
750	0	0	0	1	1	1	2	3	5	6
800	–	–	–	–	–	–	–	–	–	–
900	0	0	0	0	1	1	1	3	4	5
1000	0	0	0	0	1	1	1	3	4	5

TABLE 37	RMC FILL—ALL CONDUCTORS SAME SIZE ◆ ANNEX TC.9											
Size	Maximum Number of Conductors in THHN, THWN, THWN-2											
•	½	¾	1	1¼	1½	2	2½	3	3½	4	5	6
14	13	22	36	63	85	140	200	309	412	531	833	1202
12	9	16	26	46	62	102	146	225	301	387	608	877
10	6	10	17	29	39	64	92	142	189	244	383	552
8	3	6	9	16	22	37	53	82	109	140	221	318
6	2	4	7	12	16	27	38	59	79	101	159	230
4	1	2	4	7	10	16	23	36	48	62	98	141
3	1	1	3	6	8	14	20	31	41	53	83	120
2	1	1	3	5	7	11	17	26	34	44	70	100
1	1	1	1	4	5	8	12	19	25	33	51	74
1/0	1	1	1	3	4	7	10	16	21	27	43	63
2/0	0	1	1	2	3	6	8	13	18	23	36	52
3/0	0	1	1	1	3	5	7	11	15	19	30	43
4/0	0	1	1	1	2	4	6	9	12	16	25	36
250	0	0	1	1	1	3	5	7	10	13	20	29
300	0	0	1	1	1	3	4	6	8	11	17	25
350	0	0	1	1	1	2	3	5	7	10	15	22
400	0	0	1	1	1	2	3	5	7	8	13	20
500	0	0	0	1	1	1	2	4	5	7	11	16
600	0	0	0	1	1	1	1	3	4	6	9	13
700	0	0	0	1	1	1	1	3	4	5	8	11
750	0	0	0	0	1	1	1	3	4	5	7	11
800	0	0	0	0	1	1	1	2	3	4	7	10
900	0	0	0	0	1	1	1	2	3	4	6	9
1000	0	0	0	0	1	1	1	1	3	4	6	10

TABLE 38	RMC FILL—ALL CONDUCTORS SAME SIZE ◆ ANNEX TC.9A											
Size	Maximum Number of Conductors in Compact Stranded XHHW, XHHW-2											
•	½	¾	1	1¼	1½	2	2½	3	3½	4	5	6
14	–	–	–	–	–	–	–	–	–	–	–	–
12	–	–	–	–	–	–	–	–	–	–	–	–
10	–	–	–	–	–	–	–	–	–	–	–	–
8	3	5	9	15	21	34	49	76	101	130	205	296
6	2	4	6	11	15	25	36	56	75	97	152	220
4	1	3	5	8	11	18	26	41	55	70	110	159
3	–	–	–	–	–	–	–	–	–	–	–	–
2	1	1	3	6	8	13	19	29	39	50	79	114
1	1	1	2	4	6	10	14	22	29	38	59	86
1/0	1	1	1	4	5	8	12	19	25	32	51	73
2/0	1	1	1	3	4	7	10	16	21	27	43	62
3/0	0	1	1	2	3	6	8	13	17	22	35	51
4/0	0	1	1	1	3	5	7	11	14	19	29	42
250	0	1	1	1	2	4	5	8	11	15	23	34
300	0	0	1	1	1	3	4	6	9	11	18	25
350	0	0	1	1	1	3	4	6	9	11	18	25
400	0	0	1	1	1	2	4	6	8	10	16	23
500	0	0	0	1	1	1	3	5	6	8	13	19
600	0	0	0	1	1	1	2	4	5	7	10	15
700	0	0	0	1	1	1	1	3	4	6	9	13
750	0	0	0	1	1	1	1	3	4	5	8	12
800	–	–	–	–	–	–	–	–	–	–	–	–
900	0	0	0	0	1	1	1	2	3	4	6	9
1000	0	0	0	0	1	1	1	1	3	4	6	10

TABLE 39	PVC-80 FILL—ALL CONDUCTORS SAME SIZE ◆ ANNEX TC.10										
Size	Maximum Number of Conductors in THHN, THWN, THWN-2										
•	½	¾	1	1¼	1½	2	2½	3	3½	4	5	6
14	9	17	28	51	70	118	170	265	358	464	736	1055
12	6	12	20	37	51	86	124	193	261	338	537	770
10	4	7	13	23	32	54	78	122	164	213	338	485
8	2	4	7	13	18	31	45	70	95	123	195	279
6	1	3	5	9	13	22	32	51	68	89	141	202
4	1	1	3	6	8	14	20	31	42	54	86	124
3	1	1	3	5	7	12	17	26	35	46	73	105
2	1	1	2	4	6	10	14	22	30	39	61	88
1	0	1	1	3	4	7	10	16	22	29	45	65
1/0	0	1	1	2	3	6	9	14	18	24	38	55
2/0	0	1	1	1	3	5	7	11	15	20	32	46
3/0	0	1	1	1	2	4	6	9	13	17	26	38
4/0	0	0	1	1	1	3	5	8	10	14	22	31
250	0	0	1	1	1	3	4	6	8	11	18	25
300	0	0	0	1	1	2	3	5	7	9	15	22
350	0	0	0	1	1	1	3	5	6	8	13	19
400	0	0	0	1	1	1	3	4	6	7	12	17
500	0	0	0	1	1	1	2	3	5	6	10	14
600	0	0	0	0	1	1	1	3	4	5	8	12
700	0	0	0	0	1	1	1	2	3	4	7	10
750	0	0	0	0	1	1	1	2	3	4	7	9
800	0	0	0	0	1	1	1	2	3	4	6	9
900	0	0	0	0	0	1	1	1	3	3	6	8
1000	0	0	0	0	0	1	1	1	2	3	5	7

TABLE 40	PVC-80 FILL—ALL CONDUCTORS SAME SIZE ◆ ANNEX TC.10A										
Size	Maximum Number of Conductors in Compact Stranded XHHW, XHHW-2										
•	½	¾	1	1¼	1½	2	2½	3	3½	4	5	6
14	–	–	–	–	–	–	–	–	–	–	–	–
12	–	–	–	–	–	–	–	–	–	–	–	–
10	–	–	–	–	–	–	–	–	–	–	–	–
8	1	4	7	12	17	29	42	65	88	114	181	260
6	1	3	5	9	13	21	31	48	65	85	134	193
4	1	1	3	6	9	15	22	35	47	61	98	140
3	–	–	–	–	–	–	–	–	–	–	–	–
2	1	1	2	5	6	11	16	25	34	44	70	100
1	1	1	1	3	5	8	12	19	25	33	53	75
1/0	0	1	1	3	4	7	10	16	22	28	45	64
2/0	0	1	1	2	3	6	8	13	18	24	38	54
3/0	0	1	1	1	3	5	7	11	15	19	31	44
4/0	0	0	1	1	2	4	6	9	12	16	26	37
250	0	0	1	1	1	3	5	7	10	13	21	30
300	0	0	1	1	1	3	4	6	8	11	17	25
350	0	0	1	1	1	2	3	5	7	10	15	22
400	0	0	0	1	1	1	3	5	7	9	14	20
500	0	0	0	1	1	1	2	4	5	7	11	17
600	0	0	0	1	1	1	1	3	4	6	9	13
700	0	0	0	0	1	1	1	3	4	5	8	12
750	0	0	0	0	1	1	1	2	3	5	7	11
800	–	–	–	–	–	–	–	–	–	–	–	–
900	0	0	0	0	1	1	1	2	3	4	6	9
1000	0	0	0	0	0	1	1	1	3	3	6	8

RMC—Rigid Metal Conduit — 21 IRC — 20 NEC

- ☐ Galvanized RMC OK for direct burial or embedment w/ approved corrosion protection ______ T3801.4 — 344.10B1
- ☐ Where exposed to moisture, field-cut Fe threads req L&L compound ______ T3801.4 — 300.6A
- ☐ Provide bushing or fitting at box connection **F42** ______ 3906.1 — 344.46
- ☐ Threadless connectors not OK on threaded conduit ends __ n/a — 344.42A
- ☐ Running threads not OK for connection at couplings ______ n/a — 344.42B
- ☐ Secure in place within 3 ft. of termination EXC ______ T3802.1 — 344.30A1
  - 5 ft. where structural members prevent fastening ≤3 ft. __ n/a — 344.30A2
- ☐ Horizontal runs supported by holes in framing OK if securely fastened within 3 ft. of box, conduit body, or cabinet ___ T3802.1 — 344.30B
- ☐ Support intervals max. 10 ft. or **T41** for straight runs w/ threaded couplings & supports that prevent stresses to termination points __ T3802.1 — 344.30B2

Intermediate metal conduit (IMC) has the same rules as shown above for RMC. The NEC code citations for IMC begin with the number 342.

FIG. 42

RMC—Rigid Metal Conduit

Cut ends reamed

A bushing is required to prevent abrasion where rigid conduit enters a box, fitting, or other enclosure

Field-cut threads standard ¾-in. taper per ft.

Locknuts

Bushing

TABLE 41 — CONDUIT SUPPORT SPACING
IRC T3802.1 ◆ NEC T344.30B2 & 352.30

IMC/RMC Size	Max. Spacing	PVC Size	Max. Spacing
½ – ¾ in.	10 ft.	½ in.–1 in.	3 ft.
1 in.	12 ft.	1¼ in.–2 in.	5 ft.
1¼ – 1½ in.	14 ft.	2½ in.–3 in.	6 ft
2 – 2½ in.	16 ft.	3½ in.–5 in.	7 ft.
3 in. & larger	20 ft.	6 in.	8 ft.

EMT—Electrical Metallic Tubing — 21 IRC — 20 NEC

EMT is available as zinc-coated, stainless steel, or aluminum.

- ☐ In wet locations all supports corrosion-resistant ______ T3801.4 — 358.10D
- ☐ Listed wet-location fittings & connectors in wet locations T3801.4 — 358.42
- ☐ Couplings & connectors must be made up tight ______ 3403.3 — 358.42
- ☐ Direct burial reqs suitable protection approved for the condition, buried aluminum EMT reqs supplemental protection ___ T3801.4 — 358.10B1

*EMT does not have a specified cover depth in **T3**; other methods in that table are suitable for direct burial. Supplementary nonmetallic coatings must be evaluated for flame propagation, effect on the primary coatings, coupling fit, and electrical continuity at couplings.*

- ☐ Secure in place at intervals ≤10 ft. & within 3 ft. of termination EXC ______ T3802.1 — 358.30A
  - 5-ft. unbroken length if structure does not readily allow 3 ft. _n/a — 358.30AX
- ☐ Horizontal runs supported by holes in framing at intervals ≤10 ft. OK if securely fastened within 3 ft. of termination ____ T3802.1 — 358.30B
- ☐ Not allowed as support for boxes or luminaires ______ 3906.8.4 — 358.12
- ☐ Allowed as support for conduit bodies ______ 3906.8.4 — 358.12
- ☐ Bends must be smooth—cannot reduce internal diameter of tubing **F39** ______ 3802.5 — 358.24
- ☐ Ream cut ends to remove rough edges ______ T3802.1 — 358.28A
- ☐ Permitted as EGC EXC ______ 3908.9 — 358.60
  - EMT outdoors to rooftop AC equipment reqs wire EGC __ n/a — 440.9

FIG. 43

EMT—Electrical Metallic Tubing

Raintight wet location

Dry location

Older "raintight" fittings did not meet modern listing standards. Listed raintight connectors have identifying features such as bronze collars to indicate they contain the required gland inside the fittings.

FMC—Flexible Metal Conduit F45

FMC—Flexible Metal Conduit F45	21 IRC	20 NEC
☐ Not allowed in wet locations	T3801.4	348.12
☐ Not allowed where subject to corrosion or damage	T3801.4	348.12
☐ Trim cut ends to remove rough edges unless using fittings that thread into FMC	T3802.1	348.28
☐ Support interval max. 4½ ft. & 12 in. from boxes EXC	T3802.1	348.30A
• Where flexibility needed: 36 in. OK for sizes ½ in. – 1¼ in. 4 ft. OK for sizes 1½ in. – 2 in., 5 ft. OK for sizes ≥2½ in.	T3802.1	348.30AX2
• Lighting whip in accessible ceiling OK to 6 ft.	T3802.1	348.30AX4
☐ Cable ties to secure & support must be listed for same	3802.6	348.30
☐ Horizontal runs supported by holes in framing at ≤4½-ft. interval OK if securely fastened ≤3 ft. of box, conduit body, or cabinet	T3802.1	348.30B
☐ OK as EGC if circuit ≤20A, fittings listed for grounding, size ≤1¼ in., no flexibility needed after installation & ≤6 ft. long	3908.9.1	250.118(5)
☐ Wire EGC reqd if flexibility reqd after installation	3908.9.1	348.60
☐ Angle connections may not be concealed **F45**	n/a	348.42

FIG. 44

LFMC—Liquidtight Flexible Metal Conduit

PVC jacket

Connector

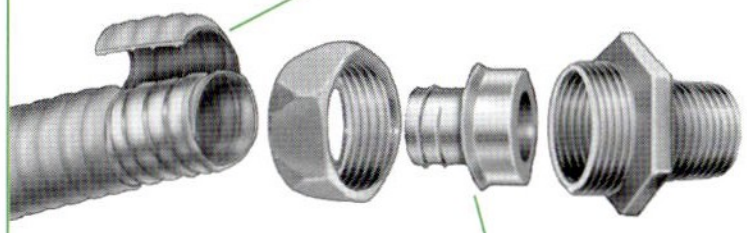

LFMC for direct burial must be listed and marked for the purpose. FMC and LFMC cannot be used where subject to physical damage.

FIG. 45

FMC—Flexible Metal Conduit

Cut ends of metal ribbon must be trimmed.

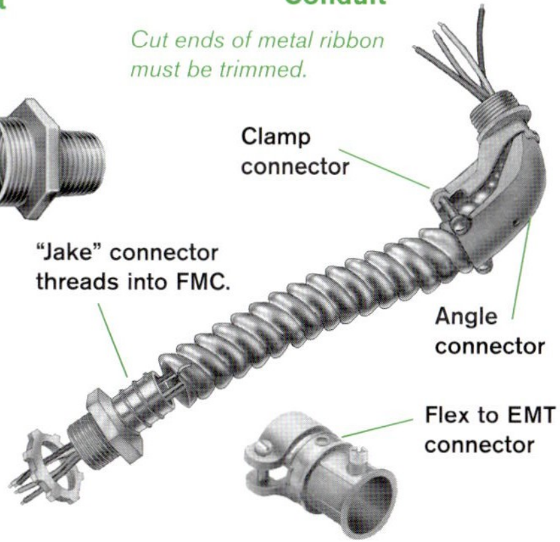

Clamp connector

"Jake" connector threads into FMC.

Angle connector

Flex to EMT connector

LFMC—Liquidtight Flexible Metal Conduit F44

LFMC—Liquidtight Flexible Metal Conduit F44	21 IRC	20 NEC
☐ OK for wet locations	T3801.4	350.10
☐ OK for direct burial if L&L for same	T3801.4	350.10
☐ OK as EGC in lengths ≤6 ft. if ½-in. conduit max. 20A OCPD or ¾–1¼ in. conduit w/ max. 60A OCPD, fittings listed for grounding & no flexibility needed after installation	3908.9.2	250.118
☐ Securing & supporting same as FMC	T3802.1	350.30
☐ Cable ties to secure & support must be listed for same	3802.6	350.30
☐ Cut ends trimmed to remove rough edges	T3802.1	350.28

LFNC-Liquidtight Flexible Nonmetallic Conduit F46

LFNC-Liquidtight Flexible Nonmetallic Conduit F46	21 IRC	20 NEC
☐ Not OK where subject to damage	T3801.4	356.12
☐ OK for direct burial or encasement when L&L for same	T3801.4	356.10
☐ OK in lengths >6 ft. if secured every 3 ft. & within 12 in. of each box, cabinet, or fitting EXC	T3801.4	356.10&30
• Unsupported up to 3 ft. where flexibility reqd (motors)	T3802.1	356.30
☐ Couplings & connectors req listing for LFNC	3403.3	356.42
☐ Cable ties to secure & support must be listed for same	T3802.1	356.30
☐ No concealed or buried angle connectors	3403.3	356.42
☐ EGC reqd	3908.9	356.60

FIG. 46

LFNC—Liquidtight Flexible Nonmetallic Conduit

Angle connector

Type B LFNC

LFNC is often used for connections to pool motors.

PVC—Rigid Polyvinyl Chloride Conduit

	21 IRC	20 NEC
☐ OK in wet, damp, or dry locations & underground	T3801.4	352.10
☐ Cover above buried conduits per **T3**	T3803.1	300.5A
☐ Not permitted in environments >50°C (122°F)	n/a	352.12D
☐ Support per **T41** w/ fastening method that allows movement from thermal expansion & contraction	T3802.1	352.30
☐ Horizontal runs supported by holes in framing OK if securely fastened within 3 ft. of box, conduit body, or cabinet	T3802.1	352.30B
☐ Cut ends trimmed to remove rough edges **F47**	T3802.1	352.28
☐ Bushings or adapters reqd to prevent wire abrasion	T3802.1	352.46
☐ Smooth bushings reqd for conductors ≥#4 **F47**	3906.1.1	300.4G
☐ Expansion fittings reqd if subject to ≥¼-in. movement **T42**	n/a	352.44
☐ Not OK for support of luminaires or boxes	3906.8.4	352.12B
☐ OK for support of conduit bodies	3906.8.4X	352.10H

FIG. 47 PVC Conduit & Connector

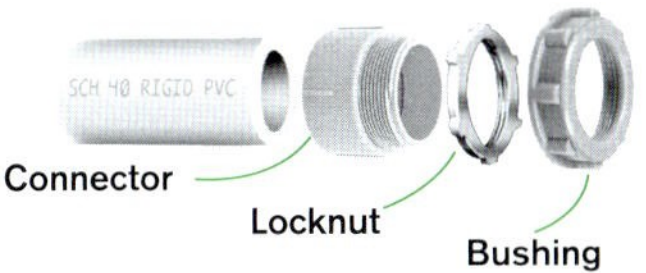

When the connector to an enclosure contains conductors ≥#4, a smoothly rounded bushing must be placed over it to prevent scraping the conductors. A locknut is also required—the bushing cannot act in place of the locknut.

TABLE 42	DISTANCE AT WHICH PVC CONDUIT REQUIRES EXPANSION FITTINGS ◆ T352.44				
Max. Temp Change °F[A]	Distance (ft.– in.)	Max. Temp Change °F[A]	Distance (ft.– in.)	Max. Temp Change °F[A]	Distance (ft.– in.)
40	15 – 5	80	7 – 9	120	5 – 2
50	12 – 4	90	6 – 10	130	4 – 9
60	10 – 3	100	6 – 2	140	4 – 5
70	8 – 10	110	5 – 7	150	4 – 1

A. The difference between the coldest and hottest temperatures to which the conduit will be exposed determines the maximum length before which expansion fittings are required.

ENT—Electrical Nonmetallic Tubing F48

	21 IRC	20 NEC
☐ ENT & fittings reqd to be listed	3403.3	362.6
☐ Must be concealed behind 15-minute finish rating EXC	n/a	362.10
• In buildings ≤3 floors above grade (or vehicle garage)	T3801.4	362.10
• In buildings w/ NFPA 13 fire-sprinkler system	T3801.4	362.10X
☐ OK above suspended ceilings w/ 15-minute rating EXC	T3801.4	362.12
• Rating not reqd if NFPA 13 fire-sprinkler system	T3801.4	362.10X
☐ OK encased in concrete w/ identified fittings	T3801.4	362.10
☐ Not allowed for direct earth burial	T3801.4	362.12
☐ Not allowed where ambient temp >122°F	T3801.4	362.12
☐ Not allowed where subject to physical damage	T3801.4	362.12
☐ Must be marked sunlight-resistant if used outdoors	T3801.4	362.12
☐ Max. support interval 30 in.	T3802.1	362.30

FIG. 48 ENT & Connector

ENT is often referred to as "smurf tubing." It is allowed for line-voltage wiring, and its most common use is for power-limited circuits & communications wiring.

CABLE SYSTEMS

Cable systems with multiple conductors contain the circuit wiring and equipment grounding conductor in an overall outer sheath. Common residential and light-commercial cable systems include nonmetallic sheathed cable(NM), underground feeder cable (UF), service-entrance cable (SE), metal-clad cable (MC), and armored cable (AC). Power and control tray cable (TC) is also used in residential, though less commonly than the others.

Protection in Framing (NM, UF, AC, MC, SE)	**21 IRC**	**20 NEC**
☐ Only NEC wiring methods are recognized as suitable	3801.2	110.8
☐ Cables through bored holes < 1¼-in. setback from face of framing members req protection w/ bushing or steel plate **F49**	T3802.1	300.4A1
☐ Notches req protection w/ min. 1/16-in. steel plate	T3802.1	300.4A2
☐ Shallow grooves intended to be covered w/ finish materials (carpet, wallboard, etc.) req min. 1/16-in. steel plate	T3802.1	300.4F
☐ Cables parallel to framing members req min. 1¼-in. setback from surface **F49,50**	T3802.1	300.4D
☐ Listed grommets reqd to protect nonmetallic cables from holes through metal framing	T3802.1	300.4B1
☐ Protect cable from physical damage where necessary w/ sleeve of RMC, IMC, EMT, schedule 80 PVC, or RTRC	3802.3.2	334.15B

Securing & Supporting to Framing		
☐ Cables to closely follow building finish or running boards	3802.3.1	334.15A
☐ Secure w/ cable ties, stackers, staples, or hangers **F50**	T3802.1	334.30
☐ Cable ties listed & identified for securement & support	3802.6	334.30
☐ Do not overdrive staples or staple flat cable on edge	T3802.1	334.30
☐ Support intervals max. 4½ ft. & within12 in. of box EXC	T3802.1	334.30
• ≤8 in. from single-gang plastic box w/o cable clamp	T3802.1	314.17B2X
☐ Max. cable length between cable entry & support 18 in.	n/a	334.30[41]

Cables in Basements & Crawlspaces (NM, SE, UF)		
☐ Install through bored holes in joists (see *p. 53*) or attach to running boards on underside of joists **F55** EXC	3802.4	334.15C
• Cables ≥8/3 or ≥6/2 can attach to underside of joists	3802.4	334.15C

41. When a conductor forms a loop or otherwise is not straight between the box and the nearest support, maximum conductor length is 18 inches.

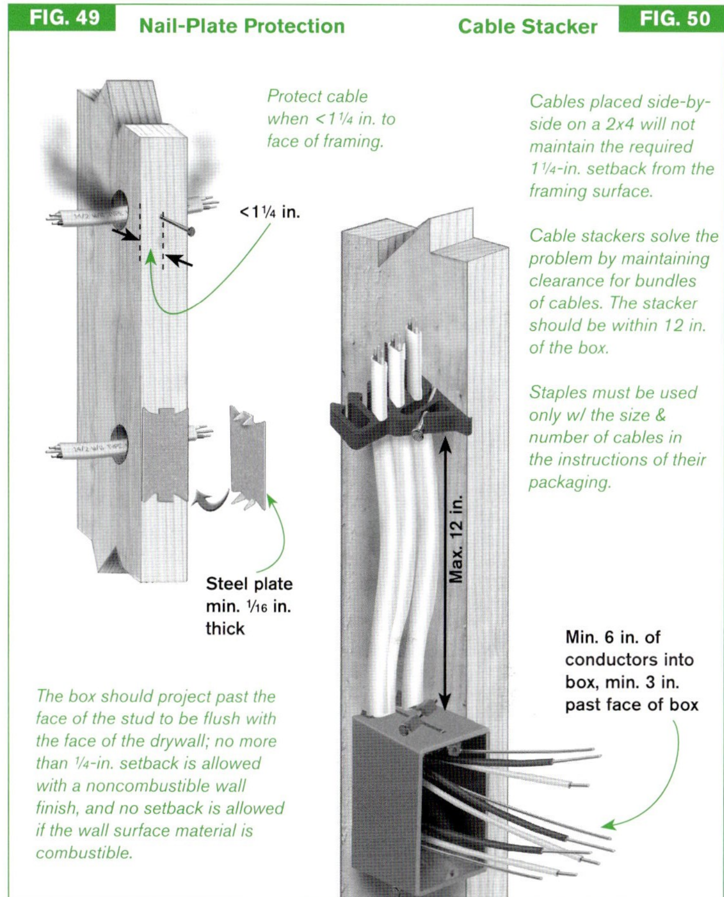

FIG. 49 Nail-Plate Protection

FIG. 50 Cable Stacker

Securing NM, UF & SE at Panels & Boxes

Item	21 IRC	20 NEC
☐ Openings for conductors entering panel must be closed in approved manner	3907.7	312.5C
☐ Clamps per L&L (chase nipples are not clamps)	3403.3	110.3B
☐ Each cable secured to panel enclosure EXC	3907.8	312.5C
• May enter top of surface-mounted panel enclosure through nonflexible raceways 1½ ft.–10 ft. in length if all the following:	3907.8X	312.5CX
1. Cable fastened ≤12 in. from outer end of raceway		
2. Raceway extends above enclosure & not penetrating structural ceiling		
3. Fitting on each end of raceway to protect against abrasion		
4. Raceways sealed or plugged at outer end		
5. Cable sheath continuous in raceway & ¼ in. into enclosure		
6. Raceway fastened at outer end & per applicable raceway article		
7. Conduit or tubing fill not exceeding allowable fill per Chapter 9 **T32**		
☐ Cable can be protected in basement walls same method as above when terminating in an outlet or device box	3802.4	334.15C
☐ Min. ¼-in. cable sheathing into box & past edge of clamp	3802.4	314.17B2
☐ Each cable secured to boxes w/ clamps EXC	3905.3.1	314.17B2
• Secured to framing ≤8 in. from single-gang box	3905.3.1X	314.17B2X

NM Cable F52

Item	21 IRC	20 NEC
☐ Normally dry locations only—not damp or wet locations	T3801.4	334.12B4
☐ Interior of underground conduits is a wet location	3803.10	300.5
☐ Interior of above-ground conduits in wet locations above grade is considered a wet location	3802.8	300.9
☐ Do not strip sheathing from cable installed in conduit	n/a	310.8A&B
☐ Min. bend radius 5× cable diameter (if elliptical cable, diameter is based on the dimension that is being bent)	3802.5	334.24
☐ NM not suitable as flexible cord or w/ plug on end	3403.3	110.3B
☐ Conductors rated 90° for purposes of derating, final OCPD selection must be based on 60° rating **T23**	3705.4.4	334.80
☐ Derate if >2 cables in fireblocked wood-frame hole or if >2 in contact w/ thermal insulation w/out spacing	3705.4.4	334.80
☐ Protect cables in attic per same rules as for AC **F53**	3802.2.1	334.23

FIG. 51 UF Cable

FIG. 52 NM Cable

UF is suitable for dry, damp, or wet locations & for direct burial; NM is only for dry locations.

Cable Protection In Attics F53

Item	21 IRC	20 NEC
☐ Provide guard strips for cables on face of floors, joists, rafters, or studs within 6 ft. of attic scuttle	3802.2.1	320.23A
☐ If attic has permanently installed stair or ladder, protect cables to height of 7 ft. in entire attic	3802.2.1	320.23A[42]
☐ Running boards or guard strips not reqd for cables on sides of framing members if set back 1¼ in. from face	3802.2.2	320.23B
☐ Cables min. 1½ in. below sheet-steel roof decks	n/a	300.4E

FIG. 53 Cables in Attics

Not allowed on face of framing or spanning across joists within 6 ft. of access opening

Setback 1¼ in. from rafter face

Bored holes min. 2 in. from surface

1 × 2 guard strips protect cable

Guard Cable Guard

Cross section

Cable bend too sharp

42. Clarification that a pull-down ladder does not trigger this more stringent requirement.

UF—Underground Feeder Cable F51

	21 IRC	20 NEC
☐ Follow NM rules when used as interior wiring	T3802.1	340.10#4
☐ OK for direct burial, depth per T3	T3801.4	340.10#1
☐ May be installed in wet or dry locations	T3801.4	340.10#3
☐ Not embedded in poured cement or concrete	T3801.4	340.12#8
☐ Not OK where subject to physical damage	T3801.4	340.12#10
☐ Protective conduit from reqd depth (up to 18 in.) & 8 ft. above grade or to conductor termination, whichever is less F54	3803.3	300.5D1
☐ Bushing reqd where underground cables exit conduit F54	3803.7	300.5H
☐ Protect where emerging from grade F54	3803.3	300.5D4
☐ Must be marked sunlight-resistant if exposed outdoors	3802.3	340.12
☐ Not OK strung through air w/o support messenger	340.12	
☐ Min. bend radius 5× cable diameter	3802.5	340.24

FIG. 54 Protecting Underground Cable

UF cable reqs protection where it emerges from the ground & to a height of at least 8 ft.

The protection should extend underground to the burial depth or 18 in., whichever is less.

Raceway protection (Schedule 80 PVC or steel conduit)

8 ft. min.

Per T3

UF

Must have bushing

SE—Service-Entrance Cable: Type USE (Underground)

	20 NEC
☐ OK as service-entrance conductor	338.10A
☐ Same rules as UF when installed underground	338.10B4b2
☐ Not OK as interior or above-ground wiring EXC	338.12B
• Where terminated inside an enclosure in an outdoor location	338.12B

FIG. 55 Cables Under Floor in Basement or Crawlspace

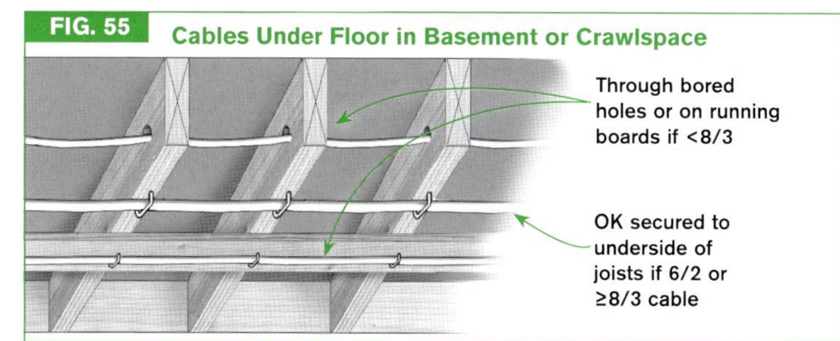

SE—Service-Entrance Cable: Type SE F56

	21 IRC	20 NEC
☐ As service-entrance conductor, see *p. 236*	3605	338.10A
☐ As interior wiring, follow same rules as NM EXC	3802.1	338.10B4
• ≤#10 60°C ampacity if contacting thermal insulation	3705.4.5	338.10B4[43]
• Derating (see *p. 266*) reqd when >2 cables in contact w/ thermal insulation, caulk, or sealing foam w/o maintaining spacing	n/a	338.10B4[43]
☐ Not OK underground, including inside raceways	n/a	338.12A
☐ Protection in attics per F53	n/a	338.10B4
☐ Uninsulated conductor only for EGC EXC	T3801.4	338.10B2
• Existing clothes dryer circuit originating from service panel	n/a	338.10B2X
☐ Min. bend radius 5× cable diameter	3802.5	338.24

FIG. 56 SE Cable

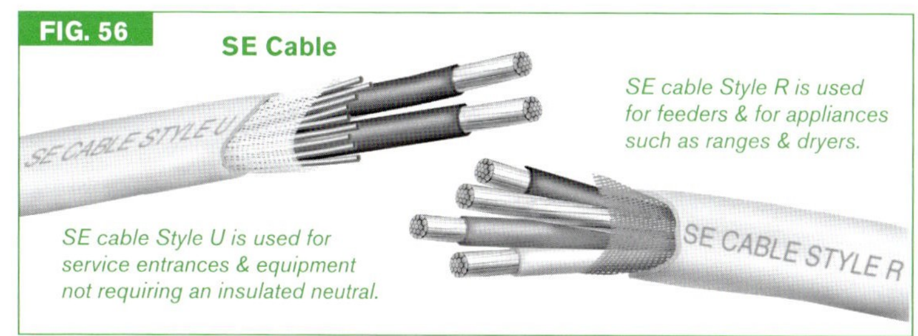

SE cable Style R is used for feeders & for appliances such as ranges & dryers.

SE cable Style U is used for service entrances & equipment not requiring an insulated neutral.

43. Small conductors limited to 60°C ampacity if in contact w/ thermal insulation.

AC—Armored Cable F58

AC—Armored Cable F58	21 IRC	20 NEC
☐ Cable & fittings must be listed	3403.3	320.6
☐ Conductors & cable armor req MFR markings	3403.3	320.120
☐ Not OK where subject to physical damage	T3801.4	320.12
☐ Closely follow surface of building finish or running boards	3802.3.1	320.15
☐ Dry locations only, not OK in wet or damp locations	T3801.4	320.10
☐ Conductors in thermal insulation req final OCPD selection based on 60° rating (90° rating OK only for derating purposes)	n/a	320.80A
☐ For attic installations, see NM cable F53	3802.2	320.23
☐ Secure ≤12 in. of enclosures & max. 4½-ft. intervals EXC	T3802.1	320.30B
• Where fished	n/a	330.30D
• ≤ 2 ft. from end where flexibility needed (motors)	T3802.1	320.30D
• Whip ≤ 6 ft. to luminaire in accessible ceiling F28	T3802.1	330.30D
☐ Allowed to be secured to underside of joists if secured to each joist & not exposed to physical damage	n/a	320.15
☐ Min. bend radius 5× cable diameter	3802.5	320.24
☐ Insulated (anti-short) bushing at terminations F58 A	3403.3	320.40
☐ Internal bond strip reqd in contact w/ cable armor F58 B	3403.3	320.100
☐ Armor is EGC—don't bring bond wire into box F58 B	3908.9	250.118
☐ Derating (*see **p. 30***) reqd when > 2 cables in contact w/ thermal insulation, caulk, or sealing foam w/o maintaining spacing	n/a	320.80C[44]

FIG. 57

MC Cable

MC cable contains an insulated EGC. When supplied with a corrosion-resistant outer jacket impervious to moisture and appropriately marked, it can be used in wet locations or buried.

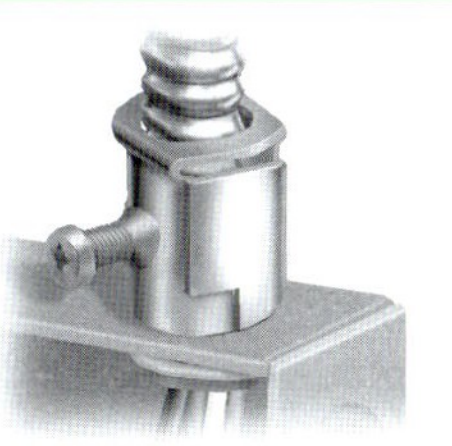

MC cable clamp (no locknut style)

FIG. 58

AC Cable

B

"Redhead" A Anti-short bushing

B

The metal sheath of AC cable, supplemented by an aluminum bonding conductor in contact with the sheath, is the EGC. The bonding conductor is not brought into the box.

MC—Metal-Clad Cable F57

MC—Metal-Clad Cable F57	21 IRC	20 NEC
☐ Cable & fittings req listing, fittings identified for such use	3403.3	330.6
☐ Dry locations only EXC	T3801.4	330.10A
• W/ corrosion-resistant jacket & conductors W rated	T3801.4	330.10A
☐ Not OK where subject to physical damage	T3801.4	330.12
☐ Secure & support at max. 6-ft. intervals	T3802.1	330.30B&C
• Holes in studs OK as support for horizontal runs	T3802.1	330.30C
☐ Secure within 12 in. of box or other termination EXC	T3802.1	330.30B
• Where fished	n/a	330.30D
• Whip ≤6 ft. to luminaire in accessible ceiling F28	T3802.1	330.30D
• ≤ 3 ft. from end where flexibility needed (e.g., motors)	T3802.1	330.30D
☐ Min. bend radius 7× cable diameter of corrugated armor	n/a	330.24B
☐ Protection in attics per F53	n/a	330.23
☐ Derating (see ***p. 266***) reqd when > 2 cables in contact w/ thermal insulation, caulk, or sealing foam w/o maintaining spacing	n/a	330.80C[44]

44. Derating required when more than 2 multiconductor cables through fireblocked opening or in contact with insulation without maintaining spacing.

OLD WIRING

From 1964 to 1971, NM cable containing a utility-grade aluminum alloy (AA-1350) was installed in millions of homes. Its UL listing was revoked in 1971, and in 1972 an improved alloy (AA-8000 series) was available and listed for use in NM cable. Precautions are needed for termination of older aluminum wire, particularly in small conductor sizes.

The insulation standard for NM cable required 90°C conductors starting with the 1984 edition. NM cable prior to that time is often subjected to temperatures in excess of the allowable rating and usually requires splicing to 90°C conductors at luminaires labeled for higher-temperature wiring.

Many of the circuit breakers and panelboards that were common even into the 1980s are now obsolete, requiring expensive specialty replacement breakers. For many of these older panels, AFCI & GFCI breakers are not available.

Aluminum Wiring — 20 NEC

- ☐ New AL wire reqd to be AA-8000 series alloy ____ 310.3B
- ☐ Switches ≤20A directly connected to AL req L&L as "CO/ALR" ____ 404.14C
- ☐ Receptacles ≤20A directly connected to AL req L&L as "CO/ALR" ____ 406.3C
- ☐ Splicing devices for dissimilar metals (AL & Cu) must be identified for the purpose & installed per their listing **F59** ____ 110.14
- ☐ Antioxidant compounds (if used) req installation AMI ____ 110.14
- ☐ Terminals (including breakers) for AL req identification for same ____ 110.14A

FIG. 59

Splicing Aluminum to Copper

Splicing devices must always be used in accordance with their listing & instructions.

This splicing device is rated for copper-to-copper, copper-to-aluminum, aluminum-to-aluminum & copper-clad-aluminum-to-aluminum. The cap is snapped closed before reinserting into a box.

Pre-1984 NM Cable (60°C rated conductors) — 20 NEC

- ☐ Derate for ambient temp ____ 310.15B
- ☐ No 60°C conductors in attics >131°F ____ T310.15B1
- ☐ No direct connection to luminaires that req >60°C conductors ____ 410.117A
- ☐ Isolate old wiring from high-temp wiring **F73** ____ 410.117B

Edison-Base Fuses — 20 NEC

- ☐ No exposed contact fuseholders **F61** (must be dead front) ____ 240.50D
- ☐ No exposed energized parts (install insulating plugs or spare fuses in any unused fuseholders) ____ 240.50D
- ☐ New Edison base (plug fuses) must have type S adapter ____ 240.52
- ☐ Not allowed in circuits over 125V between conductors unless system has a grounded neutral w/ line-to-neutral voltage ≤150V ____ 240.52
- ☐ Type S fuse **F61,80** reqd if tampering or overfusing exists ____ 240.51B
- ☐ Type S fuse adapter **F61,80** must be proper size for wire ____ 240.4D
- ☐ No fuses in neutral conductor **F61** ____ 240.22
- ☐ Fuses rated ≤15A have hexagonal window ____ 240.50C
- ☐ Screw shell to be connected to load side of circuit ____ 240.50E

Fuses are a reliable form of overcurrent protection. Most problems with fuses are from improper application or from tampering (replacement with a Lincoln fuse).

FIG. 60

Knob & Tube to NM

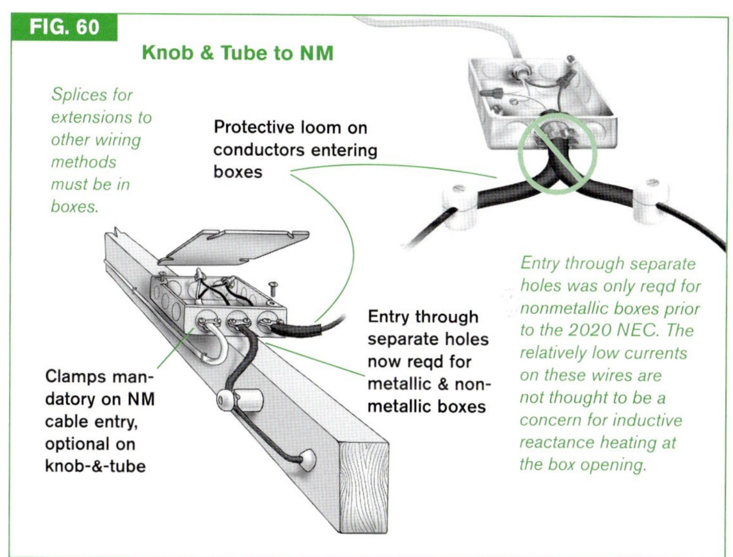

Splices for extensions to other wiring methods must be in boxes.

Entry through separate holes was only reqd for nonmetallic boxes prior to the 2020 NEC. The relatively low currents on these wires are not thought to be a concern for inductive reactance heating at the box opening.

Knob-&-tube wiring was the original wiring method when electricity first began to be used in homes. It lacked an equipment-grounding conductor, and its insulation was only rated 60°C. Over time, the insulation becomes brittle. Entirely new knob-&-tube wiring has not been allowed since the 1975 NEC; some jurisdictions banned it decades before that time. It often has improper splices or taps due to attempts to obtain more use from a system than that for which it was designed. The safety provided by older fuse systems with knob-&-tube could be defeated by installing a fuse with too high a rating or by placing a penny behind the fuse. Older fuse panels often have exposed contacts and pose electrocution hazards.

FIG. 61

Antiquated Wiring System

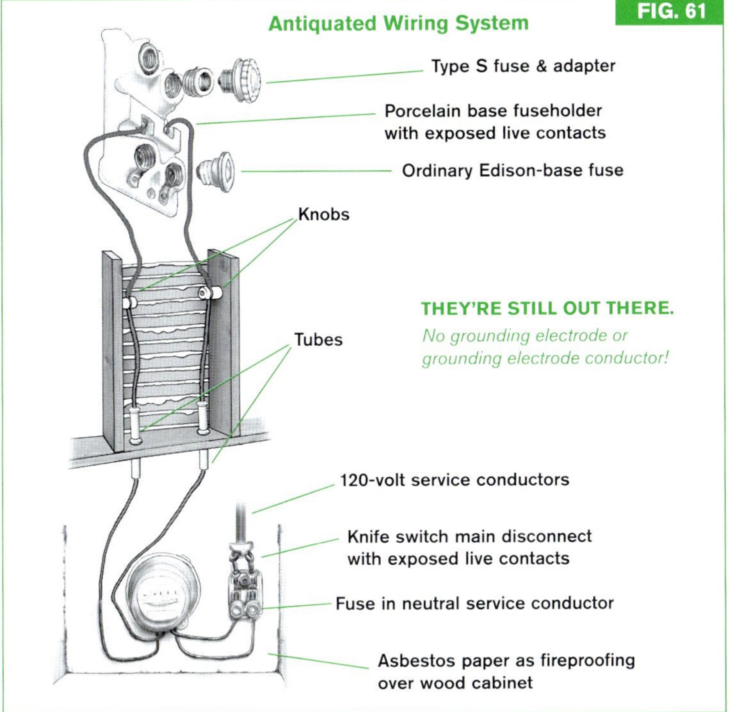

THEY'RE STILL OUT THERE.

No grounding electrode or grounding electrode conductor!

Knob & Tube — 20 NEC

Requirement	20 NEC
☐ No new K&T allowed	394.10
☐ Extension of existing K&T OK if properly protected **F60**	394.10
☐ Must enter boxes through separate holes **F60**	314.17B1[45]
☐ Loom must extend from last insulator to ¼ in. inside box **F60**	314.17B&C
☐ Do not envelop with thermal insulation in walls, ceilings, or attics	394.12
☐ Wires must be kept out of direct contact with wood framing	394.17
☐ Tubes reqd where passing through framing members **F61,62**	394.17
☐ Extend tubes 3 in. beyond wood member in plastered partitions **F61**	394.17
☐ 3 in. min. between wires, 1 in. to surfaces	394.19A
☐ 2 in. min. separation from metal raceways, signal wires, or other conductors except where protected by loom **F60**	398.19
☐ Not OK exposed on top of joists or face of exposed rafters EXC	394.23A&B
• OK on rafters or joists in attics <3 ft. high	394.23BX
☐ Protect with running boards up to 7 ft. high in attic with stairs	394.23A
☐ Provide protection where exposed <7 ft. above floor	398.15C
☐ Supports within 6 in. of each splice & at max. 4½-ft. intervals	394.30

What we typically call "knob & tube" wiring is actually referring to 2 separate NEC articles. Article 394—Concealed Knob-and-Tube Wiring—refers to wiring concealed in hollow spaces of walls & ceilings and in unfinished attic and roof spaces. Article 398—Open Wires on Insulators—refers to these same wiring methods when encountered in other areas, such as garages and barns. Such wiring can also be supported on ceramic cleats in addition to knobs & tubes.

FIG.62

Knob-and-Tube Wiring

Porcelain tube taped to wires

Head prevents tube from slipping through timbers. **F61**

Split porcelain knob

Only one side used per knob; conductor separation required except where protected by loom

The gray coating on copper wire protects against corrosion from contact with rubber insulation. It should not be mistaken for aluminum.

Tubes also used where wires cross.

45. Previous requirement for individual entries was only for plastic boxes.

BRANCH CIRCUITS

Branch circuits are the permanent wiring between the final OCPD and the outlet of the circuit. The size of the circuit is defined by the size of the OCPD. What is commonly referred to as a "dedicated" circuit is termed an "individual" circuit in the code and is defined as a circuit that supplies only one utilization equipment, such as a clothes dryer. A circuit can be "dedicated" to a specific purpose without being an individual circuit, for example, circuits dedicated for the bathroom receptacle outlets where more than one outlet is on the circuit.

Sizes & Number of Branch Circuits — 21 IRC — 20 NEC

- ☐ Min. number of branch circuits determined by calculated load **T4–T11** & size or rating of circuits ____ 3703.6 — 210.11A
- ☐ Branch circuit rating must be ≥ load it serves ____ 3701.2 — 220.18
- ☐ Min. size for branch circuit wiring #14 Cu ____ T3702.14 — 210.19A4
- ☐ Branch circuit ratings for other than individual circuits must be 15A, 20A, 30A, 40A, or 50A ____ 3702.2 — 210.18

Required Residential 20A Branch Circuits

- ☐ Min. 2-20A small-appliance circuits for receptacles in kitchen, breakfast room, dining room & pantry EXC ____ 3703.2 — 210.11C1
- ☐ Kitchen appliances (e.g., refrigerator) OK on ≥15A individual circuits ____ 3703.2X — 210.52B1X2
- ☐ Min. 1-20A circuit dedicated for laundry equipment ____ 3703.3 — 210.11C2
- ☐ Min. 1-20A circuit dedicated for bathroom receptacles EXC 3703.4 — 210.11C3
  - Other outlets OK on circuit if serving only 1 bathroom 3703.4X — 210.11C3X
- ☐ Min. 1-20A circuit dedicated for 1&2FD garage general-purpose receptacle(s) (not garage door opener) EXC ____ 3703.5[46] — 210.11C4[46]
  - May supply readily accessible exterior receptacles ____ 3703.5X — 210.11C4X

46. Previously allowed other outlets in garage above 5½ ft. such as for vehicle door opener.

Individual Circuits — 21 IRC — 20 NEC

- ☐ Individual circuit = supplying only one piece of equipment 3501 — 100
- ☐ Reqd for central heating & no other outlets EXC ____ 3703.1 — 422.12
  - Auxiliary equipment (electrostatic filter, pumps, humidifiers, related AC equipment) ____ 3703.1 — 422.12X
- ☐ Reqd for EV branch circuit(s) ____ 3702.13 — 625.40
- ☐ Reqd for cord/plug-connected range hood ____ 4101.3 — 422.16B4

Load Limitations

- ☐ General lighting & receptacles OK on same 15A or 20A except small-appliance circuits, bath-receptacle circuit & laundry circuit 3702.3 — 210.23A
- ☐ Single piece of cord-&-plug-connected equipment not permanently fastened in place max. 80% of 15A or 20A circuit **T43** ____ 3702.3 — 210.23A1
- ☐ Equipment fastened in place max. 50% of 15A or 20A circuit when circuit also has lighting or equipment not fastened in place 3702.3 — 210.23A2
- ☐ Multioutlet branch circuits for lighting or receptacles limited to max. 20A branch circuit rating in dwellings ____ 3702.5 — 210.23A–C
- ☐ Single piece of cord-&-plug-connected equipment not permanently fastened in place max. 80% of 30A circuit **T43** ____ 3702.4 — 210.23B
- ☐ Heavy-duty lampholders in fixed lighting OK in 30A circuits in other than dwelling units or utilization equipment ____ n/a — 210.23B
- ☐ Load for a single range per **T12**; load for counter-mounted unit + up to2 wall ovens per **T12** note D ____ 3702.9 — T220.55

TABLE 43 — MAX. CORD & PLUG CONNECTED LOAD TO RECEPTACLE ◆ T210.21.B2

Circuit Rating (Amps)	Receptacle Rating (Amps)	Max. Load (Amps)
15 or 20	15	12
20	20	30
30	30	24

GROUND-FAULT CIRCUIT INTERRUPTERS (GFCIs)

GFCIs provide shock-hazard protection by opening the circuit when it has an electrical imbalance, such as current returning through a person rather than a wire. Class A GFCIs allow a fault of ≤4mA and must trip when the fault is ≥6mA. GFCIs conform to the UL 943 Standard. The latest version (5th edition) of the standard was published in 2018 and incorporates several features that were not included in earlier editions. These include expansion of auto-monitoring requirements and end-of-life testing. Other improvements to the standard have been made over the years since it was first introduced, and it is prudent to update existing GFCIs, particularly if they were manufactured prior to 2017. GFCIs are available as circuit breakers, receptacle outlets, or blank-face devices. 2-pole GFCI breakers are available for multiwire branch circuits or for appliances rated 250V. Dual-function AFCI/GFCIs are also available. AFCI and GFCI devices look similar; read the label to determine its type.

General	21 IRC	20 NEC
☐ GFCI devices reqd to be readily accessible	3902.15	210.8
☐ Distance from receptacles is determined by shortest path of appliance cord w/out piercing a fixed barrier or passing through a floor, wall, ceiling, or fixed barrier	3902.15[47]	210.8[47]

GFCI Protection for Dwelling Receptacles Rated 125–250V[48]		
☐ Bathrooms	3902.1	210.8A1
☐ Garages & accessory buildings at or below grade level	3902.2	210.8A2
☐ Outdoors EXC	3902.3	210.8A3
• Circuit dedicated to non-readily accessible receptacles for snow-melting or deicing equipment w/ GFPE	3902.3X	210.8A3X
☐ Crawlspaces at or below grade level	3902.4	210.8A4
☐ Basements EXC	3902.5[49]	210.8A5[49]
• Receptacle for permanently installed (monitored) fire or burglar alarm system	3902.5X	210.8A5X

47. Distance measurements now apply even if cord would pass through a door, which confirms that garbage disposer receptacles be GFCI protected.
48. Requirements now include receptacles rated 250V & more than 20A.
49. Applies to all basement receptacles regardless of whether basement is finished or unfinished.

Dwelling Receptacles (continued)	21 IRC	20 NEC
☐ Where serving kitchen countertop surfaces	3902.6	210.8A6
☐ Within 6 ft. of top inside edge of bowl of all sinks	3902.7	210.8A7
☐ Boathouse receptacles	3902.12	210.8A8
☐ Within 6 ft. of outside edge of bathtubs or shower stalls	3902.8	210.8A9
☐ Laundry areas (including clothes dryers)	3902.9	210.8A10
☐ Indoor damp & wet locations (e.g., mud rooms)	3902.10[50]	210.8A11[50]
☐ Receptacles reqd for servicing equipment (e.g., in attic within 25 ft. of furnace *p. 184*)	n/a	210.8E[51]
☐ Listed locking support & mounting receptacles **F33** for ceiling luminaires & fans do not req GFCI protection EXC	n/a	210.8AX
• Items 210.8A4, 210.8A9 & 210.8A11 in above list	n/a	210.8AX

Other Residential Equipment Requiring GFCI Protection		
☐ Hydromassage (whirlpool) tubs	4209.2	680.71
☐ Receptacles ≤30A ≤ 6 ft. of hydromassage tubs	4209.2	680.71
☐ Sump pumps	n/a	422.5A6[52]
☐ Boat hoists	3902.13	555.9
☐ All 15- & 20A 125V receptacles at marinas & boatyards	n/a	555.35A2
☐ Dishwasher branch circuits	3902.11	422.5A
☐ Crawlspace lighting outlets ≤120V	3902.4	210.8C
☐ Electrically heated floors in kitchens, bathrooms & pool, tub, spa & hot tub locations	3902.14	424.45E
☐ Receptacles for connection of electric vehicle charging	n/a	625.54[53]
☐ Outdoor outlets rated ≤50A, such as residential air conditioners	n/a	210.8F[54]

*See **p. 298** for GFCI requirements on replacement receptacles.*
*See **pp. 306–309** for GFCI requirements at pools, spas & fountains.*

50. Reqd in all indoor damp or wet locations.
51. Receptacles reqd for service of HVAC or other equipment req GFCI.
52. All sump pumps now req GFCI protection, regardless of connection method.
53. Though redundant w/ reqs for locations where this equipment is likely to be located, this new rule ensures that all receptacles for EV charging are GFCI-protected.
54. Outdoor equipment now requires GFCI protection. A temporary interim amendment to this section exempts listed air-conditioning equipment from this requirement until September 1, 2026.

Non-Dwelling Receptacle GFCI Requirements 20 NEC

Applies to all receptacles rated 125–250V

- ☐ Bathrooms ______ 210.8B1
- ☐ Kitchens or areas with a sink & permanent provisions for either food preparation or cooking ______ 210.8B2[55]
- ☐ Rooftops & outdoors EXC ______ 210.8B3&4
  - Circuit dedicated to non-readily accessible receptacles for snow-melting or deicing equipment w/ GFPE __ 210.8BX4
- ☐ Sinks: where receptacles within 6 ft. of top inside edge of bowl ____ 210.8B5
- ☐ Indoor damp & wet locations ______ 210.8B6[56]
- ☐ Locker rooms w/ associated showering facilities ______ 210.8B7
- ☐ Garages, accessory building, service bays & similar areas other than vehicle exhibition halls and showrooms ______ 210.8B8
- ☐ Crawlspaces at or below grade level ______ 210.8B9
- ☐ Unfinished areas of basements ______ 210.8B10
- ☐ Laundry areas ______ 210.8B11[56]
- ☐ Within 6 ft. of outside edge of bathtubs & shower stalls ______ 210.8B12[56]
- ☐ Listed locking support & mounting receptacles **F33** for ceiling luminaires & fans do not req GFCI protection except in indoor damp &wet locations, locker rooms, crawlspaces, laundry areas & within 6 ft. of tub/shower ______ 210.8BX[57]

Non-Dwelling Appliance GFCI Requirements

The requirements below apply to all appliances rated ≤150V to ground, ≤60A, single phase or 3-phase. Multiple Class A devices permitted.

- ☐ Automotive vacuum machines ______ 422.5A1
- ☐ Drinking water coolers & bottle fill stations ______ 422.5A2
- ☐ Cord-and-plug-connected high-pressure spray wash machines ____ 422.5A3
- ☐ Tire inflation machines ______ 422.5A4
- ☐ Vending machines ______ 422.5A5
- ☐ Sump pumps ______ 422.5A6
- ☐ Dishwashers ______ 422.5A7
- ☐ Automotive vacuum machines ______ 422.5A1

55. The previous edition simply said "kitchens." This change addresses workplace break rooms.
56. Damp locations, accessory buildings, laundry areas & near tubs/showers added this edition.
57. Listed locking support & mounting receptacles new this edition.

*In **F63**, equal currents are flowing to & from the load. The magnetic fields generated by the current in these conductors are of opposite polarity & cancel each other. The conductors pass through a toroidal coil inside the GFCI. When the currents through the coil are balanced, the GFCI allows current on the circuit.*

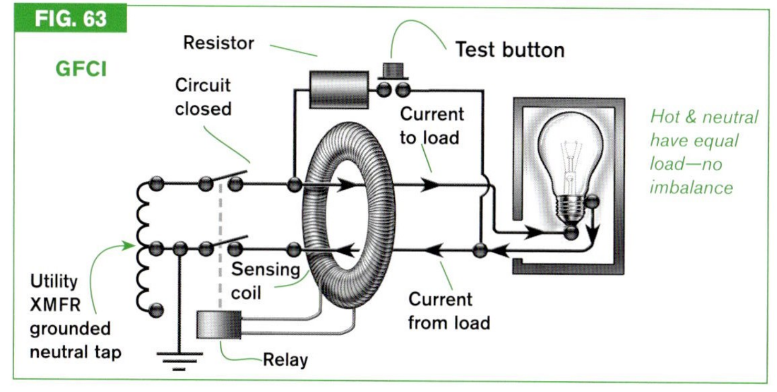

*During a ground fault **F64** more current flows to the load than from the load. This differential creates a magnetic field that induces voltage on the sensing coil. The resulting current on the coil signals the relay mechanism, which opens the circuit. The duration of the fault will be limited to approximately $^1/_{40}$th of a second.*

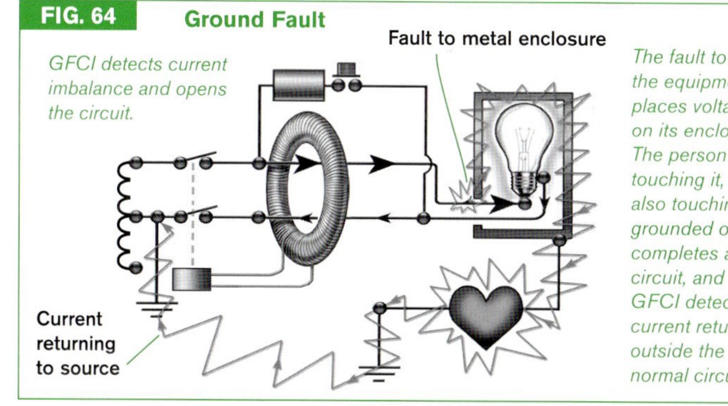

ARC-FAULT CIRCUIT INTERRUPTERS (AFCIS)

Arc-fault circuit interrupters provide fire protection by opening the circuit when they recognize the electrical "signature" of an arc. They do not protect against glowing connections. AFCI circuit breakers, receptacle outlets, and blank-face devices are rated for 120V circuits up to 20A. Cord AFCIs, such as might be installed on a room air conditioner (*p. 202*) are rated up to 30A. See the glossary on ***p. 230*** for further information on the different types of AFCIs.

Locations Requiring AFCI Protection — 21 IRC — 20 NEC

- ☐ Dwelling-unit branch circuits supplying outlets or devices in kitchens, family rooms, dining & living rooms, parlors, libraries, dens, bedrooms, sunrooms, recreation rooms, closets, hallways, laundry areas or similar rooms EXC _________ 3902.17 — 210.12A
  - An individual circuit installed with a metal-clad wiring method for an Article 760 fire alarm system _______ 3902.17X — 210.12AX
- ☐ Dormitory-unit branch circuits supplying outlets & devices in closets, bedrooms, living rooms, hallways, bathrooms & similar _____ n/a — 210.12B
- ☐ Branch circuits supplying outlets & devices in guest rooms & suites & patient sleeping rooms in nursing homes & care facilities _ n/a — 210.12C[58]

Means of Providing AFCI Protection

- ☐ Combination-type AFCI at origin of branch circuit __ 3902.17(1) — 210.12A1
- ☐ Branch/feeder-type AFCI breaker & OBC type at first outlet box on branch circuit, w/ outlet box marked as first on circuit 3902.17(2) — 210.12A2
- ☐ Ordinary OCPD supplying metal raceway or cables to first outlet, w/ OBC AFCI at first outlet _________ 3902.17(5) — 210.12A5
- ☐ Ordinary OCPD supplying conduit, tubing, or MC encased in min. 2-in. concrete to first outlet & OBC AFCI at first outlet __ 3902.17(6) — 210.12A6

In addition to the 4 methods above, the NEC also includes "supplemental arc protection breakers" & "system combination" AFCIs. These non-AFCI breakers are used in conjunction with OBC-type AFCIs as the first outlet on the circuit to create a system that is listed. As of this writing, neither of these systems are readily available. These two additional methods depend upon UL testing that is ongoing and will not work with older circuit breakers.

58. Patient sleeping rooms in nursing homes & limited-care facilities added.

AFCIs for Wiring Extensions or Modifications — 21 IRC — 20 NEC

- ☐ If branch circuit wiring extended, modified, or replaced in areas where AFCI protection currently reqd, either combination-type AFCI at origin of branch circuit or OBC AFCI at first outlet of existing branch circuit **F65** EXC _________________ 3902.18 — 210.12D
  - Extension of conductors ≤6 ft. & does not include added outlets or devices other than splicing devices; measurement does not include conductors inside enclosures or boxes _ 3902.18X — 210.12DX[59]
- ☐ Replacement receptacles req AFCI protection if located where AFCI protection currently reqd **F65** _____________ n/a — 406.4D4
- ☐ AFCI protection by installing OBC outlet, or from upstream OBC AFCI, or from combination-type AFCI breaker **F65** ___ n/a — 406.4D4

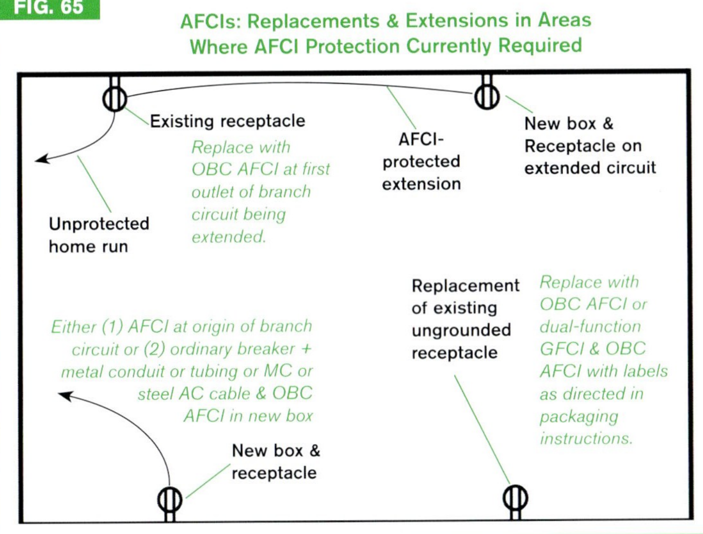

59. Clarification that conductor distance is distance between the enclosures of the terminations.

RECEPTACLE OUTLETS

Receptacles are contact devices at the outlet of a circuit for connection of attachment plugs or for direct connection of a piece of equipment **F33** designed to mate with the contact device.

Receptacles: General	21 IRC	20 NEC
☐ Grounding-type reqd on 15A & 20A circuits EXC ______	4002.2	406.4A
• Replacement non-grounding receptacles (***see p. 298***) ___	n/a	406.12X4
☐ Receptacles for specific appliances (e.g., laundry, garage door opener) must be within 6 ft. of appliance location __	3901.5	210.50C
☐ Must be mounted w/ 6–32 machine screws or AMI **F37**	4002.6	406.5
☐ Receptacles in recessed boxes to seat securely on finished surface; in flush-mounted boxes to seat securely on box ________	4002.6	406.5A&B
☐ Receptacles for direct AL connection marked "CO/ALR" _	4002.3	406.3C
☐ Face-up in countertop or work surface req listing for same	4002.16	406.5G1
☐ Metal faceplates must be grounded ________________	4002.4	406.6B

Tamper Resistant (TR) Receptacles: Required Locations	21 IRC	20 NEC
☐ All dwelling-unit receptacles specified in 210.52 EXC_____	4002.14	406.12
• Receptacles located >5½ ft. above floor ________	4002.14X1	406.12X1
• Receptacles are part of a luminaire or appliance __	4002.14X2	406.12X2
• Receptacles in space of appliance that is not readily moved (such as clothes washer) ______________	4002.14X3	406.12X3
☐ Guest rooms & suites of hotels, motels & their common areas, preschools, education facilities, business offices, & waiting rooms in clinics ______________________________	n/a	406.12
☐ Attached or detached garages, accessory buildings, common areas of MFDs, dormitory units & assisted-living facilities ___	n/a	406.12[60]

Receptacle Ratings	21 IRC	20 NEC
☐ 15A receptacles OK on 15A or 20A circuits **T44** ____	4002.1.1	T210.21B3
☐ 20A receptacles only OK on 20A circuits **T44** _______	4002.1.2	T210.21B3
☐ Single receptacle on individual branch circuit reqs rating not less than branch circuit, e.g., 20A individual circuit reqs 20A receptacle _________	4002.1.1	210.21B1

60. TR req is new for these areas in this code edition.

TABLE 44 — RATINGS FOR MULTIPLE RECEPTACLES ON 1 CIRCUIT IRC T4002.1.2 ◆ NEC 210.21.B3

Circuit Rating	Receptacle Rating	Circuit Rating	Receptacle Rating
15A	15A	40A	40 or 50
20A	15A or 20A	50A	50
30A	30		

Receptacle Locations in Habitable Rooms	21 IRC	20 NEC
☐ Reqd in any wall ≥2 ft. in habitable room **F67** _____	3901.2.2(1)	210.52A2
☐ Fixed glass panels considered as walls **F67** _______	3901.2.2(2)	210.52A2
☐ Fixed room dividers such as railings & bar-type counters considered as walls **F67** _____________	3901.2.2(3)	210.52A2
☐ Doorways, fireplaces & fixed cabinets that do not have countertops not considered as walls **F67** ____	3901.2.2(1)	210.52A2
☐ Spacing such that no point on wall measured horizontally along the floor line is >6 ft. from receptacle **F66, 67** _____	3901.2.1	210.52A1
☐ Reqd receptacles are in addition to any that are part of a luminaire or appliance, within cabinets, controlled by switches, or >5½ ft. AFF (such as television outlets) **F67** ________	3901.1	210.52
☐ Switched receptacles don't count unless "half hot" ____	3901.1	210.52
☐ Floor receptacles can be reqd receptacles if ≤18 in. from wall _________________	3901.2.3	210.52A3
☐ Receptacles built into permanently installed electric baseboard heaters OK as reqd receptacles **F83** (***see p. 305***) ____	3901.1	210.52

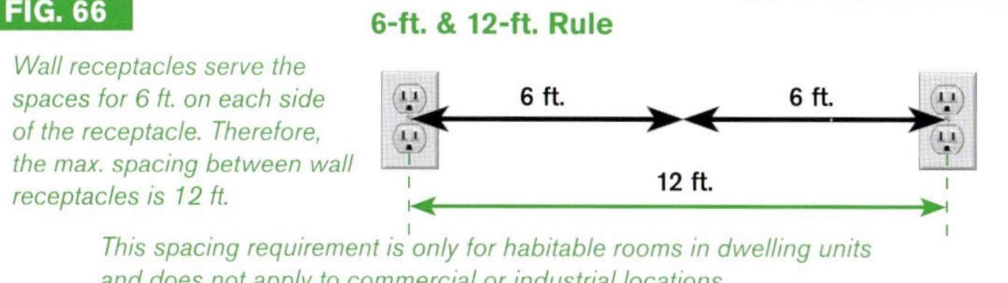

FIG. 66 6-ft. & 12-ft. Rule

Wall receptacles serve the spaces for 6 ft. on each side of the receptacle. Therefore, the max. spacing between wall receptacles is 12 ft.

This spacing requirement is only for habitable rooms in dwelling units and does not apply to commercial or industrial locations.

FIG. 67

Receptacle Locations

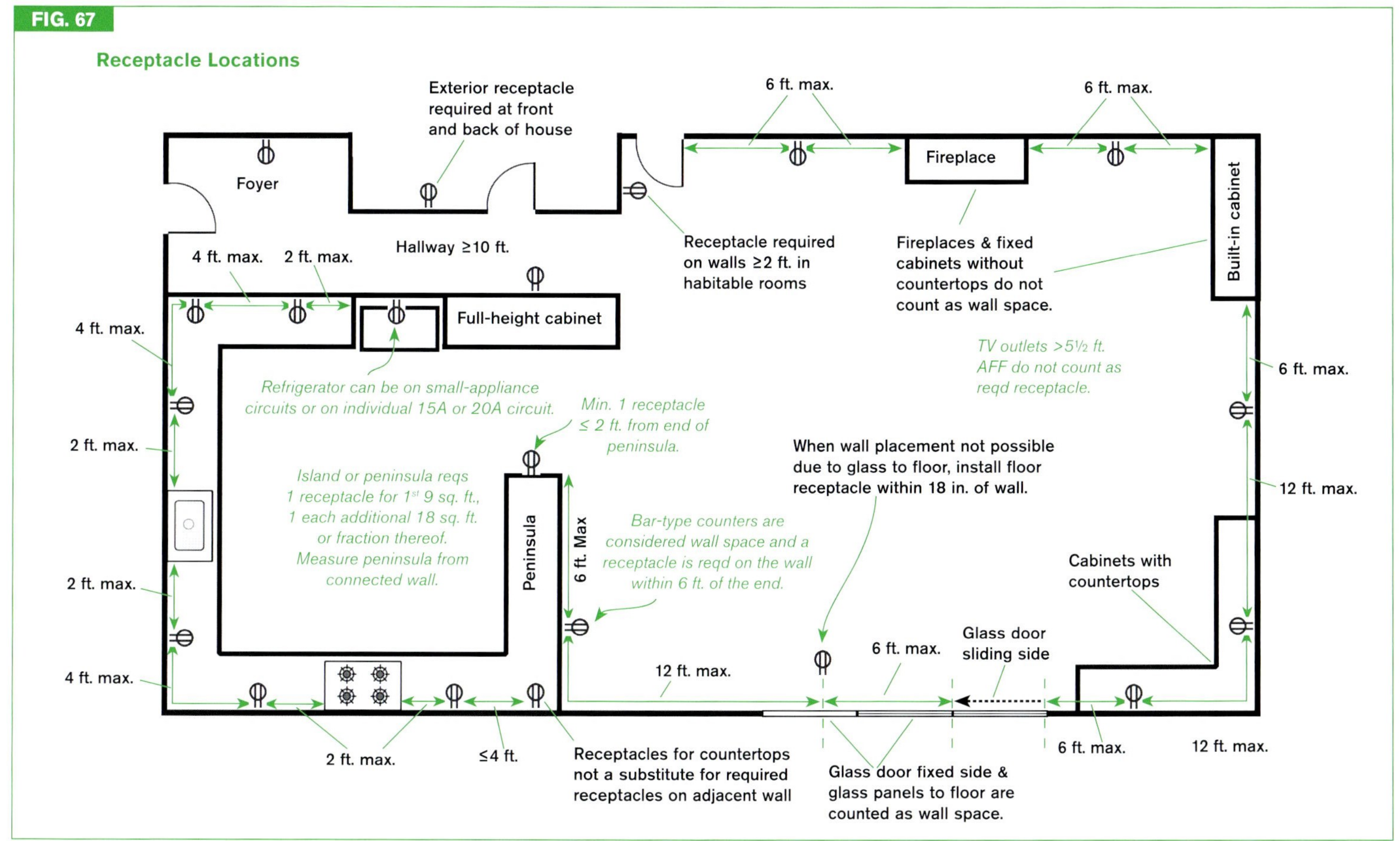

Receptacle Locations in Hallways & Foyers

	21 IRC	20 NEC
☐ Foyers >60 sq. ft. & not part of a hallway req receptacles in each wall ≥ 3 ft. EXC	3901.11	210.52I
• Sidelites extending to floor not considered wall space	3901.11	210.52I
☐ Hallways ≥10 ft. req min. one receptacle	3901.10	210.52H

Basements, Garages & Outbuildings

	21 IRC	20 NEC
☐ Min. 1 receptacle reqd each vehicle bay max. 5½ ft. AFF	3901.9	210.52G1
☐ Req for garage receptacle applicable to 1&2FD & MFDs EXC	n/a	210.52G[61]
• Not in MFD if garage space not attached to individual unit	n/a	210.52GX[61]
☐ Min. 1-20A circuit dedicated for 1&2FD garage general purpose receptacle(s) (not garage door opener) EXC	3703.5[62]	210.11C4[62]
• May supply readily accessible exterior receptacles	3703.5X	210.11C4X
☐ Min. one receptacle each accessory building w/ power	3901.9	210.52G2
☐ Min. one receptacle each unfinished basement area	3901.9	210.52G3

Laundry

	21 IRC	20 NEC
☐ Min. 1 20A circuit for laundry receptacle(s)	3703.3	210.11C2
☐ No lights on laundry circuit	3703.3	210.11C2
☐ Min. 1 laundry receptacle(s)	3901.8	210.52F
☐ Receptacle within 6 ft. of intended appliance location	3901.5	210.50C
☐ Electric dryer min. 30A circuit	T3704.2(1)	220.54
☐ Electric dryer reqs 4-conductor branch circuit EXC	3908.8	250.140
• Existing 3-wire circuits may remain if neutral min. #10 Cu or #8 AL & insulated or part of SE cable originating from service	n/a	250.140X

Outlets for Equipment Requiring Servicing *(see p. 184)*

	21 IRC	20 NEC
☐ Min. 1 accessible receptacle for HVAC equipment EXC	3901.12	210.63A
• Not reqd for evaporative coolers (*p. 202*)		
☐ Receptacle ≤25 ft. & on same level as equipment	3901.12	210.63
☐ Not on same circuit as central heating	3703.1	422.12
☐ Not on load side of HVAC disconnect	3901.12	422.12

61. Previously applied only to 1&2FD.
62. Previously allowed other outlets in garage above 5½ ft. such as for vehicle door opener.

Outdoors

	21 IRC	20 NEC
☐ Receptacle readily accessible from grade reqd at front & rear of 1&2FD max. 6½ ft. above grade **F67**	3901.7	210.52E1
☐ Balconies, decks & porches within 4 ft. horizontally of dwelling unit req receptacle max. 6½ ft. above walking surface	3901.7	210.52E3[63]
☐ 15A & 20A nonlocking receptacles in damp or wet locations req listed weather-resistant type (says "WR" on face) **F68**	4002.8&9	406.9A&B1
☐ Damp location (covered porch) reqs cover that is weatherproof when cover is closed **F68**	4002.8	406.9A
☐ Wet location covers weatherproof closed or in use **F68**	4002.9	406.9B1
☐ Wet-location box hoods must be "extra duty" **F68**	4002.9	406.9B1
☐ Receptacles other than 15A or 20A 125V or 250V in wet locations req enclosures weatherproof when closed or in use	4002.10	406.9B2

FIG. 68 Outdoor Covers

DAMP LOCATIONS

Cover that is weatherproof only when closed, not while in use

WET OR DAMP LOCATIONS

Expandable cover

Identification as "extra duty"

Not in use

In use

63. Previously required only to such areas when accessible from within dwelling. The IRC has not yet adopted this change.

KITCHENS

The required 20A small-appliance branch circuits are in addition to those for built-in or permanently installed appliances or lighting. The 2 or more 20A circuits must supply the countertops & wall spaces in kitchens, pantries, and dining rooms.

Branch Circuits

Branch Circuits	21 IRC	20 NEC
☐ Min. 2 20A small-appliance circuits reqd	3703.2	210.11C1
☐ Small-appliance circuits must serve all countertop & wall receptacles in kitchen, dining room, pantry & similar areas EXC	3901.3	210.52B1
• Additional switched receptacles	3901.3X1	210.52B1X1
• Individual branch circuits for specific appliances	3901.3X2	210.52B1X2
☐ No other outlets/lights on small-appliance circuits EXC	3901.3.1	210.52B2
• Receptacles for clock or gas range ignition OK	3901.3.1X	210.52B2X
☐ Dishwasher & disposer OK on same circuit if combined loads ≤ branch circuit rating	3701.2	210.19A1
☐ 40A or 50A 240V circuits OK for built-in cooking	n/a	210.23C
☐ Range/oven ≥8.75kW reqs min. 40A branch circuit	3702.9.1	210.19A3

Receptacles for Countertops & Work Surfaces F67

Item	21 IRC	20 NEC
☐ Reqd all wall counter spaces ≥12 in. wide	3901.4.1	210.52C1
☐ No point on wall line >24 in. horizontally from receptacle, max. spacing between receptacles 48 in.	3901.4.1	210.52C1
☐ Receptacles in appliance garages not considered as the reqd receptacles	3901.4.3	210.52C3
☐ Area behind sink or range does not req receptacle if ≤12 in. to wall or ≤18 in. to corner **F69**	3901.4.1X	210.52C1X
☐ Receptacles for counter spaces not to be considered as the reqd wall receptacles **F67**	3901.2.4 & 3901.4	210.52C
☐ Max. 20 in. above or 12 in. below countertop; max. 6-in. counter extension above receptacle on face of cabinet **F71**	3901.4.3[64]	210.52C3[64]
☐ Listed pop-up receptacle assemblies OK **F71**	3901.4.3	210.52C3
☐ Receptacles under sinks not allowed in face-up position	n/a	406.5G2[65]

See ***p. 303*** *for appliances in kitchens.*

FIG. 69

Corner Sink

If **X** <18 in. outlets not required here.

If **X** <18 in., measurement for first required receptacle within 24 in. begins here.

If ***X*** *≥18 in., countertops not considered separate spaces & the 2-ft./4-ft. rule applies to the entire countertop.*

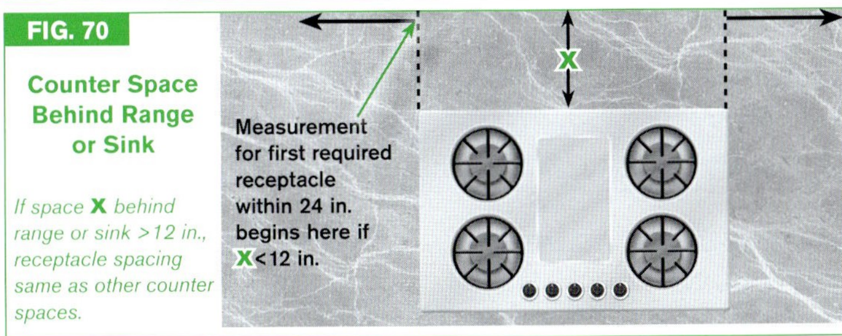

FIG. 70

Counter Space Behind Range or Sink

If space ***X*** *behind range or sink >12 in., receptacle spacing same as other counter spaces.*

Multioutlet Assemblies

Multioutlet Assemblies	21 IRC	20 NEC
☐ Max. height above countertop 20 in.	3901.4.3	210.52C3
☐ Each 12 in. of multioutlet assembly w/ >1 receptacle is considered to be one receptacle outlet	n/a	210.52C[66]
☐ Not permitted w/ cord & plug supply connection	n/a	380.12[67]

64. Receptacles below countertop now OK for all, not just islands & peninsulas.
65. New rule that receptacles not be face-up below sinks.

66. This new method of counting multioutlet assemblies would provide another way to comply with the new rules for number of receptacles at island and peninsula countertops.
67. Multioutlet assemblies must be connected by permanent wiring method, not by cord-&-plug.

Island & Peninsula Countertops

	21 IRC	20 NEC
☐ Islands & peninsulas req min. one receptacle first 9 sq. ft. plus 1 for each additional 18 sq. ft. or fraction thereof	3901.4.2[68]	210.52C2[68]
☐ Peninsulas measured from connected perpendicular wall	3901.4.2	210.52C2
☐ Min. 1 receptacle within 2 ft. of end of peninsula	3901.4.2[69]	210.52C2[69]

FIG. 71 **Island Countertop**

Island and peninsular countertops require 1 receptacle for the first 9 sq. ft. & additional receptacles for each subsequent 18 sq. ft. or fraction thereof. Receptacles can be on the side of the cabinet no more than 12 in. from the countertop surface if the overhang of the countertop does not exceed 6 in.

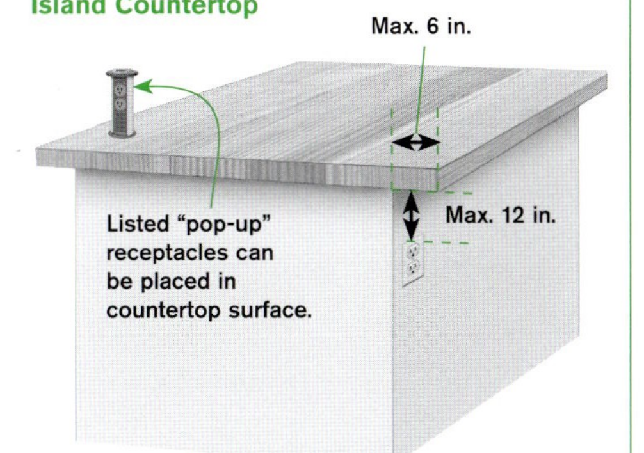

BATHROOMS

Tub & Shower Areas F72

	21 IRC	20 NEC
☐ No cord-connected or pendant luminaires, lighting track, or ceiling-suspended paddle fans within 8 ft. above tub rim or shower threshold & for zone extending 3 ft. outside	4003.11	410.10D1
☐ Luminaires < 8 ft. above tub & shower listed for damp locations (or wet locations if subject to shower spray)	4003.11	410.10D2

68. Increased number of receptacles required for islands & peninsulas.
69. New requirement for receptacle within 2 ft. of end of peninsula.

Bathroom Receptacles

	21 IRC	20 NEC
☐ Reqd within 3 ft. of each basin, located in wall or side or face of cabinet ≤12 in. below top of basin or countertop F72		210.52D
☐ No face-up receptacles on vanity countertop EXC	4002.15	406.5G1
• Listed countertop-mounted (pop-up) receptacles	4002.15	210.52D
☐ No receptacles in zone extending 3 ft. horizontally & 8 ft. vertically above top of tub rim or shower threshold EXC	4002.11[70]	406.9C[70]
• If room too small to comply, install opposite tub or shower on farthest wall within room	4002.11X[70]	406.9CX[70]
☐ Min. 1-20A circuit dedicated for reqd bath receptacles EXC	3703.4	210.11C3
• Other outlets OK on circuit if serving only 1 bathroom	3703.4X	210.11C3X
• Additional 15A or 20A circuits may serve receptacles other than the reqd receptacle outlets	3703.4[71]	210.11C3[71]

FIG. 72 *Luminaires directly above tub/shower & <8 ft. above tub rim or shower threshold must be rated for damp or wet location.*

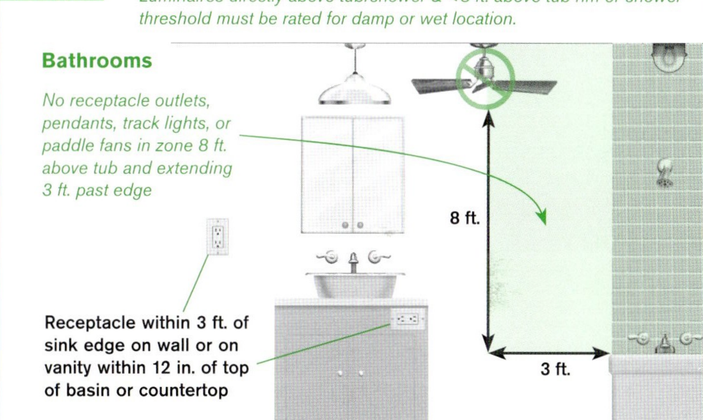

70. Receptacles were formerly prohibited only within tub/shower footprint; now prohibited in same zone where pendant lights prohibited.
71. Outlets serving the countertop & basin area req 20A circuits dedicated to that purpose. Bathrooms may have other circuits—including 15A circuits—serving receptacle outlets in other areas of the bathroom.

EXTENSIONS, MODIFICATIONS & REPLACEMENTS

Replacement Receptacles: General	20 NEC
☐ GFCI protection if located where GFCI protection currently reqd	406.4D3
☐ AFCI protection if located where AFCI protection currently reqd	406.4D4
☐ TR reqd if in areas where TR currently reqd	406.4D5
☐ Outdoor wet-location replacement receptacles must be WR	406.4D6
Replacements When Grounding Present in Box	
☐ Replacements must be 3-hole grounding type if EGC present	406.4D1
☐ Install bonding jumper from receptacle to grounded metal box EXC	250.146
• Receptacle yoke w/ secure contact w/ surface-mounted box	250.146A
• "Self-grounding" receptacles (captive metal screw from yoke)	250.146B
Replacements When No Grounding Present	
☐ EGC reqd for equipment designed w/ grounding-type plugs, including refrigerators, disposers, clothes washers, dishwashers, etc.	250.114(3)
☐ EGC can be added from box & connect to service enclosure, GEC, ground bar of panel at circuit origin, or EGC of another circuit	250.130C
☐ OK to replace non-grounding-type receptacle w/ non-grounding-type receptacle if in area where neither AFCI or GFCI protection reqd or where such protection supplied upstream of receptacle	406.4D2
☐ Not OK to jumper neutral & EGC (no "false grounds")	250.142B
☐ OK to install GFCI even if no EGC present	406.4D2b
☐ Ungrounded GFCI can protect downstream receptacles	406.4D2c
☐ No EGC from ungrounded GFCI to downstream receptacles	406.4D2c
☐ Ungrounded GFCIs req label stating "No Equipment Ground"	406.4D2b
☐ Downstream GFCI-protected receptacles req labels stating "GFCI-protected" & "No Equipment Ground"	406.4D2c
☐ Labels reqd above may be on receptacle or on cover plate	406.4D2b&c
☐ Dual-function GFCI/AFCI receptacles OK where AFCI reqd	406.4D4
Replacement Luminaires	
☐ Mechanically connect to branch circuit EGC EXC	410.44
• Replacement luminaires on ungrounded outlet may have new EGC to another EGC, GES, or panel ground bar	410.44X1
• Replacements on ungrounded outlet GFCI protected	410.44X2
• Replacement with no exposed conductive parts	410.44X2

LIGHTING

General	21 IRC	20 NEC
☐ All luminaires, lampholders & retrofit kits listed	3403.3	410.6
☐ Install wet or damp location luminaires such that water cannot enter or accumulate	4003.9	410.10A
☐ Wet-location luminaires req marking as "SUITABLE FOR WET LOCATIONS," damp-location luminaires req either that marking or one stating "SUITABLE FOR DAMP LOCATIONS"	4003.9	410.10A
☐ Listing reqd for wet- or damp-location luminaires	4003.10	410.96
☐ Screw shells for lampholders only—no plug adapters	4003.4	410.90
☐ Grounded conductor to screw shell	4003.4	410.90
Grounding		
☐ Exposed conductive parts to connect to EGC EXC	4003.3	410.42
• Incidental metal parts such as mounting screws	4003.3	410.42
• Separation by listed system of double insulation	4003.3	410.42
• Portable luminaires w/ polarized plugs & no EGC	4003.3	410.42
Required Lighting Outlet Locations		
☐ Habitable rooms, kitchens & bathrooms EXC	3903.2	210.70A1
• Receptacle controlled by listed wall-mounted control device OK in other than kitchens & bathrooms	3903.2X1	210.70A1X
• Occupancy sensors w/ manual override OK	3903.2X2	210.70A1X2
☐ Hallways, stairways & garages	3903.3	210.70A2(1)
☐ Exterior side of all grade-level doors including garages except vehicle doors	3903.3	210.70A2(2)
☐ Stairs w/ ≥6 risers req listed wall-mounted control at each level that includes an entry to the stairs **F76** EXC	3903.3.1	210.70A2(3)
• Remote, central, or automatic means OK for outdoor egress doors, hallways & stairways	3903.3.1X	210.70A2
☐ Stair lighting dimmers req full-range control at each location	n/a	210.70A2(4)
☐ Attics, underfloor spaces, utility rooms & basements w/ equipment that reqs servicing	3904.3	210.70C

Switching in the above locations is to be from listed wall-mounted control devices, a term more encompassing than "switches."

Recessed Downlights in Ceilings

	21 IRC	20 NEC
☐ Recessed incandescents req thermal protection	4003.5	410.115B
☐ Non-IC rated min. ½ in. from combustibles	4004.8	410.116A1
☐ Non-IC rated min. 3 in. from thermal insulation	4004.8	410.116B
☐ Type IC rated for contact w/ combustible material	4004.8	410.116A2
☐ Type IC rated for contact w/ insulation	4004.9	410.116B
☐ Luminaires that req >60°C wire must be marked	n/a	410.74
☐ Connect proper temp-rated wire to luminaire **F73**	n/a	410.117A
☐ Tap conductors allowed per NEC 210.19A4X1	n/a	410.117C
☐ Luminaire not OK as only access to added box in **F73**	n/a	410.118[72]
☐ Luminaire not permitted to be reconditioned	4003.14[73]	410.118[73]
☐ Retrofits installed AMI not considered reconditioned	4003.14[73]	410.118[73]

FIG. 73

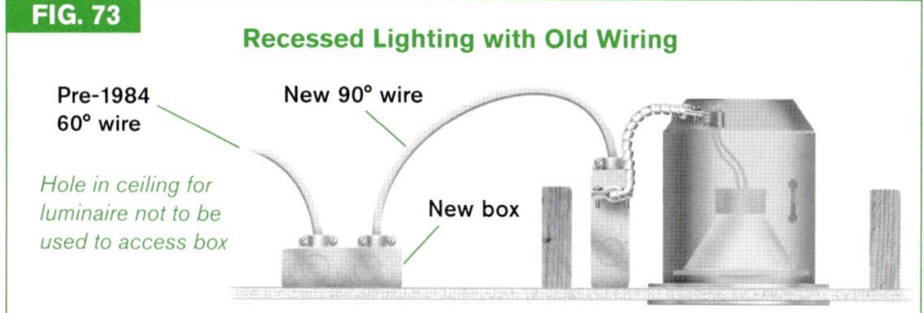

Track Lighting

The maximum length and the number of track lights on a single track is not specified; the total wattage of the installed lights cannot exceed the rating of the circuit. For example, a 15-amp circuit is allowed a maximum continuous load of 12 amps, which would mean a total wattage of 1,440 is allowed.

	21 IRC	20 NEC
☐ Branch circuit rating & connected load ≤ track rating	4005.1&3	410.151B
☐ Not OK where subject to physical damage, wet or damp locations, corrosive vapors, battery rooms, or concealed or extending through walls, or <5 ft. AFF unless <30V	4005.4	410.151C
☐ Track must be securely fastened	4005.5	410.154
☐ Track must be grounded	4005.6	410.155B

72. Boxes cannot be accessed solely through hole for ceiling luminaire.
73. Retrofit kits allowed; these are a common LED replacement item for incandescent recessed lights.

Clothes Closet Lights

	21 IRC	20 NEC
☐ Luminaires permitted in clothes closet limited to:	4003.12	410.16A
• Fully enclosed surface-mounted or recessed incandescent or LEDs		
• Surface-mounted or recessed fluorescent		
• Surface-mounted fluorescent or LED luminaires identified for installation within the closet storage space		
☐ Partially enclosed incandescent luminaires prohibited	4003.12	410.16B
☐ Pendant luminaires prohibited	4003.12	410.16B
☐ Clearance between luminaires & storage per **F74** EXC	4003.12	410.16C
• Surface fluorescent or LED OK in storage area where identified for this use—install AMI	4003.12(5)	410.16C5

FIG. 74

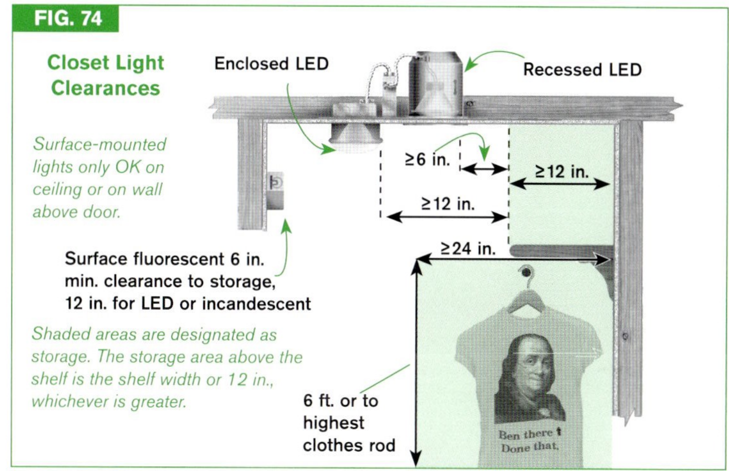

Low-Voltage Lighting

	20 NEC
☐ Can be listed system or assembly of listed parts	411.4A&B
☐ Not permitted to be reconditioned	411.4
☐ Transformer must be isolated winding type	411.3&6B
☐ Max. 20A branch circuit, power supply output max. 25A	411.3 &7
☐ Exposed bare conductors min. 7 ft. AFF unless listed for lower height	411.6C

Switches & Control Devices[74]

	21 IRC	20 NEC
☐ Switches shall be listed & used within their ratings	3403.3	404.14[75]
☐ Mounting screws 6-32 machine screws or AMI per L&L	4001.10	404.10B
☐ Faceplate must completely cover wall opening	4001.11	404.9A
☐ Snap switches directly to AL wire marked "CO/ALR"	4001.2	404.14C
☐ General-use & motor-circuit switches to indicate ON-OFF & if single-throw switches operate vertically up must = on	4001.3	404.7
☐ General-use dimmers only OK for permanently installed incandescent lights not receptacles EXC	4001.12	404.14E
• Where listed for control of other loads & installed AMI	4001.12	404.14E

Equipment Grounding

☐ Switches, dimmers & control switches req EGC & means to connect metal faceplates to EGC EXC	4001.11.1	404.9A&B
• Replacements where no grounding means present OK w/ plastic faceplate & mounting screws or GFCI protection	4001.11.1X	404.9BX
☐ Grounding OK by screws to grounded metal box	4001.11.1	404.9B1

Switches Controlling Lighting Loads

☐ Neutral reqd at switch box in bathrooms, hallways, stairways, habitable rooms, or occupiable spaces EXC	4011.15	404.2C
• In room w/ multiple switch locations, only 1 needed	4011.15	404.2C
• In raceway w/ sufficient room to add neutral	4011.15	404.2C1
• If box re-enterable w/o removing finish materials	4011.15	404.2C1
• Where lighting controlled by automatic means	4011.15	404.2C4
• Switches controlling receptacles	4011.15	404.2C5
☐ No current on EGC from electronic switches EXC	n/a	404.22
• Existing & L&L retrofit installations max. 5 on circuit	n/a	404.22X

Switches with electronic lighting controls such as occupancy or vacancy sensors are always active & req a neutral to complete the sensor circuit. Older switches with retrofit electronic controls often used the equipment ground for the return current, allowed 0.5mA by UL standards. Since January 1, 2020, such switches require retrofitting unless doing so would require removing finish materials.

Snap Switches for 277/480V Systems

	20 NEC
☐ Voltage between adjacent switches ≤300V unless barriers installed	404.22

74. In numerous locations, the code now uses the more inclusive term "control devices."
75. NEC now requires all switches to be listed.

3-Way & 4-Way Switches

☐ All switching in ungrounded conductors F75,76	4001.9	404.2A
☐ Current-carrying conductors of circuit grouped F75,76	3406.7	300.3B
☐ OK to re-identify white wires w/ tape at ends F75	3407.3X	200.7C
☐ Re-identified whites OK as supply not return F75	3407.3X	200.7C

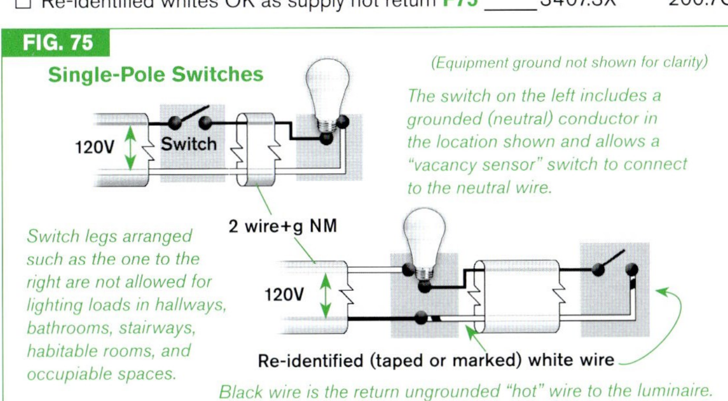

The switch on the left includes a grounded (neutral) conductor in the location shown and allows a "vacancy sensor" switch to connect to the neutral wire.

Switch legs arranged such as the one to the right are not allowed for lighting loads in hallways, bathrooms, stairways, habitable rooms, and occupiable spaces.

Black wire is the return ungrounded "hot" wire to the luminaire.

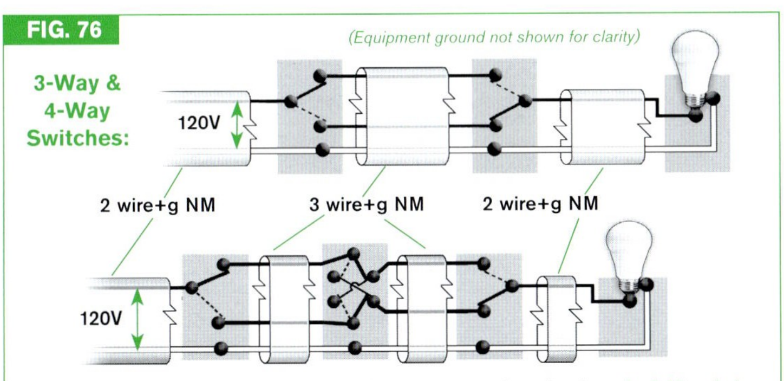

A 3-way switch connects a common conductor to one or the other "traveler." All switching must be done in the ungrounded "hot" conductors. A 4-way switch is a double-pole double-throw switch. Any number of 4-ways can be placed between the 2 3-ways.

Building Code Requirements for Suspended Ceilings 21 IBC

- ☐ Install ceiling systems AMI _______ 808.1.1
- ☐ Ceilings to conform to ASTM C635 & C636 _______ 808.1.1.1
- ☐ If fixture weight exceeds deflection capability of system, install supplemental hangers ≤6 in. from each corner of fixture __ASTM C 636
- ☐ Max. 2° rotation of runners after fixture loads imposed_______ASTM C 636

Luminaires in Suspended Ceilings in SDC C, D, E, or F

Codes and guidelines for installations in areas with high likelihood of seismic activity are provided by ASCE 7, ceiling manufacturers, the Northwest Wall & Ceiling Bureau, the Ceilings Interior Systems Construction Association (CISCA), and by ASTM 580 – a standard specific to such installations. These standards all agree on the following requirements for luminaires.

- Fixtures ≤10 lb. req one additional safety wire to fixture housing
- Fixtures >10 lb. & ≤56 lb. req 2 additional safety wires to fixture housing
- Fixtures >56 lb. req support from structure above
- Safety wires may be slack and may support wire cables
- Only heavy-duty main tees in SDC D, E & F

FIG. 77 Suspended Ceiling Luminaire

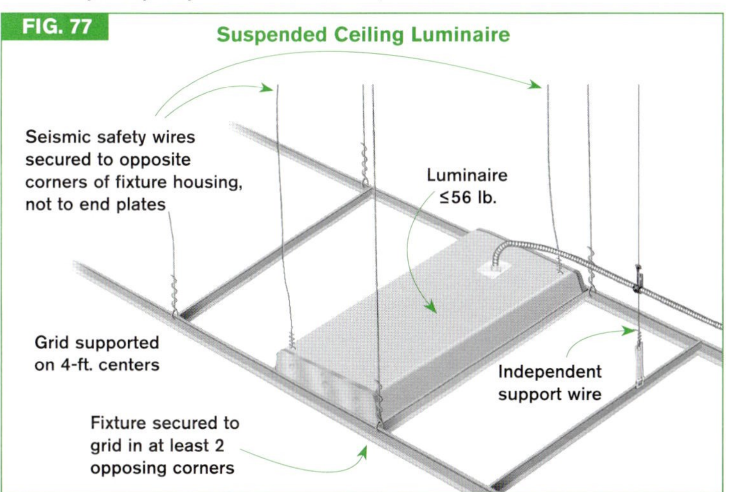

Luminaires in Suspended Ceilings 20 NEC

- ☐ Cables & raceways not to be supported by ceiling grids _______ 300.11B
- ☐ Wiring not to be secured or supported by ceiling support wires ___ 300.11B
- ☐ Independent support wires distinguishable by color, tagging, or other means (including clips made for the purpose) **F77** _______ 300.11B
- ☐ Luminaires must be securely fastened to grid by bolts, screws, rivets, or listed clips identified for the purpose **F77** _______ 410.36B

Electric Discharge Lighting ≤1,000V

- ☐ Disconnecting means reqd at or in each luminaire _______ 410.130G1
- ☐ When replacing ballast in existing fixture w/o disconnecting means, disconnecting means must be installed _______ 410.130G1
- ☐ When connected to MWBC, disconnecting means must also disconnect grounded conductor _______ 410.130G1

SIGNS

For many years, neon tubing was the system of choice for signs and outline lighting. Today, most signs use LED lighting. In a neon system, transformers raise the supply voltage to from 2,000 to 15,000 volts, whereas in an LED system a rectifier lowers the voltage, typically to 12 volts. Signs may require approval by the local planning department and compliance with energy codes.

General 20 NEC

- ☐ Signs req L&L regardless of voltage (marking on each letter of sign)__ 600.4B
- ☐ Each commercial building & occupancy reqs at least 1 outlet in accessible location at entrance to each tenant space for sign or outline lighting___600.5A
- ☐ Sign outlet reqs min. 20A circuit w/ no other load _______600.5A
- ☐ Each sign reqs disconnecting means_______600.6
- ☐ If tubular LEDs powered by existing sign sockets, warning label reqd that sign modified & not to install fluorescent lamps_______ 600.4B
- ☐ Bond all metal parts in fountains to recirculating equipment EGC___ 600.7B8
- ☐ Portable signs in wet locations req GFCI in attachment plug ______ 600.10C2
- ☐ Ballasts, transformers & power supplies in attics or soffits req access door min. 36 in. × 22½ in. & passageway min. 2 ft. wide with permanent walkway min. 12 in. wide from point of entry to each component____ 600.21E
- ☐ Attics or soffits req light w/ control provided near entry_______ 600.21E
- ☐ Suspended ceiling grids not OK to support power supply above grid_600.21F

APPLIANCES

General — 21 IRC — 20 NEC

- ☐ Appliances supplied by ≥50V req listing ______ 3403.3 — 422.6
- ☐ Install AMI ______ 4101.2 — MFR

Disconnecting Means: General

- ☐ Means reqd to disconnect all ungrounded conductors __ 4101.5 — 422.30
- ☐ If appliance reqs >1 branch circuit, disconnects grouped & identified as the multiple disconnecting means of the appliance _____ n/a — 422.30
- ☐ When disconnect switch/breaker reqd to be lockable in open position, hasp must remain in place w/ lock removed **F78** EXC___ 4101.8 — 110.25
  - Locking provisions for cord-plug connections _______ 4101.8X — 110.25X

Permanently Connected Appliances

- ☐ Appliances ≤300VA or <⅛ hp branch circuit OCPD either within sight or lockable OK as disconnect ______ T4101.5 — 422.31A
- ☐ Appliances >300VA same as above line ______ T4101.5 — 422.31B
- ☐ Motor-operated appliances >⅛ hp see *p. 313* EXC ___ T4101.5 — 422.31C
  - If appliance provided w/ unit switch that opens all ungrounded conductors, disconnect does not have to be in sight__ T4101.5 — 422.31CX

Cord & Plug or Attachment Fitting-Connected Appliances

- ☐ Accessible factory-installed cord & attachment plug or separable connector **F33** OK as disconnecting means_ T4101.5 — 422.33A
- ☐ Cord-&-plug-connected electric ranges w/ receptacle at rear of range accessed by removing drawer meets intent of above__ T4101.5 — 422.33B

FIG. 78 Breaker Lockout Hasp

The hasp for a lockable breaker must remain in place with or without a lock installed. In this example, the deadfront cover fits over the frame of the hasp assembly. Lockouts that attach only to the breaker handle are not allowed.

Flexible Cords — 21 IRC — 20 NEC

- ☐ Flexible cords w/ attachment plugs only for (1) portable luminaires, (2) appliances to permit frequent interchange, or (3) where fastening means & mechanical connections are designed to permit ready removal for maintenance & repair & appliance listed for flexible cord connection ______ 3909.1&4 — 400.10A&B
- ☐ Flexible cords & cables also permitted for pendants, luminaire wiring, portable luminaires, signs & wiring, elevator cables, cranes & hoists, prevention of noise or vibration, connection of moving parts, other areas permitted by code ______ n/a — 400.10A
- ☐ Flexible cords allowed between existing outlet & the inlet to additional single receptacle w/ approved wiring method between the inlet & the single receptacle (listed kits for wall-mounted flat-screen TV) n/a — 400.10A
- ☐ Ampacity (IRC: max. load) of cords per **T45** ______ 3909.2 — 400.5A
- ☐ Flexible cords not permitted to be (1) a substitute for the fixed wiring of a structure, (2) run through walls, ceilings, suspended ceilings, floors, doorways, windows, or similar openings, (3) attached to building surfaces, (4) concealed by walls, floors, or ceilings, (5) in raceways, or (6) where subject to physical damage_____ 3909.1 — 400.12
- ☐ Flexible cords not permitted to be spliced ______ 3909.3 — 400.13

TABLE 45 MAX. AMPACITY FOR FLEXIBLE CORDS IRC T3909.2 ◆ NEC T400.5A1

Cord Size[A-C]	3 Current-Carrying Conductors[D]	2 Current-Carrying Conductors
18	7	10
16	10	13
14	15	18
12	20	25
10	25	30

A. Size in AWG. Cord types S, SE, SEW, SEO, SEOW, SEOOW, SJ, SJE, SJEW, SJEO, SJEOW, SJEOOW, SJO, SJOO, SJT, SJTW, SJTO, SJTOW, SJTOOW, SO, SOO, SPT-2W, SRD, SRDE, SRFT, ST, STW, STOW, STOOW, STD, SV, SVO, SVOO, SVTO, SVTOO.
B. Cords with the "W" suffix are suitable for use in wet locations and are sunlight-resistant.
C. Based on ambient temperature 86°F. Apply **T25** correction factors for other temperatures.
D. Could be 3 ungrounded conductors or 2 ungrounded conductors + neutral from 208/120V system.

Appliance Circuit Ratings

	21 IRC	20 NEC
☐ Individual branch circuit ≥ marked rating of appliance	3701.2	422.10A
☐ Circuit for continuous load min. 125% appliance rating	3701.2.1	422.10A
☐ Max. OCPD per marking of appliance **F82**	4101.4.1	422.11A

Kitchen Appliances

	21 IRC	20 NEC
☐ Appliances w/ cords terminate in grounding-type plug EXC	4101.3	422.16B
• Double-insulated appliances	4101.3	422.16B
☐ Compactor & DW cords measure from rear of appliance	4101.3	422.16B2
☐ Trash-compactor cord min. 36 in. max. 48 in.	T4101.3	422.16B2
☐ Compactor receptacle in same or adjacent cabinet	n/a	422.16B2
☐ DW cords min. 36 in. max. 78 in.	T4101.3	422.16B2
☐ DW receptacle in adjacent cabinet, not OK behind DW	4101.3	422.16B2
☐ Provide bushing or grommet at opening for DW cord	4101.3[76]	422.16B2[76]
☐ Disposer cord min. 18 in. max. 36 in. to receptacle	T4101.3	422.16B1
☐ Accessible cord & plug connection for range hood + microwave allowable if individual branch circuit, cord 18 in. – 24 in. w/ grounding-type plug to accessible receptacle	4101.3	422.16B4[77]

Electric Water Heaters

	21 IRC	20 NEC
☐ Considered continuous load (125% nameplate rating)	3702.10	422.13
☐ Disconnect switch or circuit breaker within sight or lockable in open position **F78**	T4101.5	422.31B
☐ NM cable not suitable for direct connection to WH	3802.3	334.15

Central Vacuum

	21 IRC	20 NEC
☐ Individual circuit reqd if >50% of branch circuit rating	3702.3	210.23A2
☐ Branch circuit for individual motor min. 125% motor FLC	3702.6	430.22A
☐ Cord ampacity ≥ branch circuit conductor ampacity not **T45**	n/a	422.15B
☐ Bond all non-current carrying metal parts EXC	3908.19	422.15C
• Screws or rivets installed in insulating material (plastic)	n/a	422.15C

76. New requirement for a protective grommet on the dishwasher cord opening.
77. NEC clarified that this rule applies to both range hoods and microwave/range hood combinations.

FIG. 79

Hydromassage Tub (Whirlpool)

Receptacles within 6 ft. GFCI-protected

8 AWG conductor bonded to motor lug intended for bonding

GFCI-protected receptacle for cord-and-plug-connected motor. Locate ≤12 in. from opening and in direct view.

Bond to metal piping systems, grounded metal parts in contact with circulating water & metal parts of adjacent electrical devices within 5 ft.

Hydromassage Tub (Whirlpool Bathtub)

	21 IRC	20 NEC
☐ Individual branch circuit reqd	4209.2	680.71
☐ Readily accessible GFCI protection reqd	4209.2	680.71
☐ All receptacles within 6 ft. req GFCI protection **F79**	4209.2	680.71
☐ Electrical equipment (pump motor) must be accessible	4209.4	680.73
☐ Cord & plug connection receptacle max. 12 in. from hatch opening & receptacle face in view **F79**	4209.4	680.73
☐ Bond metal fittings in contact w/ circulating water, motors **F79**, exposed metal surfaces & devices <5 ft. from tub & not separated by barrier & metal-sheathed cables & raceways EXC	4209.5	680.74A
• Small conductive surfaces such as jets & towel bars	4209.5X2	680.74AX1
• Double-insulated motors	4209.5X1	680.74AX2
☐ Bonding conductor min. solid #8 Cu	4209.6	680.74B
☐ Connect bonding conductor to motor lug EXC **F79**	4209.5	680.74A
• If double-insulated motor, install bond wire from EGC to motor location for future motor swap w/ non-double-insulated	4209.6	680.74B
☐ Bonding conductor need not connect to panelboards	4209.6	680.74B

Central Heating (Forced Air & Boilers)

	21 IRC	20 NEC
☐ Central heating must be on individual circuit EXC	3703.1	422.12
• Auxiliary equipment (filter, condensate pump, etc.)	3703.1	422.12X1
• Air-conditioning equipment	3703.1	422.12X2
☐ Disconnect within sight of furnace	T4101.5	422.31B
☐ Cord & plug connection not OK unless AMI	4101.3	422.16A
☐ Lighting outlet at equipment space w/ switch at entry to space	3904.3	210.70A3
☐ Receptacle ≤25 ft. & on same level as equipment	3901.12	210.63
☐ Receptacle not on same circuit as central heating	3703.1	422.12
☐ Receptacle not on load side of HVAC disconnect	3901.12	422.12
☐ Install overcurrent protection AMI **F80**	4101.4	110.3B

FIG. 80 **"SSU" Switch**

Manufacturer's instructions may require supplementary overload protection, which can be provided by a fused switch. A furnace with instructions for 15A overcurrent protection would req this type of switch when installed on a 20A circuit.

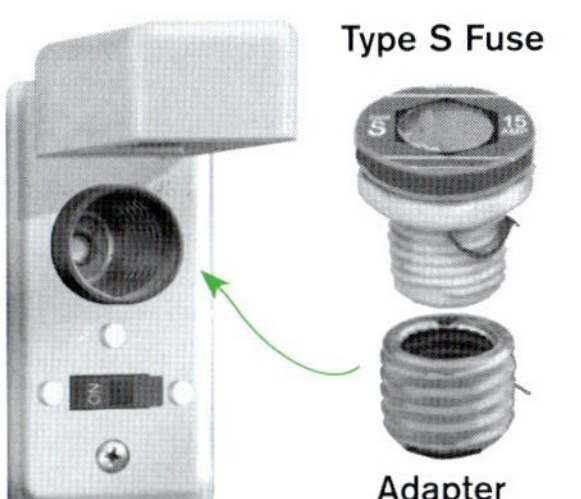

Type S adapters are required in fuseholders. They prevent replacement with the wrong size fuse.

FIG. 81 **Room Air-Conditioner Plug**

Max. wattage on shared 15A 120V circuit is 900W.

Max. wattage on individual 20A 240V circuit is 3,840W.

AFCI test & reset buttons

Central Air Conditioning & Heat Pumps F82

	21 IRC	20 NEC
☐ Disconnecting means within sight	T4101.5	440.14
☐ Disconnecting means OK on unit if not covering access panel or obscuring the equipment nameplate	n/a	440.14
☐ GFCI protection reqd	n/a	210.8F[78]
☐ Ampacity of conductors ≥ nameplate min. ampacity	3702.11	440.4B&35

*Use **T23** to determine the min. wire size based on the nameplate. The terminals in air conditioners are typically rated 75°C and that column can be used unless NM cable is part of the circuit, in which case the ampacity is limited to 60°C. The max. overcurrent device specified on the nameplate may further require a fuse or a "HACR" breaker. Always follow the nameplate instructions, including clearances.*

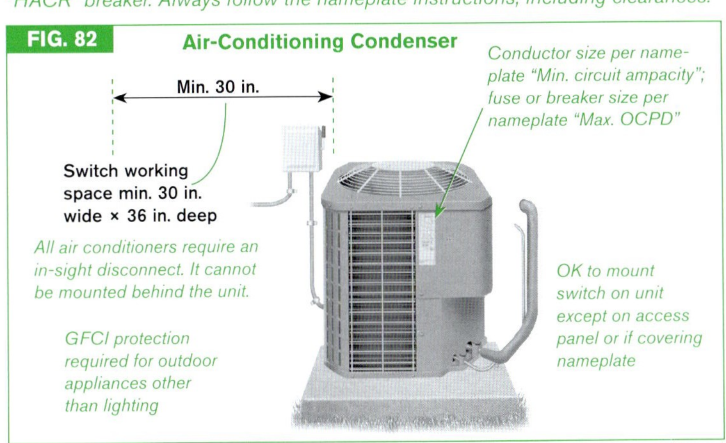

Window or Through-Wall Air Conditioners

	21 IRC	20 NEC
☐ Max. rating of unit ≤80% of individual branch circuit	3702.12.1	440.62B
☐ Max. rating of unit ≤50% of shared branch circuit	3702.12.2	440.62C
☐ Cord OK as disconnect if manual controls ≤6 ft. AFF	n/a	440.63
☐ Max. cord length 120V = 10 ft., 240V = 6 ft.	n/a	440.64
☐ Cord/plug units req AFCI or leakage-current detector-interrupter or heat-detecting circuit interrupter in cord or plug cap **F81**	n/a	440.65

78. New requirement for GFCI protection. Local adoption may vary. See change #54 on *p. 290*.

ELECTRIC HEAT

Electric-resistance heating can be in the form of central forced-air furnaces, baseboard heaters, radiant ceiling panels, duct heaters, and systems such as electric heat in ceramic tile bath floors. Electric heating is classified as a continuous load. The heating circuit wiring must be sized to 125% of the load to ensure that the wiring is not overloaded during periods of prolonged use. Heat pumps transfer heat using refrigerants and compressors and are categorized as air-conditioning equipment in the NEC (rather than as electric heating). Electric-resistance strip heaters added to heat pumps must be listed and marked.

General	21 IRC	20 NEC
☐ Circuits considered continuous load	3702.10	424.4B
☐ Circuits must be sized to 125% of load	3701.2	210.20A
☐ All electric-heating equipment must be L&L	3403.3	424.6
☐ Factory-applied nameplates must include identifying name & normal rating in volts & watts or volts & amps	1303.1	424.28A
☐ Nameplate visible or accessible after installation	1303.1	424.28B

Baseboard Heaters	21 IRC	20 NEC
☐ Must be L&L per UL 1042 and installed AMI	3403.3	424.6
☐ Provide spacing from combustibles AMI	n/a	424.13
☐ Branch circuit for 2 or more units max. 30 amps	3702.10(2)	424.4A
☐ No receptacles above heaters: integral receptacles w/ heaters can substitute for reqd room receptacles **F83**	1405.1	424.9
☐ Integral receptacles not allowed on heater circuit **F83**	1405.1	424.9

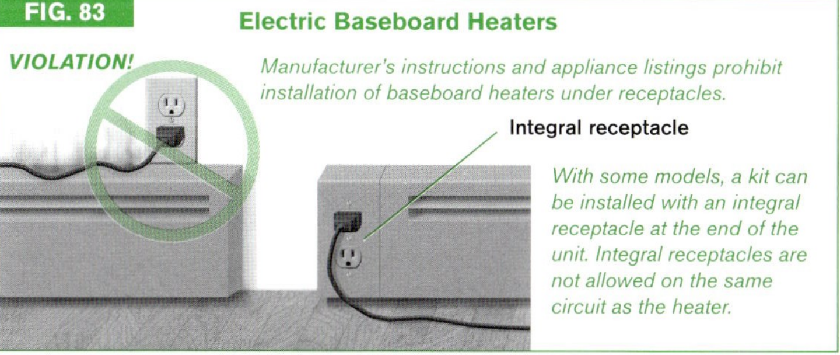

FIG. 83 Electric Baseboard Heaters

Manufacturer's instructions and appliance listings prohibit installation of baseboard heaters under receptacles.

With some models, a kit can be installed with an integral receptacle at the end of the unit. Integral receptacles are not allowed on the same circuit as the heater.

Central Electric-Resistance Heat	21 IRC	20 NEC
☐ Disconnect reqd within sight or lockable breaker	4101.5	424.19A
☐ Locking hasp must remain w/o lock installed	T4101.5	424.19
☐ If multiple disconnecting means reqd, disconnects must be grouped & identified as to conductors they control	n/a	424.19

Electric Duct Heaters	21 IRC	20 NEC
☐ Install AMI	1407.1	424.66
☐ Must be accessible for servicing	1407.4	424.66
☐ If <4 ft. from heat pump/air conditioning, both pieces of equipment must be listed & marked as suitable for same	1407.3	424.61
☐ Interlock reqd to prevent heat if fan not operating	1407.5	424.63
☐ Each unit reqs integral limit controls & manual reset	1407.1	424.64
☐ Lockable breaker reqd or disconnect within sight	4101.5	424.65

Electric Radiant Heat Panels & Sets	21 IRC	20 NEC
☐ Install AMI	1406.1	424.93A1
☐ Not permitted in/behind surfaces subject to damage, not above walls, soffits, or cupboards, not embedded in insulation	1406.1	424.93A2
☐ Install panels parallel to framing	1406.3(1)	424.93B2
☐ Fasteners min. ¼ in. from heating element	1406.3(2)	424.93B3
☐ Min. 8-in. distance from surface-mounted fixture boxes	n/a	424.93A3
☐ Min. 2-in. distance from recessed fixtures & trim	n/a	424.93A3
☐ No field modification/cutting of panels unless so listed	1406.3(3)	424.93B4
☐ Wiring not related to heating min. 2 in. above heated ceiling	n/a	424.94
☐ Other wiring above heated ceiling considered as min. 50°C ambient unless over min. 2-in. thickness of thermal insulation	n/a	424.94

Embedded Heating Cables in Concrete or Slurry Floors	20 NEC
☐ Spacing between cables AMI	424.44A
☐ Secure in place while concrete or other finish applied	424.44B
☐ Protect leads w/ conduit or EMT where leaving floor	424.44C&D
☐ GFCI protection reqd for cables in bathroom & kitchen floors	424.44E

SWIMMING POOLS, SPAS & FOUNTAINS

Conductor Clearances

	21 IRC	20 NEC
☐ Service drop < 10 ft. horizontal from pool edge reqs 22½-ft. clearance in any direction to water, 14½-ft. clearance from diving board	4203.7	680.9A
☐ Communications wires ≥10 ft. above pools & diving board	4203.7	680.9B
☐ Underground wiring RMC, IMC, PVC, RTRC, or MC, LFMC & LFNC that is L&L for direct burial use	4203.8	680.11A
☐ Not under pool unless to supply pool equipment	4203.8	680.11B
☐ Cover depth per T3	4203.8	680.11

Equipotential Bonding F84

	21 IRC	20 NEC
☐ Bonding is to reduce voltage gradients in pool area	4204.1	680.26A
☐ Equipotential grid not to be used as grounding electrode	3608.7	250.52B3
☐ Equipotential grid bond wire not reqd to extend to panels	4204.2	680.26B
☐ Bonding conductors Cu min. #8 solid	4204.2	680.26B
☐ Bonded parts to include the following:	4204.2	680.26B

1. Unencapsulated structural steel w/ steel tie wires **A** or Cu grid below pool shell if steel encapsulated **B**
2. Perimeter surface to be bonded extends 3 ft. beyond pool wall. **C** Use structural-steel reinforcement if present, or min. #8 Cu solid 18–24 in. from pool wall 4–6 in. below surface around perimeter
3. Metal components of pool structure not included above
4. Metal forming shells & mounting brackets of no-niche luminaires
5. Metal fittings, except isolated parts < 4 in. any dimension (lane rings)
6. Electrical equipment associated w/ circulating system (pumps) **D**
7. Fixed metal parts < 5 ft. horizontal & 12 ft. vertical from pool walls **E**

	21 IRC	20 NEC
☐ If double-insulated type motors, provide bond wire to area of double-insulated motor but do not connect to motor	4204.2X6.1	680.26B6
☐ If none of the bonded parts are in direct contact w/ water, provide min. 9-sq.-in. bonded metal in contact w/ pool water	4204.3	680.26C

FIG. 84 Equipotential Bonding

A or B must be installed for conductive pool shells.

Pool Cover Motors

	21 IRC	20 NEC
☐ Motors, controllers & wiring min. 5 ft. from pool EXC	4206.11	680.27B1
• Where separated by wall or other permanent barrier	4206.11	680.27B1
☐ Motors below grade must be totally enclosed type	4206.11	680.27B1
☐ Control device located so operator has full view of pool	4206.11	680.27B1
☐ Pool cover motor & controller reqs GFCI protection	4206.11	680.27B2

Other Equipment Near Pool

	21 IRC	20 NEC
☐ Other equipment (e.g., electrical panels) > low-voltage contact limit min. 5 ft. from pool unless separated by permanent barrier	4203.6[79]	680.22E[79]

79. New specified distance to other electrical equipment.

Underwater Wet-Niche Lighting F85

	21 IRC	20 NEC
☐ Lights > low-voltage contact limit req GFCI	4206.4	680.23A3
☐ Top of lens min. 18 in. below water level EXC	4206.4.2	680.23A5
• ≥4 in. OK if listed for <18 in.	4206.4.2	680.23A5
☐ Luminaire bonded & secured to shell w/ locking device	4206.5	680.23B5
☐ Must req tool to remove luminaire from shell	4206.5	680.23B5
☐ Conduit to shell red brass, stainless steel, LFNC or RNC	n/a	680.32B2
☐ Nonmetallic conduit LFNC or RNC	n/a	680.23B2
☐ Nonmetallic conduit reqs insulated #8 bonding conductor encapsulated w/ listed potting compound to terminal in forming shell	4205.3	680.23B2b
☐ EGC in cord to luminaire ≥ supply conductor size	4205.4	680.23B3

Junction Boxes & Enclosures

	21 IRC	20 NEC
☐ Pool light junction box must be L&L for pools	4206.9.1	680.24A1
☐ Deck box not to be located unprotected in walkway	4206.9.3	680.24C
☐ Box min. 4 ft. from pool wall, 8 in. above max. water level	4206.9.1	680.24A2
☐ Flush deck box OK if below low-voltage contact limit	4206.9.1	680.24A2
☐ Flush deck box min. 4 ft. from pool wall & potted	4206.9.1	680.24A2
☐ EGC to pool junction box ≥#12 insulated Cu	4205.2	680.23F2
☐ EGC unspliced except on terminals	4205.2	680.23F2
☐ Cord from underwater luminaire reqs strain relief	4206.9.5	680.24E
☐ If conduit to box or enclosure originates in corrosive environment, must be RMC, IMC, PVC, RTRC, or LFNC	4205.2	680.23F1
☐ Conductors from load side of GFCI or transformer not in same raceway or box as non-GFCI-protected wires	4206.3	680.23F3
☐ Low-voltage XFMRs L&L for pool (isolated windings)	4206.1	680.23A2

FIG. 85 Underwater Wet-Niche Lighting

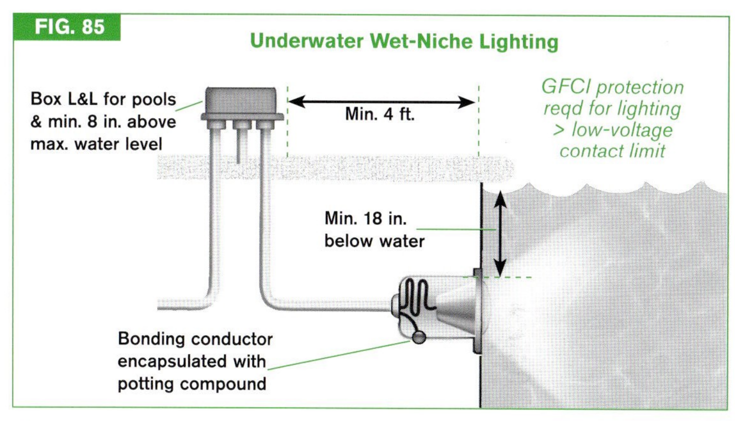

A storable pool is intended to be stored when not in use and is constructed on or above the ground. It is currently defined as having a maximum depth ≤42 in. That depth dimension is deleted from the definition in the next (2023) code edition. All applicable rules for permanent pools also apply to storable pools, and the sections below are unique to storable pools.

Storable Pools

	21 IRC	20 NEC
☐ Cord-and-plug-connected pool filter pump reqs double insulation, EGC to receptacle & GFCI protection	4207.1	680.31
☐ GFCI reqd for electrical equipment including supply cords	4207.2	680.32
☐ Luminaires must be listed as an assembly	4207.3	680.33A&B
☐ Luminaires over low-voltage contact limit req open-neutral GFCI protection	4207.3.2	680.33B

Most Class A GFCIs do not provide protection when the neutral is disconnected upstream from the GFCI device. A GFCI with open-neutral protection will open the circuit under such conditions whenever there is a ground-fault on the load side. GFCI cord-sets typically do have open-neutral protection.

Lighting & Paddle Fans near Pools

	21 IRC	20 NEC
☐ Outdoors min. 5 ft. from pool walls unless 12 ft. above	4203.4.1	680.22B1
☐ Indoor 7 ft. 6 in. above water level if GFCI-protected, totally enclosed luminaires or paddle fans identified for such installation	4203.4.2	680.22B2
☐ Low-voltage luminaires allowed <5 ft. horizontal from pool walls if supplied by XFMRs L&L for pool (isolated windings)__	4203.4.3	680.22B6
☐ Existing luminaires allowed <5 ft. horizontal from pool walls if rigidly attached, >5 ft. vertical above water & GFCI-protected	4203.4.4	680.22B3
☐ Luminaires > 5–10 ft. horizontal from pool walls min. 5 ft. above pool water level unless GFCI-protected ______	4203.4.6	680.22B4
☐ Switches min. 5 ft. from pool edge or separated by a solid fence, wall, or other permanent barrier _________	4203.3	680.22C

Receptacles

	21 IRC	20 NEC
☐ Min. 1 receptacle ≥6 ft. & ≤ 20ft. from pool walls ____	4203.1.3	680.22A1
☐ Pump-motor receptacles ≥6 ft. from pool walls ______	4203.1.1	680.22A2
☐ Min. 1 receptacle in pool equipment room, all in room GFCI	n/a	680.22A5[80]
☐ Dimensions include distance around barriers w/o penetrating a floor, wall, doorway w/ hinged or sliding door, or window opening__	4203.1	680.22A6

80. Receptacles in a pool equipment room all req GFCI protection.

Equipment Rooms & Wiring Methods

	21 IRC	20 NEC
☐ Rooms w/ electrical equipment req drainage to prevent water accumulation during normal operation & maintenance______	n/a	680.12
☐ Rooms w/ chemical storage, pumps, chlorinators, filters & confined areas under decks abutting pool are corrosive environments ____	4201.2	680.2
☐ Only RMC, IMC, PVC, or RTRC in corrosive environments	4202.2	680.14
☐ LFNC permitted for feeders in corrosive environment ___	4205.6	680.25A
☐ Feeders in corrosive environments min. #12 insulated EGC	4205.6	680.25

Pool Equipment Pump Motors

	21 IRC	20 NEC
☐ If located in corrosive environment, MC cable listed for such locations allowable w/ min. #12 EGC ___________	4205.5	680.21A1
☐ LFMC or LFNC allowable in noncorrosive environment__	4205.5	680.21A2
☐ Cord & plug OK w/ cord ≤3 ft. & min. #12 Cu EGC_______	n/a	680.21A3
☐ GFCI protection reqd for all motors ≤150V to ground & ≤60A single phase or 3-phase _____________________	4203.1.4[81]	680.21C[81]
☐ Also applies to replacement pump motors _____________	n/a	680.21D[81]

81. Now also applies to 3-phase ≤ 60A & to replacement motors.

HOT TUBS & SPAS

*See **p. 303** for hydromassage (whirlpool) tubs*

Hot Tubs & Spas: General

	21 IRC	20 NEC
☐ Outdoor spas same rules as pools plus items below	4202.1	680.42
☐ LFMC or LFNMC for package units	T4202.1	680.42A1
☐ GFCI-protected cord ≤15 ft. OK for package units	T4202.1	680.42A2
☐ Outlets supplying self-contained, packaged, or field-assembled spa/hot tub reqs GFCI (including 240V) EXC	4208.1	680.44
• Outlets supplying listed units w/ integral GFCIs	4208.1	680.44A
☐ Luminaires & ceiling-suspended paddle fans over or ≤5 ft. from indoor spa or hot tub min. 7 ft. 6 in. above & either GFCI-protected or ≥12 ft. above water	4203.4.5	680.43B1
☐ Electric-heating elements subdivided into loads ≤48A &	4208.2	680.10
☐ Electric-heating OCPD & conductors ≤125% load	4208.2	680.10
☐ Emergency disconnect clearly labeled, readily accessible, max. 5 ft. from spa/hot tub & within sight except 1&2FD	4208.4	680.41

Hot Tub & Spa Bonding

☐ Bonding not reqd for outdoor hot tub staves	4204.4	680.42B
☐ Not reqd for L&L outdoor-use package units installed AMI & top rim min. 28 in. above all perimeter surfaces ≤30 in. from unit	4204.4	680.42B
☐ Indoor tub bonding to include: 1. Metal fittings within or attached to spa/hot tub structure 2. Metal parts of water circulation in contact w/ circulating water, including motors if not part of listed self-contained unit 3. Metal raceways & piping ≤5 ft. away & not separated by barrier 4. Exposed metal surfaces <5ft. away & not separated by barrier 5. Non-current-carrying metal parts of electrical devices not associated w/ tub/spa & ≤5 ft. from such units	4204.5	680.43D
☐ Exceptions to above for small conductive surfaces not likely to be energized, such as jets, towel bars & mirror frames	4204.5X	680.43DX
☐ All electrical equipment ≤5 ft. of tub/spa & all electrical equipment associated w/ circulating water must connect to EGC EXC	n/a	680.43F
• Low-voltage equipment supplied by L&L pool XFMR	n/a	680.44FX

FOUNTAINS

Required GFCI Protection

	20 NEC
☐ Pumps, luminaires, other submersibles unless listed for operation at no more than low-voltage contact limit	680.51A
☐ All receptacle outlets ≤20 ft. of edge of fountain	680.58
☐ Permanently installed nonsubmersible pump motors rated ≤250V & ≤60A, single phase or 3-phase	680.59

Submerged Equipment

☐ XFMRs for low-voltage equipment L&L for pool (isolated windings)	680.51A
☐ No luminaires operating at >150V between conductors	680.51B
☐ Submersible pumps max. 300V between conductors	680.51B
☐ Max. length of each exposed cord in fountain 10 ft.	680.51E
☐ Equipment must be removable for relamping & maintenance—no luminaires embedded into fountain such that water level would have to be reduced or drained for relamping, maintenance, or inspection	680.51E

Cord-and-Plug-Connected Equipment

☐ GFCI protection reqd for all cord-and-plug-connected equipment	680.56A
☐ Cord immersed in or exposed to water extra-hard usage per T400.4 & listed type w/ "W" suffix	680.56B
☐ Connections w/ flexible cord permanent (not cord & plug) for equipment located in any water-containing part of fountain	680.56D

Grounding & Bonding

☐ EGC to connect to all electrical equipment (other than low-voltage) within or ≤5 ft. of fountain and to panelboard's supply equipment	680.54A
☐ Bond EGC to all metal piping associated w/ fountain, metal parts, metal raceways, metal surfaces & electrical devices ≤5 ft. from fountain	680.54B

Junction Boxes

☐ Junction boxes (other than underwater) same as on ***p. 307***	680.52A
☐ Underwater enclosures equipped w/ threaded entries or compression glands or seals for cord entry	680.52B1
☐ Underwater enclosures listed & rated for prolonged submersion, made of brass, copper, or other corrosion-resistant material	680.52B1

MOTORS

Motor circuits require two forms of overcurrent protection. Short-circuit and ground-fault protection are supplied at the source of the circuit. The conductors and motor are protected against overload by thermal devices located either in the equipment or in a separate motor controller. Motors and their associated equipment are rated in horsepower. The starting current, sometimes referred to as "inrush" current, is marked on a motor by a letter code.

FIG. 86 Motor Circuits

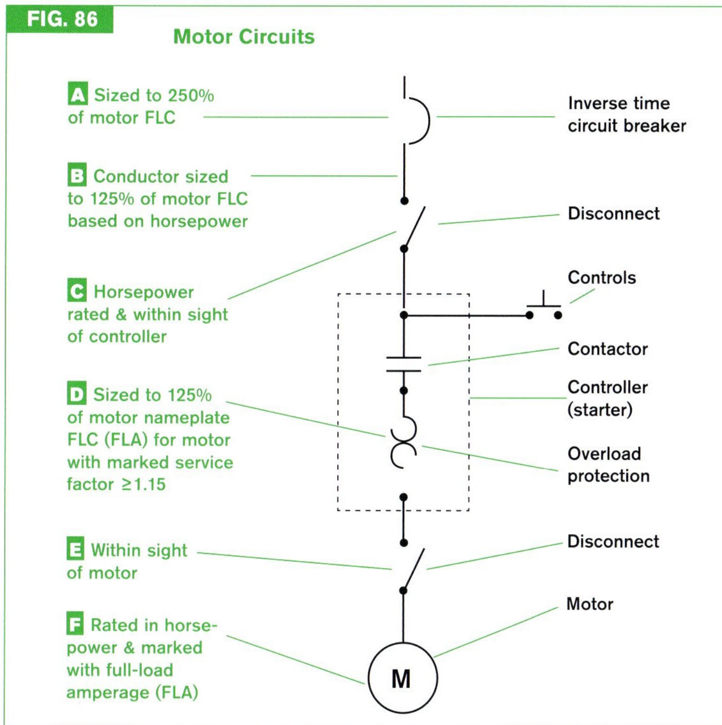

Motor Circuit Conductors — 20 NEC

- ☐ Use **T46** to determine FLC of motor EXC ______ 430.6A1
  - Where motor part of L&L appliance, e.g., air conditioner ______ 430.6A1X3
- ☐ Size conductor **F86B** for single motor to 125% of ampacity in **T23** __ 430.22
- ☐ Size conductor supplying ≥1 motor to 125% of **T23** ampacity of largest motor + 100% of FLC of other motors, + 100% of non-motor noncontinuous loads + 125% non-motor continuous load_ 430.24

TABLE 46 — AC MOTOR FULL-LOAD CURRENTS ◆ T430.248 & T430.250

Single-Phase				Three-Phase			
HP	115V[A]	208V[A]	230V[A]	HP	208V[A]	230V[A]	460V[A]
1/6	4.4	2.4	2.2	1/2	2.4	2.2	1.1
1/4	5.8	3.2	2.9	3/4	3.5	3.2	1.6
1/3	7.2	4.0	3.6	1	4.6	4.2	2.1
1/2	9.8	5.4	4.9	1 1/2	6.6	6	3
3/4	13.8	7.6	6.9	2	7.5	6.8	3.4
1	16	8.8	8	3	10.6	9.6	4.8
1 1/2	20	11	10	5	16.7	15.2	7.6
2	24	13.2	12	7 1/2	24.2	22	11
3	34	18.7	17	10	30.8	28	14
5	56	30.8	28	15	46.2	42	21
7 1/2	80	44	40	20	59.4	54	27
10	100	55	50	25	74.8	68	34
				30	88	80	40
				40	114	104	52

A. Voltages are rated motor voltages. System voltage ranges are 110 to 220, 220 to 240, and 440 to 480.

Short-Circuit & Ground-Fault Protection — 20 NEC

- ☐ OCPD **F86A** must be capable of carrying motor starting current ___ 430.52B
- ☐ Max. rating or setting of OCPD per **T47** EXC ___ 430.52C1
  - If OCPD rating or setting between standard sizes **T22,** OK to round up to next larger size ___ 430.52C1X1
  - If **T47** rating not sufficient for motor starting, following increases to table percentages are allowable: ___ 430.52C1X2
    1. Non-time-delay fuse ≤600A or time-delay Class CC fuse max. 400%
    2. Time-delay dual-element fuse max. 225%
    3. Inverse time breaker max. 400% for FLC ≤100A & 300% for FLC >100A
    4. Fuse of 601–6,000A classification max. 300% of FLC
- ☐ Instantaneous trip breaker only allowed if adjustable & part of listed combination motor controller w/ coordinated protection ___ 430.52C3
- ☐ Protective device for feeder supplying motor loads reqs rating ≤ rating or setting of OCPD for largest motor + sum of FLCs of other motors ___ 430.62A

TABLE 47 — MAX. RATING OR SETTING OF MOTOR BRANCH CIRCUIT & GROUND-FAULT PROTECTIVE DEVICES ◆ T430.52

Percentage of Full-Load Current (See **T46**)

Type of Motor	Non-Time-Delay fuse	Dual-Element Time-Delay Fuse	Instantaneous Trip Breaker	Inverse Time Breaker
Single-phase	300	175	800	250
AC polyphase[A]	300	175	800	250
Squirrel cage[B]	300	175	800	250
Design B energy efficient	300	175	1100	250
Synchronous	300	175	800	250
Wound-rotor	150	150	800	150
DC (constant voltage)	150	150	250	150

A. Other than wound-rotor motors.
B. Other than Design B energy efficient.

Overload Protection — 20 NEC

- ☐ Overload protection **F86D** determined by motor nameplate FLA ___ 430.6A2
- ☐ Overload protection not reqd if power loss would create hazard ___ 430.31
- ☐ Overload protection not allowed for fire pumps ___ 695.6C
- ☐ Continuous duty motors req one of the following: ___ 430.32A&B
  1. Separate overload device selected per **T48**
  2. Thermal or electronic protection
  3. Protective device integral w/ motor
  4. Impedance-protected motor (only applies if ≤1hp)
- ☐ Motors considered continuous duty unless nature of apparatus is such that the motor cannot operate continuously under load (e.g., elevators) 430.33
- ☐ Motors used for inherently short-time, intermittent, periodic, or varying duty can be protected by branch circuit short-circuit & GFP device ___ 430.33
- ☐ Fuses as overload protection reqd in each ungrounded conductor ___ 430.36
- ☐ Devices other than fuses reqd in locations depending upon system type & number of phases in accordance w/ T430.37 ___ 430.37
- ☐ Overload devices must open sufficient number of ungrounded conductors to interrupt current to motor ___ 430.38
- ☐ Circuit breaker may also provide overload protection if rating or setting complies w/ 430.32 ___ 430.55

TABLE 48 — MOTOR OVERLOAD DEVICE AS PERCENT OF NAMEPLATE FULL-LOAD CURRENT RATING[A] ◆ 430.32A1

Motor	Percent
Motor with marked service factor ≥1.15	125%
Motor with marked temperature rise ≤40°C	125%
All other motors	115%

A. Per 430.32C, if the table value is not sufficient to start the motor or carry the load, the value in this table is allowed to be increased by up to 15% for each motor type.

Motor Controllers **20 NEC**

- ☐ Controller enclosures req connection to EGC regardless of voltage _ 430.244
- ☐ Intent is to req suitable controllers for all motors _______ 430.81
- ☐ Branch circuit disconnect OK to control stationary motors ≤⅛hp __ 430.81A
- ☐ Plug & receptacle OK to control portable motors ≤⅓hp _______ 430.81B
- ☐ Controllers other than inverse time breakers & molded case switches req hp rating ≥ rating of motor _______ 430.83A1
- ☐ Branch circuit inverse time breaker OK as controller _______ 430.83A2
- ☐ Molded case switch OK as controller _______ 430.83A3
- ☐ Stationary motors ≤2hp controller can be general-use switch w/ ampere rating 2× motor FLC or AC-rated snap switch where motor FLC ≤80% of ampere rating of switch _______ 430.83A3
- ☐ Controller w/ slash rating only in solidly grounded circuits where voltage to ground ≤ lower of the 2 values of the slash rating _______ 240.83E
- ☐ Controller need not open all conductors to the motor _______ 240.84

Controller Disconnect

- ☐ Individual disconnecting means **F86C** reqd each controller EXC __ 430.102A
  - Single disconnecting means for group of coordinated controllers that drive several parts of a machine or apparatus _______ 430.102AX2
- ☐ Controller disconnect must be within sight of controller EXC _______ 430.102A
  - Not reqd in sight from valve actuator motor (VAM) assemblies containing the controller if such location introduces increased hazard, assembly marked w/ warning & disconnect lockable __ 430.102AX3

Control Circuits

- ☐ Conductors req overcurrent protection per **T49** EXC _______ 430.72
  - Conductors on secondary side of single-phase XFMR **F87** can be protected by OCPD on primary side if ≤ value determined by XFMR secondary-to-primary voltage ratio _______ 430.72BX2
- ☐ Control circuit XFMR reqs protection **F87** _______ 430.72C
- ☐ Arrange control circuits such that a ground fault in the control circuit remote from controller will not start the motor (install stop/start on ungrounded side) **F87** _______ 430.74
- ☐ Control circuit XFMR in controller enclosure must be on load side of disconnecting means for control circuit _______ 430.75B

TABLE 49 — MAX. RATING OF CONTROL CIRCUIT OCPD ◆ T430.72B

Control Circuit Conductor Size (AWG)	Separate Protection (not tapped from motor branch circuit)		Tapped from motor branch-circuit OCPD: Conductors within Enclosure		Tapped from motor branch-circuit OCPD: Conductors Extend Beyond Enclosure	
	Cu	AL[A]	Cu	AL[A]	Cu	AL[A]
18	7	n/a	25	n/a	7	n/a
16	10	n/a	40	n/a	10	n/a
14	T23	n/a	100	n/a	45	n/a
12	T23	T23	120	100	60	45
10	T23	T23	160	140	90	75
>10	T23	T23	note B	note B	note C	note C

A. Includes Cu-clad AL.
B. 400% of value in T310.17 for 60°C conductors.
C. 400% of value in T310.16 (**T23**) for 60°C conductors.

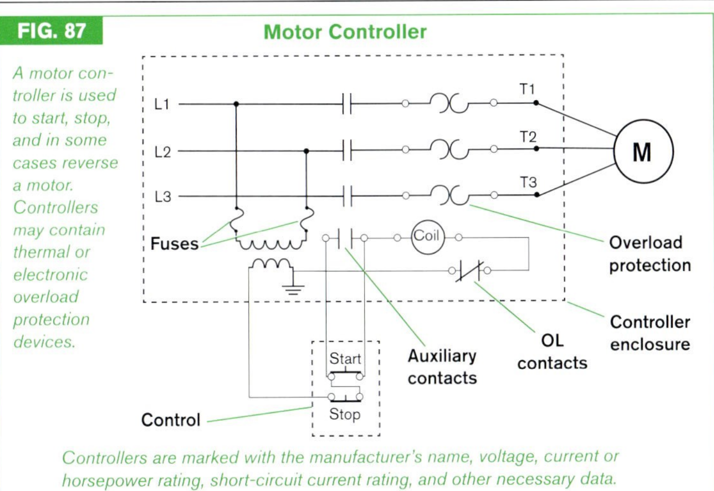

FIG. 87 Motor Controller

A motor controller is used to start, stop, and in some cases reverse a motor. Controllers may contain thermal or electronic overload protection devices.

Controllers are marked with the manufacturer's name, voltage, current or horsepower rating, short-circuit current rating, and other necessary data.

Disconnecting Means: General — 20 NEC

- ☐ Must open all ungrounded supply conductors ______ 430.103
- ☐ Must be designed so as to not close automatically ______ 430.103
- ☐ Permitted to be in same enclosure as controller ______ 430.103
- ☐ No pole to operate independently ______ 430.103
- ☐ Disconnecting means to plainly indicate "on" and "off" positions ______ 430.104
- ☐ One pole can open a grounded conductor if it cannot be opened w/o simultaneously disconnecting all conductors of the circuit ______ 430.105
- ☐ At least one disconnecting means readily accessible ______ 430.107
- ☐ Disconnect rating min. 115% of FLC ______ 430.110

Motor Disconnect

- ☐ Motor disconnect **F86E** within sight of motor & driven machinery 430.102B1
- ☐ Disconnect for controller can serve as motor disconnect when within sight of motor & driven machinery ______ 430.102B2
- ☐ Provide each motor w/ individual disconnecting means EXC ______ 430.112
  - Group of motors in a single machine or protected by 1 set of OCPDS or in single room & within sight of disconnect ______ 430.112X

Locked Rotor Current

- ☐ Locked rotor current marking on individual block on motor ______ 430.7B
- ☐ Locked rotor current indicating markings per **T50** ______ 430.7B

TABLE 50 — LOCKED ROTOR INDICATING CODE LETTERS ◆ T430.7B

Code Letter	kVA per hp	Code Letter	kVA per hp	Code Letter	kVA per hp
A	0–3.14	G	5.6–6.29	N	11.2–12.49
B	3.15–3.54	H	6.3–7.09	P	12.5–13.99
C	3.55–3.99	J	7.1–7.99	R	14.0–15.99
D	4.0–4.49	K	8.0–8.99	S	16.0–17.99
E	4.5–4.99	L	9.0–9.99	T	18.0–19.99
F	5.0–5.59	M	10.0–11.19	U	20.0–22.39

Example calculation:
Find locked rotor current for a 20hp 3-phase 460V motor with code letter G:
20 hp × 6.29 = 125.8 kVA
125.8 kVA ÷ (460 × √3) = 125.8 ÷ 460 × 1.732 ÷ 1,000 = 158A

Motor Control Centers (MCCs) — 20 NEC

- ☐ MCC reqs overcurrent protection ≤ rating of bus ______ 430.94
- ☐ MCC reqs EGC per **T16** or equivalent equipment grounding bus ______ 430.96
- ☐ Arrange high-leg systems A,B,C front-to-back, top-to-bottom, or left-to-right w/ B being phase w/ higher voltage to ground ______ 430.97B
- ☐ Available fault current & date of calculation must be made available ______ 430.99

Adjustable Speed Drives (VFDs)

- ☐ Conductor ampacity supplying the VFD ≥ 125% of input rating of power-conversion equipment ______ 430.122A
- ☐ Output conductor ampacity ≥125% of motor FLC ______ 430.122B[82]
- ☐ Separate overload protection not reqd if VFD marked as included 430.124A
- ☐ If bypass circuit allows motor operation at rated full-load speed, separate overload protection reqd ______ 430.124B
- ☐ Multiple motors from one VFD req separate overload protection ______ 430.124C
- ☐ When motor not rated to operate at nameplate FLA over speed range reqd by application, additional overtemperature protection reqd by thermal sensors, motor thermal protectors & relays ______ 430.126A

Motor Connections

NFPA 79, Electrical Standard for Industrial Machinery, includes information on recommended wiring practices, including connections to motor leads. The following are from section 13.5.9 of the 2021 edition.

- Motor-connection boxes shall enclose only connections to the motor & motor-mounted devices (e.g., brakes, temperature sensors).
- Connections in motor-terminal boxes shall be an identified method. Twist-on wire connectors shall not be used for this purpose.
- Connector insulation material cannot support combustion.
- Soldered or insulation piercing–type connectors (lugs) shall not be used.

82. This new section recognizes that the input rating of the VFD could be different than (higher than) the rating of the output conductors to the motor.

SEPARATELY DERIVED SYSTEMS: TRANSFORMERS

A separately derived system is a source of voltage, other than a service, that has no direct connection of circuit conductors to any other electrical source, other than by grounding & bonding connections. Interconnected power production sources, such as PV & wind, are not separately derived systems. Other than autotransformers, all transformers are separately derived systems in that there is no direct electrical connection between the primary and secondary conductors. A fault on the secondary conductors can overload the primary conductors even though there is no direct electrical connection. Single-phase 2-wire primary to 2-wire secondary, or 3-wire delta-delta transformers do this effectively, and their secondary conductors can be protected by the OCPD that protects the primary. Other transformers require a separate OCPD to protect the secondary conductors and the bus bars of panels supplied by the secondary conductors. The scope of the material here is limited to dry-type transformers ≤ 1kV.

Required Markings — 20 NEC

- ☐ Nameplate marking must include the following: ____ 450.11
  - Name of MFR
  - Rated kilovolt-amperes (kVA)
  - Frequency
  - Primary & secondary voltage
  - Impedance (for XFMRs > 25kVA)
  - Reqd clearances for transformers w/ ventilating openings
  - Temperature class of insulation for dry-type XFMRs

The markings above are reqd for XFMRs within the scope of Article 450, which does not include current XFMRs (CTs), XFMRs that are component parts of other apparatus or integral to equipment (such as X-ray), XFMRs for Class 2 & Class 3 circuits in Article 725, XFMRs for signs, neon & fluorescent lighting, or XFMRs for power-limited fire alarm components.

- ☐ Install marking to prohibit storage on top of XFMRs that are readily accessible & have horizontal top surfaces **F90** ____ 450.9[83]

Also see required markings of disconnecting means in right column.

83. New req prohibiting storage is consistent w/ existing MFR recommendations.

Locations — 20 NEC

- ☐ XFMRs to be readily accessible to qualified personnel EXC ____ 450.13
  - Dry-type XFMRs ≤1kV OK in the open on walls or columns ____ 450.13A
  - Dry-type XFMRs ≤1kV & ≤ 50kVA w/ sufficient ventilation for cooling OK in hollow spaces of structure (e.g., above suspended ceiling) if not permanently closed in by structure ____ 450.13B
- ☐ Room or area ventilation must be sufficient to dissipate XFMR heat w/o ambient temp rise exceeding XFMR rating ____ 450.9
- ☐ Install so ventilation openings not blocked—clearances AMI ____ 450.9
- ☐ Indoor XFMRs ≤112½ kVA req 12-in. clearance to combustible material unless completely enclosed except ventilation openings ____ 450.21A
- ☐ Indoor XFMRs >112½ kVA req room w/ min. 1-hr. fire rating unless completely enclosed except ventilation openings & Class 155 or higher insulation (typical of most XFMRs) ____ 450.21B
- ☐ Outdoor XFMRs req weatherproof enclosure **T17** ____ 450.22

Disconnecting Means

- ☐ Specific circuit source marked on XFMR disconnecting means ____ 110.22
- ☐ Disconnect within sight or in remote location EXC ____ 450.14
  - Not reqd for Class 2 or Class 3 transformers ____ 450.14
- ☐ When disconnecting means in remote location, disconnecting means lockable & location durably marked on XFMR ____ 450.14
- ☐ Transformers OK to be operated in parallel if switched as a unit ____ 450.7

Overcurrent Protection of Transformer (under 1kV)

- ☐ Primary-only protection allowed only for single-phase XFMR w/ 2-wire secondary or 3-phase delta-delta XFMR **T51** ____ 240.21C1
- ☐ Primary-only protection max. 125% of XFMR rating **T51** ____ T450.3B
- ☐ Primary & secondary protection: primary max. 250% of XFMR rating, secondary max. 125% of XFMR rating ____ T450.3B

In practical terms, protecting the conductors as required in other sections of the code will also protect the transformer.

TABLE 51 TRANSFORMER FULL LOAD CURRENTS

Single-Phase				3-Phase				
kVA	Amps			kVA	Amps			
	120V	240V	480V		208V	240V	480V	600V
3	25	12.5	6.1	15	41.6	36	18	14.4
5	41	21	10.4	30	83.0	72	36	28.8
7.5	62	31	15.6	45	125	108	54	43
10	83	42	21	75	208	180	90	72
15	124	62	31	112.5	312	270	135	108
25	208	104	52	150	415	360	180	144
37.5	312	156	78	200	554	480	240	192
50	416	208	104	225	625	540	270	216
75	624	312	156	300	830	720	360	288
100	830	415	207	400	1110	960	480	384
167	1390	695	348	500	1380	1200	600	480
200	1660	833	416	750	2080	1800	900	720

FIG. 88 Transformer Single-Line

100A
1¼-in.
EMT
T35
75KVA
480-208/120V
3Ø 4W
2½-in.
EMT
T35
225A
Panel H1
3#2 Cu,
#8G
T16,23
#2G
T52
4#4/0 Cu,
#2G
T23,52
Panel L1

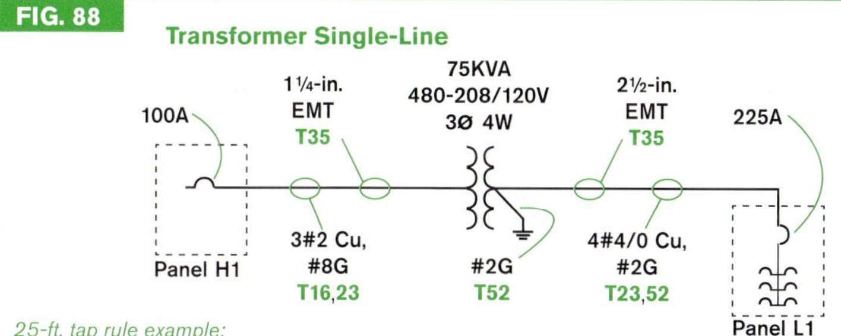

25-ft. tap rule example:

1. Ampacity ≥1/3 OCPD protecting primary × primary/secondary voltage ratio:
✓1/3 × 100A × 480/208 = 77A, 4/0 Cu conductor ampacity 230A
2. Conductors terminate in single OCPD ≤ than conductor ampacity
✓ 225A breaker ≤ 230A
3. Conductors enclosed in raceway
✓ 2½-in. EMT

Overcurrent Protection of Secondary Conductors — 20 NEC

☐ Secondary conductors ≤10 ft. OK if ______ 240.21C2
1. Ampacity ≥ supplied loads & rating(s) of OCPDs at termination
2. Conductors do not extend beyond equipment they supply
3. Conductors are enclosed in a raceway
4. Ampacity ≥10% primary OCPD × primary/secondary voltage ratio

☐ Secondary conductors ≤25 ft. OK if ______ 240.21C6
1. Ampacity ≥⅓ primary OCPD × primary/secondary voltage ratio
2. Conductors terminate in single OCPD ≤ than conductor ampacity
3. Conductors are enclosed in a raceway or other approved means

☐ Secondary conductors ≤25 ft. OK in industrial installations same as 25-ft. rule above except that secondary OCPDs must be grouped & only qualified persons service the systems ______ 240.21C3

☐ Outside secondary conductors OK w/ no length limitation if ______ 240.21C4
1. Conductors are protected from physical damage
2. Conductors terminate in single OCPD ≤ conductor ampacity
3. OCPD is integral or adjacent to disconnecting means
4. OCPD is either outside or inside nearest point of entrance of conductors

☐ Protection by primary OCPD only OK for single-phase XFMR w/ 2-wire secondary or 3-phase delta-delta XFMR OK if secondary conductor ampacity > secondary:primary voltage ratio × primary OCPD ______ 240.21C1

☐ "Rounding up" to next highest OCPD not allowed for OCPD that protects secondary conductors ______ 240.21C

FIG. 89 System Configurations

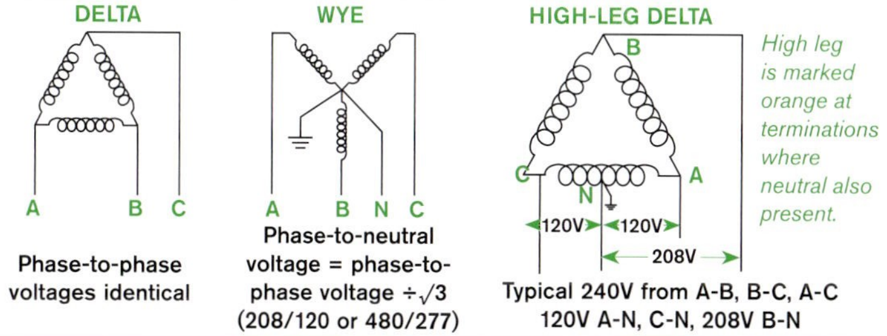

DELTA
A
B
C
Phase-to-phase
voltages identical
WYE
A
B
N
C
Phase-to-neutral
voltage = phase-to-
phase voltage ÷√3
(208/120 or 480/277)
HIGH-LEG DELTA
B
C
N
A
120V
120V
208V
High leg
is marked
orange at
terminations
where
neutral also
present.
Typical 240V from A-B, B-C, A-C
120V A-N, C-N, 208V B-N

Grounding & Bonding — 20 NEC

- ☐ Provide terminal bar for grounding & bonding **F90** EXC ________ 450.10A
- ☐ Terminal bar may not block ventilation openings **F90** ________ 450.10A
- ☐ Size primary conductor EGCs per **T16** ________ 250.122
- ☐ Size grounded conductor of secondary & SBJ per **T52** ________ 250.28D1
- ☐ Size SSBJ per **T52** ________ 250.30A2
- ☐ Size GEC per **T52** ________ 250.30A5
- ☐ GEC to connect to same GES as building ________ 250.30A4
- ☐ Multiple separately derived systems may use common GEC _____ 250.30A6
- ☐ Common GEC can be 3/0 Cu or 250kcmil AL wire, metal water pipe ≤ 5 ft. of entry into building, or bonded metal structural building frame___ 250.30A6
- ☐ Bond SDS to metal piping systems & building steel _ 250.30A8 & 250.104D

TABLE 52 — MINIMUM GROUNDED CONDUCTOR, MAIN BONDING JUMPER, SYSTEM BONDING JUMPER & SUPPLY-SIDE BONDING JUMPER SIZES ◆ T250.102C1

Largest Ungrounded Conductor or Equal Area for Parallel Conductors (AWG/kcmil)		Grounded Conductor, MBJ, SBJ, or SSBJ (AWG)	
Cu	AL	Cu	AL
≤ 2	≤ 1/0	8	6
1 or 1/0	2/0 or 3/0	6	4
2/0 or 3/0	4/0 or 250kcmil	4	2
4/0–350kcmil	> 250–500kcmil	2	1/0
> 350–600kcmil	> 500–900kcmil	1/0	3/0
> 600–1100kcmil	> 900–1750kcmil	2/0	4/0
> 1100kcmil	> 1750kcmil	Notes C & D	

A. The scope includes main bonding jumpers, system bonding jumpers & supply-side bonding jumpers.
B. Services w/ multiple service disconnect enclosures or separately derived systems w/ multiple sets of secondary conductors may size the bonding jumper based on areas of conductors in each set.
C. Min. 12½% of area of largest supply conductors or equivalent area for parallel conductors; need not be larger than largest ungrounded conductor or set of ungrounded conductors.
D. If ungrounded conductors & bonding jumper of different materials, base bonding jumper size on size of equivalent ungrounded conductors of same material as bonding jumper.

FIG. 90 — Delta-Wye Transformer

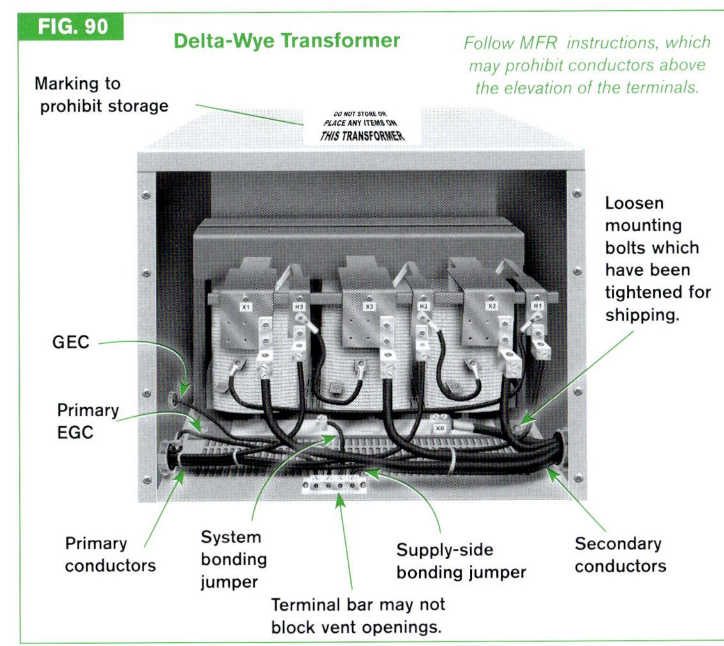

Autotransformers — 20 NEC

- ☐ Electrically continuous grounded (neutral) conductor reqd to connect to supply & derived circuits EXC ________ 210.9 & 215.11
  - OK w/o grounded (neutral) conductor for 208V:240V or 240V:208V (open delta configurations) ________ 210.9X1 & 215.11X1
- ☐ Each ungrounded input conductor reqs OCPD ________ 450.4A
- ☐ OCPD ≤ 125% of max. rated full-load current of autotransformer EXC 450.4A
  - If 125% & ≥ 9A & between standard sizes, next higher size allowed 450.4A
- ☐ OCPD not to be in series w/ between shunt-winding terminals _____ 450.4A

Transformer Energy Requirements T53

Since 2007, the US Department of Energy (DOE) has mandated the efficiency levels for distribution transformers manufactured in the US. The first DOE standard was NEMA-TP1. In 2010 NEMA introduced the CSL-3 standard that called for higher efficiencies. It was not federally adopted though it was in effect in some states. The 2016 DOE standards replaced these older standards. Individual state codes have their own rules regarding use of transformers that were in service or in the supply chain prior to 2016.

TABLE 53 TRANSFORMER EFFICIENCY STANDARDS[A]

Single-Phase		3-Phase		
kVA	TP1 & DOE	kVA	2007–2016 TP1	DOE-2016
15	97.7	15	97.00	97.89
25	98.0	30	97.50	98.23
37.5	98.2	45	97.70	98.40
50	98.3	75	98.00	98.60
75	98.5	112.5	98.20	98.74
100	98.6	150	98.30	98.83
167	98.7	225	98.50	98.94
250	98.8	300	98.60	99.02
333	98.9	500	98.70	99.14
		750	98.80	99.23
		1000	98.90	99.28

A. Based on 35% nameplate rated load.

GENERATORS

The generator and utility cannot be connected simultaneously, or there could be dangerous backfeed into the utility grid. Transfer switches prevent this potentially hazardous condition. Transfer switches can be automatic or as simple as a toggle that chooses between two breakers in an electrical panel. When the transfer switch does not switch the neutral, the generator is not a *separately derived system.* A separately derived system is one having no direct electrical connection (including a neutral) to supply conductors originating in another system.

Generators — 20 NEC

- ☐ Must be suitable for environment, rainproof if outdoors ______ 445.10
- ☐ Generators not OK enclosed indoors ______ 445.10
- ☐ Conductor ampacity min. 115% of nameplate current rating ______ 445.13
- ☐ Live or moving parts guarded against accidental contact ______ 445.14
- ☐ Disconnecting means reqd; must be lockable in open position ______ 445.18
- ☐ 1&2FD req emergency shutdown outside in readily accessible location except cord-and-plug-connected generators ______ 445.18D
- ☐ Portable generators ≤15kW req GFCI for 125V receptacles EXC ___ 445.20
  - • Generators MFR prior to 1/1/2015 GFCI portable cordsets OK 445.20BX
- ☐ Use building GES for permanently installed generators ______ 250.30A4
- ☐ Remove bonding jumper if transfer switch not switching neutral F91 _250.24A5
- ☐ MFR marking reqd indicating if neutral bonded to frame F91 ______ 445.11

FIG. 91

Transfer Switches F91 — 20 NEC

- ☐ Sign reqd at service indicating generator location ______ 702.7A
- ☐ Must prevent simultaneous connection of generator & utility service 702.5A&D
- ☐ When power inlet used for portable generator, warning sign reqd to indicate type of derived system based on transfer switch type ______ 702.7C

If the generator neutral is bonded, the sign must state "Warning: For connection of a separately derived (bonded neutral) system only." If the neutral is not bonded, it must state "Warning: For connection of a nonseparately derived (floating neutral) system only."

ENERGY STORAGE SYSTEMS (ESS)

Energy storage systems are available as assembled components incorporating batteries, charge controllers, and inverters as a single unit to provide power either to the premises or the electrical distribution system (grid). Where installed with protection against backfeed to the grid during an outage, these systems can also provide backup power to homes & other facilities. Storage technologies are now available that do not require ventilation. Fire codes regulate these systems; see section 1207 of the *2021 International Fire Code*, and NFPA 855, the *Standard for the Installation of Stationary Energy Storage Systems*. For further information, see *Energy Storage Systems,* available from iccsafe.org.

General — 20 NEC

- ☐ Installation & maintenance only by qualified personnel ______ 706.3[84]
- ☐ Nameplate to include MFR, frequency, phases, kW or kVA, available fault current, max. output & input current & voltage & interactive capability 706.4[85]
- ☐ ESS shall be listed ______ 706.5
- ☐ Multiple ESS allowed within a building or structure ______ 706.6
- ☐ Maintenance AMI, written records reqd ______ 706.7
- ☐ Disconnecting means lockable in open position, either within sight or as close as practical w/ location marked on ESS ______ 706.15A
- ☐ 1&2FD disconnect either on building exterior or remote on exterior 706.15A[86]
- ☐ Ventilation AMI ______ 706.20A

Circuits

- ☐ Circuit current is rated current on nameplate or system listing ______ 706.30A1
- ☐ Conductor ampacity ≥ nameplate rating or ESS OCPD ______ 706.30B
- ☐ OCPD ≥125% of max. calculated currents ______ 706.31B
- ☐ Systems w/ utility interactive inverters req independent means of controlling charging if primary charge controller fails ______ 706.33B3

Fire Code Requirements — 21 IFC

- ☐ Fire permit reqd for systems ≥20kWh w/ lithium ion batteries ______ 1207.1.2[87]
- ☐ ESS not allowed in sleeping units or habitable spaces ______ 1207.7.3[87]

84. Requires training and familiarity with the hazards involved.
85. Listed systems may contain integral inverters, charge controllers & communications.
86. Consistent with requirement for emergency service disconnect for service.
87. This chapter renumbered and extensively revised in 2021 edition. Check with local fire jurisdiction regarding application and enforcement.

ELECTRIC VEHICLE POWER TRANSFER SYSTEM

When adding EVSE to an existing service, first perform a load calculation per **T11** to determine if there is necessary capacity. If the electrical service does not have sufficient capacity, a demand charge controller can pause charging during times when such charging would exceed the service capacity. Note that the title of this section has changed in the NEC. It is no longer limited to charging of the vehicle; it now considers the possibility of the vehicle's battery acting as an energy storage system and possible supply source to the building.

Electric Vehicle Power Transfer System — 20 NEC

- ☐ EVSE & wireless power transfer equipment must be listed ______ 625.5
- ☐ EV outlet reqs individual branch circuit w/ no other outlets ______ 625.40
- ☐ Considered continuous—size to 125% of max. load of equipment ______ 625.41&2
- ☐ Receptacles installed for EV charging req GFCI protection ______ 625.54[88]
- ☐ Wet-location receptacle must provide weatherproof protection ______ 625.56[89]
- ☐ Indoor coupler min. 18 in. above floor, outdoor min. 24 in. above grade ______ 625.50
- ☐ Equipment rated >60A or >150V to ground reqs readily accessible disconnecting means lockable in open position ______ 625.43
- ☐ Portable equipment connects to premises' wiring receptacle ______ 625.44A
- ☐ Fastened-in-place equipment (mounted but removable w/out a tool) may also connect to premises' wiring receptacle ______ 625.44B
- ☐ Fixed equipment reqs permanent wiring ______ 625.44C
- ☐ Ventilation not reqd if listed for no ventilation ______ 625.51A
- ☐ EV as standby power source reqs L&L as utility interactive connection for the specific vehicle installed ______ 625.48
- ☐ EV standby power source operates as standby power per 702 (transfer switches) or per 705 (interconnected power production source) ______ 625.48
- ☐ AC receptacles in EV & intended to allow off-board utilization equipment must be listed, have overcurrent protection & GFCI protection ______ 625.60[90]

88. Receptacles supplying EV charging systems req GFCI protection. They are typically located in areas where such protection was already required by other code sections. If a manufacturer supplies GFCI protection in their charging unit, a hard-wired connection without a receptacle would not require a second GFCI.
89. Similar to **F68** but for higher-amperage receptacles; can be box hood or other design.
90. Scope of NEC expanded in 90.2A6 to include vehicle power transfer systems.

PHOTOVOLTAIC (PV) SYSTEMS

PV systems are regulated by the building, electrical, energy, and fire codes. Fire departments may be the AHJ for rooftop access and pathways and rapid shutdown. Interactive PV systems also require approval from the utility provider. New technologies for PV systems have greatly simplified their installation. They are often installed with battery backup systems that can provide house power during a utility outage, and interact with the utility as part of a "smart grid" system.

Definitions:

AC module. A complete, environmentally protected unit consisting of solar cells, inverter & other components to produce AC power (a.k.a. microinverters).

Array. A mechanically & electrically integrated grouping of modules with support structure, including any attached system components such as inverters or DC-to-DC converters & associated wiring.

Bipolar circuit. A DC circuit that is comprised of 2 monopole circuits, each having an opposite polarity connected to a common reference point.

DC combiner. An enclosure that includes devices used to connect 2 or more PV system DC circuits in parallel.

DC-to-DC converter output circuit. The DC circuit conductors connected to the output of a DC combiner for DC-to-DC converter source circuit(s).

DC-to-DC converter source circuit. Circuit between the DC-to-DC converters & from DC-to-DC converters to the common DC connection point(s).

Electronic power converter. A device that uses power electronics to convert one form of electrical power into another form of electrical power. Examples include inverters, DC-to-DC converters & electronic charge controllers.

Grounded, functionally. A system that has an electrical ground reference for operational purposes that is not solidly grounded.[91]

Generating capacity. The sum of parallel-connected inverter max. continuous output power at 40°C expressed in kW.

Interactive system. A solar PV system that operates in parallel to the utility.

Inverter. In PV systems, equipment that converts DC current & voltage to an AC voltage & waveform. Inverters in interactive systems must be listed to UL 1741 to ensure against backfeed of the utility. (Inverters are also used to convert AC to DC for charging batteries, typically for emergency lighting. Those inverters are not listed to UL 1741).

Inverter input circuit. Conductors connected to the DC input of an inverter.

Inverter output circuit. Conductors connected to the AC output of an inverter.

Microgrid interconnection device (MID). A device that enables a microgrid system to separate from and reconnect to operate in parallel with a primary power source.

Microgrid system. A premises' wiring system that has generation, energy storage, and load(s), or any combination thereof, that includes the ability to disconnect from and parallel with the primary source.

Module. A complete environmentally protected unit consisting of solar cells & other components designed to produce DC power.

Monopole circuit. An electrical subset of a PV system that has 2 conductors in the output circuit, one positive (+) & one negative (-).

Monopole subarray. A PV subarray that has two conductors in the output circuit, one positive (+) & one negative (-). Two monopole PV subarrays are used to form a **bipolar PV array**, which has two outputs, each with opposite polarity to a common reference point or center tap.

Panel. A colloquial term used interchangeably with what is defined in the NEC as a module. The 2017 NEC definition of this term was "A collection of modules mechanically fastened together & designed to provide a field-installable unit."

PV output circuit. The DC circuit conductors from 2 or more connected PV source circuits to their point of termination.

PV source circuit. The DC circuit conductors between modules and from modules to DC combiners, electronic power converters, or a DC PV system disconnecting means.

PV system DC circuit. Any DC circuit conductor in PV source circuits, PV output circuits, DC-to-DC converter source circuits, and DC-to-DC converter output circuits.

Solar cell. The basic PV device that generates electricity when exposed to light.

Solidly grounded. Connected to ground without inserting any resistor or impedance device.

91. Systems previously referred to as "ungrounded" have an indirect reference to ground through the inverter. "Functionally grounded" is a more accurate term. The code now recognizes this term & (usually older) "solidly grounded" systems.

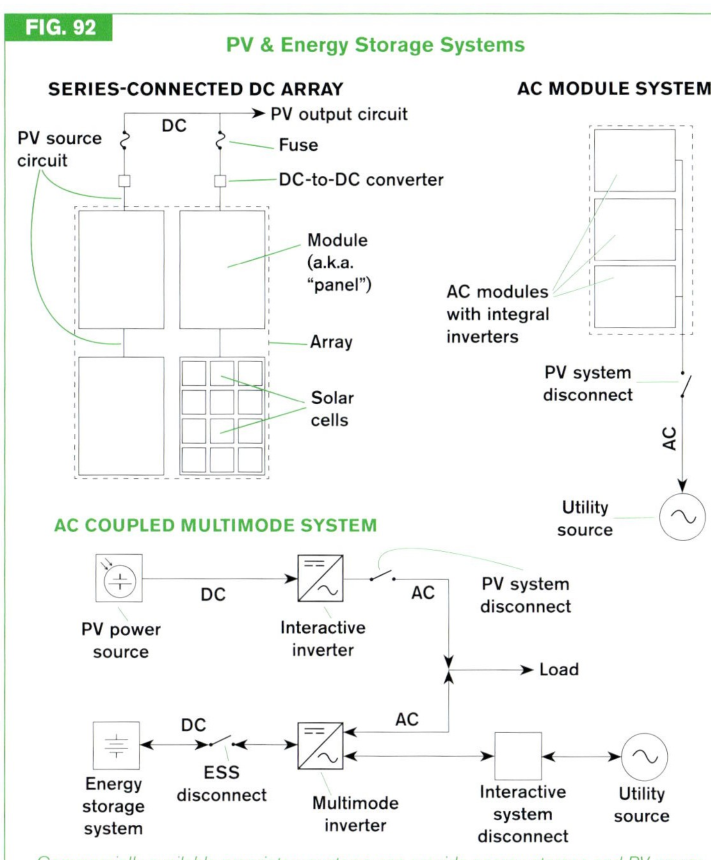

Commercially available proprietary systems can provide energy storage and PV power that can be used in "island mode" independent of the utility, providing power during a grid outage. These features can also be attained with AC module systems.

Roof-Mounted Arrays — 21 IRC

- ☐ Design system to sustain gravity, environmental & wind loads _______ 324.4.1
- ☐ Roof penetrations must be flashed & sealed **F93** _______ 324.4.3
- ☐ PV panel systems req fire rating same as roof _______ 324.4.2 & 902.4
- ☐ Panels & modules req L&L to UL 1703 or UL 61730-1&2 _______ 324.3.1

Roof Access & Pathways*

- ☐ Access, pathways & spacing reqd for firefighting access for smoke ventilation opportunities & escape & rescue EXC _______ 324.6*
  - Detached nonhabitable structures _______ 324.6X1
  - Where fire marshal determines no rooftop operations needed _______ 324.6X2
  - Roofs w/ <2:12 slope _______ 324.6X3
  - BIPV systems where cutting during firefighting operations has been determined to not expose firefighters to shock hazards _______ 324.6X4[92]
- ☐ Min. 2 pathways on separate roof planes from roof edge to ridge _______ 324.6.1
- ☐ Pathways min. 36 in. wide (18 in. each side of a ridge or valley) _______ 324.6.1
- ☐ Ridge setback 36 in. each side if PV array covers >33% roof area EXC 324.6.2
  - 18 in. each side OK up to 66% coverage if building sprinklered 324.6.2.1X2
- ☐ Minimal obstructions (conduits, vent pipes, etc.) in pathways _______ 324.6.1
- ☐ No panels or modules below escape & rescue openings _______ 324.6.3

Photovoltaic Shingles

- ☐ Deck solid or closely fitting _______ 905.16.1
- ☐ PV shingles only on roof slopes ≥2:12 _______ 905.16.2
- ☐ PV shingles L&L to UL 1703 or UL 61730-1&2 _______ 905.16.4
- ☐ Attach PV shingles AMI _______ 905.16.5

Building-Integrated Photovoltaic (BIPV) Roof Panels

- ☐ Solid or close-fit deck reqd unless designed for spaced sheathing _______ 905.17.1
- ☐ Min. 2:12 slope roof _______ 905.17.2
- ☐ PV shingles L&L to UL 1703 or UL 61730-1&2 _______ 905.17.5
- ☐ Install AMI _______ 905.17.6

Ground-Mounted Arrays

- ☐ Fire separation reqs per local jurisdiction _______ 324.7.1

* The items in IRC 324.6 are essentially repeated in fire codes.

92. New exception for local determination on hazards of cutting into BIPV.

General — 20 NEC

- ☐ Inverters, modules, panels, AC modules & AC module systems, DC-to-DC converters, DC combiners, RS equipment, DC controllers & charge controllers listed or field-evaluated for PV applications ___ 690.4B[93]
- ☐ PV panels & modules L&L per UL 1703, inverters to UL 1741 ______ 690.4B
- ☐ PV reqd to be installed only by qualified persons ________________ 690.4C
- ☐ If multiple systems installed remote from each other on single building or structure, provide directory showing each disconnect location ______ 690.4D
- ☐ PV system equipment & disconnecting means not OK in bathrooms __ 690.4E
- ☐ Output of AC module or AC module system considered as inverter output circuit; conductors & inverters considered as internal components **F92** 690.6

Interactive Inverters

- ☐ Inverters must cease exporting power in grid outage EXC _________ 705.40
  - OK as stand-alone system to loads disconnected from grid **F92** ___ 705.40
- ☐ Inverter max. currents are the rated output currents ______________ 705.28A
- ☐ Inverter currents considered continuous; size conductors to 125% of rated current or size w/ adjustment & correction factors _____ 705.28B1&2
- ☐ If neutral present, sizing same as above EXC ________________ 705.28C1
  - Neutral only for instrumentation reference sized per **F52** _______ 705.28C2
- ☐ Conductor OCPDs sized to 125% max. currents EXC ___________ 705.30B
  - Inverter output conductors connected to larger feeder can be sized using tap rules *(p. 267)* of OCPD protecting feeder **F992** ______ 705.28B3

Ground-Fault Protection

- ☐ DC circuits >30V or 8A req DC ground-fault protection EXC ______ 690.41B
  - Solidly grounded arrays w/ ≤2 PV source circuits & not on buildings (e.g., traffic sign power) __________________ 690.41BX
- ☐ Ground-fault protective device (GFPD) reqs listing for PV ______ 690.41B1
- ☐ GFPD must disconnect faulted circuits or cease inverter output & isolate faulted circuits from ground reference in functionally grounded system 690.41B2
- ☐ GFPD must provide indication at readily accessible location ________ 690.41B3
- ☐ For systems w/ GFPD, all current-carrying conductor-to-ground connections must be made by the GFPD ___________________________ 690.42

93. RS, AC module systems & DC controllers now also must be listed or field-evaluated.

System-disconnecting Means — 20 NEC

- ☐ Means reqd to disconnect PV system from all other wiring systems __ 690.13
- ☐ Disconnecting means reqd to be readily accessible _____________ 690.13A
- ☐ Where disconnecting means >30V readily accessible to unqualified persons, enclosure to be locked or req a tool to open __________ 690.13A[94]
- ☐ Each disconnecting means reqd to plainly indicate open (off) or closed (on) & be permanently marked "PV SYSTEM DISCONNECT" **F98** _690.13B
- ☐ If disconnect line & load terminals potentially energized when open, permanent durable warning sign reqd w/ wording in **F98** __________ 690.13B
- ☐ Each PV system max. 6 disconnects grouped or in one enclosure __ 690.13C
- ☐ Single disconnect permitted for combined inverter AC outputs ____ 690.13C
- ☐ System disconnect reqs AIC rating ≥ available fault current ______ 690.13D
- ☐ Disconnecting means must simultaneously disconnect all PV conductors that are not solidly grounded from all other wiring systems _________ 690.13E
- ☐ Disconnecting means must be capable of being locked open ______ 690.13E

Equipment-disconnecting Means

- ☐ Equipment-disconnecting means reqs AIC rating ______________ 690.15C
- ☐ Must disconnect all conductors that are not solidly grounded _____ 690.15C
- ☐ Disconnects not within sight or within 10 ft. of equipment req locking means w/ locking hasp that remains in place when not in use **F78** _ 690.15C
- ☐ Equipment-disconnecting means reqd for DC circuits ≥30A _____ 690.15D1
- ☐ Isolating device permitted for DC circuits <30A _____________ 690.15D2

While a PV system-disconnecting means isolates the entire system from other wiring systems, an isolating device is for the purpose of safe replacement or service of specific components. Isolating devices should not be opened under load.

Isolating Devices (Non-Load-Break Disconnects)

- ☐ Isolating devices reqd in circuits connected to equipment either within equipment or within sight & ≤10 ft. from equipment _________ 690.15A
- ☐ Isolating devices can be mating connector, finger-safe fuse holder, isolating device requiring tool to open, or other listed device ______ 690.15B
- ☐ Marking reqd "Do Not Disconnect Under Load" _______________ 690.15B
- ☐ Isolating devices may be L&L connectors, finger-safe fuse holders, or isolating switches __________________ 690.15 & 690.33

94. Prevents unqualified persons from accessing live parts.

Circuit Voltages — 20 NEC

- ☐ Max. DC voltage = highest voltage between circuit conductors or between any conductor & ground ____ 690.7
- ☐ Max. allowable DC voltage on 1-& 2-family dwellings 600V, on other building types 1,000V ____ 690.7
- ☐ 690 parts II & III n/a to listed PV equipment ≤1,500V not on buildings 690.7
- ☐ Max. voltage = sum of rated open-circuit voltage of series connected modules times correction factors **T54** for lowest cold temp ____ 690.7A
- ☐ Max. voltage of DC-to-DC converter circuits = rating per instructions in L&L of converters or, if not stated in instructions, the sum of rated outputs of converters in series ____ 690.7B2
- ☐ Max. voltage of monopole subarray in bipolar system = highest voltage between subarray conductors to functionally grounded reference ____ 690.7C
- ☐ Systems ≥ 100kW OK to use stamped documented design from registered professional electrical engineer ____ 690.7A3

TABLE 54 — VOLTAGE CORRECTION FACTORS FOR CRYSTALLINE & MULTICRYSTALLINE SILICON MODULES ◆ T690.7A

Ambient Temp °C	Ambient Temp °F	Correction Factor	Ambient Temp °C	Ambient Temp °F	Correction Factor
24 to 20	76 to 78	1.02	-11 to -15	13 to 5	1.16
19 to 15	67 to 59	1.04	-16 to -20	4 to -4	1.18
14 to 10	58 to 50	1.06	-21 to -25	-5 to -13	1.20
9 to 5	49 to 41	1.08	-26 to -30	-14 to -22	1.21
4 to 0	40 to 32	1.10	-31 to -35	-23 to -31	1.23
-1 to -5	31 to 23	1.12	-36 to -40	-32 to -40	1.25
-6 to -10	22 to 14	1.14			

PV Circuit Ratings — 20 NEC

- ☐ PV source circuit currents = 125% × sum of parallel module SCCs 690.8A1a1
- ☐ Systems ≥ 100kW OK to use documented stamped design from registered professional electrical engineer ____ 690.8A1a2
- ☐ PV output circuit currents = sum of parallel-source circuit currents ____ 690.8A1b
- ☐ DC-to-DC converter source circuit current = converter rating ____ 690.8A1c
- ☐ DC-to-DC converter output circuit current = sum of parallel-connected DC-to-DC source circuit currents ____ 690.8A1d
- ☐ Inverter output circuit currents = inverter continuous output rating ____ 690.8A1e
- ☐ Where circuit conductors protected at ≤ their ampacity, current = rated input current of electronic power converter ____ 690.8A2

PV Circuit Size & Overcurrent Protection

- ☐ Size PV system circuits for the greater of: (1) 125% of max. current before application of adjustment & correction factors or (2) the max. currents w/ adjustment & correction factors ____ 690.8B
- ☐ Common return conductor of power source w/ multiple output voltages reqs ampacity ≥ sum of OCPD ratings of individual output circuits ____ 690.8C
- ☐ DC circuits, inverter output circuit & equipment req OCPD EXC ____ 690.9A
  - Conductor ampacity ≥ max. current & currents from all sources ≤ max. OCPD rating of PV module or electronic power converter ____ 690.9A1
- ☐ Circuits rated for & connected to limited power supply & also connected to sources having available max. current > conductor ampacity req protection from overcurrent at connection to higher current source ____ 690.9A2
- ☐ Circuits ≤10 ft. in buildings can be protected on one end if in raceway or metal-clad cable ____ 690.9A3
- ☐ DC OCPDs req listing for use in PV systems ____ 690.9B
- ☐ Electronic devices listed to prevent backfeed permitted to prevent overcurrent on the PV array side of the device ____ 690.9B
- ☐ Single device can protect PV source & output circuits ____ 690.9C
- ☐ PV AFCI protection reqd for systems ≥ 80V DC EXC ____ 690.11
  - Systems not on buildings & where PV & DC-to-DC output circuits are installed in metal raceways or MC cable or underground ____ 690.11X

PV Wiring — 20 NEC

- ☐ PV source & output conductors >30V req guarding or raceway or MC cable if in readily accessible location ______ 690.31A
- ☐ Ampacity permitted to be determined by **T56** ______ 690.31A[95]
- ☐ Ampacity correction reqd if ambient > 86°F **T55** ______ 690.31A
- ☐ PV DC circuits not in same raceway or cable as non-PV EXC ______ 690.31B
  - Where separated by barrier ______ 690.31
  - Multiconductor cable identified for the application ______ 690.31BX
- ☐ Flexible fine-stranded cables terminated only w/ devices identified for the specific conductor type and class **F27** ______ 690.31C5
- ☐ Single-conductor cables in sizes #16 & #18 permitted for module interconnection where meeting ampacity of **T45** ______ 690.31C6
- ☐ Boxes must be accessible either directly or by displacement of module by removable fasteners & connected by flexible wiring system ______ 690.34

TABLE 55 — AMPACITY CORRECTIONS FOR AMBIENT TEMPERATURES ABOVE 86°F ◆ T690.31A(A)

Ambient Temperature		Temperature Rating of Conductor[A]			
°C	°F	60°C	75°C	90°C	105°C
30	86	1.00	1.00	1.00	1.00
31–35	87–95	0.91	0.94	0.96	0.97
36–40	96–104	0.82	0.88	0.91	0.93
41–45	105–113	0.71	0.82	0.87	0.89
46–50	114–122	0.58	0.75	0.82	0.86
51–55	123–131	0.41	0.67	0.76	0.82
56–60	132–140	—	0.58	0.71	0.77
61–70	141–158	—	0.33	0.58	0.68
71–80	159–176	—	—	0.41	0.58

A. PV wire is typically rated 90°C wet 105°C dry, USE-2 is rated 90°C.

95. **T56** is new.

TABLE 56 — AMPACITIES[A] OF CONDUCTORS 105°C – 125°C ◆ T690.31A(b)

Wire Size (AWG)	105°C PVC, CPE, XLPE	125°C XLPE, EPDM
18	15	16
16	19	20
14	29	31
12	36	39
10	46	50
8	64	69
6	81	87
4	109	118
3	129	139
2	143	154
1	168	181
1/0	193	208
2/0	229	247
3/0	263	284
4/0	301	325

A. For ≤3 conductors in raceway or cable. See ***p. 265*** for temperature limitations at terminations.

Mating Connectors — 20 NEC

- ☐ Must be polarized & noninterchangeable w/ other receptacles ______ 690.33A
- ☐ Must be latching & locking type ______ 690.33C
- ☐ If not rated for interrupting current w/o hazard to operator, must req a tool to open & be marked "Do Not Disconnect Under Load" ______ 690.33D

TABLE 57 — MINIMUM PV WIRE STRANDS ◆ T690.31C4

PV Wire AWG:	18	16 to 10	8 to 4	2	≥1
Minimum Strands:	17	19	49	130	259

Protection & Support — 20 NEC

- ☐ Secure & support exposed cables at max. 2-ft. intervals ______ 690.31C1[96]
- ☐ Install listed multiconductor jacketed cables AMI ______ 690.31C3
- ☐ Where not a listed assembly or in raceways, all the following: ___ 690.31C3[97]
  - Cables marked sunlight-resistant where exposed outdoors
  - Protected or guarded where subject to physical damage
  - Closely follow surfaces of support structures
  - Secure at max. 6-ft. intervals
  - Secure within 24 in. of mating connectors or entering enclosures

DC Circuits Inside Buildings

- ☐ DC circuits >30V on or inside buildings req MC cable, metal, raceways, or other metal enclosures **F94** ______ 690.31D*
- ☐ FMC <¾ in. & MC <1 in. across ceilings req guard strips & must closely follow building surface except within 6 ft. of equipment connection 690.31D1
- ☐ USE-2 inside building reqs dual rating, e.g., XHHW-2 or RHW-2 338.12B1

Labeling of DC Conductors

- ☐ Exposed raceways and box covers req labeling per **F93,94** ______ 690.31B2
- ☐ Labels must be suitable for environment where they are installed _ 690.31B2
- ☐ Labels reflective, min. ⅜-in. letters all caps white on red ______ 690.31B2
- ☐ Max. 10-ft. intervals & on every section separated by enclosures, walls, partitions, ceilings, or floors ______ 690.31B2

FIG. 93

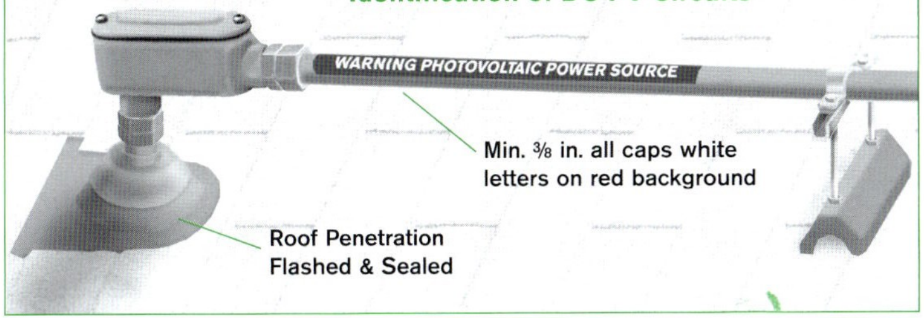

Identification of DC PV Circuits

96. Previous maximum support interval was same as for NM or SE (4½ ft.).
97. Previously only addressed listed assemblies and required support at max. 6 ft intervals.

Array Grounding — 20 NEC

- ☐ Non-current-carrying metal parts of module frames, electrical equipment & conductor enclosures req connection to EGC ______ 690.43
- ☐ Module frame bonding by mounting devices L&L & identified for PV _690.43A
- ☐ Metal support racks req bonding jumpers between sections or shall be identified for equipment bonding & connected to EGC __690.43B
- ☐ EGC in same raceway, cable, or otherwise run w/ PV system conductors where those conductors leave PV array ______ 690.43C
- ☐ Bonding per ***p. 250*** for solidly grounded systems >250 to ground _ 690.43D
- ☐ Size EGCs per **T16** EXC ______ 690.45
  - Upsizing EGC not reqd when circuit conductors upsized for VD ___ 690.45

Connection to Grounding Electrode System

- ☐ PV array EGCs must connect to building GES ______ 690.47A
- ☐ For systems that are not solidly grounded, EGC connection to associated equipment (e.g., inverter) sufficient as connection to GES ______ 690.47A1
- ☐ EGC for solidly grounded systems sized per 250.166: ______ 690.47A2
  - If neutral present, not smaller than neutral ______ 250.166A
  - If neutral not present, not smaller than largest conductor ______ 250.166A
  - Min. #8Cu or #6AL, see ***p. 248*** for sizes at rods, Ufer & ring ____ 250.166
- ☐ Auxiliary GES permitted for roof- & ground-mounted arrays ______ 690.47B
- ☐ Ground-mounted array structure meeting 250.52 (***p. 248***) OK as GES _ 690.47B

FIG. 94

Routing DC PV Circuits

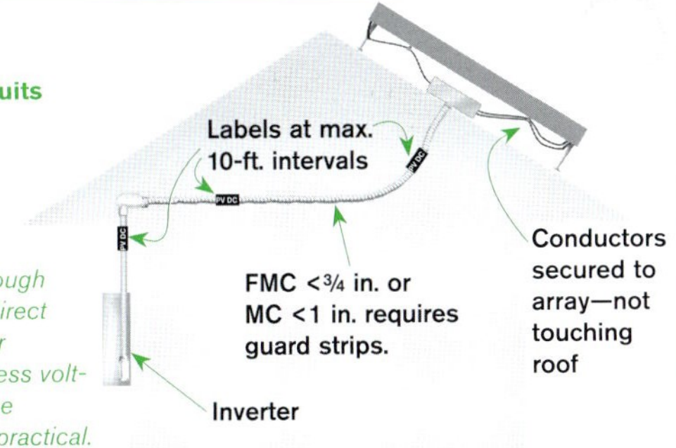

Routing the conductors through the building rather than in direct sunlight can provide a lower temperature and therefore less voltage drop. Similarly, place the inverter in a shaded area if practical.

Rapid Shutdown (RS): General **20 NEC**

- ☐ PV systems on buildings req rapid shutdown function ______ 690.12
- ☐ "Array boundary" = 1 ft. from array in all directions ______ 690.12B
- ☐ "Controlled conductors" = PV system DC circuits & inverter output circuits originating from inverters within the array boundary ______ 690.12A[98]
- ☐ Outside the array boundary, RS to limit voltage between any 2 conductors or conductor to ground to 30V within 30 seconds ___ 690.12B1
- ☐ Inside the array boundary, RS to limit voltage between any 2 conductors or conductor to ground to 80V within 30 seconds ___ 690.12B2
- ☐ In lieu of above, a listed PV hazard-control system installed AMI _ 690.12B2
- ☐ Equipment that performs the actual shutdown (other than initiation devices) must be listed for the purpose ______ 690.12D

Rapid Shutdown (RS): Initiation Device

- ☐ Initiation device must clearly indicate "off" position ______ 690.12C
- ☐ In 1&2FD, initiation device readily accessible outdoors ______ 690.12C
- ☐ For a single PV system, initiation device one of the following: ______ 690.12C
  - Service-disconnecting means
  - PV system-disconnecting means
  - Readily accessible switch w/clearly marked "ON" & "OFF" position
- ☐ For a multiple PV systems on a single service, initiation device(s) must consist of ≤6 grouped switches or sets of breakers ______ 690.12C

Rapid Shutdown (RS): Signage & Labeling

- ☐ Permanent label **F95,97** at service-equipment location must indicate location of RS initiation devices ______ 690.56C[99]
- ☐ RS initiation device reqs label **F96** within 3 ft. of switch stating RAPID SHUTDOWN SWITCH FOR SOLAR PV SYSTEM ______ 690.56C2
- ☐ Buildings w/ ≥1 RS type or w/ no RS req detailed plan-view diagram of roof showing each different PV system w/ a dotted line around areas that remain energized after RS is initiated **F97** ______ 690.56C2

98. Inverters within array boundary added to definition.
99. 2017 NEC had delayed implementation of requirement for rapid shutdown inside the array boundary.

FIG. 95 Required Label at Electrical Service

SOLAR PV SYSTEM EQUIPPED WITH RAPID SHUTDOWN

TURN RAPID SHUTDOWN SWITCH TO THE "OFF" POSITION TO SHUT DOWN PV SYSTEM AND REDUCE SHOCK HAZARD IN THE ARRAY

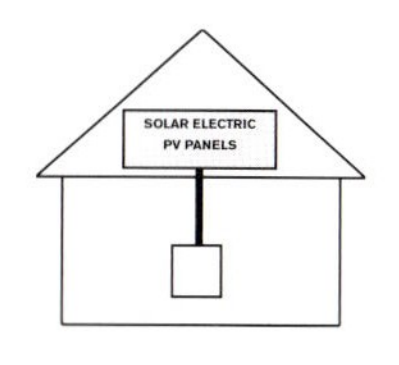

Label must be all caps, top min. 3/8 in. black on yellow, left min. 5/16 in. black on white.

FIG. 96 Required Label at Rapid Shutdown Switch

RAPID SHUTDOWN SWITCH FOR SOLAR PV SYSTEM

Label must be reflective, all caps, min. 3/8 in. white on red, within 3 ft. of switch.

FIG. 97 Label When Areas Remain Energized after Shutdown

Dotted lines required around areas that remain energized.

This label was specified in the 2017 NEC for systems allowed to remain energized inside the array boundary. All caps, top min. 3/8 in. white on red, left min. 5/16 in. black on white, red diagram of energized area.

SOLAR PV SYSTEM EQUIPPED WITH RAPID SHUTDOWN

TURN RAPID SHUTDOWN SWITCH TO THE "OFF" POSITION TO SHUT DOWN CONDUCTORS OUTSIDE THE ARRAY. CONDUCTORS WITHIN THE ARRAY REMAIN ENERGIZED IN SUNLIGHT.

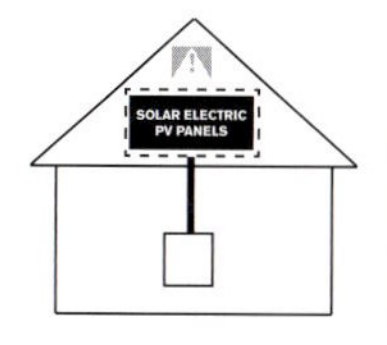

MARKINGS

Conductor & Cable Identification — 20 NEC

- ☐ DC conductors req identification by tagging, color coding, or other means at all termination, connection & splice points _______ 690.31B1
- ☐ Polarity identification by color coding or other permanent means__ 690.31B1
- ☐ White wire only OK for solidly grounded systems ____________ 690.31B1
- ☐ Type PV wire & Type DG cable must be listed _______________ 690.31C
- ☐ Single-conductor cable in exposed outdoor locations PV wire, single-conductor cable marked sunlight-resistant, USE-2, or RHW-2 ___ 690.31C1

Field-Applied Markings, General

- ☐ Must warn of hazards using effective words, colors & symbols_____ 110.21B1
- ☐ Must be permanently affixed & not hand-written EXC ___________ 110.21B1
  - Portions that are variable & intended to be filled in by installer _ 110.21B2X
- ☐ Of sufficient durability to withstand the environment ___________ 110.21B
- ☐ If line & load terminals of a disconnect potentially energized when open, marking reqd per **F98** __________________ 690.13B & 705.20

Labels are available as either "peel & stick" or phenolic. Phenolic labels are considered to meet the code intent for durability, but even those might fade when exposed to direct sunlight.

ANSI Z535.4-2011 provides guidelines for the design & durability of safety signs & labels. Many of the labeling & marking requirements of the code apply to manufacturers, and others, such as the ones on this page, apply to field installers. The examples shown on this page are not all of the ones that might be required for a particular installation.

Marking of Modules & Power Sources — 20 NEC

- ☐ Modules & AC modules to be marked in accordance w/ their listing 690.51[100]
- ☐ Permanent, readily visible label indicating highest max. DC voltage to be placed at inverter, PV disconnecting means, or at distribution equipment associated with the PV system _______________ 690.53[101]
- ☐ Interactive system points of interconnection w/ other sources to be marked at disconnecting means as a power source, marking to include rated AC output current & operating voltage____________ 690.54
- ☐ Plaque or directory denoting location of all power sources reqd at service equipment & each system disconnect **F98** ____________ 705.10

100. Previous code had a list of the specific markings that were required.
101. Previous code required a label to be placed at the disconnecting means of each DC PV power source with the maximum voltage, circuit current, and output current of charge controller or DC-to-DC converter.

FIG. 98

Labels

PV SYSTEM DISCONNECT

690.13B Each PV system disconnecting means

WARNING
3 POWER SOURCES:
UTILITY GRID, BATTERY, AND PV SOLAR
ELECTRIC SYSTEM

705.10 & 706.21 At service with plaque or directory showing location of sources

WARNING
THIS EQUIPMENT FED BY MULTIPLE SOURCES. TOTAL RATING OF ALL OVER-CURRENT DEVICES EXCLUDING MAIN SUPPLY OVERCURRENT DEVICE SHALL NOT EXCEED AMPACITY OF BUSBAR

705.12B3(3) – Install at panels that combine multiple inverter output sources. See F995

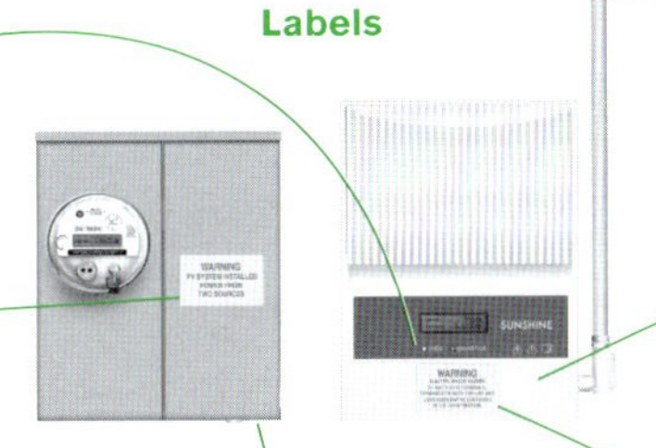

WARNING – PV OUTPUT CIRCUIT
DO NOT RELOCATE
THIS OVERCURRENT DEVICE

705.12B3(2) On deadfront cover. See F994

WARNING PHOTOVOLTAIC POWER SOURCE

690.31D2 – Label reflective, all caps, min. 3/8 in. white on red. Apply at each section of exposed raceways, cable trays, pull & j-box covers & conduit bodies with unused openings. Max. spacing 10 ft. Must appear on every section separated by enclosures, walls, partitions, ceilings, or floors.

DIRECT CURRENT MAXIMUM VOLTAGE XXX V

690.53B Install at inverter, disconnecting means, or distribution equipment.

WARNING
ELECTRIC SHOCK HAZARD
TERMINALS ON THE LINE AND LOAD SIDES
MAY BE ENERGIZED IN THE OPEN POSITION

690.13B Usually at inverter connections or at disconnect

FIG. 99

Interconnected Power Sources: Load Side Connections

FEEDER CONNECTIONS

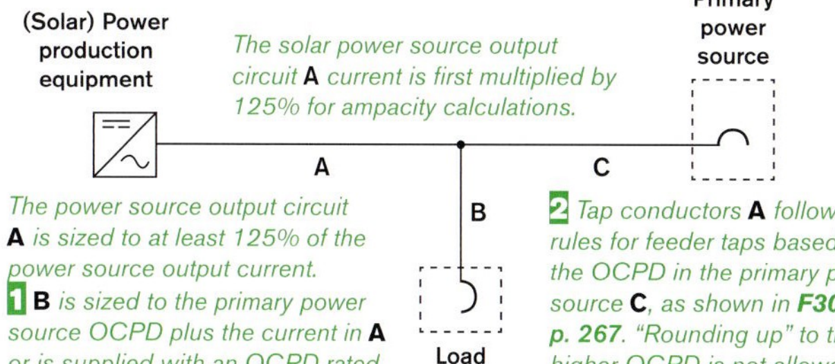

The solar power source output circuit **A** *current is first multiplied by 125% for ampacity calculations.*

The power source output circuit **A** *is sized to at least 125% of the power source output current.*

1 **B** *is sized to the primary power source OCPD plus the current in* **A** *or is supplied with an OCPD rated for conductor* **B** *at the load end.*

2 *Tap conductors* **A** *follow the rules for feeder taps based on the OCPD in the primary power source* **C**, *as shown in* ***F30*** *on* ***p. 267***. *"Rounding up" to the next higher OCPD is not allowed for feeder taps.*

BUSBAR CONNECTIONS:

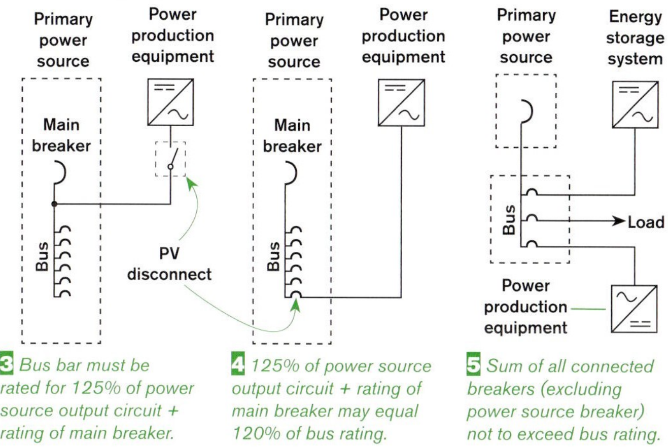

3 *Bus bar must be rated for 125% of power source output circuit + rating of main breaker.*

4 *125% of power source output circuit + rating of main breaker may equal 120% of bus rating.*

5 *Sum of all connected breakers (excluding power source breaker) not to exceed bus rating.*

See ***F93–98*** *for required permanent warning labels.*

INTERCONNECTION TO GRID POWER

Utility Interactive Systems — 20 NEC

- ☐ Microgrid systems OK to disconnect from utility for stand-alone mode 705.50
- ☐ Plaque or directory denoting location of each power source disconnecting means reqd at service equipment ________ 705.10 & 706.21
- ☐ Supply-side source connections output not > rating of service conductors, not < #6 Cu or #4 AL (meter socket backfeed reqs utility OK) _____ 705.11
- ☐ Supply-side disconnecting means reqs rating as service equipment 230.82[102]

Load Side Connections

- ☐ Load-side connection OK at any distribution equipment __________ 705.12
- ☐ Each load-side connection reqs dedicated breaker or fused switch _705.12A
- ☐ Power source output circuit current × 125% used in calculations__ 705.12B
- ☐ Connection not at load end of feeder sized ≥125% of power source output current or by OCPD sized to feeder ampacity at load side of power source connection point **F99 1** __________ 705.12B1
- ☐ Tap rules based on sum of 125% of power source output & circuit + OCPD protecting the feeder conductors **F99 2** ________ 705.12B2
- ☐ Busbar connection options: ________________________ 705.12B3
  - (a) Sum of OCPD protecting bus + 125% of power source output current not exceeding bus rating **F99 3** _______ 705.12B3(1)
  - (b) When OCPDs at opposite end of busbar or far end of center-fed bus, sum of OCPD protecting bus + 125% of power source output current ≤120% of bus rating **F99 4** _____ 705.12B3(2)
  - (c) Sum of OCPDs of load & supply (exclusive of OCPD protecting bus) ≤ bus rating (e.g., panel combining PV & ESSs) **F99 5** ___ 705.12B3(3)
- ☐ Fused disconnects considered suitable for backfeed __________ 705.12D[103]
- ☐ Fastener not reqd on backfed breaker from interactive power source _ 705.12E

Power Control Systems (PCS)

- ☐ PCS that limit source outputs can be used to limit currents & loading on bus bars & conductors ____________ 705.13[104]
- ☐ PCS-controlled circuits + all monitored circuits from other supply sources not to exceed ampacity of bus or conductors _____ 705.13A
- ☐ Access to PCS settings restricted to qualified personnel _________ 705.13E

102. A supply-side disconnecting means is required for PV, wind, fuel cell, or energy storage systems when connected to the supply side of the service and must be rated as service equipment.
103. Unless otherwise marked, a fused disconnect can be suitable for backfeed.
104. Power control systems are new in this edition. These can be used to overcome limitations of **F99**.

FIG. 100

Symbols Used in Single-Line Drawings

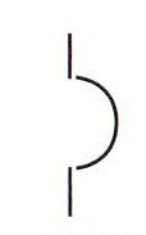
Circuit breaker

Fuse (note: this depiction reserved for high voltage in drawings that include high voltage)

Overload protection (heaters)

Switch

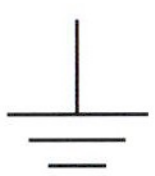
Ground

Contacts

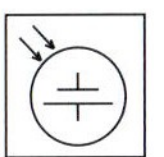
Solar PV power source

AC power source

Normally closed contacts

Battery (energy storage)

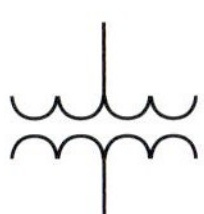
Transformer

Motor

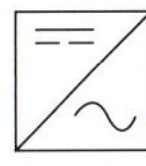
Inverter

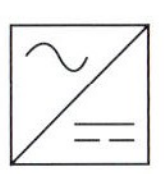
Rectifier

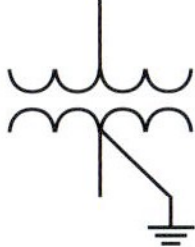
Transformer with grounded secondary

FIG. 101

The Power Wheel: Ohm's Law Formulas

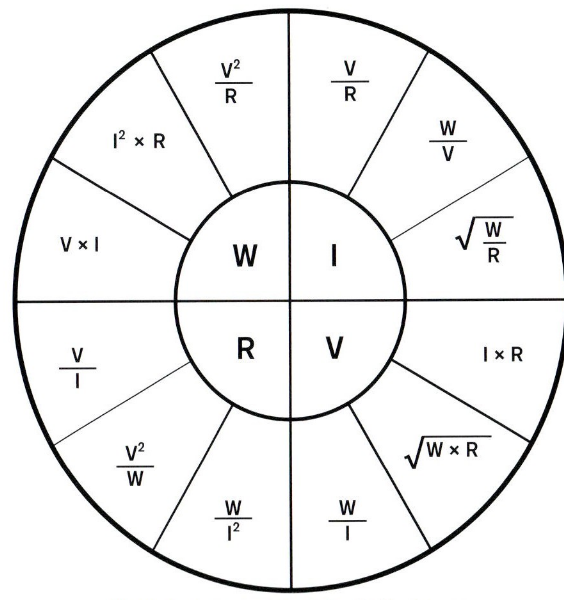

W=Watts, I=Current, V=Volts, R=Resistance

The value of the item in the inner circle is equal to each of the 3 items in the same quadrant of the outer circle.

Ohm's law example:
What is the current in a 60W light bulb?
W = V × I
60 = 120V × I
60÷120 = I = 0.5

Answer: 0.5A

Ohm's law example:
What is the resistance in a 60W light bulb?
R = V÷I
R = 120V÷0.5A
R = 240

Answer: 240Ω